GUIDANCE AND
COUNSELING IN SCHOOLS:
Foundations and Processes

McGRAW-HILL CATHOLIC SERIES IN EDUCATION
Bernard J. Kohlbrenner, *Consulting Editor*

GUIDANCE AND COUNSELING IN SCHOOLS:
Foundations and Processes

JAMES MICHAEL LEE
Department of Education
University of Notre Dame

NATHANIEL J. PALLONE
School of Education
New York University

McGRAW-HILL BOOK COMPANY

NEW YORK ST. LOUIS SAN FRANCISCO
TORONTO   LONDON   SYDNEY

FOREWORD

In 1965, the National Catholic Guidance Conference marked the tenth anniversary of the establishment of a formal organization of guidance workers and counselors who are concerned with the application of a theological-philosophical view of the nature of man to the profession of guidance. The theme we adopted for our tenth-anniversary meeting—"Citizens and Pilgrims: The Children We Guide"—is indicative of the commitment of the Catholic guidance worker. As a group, we had been concerned during the previous year with the goals and purposes of an organization such as NCGC. Brother Marion F. Belka, S.M., our president at that time, had wondered aloud whether, as our organization reached maturity, it could forgo an emphasis upon the activity phase of guidance both to seek and to spell out the commitment which underlies our professional behavior.

Since the 1955 foundation of a group of Catholic counselors and the subsequent organization of the NCGC, formal guidance services have had a real impact upon Catholic education. Of course Christian guidance, in an informal sense, is as ancient as the Christian dispensation. Yet it has been unfortunate that we, as Catholic counselors and guidance workers, have failed to provide, except on a fragmentary basis, an integrated framework for guidance theory and practice based on a religious view of man and his world.

It is to this task that Professors Lee and Pallone have addressed themselves. They have delineated the theoretical foundations upon which a Christian guidance practice is based. They have incorporated not only contemporary empirical research but also modern philosophic views into their formulation of guidance procedures. This book not only spells out what it is that the guidance worker does but it gives him reasons, both empirical and theoretical, for doing what he does.

Educators and guidance workers in Catholic schools will find herein a framework and a schema, valuable at both the abstract and the practical levels, for the guidance service. Those working in other settings will find herein both the theoretical and empirical ballasts for guidance procedures and practices and the implications of a Judeo-Christian view of man for the guidance enterprise. The results cannot but redound to the benefit of the children we guide.

There has long been a great need for this book. No other available text

v

has so adequately addressed itself to the problems and issues facing Catholics in the field of guidance, whether in public or in Catholic schools. But the authors have accomplished this task without sacrifice of professional competence. This book contains more in-depth information than can be found in other comparable works, presents more research evidence than virtually any other currently available text, focuses on issues of importance to Catholics that are ignored in most other texts, and yet admirably infuses newer Catholic philosophic and theological concepts into the foundations and processes of guidance. It belongs on the bookshelf of every Catholic counselor and guidance worker.

The authors bring to this book an unusual combination of experience and professional competence. Dr. Lee is a specialist in Catholic secondary education, with particular interests in guidance, teacher education, and religious development. Dr. Pallone is a specialist in counseling and psychological services, with interests in counseling theory and environmental structure, who brings to his task the particular vantage point of his position as editor of the *Journal* of the NCGC. They have produced together a text of the highest caliber, truly professional and truly Catholic.

(REV.) EDMUND W. OLLEY, *Executive Director*
National Catholic Guidance Conference

PREFACE

Guidance and Counseling in Schools: Foundations and Processes is intended primarily for use in colleges and universities preparing students for guidance positions in public as well as in private education. The authors trust that it will also prove valuable to in-service counselors, teachers, and administrators.

This book is addressed to three groups of readers: preservice counselors and teachers taking a basic or foundational course in a major sequence in guidance leading to the master's degree; preservice and in-service teachers and administrators enrolled in an elective course in the foundations of guidance, who may or may not take other courses in guidance; and in-service counselors, teachers, and administrators not pursuing formal course work who wish to acquaint themselves with the broad spectrum of school guidance and with newly emerging principles and techniques in this rapidly advancing field. While this book is intended chiefly as a text in graduate classes, it may also be used in upper-division undergraduate courses in guidance and in a variety of in-service activities.

It has been our intent to provide an original, integrated synthesis which offers both a sound rationale for guidance and efficient working models issuing from the rationale for the behavior of counselors, administrators, and teachers who, consciously or not, engage in the guidance enterprise. The roots of this synthesis lie in behavioral science and educational theory and tradition, set in the framework of revealed truth about the nature of man and his destiny. In executing this synthesis, the authors have endeavored to give a distinctive flavor to this book.

First, an effort has been made to provide an extensive body of in-depth information, with treatment of every major topic in school guidance. The scope and range of the book make it useful not only in an introductory course in guidance but also in the increasingly popular guidance core sequence.

Second, this work endeavors, whenever possible, to approach problems and issues comparatively. For example, there are treatments of a number of counseling theories, of the contrasting positions relative to the teacher's role in guidance, and of such issues as to whether a "Christian" counseling can or does exist. The authors have also endeavored, however, to avoid an intellectual smorgasbord; a comparative approach does not preclude our preference for one viewpoint over another.

Third, the authors have attempted a balance between theory and practice. Without a thorough grounding in the foundations of guidance inhering in educational, psychological, sociological, and philosophical theory, the practitioner can dispense little more than "patent-medicine" guidance. Yet the authors recognize the pivotal significance of technically competent professional procedures and dynamic processes in the guidance enterprise. Consequently we have endeavored to present theories sound both conceptually and empirically and, further, to spell out the application of such theories in practice.

Fourth, although guidance in secondary schools is accorded the major portion of attention, reflecting a continuing emphasis, all school levels are treated.

Fifth, this volume attempts to integrate Christian dimensions with professional guidance theory and practice, relating guidance principles and techniques to philosophical and theological foundations. At the practical level, problems and questions particularly germane to Catholic schools (for example, guidance for religiovocational development) and to Catholic counselors in public and independent schools (for example, the relationships between sin, guilt, and guidance) are outlined and discussed.

When a text is written in collaboration, occasional differences in style, word choice, or viewpoint are never totally masked. In this case, the first author was responsible for the initial writing of Chapters 1, 3, 4, 5, 7, 15, 16, and 17; the second author, for Chapters 2, 6, 8, 9, 10, 11, 12, and 14; Chapter 13 was jointly written.

In the preparation of a manuscript of this magnitude, it is usually not possible for the authors to express their gratitude to all who helped in the long process between germination and fruition. For those ideas whose precise origin is obscured in memory, we are indebted to our past teachers and our past and present colleagues and students. For very tangible assistance in reading and commenting upon portions of the manuscript, we are especially grateful to colleagues at the University of Notre Dame, Dr. Karl J. VanderHorck, Department of Education, and Dr. Peter P. Grande, Office of Guidance and Testing, and to Professor Joseph H. Maguire, chairman of the Department of Education, College of the Holy Cross. Messrs. Sereko and Gullo and the library staff at Notre Dame, Mr. Norman Wadham and the library staff at Teachers College, Columbia University, and the librarians at the University of Chicago, Northwestern University, Fordham University, St. John's University (New York), and the Catholic University of America gave invaluable assistance in locating research materials. Walter Doyle, Sister Maryl Hofer, O.S.F., and Jeffrey Blackwell graciously lent their energies in the final stages of preparation. Helen M. Weber typed the final manuscript with efficiency and dispatch. Margaret Spitz and Roger Parent gave their assistance in preparing the indices. Incalculable is our debt to Prof. Bernard J. Kohlbrenner, consulting editor of the McGraw-Hill Catholic Series in Education, for his revisional suggestions, his sound advice from the breadth of his experience, and particularly for his seemingly inexhaustible fund of patience. Finally, to his wife, Nicolina, from whose company were stolen the hours spent in research and writing, the second author owes greatest debt.

JAMES M. LEE   NATHANIEL J. PALLONE

CONTENTS

part 5

RETROSPECT AND PROSPECT

part **1**

FOUNDATIONS OF GUIDANCE

1

A SHORT HISTORY OF GUIDANCE SERVICES IN AMERICAN SCHOOLS

A general view

Guidance began to emerge as an identifiable aspect of the American educational enterprise during the first two decades of this century. A number of characteristics mark the general changes and forward advances in formal guidance programs in American schools between their inception and the present. *Then,* guidance was conceived as a helpful but not an essential facet of the school program; *now,* guidance is conceived as a necessary, crucial, and pervasive feature of the school's educative function. Then, guidance was a formal but poorly organized school service; now, a well-developed series of guidance services and personnel are systematically coordinated. Then, guidance was limited almost exclusively to occupational choice and selection; now, guidance services extend to every facet and element of the student's complex pattern of personal development. Then, attention was focused by the guidance worker only on the student's verbalized educational or vocational problems; now, emphasis is placed upon assisting the student to explore, evaluate, and ameliorate underlying dynamics of personality development as they are expressed in a variety of difficulties and problems. Then, the guidance worker was primarily a minimal data gatherer and adviser; now, among the roles played by the guidance worker are those of counselor, evaluator of human development, personality explorer, school testing specialist, home-school liaison officer, coordinator of faculty-staff guidance efforts, and curriculum consultant. Then, stress was placed almost exclusively upon the tangible results of counseling; now, there is a key concern for the process of counseling qua process, for the interaction between counseling techniques and attitudes and their value in the helping relationship. Then, the individual interview constituted the sole guidance vehicle; now, the guidance worker's armamentarium includes a vast panoply of varied individual and group guidance procedures. Then, few standardized instruments for testing and observation were utilized; now, guidance workers employ a wide variety of measurement devices and test batteries to secure a total picture of the student's aptitudes, problems, needs, interests, and personality functioning. Then, the information-gathering interview constituted the only means of securing data; now, a host of individual and group subjective and objective methods to gain a well-rounded portrayal of the student's developmental pattern are employed. Then, guidance functions were performed by teachers or administrators professionally unprepared in guidance; now, there exists in many schools and school systems a professionally prepared, state-certificated network of counselors and other specialized guidance personnel.

GUIDANCE IN THE PERIOD OF ITS INFANCY, 1908–1918

History

Guidance has been the last major educational area to develop, mature, and attain status. Indeed the guidance and personnel movement is one of the most distinctive developments in American education in this century. The guidance movement is commonly said to have begun on January 13, 1908, when Frank Parsons founded and became the first director of guidance at the Vocation Bureau of the Civic Service House in Boston. The Vocation Bureau was established to provide systematic vocational counseling to youths both on the job and out of it. In 1909 Parsons' celebrated book *Choosing a Vocation* was published posthumously.

In some respects it is not accurate to credit Parsons with founding the guidance movement, since others before him had done pioneer work in school guidance. In 1907 Eli W. Weaver began working with the Brooklyn High School Teachers Association to provide vocational guidance and occupational placement for the pupils at Boys High School in Brooklyn. In 1907 Jesse B. Davis, principal of Central High School in Grand Rapids, introduced occupational guidance into English classes on a regular basis. At about the same time, William Wheatley was attempting to bring vocational guidance into social studies courses and also to inaugurate special classes in occupations in the Middletown (Connecticut) public high school. And in Boston itself, it was Meyer Bloomfield, son of a Jewish immigrant and a Harvard graduate, who founded the Civic Service House in 1901.

By 1910 some 35 cities had worked out formal programs of school guidance or were attempting to do so. National interest in the guidance movement is evidenced by the fact that in the same year several hundred delegates from 45 cities went to Boston to attend the First National Conference on Vocational Guidance, sponsored by the Vocational Bureau of the Civic Service House and by the Boston Chamber of Commerce. In 1913, at the Third National Conference in Grand Rapids, the first professional guidance organization was founded and given the name National Vocational Guidance Association (NVGA). By the end of this period, it was evident that the principles and practices of common school guidance (elementary and secondary levels) were diverging markedly in many areas from guidance principles and practices on the college level.

Emphases and Issues

In this first period, and indeed well into the closing months of World War II, the totality of guidance was regarded as almost solely occupational guidance (Brewer, 1918). This emphasis was a natural reflection of the era. Most youths were not oriented to higher education but instead to the world of work. The National Education Association (NEA) Commission on the Reorganization of Secondary Education (1918, p. 9) gave what soon was to become a very influential definition of vocational guidance, viz., "a continuous process designed to help the individual choose, to plan his preparation for, to enter upon, and to make progress in an occupation." While the *simpliste* notion of vocational guidance as adjusting pegs to holes was discarded by the more alert leaders in the field, nevertheless vocational guidance was not regarded as anything more than "organized common sense used to help each individual make the most of his abilities and opportunities" (Bloomfield, 1915, p. 5).

Parsons' highly influential *Choosing a Vocation* (1909, p. 5) had as its central thesis the concept that a wise career choice involves three distinct factors: "(1) a clear understanding of yourself, your aptitudes, abilities, interests, ambitions, resources, limitations and their causes; (2) a knowledge of the requirements and conditions of success, advantages and disadvantages, compensation, opportunities, and prospects in different lines of work; (3) true reasoning on the relations of these two groups of facts." Parsons further stressed the point that vocational guidance must not attempt to decide for the client but rather assist the youth to decide for himself.

Program

Many of the leading figures in the early guidance movement pressed for complete integration of guidance into the warp and woof of the school's educational program rather than having it tacked on as an extra (Rockwell, 1958). Wheatley advocated the integration of classes in occupations with the citizenship development aspect of courses in social studies. In Grand Rapids, as high school principal, Davis initiated in his school a once-a-week period in English classes devoted to educational and moral guidance. His book, *Vocational and Moral Guidance* (1914), was the first of its kind to offer a systematic plan and outline on exactly how to integrate vocational guidance organizationally into the various phases of the school program. Going beyond Wheatly and the early Davis, Brewer (1918) called for a systematic guidance program in preference to incidental guidance inserted by a teacher into the social studies or English class.

In the practical order, school people began introducing guidance programs into school systems. Weaver's original activities in Boys High School were conducted unofficially and without school backing; in 1911, however, four years after he started his work, the New York City Guidance Association was organized. The efforts of Davis and Wheatley, while not organized on a systematic basis, nevertheless represented a forward step. By 1909, a vocational guidance worker had been appointed in every high school in Boston and in all but one of the elementary schools (Bloomfield, 1911, pp. 35–41). In 1911 Helen T. Wooley established the Vocational Bureau in the Cincinnati public school system. In 1913 Ella Flagg Young was appointed dean of girls in the Chicago public high schools "to organize the social life and to be a friend to every girl" (Mary H. Johnson, 1929, p. 10). By 1915 a number of school systems in large cities had begun to organize vocational guidance programs in public high schools (Treacy, 1935, pp. 256–257). In 1916 Enoch Gowin and William Wheatley published the first textbook on occupational and further educational guidance specifically designed for use by high school students, and by the end of World War I at least 30 cities had extensive, organized vocational guidance programs (Barry & Wolf, 1955, p. 52). On the level of higher education and in elementary education, however, very little was done to provide personnel or guidance services to the students during this period.

Techniques

The concept of guidance procedure was that of directive advisement, i.e., asking the student to identify his needs and interests, making an appraisal of the student, examining job opportunities, and then telling him the best course of action (Bloomfield, 1912, pp. 109–116).

Personnel

Professionalization of guidance personnel started in 1909, when the Vocational Department of the Boston Young Men's Christian Association (YMCA) established a school to train vocational counselors. The first course ever offered in vocational guidance to train secondary school teachers was given in 1911 by Harvard University. By 1913 at least five universities around the nation were offering such courses.

The first professional school guidance association was the Vocational Guidance Association of Brooklyn, established in 1908 (Anna M. Jones, 1959). In 1913 the first national guidance association was organized and given the title National Vocational Guidance Association, with branches in various cities and states throughout the country (Norris, 1954). The 30 cities which by the end of World War I had extensive organized guidance programs also employed guidance counselors (Barry & Wolf, 1955, p. 52). In addition, guidance specialists began to appear in the schools during this period. The first such specialist was the school psychologist, a position which originated in 1915 when the Connecticut Board of Education appointed Arnold Gesell to conduct a testing program to identify the mentally retarded, the emotionally disturbed, and other types of deviant children in the public schools.

On the college and university level, the post of dean of women had clearly evolved by the turn of the century. Deans of women began to meet regularly after 1903 to discuss professional problems, and in 1916 the National Association of Deans of Women (NADW) was formed.

The first large-scale professional publication was *The Vocational Guidance News-letter,* begun in 1911 under the sponsorship of the Boston Vocational Bureau. In 1915 this little professional organ became a national journal entitled *Vocational Guidance Bulletin,* but in 1918 it was discontinued because of the war.

Catholic schools

History

There is extremely meager evidence on the history of guidance in Catholic schools in this early period. They tended in those days, as they do even down to the present, to be quite isolationist and hence reluctant to release any information about themselves except in cases of necessity, such as by demand of an accrediting association. Therefore much of what is said about guidance in Catholic schools in this and subsequent periods must be inferential from the literature. Even this does not present a totally accurate picture, since the literature tends to reflect more advanced Catholic guidance thinking and so is not truly representative of the actual condition of guidance in the schools.

Emphases and Issues

During this period those Catholic educators who gave consideration to occupational guidance were inclined to equate it with vocational education. In general, the priests contended that vocational education "debauched" or "dehumanized" true education (McLaughlin, 1915, p. 315). In opposition to this view, many teaching brothers argued that vocational training was a legitimate aim of Catholic education and should take its rightful place in the Catholic school curriculum (Brother Baldwin, 1917).

Despite the insights provided by psychology and the newer educational theory, Catholic schoolmen seemed to think that very strict discipline and close surveillance of the students were two of the most effective and valuable guidance vehicles ever devised. Religiovocational guidance to the priesthood and religious life received much-deserved emphasis during this period. A few prominent Catholics such as Dom Thomas Vernor Moore advocated incorporating the newer scientific methods of psychology into Catholic education, but these men were usually bitterly opposed by most Catholic educators (J. J. Ryan, 1913, p. 267).

Program

Catholic education in the United States has always been alert to the need for religious guidance in the school program (Sister Estelle, S.S.N.D., 1951). As a result there was a tendency to regard guidance as flowing automatically from the educational program, requiring no special organized program of its own. No Catholic school system had a formal program by the end of this period. Furthermore there is not a single reference to existing, proposed. or ideal guidance programs in the literature.

Techniques

The exclusive technique was the explicit and definite direction of the student by the guidance worker, most commonly evidenced in the traditional, age-hallowed practice of spiritual direction. This advisement system was perhaps succinctly summed up by Fr. McLaughlin, S.J. (1915, p. 320), one of its champions, when he remarked that youths are "in the waxen age where the gentle pressure is exerted, there it yields." Guidance technique, then, was regarded as "molding" and "forming" the docile, plastic student.

Personnel

By 1918 there was still no special course or series of courses in guidance in any Catholic college or university, although there is evidence that guidance was given some consideration in the education courses at the University of

Notre Dame, Catholic University of America, and St. Louis University (Sister Teresa G. Murray, O.S.B., 1938, pp. 23–24). There was no discussion in the literature of professional preparation of guidance workers. Perhaps this was due to the concept that in a Catholic school every clerical and religious teacher is automatically a competent guidance counselor; hence special preparation would be superfluous.

Catholic educators made no attempt to form a professional guidance association, nor was any formal effort made to cooperate or otherwise work with NVGA. No special guidance publication appeared. There were no reports of scientific research on guidance or personnel work in Catholic schools. What guidance-related articles appeared in the Catholic literature were written for the most part by priests and religious. The role of the laity in Catholic education was very remote in this period.

GUIDANCE IN THE PERIOD OF EDUCATIONAL SURGENCY, 1918–1929

History

During this period serious efforts were made further to individualize education. As a result, the vital role of guidance and personnel services in the school enterprise became increasingly recognized by educators. Nowhere was this more evident than in the organized standardized testing programs which began to mushroom in public school systems all over the country. Encouraged by Terman's famous, massive study (1919) of the intelligence of schoolchildren (which included a chapter on the use of intelligence tests in vocational and scholastic guidance), many important educators, including Brewer (1924), Griffits (1924), and Proctor (1923), wrote works suggesting how measurement devices could be utilized to great advantage in school guidance programs.

Immediately after the war, the Federal government set up vocational rehabilitation centers for veterans which provided, among other things, a vocational advisement service. This service was not very successful for several reasons, such as the fact that the advisers had neither sufficient training nor adequate guidance tools.

The school guidance movement continued to be spurred on by organizations and foundations, e.g., the Commonwealth Fund. The American Psychological Association (APA), founded in 1892, became incorporated in 1925 and indirectly exerted considerable influence in developing in both schoolmen and guidance workers a deepening awareness of the importance of a sound psychological basis for every phase of the school program. In 1924 the NVGA sponsored research which led to the development of the first standards for preparing and evaluating occupational materials.

The guidance concept and guidance movement soon spread from the

United States to other countries. While vocational guidance in some European countries had faint and scattered beginnings before World War I, it was generally not until the years immediately following the war that these countries began to adopt school guidance programs. Of particular interest to American educators and guidance workers is the fact that vocational guidance in European schools, notably in Austria and Germany, was sponsored by and centered in a governmental, nonschool agency (Brewer, 1942, pp. 219–236; Keller & Viteles, 1937; Papanek, 1962, pp. 89–90).

Emphases and Issues

The issue of whether vocational guidance should comprise the totality of guidance or form only one segment raged with intensity throughout this period and became particularly prominent as a result of two developments. First, vocational guidance workers in schools increasingly found themselves performing a host of varied tasks, many of which were related more closely to scholastic guidance than to vocational guidance, e.g., administering and interpreting intelligence tests for grade-placement purposes and counseling students on how to succeed in academic work. Second, the only national professional organization to which school guidance workers could belong was NVGA, which steadfastly took the position that all guidance was vocational guidance. The separatists, who maintained that there were distinct types of guidance, attempted in vain in 1929 to broaden the NVGA's exclusively vocational emphasis.

During this period emphasis began to focus on the inner personality dynamics of the individual. Much of the impetus for this emphasis came from Edward L. Thorndike's research-based book (1923) which had as its central thesis that the aim of human life is the improvement and satisfaction of wants. This work had great impact on both the curriculum and the guidance movements, as is evidenced by Kitson's important guidance book which appeared two years later. Kitson's work, the first comprehensive treatment of vocational adjustment, gave some attention (though by no means the major emphasis) to the role and importance of self-involvement in the environment as the genesis of vocational interests. It recognized, perhaps a bit hazily, that occupational interest is an attempt of a person to identify himself with the job (Kitson, 1925). Three years later E. K. Strong published his famous Vocational Interest Blank, which gave an added dimension to the school's vocational guidance program. To round out the picture, the entire climate of the educational enterprise during this period was profoundly affected by the newer theoretical approaches of progressive education, which emphasized a focus on the schoolchild as he is, a person here and now, rather than one who is preparing for life or for a life's work. Progressive education also stressed the necessity of bringing guidance into the very structure of the curriculum rather than having it exist as a separate service. The "case study" approach to guidance and counseling made its initial appearance in guidance circles at this time, due to the influence of Brewer (1926), who first introduced this process into his guidance classes at Harvard.

Program

Guidance programs in the nation's public secondary schools were growing by leaps and bounds. Often these programs were organized in a haphazard, nonprofessional manner. Many metropolitan communities established departments of vocational guidance, frequently under the sponsorship of and with the financial assistance of local civic associations. Eventually the local boards of education assumed control of these departments.

In 1923, among American cities with a population of 10,000 or more, there were only 143 communities (having a total of 124 full-time counselors) in which at least one public school attempted to provide some sort of organized program of vocational or scholastic guidance, or both (Edgerton & Herr, 1924, pp. 3–27). By the end of the period, vocational guidance programs had begun to spread from large city school systems to smaller systems. Schools also began on a wide scale to initiate standardized testing programs.

College personnel services made considerable headway in this postwar period, probably stimulated in large measure by the occupational investigations of the armed services. A new element was evolving within the college complex, viz., the guidance personnel office (Maverick, 1926, pp. 32–61). The larger state universities tended to provide the most complete and varied programs of personnel services. Of interest is that by the end of this period no regional accrediting agency saw fit to judge a college's program of personnel services worthy of official recognition.

Techniques

The concept of good guidance procedure remained that of directive advisement through the integrating interview. Test data were utilized more and more by the guidance worker in learning about the client so as to evaluate and advise him in a better way.

Personnel

Courses for the professional preparation of guidance workers became more numerous as the period progressed. By 1926 a prospective *vocational* guidance counselor could find *courses* (not necessarily degree programs) in his field of interest at more than 40 universities around the country (Barry & Wolf, 1957, pp. 82–83). These became sufficiently specialized so that distinct courses were offered in the area of school guidance, as contrasted with the separate though related area of personnel work in higher education. As late as 1925, Teachers College, Columbia University, was the only institution offering organized programs preparing students for the post of dean of women in higher educational institutions.

During this period, NVGA became a very powerful organization. In 1920 it reorganized itself into a federation of seven regional branch associations, but its officers were elected by the membership at large. By the end of the period educators and schoolmen gained the ascendancy in NVGA, with representatives of nonschool vocational agencies becoming a minority.

In 1924, New York became the first state to issue special certification requirements for school guidance counselors. NVGA did not take an official stand on certification of guidance workers in educational institutions.

On the college level, this decade saw the establishment of several new college personnel organizations and the strengthening of the existing one. In 1919 six deans of men from various colleges met to discuss common problems, and in the following year they officially organized the National Association of Deans and Advisers of Men or NADAM (Findlay, 1937, pp. 104–121). In 1924 the American College Personnel Association (ACPA) was established to coordinate personnel services on the college level. The same year the National Association of Appointment Secretaries was founded to meet the needs of college placement officers; in 1929 it changed its name to the National Association of Placement and Personnel Officers. In the first period the NVGA had the leadership of college personnel workers. From 1918 to 1924 this leadership was exercised by NADW, and after 1924 by the American College Personnel Association.

Guidance specialists began to appear on the college scene. Probably the first incorporation of psychiatrists into the college personnel services program occurred in 1920, when Karl Menninger inaugurated a counseling system at Washington Municipal University, Topeka, Kansas. The same year a psychiatrist was appointed to care for the students at the United States Military Academy at West Point. In 1921 Dartmouth College established psychiatric services as part of its student health program, followed by Vassar College and Yale University in 1923 and 1925, respectively.

The publication of the official NVGA organ, the *Vocational Guidance Bulletin,* was suspended during the war and was never revived. In 1921 NVGA began publishing its new official magazine, *The National Vocational Guidance Association Bulletin.* Two years later, control of this publication was turned over to the Bureau of Vocational Guidance of the Graduate School of Education, Harvard University. Reflecting this change, the journal altered its name the following year to *The Vocational Guidance Magazine.* During this period the American College Personnel Association, the National Association of Deans of Women, and the National Association of Deans and Advisers of Men published annual reports of their yearly conventions.

Catholic schools

History

The postwar period was a time of great expansion in the number of Catholic high schools. Little thought, however, seems to have been given to the guidance services and facilities of these schools.

The arguments about the merits of standardized psychological testing continued to be hotly debated in Catholic educational circles. Most Catholics tended to resist objective standardized testing instruments because they thought that either they somehow interfered with the operation of Divine grace or that the measurement instruments were superfluous frills. A few Catholic educators like Fr. John A. O'Brien and Leo F. Kuntz spoke out in favor of testing programs, but they were either ignored or denounced.

Emphases and Issues

The battle among Catholic educators on the introduction of vocational education into the Catholic school program continued to rage during this period. As in the preceding period, most guidance emphasis in Catholic schools was in the area of religious and religiovocational guidance. Both the literature and that which can be inferred from school practices gave scant recognition to the areas of personal, social, or even scholastic development guidance. Chouinard's investigation of Catholic high schools (1927) revealed that their administrators perceived the principles and outcomes of the guidance program and the extracurricular activities program to be the same. Since extracurricular activities were still considered as a marginal and in many cases a useless (Brother Barnabas, F.S.C., 1925; Editorial Comment, 1926) segment in the Catholic educational program, the same apparently held true for guidance.

Rigid discipline continued to be stressed as the primary guidance vehicle. This viewpoint was grafted onto the concept of the supernatural meritoriousness of total docility and unquestioning obedience of the student to the teacher.

Program

During this period Catholic schoolmen predictably were advised by their leaders not to experiment with guidance programs but rather to wait and see the results of the newly formed public school guidance programs (Editor's Note, 1921, p. 13). Toward the end of the period a study sponsored by the National Catholic Educational Association and executed by Fr. (later Msgr.) Sheehy (1929) concluded that there was a notable lack of organized and professionally implemented guidance and counseling programs in Catholic colleges.

In 1928 the diocese of Pittsburgh inaugurated an organized guidance service and appointed as director a priest who had received advanced professional training at Harvard and at Notre Dame. This pioneer guidance program became a frequent topic for discussion at meetings of Catholic educational groups.

Techniques

Spiritual direction and religious or occasionally scholastic advisement to a pliant student continued to be the almost exclusive guidance technique during this period.

Personnel

During this period the University of Notre Dame, the Catholic University of America, and St. Louis University developed master's degree programs in guidance. Notre Dame's celebrated Boy Guidance program gave an indication that forward-looking Catholic educators at least implicitly recognized that guidance is essentially concerned with the pupil's entire personality structure. The program's short life was also reflective of the prevailing Catholic attitude of the time.

By 1926 there were 35 Catholic central high schools in America, but only 2 of these had a guidance counselor (Fr. C. J. Ryan, 1927). Of all Catholic schoolmen, the Jesuits seemed most aware of the necessity of counselors in Catholic schools. In Jesuit high schools part-time pupil advisers were introduced (Fr. Garesché, S.J., 1928, p. 546; Fr. McGucken, S.J., 1932). The awareness of the suitability of a lay counselor was not grasped by Catholic schoolmen of this period.

Toward the end of the period, Fr. Sheehy (1928, p. 180) proposed that in small Catholic colleges the ratio of professionally trained, full-time counselors to students should be 1:100. In the practical order there was nothing even faintly resembling either this ratio or the professional training recommended.

As in the preceding period, Catholic educators made no attempt to form a professional guidance association, nor was any effort made formally to cooperate or otherwise work with NVGA, ACPA, or NADAM. No special guidance publication appeared.

GUIDANCE IN THE PERIOD OF
ECONOMIC UNCERTAINTY, 1929–1945

History

In these years guidance did not expand in the nation's public schools nearly so much as it did in the preceding period. There were two basic reasons for the slower pace. First, most of the possible penetration of guidance services into the schools had been made in the preceding period, so that strengthening existing services and personnel rather than introducing new ones was the more urgent need. Related to this, an expanded theoretical rationale for guidance was earnestly being sought. Second, and perhaps more important, the Great Depression of 1929 caused school budgets to be drastically reduced, with guidance suffering the most since it was still regarded in many educational and community quarters as a nonessential or even a frill in the school program. Many guidance directors and counselors lost their jobs (Bogan, 1935, p. 103).

In the economically troubled decade of the 1930s, the guidance movement was aided by two outside sources. The first assistance came from the Carnegie Corporation, which in 1933 financed the National Occupational Conference (NOC). The threefold purpose of the NOC was to assemble and disseminate to guidance workers information about occupations and careers; to encourage studies and research in areas in which occupational data were incomplete, fragmentary, or nonexistent; and to maintain a central index of all published data on all occupations and lines of work. The NOC terminated its existence in 1939. The second assistance to the guidance movement came from the Federal government, which in 1938 established the Occupational Information and Guidance Service in the Vocational Education Division of the U.S. Office of Education, appointing a director (Harry A. Jager) and two specialists. The Service promoted throughout the nation the need for occupational information as an integral part of school programs, gathered and published such information, and engaged in research and field services. Other important assistance came from the Federal government in 1938, when the Commissioner of Education made a formal ruling that Federal funds to schools having vocational educational programs subsidized by the Smith-Hughes and George-Deen Acts could be used for vocational guidance as well as for vocational education properly so called. In 1939 the U.S. Department of Labor first published *The Dictionary of Occupational Titles* (DOT), which with each updated edition has increasingly become the standard reference for job descriptions and coded job titles. Also, the United States Employment Service was organized during this period to provide vocational guidance for adults and entrants into the labor market.

Emphases and Issues

Because this period lay either in the Great Depression itself or in its long, dark shadow, the issue of the primacy of vocational guidance as contrasted with other types of guidance in the school setting was not controverted.

It was not until this period that deep or serious guidance theories began to evolve. Impetus for developing guidance theory came from psychology and psychoanalysis. E. L. Thorndike (1935) elaborated significantly on his theory of the centrality of wants in human nature, and other psychologists began seriously to explore man as a need-centered organism. Men like Gordon Allport and Kurt Lewin started to explore human behavior from the matrices of drive, attitude, and other personality causative factors. These developments in psychology were accompanied by a widespread interest in psychoanalysis, which stressed disorders in the deepest regions of the personality structure as the genesis of human behavior. This interest was paralleled by the development of ego psychology by such psychoanalysts as Anna Freud, herself a former schoolteacher in Vienna. Some of this emphasis spilled over into the mainstream of the guidance movement. In the early 1940s, first with Harold D. Carter (1940) and then with J. G. Darley (1941), Ralph F. Berdie (1943), and Edward S. Bordin (1943), depth theories of vocational choice began to be developed. It was at this time that D. E. Super began his pioneer thinking on career development patterns. These theories mainly hinted at vocational interest and choice as a basic thrust of the person's total personality, something which must be regarded in terms of personality fulfillment. Unfortunately these new emphases did not have a noticeable impact on school guidance practice during this period.

Guidance and curriculum were continuing to merge. The increased interest in progressive education, with its emphasis on building the entire curriculum around the learner's needs, and the significant conclusions of the Eight Year Study, out of which developed a new type of curricular design (the core curriculum), had a decided effect in bringing guidance into the very heart of the classroom learning experience itself.

An issue of great concern in this decade was the definition of terms. What was the difference between guidance, advisement, personnel work, counseling, and so forth? There was no consensus, and the debate continues to the present day.

In 1932 the ACPA published an influential statement called *College Personnel Principles and Functions*. Often known as the Clothier Report, after the name of the committee head, the statement defined college personnel work as assisting each individual student to develop himself through his own efforts to the limit of his capacity for growth. The Clothier Report was followed in 1937 by the famous document issued by the Committee on Student Personnel Work of the American Council on Education and entitled *The Student Personnel Point of View* (revised in 1949). The ACE statement urged colleges to develop and implement their personnel programs and to give increased attention to "the personnel point of view."

Program

Guidance leaders began to develop the concept of an integrated, coordinated, pervasive all-school guidance program. This concept probably arose as a reaction to the almost exclusively vocational emphasis of guidance workers and school programs in this economically disturbed era. Indeed the Sub-committee on Vocational Guidance, White House Conference on Child Health and Protection (1932, pp. 43–64), found that during this period there were few well-organized public school system guidance programs. Another study (Altstetter, 1938, p. 513) conducted the same year concluded that guidance services seemed less well organized and less effective than any other phase of the secondary school's overall educational program.

A 1940 nationwide study (Eugenie A. Leonard & A. C. Tucker, 1941) of public secondary schools having at least one half-time counselor disclosed that 44 per cent of the responding schools reported insufficient time for guidance work; in more than 75 per cent of the schools the administration rather than the guidance personnel determined what psychological tests were to be given; and intelligence tests were administered in 87 per cent of the responding schools, while only one-third of these institutions gave aptitude tests.

The research data for the period indicate that personnel services in colleges and universities were more often than not poorly organized, without form, and conducted in a haphazard fashion. These studies almost unanimously recommended tightening the organization through centralization (Barry & Wolf, 1955, p. 266).

Techniques

Guidance techniques began to develop and mature. The early 1930s witnessed the introduction of depth psychology tests in the United States, particularly the Rorschach test employing inkblots, basically a test of projection. Several radically new techniques in group guidance appeared, most notably the psychodrama, or sociodrama, a device invented by Jacob L. Moreno, a Rumanian-born, Vienna-trained psychotherapist. In 1936 the American Association of Group Work was founded.

But it was in counseling that the most momentous advances in technique took place. In 1939 E. G. Williamson published *How to Counsel Students,* which was the first systematic, psychologically rooted work dealing with the various phases of the precounseling and counseling interview. The real revolution in counseling techniques, however, occurred in 1942, when Carl R. Rogers published *Counseling and Psychotherapy.* In this work Rogers advo-cated a totally new counseling technique, called the client-centered or non-directive method, in which the client rather than the counselor totally controls the flow of communication in the interview. Rogerian technique profoundly altered the entire concept of counseling and turned tremendous attention to the psychodynamics and technique of the interview situation. During this period Rogers's influence was restricted chiefly to psychotherapists. It was not until the postwar era that nondirectivism was widely utilized in school counseling.

Personnel

By 1931 there were 124 institutions of higher learning in 37 states offering courses in guidance (Rose, 1932). Following the lead of Teachers College, Columbia University, universities preparing guidance workers in the 1930s inaugurated the guidance laboratory as part of the normal training program. By the end of the period, most American universities offering graduate degrees in education had a sequence in guidance.

The first concrete attempt to coordinate the seemingly myriad guidance organizations was the formation in 1934 of the American Council of Guidance and Personnel Associations (ACGPA), a confederation of separate, autonomous associations joined for the purpose of cooperative effort and integrated action. The ACPGA was composed of the NVGA, ACPA, and NADW, plus the National Federation of Bureaus of Occupations, the Personnel Research Foundation, the Southern Women's Educational Alliance, and the Teachers College Personnel Association. In keeping with its isolationist policy, the NADAM never joined the Council. In 1941 the ACGPA reorganized slightly, changing certain regulations and also its name (the first word of the old title was dropped).

It was only after 1940 that many states began to establish certification requirements for school guidance counselors and specialists. In the 1930s, it was NVGA which took the lead in certification and related professional requirements. In drawing up these standards, NVGA worked through its own membership, through state departments of education, and after 1938 with the Occupational Information and Guidance Service of the U.S. Office of Education. In 1941 NVGA published its policy statement *The Preparation and Certification of the School Counselor*. NVGA therefore, in effect, was certifying its own members, in much the same way as the American Medical Association.

In 1931 one-third of the nation's public school systems located in cities with a population of 25,000 or more had no full-time or part-time guidance counselors. In only 38 per cent of those systems having a counseling program was the counselor a full-time specialist. A mere 14 per cent of all the counselors had any special training in guidance (Subcommittee on Vocational Guidance, 1932, pp. 43–64). A 1938 study of 23,000 high schools throughout the country disclosed that there was a total of 2,286 half- or full-time counselors employed in only 1,297 of these schools. Only 5 per cent of the high schools surveyed had officially designated counselors. The heaviest concentration of counselors was in the densely populated industrial areas (Brewster & Greenleaf, 1939, pp. 83–89).

On the college level, ACPA had clearly become the principal professional association for college personnel workers. That it exercised considerable leadership is evidenced by its sponsorship and publication of the Clothier Report.

In the early 1930s, the college deans of men "had little or no training in the personnel field and possibly had little idea of the actual content of personnel courses" (Barry & Wolf, 1955, p. 281). By the middle of the period, however, NADAM undertook for the first time seriously to examine the training program for the deanship.

In 1931 the Student Personnel Association for Teacher Education (SPATE) was founded, ostensibly to serve the special interests and needs of personnel workers and counselor educators in teacher training institutions. In 1940 the American Association of School Personnel Administrators (AASPA) was organized, thus once more proliferating associations of college personnel workers. Meanwhile, NADW had become quite defensive and conservative by the end of the 1930s. By the end of the period a definite shift in college guidance had occurred. The positions of dean of men and dean of women had by and large become administrative posts. Hence the deans more and more became administrators of other personnel workers and less and less personnel workers themselves.

The withering finger of the Great Depression touched everything. In 1932 Harvard, mighty bastion of collegiate wealth, stopped subsidizing *The Vocational Guidance Magazine*. The National Occupational Conference agreed to sponsor the publication and in June, 1933, fittingly renamed it *Occupations, subtitled The Vocational Guidance Magazine*. When the NOC itself breathed its last in 1939, the NVGA was fiscally strong enough to resume sponsorship. The official organs of the other guidance and personnel associations retained the same titles and emphases as they had in the preceding period.

Catholic schools

History

In 1930 several prominent, forward-looking Catholic educators formed a Life-Guidance Conference. This Conference subsequently requested affiliation with the National Catholic Educational Association, but the conservative NCEA refused. As a last resort the Conference requested the Secondary School Department of the NCEA to make provision for discussion of vocational and scholastic guidance. This department then formed the Standing Committee on Vocational Guidance, whose members consisted of the original group of petitioning Catholic educators. Soon afterward, the committee evolved into the Catholic Vocational-Counsel Conference (CVCC), which lasted from 1930 to 1934. The aims of this Conference were to inform Catholic parents and schoolmen of the importance of guidance and to formulate definite programs adaptable to Catholic schools and other Catholic agencies for the purpose of assisting these groups in their advisement work (Catholic Vocational-Counsel Conference Proceedings, 1931). It attempted to promote vocational counsel sections in Catholic school systems. Though unfortunately short-lived, the CVCC represented a significant advance in Catholic guidance activity.

During this period some of the more alert Catholic diocesan school systems began establishing some sort of loosely organized guidance services. Notable among these were Milwaukee, Philadelphia, Boston, and St. Louis, followed by New Orleans, Ohio, and San Francisco. Vocational guidance still consisted chiefly in occasional talks by persons in the professions (Sister M. I. Biehn, S.C.C., 1933).

A few outstanding Catholic educators with backgrounds in psychology, such as Dom Thomas Vernor Moore (1930), proposed that Catholics sponsor special classes and special schools for the emotionally disturbed. As late as 1935 only two dioceses were sponsoring Catholic psychiatric clinics (A. G. Schmidt, 1935, p. 233). By the end of the period, the Catholic Charities and Catholic Youth Organization (CYO) divisions of some dioceses began providing guidance and psychological services to Catholic youths.

Emphases and Issues

In this period considerably increased attention began to be given to guidance in the convention speeches of the NCEA, but it is important to remember that the advanced or innovational ideas expressed in these speeches were not reflections of the actual guidance picture in Catholic schools of the time. This can be demonstrated, for example, by a 1932 nationwide study (Sister Teresa G. Murray, O.S.B., 1938, p. 105), which indicated that only 5 per cent of the surveyed Catholic secondary schools reported that the source of their interest in formal organized guidance lay in NCEA speeches and activities.

A nationwide survey near the beginning of the period by the Subcommittee on Vocational Guidance of the White House Conference on Child Health and Protection (1932, p. 281) concluded that Catholic high schools were beginning to provide vocational guidance to their pupils. The available research evidence indicates that not only were these beginnings small and scattered, but also that even by the end of the period not much substantial progress had been made. The 1932 study of Catholic high schools by Sister Murray observed that these institutions tended to regard occupational talks during assembly periods as comprising the totality of the vocational guidance program. A nationwide study by Sister M. Mildred Knoebber, O.S.B. (1937), of girls in representative high schools, most of which were Catholic, concluded that the girls expressed disappointment that their schools did not provide them with adequate vocational guidance.

Sister Murray in her study (1938, p. 142) concluded that Catholic high schools seemed fallaciously to think that all guidance ranging from occupational to social is adequately taken care of in religion class. Nonetheless it is true that for the first time Catholic educational theorists began to discuss personal guidance in deeper than "commonsense" fashion.

Throughout this period only a few perceptive Catholic educators (among whom were Fathers E. J. Goebel, F. X. O'Connell, and M. S. Sheehy, Sister M. Madeleva, C.S.C., and Francis M. Crowley) recognized that guidance was an essential part of the school program and were aware that Catholic schoolmen had much to learn from their non-Catholic contemporaries in this regard. Fr. (later Msgr.) Sheehy's book (1929) even outlined constructive measures which Catholic colleges should take to make guidance an integral part of the school program. In 1941 Msgr. Goebel (1941a, p. 374) observed from his wide Catholic school experience that far too many Catholic school people not only believed that guidance was a separate rather than an integrated part of the school program but also felt that it was a modern fad or frill. There was still heavy emphasis on strict school discipline as the primary guidance device. Restrictions on social life remained quite rigid, particularly in girls' high schools and women's colleges.

Program

While a few forward-looking Catholic educational theorists were concerned with organizing formal, comprehensive guidance programs in Catholic schools, comparatively little was done in practice. Thus, for example, in 1932 Fr. Clifford J. LeMay, S.J. (pp. 266–267), decried the fact that "in the field of guidance, there is not even a semblance of organization" in Catholic schools. He called for the establishment of diocesan branches of a National Catholic Guidance Conference to coordinate guidance activities. But it would be thirty years before such an organization was finally formed.

Localized studies (Sister M. P. Freidel, S.N.D., 1933; Sister M. C. Friesenhahn, 1930; Sister M. C. Gansirt, O.P., 1933; Fr. McGuire, 1932; Sister Teresa G. Murray, O.S.B., 1938; Rooney, 1931) of guidance offerings in various dioceses in the early 1930s showed that there were practically no organized guidance programs or adequate guidance activities in any but informal fashion, and even these were minimal. A 1940 national study (Sister A. Cawley, O.S.B., 1941a, p. 225) of Catholic high schools concluded that only half of the schools made the cumulative record available to the teachers. In this regard larger schools were found to be superior to the smaller ones.

On the college level, a 1940 nationwide survey (Sister A. Cawley, O.S.B., 1941b) of Catholic institutions revealed that organized programs of guidance in institutions of higher learning were of comparatively recent introduction and still not universally accepted. The Catholic colleges studied apparently did not provide adequate vocational guidance or placement services. A 1942–1943 national study by Eugenie A. Leonard (1943) concluded that Catholic women's colleges were doing considerably less than their non-Catholic counterparts in the areas of guidance-mindedness, placement services, school government, and specific guidance courses but had more numerous provisions for disciplinary services.

Techniques

As in the preceding periods, the guidance techniques in Catholic schools remained those of direction and advisement. There is no available evidence that Catholic educational theorists discussed the new nondirectivist procedure.

Personnel

A nationwide survey (Sister Teresa G. Murray, O.S.B., 1938, pp. 98–126) of Catholic secondary schools made in 1932 indicated that only ¼ per cent of all the schools studied had full-time guidance counselors; 16 per cent had other than full-time counselors. Nearly 80 per cent of the actual "counseling" done in these schools was performed by the school administrators. Many Catholic educators (cf. Cummings, 1939, p. 17) thought that it was not at all necessary to employ trained guidance counselors, apparently since they believed good classroom instruction of itself was good and sufficient guidance. The school or college chaplain tended to play a large role in religious direction. Virtually none of these priests was professionally trained in guidance, since it was the common belief that seminary training fully equipped the cleric for any and all types of counseling (Sister Teresa G. Murray, O.S.B., 1938, p. 142). Most Catholic school people (cf. Sister M. Annetta, S.L., 1940, p. 106) seemed to believe that the Catholic lay teacher was considerably inferior to the religious in the area of counseling in Catholic elementary and secondary schools.

Other than the proceedings of the CVCC which were published in the *Bulletin of the National Catholic Educational Association,* no special guidance publication appeared during this period. Of interest is that during this period the laity began to publish more widely on the topic of guidance in Catholic educational journals.

GUIDANCE IN THE MODERN PERIOD, 1945–PRESENT

History

World War II gave great impetus to the development of the guidance movement. During the war years the Armed Forces requested high schools and colleges to offer guidance to prospective recruits, so that the military could concentrate its efforts on the combat phase of recruit training. In 1945, at war's end, Veterans Administration (VA) guidance centers began operating in quite a few (but by no means the majority of) colleges and universities

(McCully, 1957). The purpose of these centers was to provide continued and continuing guidance to veterans attending school. In 1951 the Advisement and Guidance Service was formally renamed the Counseling Service, thus indicating a new ideational orientation.

Federal support, direct and indirect, of guidance activities was extended to other areas. In 1946 the passage of the George-Barden Act allocated Federal funds to states which provided vocational guidance services in public vocational secondary schools. The U.S. Office of Education did much to promote guidance by collecting and disseminating school guidance statistics, by publishing influential guidance booklets, and by assisting states to develop their guidance programs. During this period the status of guidance within the U.S. Office was often uncertain. Its Occupational Information and Guidance Service was discontinued in 1952. The next year a Pupil Personnel Services organization was established, but in an obvious de-emphasis it was placed in the Division of State and Local School Systems. Pressure from professional groups brought about the creation in 1955 of a Guidance and Personnel Services Section. A few years later, this title was changed to the Guidance and Counseling Programs Branch.

More important than the establishment of VA counseling services, the GI Bill of Rights guidance benefits, passage of the George-Barden Act, and U.S. Office activities was the Federal government's passage in 1958 of Public Law 85-864, the National Defense Education Act (NDEA). This act represented the greatest single external impetus the guidance movement has ever received. NDEA provided for massive, overall Federal financial support of guidance services in public secondary schools. (Originally, Catholic high schools were not permitted to share in these benefits, except in a most limited way.) Since NDEA, the status and quality of public school guidance programs have probably risen more than in all the preceding years combined. Title II of the Economic Opportunity Act of 1964 extended Federal support of guidance activities, particularly in relation to early school leavers. Major social legislation in 1964 and 1965 supported guidance services for disadvantaged youth and adults. In 1965, NDEA was extended to cover both elementary and college levels.

The mainstream of American public educational thought was becoming increasingly aware of the importance of guidance in the total work of the school. In 1947 the National Association of Secondary-School Principals issued the statement *The Imperative Needs of Youth of Secondary-School Age,* which emphasized the necessity of meshing the school program with the pupils' developing physiopsychological structure. In 1951 the Educational Policies Commission of the National Education Association officially urged the public schools to provide their pupils with moral and spiritual guidance. The 1959 Conant Report on the American public high school placed great stress on improving guidance services. The important 1961 Trump Report, which will influence public secondary education for the next few decades, gave special emphasis to developing the school guidance program through both specialists and teachers.

Emphases and Issues

The full awareness that school guidance encompasses the whole range of pupil problems and needs developed in this period. As a result, guidance theory and emphases moved away from exclusive or even primary stress on vocational guidance to a deeper consideration of all the student's guidance needs, personal, social, and spiritual, as well as vocational and scholastic.

Development and refinement of individual counseling theories and practices probably constitute the most important single guidance emphasis during this period. The directivist theorists of the University of Minnesota group stressed the diagnostic element, whereas the Rogerian school emphasized the clinical approach and counseling qua process. Counseling became the central concern of the guidance movement and the heart of the guidance process. In 1962, the Commission on Guidance in American schools of the American Personnel and Guidance Association published an important document entitled *The Counselor in the Changing World,* which attempted to define the counselor's role in the school setting.

A growing trend in certain hard-core segments within psychological and guidance associations is the view that the only adequate guidance is that provided by professionally trained counselors or specialists. This position tends to denigrate the essential guidance role of the teacher-counselor and the teacher. A counterdevelopment, led by Ruth Strang and Dugald Arbuckle, however, sees the guidance-aware teacher as the heart of the school's guidance program, with the counselor as the prime referral person.

The work of psychologists became directly injected into the bloodstream of the guidance movement during this period. The phenomenological-self theory, developed and elaborated by such men as Carl R. Rogers, Donald Snygg, and Arthur W. Combs, led to an awareness by guidance workers of the fact that problems and needs are reflections both of one's inner self and of one's own evaluation of one's inner self. Robert J. Havighurst and associates stressed developmental tasks which all children and youth must accomplish successfully on their road to maturity. Robert H. Mathewson was in the forefront of those guidance theorists who underscored the necessity of integrating the many and varied elements of the self for successful living. Finally, the emphasis on the experimental study of human development led to a moving away from armchair philosophizing about the nature and growth of people to a more exact understanding of human behavior and its causes. Psychologically rooted theories of vocational choice, developed by Eli Ginzberg, Anne Roe, and particularly Donald E. Super, opened entire new avenues of thinking and practice to both theorists and guidance workers in the field. It is impossible to overemphasize the impact of psychological developments on the guidance movement.

The more alert leaders in the field increasingly see guidance in the total educational setting, interwoven with curriculum and teaching. The counselor is being viewed as an educator within the school setting, and guidance is being conceived as more than just interviewing and testing. In 1949 the ACE revised *The Student Personnel Point of View,* reflecting these emphases.

Program

Fairly well-developed guidance programs became a regular part of the overall school program in most medium-sized and large urban school systems by 1952. Often the wealthier suburban school systems took the lead in this area. Insufficient attention still was accorded to guidance programs in elementary schools.

A mid-World War II poll (F. J. Brown, 1943, p. 181) of non-Catholic colleges and universities by the ACE revealed that these institutions pledged to expand their counseling services and to develop the personnel point of view among their faculties in the postwar years. Another investigation (Eckelberry, 1944) made a year later, however, showed that only a small percentage of institutions of higher learning seriously intended to develop a guidance program or improve the existing one in the postwar years. A 1945 study (Committee on Postwar Education, 1946) of colleges by the North Central Association revealed that the expansion of guidance facilities represented the area of greatest concern to the surveyed institutions. The Association recommended to member colleges that they study their existing personnel programs intensively for the purpose of clarifying objectives, broadening and deepening services, and upgrading counselor standards. During the years following the war, personnel services in colleges grew and became increasingly separate from the curricular and instructional facets of college life (Barry & Wolf, 1955, p. 419).

Techniques

This period was one of guidance and counseling techniques par excellence. Williamson refined his theory of counseling, particularly in his 1950 book *Counseling Adolescents,* in which he delineated his famous steps of the counseling process. But it was the Rogerian nondirectivists who swept the field, so that today practically all counseling psychologists and most guidance workers *theoretically* align themselves with nondirectivistic methodology. In the actual school setting, however, most guidance workers employ the eclectic approach advocated by Frederick C. Thorne (1959) and others on the ground that there is insufficient time or atmosphere for application of a pure nondirectivist approach.

Successes in psychiatric hospitals with group psychotherapy had implications for school guidance. Multiple counseling, as developed by Helen I. Driver and others, was advocated as a method of group cooperation in the solution of problems of pupil personal and social adjustment. New and improved group guidance books for high school students were published. Psychodrama and sociodrama were employed in forward-looking schools.

Personnel

The number of guidance courses and degree programs offered by universities multiplied, chiefly because of the convergence of three outside forces. First, upgraded certification requirements for counselors and guidance specialists created the demand for courses and programs. Second, professional psychological and guidance associations began exerting pressure for both drastically improved standards for guidance personnel and university programs to prepare such personnel. Third, the NDEA authorized the appropriation of Federal funds to universities sponsoring approved guidance institutes, both in the regular academic year and in summer sessions. These funds benefited the sponsoring university and the institute students as well. Counselor preparing institutions began to require supervised counseling experience, often referred to as the *practicum,* for the degree program.

After the war, NVGA became quite vigorous and indeed assumed leadership in the guidance movement, primarily because no other guidance organization was so large, the other organizations tended to be too provincially minded, and no other organization received so much support financially or otherwise from the Federal government. Notwithstanding, by 1949 less than 10 per cent of NVGA members were "professional members" (Speer, 1949, p. 312). Meanwhile, in 1945, the American Psychological Association reorganized and created the Division of Counseling and Guidance (Division 17). In 1952 the name was changed to Division of Counseling Psychology, reflecting the fact that Division 17 had divorced itself from the guidance function to concentrate on the counseling function.

The dream of unification of guidance associations became a reality during this period. After much haggling, a name for the new organization was selected: American Personnel and Guidance Association. Its chief objective is to "foster a continuing improvement of sound personnel and guidance philosophy, principles, policies, and practice in education" and in other social and governmental agencies (Buchwald & Froehlich, 1951). On April 1, 1952, the new organization began its existence with five divisions: Division I, American College Personnel Association (ACPA); Division II, National Association of Guidance Supervisors and Counselor Trainers (NAGSCT); Division III, National Vocational Guidance Association (NVGA); Division IV, Student Personnel Association for Teacher Education (SPATE); and Division V, American School Counselor Association (ASCA). In 1957 Division VI, Rehabilitation Counseling, was added. In 1961, Division II changed its name to Association for Counselor Education and Supervision (ACES), and in 1962 Division VI altered its title to American Rehabilitation Counseling Association (ARCA). As their titles indicate, each division represents a particular interest in some specialized aspect of the guidance movement. APGA is a confederation of separate divisions rather than a single organization; hence it is an example of a working coalition, not of opposite memberships but of groups with similar yet divergent interests. An individual cannot belong to APGA itself but only to one of its constituent divisions. APGA thus serves to unite many varied guidance groups into one effective, coordinate, cooperative group. The creation of APGA has given enormous stimulation to the guidance movement.

By 1950 only 23 states had established mandatory certification requirements for school counselors, 18 of them having done so between 1946 and 1950. By 1955, 27 states had certification requirements. Two years later the number jumped to 34 states, and by 1963 all but 5 states had mandatory certification. By 1960, however, only 25 per cent of the states had mandatory certification requirements for school psychologists.

Within the profession there has been renewed vigor throughout this period for upgrading the preparation of school counselors. In 1945 the Sixth National Conference of State Supervisors of Guidance made recommendations for the professional preparation of prospective counselors, as did the 1945 Chicago and Raleigh conferences, which represented counselor preparing institutions and interested state supervisory personnel. In 1949 the influential booklet *Counselor Preparation* was prepared by eight professional organizations, including NVGA, ACPA, APA Division 17, and the U.S. Office of Education. In 1952 APA Division 17 issued two statements, *Recommended Standards for Training Counseling Psychologists at the Doctoral Level* and *Practicum Training of Counseling Psychologists*. In 1960 APGA's Division II sponsored a five-year investigation called the Cooperative Study of Secondary School Counselor Education Standards. In 1962 the Johnson committee of the APA published its report on psychology in the training of school counselors. The professional associations also developed codes of ethics for their membership in practice. The APA code appeared in 1952; the APGA published its code nine years later.

In 1946 a survey (Froehlich, 1948) of the nation's public secondary schools disclosed that only 8,299 persons were designated as counselors or guidance officers. By 1959, a year after the passage of the NDEA, the number had risen to 13,300, while by 1963 the figure had climbed to 26,947 (R. J. Becker, 1963, p. 4). The 1960 Golden Anniversary White House Conference on Children and Youth recommended 1 counselor for every 250 secondary school students, 1 counselor for every 600 elementary school pupils, and 1 school psychologist for every 2,000 students. By 1963 there was 1 counselor to every 537 pupils in public secondary schools. The number of school psychologists has grown at a much slower pace. In 1948 there were only 88 school psychologists in the APA Division of School Psychologists, but in 1954 there occurred an important development in school psychology, viz., the convocation of the Thayer Conference at West Point. This Conference represented the first major self-appraisal by school psychologists and considered the role and function of school psychologists qua *school* psychologists.

On the college level, the National Association of Deans of Women elected not to join APGA. In 1956, however, it changed its name to the National Association of Women Deans and Counselors, indicating its broader interests. After the war and continuing to the present, the National Association of Deans and Advisers of Men increased in both membership and isolationist policies. In 1952 it altered its title to the National Association of Student Personnel Administrators (NASPA), reflecting the fact that most deans of men are really administrators rather than counselors.

Specialized personnel services expanded in colleges and universities during this period, so that by 1963 there were nearly 600 school psychiatrists who were either full-time or part-time consultants.

APGA publishes its own monthly journal, *The Personnel and Guidance Journal,* the most important professional magazine in the field. (This magazine replaced *Occupations* in 1952, when APGA was organized.) In addition, each division of APGA publishes its own quarterly magazine. Certain members of the APA Division of Counseling Psychology banded together in 1954 to publish a quarterly bulletin, *The Journal of Counseling Psychology.* The other guidance organizations publish journals and bulletins much as they did in the preceding period.

Catholic schools

History

In the late 1950s the Catholic guidance movement arose from its deep, deep slumber and showed signs of life, but from 1945 until that time apparently little development had occurred beyond the preceding period. By mid-century, only 4 of the 107 archdioceses and dioceses had laymen on their school boards, thus hindering infusion of new ideas from nonclerical circles (Msgr. C. J. Ryan, 1951, p. 141). Even by 1966 no special section for guidance comparable to that of the U.S. Office of Education has been set up either in the Department of Education of the National Catholic Welfare Conference (NCWC) or in the National Catholic Educational Association, although NCEA appointed in 1965 a special consultant on guidance services at all school levels.

Several factors hastened the development of guidance in Catholic schools. With the increased student population due to new buildings, more mature

Catholic educators began to be aware of the need for professionalization in all areas of the school program. Beginning in 1955 with the article by J. T. Ellis, informed and articulate Catholics began publishing searching criticisms of Catholic education on the popular level. At first the criticisms were confined to Catholic higher education, but soon they spread to elementary education with the widely publicized McCluskey speech (1960) and finally to the secondary level with the Lee *Catholic World* article (1961a). These constructive criticisms pleaded for a dramatic upgrading of Catholic education in all its aspects. In 1954 a giant forward step was taken with the establishment of the Sister Formation Movement, which seeks to bring about a long-needed reform in the professional preparation of women religious. Correlative to this, the late 1950s witnessed the development of psychological inventories to screen unsuitable candidates from the religious and clerical life.

Emphases and Issues

Most of the Catholic guidance literature and practice still tends to be primarily vocational and religious, with the other areas of guidance being relatively neglected. In many Catholic schools vocational guidance even now means primarily recruitment of candidates for the religious life. Among such psychologically oriented theorists as William C. Cottle, Alexander A. Schneiders, Robert B. Nordberg, and others, however, the emphasis has begun to shift from guidance as character molding to guidance as fostering the growth and development of the entire personality at its deepest levels.

Strict discipline still tends to be stressed as a principal guidance vehicle, but most diocesan school offices urge teachers and guidance workers to refrain from administering corporal punishment. Restrictions on social life in Catholic high schools and colleges seem to have been eased somewhat, but on the whole they continue to be rather strict and sometimes unrealistic, except possibly in some of the larger Catholic universities.

Program

Eugenie A. Leonard's 1945 nationwide study (1946) of Catholic secondary schools revealed that only 35 per cent of the schools surveyed had some type of homeroom guidance; less than one-third of the schools allotted a special time during the school day for individual counseling, group guidance, or both, other than in the homeroom period; vocational guidance usually excluded occupational guidance and placement services of both early school leavers and alumni; and 87 per cent of the schools gave intelligence tests, 72 per cent standardized achievement tests, and only 37 per cent some kind of aptitude test. In 1946 an informed religious observer (Fleege, 1946, p. 357) concurred with the observation that at least 75 per cent of the youths in Catholic secondary schools were not receiving adequate guidance even by minimal standards. The NCWC's 1947 national survey (Sister M. Janet,

S.C., 1949) of Catholic secondary schools revealed that only 33 per cent of the reporting schools stated that in their opinion they had a reasonably well-organized and adequate program of guidance. A 1951 review (Cribbin, 1951, p. 352) of both the literature and the field concluded that there was a singular lack of organization of and in Catholic guidance and personnel work. Three years later, Cribbin (1954) suggested that Catholic colleges did not have a clear concept of the role of guidance in the total school program. Scanlon's study (1955) revealed the not surprising finding that student government in Catholic women's colleges was more tightly controlled by administration and faculty than was the student government in nonsectarian colleges. This close supervision hindered the development of valuable exploratory behaviors, self-actualization, and independent action. A host of studies (see Chapter 5) in the late 1950s concluded that guidance and counseling programs in Catholic secondary schools and colleges are in dire need of improvement. There is, however, a definite trend toward upgrading guidance programs in Catholic educational institutions.

Most Catholic high school plants lack adequate professional facilities for the counselor's office. Brother Philip Harris, O.S.F., was the most vocal Catholic to urge that a division of guidance and pupil personnel services be set up in each diocesan superintendent's office, but many superintendents are apparently still not interested in such a division (Fr. Drolet, 1959, p. 82). Some forward-looking Catholic educators, such as Fr. Moynihan, S.J., have emphasized the need for additional Catholic school guidance clinics. By 1965 some of the more alert and larger Catholic colleges and universities had established comprehensive guidance programs as well as counseling centers.

Techniques

In the early part of this period, most Catholics continued to think of guidance almost exclusively in terms of direction and advisement, but as alert and dynamic Catholic thinkers became psychologically educated, the impact of nondirectivism became more marked. The Catholic pioneer in this area was undoubtedly Fr. Charles A. Curran. Meanwhile Fr. James F. Moynihan, S.J., was writing articles espousing nondirectivism. While at the more advanced Catholic levels there was a definite turning away from the old techniques of advisement and heavy-handed direction, character molding and advisement still prevailed on the level of Catholic school practice.

Personnel

During this period, especially after the passage of the NDEA, practically all the larger Catholic universities offered course work or degree programs in guidance. Catholic school people flocked to these courses. This growth was in large measure due to outside forces, including state certification requirements, regional accrediting associations, and increased professionalization of public school guidance workers. Forward-looking priests began to specialize in guidance, and by 1960 summer courses in guidance were filled with women religious. Unfortunately, too few Catholic universities have availed themselves of the opportunity of establishing NDEA guidance institutes in the summer and, particularly, in the winter sessions.

Eugenie A. Leonard's (1945) nationwide study of Catholic secondary schools concluded that only 21 per cent of the surveyed institutions had specialized counselors. Moreover, no information was given as to whether or not these counselors were trained. Since that time, Catholic schools have slowly endeavored to improve the quality of their guidance workers. A 1945 nationwide study (Mary B. Walsh & Eugenie A. Leonard, 1946) of Catholic women's colleges revealed that only 34 per cent of the responding institutions had lay counselors, whether trained or untrained. There was mixed opinion among Catholic women's college administrators who employed lay counselors as to the desirability of hiring lay people as counselors. Even at the present time, most deans of men, deans of women, hall prefects, housemothers, and chaplains at Catholic institutions of higher learning have little if any professional preparation in guidance. Practically all the studies show personnel services in Catholic colleges to be uncoordinated, excessively limited, and carried out by professionally unprepared personnel.

The hope of establishing a national Catholic psychological association and a national Catholic guidance association came to fruition during this period. In 1948 the American Catholic Psychological Association (ACPA) was founded to infuse the Catholic dimension into psychology and to interpret psychology to the Catholic community. The beginnings of a national Catholic guidance association took place in New York when the Catholic High School Guidance Council of the Archdiocese of New York was formed in 1951 (Brother J. M. Egan, F.S.C.H., 1956). By 1958 there were 10 diocesan guidance councils in various parts of the country, and it was decided to form a national coordinating agency, the National Conference of Catholic Guidance Councils (NCCGC). Meanwhile a parallel development was taking place. In 1955 a few Catholic counselors attending the annual APGA meeting decided to hold a session at that time to discuss special problems and interests of Catholic counselors. Thus a second organization, Catholic Counselors in APGA, was born. A third parallel development was the formation of the editorial board of the newly established (1956) national Catholic guidance journal, the *Catholic Counselor*. The majority of this board was composed of Catholic Counselors in APGA. In 1962 these three groups were unified into a new national Catholic guidance organization, the National Catholic Guidance Conference (NCGC), which subsumed all their functions. In so doing it provided the leadership in professional guidance lacking in previous decades. NCGC sponsors a national meeting which convenes every

Palm Saturday and Sunday, on the two days before and in the same city as the national APGA meeting. Early leaders in the new organization included Brother John M. Egan, F.S.C.H., Brother Philip Harris, O.S.F., Edward Daubner, Norbert Riegert, Fr. Edmund W. Olley, Fr. George H. Moreau, O.M.I., and Brother Marion F. Belka, S.M. (Editorial Staff, 1963).

In 1950 the American Catholic Psychological Association started to publish its bimonthly *Newsletter*. Some years later it began to publish at irregular intervals the *Proceedings* of its meetings, and in 1963 it commenced to issue its semiannual journal, *The Catholic Psychological Record*. In 1956 the first national Catholic guidance journal, the *Catholic Counselor,* appeared thrice annually. The chief purpose of this new journal was to act as an organ of communication for Catholics engaged in guidance. Initially, much of its content was informational rather than professional in intent. When the NCGC was formed in 1962, a *News Digest* was inaugurated on a quarterly basis, subsuming most of the communicative functions of the *Catholic Counselor*. In 1964, this publication was suspended and succeeded by the *National Catholic Guidance Conference Journal,* "a professional journal of theory, research, and opinion" published quarterly. Each year, in its autumn issue, the *Journal* publishes the proceedings of the annual NCGC meeting.

Books on group guidance for Catholic high school students made their appearance in this period. Begun in 1957, the first and probably the most comprehensive of these was the Insight Series of four books, one for each year of high school, written by James J. Cribbin, Brother Philip Harris, O.S.F., and Fr. William J. McMahon. In 1958 Brother Joseph J. Panzer, S.M., edited *Group Guidance for Boys,* a series of four workbooks in group guidance for use by Catholic high school students.

2

THE DEVELOPING PERSON:
A FRAMEWORK FOR GUIDANCE

The task of self-knowledge

The essence of Socrates's admonition to the youth of Athens, in an era which had not yet learned to call itself the "age of anxiety," is distilled in the familiar maxim "Know thyself." Self-knowledge constituted, for Socrates, not only the beginning and end of wisdom but a positive virtue in the practical order, since adequate self-knowledge enables a person to cope effectively with the tasks of daily living. Indeed Polonius assumed adequate self-knowledge as a prerequisite to facing life when he urged Laertes: "This above all, to thine own self be true." And it well may be that the fulfillment of the goal of self-knowledge, of the formation of a meaningful personal identity of the self, was accomplished more easily in ancient Greece or medieval Denmark than is possible in modern America. The self-identity of the Athenian or of the Dane was rooted in his birthright as the offspring of the nobleman, the freedman, or the slave. But American society strives to afford manifold educational, occupational, and social alternatives to the definition of self.

33

Formation of a meaningful personal identity, i.e., the task of self-knowledge, circumscribes the human predicament. Such contemporary psychologists as McArthur (1961, p. 59) have abandoned the Socratic imperative in formulating as the cardinal developmental need of the human person an adequate and meaningful response to the question "Who am I?" McArthur has observed that, in the process of forging a response to this prime question, the individual undergoes "diffuse agitation over who on earth he may be," as he seeks an identity in an age which has indeed learned to call itself the age of anxiety. Erikson, the distinguished psychoanalyst who has lucidly portrayed the "identity crisis" attendant upon the threshold of adulthood (1959, pp. 101–164), has observed that contemporary behavioral scientists, counselors, and guidance workers have focused their attention on self-identification as the prime task of human development and that "we begin to conceptualize matters of identity at the very time in history when they become a problem" (1950, p. 242).

For it is at this point in world history, characterized by corporate identities, by manifold alternatives to self-definition, by global conflicts imperiling the continued survival of the race, and by the assumption by governments of enormous powers over individual destinies, that man has come to question most deeply the meaning of his individual existence. It is from these considerations, from continued probing into the meaning and worth of the individual person's existence, that the most characteristic of anxieties present in the modern age of anxiety, "existential anxiety," arises, since existential anxiety is precisely "the anxiety of a man facing the limits of his existence with its fullest implications" (Ellenberger, 1958, p. 118).

Primacy of Self-identity

At first glance, the response a person renders to the question "Who am I?" appears far too susceptible to an overfacile and perhaps superficial answer to occupy the position of psychological import assigned to it. Indeed, in simplest outline form, responses to this pivotal question can be found in the first few pages of the Baltimore catechism.

But the formulation of a clear and adequate identity is no easy task. As Wheelis (1958, p. 18) has suggested, upon the answer given to the question "Who am I?" hinge the responses to two additional significant questions: "Where am I going?" and "What is the meaning of life?" Echoing Erikson's view with the observation that "Nowadays, the sense of self is deficient," Wheelis (1958, p. 19) has provided a cogent but nontechnical definition of "identity" in its salient psychological sense:

> Identity is a coherent sense of self. It depends upon the awareness that one's endeavors and one's life make sense, that they are meaningful in the context in which life is lived. It also depends upon stable values, and upon the conviction that one's actions and values are harmoniously

related. It is a sense of wholeness, of integration, of knowing what is right and what is wrong and of being able to choose.

An indication of the centrality of the problem of self-identification, of the formulation of a clear sense of self-identity, was suggested by Cottle (1963, p. 3), a Catholic psychologist, when he declared that "the answer to the question 'Who am I?' . . . requires clarification of interests, goals, values, feelings, and attitudes"; he emphasized that this clarification "must occur before the client is in a position to make life choices, large *or* small." Self-identification is prime among the tasks to be met on the road to adulthood precisely because *a person behaves in a manner consistent with the way he identifies or "defines" himself*. It is commonplace for teachers to encounter students who possess a high degree of intelligence but who are unable to perceive or define themselves as "good students" and who consequently fail to achieve their academic potential. The example can be multiplied infinitely in work and in social situations.

In the answer each person formulates to the question "Who am I?" is to be found not only his attitude toward the meaning of life but his *perception of the world and of himself in relation to it*. A person bases his life choices and his behavior on this perception or set of perceptions. Psychologists have given the term "self-concept" to this set of complementary and intersecting perceptions of the world and of self, perceptions in response to the inner imperative of formulating a personal self-identification. Indeed, many psychologists contend that the self-concept is the principal factor influencing a person's behavior. In other words, the response to the question "Who am I?" determines the manner in which one is ready to relate to the world, a world he views refracted through the prism of self-concept.

Self-identity and personality function

The self-concept constitutes the core of a person's perceptions and feelings *about himself, as perceived by himself*. It comprises that core of perceptions and feelings which a person identifies as *what is really "me."* All the strongest, most lasting thoughts, feelings, and emotions a person has about himself, all his hopes and aspirations, he perceives as "what is really me." This group of perceptions which he has about himself, what he can call "really me," is his self-concept. As the person develops psychologically from childhood to adulthood, he begins to distinguish and separate his closest feelings about himself—what is really me—from everything else of which he is aware in any way whatever. Psychologically, the arena of consciousness, of everything of which the person is aware in any way whatever, is termed the *perceptual* or *phenomenal field*. The phenomenal field contains every perception which he can in any way call "mine" (his family friends, school, job, possessions, teachers, religion, values, even his most intimate thoughts and emotions).

In the center of this field stands his self-concept, through which he relates his self to every other perception in the field and through which he organizes the phenomenal field meaningfully for himself. In so doing he seeks to organize his experience into meaningful patterns.

Though the notions of self-concept and of phenomenal field contain much in common with a "commonsense" approach to the study of human behavior, the perceptual or phenomenological theory of human behavior and personality organization is a relatively recent development (cf. Combs & Snygg, 1959; Snygg, 1941). Among the many psychologists and counseling theorists who have focused their attention on the elaboration of a phenomenological view of behavior, Combs and Snygg, as well as Rogers (who developed a system of counseling based on this approach), have had wide and decisive influence on counseling and guidance. The counselor following a phenomenological approach to the study of behavior attempts to understand the attitudes, feelings, and behavior of his client through *empathy*. To this end, the counselor endeavors to insert himself, both intellectually and emotionally, into the client's phenomenal field and, as it were, to see through his eyes, to perceive and experience the world of "valenced" objects and values as that world appears to the client. The counselor strives to experience for himself both the client's perceptions and his predispositions to perceive certain types of persons, objects, and events in certain ways. In the words of Combs and Snygg (1959, p. 11), "This approach seeks to understand the behavior of the individual from his point of view," because "people behave as they do in consequence of how things seem to them." In this frame of reference (C. R. Rogers, 1951, p. 494) behavior is seen as a function of human perception, specifically of the person's perception of himself in relation to the phenomenal field: *"The best vantage point for understanding behavior is from the internal frame of reference of the individual himself."* The phenomenologically oriented counselor strives to enter the perceptual field of his client in order to comprehend the motives governing and influencing his behavior. This approach is based on the highly significant assumption that human behavior is purposive, that, to the behaver, his behavior appears a reasonable mode of acting based upon the situation as he perceives it. "Behavior is a reaction to the field as perceived," Rogers (1951, p. 494) has suggested, and "there is then no such thing as random trial-and-error behavior," because "behavior is always purposeful and in response to reality as it is perceived."

Nature of the Self-concept

At the psychological "center" of the person's perceptual field, according to phenomenological theory, stands a group of percepts which gradually become differentiated from what is perceived as not "really me." This core of self-percepts forms the self-concept, the phenomenal self, which can be described as a sort of perceptual prism through which the person perceives every "object" in the phenomenal field, including himself. The person tends to accept and incorporate into the field those percepts which are consistent with his self-concept and to reject those which are inconsistent. Through the prism of the self-concept, he attaches positive or negative valences to the objects of his perceptual experience. A student who thinks of himself as a class leader, for example, may perceive other students who show leadership qualities as threats to the realization of his own ambitions. He attaches negative valences to his perceptions of these presumed rivals. Consequently, he searches for their faults to justify his negative perceptions of them. He is likely to behave with hostility and unfriendliness toward these presumed rivals, even though he and they may have many common interests.

The self-core or self-concept thus becomes the unifying element in the perceptual field. As the psychological center of the field, it is the prime "agent" in behaving: *"Most of the ways of behaving which are adopted by the organism are those which are consistent with the concept of self"* (Rogers, 1951, p. 507). Conscious behavior is interpreted in phenomenological theory as an attempt to project the self-concept into reality, a notion which holds manifold implications in the guidance situation, for "Since it is always the self which is perceived as behaving, behavior must always be appropriate to the phenomenal self" (Combs & Snygg, 1959, p. 44). Thus, for example, a female high school student may perceive herself as rather plain and unattractive. Her younger, blue-eyed, blonde sister has always been referred to by neighbors and relatives as "the pretty child." Though less attractive than this younger sister, the student has regular features and a pleasant appearance and by wider than family standards could not be considered homely. Yet she thinks of herself as unattractive. Therefore she might spend little time in improving her appearance, might select clothes haphazardly, might fail to take care with personal grooming, and the like. Her behavior is predicated upon her perception of herself as unattractive. Since her appearance (behavior) is a direct consequence of the ways she perceives herself (phenomenal self), she is perceived by others as rather unattractive. The reaction of others tends to reinforce her perception of herself. The reactions of others are incorporated into her phenomenal field since they are consistent with her self-concept. Thus the self-concept directs behavior, and self-directed behavior tends to reinforce the self-concept. Rogers (1951, pp. 36–37) offered an empirically derived definition of the phenomenal self in relation to the perceptual field:

> If a definition seems useful, it might be said that clinical experience and research evidence would suggest a definition along these lines. The self-concept, or self-structure, may be thought of as an organized configuration of perceptions of the self. . . . It is composed of such elements as the perceptions of one's characteristics and abilities; the percepts and

concepts of the self in relation to others and to the environment; the value qualities which are perceived as associated with experiences and objects; and goals and ideas which are perceived as having positive or negative valence.

Consistency in the Self-concept

In the determination of behavior, the person's self-concept thus forms the decisive *frame of reference* (Sherif & Sherif, 1956, pp. 77–114) through which he perceives and responds to the elements of his experience. But neither the self-concept nor the perceived world is static. Both are subject to constant modification and revision as new and diverse percepts are encountered. As new situations confront the self, the person reorganizes the phenomenal field to accommodate his perceptions of both self and situation, either by accepting and incorporating those perceptions which are consistent with his self-concept or by reacting defensively to them (e.g., denying their relevance for self) so as to maintain the stability and consistency of the self-concept (Lecky, 1945, pp. 12–18). Perceptions which threaten the consistency of the self-concept are not incorporated unless the person has developed a reasonable degree of flexibility in self-perception. Thus, for example, the female student referred to earlier who is told by a friend or a teacher that she really is a pleasant and attractive girl is likely to reject this perception of herself unless she is open to experience not in consonance with her perceptual field. *The rigidity or permeability of the phenomenal field in regard to new perceptions is a major factor in determining one's behavior and ultimately the quality of one's psychosocial adjustment.*

Even behaviors which appear to the observer as "wild and fluctuating" are interpreted by phenomenological theory as attempts of the self to maintain the consistency of the self-concept, i.e., as purposive responses to the field as perceived. Such apparently fluctuating behaviors, however, are not fully understandable until the observer shares with the behaver the behaver's perceptions of himself and the world (Rogers, 1956, p. 1063). Without exception, Rogers (1951, p. 486) has maintained, *"The organism reacts as an organized whole to the phenomenal field,"* and "one of the most basic characteristics of organic life is its tendency toward total, organized, goal-directed responses." Attracting forces which induce the self to behave toward an object or person are the *valences* attached to the figures in the field by the self (Bischof, 1964, pp. 582–583). The strength of attraction or of repulsion of a percept in the field constitutes its valence. As new objects enter the field, especially when the person is not rigidly closed to new perceptions, valences attached to other percepts may change. Thus the perceptual field is constantly in the process of dynamic reorganization. A high school senior, for example, may be experiencing a conflict within himself occasioned by his attraction to the fields of art and of biology. A research career in biological science holds a positive valence for him; so does a career as a creative artist. When he learns (perhaps through the provision of career information by a school counselor) of opportunities in the field of medical illustration, both art and biology considered in themselves seem less attractive; i.e., their valences change as a new percept enters the field. Many conflict situations in daily life can be solved relatively easily when the person is open to new information and experience and when he has the capacity to reappraise and reorganize his phenomenal field and himself in relation to it. "By the perceptual field, we mean the entire universe, including himself, as it is experienced by the individual" (Combs & Snygg, 1959, p. 20) at a given moment, subject to reorganization and revision in the next moment in response to new perceptions of self and situation. Thus, "there is no behavior except to meet a present [perceived] need" (Rogers, 1951, p. 492).

Self-experience, self-acceptance, and mental health

Self-concept psychology thus places the highest premium on self-knowledge, since it regards the self-concept as the primary factor in influencing both behavior and the frame of reference through which the person perceives the world of reality (Rogers, 1953, pp. 48–63; Rogers, 1961, pp. 243–272). The issue of *adequate* self-knowledge, however, transcends the question of the self-concept. The self-concept held by the bright but academically undistinguished student (alluded to earlier) definitely influences his behavior in response to the phenomenal field as he perceives it, as does that of the female student who perceives herself as a "plain Jane." But their self-concepts are unrealistic. The underachieving student refuses to define himself as an intellectually superior person who can demonstrate his intellectual adequacy in the classroom situation. To that extent, his self-concept fails to conform to reality, and his self-knowledge is inadequate. In the second case, the girl refuses to accept the judgment of others about her attractiveness, and her self-knowledge is similarly inadequate. As Schneiders (1955, p. 75), a Catholic psychologist, has observed, "*Self-knowledge requires an intelligent inventory of personal assets and liabilities,*" in congruence with "reality" and free from the necessity of deceiving oneself, either through positively or negatively distorting one's own self-picture.

The converse of the bright but academically undistinguished student might be the person of limited mental ability who has developed a perception of himself as intellectually brilliant. His parents, members of a social or ethnic upper-middle-class group which prizes academic achievement, have urged him to excel in school and perhaps have made unrealistic demands upon him. His teachers anticipate that a child from a culturally "privileged" home will excel in school. These forces act on him in such a way as to curtail the available alternatives to self-definition. He is led to define himself as an intellectually brilliant student and to attempt to behave in accordance with that perception. As long as his competition from classmates is limited, he may succeed in implementing the role of the high achiever. But eventually he will begin to exhibit frustration as he encounters intellectually more able classmates homogeneously grouped in his high school years. Those frustrations will cause tensions and anxieties, which are objectively needless since they are rooted in an inaccurate knowledge of self-capabilities. Unless he opens himself to re-evaluation and reorganization of the phenomenal field, he may be led to employ crippling adjustive mechanisms to defend the consistency of a faulty self-concept, in the face of *self-experience* incongruent with self-perception. His self-concept is as unrealistic as that of the bright student who thinks of himself as an average achiever. But in this case the self-concept will be more difficult to maintain as he experiences failure instead of success. His self-experience is likely to be incongruent with his self-perception. The inevitable corollary to the *self-as-perceived* is the *self-as-experienced,* the self inferred from the reaction of others toward the self. For healthy growth and development, realistic self-knowledge based upon openness to the meaning of one's self-experience is demanded.

Shaping One's Experience

There is some disagreement among phenomenological theorists concerning the sequential relationship between self-perception and self-experience, since the person tends to shape his experience in consonance with his perception of himself, in reacting to the field as perceived. It seems reasonable, however, that self-experience is initially antecedent to the formulation of a self-identity. Staton (1963, p. 30) has suggested that the self-concept "probably grows out of the particular experiences the individual undergoes." Brammer and Shostrom (1960, p. 37) clearly regard the self-concept as issuing from self-experience: "The concept of self is a learned attribute, a progressive concept starting from birth and differentiating steadily through childhood and adolescence like an unfolding spiral." The individual, in reflecting on his experience of self—the reactions of his parents, peers, teachers, and casual acquaintances to his behavior, the evaluations they place on his behavior, the manner in which "reality" responds to him—gradually distinguishes those *self-definitions* which are mirrored in his self-experience. Initially, the self-concept is formed by the person through reflection on his growing awareness of his distinctiveness, of the modes of behavior which make him peculiarly aware of himself, of the ways of behaving, relating, and reacting which he comes to regard as characteristic of "I" or "me." Once established and reinforced through experience (i.e., through the appropriate response of others and of reality), the self-concept can proceed largely to create its own self-experience. The person tends to place himself in situations in which he perceives he can successfully "play the role" dictated by his self-concept. Available alternatives to self-definition may thus be limited by the need to defend oneself against one's self-experience. If one's perception of himself is not grossly distorted and is reasonably congruent with reality, his self-directed self-experience is likely to prove successful and his perception of himself is reinforced. Even the person whose self-concept is unrealistic, who has not appraised himself properly, attempts to create and direct his own self-experience and often succeeds in doing so. The hypothetical student who has high ability but perceives himself as a person unable or unwilling to achieve academic superiority is likely to behave in such a fashion that he indeed fails to attain academic excellence. His parents, peers, and teachers then come to regard him largely in the same way he regards himself, as a person incapable of academic accomplishment, and they will react to him accordingly. In this wise, his self-perception is reinforced by his self-experience, a self-experience largely self-directed and self-initiated as he behaves in accord with his perception of himself.

In short, initially "we learn the most significant and fundamental facts about ourselves from . . . inferences about ourselves made as a consequence of the ways we perceive others behaving toward us. We learn who we are and what we are from the way we are treated by those who surround us" (Combs & Snygg, 1959, p. 134). Once a person learns who he is, his self behaves in such a manner as to maintain the consistency of the perceived self, and this implies that he largely creates his own self-experience in congruence with the way he perceives himself.

Openness to Meaning of Experience

Persons who perceive themselves realistically, who are open to self-experience, and who have little need to distort their perceptions of themselves or of figures in the field are regarded by phenomenological and other psychologists of personality function and dysfunction as mentally healthy. On the other hand, persons who seriously distort or deny their perceptions in order to maintain a faulty or unrealistic self-percept are regarded as emotionally maladjusted (Shaffer & Shoben, 1956, pp. 286–287). The modes of behavior exhibited by poorly adjusted persons in order to defend the integrity of ill-formed self-pictures constitute the "mechanisms of defense." The salient point is that *self-acceptance* of self-experience is central to sound personal adjustment and mental health (Rogers, 1961, pp. 87–90). The person who needs to distort his perception of reality or of his self-experience needs to do so precisely because he cannot accept himself as he is but must attempt to maintain a distorted, elevated, depressed, or skewed core of self-perceptions. He is driven to distorted perceptions of other figures of the field and of the objects and persons of his experience precisely because the elements of his self-experience are too threatening to his faulty self-picture. The person who has formed a realistic picture of himself, however, and who has learned a degree of flexibility in his thinking about the inner core of "what is really me," has no similar need to deny or distort his self-experience, because his degree of self-acceptance is such that he can accept and incorporate even highly threatening and psychologically noxious self-experiences without damage to the internal security of his perceived self-core. In modern phenomenological terms, *adjustment* (or *mental health*) and *maladjustment* hinge on the relationship between self-perception, self-experience, and the ability to appraise the self realistically.

The self-concept denotes the self-as-perceived-by-the-self. Self-experience denotes the self as inferred from a realistic perception of the reactions of others to oneself, i.e., the awareness of the self as judged by others. Self-acceptance denotes the ability to integrate the self-concept and self-experience. As Schneiders (1955, p. 77) has suggested, "Self-acceptance is the opposite of self-negation and is based on an objective knowledge or appreciation of self. It does not mean self-condonement nor complaisance about one's weaknesses" but rather implies a readiness to structure one's self-picture in accord with one's self-experience in a normally flexible manner. Zeller (1963, pp. 41–48), a psychiatrist, has emphasized that self-knowledge precedes self-acceptance and acceptance of others and is essential to positive mental health.

Accurate Self-appraisal

This is the psychological portrait of the well-adjusted person, who can face the realities of life with little need to deceive himself, who has developed a secure self-knowledge free from distortion, and who is able to integrate his closest feelings about himself with the world of experience.

A false notion of humility among many Catholics, especially religious, tends to impede accurate self-appraisal. In this distorted sense, humility is confused with self-depreciation or self-negation. Misunderstanding Christ's admonition to die unto oneself, many Catholics tend to undervalue their own capabilities and their own worth as persons. Such a false concept of humility, masquerading behind piety, begets what Fr. Ramirez, O.F.M., has termed the "negative [self-] regard complex," which he believes lies at root in many personality disorders. True religious humility is identified with realistic self-appraisal. As Fr. Ramirez (1959, pp. 161–202) remarked, "The most realistic and truthful approach to God is . . . the most humble." False humility not only impedes accurate self-knowledge but also impedes the development of a mature religious outlook and often causes Catholics to retire from active participation in the affairs of Church or community.

Developmental life experiences

The interplay between self-concept and self-experience, i.e., the formation of secure self-identity, suggests the importance both of the ability to abstract the sense of self from the world of experience and of the quality of life experiences encountered by the developing self. Staton (1963, pp. 28–32) and others (Bonner, 1961, pp. 429–455) maintain that the sense of self develops as the cumulative inference of the reality of self-identity from the experiences of one's life. Consequently it may be expected that supportive, identity-fostering experiences in childhood and adolescence tend to lead to fully functioning, flexible, self-accepting, reasonably well-adjusted adult "selves." On the other hand, experiences which threaten the security of the developing self tend to produce rigid, constricted, poorly functioning adult selves who need to make frequent use of crippling and disabling mechanisms to distort their perceptions of themselves and of reality. Some kinds and qualities of life experiences seem to produce well-adjusted, integrated persons capable of meeting life on realistic terms, while others tend to produce persons prone to psychosocially maladaptive behavior. One of the present challenges to developmental psychology is the determination and cataloguing of favorable and unfavorable life experiences. Since the process of empirical investigation, in behavioral sciences no less than in physical and biological sciences, is slow and arduous, there is presently little uniformity of belief regarding the precise conditions and experiences which foster optimal self-development. Nevertheless, many developmental psychologists have attempted partial catalogues, and there is some evidence that a synthesis will emerge as a result of improved methods of observation and experimentation and an increase in longitudinal studies of the development of normally integrated personalities (cf. Nurnberger, Ferster, & Brady, 1963, pp. 108–134).

Concept of "Developmental Tasks"

A cornerstone in the emerging synthesis is likely to be the concept of *developmental tasks,* a theoretical construct which appears viable enough to serve as a general conceptual matrix into which the results of empirical research in human developmental patterns might be arrayed. The developmental-tasks concept was first observed in scientific studies of the physiological development of animals and is analogous to certain features of the psychoanalytic schedule of development elaborated by Sigmund Freud and his followers (cf. English & Pearson, 1945, pp. 15–19). The concept has been outlined clearly by Erikson (1950, pp. 61–62), an ego psychologist in the psychoanalytic tradition, who (1956) added the concept of phase-specific developmental tasks, and by Havighurst, an educational psychologist specializing in human development. It is Havighurst's formulation (1953, p. 2) of the developmental-task construct which probably has most directly influenced practitioners in guidance and counseling: "*A developmental task is a task which arises at or about a certain period in the life of the individual, successful achievement of which leads to his happiness and to success with later tasks, while failure leads to unhappiness in the individual, disapproval by the society, and difficulty with later tasks."* Inherent in the concept of the developmental task is the notion of a series of common experiences in the process of maturing into adulthood, through which the person achieves satisfaction or happiness within himself, social approval, and facility in mastering the situations which life presents. In short, the end product of the successful meeting of the demands of the tasks encountered at each stage of development is the formation of the secure, adequate self-identity. As Erikson (1959, p. 52) has expressed it, ". . . this [epigenetic] principle states that anything that grows has a *ground plan,* and that out of this ground plan the *parts* arise, each part having its *time* of special ascendancy, until all parts have arisen to form a *functioning whole."* The "time of special ascendancy" for each part or element of the developing personality has been identified by Erikson as the *critical stage in development,* during which the developmental tasks related to the particular element of personality in question must be satisfactorily resolved. Failure to execute the phase-specific developmental task satisfactorily during the critical period of its ascendancy results in an immature organism unable to cope successfully with succeeding tasks of development (cf. J. P. Scott, 1958, pp. 42–54). As Havighurst (1953, pp. 2–4) has suggested. "The tasks which the individual must learn—the *developmental tasks* of life—are those things that constitute healthy and satisfactory growth in our society . . . if the task is not learned, the failure will stand in the way of learning a series of later tasks." In phenomenological terms, faulty self-experience reinforces faulty self-identity and inhibits satisfactory psychosocial adjustment.

Origins of Developmental Tasks

Little agreement exists among behaviorial scientists concerning the specific developmental tasks which arise at critical life stages. Some psychologists (cf. Mussen, 1963, pp. 21–24) investigating human development have tended to become excessively concerned with such activities as psychomotor coordination, neuroanatomical maturation, and the production of catalogues and scales which purport to cite the typical age at which the "normal" child learns to crawl, lifts his head to his shoulder, is able to sit alone for thirty seconds, and the like. Others have focused attention primarily on interpersonal relationships and the learning of appropriate social roles. Indeed, each phase of human behavior presents its particular set of developmental tasks, so that the tasks set for the developing biological organism are couched in terms of physical maturation, while those set for the developing psychosocial organism are couched in terms of the maturation of adequate self-identity. "Thus," says Havighurst (1953, pp. 4–5) "development tasks may arise from physical maturation, from the pressure of cultural processes upon the individual, from the desires, aspirations, and values of the emerging personality, and they arise in most cases from combinations of these factors acting together." While recognizing the importance of psychobiological factors in human development, theorists and practitioners in counseling and guidance tend to center their concern on tasks and critical stages in educational, vocational, social, and often emotional development. Doubtless this concern is related to the nature of the educational setting in which they work. Therefore counseling and guidance theorists have sought to identify the broad major developmental tasks of childhood and adolescence and to develop methods to assist students to meet adequately developmental life experiences. Mathewson (1955, pp. 62–63) has in this vein identified five broad "need areas" which correspond to major developmental tasks: (1) the need for appraisal and self-understanding; (2) the need for adjustment to the self as well as to present and future environmental realities; (3) the need for orientation to changing environmental conditions; (4) the need for development of personal potentialities; and (5) the "ultimate need," development toward an ideal, specifically, "a spiritual ideal, independent of circumstance, to which man can relate his individual and social existence and performance." To each of these need areas, Mathewson (1962, pp. 16–17) suggests, corresponds a "guidance process area" through which counselors help students satisfy developmental needs.

Prime Task: Self-actualization

Each of these specific needs may be considered an aspect of the principal need for *self-actualization* or *self-realization* in the varied spheres of human behavior. In this light, the fifth of Matthewson's needs, development toward a spiritual ideal, assumes an importance which organizes and orders other needs. Epigenetically and teleologically, spiritual development toward a participated similitude in the Divine Being constitutes the ultimate self-actualization. Thus spiritual development needs assume an ordering importance. As Dom Thomas Verner Moore, O.S.B. (1950, p. 409), a pioneering priest-psychiatrist, expressed it, "If man is a member not only of a family and of a state, and perhaps too of a supra-national society of peoples, but also a citizen of the universal society in which God is the supreme intelligence in a world of intelligible beings, he must not only be adjusted to and live in harmonious relations with his family, his state and the supranational society, but also be adjusted to and live in harmonious relation with God, the Supreme Intelligence . . . to bring about a harmonious organization of human life." It is in this vein that Fr. Joseph Nuttin (1962, pp. 246–250), the noted psychologist at the University of Louvain, regards spiritual development needs as the "universal integration" of all other human needs. What is highly significant, however, in the thought of Fr. Nuttin and of such writers as Fr. Teilhard de Chardin, S.J., is that man satisfies his need to grow toward God precisely *in and through* his growth and development in the natural order. Mother Marygrace McCullough, R.C.E. (1963, p. 25), has observed that "The deepest response-to-value is response to God, in whom all other forms of response-to-value are contained." Spiritual needs become satisfiable only through the satisfaction of other human needs. In this fashion, spiritual self-actualization, i.e., growth toward God, is the epigenetic culmination of physical, emotional, rational, and social development. Spiritual development is not other than, but dependent upon, satisfactory human development, i.e., growth in the world. Yet it is interesting to note that many Catholics, especially Catholic educators, fail to grasp the essentially developmental nature of spiritual life, expecting youth to hold mature spiritual attitudes and values without the reversions, indecisions, and uncertainties which are inevitably encountered in the process of development.

To provide appropriate guidance services in the school setting geared to the fundamental needs of students and to assist students in executing successfully the developmental tasks they face, guidance workers need a broad general knowledge of developmental life experiences, an orientation to developmental psychology, and the technical skill necessary to understand, interpret, and translate into practice continuing empirical investigation of human developmental patterns.

Childhood and socialization

Most psychologists consider *socialization* the chief developmental task of the years of life between birth and the onset of puberty. The child at birth is almost exclusively oriented toward the satisfaction of his own bodily needs, since the alternative is death. His principal "attention" is centered within himself. He makes constant demands on the environment, which for him consists of a mother and a father. The well-adjusted adult, on the other hand, is altruistic, attentive to the needs of others, and lives in harmony with the psychological and social environment. The gradual process through which the child moves toward adulthood is socialization, *"the process by which someone learns the ways of a given society or social group so that he can function within it"* as a responsible adult (Elkin, 1963, p. 4). Subordinate to socialization as the principal developmental task of childhood are many other developmental tasks, ranging from physiological maturational tasks to intellective-educational tasks.

The child emerges at birth into a world which consists for him essentially of a mother or mother substitute, in the sense of the person who cares for his physical needs, furnishing food, shelter, and warmth, introducing him to pleasurable body satisfactions, and, for his psychological or emotional needs, providing security and love. It is only later that the child learns to recognize and respond to father, because mother, during the first months of life, indeed forms the social milieu for the child. Strang (1959, pp. 97–99), a pioneer in developmental guidance, has suggested that it is precisely during the first few weeks of life that the child starts to make his first evaluation of the world into which he has been born as a friendly, supportive environment in which his needs are met and begins to orient himself accordingly. The English psychiatrist Bowlby (1961, pp. 12–19), in research sponsored by UNESCO, has demonstrated that complete or partial maternal deprivation lies at the root of serious maladjustments in later life. Psychoanalysts generally (cf. A. Freud, 1960b, pp. 26–29), following the schedule of development elaborated by Sigmund Freud, have assigned to early childhood a crucial role in the development of the adult personality.

Sense of Basic Trust

It is probable that the child's first "lesson" in socialization occurs with the introduction of feeding schedules during the early months of life. Before the family physician is likely to suggest a feeding schedule as an alternative to instant gratification of the child's needs, the child's physiological, especially gastric, organs must be developed sufficiently to be able to tolerate less frequent feedings. Thus this first social developmental task is based on the prior accomplishment of physical developmental tasks. But far more than the satisfaction of the need for food is involved, for the child learns that the environment too has its own special demands and that his needs can be satisfied only as the demands of the environment are satisfied.

Similarly, this early experience teaches the child a basic sense of trust that mother, or the social environment, is ready and willing to fulfill his needs. Many psychoanalysts (cf. Spitz, 1959, pp. 14–20) suggest that, in feeding, the child first develops a genuine sense of identification with his mother, an identification which serves as a paradigm for later identifications with the larger society which mother represents to the child. In short, "the first demonstration of social trust in the baby is the ease of his feeding" (Erikson, 1950, p. 58). It is precisely on this basis that Erikson (1959, pp. 55–56) has suggested the development of a sense of basic trust or security as the first task in the process of socialization: "For the first component of a healthy personality I nominate a sense of *basic trust,* which I think is an attitude toward oneself and the world derived from the experiences of the first year of life."

Whether indeed the sense of basic trust and security is consequent upon the introduction of feeding schedules into the life of the child is a matter which most probably must await further research for a full exposition. Yet it seems clear that the perception of the world as supportive and responsive to the needs of the individual antecedes later psychological and social development, and, for this reason, Erikson (1950, pp. 219–234) has identified the experience of trust versus mistrust as the first developmental "crisis" in what he has called the "eight stages of man," which form useful theoretical constructs through which to consider the patterning of developmental tasks.

Autonomy and Self-awareness

Once the child has developed a basic orientation or expectation of the supportiveness of the universe, his experiences in infancy involve progressive and successive behaviors independent of direct intervention by mother. The child begins to become more active; he no longer responds to the environment; instead he seeks to reach out toward the environment and begins to seek active mastery over it. This developmental stage is expressed behaviorally in upright posture, walking, running, attempts to dress himself, and the like, indicating a higher level of development in psychomotor coordination. Of the child at this developmental stage, Woodcock (1941, p. 31) observed that "his impulses are to move and explore; to react to experience that he meets by some direct, overt behavior; to affect his environment by such changes as he can bring about in it." As the child finds some elements of the environment malleable to his efforts and as he finds that the human environment responds more readily to progressively more active behavior, he begins to develop a sense of *autonomy,* "in the sense both of the wish and the ability to be independent" of passive reliance upon adults (L. J. Stone & J. Church, 1957, p. 112). Concomitant with the sense of autonomy are the child's growing awareness that at least some of his behaviors are subject to his control (Freudian theorists tend to pinpoint the eliminatory function as the specific behavior crucial in developing autonomy) and a *growing awareness of self.* Stone and Church (1957, p. 115) have further observed that "his experience has become differentiated to the point where he has some sense of being a person separate from other people and from the physical environment." Often, this embryonic self-identification is self-reinforced by negative attitudes and behaviors, which tend to demonstrate to the child his growing autonomy. It is evident that "to develop autonomy, a firmly developed and a convincingly continued stage of early trust is necessary" (Erikson, 1959, p. 68).

Initiative and Independent Behavior

The sense of autonomy developed by the child in the second and third years of life, paralleled by continuing biological maturation, make it possible for him to control and direct his behavior more firmly and to become successively less dependent upon his parents. Indeed, "(1) he learns to *move around* more freely and more violently and therefore establishes a wide and, so it seems to him, an unlimited radius of goals; (2) his sense of language becomes perfected to the point where he understands and can ask about many things just enough to misunderstand them thoroughly; and (3) both language and locomotion permit him to expand his *imagination* over so many things that he cannot avoid frightening himself with what he himself has dreamed and thought up" (Erikson, 1959, p. 75). His play now needs little or no supervision for physical maintenance, he spontaneously joins groups of his peers, and he exhibits greater self-reliance in satisfying his personal needs. More and more, the child begins to follow his own inclinations and wishes, especially in exploring and manipulating elements of the environment. Often he is resentful of limitations placed upon his independence; to be sure, children in this developmental stage tend to feel that they are capable of greater independence than their parents are willing to grant and to rebel against restrictions placed upon behavior (Hurlock, 1959, p. 133). Independence in planning and executing their own activities seems vital to children in this stage, for they are learning a *sense of initiative*. The burgeoning self-concept, developed along with the sense of autonomy, is seeking to project itself actively and on its own terms into the environment. For most children, the early striving for initiative in behavior control immediately prior to entering school presages the dynamisms through which the adult in later life seeks to create his own self-experience and maintain the integrity of his self-concept. Children (as well as adolescents) typically tend to overevaluate their resources and capacities. This tendency is appropriate in late infancy and early childhood, but it becomes pathological if it persists into adulthood. Though the parent may regard the behavior of the four- or five-year-old who fails to adhere to the limits imposed upon him as naughty or disobedient, his behavior should be understood as a demand for autonomy (an autonomy that he is obviously yet unready to cope with fully), which is regarded as a major force in the development of the preschool child (Allport, 1955, p. 35). It is in seizing (often prematurely) the initiative for planning and executing his own behavior that the child demonstrates to the environment his growing sense of self.

Effects of School

The social environment of the child at birth has been considered to be constituted essentially by one other person, mother, who represents in varying degrees the archetype of later social structures which the child will meet. Gradually, the child learns to adjust his needs to those of other persons in the family, the play group, and the neighborhood group; and he learns to operate efficiently, in terms of internal need satisfaction, within the structure of these primary societies or *primary social groups* (Krech, Crutchfield, & Ballachey, 1962, pp. 195–197, 214). When the child has successfully mastered each of the developmental tasks subordinate to the principal developmental task of childhood, viz., socialization, he is psychologically ready to undergo an experience which first appears as a "test" of the strength of the socializing influences previously incorporated. Such a test ultimately provides the vehicle through which earlier developmental tasks are consolidated. Full-time attendance at school makes new demands on the child, especially in terms of initiative, self-mastery, and self-control. The school as a social structure, although it is essentially "the family writ large," gears itself to the accomplishment of specific learning tasks important in themselves but also highly significant in the course of development toward adulthood (Prescott, 1957, pp. 48–50).

Sense of Industry

While the child in the primary social group may have assumed certain responsibilities, chiefly related to his own behavior, he finds that the *secondary social group,* represented by the school, unequivocally assigns him responsibilities involving behavior control oriented to the task of learning specific educational and social skills. And this control is accomplished under conditions which tend to diminish the centrality of the position of the individual child within the secondary group. The well-being of the group now necessarily assumes greater importance than the needs of the individual child, for it is prerequisite to effective teaching and learning. Similarly, he finds that he must accommodate himself to the accomplishment of tasks set for him by the educational structure and reinforced by family members at a level of achievement not grossly discordant with his ability level. In short, the child in the elementary school is placed in a social role which demands of him (1) constructive, cooperative activity shared with fellow pupils, assigned on a basis quite different from the avenues of admission to the neighborhood play group; (2) occasional subordination to the well-being of the group; and (3) a rather definite level of productivity in accord with his capacity for meeting successfully intellectual challenges. The child who meets these demands develops what Erikson (1959, pp. 82, 86) calls the *sense of industry* and what Staton (1963, p. 47) terms the *sense of accomplishment and duty.* In resolving these demands, the child strengthens the primal elements of self-identity. He becomes increasingly more capable of responding to situations productively, with the expectation that he will be adequate to meeting both intellectual and interpersonal challenges without fear of frustration. Similarly, he feels more secure in the knowledge that his own well-being is not antagonistic to, but dependent upon, the well-being of others. In a very real sense, the classroom group is the psychosocial reality in the "natural order" which demonstrates concretely to the growing child the essential character of the theological concept of the Mystical Body. In the natural order, the classroom demonstrates the interdependence of its members necessary to the good of all, i.e., to the accomplishment of the learning task. Such interdependence in a sense prefigures the interdependence of the members of the Mystical Body or, in the newer idiom, the People of God.

Those psychoanalysts who have addressed themselves to education also employ the notion of learning readiness in discussing the development of children during elementary school years. If they are of the Freudian school (cf. A. Freud, 1960b, pp. 80–83), they tend to regard as the foundation of such readiness the successful resolution of the fabled Oedipal or Electra situations, considered the apices of infantile sexual life, during which (it is presumed) the child ardently desires the death of the same-sex parent so that he can enjoy the undivided attention of the opposite-sex parent. Such theorists as I. D. Harris (1959, pp. 23–24) also see the foundation of learning readiness in a high degree of infantile genital exploratory activity which is, quite mysteriously, converted into intellectual exploration. It is evident that behavioral scientists attuned to a developmental orientation regard learning readiness as the positive culmination of the successful completion of earlier tasks in the epigenetic pattern. Educational psychologists oriented to a phenomenal viewpoint regard learning readiness as the culmination of a developmental process in which the child comes to regard himself perceptually as adequate to the tasks and challenges of the school.

Task Patterns

The developmental-task orientation is of its nature teleological. Each successive task is directed toward the accomplishment of preparation for the assumption of adult psychological, social, and biological roles within a sociocultural context. Characteristics of adulthood in Western society are a certain independence of action based on security and a firm sense of self-identity, a readiness to accept the responsibility for and the consequences of one's behavior, and a willingness to behave in a fashion which does not impede the goal-directed behavior of others and occasionally assists others in the achievement of their ends. Central to each of these characteristics are (1) the ability to reflect on and to integrate the meaning of one's self-experience and (2) the flexibility of the self-concept in order to incorporate and integrate reality (i.e., self-experience).

Infancy and childhood pose for the developing person certain psychological, social, and biological tasks. Each of these tasks is subordinated to the major overriding developmental task of socialization. The accomplishment of each task represents a successful attempt at socialization at a particular developmental level. As Kowitz and Kowitz (1959, p. 7) have observed, for the child qua child, "the best preparation for adult life is to live and enjoy childhood." Children whose behavior and self-identification fall within a normal range (which does not imply a single standard or unique point, but includes a wide latitude) may be expected by the end of childhood to be ready to undertake the intensive experiences of adolescence, which culminate in adulthood. These persons have successfully met the major developmental task of socialization and are potentially constructive members of their society. They have passed from the first (originally biological) world of the family to the second (primarily social) world of the school. A high degree of *plasticity* inherent in the human person has permitted profound changes in important psychosocial and physical dimensions between birth and the period immediately preceding the onset of puberty. Tasks appropriate to critical periods in development have been successfully mastered, and a capacity to tolerate the developmental crises inherent in the nature of the adolescent experience has been strengthened.

Adolescence: preparation for independence

Adolescence is the term used to bracket conceptually the period between the profound biological changes which occur at pubescence and the assumption of adult roles. It is the bittersweet time of heightened self-awareness, of impatience with oneself, with one's parents, and with one's associates. Adolescence is the greengage period of intense longing for emancipation from the control of one's elders and of equally intense longing for a return to the halcyon days of childhood, when reality seemed less fraught with demands.

Just as the principal developmental task of childhood is socialization, so the principal developmental task of adolescence is *preparation for independent adult behavior,* to which other salient tasks are subordinated. And as plasticity is the principal developmental characteristic of childhood, so *emotional lability* is the principal developmental characteristic of adolescence. The celebrated adolescent of fiction and experience (e.g., Holden Caulfield) customarily exhibits wide vacillation in behavior, interests, and emotional control. His oscillations seems unintelligible to observers, who fail to see in his behavior intense exploration directed toward the formation of a mature self-identity. He wishes to renounce and often loudly denounces the dependence upon others typical of childhood, though he must depend in varying degrees upon his parents and teachers. Yet he longs for and sometimes asks for direction and other-imposed behavior control. His sporadic behavior appears peculiar and contradictory, but, in fact, it is quite normal and perhaps inevitable when one considers the developmental tasks which face the child as he grows through adolescence on the way to adulthood. The child at the beginning of adolescence faces the problem of learning new, more appropriate social roles, a problem precipitated not only by his altered physical composition but by altered conditions of schooling in most American communities. A modern industrial society seems less well organized to provide appropriate role models than do primitive societies in which regimented and ritualistic patterns of preparation for adult roles were imposed (Mead, 1958). School is typically no longer the neighborhood school, essentially the family writ large, but rather an adult microcosm, which brings the early adolescent into contact with others from outside the neighborhood or the immediate sociocultural unit. The conditions of instruction, indeed, have altered so that the child no longer learns to identify himself with a single teacher with whom he shares the school day. Against this backdrop, the adolescent is thrust into the position of making several *critical life decisions* relative to his education and his future vocational career, beginning with what first appear to be no more than minor choices of a curriculum or course of studies and culminating in the choice of an occupation or work of life and a way of life (i.e., the married, single, or religious lifeways).

A number of commentators (cf. Britton & Winans, 1958, pp. 58–90) have offered catalogues of developmental tasks appropriate in preadolescence and early, middle, and late adolescence. More broadly oriented catalogues have been offered by Havighurst and by Sister Annette Walters and Sister Kevin O'Hara. Havighurst (1953, pp. 111–148) suggested 10 developmental tasks specific to adolescence: (1) achieving new and more mature relations with age mates of both sexes, (2) achieving a masculine or feminine social role, (3) accepting one's physique and using the body effectively, (4) achieving emotional independence of parents and other adults, (5) achieving assurance of economic independence, (6) selecting and preparing for an occupation; (7) preparing for marriage and family life, (8) developing intellectual skills and concepts necessary for civic competence, (9) desiring and achieving socially responsible behavior, and (10) acquiring a set of values and an ethical system as a guide to behavior.

In the same vein, Sister Annette Walters and Sister Kevin O'Hara (1953, pp. 480–497) have suggested six developmental tasks, some of which subsume those mentioned by Havighurst: (1) formation of new relationships with adults, (2) formation of healthy boy-girl relationships, (3) acceptance by other adolescents, (4) realistic occupational adjustments, (5) establishment of a role in the community, and (6) development of a mature religious and philosophical outlook.

Exploration, Projection, Definition

From a phenomenological vantage point, it is possible to perceive the varied specific tasks of adolescence as subordinated to the principal task of preparation for the impending assumption of adult roles. These tasks, then, are specifications of two primary tasks of adolescence which are superordinate to specific adolescent tasks but subordinate to the principal task: (1) *self-definition* and (2) *self-projection*. Each specific task may be considered to function as an avenue through which the adolescent fulfills the primary task, i.e., learns to project into reality, into the realm of self-created self-experience, a realistic, mature self-concept.

In playing a succession of roles, ranging from that of the dependent child who shuns self-direction to that of the self-willed egocentric adult who demands absolute self-direction and regards his parents and teachers as antediluvian martinets who refuse to recognize his autonomy, the adolescent displays exploratory behavior. In effect, in what is essentially a process of *exploration of usable self-roles,* the adolescent "tries on" a number of diverse self-concepts while seeking an appropriate self-definition. Initially, he identifies himself rather vaguely in terms of tentative self-roles carried over from the fantasies of childhood. Such self-roles may bear little resemblance to the realities of his capacities, his past experience, his educational history, and so forth. Indeed, the intellectually deprived high school freshman may still perceive himself in fanciful self-projection as a lawyer or an Indian chief, despite a level of intellectual capacity which makes such self-roles inappropriate. An intellectually gifted high school student who comes from a family with limited income may perceive himself as a future physician, notwithstanding the staggering costs of medical education. Later, he abandons these fantasy-derived roles in favor of roles more realistically anchored and appropriate to his unfolding self-experience. The question of the choice of an occupation, as McArthur (1961, pp. 58–60) has observed, is an apt illustration of the "identity crisis" prevalent in adolescence, since career choice is one special issue seized upon in the adolescent's apparently random thrashing about in search of a clearly defined identity. Regardless of their basis, however, these tentative self-roles exert an attracting and prescriptive influence on adolescent behavior; they induce the adolescent to behave in certain ways which he believes conform to a fantasied self-role. To the poet Allen Tate is attributed the remark, "Lacking a usable past, distrustful of the present, which momentarily becomes the past, we build our standards on an imaginative construct of the future." This observation seems particularly apt in discussing the fantasy life of adolescents.

Behavior as Self-projection

The adolescent structures a role for himself, a role issuing from childhood fantasy or from chance selection in random thrashing about. This role involves certain internally determined behavior prescriptions which are rooted in his perception or even fantasy of the role. Typically the self-role corresponds to the future adult roles the adolescent wishes to play. He behaves in accord with his perception of those roles. His behavior is thus future-oriented, rooted in his perception of himself, not as he is in the here and now, but as he would like or fancies himself to be, as he is ideally, in that future time when he will have achieved adulthood. Behaviors issuing from self-projected role perception which seem to be accepted by others are reinforced and therefore likely to be repeated. Those which are not accepted are nonreinforced and therefore extinguished. But it is probable that the adolescent's behaviors are likely to be accepted by some "others," e.g., members of the adolescent peer group, and not accepted by some other "others," e.g., parents and teachers. In this situation, the behavioral patterns are intermittently reinforced and are likely to recur. Modern experiments (Mowrer, 1960, pp. 457–468) on human learning have amply demonstrated that behaviors which are said to be "maintained" on a schedule of intermittent

reinforcement tend to hold considerable tenacity in one's repertoire of behaviors. The horseplayer who occasionally wins on a $2 bet, although his
winnings scarcely equal what he has lost in the periods between such wins,
is an apt example. An earlier poetic expression had it that hope springs
eternal in the human breast. The strength of such intermittently reinforced
behaviors depends upon the psychological salience at any given moment of
the "significant others" approving or disapproving the behaviors.

Formation of Ideal Self

A series of future-oriented perceptions of self-as-adult controls and establishes goals toward which the adolescent strives. Similarly, a series of rapidly
changing perceptions (intermittently reinforced) of self-as-adult implies rapidly changing goals for adult life, each of which, for a time, exerts an attracting force inducing the adolescent to behave in accord with tentative self-roles.
"This urgent desire to define one's own life in terms of goals is a sign
of the reorganization of the self which takes place and which is fostered
constructively if the adolescent comes in contact with rich, realistic experiences" (Blos, 1951, p. 295). Each of the successive perceptions of self as
self wishes to be constitutes a tentative precursor of what perceptual psychologists call the *self-ideal* or ideal self (Rogers, 1961, pp. 77–103) and what
the psychoanalysts call the ego ideal (Blos, 1962, pp. 184–186). The formation of the appropriate mature ideal self (which includes the hopes, aspirations, and ambitions the adolescent holds for himself) involves the consolidation of ideal self-identifications developed earlier in life. This is a task which
is likely to extend over the entire adolescent period. Initially, the early adolescent is likely to feel that a vast incongruence exists between the self-as-
perceived in the here and now (self-concept) and the self-ideal.
Consequently, both the self-concept and the self-ideal are likely to be modified through reinforcement or extinction in the face of the adolescent's unfolding self-experience and, importantly, his reflection on it. The process
through which both self-as-perceived in the here and now and self-as-perceived in terms of future aspirations are altered and become more congruent
is called *self-definition*. It must be noted that self-definition occurs within
the matrix of the self-experience and integrative reflection. Concomitant with
self-definition is the formation of a realistically anchored self-identity. Successful completion of the task of self-definition in adolescence issues in goal-
directed behavior free from vacillation and emotional lability.

The rapid succession of tentative self-roles is one of the prime characteristics of the adolescent period, since the process of exploration extends
throughout the course of adolescence and touches virtually every facet of
sociocultural activity and biologic functioning. Else Frenkel-Brunswik (1963,
pp. 161–171), interpreting the theoretical contributions of Charlotte
Buehler for an English-reading audience, observed that the adolescent's life

stage is primarily exploratory in character. Adolescent exploration involves developing greater self-understanding, playing the role of prospective adult, establishing, at least in fantasy, tentative occupational and marriage choices, and searching for one's place in the community. Super (1957, pp. 80–82), adapting Buehler's conceptual paradigm to the investigation of the dimensions of vocational development, has provided apt illustrations of the process of adolescent exploration in connection with the choice of a career. The process of exploration eventuates in the attempted projection of tentative self-roles into experience. School activities, both educational and social, provide a common cultural experience as well as a social testing ground in which adolescents attempt to project self-determined roles, thus underscoring the school's function as an adult microcosm (Ausubel, 1954, pp. 480–482). The school commonly serves as the focus of adolescent social activity and the home ground for the adolescent peer culture, since it provides (whether intentionally or not) its own role models, in the form of faculty and other students, and a convenient social testing ground for the self-roles perceived by the adolescent.

Self and Social Structure

Correlative to the task of self-definition is the task of *self-projection,* whereby the adolescent seeks to implement in the "real world" the roles and behaviors central to his phenomenal and ideal selves. These self-roles are likely to be those "selected" from fantasy or from randomly reinforced behaviors. Such roles are now adopted as more cohesive repertoires of behaviors which the person believes to be suitable for him as he seeks to cope actively with the problems attendant upon his approaching adulthood. The extent to which he is able to implement in behavior his perceptions of himself as he is and as he wishes to be appears to be a function not only of the realistic anchorage of the phenomenal field but also of the tolerance of the social structure for adolescent exploration. Some social structures are less malleable, more rigidly organized, and hence less tolerant of exploratory trial behavior. A series of tentative self-projections inevitably eventuates as the adolescent successively adopts and discards tentative self-roles until a mature self-identity is formed and reinforced through self-experience.

The necessary condition for the successful completion of adolescent developmental tasks is "the freedom to become." In this view, the adolescent is perceived essentially as a person-in-transition, who needs both the freedom to explore widely and to behave in seemingly bizarre fashion as he searches out a realistically perceived and realistically projectable self which will serve him as the core of his adult self-concept. The freedom to become, however, does not imply the abrogation of adult responsibility for overseeing optimal development in the adolescent. Erikson (1950, p. 228) has suggested that the "danger of this stage is role diffusion." The consolidation of self-identity is impeded equally by social structures which burden the adolescent with freedom beyond his capacity to cope effectively with it. To complete his tasks adequately, the adolescent needs *training* in independence rather than independence itself. Thus, the adolescent requires a degree of emancipation from the home and a greater latitude in choice than that accorded a child, in order to develop meaningful identifications with adults (chiefly, his teachers) outside the home and so undergo exposure to a greater number of role models. Indeed there is partial evidence that more constricted, authoritarian home and family environments provide greater stimulation for self-identity by giving adolescents "boundaries against which to rebel."

College and Ambiguity

Special developmental problems are posed in late adolescence for persons of college age, because higher education represents a prolongation of the economic dependency of adolescence after biological and social maturity has been reached (Mead, 1960). Familial as well as school pressures placed upon the college student usually favor cessation of adolescent exploration. But *intellectual* exploration in college demands greater freedom in order to engage the life of the mind at its highest level of development. Nevitt Sanford (1962, p. 281) has described the added developmental task of the college student in prolonged adolescence: "The problem for the student is how to wait; how to tolerate ambiguity and open-endedness in himself while he is preparing for adult roles." Further problems may be posed for early adolescents as the social culture lowers the age at which social, rather than biological, adolescence officially begins, while at the same time raising the upper limits of adolescence by prescribing college education as desirable for all American youths.

The second plateau toward the horizon of adulthood is well traversed when the self has been adequately defined and the adolescent has learned to test the reality of his self-perceptions through self-projection, since the core of the mature self-concept has been formed by this time. In terms of ego psychology (Erikson, 1959, p. 89), "The sense of ego identity, then, is the accrued confidence that one's ability to maintain inner sameness is matched by the continuity of one's meaning for others." Having accomplished the developmental tasks of adolescence, the person need no longer be preoccupied with himself or with the implementation of self-roles in fantasy or reality. He is ready to make sound decisions respecting his own life situation and that of the significant others around him, and he is free to divert psychological attention away from concern with his own development and into socially useful, constructive channels.

Maturity as Relative

Throughout this chapter frequent mention has been made of the gradual progression of the person-in-transition through a series of experiences which in a modern industrial society commonly culminate in an integrated, flexible personality capable of coping adequately with the pressures, frustrations, and difficulties inherent in the condition of industrial man. In every part of this treatment the epigenetic and teleological aspects of human growth have been considered as basic thrusts in the individual's developmental tasks. Many behavioral scientists adhere to the conviction that there are crises attendant upon the completion of the various developmental tasks and to the further conviction that failure to meet each task within a certain, fairly rigorously defined, critical period will eventuate in an immature organism. Such an organism will perhaps be incapable of achieving maturity in later life. Evidence from recent research (cf. Bettye M. Caldwell, 1962), however, indicates a trend which challenges these convictions and suggests instead that developmental patterns are virtually unique, so that the timing and sequence of events in development may show considerable individuation from person to person. Persons-in-transition who meet supportive, tolerant social environments favorable to the facile accomplishment of developmental tasks may be expected to "mature" more rapidly and with a lower incidence of crisis, but those who meet environments not conducive to favorable development need not be incapacitated in the process of maturation. "Maturity is a relative term, denoting the degree to which, at any juncture of his life, a person has discovered and is able to employ the resources that become available to him in the process of growth" (Jersild, 1963, p. 9). Barring the onset of major psychopathologies, persons whose social environments make reality hard to deal with usually mature at a rate and in a sequence appropriate to their own specific developmental patterns. In human development there are few absolutes. The only appropriate standards are those which "fit" the specific developmental pattern of the individual person in his unique history. This capital point must suffuse every aspect of the guidance worker's relationships with students.

The school and human development

As an agency established and maintained by an organized society, the principal role of the school is to perform those duties assigned it in order to assist society to maintain itself. It shares with the family and the church its character as a formal institution whose principal purpose is to socialize the next generation in accord with the norms and the values governing the society which maintains it. Specifically, the school is charged with the task of developing in the student the truth, "whole and entire." Its proper role is to foster coequally the intellectual and moral virtues, a role which in precise Scholastic terminology would be regarded as fostering the development of *prudence*. Flowing from this primary proximate function, the school provides services which facilitate the student's growth in those educational and vocational skills necessary for effective social performance, much as the family is charged with the development of social skills.

Anna Freud (1960b, p. 45) expressed the common framework for the perception of the role of the school when she suggested that the universal aim of the school is "always to make out of a child a grown-up person who shall not be very different from the grown-up world around him." Tasks involving the development of intellectual, educational, vocational, and some social (especially when these pertain to the classroom group) skills are accomplished by the student more easily within the structure of formal education. These tasks pertain directly to the school's primary proximate area of responsibility. In Havighurst's view (1953, p. 5), "Education may be conceived as the effort of the society, through the school, to help the individual achieve *certain* of his developmental tasks." Indeed, those developmental tasks whose achievement is promoted by the school are precisely those whose achievement is related to the student's growth in truth, whole and entire, or prudence (to use the Scholastic term).

"Teachable Moment"

The epigenetic, teleological character of the developmental-task construct emphasizes the prior accomplishment of certain tasks at a lower level of existential integration in order to develop readiness for undertaking the succeeding task, a notion encapsulated in Havighurst's "teachable-moment" construct (1953, p. 5): "When the body is ripe, and society requires, and the self is ready to achieve a certain task, the teachable moment has come." For the school to be able to do its job well, the student needs to be developmentally disposed toward efficient learning. His prior developmental tasks, upon which the readiness to learn at various educational levels depends, need to be accomplished successfully. Thus the guidance of human development is an appropriate role for the school to undertake, not by default, but as its positive obligation, in order to assure its effectiveness in fulfilling its function of developing within the student truth, knowledge, and action coequally.

While focusing on the student in the academic situation, efficient school guidance services direct their attention to the developmental pattern of the individual student, in its multifoliate aspects, as it impinges on the self in the total life situation. From a phenomenological vantage point, Havighurst's comment might be amended to read "*only* when the self is ready"—or suitably disposed by the favorable process of psychosocial growth and development—to achieve a certain task has the teachable moment arrived, and only under these circumstances can the school properly discharge its obligation to society.

Guidance for Development

Similarly, the very nature of the school as essentially a social activity places it in the forefront as the typical context in which the individual learns a pattern of social behavior. From the first grader who learns to respect the rights of his schoolmates by not distracting them at will, to the senior high school and college students whose courtship and precourtship behavior takes its impetus from social activities organized and chartered by the school, social behavior is learned primarily in school. In adolescence, the typical comprehensive high school eases the task of emancipation from parental controls by providing parental substitutes and gives the student the opportunity to develop the ability to make appropriate decisions by placing him in positions in which minor and major choices are necessary (Ausubel, 1954, pp. 473–485). In terms of vocational development, schools deliberately and casually provide occupational role models which stimulate occupational self-identification. In short, the school is deeply involved in the psychosocial development of the student, and the accomplishment of its primary role which depends upon the prior readiness of students to undertake intellectual tasks, largely relies on how well it meets its positive obligations in providing developmental guidance.

School guidance services oriented to developmental theory seek to provide continuing opportunities for positive assistance to the student in the normal accomplishment of his developmental tasks. A key feature of school counseling oriented to developmental theory is the provision for counseling for self-insight, in terms of the ability to reflect on the meaning of one's self-experience and to incorporate these reflections into the developing self-concept. Self-insight is, of course, a means toward the attainment of the ultimate objective of counseling, viz., self-actualization. Other guidance services seek to provide positive opportunities for self-actualization through exploration, both socially and occupationally, via planned and casual experiences. Counselors attuned to a developmental orientation play active roles in the establishment and maintenance of school policy and procedures which foster and tolerate self-exploration as an avenue toward self-actualization. In this way a school atmosphere is created which is conducive to the successful accomplishment of developmental tasks at all levels of education.

The self-system: a glossary

Guidance is essentially the facilitation of optimal human development within the context of the school-community-family environment. The product of satisfactory development is the mature, integrated, actualized adult self. With cogency, Hamburger (1962) regards guidance policy as the strategy for positive intervention in human development and guidance procedures as the tactics for developmental intervention. Hence, guidance is concerned directly with fostering the development of integrated selves in the students it serves. Since a number of somewhat technical terms for elements of the self-system, introduced in this chapter, are used with considerable frequency throughout this book, it seems appropriate to conclude the discussion of the self-system in relation to developmental patterns with a brief "glossary" of these terms.

The term *self-system* is the most inclusive, designating the totality of forces inhering in the self. Principal components of the self-system are the perceived self, the aspirational self, and the experiential self.

Self-perception or the perceived self designates the self-concept, the self-as-perceived-by-the-self in the here and now, the picture the person holds of himself, his characteristic abilities, his value system, his habitual patterns of behaving, of those things he calls "really me."

An important element in the perceived self is the *aspirational self*. This term designates the totality of those perceptions the persons holds of himself, not in the here and now, but as he would like to be, as he is "ideally." It is characteristic of mentally healthy persons that the aspirational self is both realistically anchored and realizable in the present or future. This implies that well-adjusted or mentally healthy persons hold few fantasied aspirations which are not likely to be realized.

The *experiential self* is the self-as-it-is-experienced, the self inferred from "feedback from reality," from the behavior of others, especially significant others, toward oneself. The greater the incongruence between the self-as-perceived (including the aspirational self) and the self-as-experienced, the greater the need for the use of crippling and disabling mechanisms of defense to thwart threatening perceptions of self issuing from self-experience.

A number of terms describe the *relations among* the elements of the self-system. *Self-acceptance* designates the optimal relationship between the experiential self and the perceptual self. The mentally healthy, secure person tends to accept his experiences of himself without the need for distortion and to order these experiences into his perceptual self. The "line" separating the perceived from the experiential self is, for the mentally healthy person, a "permeable membrane," not a rigid wall.

Self-definition refers to the relationship between the perceived and the aspirational self. It occurs when the elements of the self as perceived now and the ideal self as perceived in the future reach a high level of congruence. Stability is implied both in each self-element and in the relationship between these self-elements. Thus self-definition implies a stable self-concept, a stable ideal self, and a stable self-ideal relationship.

Self-organization designates the relationships obtaining between the perceived, aspirational, and experiential selves, particularly in terms of the readiness of the self to undergo developmental experiences or developmental tasks.

When self-organization has reached an optimal level, that is, when the person has accepted himself and ordered his self-experience into his self-perception and self-aspiration, the term *self-integration* is applied. Self-integration, characterized by a high degree of self-acceptance and optimal self-organization, is an earmark of the mature self.

Self-projection is a term which describes the *relations between* the self-system and "reality." Self-projection eventuates in behavior; in effect, the person is trying out a novel perception of himself, or, more accurately, testing the reality of a particular self-aspiration. A series of tentative self-projections is characteristic of the process of development. One "finds out" whether one is really as one perceives oneself to be only through feedback from reality.

When the person has accepted himself, integrated the self-system, developed the capacity to read feedback from reality accurately, and, most important, developed an awareness of the relationships among the elements of his self-system and between the self-system and reality, he has developed *self-insight* or *self-knowledge*. It is at this point that he can supply an adequate answer to the question "Who am I?" These terms are often used interchangeably with the term *self-identity*.

Self-actualization represents, in an hierarchical order, the most elevated term used to describe the self. In its simplest form, this term suggests that the potentialities inhering in self—with its relations among and between—have been "reduced" to "act." But what does it mean to actualize one's potentialities as a person? The answers often tend to the ephemeral. Maslow (1954) contends that what a man can become he must become in order to achieve self-actualization. McCall (1963) regards the maximization or realization of self as the equivalent of self-actualization. Indeed, it is likely that the definition of self-actualization must vary with the particular developmental stage and history of the person. While the present authors agree generally with Maslow and McCall, they feel constrained to provide a notion of self-actualization useful in describing the development of students in an educational setting, whose opportunities for becoming what they must—and perhaps in time will—become are circumstantially constricted, both by the environmental context and their developmental stage. Hence, self-actualization is used in this book to designate the optimal integration of self-forces, optimal self-knowledge, and the relations among and between, in terms of the *readiness to profit optimally from developmental experiences*. Succeeding developmental experiences provide progressively greater opportunities for ultimate actualization of self-potentialities. Guidance aims at assisting students so to organize the network of realities of self and existential situation that optimal resolution of developmental tasks is facilitated and, in this fashion, facilitates ultimate self-actualization.

3

SCHOOL GUIDANCE:
ITS NATURE AND ROOTS

Some fundamental definitions

Since the 1920s there has been considerable controversy in professional guidance circles over the meaning of such terms as *pupil personnel work, guidance, counseling,* and *advisement.* What Dietz (1937, p. 692) said of the situation in 1936 still holds true today, viz., "The tower of Babel had nothing on the guidance and personnel field when it comes to a need for a common language. We must agree among ourselves on what we are talking about." Some guidance experts have changed their own definitions with nearly every revision of their basic guidance textbooks. In this section of the chapter, the authors present what they believe the most satisfactory definitions of various terms. Throughout the rest of the book these terms are used in accordance with the definitions presented.

Education

Formal education is the totality of experiences which the school directly or indirectly furnishes the student to enable him to develop and mature.

63

These experiences include intellectual learning, motor learning, appetitive learning, appreciational learning, moral conduct, social skills, emotional growth, spiritual satisfaction, personnel services, and guidance.

Personnel Work

Personnel work is the totality of the helping services which a school makes available to the pupil. A vital component of education, it is nonetheless a unique school service distinct from classroom instruction. Personnel work includes four elements: an organized program, facilities (e.g., adequate office space), professional staff, and a series of specialized services, such as orientation, guidance, health, housing, and financial aid. In the literature, however there is also another commonly accepted meaning for personnel work; viz., it is a synonym for guidance at the college or university level.

Guidance

Guidance is that assistance which the school gives the pupil to aid him in fulfilling his potential, negotiating the tasks of development, and solving his special problems. It constitutes the most important aspect of pupil personnel work. Usually it necessitates personal contact between the guidance worker and the student, while personnel work may or may not require such personal contact. Guidance connotes a planned and organized program of school-wide assistance to aid the individual to self-actualize, to develop his full potentialities. But guidance is more than a service; it is also a point of view. Indeed it is a basic orientation toward working with students, whether in the capacity of teacher, administrator, counselor, or guidance specialist. Thus not only counselors and guidance specialists but also teachers in the classroom have a role in guidance insofar as they foster the guidance point of view, as they assist the student to develop as a person. This is not to say that guidance *is* the same thing as education, as was held by many guidance experts in the 1930s, but rather that guidance services are an integral and necessary component of the total educative process and that the guidance point of view should permeate every aspect of the school's program. There are five basic directional thrusts of guidance, viz., personal, social, religious, vocational, and scholastic. Thus guidance is far broader than vocational selection, a position held for years by the National Vocational Guidance Association.

Counseling

Counseling is the relationship between two persons in which one of them attempts to assist the other in so organizing himself as to attain a particular form of happiness, adjustment to a life situation, or, in short, self-actualization. Counseling always involves a one-to-one relationship, that is, one client and one guidance worker in a formal or an informal interview situation. It is the central and most important aspect of guidance. Counseling stresses almost exclusively the process of assistance, while personnel work tends to emphasize services and guidance usually accentuates both helping services and the process and purpose of assistance. Furthermore, counseling must be distinguished from advisement. *Advisement* is that relationship in which one person listens to the problems of another person and on the basis of his presumed knowledge and maturity gives that person specific practical suggestions and directions which he deems will aid in the solution of the problem. Like counseling, advisement is part of guidance, but it partakes more of direct instruction than does counseling. Unfortunately many guidance workers in public schools and particularly in Catholic schools knowingly or unknowingly are not engaged in counseling but rather in advisement. Counseling, as Fr. Curran (1956) has noted, aims at developing in the client self-insight and the readiness for self-actualization, while advisement seeks merely to offer a solution. The student in the counseling situation is usually referred to as either the *client* or the *counselee*. Neither term is particularly accurate. The term *client* has been imported into school guidance from Rogerian psychotherapy, and therefore to some guidance experts it connotes a pupil's undergoing an interview of greater depth than is possible in the customary counselor-student relationship in the school setting. On the other hand, the term *counselee* clearly suggests a passive student, one who is receiving counsel from the guidance worker, and to receive counsel means that advisement, not counseling, is taking place in the interview. A new term for the student seeking assistance is urgently needed. In the absence of this new term, the word "client" is preferred, since "counselee" savors too much of the passive, overdependent student rather than of a student who actively participates in the counseling relationship. Moreover the word "client" has an additional advantage since it tends to focus on the capital fact that every pupil problem, every lack of complete self-actualization, is rooted in the total developmental structure of the student. Thus, for example, a student's scholastic problems are deeply related to his personal development and to his complete fulfillment as a person.

Group Guidance

Group guidance is that relationship in which a guidance worker attempts to assist a number of students to attain for themselves satisfactory development or adjustment to their respective individual or collective life situations. It occurs in a setting in which one or more guidance workers encounter students as a group. Group guidance differs from *group advisement* in the same way that counseling differs from individual advisement.

PERSONNEL AND
GUIDANCE SERVICES

Even a minimally adequate school provides three services, viz., instructional services, administrative services, and personnel services. While each of these services has its own distinct aspects and emphases, each nonetheless contributes its share to the total school education of the student.

Personnel services

Personnel services are those specific assistances which the school makes available to the pupil as part of its total program of personnel work. Thirteen principal personnel services are offered in well-organized schools and colleges. *The admissions service* is designed to assist the student and the school to ascertain whether a specific educational institution, a particular program within that institution, or both are suitable for the furtherance of the student's interests, aptitudes, and needs. It is the first step in the school's continuous program of personnel work on behalf of each student. *The scholastic orientation service* is intended to acquaint the student and his parents with the school's requirements for success, its program of services, and its ability to satisfy his personal, social, vocational, religious, and scholastic needs. The orientation service perdures minimally throughout the student's first term in the school and ideally for one full year after his admission. *The attendance service* is designed to promote the daily presence of the student so that he will be in a position to receive all the broad benefits which the school can provide him. *The financial service* is aimed at assisting needy students so that they may remain in school or at orienting them to budget their funds and to develop fiscal responsibility, or at both functions. *The housing service* is intended to help the student obtain that type of living facility most conducive to the furtherance of his educational and personal goals. It also assists him continually to realize his goals while he is situated in his particular housing. In general, there are three types of student housing according to the type and level of the school: the student's own home, the school dormitory, and the off-campus rooming house or apartment. *The food service* is designed to provide the student with nourishing, well-balanced meals in the school cafeteria and snack bars, so that he can pursue his educational and personal goals in good health. This service is often designed to give the student educational experiences in what constitutes an imaginative cuisine, a well-balanced diet, and the social graces at table, all of which he can carry over into his postschool life. *The health service* aims at preserving and developing the student's physical well-being. Hence it is concerned not only with temporary or prolonged care and treatment of students in the office of the school nurse or in the school infirmary but also with the institution of a program of preventive medicine and hygiene development.

The remedial service is intended to render special assistance, usually by means of distinctive programs, to those students having deficiencies in such areas as reading, speech, and study habits. *The guidance service* offers personal help to the student to aid him in solving special problems and in fulfilling his potential. It is the most important of all personnel services. *The psychological service* gives assistance to students who manifest mental or emotional disturbances which fall outside the normal range. This service utilizes such specialists as the school psychologist and school psychiatrist, who usually treat students referred to them by the guidance staff. *The spiritual activities service* endeavors to provide the student opportunities for spiritual and moral development. In public schools the school itself is restricted to fostering nondenominational spiritual development, but it can and should cooperate actively with local church agencies as part of its overall program of positively encouraging pupil spiritual growth. The church-related school, e.g., a Catholic school, should be characterized by a deep, pervasive, relevant, and continuing religious and spiritual service. *The recreational service* is designed to enrich the student's leisure-time activities by providing him with opportunities for engaging in nonscholastic interests, such as sports, avocations, and social life. *The vocational orientation service* is intended to assist the student both in attaining an adequate understanding of the world of work and in securing a satisfactory and self-fulfilling position in that world. Such a position may be, first, part-time employment while he is a student in order to defray personal or school expenses, to ease the transition from school to the world of work by such activities as high school work-study programs, or to provide exploratory experiences in the world of work through planned and casual observation and summer employment or an after-school job; or, second, full-time employment when the student has terminated school, either by graduation or by dropping out before graduation. *The coordination service* aims at harmonizing and synchronizing the efforts of the administration, teachers, guidance workers, and staff to further the goals of the pupil personnel program. It is initiated and directed by the pupil personnel office.

Guidance services

One of the most important characteristics of a profession is service. A guidance worker is a professional who ministers unto the needs of his clients. He never forgets this ministerial function, this service aspect. And when two different service occupations are united in a single person, as in a priest who is also a counselor, a double measure of humility and subsidiarity is incumbent on the minister of the service. Unfortunately some guidance workers, and some priest-counselors, overlook the fact that their duty is to serve the student and not to be served by the student. Indeed it sometimes happens that priests and religious build up in the minds of the laity such a concept of the superiority of the priestly and religious office that students forget the basic ministerial aspects of the guidance profession and become afraid to approach the priest or religious with their problems. Guidance, like the priesthood and religious life, is a helping profession, not a commanding one.

Guidance services do not stand isolated from one another; rather they are woven into the seamless garment of a unified program. A guidance program might be defined as a series of organized services and school guidance-mindedness designed to provide planned, systematic, pervasive, and continuous assistance to all students from kindergarten through graduate school. Hence guidance is at once services and a point of view.

What is the goal of the school's program of guidance services? At first blush this might appear to be a simple question. For example, it would seem apparent that the goal of scholastic guidance with a student who is failing his courses is to help him raise his marks and keep him in school. For a particular student, however, perhaps the appropriate plan might be to drop out of school to enter the world of work because the school's existing program is neither adequate nor appropriate for him (Lee, 1959). Thus the goal of the guidance program cuts far deeper, to reach the inner level of unique developmental pattern so as to assist the student to self-actualize. For example, one student might achieve self-actualization by going to college; for another student attendance at college might be disastrous even though he is intelligent enough to do well there. Regrettably, all too frequently school guidance programs are evaluated chiefly on the external, superficial aspects, such as the number of students going on to college or the holding power of a school with a traditional curriculum. These factors are indeed easier to measure, but they are not the goal of the program of guidance service.

An effective guidance program, to be minimally successful, includes the following services:

1. *The counseling service* establishes a relationship between guidance worker and student in which the worker attempts to assist the student in achieving optimal educational, vocational, personal, social, and religious development, or, in short, self-actualization. The counseling service may be performed by the counselor himself, by the teacher, by the teacher-counselor, or by any other member of the school staff who has had adequate guidance training. This service is typically performed in a one-to-one situation, i.e., in an interview. During the interview situation, the counselor is usually called on to perform other duties or to engage in roles somewhat tangential to counseling as delineated later. Some of the more important roles, direct and tangential, which the counselor assumes during the interview include engaging in friendly discussion, gathering information, diagnosing, listening, supporting, asking for elaboration, reflecting, posing the focusing comment, offering a brief interpretive comment or making the integrative remark, giving pertinent information, participating, advising, rejecting, tutoring, and

structuring and focusing the topic (cf. A. E. Hoffman, 1959, p. 62). Thus the interview comprises more than counseling. The counseling service is the most important and certainly the most distinctive of all the guidance services. Consequently the American School Counselor Association (1963b, p. 201) has officially recommended that the guidance counselor devote at least 50 per cent of his assigned time in individual or multiple counseling. In many schools routine duties unfortunately prevent him from devoting sufficient time to the counseling service. To alleviate this problem, counselor aides could be hired to perform routine, nonprofessional tasks, e.g., scoring tests, filing tests, ordering occupational literature, duplicating transcripts for college entrance, and the like. A similar waste of counselor manpower occurs when counselors are assigned to perform functions which properly fall within the province of the administration, such as meting out punitive discipline.

2. *The group guidance service* provides for the establishment of a relationship between the guidance worker and a group of students in which the worker attempts to assist these students to attain optimal self-development through adjustment or problem resolution. There are five chief forms through which the service may be offered, viz., group discussion, sociodrama, multiple counseling, group therapy, and brainstorming. The teacher and teacher-counselor adequately trained in group dynamics are competent to engage in group discussion, sociodrama, and brainstorming, while the counselor usually receives additional training in multiple counseling. Group therapy is normally handled by a trained group therapist, e.g., a psychologist or psychiatrist. Super (1949) has delineated four contrasting methodologies, which, when utilized separately, determine the particular form taken during the discussion session, the multiple counseling session, or the group therapy session. These four methodologies are the cathartic-supportive, the nondirective, the group development, and the interpretive. Group guidance is treated in detail in Chapter 12.

3. *The information service* supplies pertinent facts and data to individual students, groups of students, or the school at large. The emphasis in the literature on the dynamics of the counseling relationship has led to an unfortunate neglect of the information service, especially of the counselor's role in this service. Pupils need accurate, current information to make intelligent choices. Indeed some students' problems may disappear when they are supplied with relevant information. In giving guidance information to individuals or to groups of students, the counselor functions much as a teacher and should therefore know the principles and methods of the teaching process. Many counselors and counselor educators (cf. G. D. Moore, 1960, p. 358) seem to have little knowledge of the teaching process, regarding it as "imparting information." (It is, of course, impossible to impart information, as any student of the teaching process knows.) To be relevant and effective, information must be integrated by the student into his perceptual field. Effective guidance vehicles for the provision of appropriate information relative to the common developmental needs of students include special assemblies, lectures, guidance "courses," such as how-to-study and orientation

courses, information interviews, bulletin boards, and well-organized information libraries.

4. *The educational and occupational planning service* aids the pupil and his parents in relating his interests, aptitudes, and abilities to current and future educational and occupational opportunities and requirements. The guidance worker supplies this service by furnishing the pupil and his parents with a carefully planned sequence of assistances, including interviews, group discussions, special programs, talks by representatives from higher educational institutions and the occupations, occupational and educational files, guidance newsletters, bulletin boards, and visits to educational institutions and industrial settings. This service also helps the pupil to learn how to apply for admission to higher educational institutions and how to plan the financing of his further education. The educational and occupational planning service constitutes far more than merely providing the student with pertinent educational and occupational literature; rather it also consists in working with him to plan a program for advanced educational or career entry which will fulfill his personality thrusts and further his self-actualization.

5. *The appraisal service* assists the student to obtain a realistic picture of his abilities, his aptitudes, his interests, his personality characteristics, and his school achievements, in short, to get to know himself on a *sociocomparative* basis. It also is designed to facilitate identification by the educational institution of a pupil's personality matrix and special characteristics, so that the most appropriate school program may be planned for him. Appraisal is made in two ways, viz., by the personal, "clinical" judgment of guidance workers, teachers, administrators, and staff; and by measurement instruments. Measurement instruments devised for pupil appraisal usually fall into one of four categories: nationally standardized tests, school system tests, school testing programs, and individual testing programs. The most commonly used appraisal instruments are intelligence tests, aptitude tests, personality tests, personal and social adjustment tests, attitude and values tests, and achievement tests.

6. *The records service* assembles and gathers in a central location the available data concerning the pupil's aptitudes, interests, abilities, achievements, and personality characteristics. The guidance record usually contains more information than the standard cumulative record kept on file in the administrative office and in the homeroom teacher's records. An important part of the guidance record is a confidential record made by the counselor of privileged material discussed in the interview or gained from confidential or semiconfidential sources. The records service facilitates interpretation and evaluation of the pupil in terms of the perspective of his entire past development.

7. *The referral service* recommends and indicates to the student a more specialized person or agency which can give him better help than he is presently obtaining. The necessity for referral originates with a student who has needs too specialized for a teacher or counselor to handle adequately. Neither the teacher in his capacity as guidance worker nor the counselor

can provide for every distinctive pupil need. Referrals are made to specialists within the school (e.g., the school psychologist), to specialists within the school system (e.g., the child guidance clinician), or to specialists in non-school agencies (e.g., a psychiatric social worker attached to a community social service agency). The counselor follows up a student whom he has referred for more specialized treatment, and he maintains a close working relationship with referral persons and referral agencies so that he can utilize them optimally. He assists in the development of referral procedures within the school and the school system, as well as with outside agencies.

8. *The placement service* assists the student in situating himself in the proper scholastic "track" (e.g., college preparatory), in the proper course (e.g., trigonometry), and in the proper postschool environment (e.g., a suitable college or a suitable occupation). It helps all pupils—the normal, the intellectually gifted, the emotionally disturbed, the mentally retarded, and the artistically talented—to find their appropriate niches in the school and vocational setting. An effective placement service has established procedures for appropriate track and course selection, as well as for further educational and occupational choices. The service accepts appropriate data from sending schools and transmits pertinent information to receiving schools and to prospective employers. In addition, it maintains close contact with admissions officers of colleges and graduate schools, as well as with personnel managers in business and industry.

9. *The follow-up service* continues to assist the student after he has been placed in what he and the guidance worker have deemed the optimal school, further educational, or occupational setting. The service is the school's recognition that its guidance obligation to the student does not cease once he has been placed. It is maintained by follow-up interviews with the student and those involved in his new setting, e.g., his employer; follow-up questionnaires to the student asking his degree of satisfaction in his new setting; and follow-up guidance bulletins giving him relevant information helpful in achieving self-actualization in his new environment.

10. *The developmental service* provides total and coordinated assistance to the student through the development and organization of appropriate guidance procedures, activities, and emphases on a school-wide level. This service needs to be perpetually updated since new techniques, procedures, approaches, and assistances must be constantly injected into the guidance program both to meet adequately the emerging needs of the students and to improve the quality of the existing program.

11. *The staff service* aids the student through integrating and harmonizing the efforts of all the school personnel directly or indirectly involved in the guidance program. It also aims at increasing the number and efficiency of referral specialists and referral agencies so as to render more comprehensive assistance to every student, however exceptional.

12. *The parent and community service* provides assistance to parents and members of the community who have problems or who wish to improve their level of self-actualization. Occasionally parents have serious mental or emotional disturbances which consciously or unconsciously affect the psychic

functioning of their offspring. The successful solution to the problems of the offspring or the prevention of psychic disorders among them might well necessitate referral of their parents to specialized community helping agencies for psychological or psychiatric treatment. On occasion the counselor or other guidance worker might lecture community groups on positive mental hygiene or on the operation of the school's guidance program so that these groups can assist the school in its guidance efforts (Bennett, 1959, p. 109; W. O. Williams, 1954, pp. 129–151).

13. *The research service* investigates and evaluates the effectiveness of the various aspects of the guidance program so that the students will be assisted in an increasingly superior manner. The research should be undertaken not only by the school system but by each individual school under the leadership of its guidance director or head counselor (Campanelle, 1963). The service attempts to examine both the personnel in the school guidance program and their techniques of guidance. Evaluation of personnel and techniques can be made by clients, guidance and counseling experts, later teachers, fellow students, employers, parents, and community people. Methods used in evaluation include the following: external criteria; before-and-after comparisons; client opinion; opinion of knowledgeable others, e.g., guidance experts or parents; two- or three-group methods, i.e., control group and experimental group or groups; follow-up studies; and case studies (Froehlich, 1949; F. W. Miller, 1961, pp. 228–247). Of course, school system guidance officers as well as guidance research specialists utilize more sophisticated techniques than these. Research and evaluation, whether conducted locally by the school counselor or on a system-wide level, present many formidable problems, such as the establishment of valid criteria and the allotment of sufficient time to carry out the research (Humphreys, Traxler, & North, 1960, pp. 224–237). Nonetheless, the importance of the research service cannot be overestimated, because it provides the only sound, empirical basis on which to develop and improve every aspect of each guidance service and indeed of the entire guidance program.

SOME WELLSPRINGS
OF GUIDANCE

Guidance is an art-science, and no art-science is an island unto itself. For much of its direction, development, and fructification, guidance receives continual nourishment from many deeper wellsprings. To perform his function properly and fruitfully, the guidance worker must be familiar with the content, spirit, methodology, and literature of the four principal wellsprings of guidance, viz., theology, philosophy, psychology, and sociology.

Theological wellsprings

Are guidance and counseling totally objective sciences, or do they derive some of their strength from value wellsprings, both theological and philo-

sophical? This is a hotly debated point among non-Catholic guidance specialists and counseling theorists, as can be illustrated by the controversy in the
late 1950s between Orville S. Walters (1958) and Myron Brender (1959).
Walters argued that counseling and therapy are existentially and therapeuti-
cally impossible without the substrata of religion and philosophy as the guiding values. Brender countered that such a view exemplified "the recrudescent
retreat from empiricism increasingly characteristic of our age." Walters asserted that empirical science is quite limited, in that it cannot tell the client
anything of reality beyond the reach of science. Brender answered that "a
minimal definition of reality might be all that which manifests in some aspect
the property of extension in space and time." Walters contended that therapy
and counseling plunge immediately into theology and philosophy because,
in dealing with persons, scientific precision is perforce lost and the realm
of values becomes crucial. Brender replied that therapy and counseling do
not deal with values but rather attempt to make clear to the client the causes
and consequences of his behavior with a view to assisting him in working
out a solution.

Despite Brender's highly positivistic position, it is obvious that guidance
and counseling are and indeed must be based on such nonempirical values
as the worth of the individual. Natural science cannot determine value but
merely observes, describes, and classifies *what is* and attempts to predict what
will be. It cannot decide *what ought to be*. In fact, it cannot even determine
whether the scientist's knowledge of what is, is epistemologically valid.
Conant, an eminent chemist, holds that natural science as a conceptual entity
is manifestly inadequate to account for everything in the universe. Natural
science is incomplete because, among other things, it fails to explore or provide for the altruistic side of human nature (Conant, 1955). A careful analysis of the mental-hygiene movement by K. Davis (1958, p. 65) concluded
that the role of those concerned with the prevention and treatment of the
mentally troubled is not so much that of a scientist as that of a practicing
moralist operating out of a scientific, mobile context. Commenting on Davis's
opinion, Shoben (1961, p. 347) remarked that considerations of mental
health and personality adjustment are problems of how a person should live,
"a moral problem of how conflicting needs and values may best be reconciled
within individuals and between persons and groups, the ethical problem of
how a man may properly judge the 'rightness' or 'goodness' of his own
conduct and that of his fellows." These questions are in the domain of
religion and moral philosophy, both of which consider what man ought to
be, while the behavioral sciences examine what man is. The behavioral sciences need integration with theological and moral sciences to achieve the
total goal of helping man.

In addition to positivism, Freudianism has tended to deny the relevance
of theology and religion. Indeed classical Freudianism leans toward libidinal

reductionism. But surely the quest for holiness is more complex than—and perhaps totally unrelated to—reaction formation against one's childhood "castration fear." Gordon Allport (1955, p. 94) has noted that any theory which holds that adult religion is merely the repetition of one's childhood experiences is a "trivial view," since the most comprehensive units in one's personality are broad, intentional, future-pointed dispositions.

From the Catholic point of view, religious experiences are necessary to promote all aspects of personal growth. A warped or distorted view of Catholicism has regrettably led many Catholics to regard their religion as a restraining rather than as a liberating force in their daily lives. Much of this view is due to the persistence within the Church of the influence of Manichaeanism and Jansenism, heresies which created a tremendous chasm between natural and supernatural, which looked on matter and the world as hindrances to spiritual perfection. A reaction to this erroneous concept of religion gave impetus to much of John Dewey's thought, particularly that great respect for physical matter which constitutes one of the finest elements in his philosophical system. More advanced theologians, perhaps influenced by Fr. Teilhard de Chardin, S.J., affirm the oneness of man's experience and are reuniting God, nature, and man (Fr. R. J. Roth, S.J., 1963). The fruitful doctrine of all creation's participation in God is the keystone to this new yet pristine theology. Fr. Teilhard de Chardin (1960, p. 36) could thus speak of physical matter as "the great and universal Host" which should be prepared and handled in a spirit of adoration. All reality is God-soaked, oozes God, for as Teilhard de Chardin (1960, p. 34) has noted, "by virtue of the Creation, and still more of the Incarnation, *nothing* is profane [i.e., secular] for those who know how to see." Thus Georges Bernanos, the deeply spiritual French Catholic author, could write from a thoroughly Catholic point of view:"When I am dead, tell the sweet Kingdom Earth that I have loved it more than I would ever dare express." For God is incarnated everywhere; Christ walks every street eternally, from the clean-swept Schwarzspanierstrasse in Vienna to the litter-strewn Bowery in New York City.

This new theological view of the world should produce a kerygma of the guidance movement. "Kerygma," which freely translated means "the good news of salvation," has been the driving force behind the Catholic renewal in the improvement of the teaching of religion. The Incarnation is the core of the kerygma, and the kerygma should be the core of Christian guidance. What Dorothy Day (1952, p. 285) has termed the Christian "duty of delight" should underlie the Catholic guidance worker's relationship with the student. The theological wellsprings, or more precisely this kerygmatic thrust, can and must make guidance in the Catholic school a far richer experience for the pupil than guidance in the school which implicitly or explicitly ignores the kerygma and hence denies its relevance to the optimal development of students.

Catholic theology has been and still is often misused insofar as it is conceived as explaining all reality solely in its own terms rather than viewing God's interpenetration in reality as varying according to the specific mode of the reality. Thus, for example, to offer theological causes as total explanations for personality maladjustments or for difficulties in maintaining an adequate social life is patently ridiculous. Yet this concept is still quite prevalent today, as can be evidenced by the following statement of a priest-counselor (Saalfield, 1958, p. 29) recognized in some circles as a guidance expert:"The best qualification for a Catholic guidance worker is the possession of the *gift of counsel* which comes from the abiding presence of the Holy Spirit. This point cannot be stressed too much in Catholic guidance." More advanced Catholic thinkers would hold that professional competence integrated with a Christian *Weltanschauung* is the *best, but by no means the only,* qualification for a Catholic guidance worker. Lack of a proper theological balance often has hindered guidance in Catholic schools. Thus Msgr. Fuerst (1954, p. 254) has noted that "the logical pursuance of a supernatural destiny [by the Catholic school] might give rise to a certain weakness, not intended, but produced incidentally. Teaching personnel may by too complete insistence on blind obedience to rule and strict acquiescence to precept rob the child of originality and prevent self-expression." This was further demonstrated in an empirical investigation by Fr. Roesch, S.M. (1954, p. 364), of Catholic youths who transferred from a Catholic to a public school. These youths declared that the greatest advantage of the new school environment was freedom—freedom from strict and often ultrastrict and detailed regulations and harsh enforcement, freedom to choose their own curriculum, freedom from discrimination, in short, freedom *to be* and *to become.*

The emphasis in Catholic theology on man-to-God relationships has sometimes led to neglect of a realization of the Christian import of man-to-man relations. Indeed non-Catholics and atheists in the last 200 years have carried the banner of Christ with respect to furthering humanitarian causes far more often than have the Catholics. Jacob's study (1957, pp. 19–20) of youths in non-Catholic colleges discovered that the less religious youths tended to be more humanitarian than the more religious ones. Fr. Charles F. Donovan, S.J. (1960, p. 91), has perceptively remarked in this connection:

If we [Catholic educators and guidance workers] are not loyal to the rich content of Christian humanism, our secular colleagues will be more successful than we. An educator who sees no religious dimension to life but who is impressed by his own finitude may honestly come to view himself as no better, no more important than the youngster in front of him. The bleak finality of life on earth may give life a poignancy and importance that make such an adult almost apostolic in his urge to help young men and women get the most out of it, to guide them to live fruitfully and with satisfaction these threescore years which are the be-all, and alas the end-all of existence. Here is no supernatural charity, here is none of the spirit of Christ, but here *is* a genuine human concern for the student as a person—perhaps as a wayfarer homeless in search of a home, as the existentialists say. And compared to this secular gospel of service, compared to this obviously sincere involvement in the interests and welfare of others, the Catholic counselor, who may be preoccupied with his own spiritual perfection, who may be over-concerned with legalism, who is confident that God is the child's ultimate guide and goal, who believes that this life is of minor significance compared to the next, such a Catholic counselor comes in a poor second.

Philosophical wellsprings

Guidance deals with human beings and therefore finds nourishment in philosophy, the science which probes the deepest and most ultimate roots of human existence. The growth of the behavioral sciences and the social sciences, such as education, guidance, and psychology, in both power and prestige has led to a divorce between humanistic and philosophic traditions and these new sciences (Riesman, 1956). In turn, philosophers (cf. V. E. Smith, 1960) and the litterateurs (S. G. Molnar, 1961) have tended too easily to dismiss the new sciences as unworthy of serious attention. A rapprochement where philosophical wisdom can enrich the behavioral and social sciences, and vice versa, must be reached.

Perceptive Catholic and non-Catholic psychologists and guidance experts have affirmed the necessity for seeing the philosophical wellsprings of all aspects of guidance. Zilboorg (1955, pp. 107–110), a Catholic psychiatrist, holds that man's fundamental problems arise from anxiety and conflicts about his basic self, his oughts, his personness, all of which are intimately bound up with ontology (as well as with theology). O. S. Walters's review (1958, p. 245) of the theorists of neuroses concludes that "efforts to understand neurosis apart from an ontology of anxiety have been disappointing." Allport (1953, p. 347) has contended that "whether he knows it or not, every psychologist gravitates toward an ontological position," whether positivism, idealism, realism, or personalism. Harry Stack Sullivan (1953, pp. 53–55) maintains that anxiety is limited to human beings. Allers (1955) holds that a person's metaphysical difficulties usually erupt in the form of psychological problems. Some more alert public school educators and public school systems, such as the Oregon State Department of Education (1961), have recognized the philosophical wellsprings of guidance and have recommended that every school guidance worker be "thoroughly grounded" in the philosophy of education.

The impact of existentialist psychology has done much to awaken the counseling aspect of guidance to its philosophical underpinnings. From this font flowed the concept of the counselor as one who is existentially oriented, whose concern is for the client as an immediate, emerging person. The counselor meets the client in an interhuman, existential encounter, in an open relationship, as person to person in which the dichotomy of twoness is not emphasized; rather emphasis is placed on two beings working together toward common understanding (May, Angel, & Ellenberger, 1958). The counselor "allows what is to be, so that it can reveal itself in the essence of its being, and then proceeds to elucidate what he understands" (Hora, 1960). The counseling encounter thus stresses two persons as together, affirming and confirming the existence of each other by total acceptance. This infusion of philosophy into the aorta of the guidance movement has given the latter new dimensions, new depth, and above all new relevance.

The increased emphasis in guidance theory on man's rationality and goodness is in some way a restatement of an older, traditional philosophical position. Thus Wild (1953) notes that the traditional concept of the natural law implies that goodness lies in the realization of essential human tendencies, while it was Thomas Hobbes and John Locke who believed that the natural law arose from society's wish to curb man's desires. The Puritan and Jansenistic attitude toward keeping the student's striving for self-actualization in constant check owes more to the Hobbesian than to the Thomistic concept of the natural law. Belief in man's essential goodness, a philosophical position, has been expressed well by C. R. Rogers (1957b, p. 202): "Man's behavior is exquisitely rational, moving with subtle complexity toward the goals his organism is endeavoring to achieve. The tragedy for most of us is that our defenses keep us from being aware of this rationality, so that consciously we are moving in one direction while organismically we are moving in another." This is reminiscent of St. Paul's concept of the struggle between the various aspects of the human being, the "war of the members."

While Thomism is the "official" philosophical system of the Church, it would be lamentable if Catholics restricted their philosophical orientation to guidance solely to this system. Regrettably too many Catholics (cf. Cavanagh & Fr. McGoldrick, S.J., 1958, pp. 80–94) tend to judge guidance, psychology, and psychoanalysis totally according to Thomistic norms, failing to realize that there are other philosophies, even other Christian philosophies, which have given valuable insights into reality. Thomism is not revealed truth but instead a provisional philosophical system which, like Augustinianism before the thirteenth century, might be seriously modified or even be replaced with the advent of new knowledge and new insights into reality. The *Summa Theologica* is not the seventy-third book of the Bible. "It is to the Gospel, and not to Scholasticism, that God from on high has promised indefectibility" (F. Arnold, 1957, p. 60).

There are many areas of vital interest to modern life which St. Thomas did not treat. An outstanding example of such a lacuna is the role of intuition in the thinking process. Intuition is direct experiencing, as contrasted with abstraction, which "slices up" reality for analysis. Studies conducted at the

Institute for Personality Assessment (Rowan, 1961) concluded that the highly creative people in all fields are overwhelmingly intuitive and that creative people are more open to experiences both within and without. Recently Zen Buddist philosophy has been in evidence in guidance literature. Zen philosophers propose the doctrine of no-thought, a process in which a person allows "the mind to function on its own, free of thought about the environment, free of any object of consciousness, free of ideas, of good and bad, free of established forms of practices" (Berger, 1962, p. 123). Somewhat allied to this is the Idealist notion of rational thought as essentially nonconceptual (Radhakrishnan, 1937). Both counseling theory and psychoanalytic theory stress the role of intuition in the process of counseling and therapy. Hence there are many fruitful but non-Thomistic philosophical wellsprings of guidance.

Finally, there is an issue of capital importance, viz., that man is a supposit, a person. Because he exists in himself and is endowed with a human nature, he possesses dignity *in se,* a dignity which carries with it a *right* to self-direction. Every person is given free will to direct his life as he wishes. It is the function of the guidance worker not to thwart the Creator by using guidance subtly to deprive the student of his free will through maneuvering him or steering him but rather to cooperate in assisting the student fully to direct himself.

Psychological wellsprings

The client's psychic processes are influenced by many conditions immanent to each client. First, age has a profound effect on the personality of the client. A child client is typically a happy, expansive, discovering person, but as an adolescent the same human being may be quite different. Teen-age is the border region of reality where *joie de vivre* and gloom, the ridiculous and the sublime, hell and the happy isles converge, where champagne is often as not tears. Second, sex is an important conditioner of personality. Boys learn differently than girls, have different personality thrusts. As Reik (1963, pp. 11, 82) has noted, girls want to be loved for what they are, and boys for what they accomplish. A boy must have dedication and concentration to something outside himself, such as a cause or a task, while such a psychological necessity may not exist for a girl. Third, the intelligence of the client makes a radical difference in how he views the world, how he functions as a person. Fourth, the specific needs of the client, arising out of developmental tasks, physical maturation, and so forth, have a vital impact on the client. Fifth, the client's individual problems leave their mark and indeed shape the general contours of his personality. Sixth, the client's self-concept and self-acceptance are of great importance. Brother John M. Egan, F.S.C.H. (1961b, p. 82), has noted that various research investigations have demonstrated a relationship between levels of self-acceptance and the wholesomeness or unwholesomeness of behavior. Seventh, personality structure does much to condition a person's present and future human functioning. Thus, for example, it has been found (Cavanagh & Fr. McGoldrick, S.J., 1958, p. 403) that a rigid personality structure is often characteristic of the prepsychotic state of a seriously disturbed person.

From the psychological standpoint, the student's perception of reality is far more important than is the objectivity of that reality. Consequently, whether the school, the teacher, or the counselor accepts or rejects the client as a person is not so important psychologically as whether the student *perceives* himself as accepted or rejected by these others. Clients are subjective entities, not masses of ambulatory objectivities. The emphasis by Catholics on objective reality and objective truth has often blinded them to this crucial psychological fact.

Man is a psychologically integrated being, i.e., a psychic thrust of whatever kind exists in the person not in isolation but always in an affected-affecting relationship with other mental and emotional thrusts. Thus, for example, one's interest in a particular occupation is an extension of one's self-concept, not merely an isolated concern of the individual. Hence Super (1954, p. 61), reviewing Fr. Curran's otherwise outstanding book *Counseling in Catholic Life and Education,* observed that this widely used volume does not even index the terms *occupation* and *vocation.* He remarked that some guidance theorists "still deny the reality of work and occupation as parts of the lives of our clients."

In an attempt to fathom more meaningfully the psychological wellsprings of guidance, personality theories have been briefly summarized in Chapter 2. None of these theories is "right" or "wrong" but rather represent different ways of looking at man's psychic structure. Each theory sees the person from a different perspective, with none offering the total view. Hence guidance or counseling based on one personality theory alone might be effective in helping John Jones but ineffective in assisting Sara Smith. Personality theories are like spotlights thrown from different angles, each illuminating some aspects of the human personality which another theory does not reveal. Therefore the doctrine of concurrent truth applies to personality theory; i.e., each of them may be "true" at the same time, although they do not agree with one another.

Sociological wellsprings

Man becomes what he is through interaction with his milieu. His widest cultural context as well as the specific social setting in which he lives have considerable impact in forming his lifeway, his attitudes, his goals, his entire personal *modus operandi.* Kardiner's researches (1939) concluded that where children are regularly cared for in a specific manner within a given culture, most of them are likely to develop a similar "basic personality." Thus, for example, it is possible to speak with some validity of "the Belgian way of thinking," as contrasted with "the Italian way of thinking," as contrasted in turn with "the American way of thinking." A study by Mother Hortense Doyle, R.S.C.J. (1960), of American and Canadian teen-age pupils revealed that students' self-concepts were positively influenced by the culture in which they lived. Further, subcultures have a great effect on the developing student, particularly the three subcultures of socioeconomic milieu, religious atmosphere, and school setting.

Socioeconomic environment, in the totality of the term, has enormous influence on the developing person. Youths from a low socioeconomic subculture develop values which are quite different in many respects from those of youths from a high socioeconomic subculture; e.g., socioeconomically disadvantaged youths usually react favorably to behaviors involving overt hostility such as fist fighting on the street, while socioeconomically advantaged youths usually look down on such behaviors as exemplifying rowdyism and lack of gentlemanly conduct. A celebrated investigation by Bruner and Goodman (1947) disclosed that poor children visually overestimated the size of coins, while wealthy children underestimated their size. This illustrates the effect of socioeconomic environment on visual perception. A study by Brother Clement Cosgrove, S.C. (1955, p. 295), revealed that the socioeconomic status of the Catholic elementary school children investigated had a significant influence on the extent of the children's theoretical and practical knowledge of religious and moral truths. A study by Singer, Stefflre, and Thompson (1958) of 672 male high school seniors concluded that there was a definite relationship between the socioeconomic status of a father and his son's temperament; i.e., boys from professional homes tended to be more friendly and more active than the rest of the group, boys from skilled workers' homes more active and less restrained, and boys from agricultural and unskilled workers' homes less active, less restrained, and less thoughtful. A comprehensive study (Ugurel-Semin, 1952) of Turkish youths revealed that poor children were the least selfish and ranked high in generosity, rich children tended to be generous rather than equalitarian, and middle-class children were the least generous and the most selfish.

Religious affiliation and religious environment in general have a sizable effect on a person's basic attitudes and life-style. Research investigations by J. D. Donovan (1963), Lenski (1961), and Rosen (1959) have found that the Catholic milieu does not encourage, and perhaps indeed inhibits, the achievement motive in its members as contrasted with members of non-Catholic milieus. These empirical studies buttress the contentions of figures like Msgr. Ellis (1955) and O'Dea (1958) that American Catholicism so emphasizes original sin, a false concept of humility, a misconception of docility, and an ultraconcentration on the otherworldly that American Catholics have made relatively little contribution to the intellectual or cultural life of their homeland. Pallone's investigation (1963e) of the dynamics of perception among students in a male Catholic college disclosed these students were so docile to clerical authority that when a nonpunitive, unknown person in clerical garb told them that a certain projected clear geometric figure was grossly larger than it obviously was, there was significantly high agreement with this perceived clerical authority. This finding is cognate to a study of professed women religious by Sister Marie Francis Kenoyer, S.L. (1961), which revealed that nuns perceived themselves as more submissive and more shy than a matched group of lay persons. Sister Marie Francis concluded that this difference was due to the effect of convent life on the nuns, chiefly because these women religious were matched with the lay people before they entered convent life.

The school itself is a social setting. A review of the pertinent research by Lee (1963b, p. 531) concluded that in the case of maladjusted pupils the school is often a major factor in contributing to maladjustment. Indeed the school contains a number of predisposing factors to juvenile delinquency. J. S. Coleman's investigations (1961) found that the school climate or environment can stimulate or stifle student effectiveness and development. His study of the effects of differing school social climates highlights the influence within a school of peer groups on a student's motivational level and direction, as well as on his performance. A study by Torrance (1962a), comparing the attitudes of students in a public Midwestern college in terms of place of college residence, concluded that students living in private homes made the greatest gain in positive attitudes toward responsibility, while those living in the dormitory made the least change. Students living in fraternity houses assumed responsibility in an authoritarian atmosphere with an authoritarian attitude. Both the student's basic culture and the various subcultures out of which he operates have a decided influence in the shaping of his personality.

THE "ESSENCE"
OF GUIDANCE

The role of guidance in the school

Conant (1958, p. 5) remarked that the success or failure of the school depends in large measure on the success or failure of its guidance program. Certainly it is impossible for the school to fulfill its total educative function without an organized, pervasive, overall guidance program.

The crucial importance of the school guidance program can be partially appreciated by noting six major contributions which it makes to the educational enterprise. *First,* guidance assists the student to develop as a total person rather than emphasizing growth in one specific human area, such as the mind or will only. Provided in the classroom situation by the teacher or in the guidance office by the counselor, guidance concentrates on the unfolding of the pupil's total personality in accordance with the developmental pattern unique to that student. As Mounier (1938, p. 22) noted, this concentration on the total personal development of the student aims at a "profound transformation" of the work of the school, particularly the work of the school as "traditionalists" view it. *Second,* guidance helps the student to build the capacity to solve problems which perhaps might otherwise go unsolved. A student with a personal problem gets no aid from a teacher who simply gives instruction in his subject. If this teacher injects the guidance point of view into classroom or extraclassroom activities, however, or if the student takes his problem to the counselor, then there is considerable hope that the pupil will be helped. *Third,* guidance assists the student to know more about himself through measurement and appraisal. This appraisal is much more comprehensive in scope than the measurement for academic achievement utilized in traditional classroom situations. Rather, guidance appraisal encompasses all aspects of pupil growth and development, ranging from personality to vocational aptitude. Thus the student is enabled to get a total picture of himself as derived from the composite of measurement and particular appraisal. *Fourth,* guidance assists the student to develop a self-identity free from distortion so that he can organize his own life in such a manner as both to cope effectively with those situations which life presents and to attain total self-actualization. As was indicated in Chapter 2, a realistic self-concept is crucial not only to fruitful living but also to the effective performance of one's tasks, including academic tasks. Guidance is the only school service which has as one of its direct objectives the development within the student of an adequate self-concept. *Fifth,* guidance helps the student to develop insight into the dynamics of his behavior. Self-insight is both a process and a product. The process of self-insight is an operation which the student must use constantly throughout his lifetime and is developed only by the actual probing and penetration of one's very self. Self-insight as a product refers to the understanding of self which one finally arrives at after the probing and penetration of self. Guidance is the only school service which directly fosters in the pupil the process and the product of total self-insight. *Sixth,* guidance assists the student to self-actualize both his present capacities and those inherent in his developmental pattern. Indeed this is the very purpose of the guidance effort; all other guidance endeavors, such as developing self-insight, assistance in the solution of problems, and so forth, are means to the final end of self-actualization. Other school activities, such as classroom instruction (as distinct from teaching), seek to help the pupil to actualize only *part* of himself. Guidance aims at *total* self-actualization.

Guidance, like every other aspect of the school's program, is rooted in the educational philosophy of the school. Many Catholic (cf. Kerins, 1957) and non-Catholic (cf. Bowles, 1959) educators who hold that the goal of the school is primarily or exclusively the development of the pupil's intellect regard guidance as tangential to the school's role and therefore of little importance. What guidance there is, is almost exclusively scholastic guidance. Those Catholic (cf. Fr. K. J. O'Brien, C.SS.R., 1958) and non-Catholic educators who contend that the purpose of the school is primarily or exclusively character development, moral training or both, regard spiritual or religious guidance as the only necessary type of guidance. This explains why Catholic schools, chiefly based on and organized around the moralist position, have woefully neglected all forms of guidance except religious and possibly scholastic guidance. Educators who contend that knowledge and action are coequal goals of the school (the virtue called "prudence" by the Scholastics) believe that all types of guidance are necessary to fulfill the school's total educative function (Aquinas, *Summa Theologica,* II–II, qq. 47–56; Lee, 1963b, pp. 65–70; Pallone, 1962a; Policies Committee, 1958).

Approaches to guidance

When a guidance worker engages in school guidance, he does so within the context of his perception of what guidance ought to be, of what guidance should accomplish. The attitude of the worker toward his task, i.e., his basic approach to his role, has important, direct ramifications on the type of guidance which takes place. Barry and Wolf (1957, pp. 39–52) have suggested eight distinct approaches to guidance:

THE EDUCATIONAL-VOCATIONAL APPROACH.   This approach regards the student primarily as a future worker, whose fulfillment in life comes through his occupation. Therefore school guidance focuses chiefly on helping him find his proper place in the world of work, a place eminently suitable both for the fulfillment of his own needs and for the welfare of society.

THE SERVICES APPROACH.   This approach regards the student primarily as an entity composed of many need segments, such as health needs, intellectual needs, emotional needs, and so forth. Therefore school guidance is a confederation of services the combination of which helps the student meet all the various segments of his total need structure.

THE COUNSELING APPROACH.   This approach regards the student primarily as a person who has a number of unresolved psychological problems. Therefore school guidance chiefly if not exclusively comprises counseling sessions or psychological interviews in order to help the student to harmonize both with himself and with society.

THE ADJUSTMENT APPROACH. This approach regards the student primarily as a member of society, one who either fits or does not fit in well with his group and with the larger society. Therefore school guidance concentrates not on pupil self-development but rather on assisting the individual to adjust and conform to the demands and exigencies of both his own group and the larger society.

THE PROBLEM-CENTERED APPROACH. This approach regards a student as normal unless he manifests needs which put him outside the range of "normal students," thereby presenting special or abnormal problems, e.g., special needs for college preparation, for the emotionally disturbed, for the artistically gifted, for cases of misbehavior. Therefore school guidance concentrates almost exclusively on those with special problems since only they really need help.

THE EDUCATIVE APPROACH. This approach regards the student as essentially a learner who "needs" guidance not in a special setting (i.e., in the counselor's office) but rather meshed with his other learning experiences. Therefore school guidance consists chiefly in efforts in the homeroom as well as in the classroom by the teacher during the very process of teaching, with only certain extreme cases being referred to the counselor.

THE DEVELOPMENTAL APPROACH. This approach regards the student primarily as a constantly growing self who can substantially benefit from assistance at stages of his development in order to attain self-fulfillment. Therefore school guidance should be continuous at all grade levels and not available only at crisis points when a pupil exhibits marked or abnormal problems.

THE INTEGRATED APPROACH. This approach regards the student not only as he is in himself but also as he is in the school setting, interacting with teachers, clerical staff, administrators, and fellow students. Therefore school guidance not only centers on the pupil but involves each member of the school community in order to create a school-wide atmosphere which favors the personal growth and development of everyone in the school.

Barry and Wolf emphasize that these eight approaches are not intended to be all-inclusive but rather indicative of the chief guidance approaches. Further, each of these views has validity, albeit some more than others; it is not a question of branding any one of them as totally acceptable or totally unacceptable.

Another useful, although not completely different, delineation of guidance approaches has been made by Mathewson. Drawing on a tentative model (1961), Mathewson identified (1962, pp. 97–104) seven basic approaches to guidance in terms of dichotomies. Between each pole of the dichotomy is a continuum, so that a guidance worker's individual approach could be at either pole or somewhere in between.

EDUCATIVE-DIRECTIVE APPROACH.   At the educative pole, guidance is regarded as a learning process in which the student develops self-insight and the ability to make his own decisions. At the directive end of the continuum, guidance is conceived as diagnosis by the guidance worker of the student's problem, followed by recommendations by the worker on how the pupil can best solve his problem.

CUMULATIVE–PROBLEM-POINT APPROACH.   At the cumulative pole, guidance is regarded as a continuous process of assistance to students at every educational level. At the problem-point end of the continuum, guidance is conceived as necessary only at those times in the lives of the students when special problems erupt or crucial decisions must be made.

SELF-EVALUATIVE–MENTOR-EVALUATIVE APPROACH.   At the self-evaluative pole, guidance is regarded as freeing the student to integrate by himself his own personal perceptions and constructs into a paradigm of effective self-definition and self-identity. At the mentor-evaluative end of the continuum, guidance is conceived as placing the student in a relationship with a mature, professionally experienced individual who will be able to assess objectively and skillfully both the individual himself and the self-in-situation.

PERSONAL VALUE–SOCIAL VALUE APPROACH.   At the personal value pole, guidance is regarded as being almost solely concerned with the satisfaction of each student's unique needs, purposes, and values. At the social value end of the continuum, guidance is conceived as almost exclusively concentrating on societal or institutional needs.

SUBJECTIVE-FOCUS–OBJECTIVE-FOCUS APPROACH.   At the subjective pole, guidance is regarded as directed toward the internal psychological events, processes, feelings, and thoughts of the student. At the objective end of the continuum, guidance is conceived as the evaluation and interpretation of the student almost solely on the basis of the objective tests.

MULTIPHASIC-UNIPHASIC APPROACH.   At the multiphasic pole, guidance is regarded as a comprehensive process in which all but extremely deep problems requiring psychotherapy may be handled by a general practitioner of guidance, viz., the trained counselor. At the uniphasic end of the continuum, guidance is conceived as requiring concentration by highly skilled specialists on only one or another segment of guidance, e.g., vocational guidance, personal guidance, and so forth.

COORDINATIVE-SPECIALIZED APPROACH. At the coordinative pole, guidance is regarded as a cooperative affair in which every member of the school staff plays an important role in the overall school guidance program. At the specialized end of the continuum, guidance is conceived as conducted almost exclusively by trained professional specialists with little or no help from teachers, administrators, and other school staff members.

Degrees of depth in guidance

In reference to degrees of depth, it is important to distinguish three areas of guidance which the school provides for the student, viz., general all-school guidance; individual, or personalized, guidance; and group guidance.

General all-school guidance consists in nonpersonalized assistance which the school offers the student in an effort to help him self-actualize. Examples of this type of guidance include the establishment within the school library of a special section devoted to occupational and educational literature and the setting up of career days, college nights, and so forth. Because of its general, all-purpose nature, there are no definite levels of depth in this area of guidance. General all-school guidance inheres in the development-facilitating social structure of the school.

Individualized, or personalized, guidance has three degrees of depth levels, viz., advisement, counseling, and psychotherapy. *Advisement* is the supplying of information of one kind or another to the client in order to fill in some gap in his knowledge or to broaden his horizons (e.g., giving the student a list of occupations which the guidance worker thinks might be of use or interest to him). *Counseling* refers to assisting the pupil to develop optimal self-actualization by the effective utilization of his present resources and by the elimination of the more elemental blocks to the use of these resources. In phenomenological terms, counseling helps the client to clarify, modify, and subsequently to reorganize the valenced figures in his perceptual field for optimal personal functioning. *Psychotherapy* (or *therapy,* as it is usually called) aims at a personality change, a basic restructuring of some sort. This change and restructuring aim at alleviating profound distortions or psycho-pathologies within the personality, while counseling aims at optimal development of the reasonably healthy or minimally unhealthy personality. Unlike therapy, counseling does not attempt to delve into the sources of more deeply rooted conflicts but rather tries to discover some unblocked path through which the person can move toward fruitful living or to help him erect a healthy (or perhaps even a minimally unhealthy) defense against some anxiety or conflict inhibiting fruitful living (Tyler, 1961, pp. 221–224). Psychoanalysts contend that psychoanalysis comprises the deepest level of psychological helping relationship, for it aims to help the patient explore the inmost recessed, unconscious sectors of his existence, with the goal of effecting a profound alteration of his personality. Psychologists tend to regard analysis as a type of therapy, while psychoanalysts generally believe that it constitutes a deeper level of treatment distinct from therapy. Therapy is offered properly only by a duly qualified and trained counseling psychologist, clinical psychologist, social worker, or psychiatrist who has had postdoctoral training in psychotherapy. The distinction between counseling psychology and clinical psychology is not accepted by many writers, including Hahn and MacLean, Patterson, and Williamson and Darley. Notwithstanding, there are separate divisions in the American Psychological Association for counseling and clinical psychology, thus indicating that the official body does in fact recognize the difference. On this point, the reader should see Gustad (1953, p. 5). Analysis can legitimately be performed only by a trained psychoanalyst. If the school counselor believes that the client's problem is too serious for counseling, he makes a formal referral to someone competent to treat the problem, e.g., the school psychologist, the school psychiatrist, or a community agency mental-health specialist. The imposition (possibly excessive at times) of clinical counseling theory on school guidance should not delude the counselor into thinking he is a therapist. To do so results in psychological harm to the client.

Group guidance has four depth levels, viz., group advisement, group guidance in species, multiple counseling, and group therapy. The goals of group advisement and of group guidance are generally equivalent on a group level to individual advisement and counseling. Multiple counseling is a small-group guidance situation involving 3 to 10 students who work together toward the solution of some common pressing problem. Group therapy is a distinct type of psychotherapy. A guidance-trained teacher can use group advisement and group guidance in species with effectiveness. A counselor can utilize group advisement, group guidance in species, and multiple counseling. Group therapy should be left to specialists.

The counseling subprocess

When psychology and later guidance were struggling to become recognized and gain prestige as sciences, an almost purely empirical viewpoint and approach were embraced "with a vengeance" (Borow, 1956, p. 292). Now that both psychology and guidance have been accepted on their merits, they need to mature to include the human (as opposed to the statistical) dimension, else the poets will tell students more about themselves than will psychologists and guidance experts.

The humanization of guidance can be well illustrated by examining what has happened to its most important subprocess, viz., counseling. Perhaps more than anyone else, Carl Rogers diverted the direction of counseling (and thence guidance) from a purely scientific approach to that of an "artistic" relationship between the counselor and the client (although he did so on the basis of considerable empirical evidence). His emphasis on the necessity of establishing a warm, giving relationship with the client, of the dynamics of the relationship itself, helped move counseling away from its statistical, definitely predictive, careful step-by-step system of analysis and interviewing. Many counseling theorists and practitioners still prefer the old, sequential methods of counseling. Patterson (1960, p. 12) describes a typical use of this method in occupational rehabilitation counseling which can be extrapolated to the other types of counseling: "He [the counselor] determines the eligibility of clients as clients and the feasibility of their rehabilitation; he *appraises* the client's vocational potential and the probability of his success; he *evaluates* the suitability of various jobs; he *interviews* the client toward realistic (as defined by himself) goals; he *develops* a vocational rehabilitation plan with all its parts; he *carries out* the plan, implementing and administering its various aspects; he *makes referrals* to related services. One might ask: What is the client doing all this time? Too often he is literally doing nothing except what he is told to do by the counselor, who, of course, is evaluating him in fine empirical fashion." This method is quite in harmony with the early Williamson theory and technique (1939; 1950), which are decidedly clinically oriented.

Effective counseling partakes of both art and science and should render the question "Is counseling persons an art or science?" a false dichotomy. The counselor is an artist, not in the sense in which a sculptor is the molder of an inert and pliable lump of clay, but in the sense of the conductor who brings out the full richness of the orchestra. The modern person-centered spirit of counseling has spilled over and penetrated other guidance functions and services. Consequently emphasis on guidance as artistry, as deeply concerned with the personal element, has spread beyond counseling itself to group guidance, to advisement, and even to the mechanical, non-personalized aspects of guidance, e.g., the tenor of the school's weekly guidance bulletin. The counselor is also a scientist, for his knowledge of the scientific basis and process of counseling gives him cues as to precisely what behavior to employ in the interview at a given moment.

The five major foci of guidance, viz., personal, social, religious, vocational, and scholastic, are not separate but intimately intertwined. For example, realistic occupational planning is an outcome of the student's self-concept, experiences, and personality dynamics, which include his vocational aptitudes and interests, and not merely of job openings. These in turn are influenced by his social relationships with others, as the studies of Berger (1952) and Brownfain (1952) indicate. Thus the counselor of necessity engages in personal and social counseling even if he is in relationship with a student who exteriorly wishes only occupational or scholastic guidance. In Catholic schools, religious problems very often have their genesis in the pupil's lack of personal and social self-actualization, thus forcing the Catholic counselor to intertwine these considerations in the very core of the interview.

School Counseling

Guidance workers, be they counselors, teachers, or school psychologists, are ever mindful that they practice their art in a school setting. There is considerable difference between guidance *in se* and guidance in the school situation and between counseling *in se* and counseling in the school guidance context. In the school milieu, guidance is but one service within the educational context; counseling is only one service of school guidance. Thus neither guidance nor counseling is an isolated service, but both are deeply related to and indeed further the school's total educational program. This relation of counseling both to school guidance and to education is easily grasped by teachers and teacher-counselors, but it is not apparent to some counselors and guidance specialists. There is a growing movement among some counselor educators to make of school counseling a special service whose relation to the school would consist solely in its being housed there. G. E. Hill's review (1961, p. 356) of the pertinent literature indicates that this separatist, ultraprofessional movement is still quite small in terms of numbers; indeed there has been a strong resurgence of emphasis in the literature on the role of the school counselor as a special type of educator working to achieve educational goals as defined by the school.

Because the school counselor is faced with a heavy case load and resultant paucity of time for each client, most school counseling consists in what Goldburgh and Penney (1962, p. 134) have termed "sector counseling," i.e., focusing on the symptom, its causes, and cure rather than on the basic underlying problem. In sector counseling, for example, handling a scholastic problem of underachievement is concerned with helping the student to study more effectively and perform better on examinations rather than in removing the basic personality, or self-in-situation, cause of the scholastic underachievement (e.g., hostility). In this type of counseling, (1) the material treated in the interview is confined to the boundaries of the specific problem itself (e.g., scholastic underachievement); (2) the counselor merely tries to assist the client to help himself eliminate the external symptom rather than to go deeper to the ultimate or even penultimate cause; and (3) the primary concern is the speedy solution of the surface problem. Sector counseling is certainly not ideal counseling, but it is often the best a counselor can do within the limits of the very heavy case load assigned to him by public, and even more so by Catholic, school officials. Guidance workers and administrators are obliged to urge school boards and diocesan superintendents to provide counselors with a realistic case load to enable them to work properly with students.

Another problem confronting school counselors is that they must bear the brunt of criticism from two other social service professions, viz., psychoanalysts and teachers (Kate H. Mueller, 1959, p. 411). Some psychoanalysts declare that it requires a minimum of $10,000, three years of daily sessions of one hour's duration, and an intelligent client to come to grips with his total personality through psychoanalysis. Because of the exuberance and confusion characteristic of adolescence, the task with this age group is even more difficult. Thus psychoanalysts are aghast that school counselors with considerably less training attempt to assist a student to solve problems at the rate of a single half-hour interview per month for one or two semesters. Teachers believe that, through their classroom instruction and continuous process of scholastic evaluation via marking practices, they are hastening the students' growth and development as rapidly as any counselor. Hence, according to their critics, counselors sail in an uneasy bark between the Scylla of teaching and the Charybdis of psychoanalysis.

The school counselor is committed to the student as no other member of the educational enterprise is. He helps the student appraise himself but does not judge him. He works with disturbed children and youths with problems but does not evaluate. He works with misbehavior cases but does not punish. He gives information but does not give directions on its precise use. And yet despite all this, the school counselor's role is often misunderstood. Some administrators have succumbed to the mania that every student should undergo a little counseling, and so there is an endless parade into the counselor's office, with scarcely any time for each client. Still other administrators regard as the counselor's role solely that of dealing with misbehavior cases and students with other abnormalities. As a result, into the counselor's office come only the walking wounded, the unofficial dead of an affluent bourgeois society. The counselor's office is looked upon as the wastebasket for crumpled lives. Both of these views are incorrect, for the counselor's role is to give help to *anyone who needs it.*

Because guidance and counseling are functions of a social agency, they are of necessity concerned not only with the good of the individual but also with the welfare of society. Often this dual role is considered as a conflict in the guidance worker's function, whether the worker be counselor, specialist, or teacher. This conflict dissolves, however, if it is recalled that when the worker assists the individual to self-actualize (and this is the basic purpose of guidance), he is at the same time contributing to the improvement of the individual and thus automatically to the betterment of society (Berdie, 1960). In Catholic schools, the total fulfillment of the individual which Catholic guidance and counseling are in a position to provide is the best and most efficient way of improving the Church which sponsors the school.

The Process of Counseling

Counseling is essentially a process. When the guidance worker is engaged in counseling, he concentrates on the counseling process and not merely on the end result, whether that result is self-actualization or simply the solution of the client's problem. Catholic guidance workers often fail to appreciate this process emphasis, because in Catholic colleges process philosophy is frequently looked upon with great distrust if not with open hostility. Yet counseling is first and foremost a process, a *learning* process whereby the client discovers himself and learns to utilize himself. It is something *which goes on* between the worker and the client. In the counseling situation, the guidance worker does not so much try to solve the client's "problem" as to create an atmosphere which facilitates the client's developing total self-actualization (Arbuckle, 1950, p. 6). The dynamics of the counseling relationship are suffused with the atmosphere of positively oriented process, of that which assists the client to become himself during the interview itself. Such a positively oriented process atmosphere does not, however, necessitate that the guidance worker take an overtly active role during the counseling relationship. Indeed, Fr. Curran (1960b) emphasizes that the worker's listening in a fully attentive and sympathetic manner is in itself an important process attribute in helping the client come to self-insight and to eventual resolution of his problem. He quotes one client who said of his counselor: "I've never been listened to so well—no one before ever cared so much about what I was saying. I have confidence in speaking. Even if what I say is stupid or foolish, I am not made to feel stupid or foolish myself. I trust the counselor to hold what I say and not to let it slip or become blurred. In such a situation I can react to myself and my own thoughts and feelings much as I might react to those of someone else. There is an objectivity about the counselor's responses that is freeing." Frs. Hagmaier, C.S.P., and Gleason, S.J. (1959, pp. 31–50), have emphasized the role of the priest-counselor as a listener, something which is difficult for clerics because of their customary conception of the role of the priest as the giver of commands and of advice. Even listening has to be a perceptive process; in the interview the guidance worker must "listen with the third ear," to use Vienna-trained Reik's phrase (1948). Counseling, like guidance, is much more a process than a statement of goals.

Counseling and Teaching

There are many basic similarities between counseling and teaching. This is to be expected, since both are fundamentally social learning experiences in which a guidance worker and a student are involved. *First,* the purpose of both counseling and teaching is to effect a change in the thinking and behavior of the student. *Second,* the method basic to each is stimulating the student to mental and indeed to personal self-activity. Guidance, like teaching, is not imparting. Unfortunately many guidance theorists who posit a yawning chasm between teaching on the one hand and guidance and counseling on the other fail to grasp this cardinal point. Thus, for example, Tiedeman and Field (1962, p. 495) assert that "teaching involves a communication of *other's* experience—data and conclusions," while guidance and counseling constitute "primarily an examination of the individual student's experiences—data and the *process of forming* conclusions about them." This faulty concept of teaching has been opposed by such diverse thinkers as St. Thomas Aquinas (*De veritate,* 8:11) and John Dewey (1916). Teaching stresses the process, the activity, whereby the teacher assists the student to learn things by himself, to learn things by and through self-discovery. Imparting of information, or attitudes, or anything else is impossible; there can be no direct transfusion of learning as there is transfusion of blood. *Third,* the processes of teaching, guidance, and counseling, as Gardner Murphy (1961a) has pointed out, are designed to develop self-discovery in the student so as to release his potentialities, to look inward and discover his joyful and wonderfully thrusting self. In Thomistic terminology, teaching, guidance, and counseling assist the student to pass from potency to act. *Fourth,* both teacher and counselor are only secondary proximate causes of the student's learning, with the student himself the primary proximate cause (Lee, 1963b, pp. 228–234). *Fifth,* both counselor and teacher are merely agents or ministers to the student and undertake to "teach" only what is specifically determined jointly by counselor (or teacher) and student (Giles, 1941; Lee, 1963b, pp. 269–285; Sulzer, 1962). Counseling and teaching are both joint searches for truth, for meaning, between the counselor (or teacher) and the student. *Sixth,* in both counseling and the classroom situation, the staff member is the teacher and the youth is the student. The teacher and the counselor in this learning situation merely facilitate learning in the student. This facilitation usually comes about by creating an atmosphere conducive to student learning, by developing empathic oneness, by stimulating the student to self-activity, and occasionally by providing information, e.g., occupational data (Schwebel, 1960). *Seventh,* both teaching and counseling are done in a social setting, i.e., an experiential situation involving an interpersonal encounter, a relationship involving a "we." *Eighth,* the sole criterion of success is the fulfillment of the original joint agreement by student and teacher, by client and counselor, on what was to be the learning outcome. What Karl Menninger (1961, p. 30) stated about psychoanalysis is equally true for both counseling and teaching, viz., that it is a two-party contractual relationship in which each party expects something of the other, to be delivered over a specified period of time. Client and counselor, student and teacher, are in a situation which involves the joint working together toward a common goal. *Ninth,* when asking questions, making interpretive remarks, or otherwise stimulating the pupil to self-activity and self-actualization, both counselor and teacher must be ever mindful of students' individual differences.

While there are marked similarities between counseling (and guidance) and teaching, there are also dissimilarities. Perhaps the most important difference is that guidance and counseling are interested in the student primarily as a person; teaching, on the other hand, is concerned chiefly with the student as less than the whole person, one who grows in truth, who acquires the Scholastic virtue of prudence, who develops coequally intellect and will. The other aspects of the pupil's personality must of necessity also be considered in the classroom situation, but not in a direct, primal way, as is the case in guidance and counseling. Hence both guidance and counseling are focused on the *whole* student, his total self, whereas classroom teaching focuses only on his need to develop within himself truth, whole and entire. This is a capital difference and indeed serves to distinguish the school's teaching function from its guidance function.

The Purpose of Counseling

What is, or at least what should be, the fundamental purpose of counseling? There are as many answers as there are experts. Carl Rogers (1951) contends that the basic purpose is to liberate the innate growth tendencies in the client. Mowrer (1960) asserts that it should aid the client to clarify and live up to his own conscience and system of values. May (1958) holds that at bottom it should increase the person's sense of responsibility to himself as a unique being. Tyler (1961) believes that it should help the student to form habits of informed and thoughtful decision making. The present writers, while not disagreeing with these opinions, nonetheless believe that it is more precise to say that the basic purpose of counseling, and indeed of guidance also, is self-actualization. Actually the purposes as listed by Rogers, Mowrer, May, and Tyler can be considered as either aspects or dimensions or divisions of self-actualization. Counseling, like guidance, liberates the person as a person, to facilitate his becoming what *his* human nature must be. Every guidance service, and particularly counseling, aims at assisting the student to actualize all his potentialities, both latent and manifest. Self-actualization is here considered not only in regard to the eventual or long-term outcome of guidance and counseling; rather every guidance or counseling encounter should *itself* be a self-actualizing experience for the student. Counseling is basically a releasing process whereby the client can become himself, and talking helps more than anything else in effecting this release.

Counseling, and indeed all of guidance, is a freeing experience, i.e., one which frees the individual from the entangling net of his lack of total self-actualization and permits him to make adjustments in personality, outlook, behavior. Fr. van Kaam, C.S.Sp. (1962, p. 403), has written that "counseling is essentially a process of making-free, a humanizing of the person who has lost his freedom in sectors of his existence where he can no longer transcend his life situation by freely giving meaning to it." If counseling is to be this kind of creative, liberating experience between the guidance worker and the client, then the counselor must be personally involved in the interhuman interview relationship. Scientific counseling does not imply "scientific" detachment on the part of the guidance worker. An important aspect of the "freeing" concept of counseling is helping the student to shift his focus first from exclusive love of himself to the love of his neighbor, then to the love of his neighbor as himself, and finally to the heroic, to the saintly, stage of love of his neighbor more than himself. Another key dimension is assisting the student to free himself from the narrow range of his childhood or adolescent interests, so that he is properly oriented to life in the outside, nonschool, nonfamilial world. Maturation can come about only by this liberating, this freeing, which guidance and counseling facilitate.

There is some evidence (cf. Sister M. R. Fahey, 1960, pp. 118–119), both historical and empirical, which suggests that Catholic institutions often apply the Ignatian principle of *agere contra* to self-actualization, not only of students, but of religious teachers as well. While the *agere contra* (literally "to go against one's inclinations") has certain roots in Catholic ascetical theology, it must be applied with great care and discretion; indeed the *agere contra* can be a strong hindrance to self-actualization. It probably is the wiser course to apply the *agere contra* as a general rule of life to a student or religious only after he or she has achieved a fairly high level of self-actualization.

Above all, counseling, like guidance, is not steering, is not maneuvering, is not even urging a pupil. As far back as Frank Parsons (1942, p. 304) the primacy of self-direction has been recognized. The student must always decide for himself; the guidance worker can never decide for him. Counseling is not a superior-inferior relationship; it is a creative *partnership* in the sense of freeing, of liberating. Yet creative partnership is not always the case. Pohlman's review of the research (1961), plus his own investigation, concluded that by the end of counseling the client's tastes and preferences tended to move nearer to those of the counselor than they were initially.

Brayfield (1962, p. 3) has commented that since World War II counseling theory has tended to emphasize what he terms "tender ego psychology," i.e., an excessive concern for the client's self-actualization, need fulfillment, and creative self-expression. Such an overemphasis can lead to a traumatic experience when a client counseled in such a manner enters the outside world, which places almost exclusive emphasis on performance, whether in terms of job achievement or of a girl's good looks. Employers and people in general are not concerned with a person's self-actualization or his difficulty in reconciling his id striving but rather with his objective performance. Certainly the client's self-actualization in the school guidance process must be delicately balanced with outside, nonschool reality. As Patterson (1962, p. 179) has commented, "The counselor does not protect the client from reality, but accepts the assistance of reality." A counselor should be softhearted, but this does not mean that he should also be softheaded.

The Counseling Relationship

All counseling, because it involves people in confrontation, is suffused with the dynamics of human relationships. Indeed Rogers (1962) has called the interpersonal relationship between guidance worker and client or clients "the core of guidance." Counseling is essentially a living relationship, a guidance worker and client coexperiencing. The worker not only perceives the world as the client perceives it but as far as possible experiences the world as the client experiences it. The mystery of the Incarnation, with its emphasis on the necessity of God Himself experiencing the human condition in its existential form so as to understand men better (Merton, 1961), provides food for reflection for the Catholic counselor. This is why not the Father nor the Spirit, but Christ, the Word Who was incarnated into the human milieu, will judge the living and the dead.

In the interview situation, the counselor and the client form a single, existential bond, two persons in one encounter, an "us is" situation. The counselor and client, their existential dialogue, and the deepening togetherness which such a relationship produces result in growth in self-understanding, insight, orientation to more adequate goals, and self-actualization.

Counseling is a dynamic relationship of the giving or withholding of the selves of both client and counselor, of the sharing of each other's being, of an intense mutual sense of acceptance. But it is the counselor who first gives himself. Fr. Curran (1958, pp. 4–5) has noted that the counselor needs first to give himself and to be acceptant. Unhappily for Catholic students, much of contemporary Neo-Thomism accords insufficient attention to love. In its overconcern with knowledge and the supreme value of the intellective processes, much of Neo-Thomism seems to lose sight of the fact that St. Thomas held that love is the principle of creativity as well as the force which moves all things to God. In the counseling situation, counselor giving and acceptance are but forms of love.

Counseling is a to-and-fro relationship. As such, it follows the irregular contours of any living reality. Regularizing the flow of the relationship simply for the sake of methodological purity may render the relationship more methodological, but it will probably also rend it. Nor should regularization take place by subverting counseling into a series of directives by the guidance worker. As a client once said to his school counselor, "We ought to respect each other a lot" (Southard, 1960, p. 618). Counselors need not fear that such respect on their part for the client is tantamount to abdication of the authority of their position.

The counselor's personality or, even more precisely, the counselor himself probably is more important than any set of specific techniques designed to establish the proper relationship. As Williamson (1962) noted, the counselor himself *is* technique. Gardner Murphy (1955, p. 8) similarly observed that a great deal of what the counselor communicates to his client is not what the counselor says but what he is. In Thomistic phraseology, act follows being. This is not to imply that technique is worthless but rather to put it in proper perspective. Emphasis on the counselor's personality, on his *being* rather than on his *doing*, does not suggest that the counselor is virtually inactive during the relationship. Even Carl Rogers (1957a; 1959b) has broadened his nondirectivist concept to include more activity on the part of the counselor. Formerly, nondirectivists regarded reflection of feeling as a looking glass on which the client's feeling is perfectly mirrored so that he can see that feeling bounced off another person. Now, the counselor (whose basic tasks still include the reflection of feeling) is told by Rogers to display three attitudes, viz., empathic understanding, unconditional positive regard, and genuineness. These attitudes of the counselor are conveyed in a wide variety of conscious and unconscious behaviors during the interview. Hence the counselor is very active in the interview situation, not necessarily in the overt sense, but in the deeper, nonverbal sense of communicating one's psychic being to another (Whitaker, Warkentin, & Malone, 1959). Since counseling is a social relationship, the personality of the client has much to do with its success. This point was illustrated by Taulbee's study (1958), which revealed that clients who terminated their therapeutic interviews prematurely were more defensive in personality structure than those who continued to completion.

Do the theoretical considerations mentioned in the past few pages actually lead to more effective counseling? A summary of the pertinent empirical research by Rogers (1961) concluded that if the counselor provides a relationship in which he is genuine and acceptant, prizes the client as a person of worth, and attempts empathically to understand the client's private world of feelings and attitudes, then certain positive changes occur in the client. Some of these positive changes include the client's becoming: "(a) more realistic in his self-perceptions; (b) more confident and self-directing; (c) more positively valued by himself; (d) less likely to repress elements of his experience; (e) more mature, socialized, and adaptive in his behavior; (f) less upset by stress and quicker to recover from it; (g) more like a healthy, integrated, well-functioning person in his personality structure."

Values in Counseling

Do values enter into the professional relationship, the ongoing process, the interaction between the counselor and the client? The problem this question poses for counseling in a public school in a pluralistic society has caused some counseling experts to contend that the counseling relationship is and in fact must be value-free. Such an opinion hardly seems well founded.

First, the counselor himself is value-laden; he cannot hope to escape values, since values are of the warp and woof of his own concrete, existential situation. The counselor has values, and it is psychologically and metaphysically impossible for him not to bring these into the interview situation. In his review of the literature and pertinent research, Patterson (1958b) concluded that there is a growing opinion among theorists, plus some empirical evidence, that it is indeed impossible for the counselor not to influence his client in value structure. Wolff (1956, p. 263) noted that half of 43 leading psychoanalysts surveyed declared that in their opinion therapeutic counseling does in fact, and indeed should, directly transmit or develop value concepts in the clients, while an additional one-fourth thought that therapy directly develops values in the clients. Rosenthal's investigation (1955) concluded that, in general, clients' scores on a moral values test changed during therapy, with those clients who were rated as improved moving closer to the values of their therapists, with those rated as unimproved tending to share less of their therapists' moral values. Further, it must be noted that the counselor's values also enter into his nonpersonal guidance activities. Thus, for example, the very material he chooses to insert in the weekly school guidance bulletin is a result of his value structure, e.g., his emphasis on certain student problem areas rather than on others.

Second, the client himself is value-laden, is a person who has values. Above and beyond this, he has an inner value system working toward the good, a value system which manifests itself in the very innards of the counseling relationship itself. This is not a denial of original sin but a realization of the positive thrust of one's metaphysical goodness plus the additional radical impetus effected in each person by the Redemption. Fr. Curran's analyses (1958) of counseling relationships over the years led him to observe that in the interview the client constantly attempts to preserve his value system (especially the more newly acquired elements of that system which may have generated his problem) and simultaneously to resist with vigor the attempts of the counselor to impose values on him from the outside, however surreptitiously.

Third, the very process and the relationship of counseling, its structure and rationale, have roots in democratic principles, e.g., belief in the dignity and worth of each person, affirmation of the individual's freedom (A. W. Green, 1946). In Catholic schools these values are given full dimension by virtue of the overtly religious conception. Indeed as Williamson (1958b) has observed, a prime purpose of the very establishment of the counseling relationship is to "teach the counselee how to understand more clearly his own value orientation and how to guide his behavior more rationally and consistently in terms of the standards he [the counselee] has chosen."

What relevance does Catholicism have to guidance in general and to counseling in particular? Does Catholicism add anything, infuse anything, or change anything in personnel work, in guidance, in counseling? Arbuckle (1958, p. 212) raised this question in connection with existence of the

Catholic Counselor (now the *National Catholic Guidance Conference Journal*) and answered it in the negative. Is there any such thing as Catholic guidance, Catholic counseling? The answer would seem to be yes. Certainly there is such a thing as a Christian understanding of guidance practices, of counseling theory, of the nature of the client. The Catholic guidance worker is distinct from the non-Catholic worker in that he is aware of the divinized context of life and the universe, of man's first and last end, of the existential ramifications of God's existential plunge into the human milieu in the Incarnation (Fr. Teilhard de Chardin, S.J., 1960). He sees how, through creation, God impregnated Himself in all reality, giving everything a share of the Divine. Though the guidance worker can never impose his values on the student, nonetheless these values form the framework out of which the Catholic guidance worker operates, a value framework which vitally affects the client's values. Nordberg (1963c) has similarly argued that there is a Christian counseling on the ground that Christian humanism underlies the "true and right" counseling relationship. As Cribbin (1951, p. 456) has observed, however, "Christian guidance must be scientific without ceasing to be human or divine." This is a capital point. All too frequently guidance and counseling in Catholic schools are assumed to be good because they are done in a Catholic school by a priest or religious—without any tethering to the scientific or the artistic principles of guidance. Indeed inadequate guidance or counseling performed by an untrained counselor constitutes a grave moral evil because of the effect which guidance has on the client's resultant way of living. Moreover, guidance in a Catholic school should not be merely secular guidance with some religion tacked on. The Catholic dimension should suffuse not only counseling but every aspect of the entire guidance program; if it does not, then the school is tacitly admitting that Catholicism does not have anything to say to vast segments of human life.

The helping act is in itself a Christian act, since it is an act of charity to aid one's neighbor, whether the helper overtly relates this act to God or not. Besides, both spiritually and psychologically, the counselor as a person is helped when he helps others. Martin Buber's (1937) I-Thou dimension, the mutual enriching of the human encounter as compared with the I-It, reveals how richly sanctifying both in grace and in personal development the guidance and counseling relationship in fact is.

Fr. Curran (1952, pp. 19–52), following St. Thomas, has shown how the Christian virtue of counsel facilitates the development of prudence in the client, i.e., aids him in growth in both knowledge and action. Now this is precisely the goal of the school, to develop in the student truth, whole and entire, or what the Scholastics termed prudence. Catholic counselors, who received a superabundance of this gift of counsel (one of the seven gifts of the Holy Spirit) at Confirmation, are in a uniquely favored position to fructify the virtue of counsel in their counseling activity. Catholic counselors cannot, however, take an overspiritualized view of this gift of counsel, as did one clerical director in a Catholic school (Saalfield, 1958, pp. 55–56): "The operation of the Holy Spirit is even more pronounced in counseling the individual than it is in the guidance of the group." How this priest could measure the differences of the operation of the Holy Spirit in the two different situations is as unclear as it is tenuous. Certainly it is dubious if he devised a scientific instrument to appraise the degree of the Divine indwelling.

If Catholicism adds a deepening dimension to the counseling relationship, it is equally true that a misconception of Catholicism injures counseling, as has sometimes happened in Catholic schools. Fr. Charles F. Donovan, S.J. (1960, p. 90), has decried the fact that Catholic counselors and other guidance workers often put a limit on the "amount" of Christian humanism and charity which they permit to enter into their relationships with the students. Such workers seem to think that pupils must learn discipline and respect for authority the hard way, thus overlooking the full sweep of the Catholic notion of human and Divine love. A second misconception is the dichotomy which many Catholics think their religion posits between the natural and the supernatural. This dichotomy is illustrated by Cribbin's statement (1951, p. 255) that "Christian guidance is Christ-centered, not merely student-centered." Such a tragic dualism ignores the Divine indwelling in all reality. When counseling is student-centered, it is perforce Christ-centered, just as St. John's Gospel is the most Divine of the four Gospels because it is the most human. The distinctiveness of Catholic guidance and counseling lies not in a denial of the interpenetrability of the human and the Divine, the natural and the supernatural, but rather in that they make this interpenetration more conscious, more overt, and consequently more effective. Catholicism is not purely transcendent but instead a transcendental vitally enmeshed in life, social order, love—and in education and guidance too. Catholicism incarnates the transcendent, making the Word flesh to dwell among us (Suhard, 1950). If the Church has failed the modern world, if the Catholic schools have failed their students, it is because the transcendent has not been incarnated into their daily lives, into actual living (Lepp, 1962).

The Catholic dimension has caused certain conflicts between guidance and counseling concepts as propounded in this chapter and the Catholic concept of morality, particularly with regard to priest-counselors. Nowhere can this clash be more clearly seen than in the case of the client whose problems are materially (as contrasted to formally) sinful (e.g., masturbation). Thus Frs. Hagmaier, C.S.P., and Gleason, S.J. (1959, p. 43), have written that the "clergyman can never forget that he is a priest first and a counselor second" and that at certain times during a counseling interview a priest must "suspend his role as counselor and assume that of instructor in the faith or of admonisher." Fr. Grau, S.J. (1958, p. 34), attempting to buttress this position with philosophical considerations, has noted that the counselor can never really be nonjudgmental, no matter how hard he tries. It would seem, however, that even this conflict between the counselor's remaining nonjudgmental and his duty to lead the client away from sin toward virtue is not a real conflict. To remain silent merely means to remain silent; silence neither condones nor does it condemn. The question is not whether to let sin go without admonition but rather *how* the client will best learn to rid himself of sin and attain virtue. Both sound learning theory and counseling theory are agreed that, in this area, counselor admonitions, counselor telling, will be of little or no avail. Pupil self-discovery is the only effective learning.

It is the warmth of the counselor, his existential response to the client as a person with a special personality, problems, and needs which contribute more to the success of the counseling relationship than any theoretical technique employed. This does not diminish in any way the theoretical and practical advantages of the self-interpretive model; rather it serves to emphasize that technique does not exist in a vacuum. Indeed technique flows through a person in the counseling process. Probably a warm, deeply client-related counselor who uses heavy-handed "directive" techniques will be more successful than an impersonal, problem-related counselor who employs nondirective procedures.

4

GENERAL GUIDELINES FOR
EFFECTIVE SCHOOL GUIDANCE

The preceding chapters have examined concepts underlying and involved in school guidance. From this treatment it is now possible to formulate some guidelines for effective school guidance.

GUIDELINE 1: EFFECTIVE GUIDANCE INVOLVES A LEARNING SITUA-TION. Learning is that form or process of self-activity through which, by means of experience, conscious or overt behavior is changed. Guidance partakes of each of the four elements of this definition. First, the form or process of guidance learning is realized in the dynamic encounter between the guidance worker and the client or clients. Second, the self-activity of guidance "learning" is effected by the dominant role of the client or clients during the interview or in the group setting, a role in which the worker's function is to facilitate the client's self-actualization in the very guidance situation itself. When non-personal-contact guidance is occurring, e.g., when the student is reading the guidance bulletin board, then it is obvious that the student, rather than the worker who posted the material, has the

101

dominant role. Third, experience in guidance "learning" comprises the sum total of all which the client undergoes, which flow into him and from him during the guidance encounter. Fourth, in guidance "learning" both consciousness and overt behavior are usually changed in some way so that the client may function as a person more adequately and more fruitfully. This change may be only minimal or it may radically affect the deepest layers of the client's personality and self-organization.

The learning aspect of guidance cannot be overstressed. Guidance is a learning process in which the pupil discovers himself, finds out who he really is; it is a process in which he learns to utilize himself to the maximum degree. Indeed personality is usually defined as the particular ways in which an individual learns to react habitually to life situations. Guidance assists him to learn to cope with life situations in a healthy, fruitful manner so that he can actualize every sector of his being.

Because both guidance and teaching are primarily concerned with the facilitation of learning in the pupil, with the stimulation toward maximum self-activity, there are many similarities between the two processes. Hence the guidance worker utilizes some of the more effective methods of "good" teaching, with especial attention to an abiding awareness that the guidance worker, like the teacher, is only the secondary proximate cause of learning. The student himself is the primary proximate cause (St. Thomas Aquinas, *De veritate,* a. 1; Lee, 1963b). The emphasis in the guidance relationship is therefore on the student's experiencing, on the student's developing insight by himself, on the student's actualizing himself. Because guidance is a learning situation for the student, it constitutes one of the indispensable and primary prongs of the school's total educational program.

GUIDELINE 2: EFFECTIVE GUIDANCE ASSISTS THE STUDENT TO DEVELOP AN ADEQUATE AND REALISTIC SFLF-CONCEPT. One of the key goals of guidance and particularly of counseling is to assist the client to bring his self-perception into closer congruence both with his experiental self and with objective, external reality (Layton, 1961; Wrenn, 1958). As was indicated in Chapter 2, a person cannot function productively as a person if his self-concept is not reasonably well aligned with both of these actual impinging existences. Just as the development of insight is necessary before the client attains an accurate self-concept, so in turn is a realistic self-concept necessary both to optimum self-actualization and to the ability to make those intelligent choices and commitments which further self-actualization (Tyler, 1958, p. 8). To be sure, of the five basic goals of the counseling process which the Committee for Counselor Preparation of the American Personnel and Guidance Association (1958, p. 163) adopted from the University of Michigan Conference of the Institute of Human Development, three were concerned with the development of an accurate self-concept.

The self-concept is a psychological construct, not a biological given. Therefore it is subject to change and development. Because the self-concept is psychological in origin and nature, many contemporary psychologists regard it as the most important influence on a person's behavior. A person thinks and behaves as he perceives both himself and objective reality to be, not as he really is or as objective reality really is. This does not minimize objective reality and espouse epistemological relativism; rather it states a crucial psychological fact. The primacy of the subjective has profound implications for individual value structure, guilt, and the concept of morality in general (Zilboorg, 1950, pp. 744–747). Those Catholics who might be startled and even fearful of exploring this fecund notion may gain some courage from Martino's investigation (1963), which disclosed that the self-concept, properly developed, can become an excellent psychological foundation for the spiritual formation of the Christian virtue of humility.

One of the marks of successful guidance and counseling is the development within the client of an accurate self-concept. Rosalind D. Cartwright's careful investigation (1957) concluded that the client's self-concept in relation to each of three important other-realities became more consistent after nondirective counseling which had been judged successful by selected experts. J. E. Williams's review (1962) of the pertinent research concluded that effective counseling with clients on problems in personal and social adjustment in fact effected a change in the clients' self-concepts, particularly in helping close the gap between the ideal self and the perceived self.

GUIDELINE 3: EFFECTIVE GUIDANCE HELPS THE STUDENT TO SELF-ACTUALIZE OPTIMALLY. Actualization is the fulfillment of one's potential. In every person there is an urgent need toward self-actualization, toward the realization of the fullness of being. Act follows being, and as Fromm (1947, p. 219) has observed, "the power to act creates a need to use this power, and failure to use it results in dysfunction and unhappiness." Hence a person has no alternative but to self-actualize; to use Maslow's forceful phrase (1954, p. 91), "What a man *can* be, he *must* be." This notion compares with what the great Jesuit poet Fr. G. M. Hopkins (1948, p. 95) wrote: "Each mortal thing does one thing and the same; . . . *myself* it speaks and spells; crying *what I do is me: for that I came.*"

Every person has an inner tendency toward growth and maturity. The basic nature of the human person is good, positive, constructive. When he is freed from defensiveness, anxieties, and fears, his reactions inevitably move in this positive, fulfilling direction. Man was created good; he fell, but not substantially so, with Adam's sin; and most important, he rose again triumphant with the Redemption by the new Adam. Regrettably those Catholic guidance workers and theorists who have been consciously or unconsciously influenced by Manichaeanism and Jansenism tend to deny, in practice at least, this basic goodness of man's personality. St. Thomas holds that neither the theological virtues nor the intellectual virtues are sufficient to aid a person to live "the good life." The virtues of action, the cardinal virtues, are also necessary. Commenting on this Thomistic position, Brother Lawrence Joseph, F.M.S. (1958), has stated that both teacher and guidance worker assist their pupils in that cooperation with grace which is necessary for growth in the cardinal virtues. *The* primary proximate goal of the school is the development within the pupil of knowledge and action coequally; this also is *an* aim of guidance. The development of self-knowledge and particularly of self-action is inherent in the development of self-actualization.

The development of self-actualization is not regarded as either automatic or easy. Jung (1954, pp. 167–186) thought that the total actualization of self is an achievement of heroic proportions. He believed that most people are content to live their lives considerably less than actualized, preferring to remain within the confines of convention. Adler (1956, pp. 101–105) contended that as an infant the individual is both helpless and deeply aware of his helplessness; in childhood, adolescence, and adulthood he retains his basic feeling of inferiority which he is constantly attempting to master. In Adler's view the drive to *be,* the drive to self-actualization or mastery, is at the very base of personality. But, confronted with the early and powerfully conditioning effect of childhood helplessness, self-actualization is a constant and difficult struggle.

One of the most important avenues—and indeed a necessary one through which an individual actualizes is *experiencing.* The wider and more fruitful the range of a person's experiences, the more opportunity he has to develop his potential. Meaningful experience, grasped and integrated into the developing personality, is the key. It is through experiencing joy, for example, that a person becomes more "Divine"; it is through experiencing suffering that he becomes more human. But the greatest experience, the one which helps a person actualize more than any other, is love. Man's supreme perfection, as Maritain (1943, p. 7) has observed, consists in loving. What Clutton-Brock (1943) said of education is true of one of education's prime components, guidance: "Education ought to teach us how to be in love always, and what to be in love with. The great things in history have been done by the great lovers, by saints and men of science and artists."

Self-actualization should not be regarded as a product to be gained as a result of guidance after the relationship has been terminated. Rather, it is an organic part of the very guidance encounter itself. Guidance is a freeing experience for the client, an experience in which his potentialities are liberated.

If any guidance encounter, be it face to face or in a group, is to be a liberating experience for the student so as to further self-actualization, it must be characterized by a permissive climate. Permissiveness is indispensable, for it establishes an atmosphere in which the client can become open, honest, revealing himself, as he really is, to himself. Actualization is based on a person's "isness," denuded of those external psychological trappings which he presents to others. The mask is discarded, and the persona revealed. Only in a permissive, acceptant climate can the client learn himself.

Self-actualization takes place not in the inner encounter of self with self but rather in the confrontation of self with other, in a social milieu, in the reciprocal relationships which a person experiences while in living contact with external reality. It therefore is accomplished by and through a person's relationships and dynamic encounters with external reality, for only in this manner can he see himself "bounced off," mirrored from a nonsubjective entity. This psychological process has direct relevance to the actualizing of a Catholic in virtue, for as St. Catherine of Siena (1964) noted: "There can be no perfect virtue, none that bears fruit, unless it be exercised by means of our neighbor."

The school is an important social milieu in which a student's self-actualization takes place, or more precisely in which his self-actualization is helped or hindered. Indeed the Gluecks (1952, pp. 69–80) have noted that the elementary school is the child's first testing ground outside the secure atmosphere of his home. Yet the school, the very place where self-actualization could be constantly and sympathetically promoted, often presents the greatest blocks to a child in his attempts to develop the full potentialities of his being. Anna Freud (1960b) commented in this connection that elementary education has traditionally been directed at inhibiting the child's aggressive impulses by punishment and withdrawal of love. Such callous suppression results in the child's repression of natural feelings, thereby preventing him from achieving total self-actualization.

When the school stresses exterior conformity to its rules in the hope that such compliance will develop interior submission in the student, it often thwarts self-actualization and obstructs personal growth. It is the task of guidance to assist the student along the narrow path beset with brambles of excessive self-concern on the one side and with the chasm of conformity on the other. Morris (1959) has suggested that school guidance might be expected to be on the side of individual self-actualization; *de facto,* however, it strongly supports the organization-man principle. Actually there is such a value as fruitful nonconformity which aims at freeing the person from the bondage of sameness, of externally imposed ideas, values, and behavior. Unfortunately religion is utilized by some of its adherents for promoting life-killing conformism. But true religion promotes freedom, not conformity. The Church has established myriad types of devotions, myriad types of religious orders, myriad types of methods for attaining sanctity in its attempt to make religion a freeing experience, an experience which encourages self-actualization on the individual's own terms. Nor does conformity to God's will necessitate passivity, inaction, or ultradocility. Regrettably some religionists fail to grasp this freeing, this anticonformity aspect of the Church's working in the world.

In effectively fostering self-actualization, both the school and the guidance worker operate within the context of the individual student's limitations. While it remains ever true that a climate of client self-satisfaction and self-realization promotes actualization far more than does a debasing climate, nevertheless it is quite possible that such a climate may operate to induce in the client expectancies he will be unable to realize (Brayfield, 1962, p. 3). Nor should the school so shelter the student from the real world that it provides him only success experiences. No person can live a fruitful life either by expecting more than his abilities warrant or by remaining untutored by defeat. The guidance worker in dealing with a client adopts the Roman motto *"Ubi nihil potes, nihil tentas"* (Do not attempt anything which cannot be done).

GUIDELINE 4: EFFECTIVE GUIDANCE PROMOTES SELF-DIRECTION. It assists the student in making *his own* choices and decisions. Guidance is not a process whereby the pupil is gradually conditioned to accept the advice of the counselor or other school person.

Every student needs, and in fact is usually eager to assume, an increasing degree of self-direction and personal responsibility as he advances in age (Lloyd-Jones, 1940, p. 19). But, as von Hildebrand (1953, p. 171) has noted, responsibility essentially presupposes freedom. If the school does not give the student a wide measure of freedom, it can hardly expect him to grow in responsibility and self-direction. Many schools, both public and particularly Catholic, however, seem unwilling to give students freedom or to expend the additional effort involved in structuring conditions which help them use this freedom wisely. As Fr. Cunningham, C.S.C. (1953, p. 233), commented, giving students more responsibility "supposes much more education on the part of the students, much greater effort on the part of the teachers, and subjects administrators to greater hazards than the current 'safe' approach." The school must decide whether its educational (and guidance) efforts are primarily for the establishment of "safe" rules or primarily to further student-self-actualization through increased self-direction.

While most children and youth seek freedom and self-direction, the school cannot delude itself into thinking that youths are ready to cope with full self-direction. As Fromm has pointed out, freedom and self-direction take the child or youth away from the security of authority and place him in the position of deciding, of having the responsibility to decide without help on a clear course of action. If the child develops fear in these initial attempts at self-direction, he becomes frightened and all the more seeks rules, orders, and specific fiats of superior authority. As a result he never develops self-direction. Hence not only guidance encounters but also every aspect of the school's program can give the student *Lebensraum* for the exercise of freedom, responsibility, and self-direction.

Effective guidance, then, accords the student as much freedom as possible. Certainly guidance does not consist in the school's banning and prohibiting. Long sets of rules and prohibitions seem to encourage their violation by pupils; this is particularly true when the rules are silly, petty, nonsensical, and arbitrary, as they often are. All school rules are burdens and should be enacted only when necessary to further, not restrict, the pupils' growth in self-direction. The school governs best which governs least. Nor should the school think that the constant drumming into the students of principles and modes of behavior serves the cause of good guidance. As Fr. McGucken, S.J. (1942, p. 20), testified, "objectives of conduct are not obtained by irrational, mechanical drill."

Self-discipline or self-control is a crucial ingredient in self-direction, and the entire school program can be guidance-oriented to promote this. A tight and total system of external controls, an elaborate surveillance procedure or similar device, however, does not encourage self-control, a fact which many public and Catholic schools have yet to learn. The contemporary concept of self-control is the ideal of the strong, silent, nonemotional type. This notion perhaps can best be exemplified by the mottoes which appeared on Nazi school walls for the inspiration of the German youth: *"Gelobt sei was hart macht"* (Praise be that which makes one rugged) and *"Jammer nicht, sei stolz und schweige"* (Don't cry! Remain proud and silent!). But as Jersild (1952, p. 39) noted, such an ideal "is not healthy, but false, insidious, and morbid." Rather self-control means satisfactory adjustment of one's particular emotions (which vary according to different persons) for fruitful living. Control means the proper, effective use of emotions rather than blocking or stopping them. In the words of Jersild and Helfant (1953, p. 9), "emotional control is not the same as emotional maturity."

The practice of autocracy on the part of the school is probably the most effective means of hindering pupil self-direction. To command is not to provide guidance. Effective school leadership for pupil self-direction consists not in herding pupils but in sharing some leadership functions with them. Guidance is not doing something *to* the pupil but *with* him. If the school wishes the pupil to develop responsibility, it must give him the opportunity to exercise some responsibility. If it wishes him to develop self-direction, it must allow him some share in the direction of his life and of those areas which intersect his life, such as representation in the management of the school. Pupils should also be permitted free choices without fear of reprisals from school officials. Such democratic concepts considered from the religious standpoint can be regarded as an implementation of the doctrine of the Mystical Body and therefore as the fulfillment of the deepest facet in Catholic theology.

Pupils fail to develop a respect for authority if that authority is self-mandated and hence undemocratic in origin. Nothing hurts true authority more than the practice of authoritarianism by its possessor. Unhappily Catholic schools are at the present time generally in the lead in the practice of autocratic controls, usually in the name of inculcating self-discipline. In these institutions, self-direction is usually not only not encouraged; it is forcefully discouraged. The *magister dixit* attitude prevails. The cause of Catholic schools' treatment of students may be in large measure due to the fact that members of religious communities are themselves often treated as children, as Fr. A. Leonard, O.P. (1963), has suggested. They are permitted little or no initiative and are seldom given authority, and so they become aged children. In their turn, they impose a similar code of life on those whom they teach and guide. A study of seminary life made by Fr. Brooks, O. Praem. (1961, p. 49), indicates that much the same holds true in the education of priests. Perhaps the only lasting and effective remedy is a drastic reform of convent and seminary education. But in any event, as Fr. Lepp (1962, p. 87) has observed, "more and more of the faithful are beginning to realize that in comparing them to sheep, Our Lord did not intend them to be merely a bleating flock resigned to being slaughtered." The encouragement of pupil self-direction in the Catholic school is vital if this type of school is to produce lay leaders. Thus Fr. Michonneau (1948, p. 22) could justifiably observe that priests complain about the passivity of Catholic laymen, but where could these laymen possibly get any ideas about, much less any participation in, leadership and self-direction?

In his book *Walden II,* Skinner (1948, pp. 218, 243), an experimental psychologist, states: "We [psychologists] can achieve a sort of control under which the controlled, though they are following a code much more scrupulously than was ever the case under the old system, nevertheless *feel free.* They are doing what they want to do, not what they are forced to do. . . . By careful cultural design, we control not the final behavior, but the *inclination* to behave—the motives, the desires, the wishes." Thus the goal is to mold personalities, for as Skinner goes on: "What do you say to the design of personalities? . . . The control of temperament? Give me the specifications, and I'll give you the man." Is this what educators, whether public or Catholic, really and secretly wish to accomplish through the school environment? Is this manipulation, or is it guidance in self-direction?

GUIDELINE 5: EFFECTIVE GUIDANCE FURTHERS EXPLORATION. The purpose of exploration is to get to know oneself in order that one may become that self whom one can become. A person cannot truly know himself by merely introspecting; rather he can really know himself only through encountering external reality. In this encounter two elements occur: first, one sees oneself bounced off, mirrored from a nonsubjective entity; and, second, external reality extracts from the individual traits which otherwise would never have been brought to the surface. Thus exploration, which involves a wide array of personal experiences, is crucial to self-knowledge and self-actualization.

These experiences cannot be so restricted and hemmed in by the home or the school that they constitute a narrow, predetermined directional path rather than the free, uncharted sweep which is inherent in any exploration. Such unhampered exploration of necessity involves risks on the part of the student. But as Cardinal Suhard (1950, p. 90) has observed, "there is no human action without dangers or setbacks." Students must be given freedom to explore the contours both of their own personalities and of the external world, even if this means, as it often does, the freedom to make mistakes (Fr. Greeley, 1961, p. 116). The school's task is not to shield the student from all error and mistakes, or even from sin, but to help him grow and live fruitfully. In Mounier's words (1938, pp. 117–118), "the child must be educated as a person, along the path of personal experience and of apprenticeship in free actions."

The school promotes an openness to *being* (Marcel, 1960) as a prerequisite to productive exploration. A lack of openness to being results in the failure of a person to allow himself to flow freely into the external world, with the consequence that he erects defense systems. Excessive defense systems lead directly to neurosis. Defense systems, or the lack of openness to being, result in rigidity, a personality trait characteristic of the seriously disturbed person (Cavanagh & Fr. McGoldrick, S.J., 1958, p. 403). Prejudice, which is nothing more than rigidity about one's own group vis-à-vis outgroups, is so pervasive in its effects that it even significantly affects a person's sensory perceptions. Experiments (cf. Block & Block, 1951) have demonstrated that the more strongly a person is prejudiced, the less able he is to tolerate ambiguity or uncertainty in a situation. Rigidity and prejudice usually result from a lack of a wide range of experiences; exploration can do much to prevent rigidity and prejudice.

The whole school program, and not merely the guidance service, should actively promote a wide range of exploratory activities for the student (Johnson, Busaker, & Bowman, 1961, pp. 138–156). This is particularly important for Catholic schools, which sometimes seem to be training pupils for the eremitical life rather than for life in the world.

GUIDELINE 6: EFFECTIVE GUIDANCE IS DEVELOPMENTAL. If guidance does little else, it helps the student grow and develop; it should be the school's primary means of actively facilitating growth and development. Effective guidance provides the context in which the individual has the latitude first to *become,* then to *be.* The guidance worker realizes that the client is in the stage of becoming. Hence he does not expect the student to be a "finished product" either before that student enters the guidance relationship or when he leaves it. Rather the worker inwardly and outwardly confirms the client's potentiality, his ability to become, his capability of growth and development in humanhood and in sainthood. Further, the worker permits the client the freedom to be, to be a separate entity from the worker. The worker accepts the client as he is, with his faults and virtues, so that the client is truly free to be. If the client is not permitted the freedom to be, it is doubtful whether he will gain the encouragement and strength to strive toward development, toward better being, toward being better. If his present being is rejected, why should he strive for another type of being? Catholic guidance workers should not fear this acceptance of the client's being, of his existential situation. Fr. Charles F. Donovan, S.J. (1960, p. 92), has sympathetically written in this connection:

> Too often adults adopt the insufferably arrogant position that the child's lack of development is a total, and indeed an almost reprehensible negation. The privative nature of the child's or young person's status is harped on. What the student lacks is spelled out; he is compared unfavorably with older persons who represent a state of accomplishment. This is merely negative and discouraging.

Consequently the essentially developmental nature of childhood and adolescence must be understood by the guidance worker who sees students from the vantage point of that relatively stable existential situation which comprises adulthood. Lability is, however, a cardinal characteristic of adolescence. The worker does not expect youths to be emotionally constant but rather to fluctuate widely; further, he expects wide and sudden spurts and dips in youths' everyday lives. Teen-age is a fluid champagne and tears, with the percentage of its ingredients varying from day to day, from circumstance to circumstance.

A vital element in the development of the child or of the adolescent consists in his defining his role in contemporary adult-dominated American society. Once he has arrived at and formulated this definition, he is faced with the additional task of both living this definition and adjusting it to meet new and different circumstances. It is one of the tasks of the guidance worker to assist the child or adolescent to define his role and *to provide situations in which he can test this definition.*

If the practice of Catholic guidance workers is sometimes inimical to this concept of development, preferring instead to superimpose the stability of adult life on young persons, it may be due to a misconception of the Church as a fixed, static entity. But, as Cardinal Suhard has noted, the Church is a living organism; because she is such, she cannot and does not remain stationary. Rather the Church is in a perpetual state of development, change, and growth (Suhard, 1950, p. 39). Alert Catholic guidance workers view development with confidence, believing with St. Paul (Romans 8:28) that "For those who love God, all things work together unto good."

GUIDELINE 7: EFFECTIVE GUIDANCE IS PREVENTIVE. Guidance is not primarily a salvage effort, an attempt to rescue and rehabilitate the misbehavior cases. To be sure, guidance is concerned with pupils who have pressing problems, but it is even more concerned in preventing these cases from arising, in so helping students to develop and self-actualize that they are not burdened with overwhelming problems. Guidance assists students with difficulties arising from their developmental needs before these "difficulties" erupt into "problems." Because the school is a manipulable environment, it is in a uniquely favored position to foster proper development and thereby inhibit the onset of many problems. As Pallone (1961c) has pointed out, the fact that the school is precisely a controlled setting enables it purposefully to surround the student with those situations which further his optimum self-actualization and reduce his anxieties. Conversely, the school should not itself bring about the onset of pupils' problems by blocking their creative thrusts, by issuing numerous and strict rules, or by promoting a punitive school or classroom atmosphere. The school cannot be so rigid as to fail to facilitate the negotiation of developmental tasks through self-exploration.

GUIDELINE 8: EFFECTIVE GUIDANCE IS IMMEDIATE. It attempts to solve today's "problems" today. Problems have an urgency which calls for instantaneous help.

It is inadequate both theologically and psychologically to give as a *total* response to a young person's problem, "Offer it up." This is not to deny the importance of spiritual victimhood, a pivotal and enriching wellspring of sanctity, but rather to emphasize the necessity of assisting the troubled student here and now with the resources at the guidance worker's disposal.

The basis for viewing guidance as immediate is that the client is a *present* person. Too often the school is looked upon as preparation for life instead of as life itself. In the light of the future, a student's problem might seem quite inconsequential; in childhood and particularly in teen-age, however, every problem, no matter how objectively insignificant, seems momentous to the student. Therefore the guidance worker avoids communicating to the student: "Don't worry; it's a small problem, and you'll get over it soon." To the student, in his phenomenal world, the problem is not a small one at all, and that is what counts. Moreover, he might not "get over it" soon, for if the problem remains unresolved, it could develop into a far more serious difficulty.

GUIDELINE 9: EFFECTIVE GUIDANCE IS BASED ON UNDERSTANDING. The underlying spirit of every aspect of the guidance program is charity, the love of one's neighbor as oneself or, in the highest degree, more than oneself. Guidance in Catholic schools should be particularly characterized by a spirit of human understanding rather than by severity and rigid discipline. As von

Hildebrand (1955, p. 21) has noted: "The pharisee hates mercy. He refuses mercy to other people and uses the rigid scale of the letter in order to condemn them."

Kindness, warmth, and charity are never wasted on anyone, even when results are not immediately apparent. This was demonstrated empirically in an investigation by Dittes (1957), which revealed that the degree of a client's registered physiological changes, as measured by a psychogalvanometer, depended on the warmness and permissiveness of the counselor. Hence even on the physiological level, the human organism responds to warmth and understanding and organizes itself against nonacceptance and nonunderstanding. An example of the lack of understanding is found in the statement of a clerical guidance director of a Catholic high school (Saalfield, 1958, p. 210): "Some pupils never make a success in school because they never make any effort to get along with their fellow students and teachers." A nonunderstanding attitude never probes the deeper reasons why some students do not get along with agemates and teachers. Understanding lay students is in all probability an especially difficult problem for guidance workers who are priests and religious, for frequently they are removed from the concrete realities and problems which beset the lay life.

The guidance worker with a religious commitment should for that very reason be even more understanding than his secular counterpart. Most religious have as one of their central teachings the Divine character of mercy and compassion. Yet paradoxically it sometimes happens that religious guidance workers utilize religion in such a way as to cause deep guilt feelings in the client. To illustrate, a boy with a problem of masturbation might be counseled in such a way as to have added to feelings of inferiority which produced this problem the further impact of feeling totally sinful in the eyes of God. The fact of the matter is that, because of the force of the habit and its pathogenic origins, the boy might not be sinning formally at all. Often a person is not formally guilty of material sins he commits. Hence understanding on the part of the religious guidance worker is crucially important.

The guidance worker does not regard children and adolescents as somewhat inconsequential because of their youthful ages. Nor does the counselor subscribe to the old saying "Children should be seen but not heard." And as far as teen-agers are concerned, guidance seeks to assist the hopeful young, that group of people who are often described—and discarded—by adults and school people as "adolescents." The guidance worker does not take young people lightly. When the teen-age girl tearfully says that she would rather be dead than wear out-of-date, hand-me-down clothes, she means it literally.

In the guidance encounter, the client should be encouraged to talk about anything and everything he would like to talk about, however subjectively or objectively remote it may seem to be. The mere fact of expressing hostile, aggressive, fantastic notions without fear of rejection or exhortation is itself a growth-facilitating experience.

GUIDELINE 10: EFFECTIVE GUIDANCE IS CONSISTENT WITH RESPECT FOR THE STUDENT. A natural outcome and in fact a correlate to respect for the pupil is the guidance worker's *unconditional* acceptance of the client. This acceptance must be unconditional and include all the pupil's faults and failings, all his sins and transgressions. Fr. McKenney, S.J. (1951, p. 56), attempts to infuse the Christian dimension into acceptance of the client despite repugnance to some of his actions. Developing this thesis, Fr. Grau, S.J. (1960, p. 71), has observed that in a guidance situation a counselor has before him not merely a client but rather a son of God, a brother in Christ's blood. Christ died as much for the client, however sinful, as for the guidance worker, however saintly. Whether the client is a rapist, a drug addict, or just a "mixed-up kid," he has God-given rights which are transcendent and which no guidance worker, lay, clerical, or religious, can take from him. Guidance workers respect the client as one for whom Christ Himself shed His blood. No matter what the source of the client's self-rejection or rejection by others, he is still accepted by God. Theological systems which deny or minimize this acceptance by God of a troubled or sinful person not only negate God's mercy but use religious constructs to undermine the person's mental health by inducing added guilt feelings.

Effective guidance workers strive to recognize the positive attributes of the client, his strengths and assets as well as his weaknesses, fears, and hostilities, even if the negative attributes seem at first to be more evident (Witryol & Boly, 1954, pp. 63–68). Such acceptance of the worth of the client can of itself do much to assist him. A study by A. Baldwin, Joan Kalhorn, and Fay H. Breese (1945) of the effect of parental attitudes on the behavior of their children revealed that the parental attitude cluster "acceptant-democratic" seems to facilitate psychological growth the most. Children of these "warm" parents showed an accelerated intellectual development as measured by increased IQ score, more originality, greater emotional security and control, and less excitability than children of other parents. This investigation also concluded that when parents' attitudes were classified as "actively rejectant," a deceleration in the child's development in these areas was noted.

Misplaced emphasis on original sin and the fallen aspect of man's nature had led many Catholic guidance workers to become so preoccupied with the eternal as to de-emphasize and devaluate the temporal. Thus quite a few Catholics in education would probably agree with Sister Margaret Marie Doyle (1932, p. 65) who wrote: "The philosophy of Catholics can be summed up in the statement that temporal things exist for the eternal." They would similarly concur with Redden and Ryan (1956, p. 141), who stated that Catholic philosophy clearly implies that in true education (and therefore in guidance also) *all* necessary adjustments to the realities of material life are at all times secondary and subordinate to the goal of attaining salvation. Unfortunately this somewhat unbalanced view had led some Catholics to neglect and even despise temporal realities, including students and the world in which students live. As a result these Catholic school people not only have caused their own spirituality to become narrow but also have lost to the Church many students who had the ability to see the temporal as beautiful and lovable. Such Catholic school people neglect to see God in the temporal. He is, however, in the temporal in such a way that one loves the temporal *as it is temporal,* for in so doing one perforce loves God, whether he realizes it or not. To love man for man's sake and not for one's own sake is to love God. *Not to love man but rather only to love the Christ in him is neither to love man nor Christ. Not to love the world but only the God in it is neither to love the world nor God.* Views exemplified by Sister Margaret Marie and by Redden and Ryan, while aiming at what they sincerely believe to be spiritual perfection, almost inevitably end by scoffing human advances, which are fundamentally advances of Christ immanent in the world.

In respecting the client, in accepting him unconditionally, the guidance worker remains nonjudgmental. The worker listens; he does not blame. Such behavior has been shown empirically to produce effective results (Benz, 1948, p. 28). Further, the guidance worker remembers that differences in pupil talent in no way reflect differences in pupil worth, particularly supernatural worth.

Respect for the student implies that the guidance worker thinks *with* the student; he does not think *for* the student. The worker is a partner with the student in the guidance encounter. Gardner Murphy (1961b) observed that such a partnership requires the counselor to be guided by the client in much the same way as the client is being guided by the counselor; i.e., just as the client learns to recognize the skills forming together into the unity by which the counselor offers something of value to him, so too the counselor begins to note the skills by which the client manages to teach and to guide the counselor to perform his specialized guidance function more effectively. And, above all, respect for the pupil demands that the guidance worker refrain from prying or "pumping."

Respect for the student also means that the guidance worker at all times treats him as a human being, as a *person.* Betz and Whitehorn's investigation (1956) of young resident physicians working with schizophrenic patients in a psychiatric ward revealed that the most improved patients had as their physicians men who regarded them as human beings and treated them as persons, while the least improved patients had as their physicians men who treated them as "objects," in the spirit of scientific detachment. Although the investigators emphasized that their findings applied only to the treatment of schizophrenics, Carl R. Rogers (1958, p. 7) suspects that similar results would be found in almost any class of helping relationship, including guidance.

Counseling can easily degenerate into the control of the client by the counselor. Indeed the counselor can subtly mold the client into an imitation either of himself or of what he wishes the client to be. Such molding, formerly regarded by many Catholics as the very purpose of the guidance function, violates the inalienable integrity of the client. Farson (1955) found that the less adjusted and the less competent a guidance worker is, the more he tends to induce his clients to model themselves after him, to conform to his wishes.

GUIDELINE 11: EFFECTIVE GUIDANCE TAKES INTO ACCOUNT THE WHOLE STUDENT. Guidance is organic since it focuses attention on all areas of development. Thus, for example, in scholastic guidance the emphasis (in an ideal situation in which the counselor has time to work with the pupil) is not only on helping the student to improve academically but also on dealing with whatever failure to resolve developmental tasks adequately is causing both low academic achievement and the social maladjustments which result from poor scholastic performance. This organic nature of guidance is derived from the notion of *homo integer,* that all man's tendencies and needs are deeply interrelated so as to form one unified person. "Problems" in any area of human development have ramifications in other areas as well. For purposes of explication and analysis, this textbook treats of five foci of school guidance, viz., personal, social, religious, vocational, and scholastic. In the concrete existential order, however, no such clear boundaries can be delimited, for all are intermingled in the flowing unity of the pupil's personality. Treatment is separated for the sake of conceptual analysis and discussion.

It is a mistake to separate man's animal nature from his spiritual nature, as in certain heresies, or to deny one or the other, as in certain schools of scientific thought. Concerning the first, Fr. A. Leonard, O.P. (1963), has observed that Catholics tend to ignore the driving force of instincts which profoundly influence human behavior. There is also a tendency on the part of many Catholics in education (perhaps still unknowingly under the sway of a Jansenistic mentality) to devalue emotions. But to know and to understand oneself, as well as to be oneself, a person must be able not only to think but also to feel (Jersild & Helfant, 1953, p. 9). On the opposite side of the fence, some educators seem to overemphasize the physical side of man's nature. Man is not an impulse-ridden, id-driven organism, nor is he totally a rational, conscious, intellectually affected being (L. S. Levine & R. E. Kantor, 1962). These elements are so deeply intertwined that man does not function as a human being unless they are operating simultaneously.

The goal of the school determines whether in a particular educational setting the guidance function is or is not regarded as organic. Those educators such as Bowles (1959) and Conant (1959) in public school contexts, and such as Kerins (1957) within Catholic schools, who hold that the school's primary and perhaps exclusive proximate goal is to cultivate the intellect usually view guidance solely in terms of scholastic counseling and college entrance advisement, of identification, selection, and assignment in the school curriculum. On the other hand, if the goal of the school is to help the student grow in truth, whole and entire, then guidance tends to become organic, treating of the whole spectrum of pupil needs.

Because of the organic nature of guidance, the guidance worker cannot allow himself to become so deeply absorbed in one facet of the client's functioning that he neglects its other aspects and ramifications, e.g., concentrating solely on failing marks and overlooking the hostility which might be tied with poor academic performance. Nor should a counselor regard his basic function as treating only one or another type of pupil problem, e.g., scholastic difficulties rather than the total range of pupil needs. That this unfortunate situation does exist and indeed spills over into the students' perception of the counselor's role can be seen from a New York State study (Hartley & Hedlund, 1952, p. 14) which disclosed that in the high schools investigated seniors saw counselors as concerned with providing assistance in educational-vocational but not social-personal matters.

GUIDELINE 12: EFFECTIVE GUIDANCE PROVIDES FOR INDIVIDUAL DIFFER-ENCES. No two students are exactly alike; the needs of students are not identical. Hence there is no such thing as a routine guidance case. Somewhat apropos, Martin Buber (1947, p. 83) has written: "In spite of all similarities, every living situation has, like a newborn child, a new fact that has never been before and will never come again. It demands of you a reaction which cannot be prepared beforehand. It demands nothing of what is past. It demands presence, responsibility; it demands you."

There are no stock answers or solutions which can more or less take care of every client's concerns. Brother John M. Egan, F.S.C.H. (1960, p. 126), has labeled such an approach "prescriptive guidance," i.e., that in which the client tells his problems to the guidance worker, whereupon the worker gives the student patent-medicine advice to cure all ills. An example of this prescriptive or "aspirin" guidance is the current frenzied fostering by schools and some guidance workers of the notion that every student possessing a reasonable amount of mental ability should be encouraged to enter college. It might well be that such a pupil, for self-actualization, should not attend college at all. Again, in some cases, it might be wiser for that student to terminate his school career before high school graduation if the school's program is neither adequate nor appropriate for him (Lee, 1959). Nor should all Catholic students be encouraged to attend a Catholic college. A. C. Riccio (1962a, p. 237), a Catholic guidance specialist, has observed that some Catholic students function better at a non-Catholic than at a Catholic college. Students in this category include not only sensitive individuals who have difficulty in reconciling the social encyclicals with the un-Christian manner in which some Catholic employers in both educational and noneducational institutions treat their employees but also students for whom a sheltered education is not suitable.

Guidance is necessarily client-centered; the individual student qua individual is its axis and focus. Thus the type of counseling interview, its length, and the techniques employed are determined by the client and by the counselor's perception of him, a perception modified by renewed contacts. The specific nature of the client's concern, the level of his anxiety, his ego strength, age, intellectual level, case history, the urgency he feels, his defense mechanisms must be taken into account by the guidance worker during his encounter with the client. Some students regard counseling itself as a threat, something which brings with it fear of exposure, revelation of hidden longings, humiliation.

The efficient counselor is literally prepared for anything during the interview. One college personnel worker (W. S. Lee, 1959, p. 28) reported that during an interview a student pulled out a fully loaded revolver and aimed it at him, saying, "Sorry to have to do it this way." While such clients are happily not common, the story serves to illustrate that the alert guidance worker must constantly be prepared for the unexpected.

To be in a position to minister best to the individual needs of each client, the guidance worker begins the process of identification as early as possible. Tests may be used at the outset, but the knowledge derived from them constitutes only the beginning of pupil identification. Although tests are important, they are not enough, for as Recktenwald (1957, p. 23) has noted, guidance must get beyond the visible data. The counselor considers also the psychodynamics manifest in the guidance encounter. Clients handle the counseling situation in basically the same way as they deal with their life experiences; viz., if they are dependent in their social milieu, if they are maladjusted, they exhibit these characteristics in the counseling encounter. The perceptive counselor often learns more about a client by observing psychodynamics in the interview than from test data or even from what the client verbalizes.

Above all, the guidance worker remembers that there is no case so far gone that it is absolutely hopeless. St. Augustine's treatise on the theological virtues contains 113 chapters on faith but only 3 on hope. In St. Thomas's *Summa Theologica* there are 604 questions, with only 2 on hope. Similarly late Scholastic theology badly neglected hope, and it remained for the "human" sciences of the Renaissance to fill this void (Brother G. Moran, F.S.C., 1963, p. 307). Despite this theological neglect of hope and optimism, despite the constant reminders in prayers that life is a "vale of tears," the guidance worker is ever filled with a spirit of optimism. There are some students for whom everything seems to go wrong, and there are others who, as Camus (1963, p. 34) wrote, make a failure of everything, even of death. Though these are tragic figures, it is the task of the guidance worker to help as much as he can, in what ways he can.

GUIDELINE 13: EFFECTIVE GUIDANCE IS FLEXIBLE.   It is adapted to all types of pupils and all types of problems. Normal and abnormal children and youths, personnel and scholastic problems, all fit under the guidance umbrella. Further, no one technique is used exclusively in guidance. Thus in counseling, for example, some clients might respond best to the nondirective technique, while with others advisement may be more appropriate. Even with the same client, procedures vary according to his immediate needs and state. Group guidance is not to be used exclusively, as sometimes happens in under-staffed public and Catholic schools; flexible guidance calls for individual counseling as well. Even the proposed ratio of 1 counselor to 300 pupils (or 1:250, depending on whose recommendations one reads) is not intended to cover all situations, for as the Wrenn Report (1962, p. 156) noted, such a ratio might well be too high in some schools and possibly too low in others.

Nothing is more inimical to flexibility than a spirit of rigid precision. Because of the emphasis on a fixed rule of life and what Fr. Ong, S.J. (1957, pp. 39–44), has identified as "tradition-directedness," religious seem to have a tendency toward rigidity more than do most other school people. This attitude often arises from a concept of tradition which is too narrow or which is defined as complete, static, ready-made (Lawler, 1959, p. 35). If tradition and indeed the religious rule are seen not as historical fixities but as vital, living, adaptive entities, they cause the religious guidance worker to be deeply and more truly flexible.

GUIDELINE 14: EFFECTIVE GUIDANCE IS PERVASIVE.   Every aspect of the school's total educational program should be permeated with the guidance point of view. Guidance can infuse the school's curricular program. In the classroom situation the alert teacher nurtures rather than thwarts the guidance function. To be sure, guidance may be incarnated into the very lesson itself. This is comparatively easy in the core curriculum, inasmuch as that curricular design builds guidance into each lesson (Faunce & Bossing, 1958; Lee, 1963b, pp. 190–208). While it is admittedly more difficult to bring guidance into a subject-centered curriculum, a guidance-oriented teacher can seize opportunities to promote guidance even in this rigid curricular design and "bootleg" it into the lesson.

The alert school administration similarly encourages school-wide conditions which foster the guidance point of view. This is especially true in allowing students freedom to develop mature self-responsibility (Mallery, 1961). The emphasis on the administrator, teacher, and guidance worker *in loco parentis* has unfortunately been almost exclusively interpreted by many school people to mean the right to exercise power and disciplinary authority over the child. The *parental* aspect of fostering individual growth in all areas, in which the school person should also stand *in loco,* has been forgotten or at least overlooked. It is indefensible for school people to deprive students of freedom on the pretext that pupils are using it wrongly. Fr. Kohake, O.S.B. (1963), has used the term "the theology of student responsibility" to highlight the duty of school people in this regard. It is unfortunate that many public and Catholic schoolmen seem passionately devoted to out-of-date ideas and thwart guidance by severely restricting or otherwise suppressing student freedom. Williamson (1961b) has noted that within this century student rights to free expression, free discussion, and freedom to advocate a point of view have been and are now being slowly won in the forge of incidents, crises, protests, and, in some instances, revolts. Protests against the mass conformity promoted by the school are coming to the fore in "beatnik" dress, teen-age argot, and the like. The task of all school people, and of guidance workers in particular, is to defend freedom of student expression whenever and wherever it is suppressed in the name of "order" or "prudence."

GUIDELINE 15: EFFECTIVE GUIDANCE IS CONTINUOUS.   Guidance is wed to education at all grade levels, from kindergarten through graduate school, and at all times during the student's progression through a particular grade level. Many public and Catholic schoolmen regrettably regard guidance as necessary only on three occasions: (1) when a student gets into trouble or grave difficulty; (2) when a student has a serious problem; and (3) when students reach certain pivotal points in their school careers, such as the end of the academic year, in planning the course of study for the following year, or the senior year of high school, in preparing for a suitable job. As a result, guidance is usually sporadic rather than continuous. School guidance often is a crash program at certain intervals, "hit-and-run" guidance. Long-term guidance is virtually unknown in many schools, and even short-term guidance often becomes little more than "one-shot counseling" featured by a "bullet interview."

Compounding this difficulty is the fact that many administrators and teachers consider the guidance office a combination of medieval alchemist's studio and modern automotive repair shop. The counselor is thought to be the possessor of magical properties and hence the miracle man in the school who can "patch up" a student problem or difficulty. Superimposed on this situation is what Feder (1961, p. 8) has termed the new educational rocket of "Conantism," which implies that guidance workers hold the "right" answer for every student in the school. Thus the concept of sporadic rather than continuous guidance is reinforced.

Guidance is intended for all students, not merely those who misbehave or have problems. Even in so-called misbehavior cases, the emphasis in guidance circles has turned *from* problem students *to* students with problems. "Troublemakers" are usually such because they are troubled. Guidance seeks to prevent problems and misbehavior from arising by promoting positive development. Prevention can come about only if guidance is continuous.

Administrators and teachers commonly expect counselors to assume a major role in handling misbehavior cases. The counselor's office is thus regarded as the wastebasket into which to deposit the troublesome student. The counselor's role, however, is not that of administering punitive discipline. The guidance and disciplinary functions are by their very natures quite separate and distinct. Guidance is internal, not directive, and nonthreatening, whereas punitive discipline is perforce external, directive, and threatening (Lee, 1963a, p. 115). The administrator, not the counselor, is responsible for punitive discipline in the school. A survey (Winfrey, 1962, pp. 36–37) of the most influential figures in the American School Counselor Association disclosed that 95 of these leaders thought the counselor should not be responsible for punitive discipline, while only 2 held the opposite view. A review of pertinent research by Reed and Stefflre (1963, p. 159) concluded that one function unacceptable to school counselors is handling punitive discipline. If in a given school situation the administration thrusts misbehavior cases on the counselor, the professional counselor refuses to be so "used," on the ground that such action is unprofessional behavior which could preclude the opportunity to self-actualize. The basis for this position is that the meting out of punishment by the counselor almost inevitably destroys in the student's eyes the image of the counselor; hence the counselor is unable to enter into that relationship or achieve that rapport necessary for assisting the pupil to get at the root of whatever occasioned the original misbehavior.

Continuous guidance at all age and grade levels does not imply that guidance at these levels is much the same. Quite the contrary; there are significant differences in guidance understanding and practice, so much so that it seems unwise to issue a single guidance certificate to a counselor valid for all school or grade levels. There are several radical differences between elementary school children, on the one hand, and secondary school and college youths, on the other. These differences necessitate a substantially different kind of guidance for each group: (1) the problems and needs of each age group are very different; (2) the elementary school child sees himself primarily in present, while the adolescent views himself as having an extension into the future; (3) the elementary school child is more dependent on his parents and immediate home environment; (4) the elementary school child does not operate with the same verbal fluency as the high school and college youth;

(5) major choices are not normally involved in the elementary school program; (6) vocational counseling with an elementary school child differs substantially from that of a high school or college youth; (7) the elementary school class is normally self-contained, so that the teacher knows the pupils much more intimately than is possible in the departmentalized secondary school and college.

GUIDELINE 16: EFFECTIVE GUIDANCE IS DISTRIBUTIVE. Each member of the school staff in one direct way or another is involved in the guidance function within his particular educational role. Every school person is a guidance worker, with the counselor as the specialized guidance generalist and the school psychologist, psychiatrist, social worker, and so forth comprising the team of guidance specialists. Some theorists resent or reject the concept that every school person is a guidance worker, but teachers, administrators, and staff are and in fact must be guidance workers if they are to further the school's total *educational* function. Moreover, these theorists overlook the fact that an essential part of the client's successful adjustment, or even "cure" in appropriate cases, occurs outside the counselor's office. Away from the office, as Alexander and French (1946) have noted, the client continues to examine himself, to gain insight, to "release," all with the conscious or unconscious help of various school people and age mates.

If all staff members are guidance workers by virtue of their specific school function, then it follows that they all need some guidance competence. Indeed competence is a grave moral obligation because of the serious personal consequences incompetent guidance has on a student. Every teacher and administrator needs at least one undergraduate or graduate course in the principles and foundations of guidance and one graduate course in interview techniques, with some opportunity for supervised laboratory experience. Such course work constitutes the minimum requirements, certainly not the desideratum. It is assumed that all teachers as part of their general requirements take at least one graduate course (appropriate to their level of school service) in the dynamics of human development.

The homeroom period provides the teacher with excellent opportunities for group guidance (Hutson, 1958, pp. 287–323). During classroom lessons, even in a rigid subject-centered curricular design, the teacher can promote human relations skills. A review of the pertinent research by Ojemann (1958, p. 199) concluded that in the homeroom elementary and secondary school children can learn both to understand some dynamics of human behavior and to apply this knowledge in their relationships with others. The teacher can effect a fusion of instructional and guidance functions in the course of the lesson. For example, during the "story" period in a primary-grade classroom, the teacher reads a narrative in which the children consider some human relations problem, e.g., two boys fighting in the schoolyard. The story describes how one of the boys got into the fight; viz., he had been teased by other boys because he never played with them but instead went directly home after school. The story, however, also relates why he went home. He came from a poor family and had to take care of his baby sister while his mother went to work as a part-time laundress. Emphasis is on recognizing human relations dynamics and, even more important, on helping students improve their own interpersonal relationships with schoolmates and peers.

The alert school enlists the cooperation of the home and community in distributing the guidance function to all areas of the student's life. The community should be actively engaged in fostering mental hygiene (W. E. Hall, 1958). The home should be a source of support and understanding for the student.

GUIDELINE 17: EFFECTIVE GUIDANCE IS PERMEATED WITH VALUES. Like the philosopher von Hildebrand (1953), the counseling theorist Williamson (1959, pp. 6–8) contends that all human behavior is deeply rooted in a conscious or unconscious commitment to values. Psychological conflict arises when there is a clash between values and the direction which a person's behavior is taking. Thus the basic problem of human development and fulfillment is that of enabling a person, first, to discover the values which are fundamental to him and, second, to incorporate these values into the mainstream of his daily living. Of course the interpretation, the living out of these values, is a subjective matter, which differs from one person to another. What is one individual's manner of serving God, for example, may not be another's. What is one person's moral code may not be the moral code of another, although each indeed has a moral code. Thompson (1963) has noted that both empirical evidence and theoretical speculations have indicated that human nature appears to have a *need* not only for values but for a variety of values. Both specific values and their variety are greatly influenced by the particular student's culture, background, and personality. This does no violence to the idea of absolute values but rather preserves such values while upholding the individual's personality as a distinct, inviolable entity, the forum of ultimate recourse.

Consequently, if student development is to be furthered optimally, values must suffuse guidance. The guidance worker does not impose his own value system on the student; this in fact violates the ultimate bases of guidance. Rather the guidance worker helps the client clarify his own values so that he may self-actualize from that framework. From such examination and clarification comes either an alignment of behavior and values or a change in either behavior or previously held values.

Many counseling theorists and guidance workers in the field neglect or deny the pivotal value underpinnings in guidance. Thus Wrenn (1952, p. 176) was able to remark: "If this profession [of counseling] is in want of anything, it is in a neglect of the proposition that man is spiritual as well as intellectual in nature; it is in a failure to recognize that man has a relationship to the Infinite as well as to other men."

GUIDELINE 18: EFFECTIVE GUIDANCE IS BASED ON A PERSONAL RELATIONSHIP BETWEEN GUIDANCE WORKER AND STUDENT. Guidance is not a bag of tricks which the worker uses with the student; rather it is the total giving of self and unconditional acceptance of the student. In short, it is the forming of a deep, personal existential bond, an I-Thou, an "exchange" of selves. It is a prizing, a "loving," of the student on the part of the worker.

Several significant empirical researches can be cited to illustrate the necessity of a warm, personal relationship between guidance worker and student for optimal assistance. A study by Halkides (1958) revealed that the following were necessary and sufficient conditions for beneficial change in the client: the degree of empathic understanding of the client manifested by the guidance worker; the degree of positive affective attitude toward the client manifested by the worker; and the degree or extent to which the worker was genuine, i.e., his words were congruent with his internal feelings. Seeman's investigation (1954) disclosed that success in psychotherapy is closely linked with a strong and growing mutual liking and respect between client and therapist. Heine's study (1950) of individuals who underwent psychotherapy with practitioners of different psychoanalytic schools disclosed that despite the theoretical differences and allegiances of the therapists, the therapists' attitude accounted for constructive growth changes. When the therapist was warm and personal, constructive growth changes occurred; when the therapist was remote and distant, that growth was not facilitated. A celebrated study by Spitz (1945, pp. 53–74) of babies born to unwed mothers dramatically reinforces the thesis developed here. Two groups of babies were separated for investigation. The babies in group A were cared for by their own mothers or by adequate mother substitutes. The babies in group B were cared for by trained nurses in accordance with high professional medical standards. Indeed the babies in group B were cared for in a more professional manner and with higher medical standards than those in group A. At the end of the study, group A babies had made normal progress, while group B babies were tragic on all counts. Of 91 babies, 34 died (despite elaborate medical precautions), while the rest were apathetic and had regressed in intelligence; only 5 could walk unaided. Spitz concluded that mothering, the personal bond between the mother or mother substitute and the baby, is far more vital than impersonal attention, however professional. Certainly the study bears out the contention of Reik (1963, p. 22): "The unloved child dies, and if it does not die, maybe it is better that it did."

Even lower animals have the need for close relationships to one of their own kind. In this connection a classic study by Harlow and Zimmerman (1958) is of especial interest. Infant monkeys removed from their mothers almost immediately after birth were presented with two objects. One, called the "hard mother," consisted of a sloping cylinder of wire netting with a nipple from which the neonate might feed. The other, termed the "soft mother," consisted of a cylinder made from foam rubber and terry cloth. Even when the neonatal monkey received all its food from the hard mother, he clearly and increasingly preferred the soft mother. Of this investigation, C. R. Rogers (1958, p. 9) remarked: "Of the many interesting and challenging implications of this study, one seems reasonably clear. It is that no amount of direct food reward can take the place of certain perceived qualities, which the infant appears to need and desire."

The personal relationship between guidance worker and client is often called *rapport*. Rapport consists not in a series of psychological devices but in the warm giving of self and unconditional acceptance of the client. In the counseling relationship, the client contributes to rapport not because he knows that the counselor is professionally competent to assist him but because the counselor is warmly acceptant (Oppenheimer, 1954). The counselor must do more than *think* with the client. As Brother Austin Dondero, F.S.C. (1961, p. 42), expressed it, he must *"feel* with the client."

In order to enter into a deeply personal relationship with the client, the counselor himself must be well developed as a person. He must be secure, self-acceptant, possess a realistic self-concept, have self-actualized to a significant degree, and be reasonably adjusted. Counseling, like teaching and other helping professions, often draws to its ranks persons who wish to work out their own personal problems through clients.

GUIDELINE 19: EFFECTIVE GUIDANCE IS PROFESSIONAL.   Guidance performed in a haphazard manner by well-intentioned but untrained guidance workers in an unselected setting is haphazard guidance. Effective workers are professionally trained *before* they enter service. They continue to professionalize through appropriate in-service work. Counselors need the kind of training suggested in the recommendations of the American Personnel and Guidance Association. Guidance specialists such as school psychologists need the kind of training suggested in the recommendations of the appropriate professional organization, e.g., the American Psychological Association. Because teachers and administrators function as guidance workers, they too need training commensurate with their guidance function. It was suggested earlier that this training include, as a minimum, courses in the principles and foundations of guidance and in interview techniques with supervised laboratory experience. These are in addition to the graduate course, appropriate to the level of school service, in the dynamics of human development which is now (or should be) required of all teachers. Guidance courses should be expressly tailored *to the needs of teachers and administrators* rather than of counselors. Some states have incorporated such a requirement into their certification laws. In Catholic school systems, such professional work for teachers and principals is all too rare.

Professional counseling is conducted in a professional setting. A specially designated and equipped counseling office is provided for each school counselor, warmly furnished, with an adequate file cabinet for student records, another cabinet and bookshelf space for test materials and occupational-educational information, and a reception room for waiting clients. There should be one counselor aide for every two or three counselors to assist with the routine nonprofessional aspects of the counselor's function. The maximum counselor-pupil ratio is normally from 1:250 to 1:300. Both an adequate staff of personnel specialists (e.g., school psychologists) and adequate professional offices for these specialists are provided in a comprehensive guidance program.

Like teaching, guidance and counseling are more art than science. This is not to minimize the scientific aspect of guidance but to place it in proper perspective. Counselors must beware of overpsychologizing or of engaging in pseudoanalysis, each masquerading as a "scientific approach" to counseling (Brother J. M. Egan, F.S.C.H., 1958, p. 79).

Counselor educators in universities should carefully screen counselor candidates so that ineffective and nonprofessional aspirants are encouraged to seek occupational self-fulfillment in other areas. Like teacher candidates, counselor aspirants are too often weak personalities seeking either the security of a tenured position which offers automatic increments or the psychological support of a position of authority over pupils.

GUIDELINE 20. EFFECTIVE GUIDANCE IS ORGANIZED AND SYSTEMATIC. A school which promotes guidance passes through three successive stages, viz., guidance-conscious, guidance-active, and guidance-organized. Without careful organization, its guidance efforts are haphazard, uncoordinated, and generally ineffective. In a school system well organized for effective guidance, a guidance director supervises formal services in the system. Each large school also has a pupil personnel services coordinator who synchronizes personnel services and guidance efforts in that school. There are an organized records service, referral procedures, an in-service program, and systematic principles for evaluating the guidance program (Froehlich, 1958, pp. 18–21). Catholic schools are especially weak in the area of guidance organization.

An investigation by Sister M. Eugenia Ziegler, C.S.A.C. (1958, p. 336), of selected Catholic high schools concluded that there is "a definite need for a more highly organized program of group guidance and individual counseling. This need is especially urgent in Catholic schools whose personnel have too long relied upon an informal program of guidance and considered its results sufficient." Public and Catholic schools cannot believe that because administrative and instructional services are well organized and systematized, the same is automatically true of the guidance service.

part 2

GUIDANCE ORGANIZATION: PERSONNEL AND POLICIES

5

THE TEACHER'S ROLE
IN GUIDANCE

THE RELATIONSHIP BETWEEN
TEACHING AND GUIDANCE

Teaching shares a number of important characteristics with guidance and with counseling, for they are all fundamentally learning experiences for the student. The basic method in both teaching and guidance is stimulating the student to self-activity, not imparting information. Both teacher and guidance worker are only secondary proximate causes in learning; the student himself is the primary proximate cause. The function of both teaching and guidance is so to facilitate situations that the student is stimulated to self-activity. Finally, teaching and guidance involve joint searches for truth. The student has a pivotal role in planning and in sharing in the learning experience, whether in learning cognitive content or in learning the contours of self.

The major cause of lack of awareness of the relationship between teaching and guidance is that often what purports to be teaching is at best inferior and at worst not really teaching at all. As Torrance (1962b, pp. 179–182) has noted, much of what passes for teaching today is a stimulus-response approach in which the teacher attempts either to get from or to give to the student a single answer, rather than assist him to engage in mental self-activity. Teachers frequently attempt to "impart" information by lecturing or by telling, rather than by so structuring the learning environment that the student is assisted to learn by and through himself. The teacher is often a god, not a guide, and the goal of a joint search for truth becomes neither "joint" nor "search."

Like guidance and teaching, counseling and teaching are also interrelated. As Combs (1954, p. 31) has stated, "There can be little doubt that counseling is, in essence, a learning process." Teaching, like counseling, is defined only in terms of what the student involved actually learns; i.e., if there is no learning, then there is no teaching, there is no counseling (Arbuckle, 1957b; Lee, 1963b, pp. 228–238). Both teaching and counseling are vitally concerned not merely with the *product* learning outcome (e.g., learning that 18 multiplied by 26 equals 468 or attaining the solution of a personal problem) but, more important, with a *process* learning outcome (e.g., the critical thinking involved in arriving at the answer to a mathematical problem or the self-actualizing which takes place while resolving a personal difficulty). Because teaching and counseling effect product and process learnings in the student, it is possible for Williamson (1958b) to say that counseling is a "teaching-learning" situation in that the counselor as teacher can either "instruct" or assist the student. Counseling is more concerned with process learning than with product learning; thus counseling has been considered "deeper teaching." Deeper teaching avoids giving the student a direct response or a ready solution but rather so structures the situation that the pupil is encouraged to discover for himself the ways and means of meeting problems.

While guidance and counseling are strongly related to teaching, classroom teaching as a process is quite distinct from guidance and counseling. Guidance and counseling are concerned with helping the student to grow as a person, while classroom teaching is concerned with assisting him to grow in truth. The teacher is concerned primarily with the whole student in order to help him self-actualize in truth, while the guidance worker is concerned with the whole student in order to help him self-actualize as a person. If the teacher is genuinely concerned with the whole student, he is perforce concerned with guidance in the classroom situation and indeed in all his professional relationships with students. If the teacher adopts not only the "guidance viewpoint" but also guidance practices in his classes, he comes closer to realizing some of the cardinal goals of the *teaching* process.

THE TEACHER AND THE
GUIDANCE TEAM

Guidance worker as a generic term applies to anyone who performs guidance functions in a school setting or in a school-related context. There are four chief school guidance workers, viz., the teacher, the teacher-counselor, the counselor, and the personnel specialist. The teacher is the pedagogical leader in the classroom or classroom-related milieu who performs guidance functions in those aspects of the school program in which he is directly or indirectly involved. To perform effectively his minimal, though crucially important, guidance function, every *teacher* should complete at least two guidance courses especially designed for teachers, viz., a graduate or undergraduate course in principles and foundations of guidance and a graduate course in interview techniques for teachers with supervised laboratory experience. This presumes that he also has taken the standard course, appropriate for his level of service, in the dynamics of human development. The *teacher-counselor* is a regular teacher whose assignment includes spending one-third to one-half of his time as consultant to students, with a proportionate reduction in his class teaching load. In some schools the teacher-counselor is referred to as the *grade adviser* because he handles the occupational and further educational plans or problems of pupils at a particular grade level. The teacher-counselor needs a course in educational and occupational information and a course in the dynamics of vocational orientation, in addition to those guidance and psychology courses which every teacher should take. The *counselor* is a member of the school staff whose full-time assignment consists in assisting the students to self-actualize in the developmental patterns unique to each. While at least 50 per cent of his time is spent in interviewing, he has a host of other guidance duties, ranging from group guidance to management of the guidance bulletin board and to planning career nights. The counselor should meet those course and experience requirements set forth in the latest APGA recommendations. The *guidance or personnel specialist* is a member of either the school staff or the school system. His assignment is such that he usually deals with exceptional students, i.e., those in need of detailed psychological examination, psychotherapy, and so forth. The guidance specialist should have attained the level of professional training recommended by the appropriate professional group for his position. None of the four types of guidance worker has a monopoly on guidance in a school; each worker engages in the type and level most in keeping with his specific assignment and level of training.

THE TEACHER AS
GUIDANCE WORKER

There are two reasons why every teacher is a guidance worker. First, the nature of teaching demands that he be a guidance worker. Teaching is not imparting, nor is it mere verbal instruction. Teaching is "causing" the whole student to learn (Turner, 1963), and it utilizes guidance in effecting this causality. Many vectors bear on the teaching function, and not the least of these is the guidance responsibility. It is not surprising that one's philosophy of education, or more precisely one's philosophy of teaching, has considerable impact on the amount and degree of interpenetration of the guidance function in the teaching encounter. For example, Schneiders (1960, pp. 96–97), a Catholic psychologist who seems to hold an intellectualist view of both education and teaching, well summarizes the view that even positive mental hygiene lies outside the direct role of the teacher:

> The primary and essential end of a college or university is to teach, and thereby to promote intellectual growth. Through this growth, each student should mature spiritually, morally, and socially. If he matures emotionally, so much the better; but it is not the purpose of higher education to utilize the classroom situation for the purpose of emotional development. The classroom and the clinic, the couch and the lectern are distinct entities whose purpose and functions belong to different aspects of human service. . . . The teacher is primarily a custodian of truth, a purveyor of knowledge.

Fr. Charles F. Donovan, S.J. (1960, p. 93), appears to have offered an excellent rebuttal of such a position when he said on another occasion: "I thought we long ago disposed of the arbitrary dilemma that the teacher must teach either subjects *or* people." Most intellectualists seem to believe that intellectual growth takes place in a vacuum, without simultaneous growth and development of emotions, will, or other personal-social facets of man's nature. The student is an integer; his intellect cannot be isolated by the teacher.

The second reason why every teacher is a guidance worker is more concretely rooted. Every teacher, whether he wishes to or not, "does" guidance of some sort in both his classroom and his classroom-related activities (Willis, 1957). The teacher deals with students, with human beings. His existential situation thrusts the guidance function on him. The teacher, however intellectualist a position he may hold in theory, is *de facto* a guidance worker. The guidance role in teaching can be compared to the Romans' notion of fate; viz., it leads the willing, drags the unwilling. Many teachers are unfortunately not aware of their guidance role; when they learn of it, however, most greet it with enthusiasm. Thus a study by H. E. Williams (1958) concluded that when guidance concepts and principles were presented to elementary school teachers, these teachers recognized them as part of their work as teachers.

While many educators highlight the crucial role of the teacher in the school's guidance program, too little empirical research has been done in this area. One of the few germane studies is that of J. A. Stewart (1961) on teachers in the state of Washington. He concluded that teachers were in fact participating very actively in guidance activities, there were significant differences in the degree to which individual teachers engaged in such activities, married male and female teachers participated in guidance activities to a significantly higher degree than did unmarried male and female teachers, women teachers had significantly higher attitude-toward-guidance scores than did male teachers, and optimal predictors of teacher guidance participation were teachers' attitudes and experience. Favorable attitudes toward guidance are crucial, for as Sister Mary Agnes, C.R.S.M. (1958, p. 218), has observed, if the teacher has no positive attitude toward or interest in guidance, he is ineffectual in whatever guidance activities he may undertake, e.g., in the homeroom. Because teachers are unaware of or uninterested in their role as guidance workers, they frequently fail to work with their pupils in an effort to assist them in achieving total self-actualization.

Sister Teresa Gertrude Murray, O.S.B. (1940, p. 378), one of the pioneers in Catholic school guidance, remarked that even if a public or a Catholic school system had all the counselors and guidance specialists it needed, the teacher would still perform half of the school's guidance work. This is even more applicable in the elementary school than in the secondary school and college, since lower grades are characterized by a self-contained classroom. This type of organization enables the teacher to get to know the pupil on a more intimate basis than is possible in the departmentalized secondary school and college and so places him in a uniquely strategic guidance position. In all schools at every level, the counselor is the "nerve center" of the guidance program, while the teacher remains the "heart."

There are five principal ways in which the regular teacher serves as a guidance worker: (1) in formal classroom activities, (2) in homeroom activities, (3) in student activities (formerly referred to as extracurricular activities), (4) in other allied school activities, and (5) in interview activities.

Guidance in formal classroom activities

A guidance-aware teacher in the classroom itself fulfills his function as a guidance worker in a variety of ways. For purposes of clarity, these classroom guidance activities have been synthesized and condensed into minimal "imperatives."

KNOW EACH STUDENT. Like good teaching, effective guidance cannot operate out of an ignorance of student needs and the developmental pattern unique to him. The teacher comes to know each student better by reviewing his cumulative record, by conferring with his other teachers and his counselor, and particularly by analyzing his behavior in class. Because the teacher deals with the student more directly than does any other school person, he can come to know the student best, but only if he wishes to come to know him. This daily relationship of teacher and pupil forms the *raison d'être* for the teacher's guidance role. As the American Council on Education (1948, p. 11) officially declared, "Specialized personnel services can never replace the day-by-day intimate contact of teacher and student." In the self-contained classroom in the elementary school, the teacher has an excellent opportunity for systematic observation of each student's behavior pattern. A guidance-aware teacher watches for "danger signals" in the pupil's normal developmental maturation, e.g., the existence of patent disturbances, problems in getting along with classmates, marked withdrawal tendencies, over-aggressiveness, compulsive conduct, or persistence of a difficulty (I. J. Gordon, 1956, pp. 297–298). Many psychological problems which erupt during adulthood can be traced to unhealthy defense mechanisms during elementary and secondary school years. These mechanisms at first protect and bolster, but in later years destroy, the person; they prove costly palliatives. Every teacher should not only work with the student in developing himself as a person but also make sure that the classroom situation itself does not cause difficulties in development, e.g., by failing to provide opportunities for exploration, by subjecting students to experiences which weaken confidence in themselves. The teacher is usually in a position to know the student better than is any other school guidance worker, including the counselor. L. R. Pierson's study (1958) investigated the question of whether the scholastic success of a selected group of college students was better predicted by their high school counselors or by their high school teachers. Counselors in this study knew the students for their entire high school careers, while teachers in most instances first became acquainted with them during the senior year. Counselors had access to all marks in the school record, as well as results of all standardized intelligence, achievement, aptitude, and other tests taken by the students. Nonetheless, counselors were not able to predict college scholastic success as well as classroom teachers. Teachers saw pupils in a variety of situations in day-to-day classroom experience and so had more experiential knowledge of their adaptive dynamics than did counselors.

UNDERSTAND EACH STUDENT.   Knowing the student is preliminary to understanding him. Understanding is that deeper comprehension, that more profound grasp of what the student is really like, of why he is the way he is. St. Thomas Aquinas (*Summa Theologica*, II–II, q. 8, a. 1, AD. 1) held that knowledge pertains merely to the apprehension of the truth, while understanding refers to penetrating and discerning judgment about the truth.

Therefore understanding perfects knowledge (Aquinas, *Summa Theologica,* I–II, q. 68, a. 4). St. Thomas also maintained that there are two ways of attaining the truth, viz., through study and through experience (*Summa Theologica,* II–II, q. 8, a. 6; q. 45, a. 2). Commenting on these passages, John of St. Thomas suggests that perhaps another, more concrete, reason why understanding is superior to knowledge is that, unlike knowledge, it can be gained only through *experiencing* (1951, pp. 97–98). Knowledge can be gained vicariously, while understanding can be attained only by a direct encounter, a personal confrontation.

The guidance-aware teacher strives to understand the student. This involves plunging himself into the student's world, tasting of its joys and bliss, its gall and wormwood. It means listening to the student's music, going to his movies, visiting his "hangouts," and bringing this understanding into classroom situations. Such an "incarnation" into the student's world is often lacking in religious teachers in Catholic schools, doubtless because of the relatively sheltered life which teaching religious often lead. Thus Pope Pius XII (1951, p. 25) stated that the teaching sister and the modern girl do not understand each other very well. The nature of the teaching apostolate *demands,* however, that the religious plunge himself or herself into the student's world so that effective teaching and guidance ensue in the classroom. If the constitutions of a particular order or congregation engaged in teaching are so written that religious cannot immerse themselves in the student's milieu for more fruitful exercising of the classroom mission, that order or congregation might profitably modify its constitution or seriously examine its suitability to engage in the educational apostolate. Nor should existing constitutions be interpreted so stringently and so myopically as to choke whatever milieu plunging is possible within their legitimate framework. An example of such rigoristic interpretation was provided by one woman religious (Sister M. Vernice, S.N.D., 1959, p. 296), who wrote that the religious teacher should not read "frivolous stories" in modern magazines because it would open the mind of the religious to the "contamination of the world." While this statement is no doubt based on a legitimate and praiseworthy constitutional interpretation of the necessity of single-minded striving for perfection, nonetheless adequate guidance is nigh impossible unless the teacher understands the student's world, however "contaminated" it might seem. Indeed reading about something yields only knowledge, which is not understanding but merely a preliminary to it. The essential Christian *Weltanschauung* regards the world as sacramental, as an extension of God's creative force, as a capsule participating in Divine life.

EMPATHIZE WITH EACH STUDENT. Knowledge and understanding are not enough for the teacher who wishes to be effective in guidance work in the classroom; his whole being must be involved. Only through *empathizing* can the teacher feel as the student feels, structure the world as the student structures it, and, in short, become the student as far as he is able. Empathy is the ultimate step which a teacher can take in grasping existentially the vitals of what a student is actually living. Understanding yields judgment about the person or thing experienced; empathy yields those raw data of life which by their very nature do not submit themselves to intellectual judgment.

BE WARM TO EACH STUDENT. A teacher who does not treat each student warmly fails both as guidance worker and as teacher. A review of the pertinent research by Sister Mary Agnita Spurgeon, G.N.S.H. (1959, p. 151), concluded that academic learning is not an adequate predictor of teacher effectiveness; the teacher's personality, warmth, and kindness toward students are more important predictors. A. J. Becker's study (1962) of teaching sisters ten years professed who were judged to be successful by their superiors concluded that these nuns were warm, cooperative, and empathic in the classroom. Unfortunately, in place of warmth, some teachers have developed and refined a new guidance vehicle, viz., "shout" guidance. Shout guidance consists in yelling at the top of one's voice at a student who doesn't understand a point in the lesson or whose personal problems are such that he "misbehaves" during the lesson. Shout guidance operates on the principle that the guidance-aware teacher helps the students more by vinegar than by honey. It is particularly suitable for use by teachers who wish to make it impossible for students to fulfill their imperative developmental tasks adequately, thus helping to ensure a steady and never-ending stream of customers for mental-health clinics, prisons, and neuropsychiatric wards.

ACCEPT EACH STUDENT COMPLETELY. The teacher must accept each student without reservation, no matter how intellectually incapable he is, no matter how many "sins" or other misbehaviors he has committed. Accepting a student totally does not imply that the teacher approves or even fails to disapprove of the student's "misdeed" but rather that he makes the legitimate and necessary separation between the student and his offense. As Erasmus (1962b, p. 129) wrote, "Let him love the pious in Christ and the impious for Christ's sake." How acceptant are Catholic teachers, clergy, religious, or laymen of students, especially those who misbehave? Catholic teachers accept Mary Magdalen as a saint according to the Gospel, but what would happen if she were to walk into one of the classes in a Catholic school?

ESTABLISH A FRIENDLY, PERMISSIVE CLASSROOM CLIMATE. The atmosphere of a classroom and the tone which pervades the formal learning situation exert definitely either a positive or a negative guidance influence (E. Caldwell, 1960, pp. 11–12). A permissive classroom atmosphere is conducive to the promotion of optimum student development, while a punitive or an autocratic atmosphere stunts and stifles growth. The classroom climate is so pervasive that it colors and affects all the student's thoughts and activities while he is in that environment. A Catholic psychiatrist (Cavanagh & Fr. McGoldrick, S.J., 1958, p. 21) has stated that the teacher is the person "most strategically situated in the educational system to contribute to the maintenance of the mental health of the child." A strict, punitive, authoritarian classroom climate can easily cause problems. In any event, such a climate is conducive to neither mental hygiene nor learning.

GIVE EACH STUDENT THE FREEDOM BOTH TO BE AND TO BECOME.   The teacher is a child developer, not a child keeper. His role in the classroom is to facilitate growth and development. The alert teacher provides as many exploratory experiences as possible. Students should be encouraged to explore within the framework of those subject-matter or problem areas encountered in a particular class. When teachers or curricula consciously and actively promote exploration, these teachers and curricula make education truly rigorous, place the center of classroom effort directly in the students, assist them to achieve their potential through their own activity, and help bring their minds and personalities from potency to act. Exploratory activities are challenging educationally. Effective teachers also provide their students with sensory experiences of an exploratory nature. One research experiment (Bexton, Heron, & Scott, 1954) demonstrated that if the channels of sensory communication are cut off or even muffled, abnormal reactions resembling the psychotic ensue. Unfortunately Puritanism has so influenced some public school teachers, and Jansenism has so gripped some Catholic school teachers, that many pupils are not provided with adequate sensory experiences. Sensations are not possible paths to temptation and sin but gateways to fruitful becoming as person and learner.

Guidance-aware teachers do not attempt to foster conformity or de-emphasize or punish creativity. Conformity places a pupil into a preconceived mold and prevents him from attaining the full amplitude of his personality. A study by Torrance (1959) revealed that highly creative pupils were considered by their teachers less desirable as pupils than conforming students whom the teachers judged to be of higher mental ability, despite the fact that the two groups of students did not differ on standardized achievement tests. Further, the teachers believed that creative students were less hardworking and studious than conforming youths. Perhaps creative youths often work and study in a somewhat different fashion from that which the teacher has come to expect as the normal, and indeed the only acceptable, pattern of work and study.

Catholic teachers, precisely because they are Catholic, have an added reason for according the student optimal freedom to be and to become. As de la

Bedoyère (1954, p. 89) has noted, "We have been created *free* personalities, and our free cooperation in a responsible way is the absolute condition of our sharing in the divine order." Unless the student is given freedom to be and to become, he never learns freedom and is prevented from furthering God in the world. Unfortunately all too many teachers in Catholic schools allow students very little freedom, doubtless in the fear that such freedom is a danger both to rigid classroom order and to the absolute nature of the dogmas of the Church. Fr. Congar, O.P. (1960, p. 27), the French theologian, has noted that freedom calls for open discussion and disagreement and consequently poses a serious threat to dogmatism (as distinct from dogma). Freedom, as he observes, "involves the acceptance sometimes of uncertainties and hazards; these are things that alarm a short-sighted authority, or one that is too self-conscious, an authority that is inclined to paternalism." Growth and development necessitate freedom, and freedom involves risks and hazards; the teacher who eliminates student risks and hazards does havoc to pupil development. In the modern age, the Church is dependent on the initiative and activity of the layman, but many agencies of the Church, including its schools, usually do not grant him the freedom necessary to the development of such initiative. As Callahan (1962, p. 88) has noted, "The layman has been incited by the Church to ask for, and anticipate, a freedom and responsibility which, in the end, the contemporary Church is hardly prone to give him." What is needed is a radical reform in theology, in canon law, and indeed in a fundamental attitude vis-à-vis the layman. The Catholic schools can prepare for that day by *now* according students the freedom to be and to become, so that the young people of today may become the dynamic lay leaders in the Church of tomorrow.

UTILIZE DISCIPLINE TO HELP EACH STUDENT GROW AND DEVELOP. Discipline is often regarded as the maintenance of order or the punishment of a student's misbehavior (Sheviakov & Redl, 1956). This is not an accurate concept; discipline is a *positive,* not a negative force. Classroom discipline is that combination of the constructive influences exerted on the pupil by his teacher, his peers, and the specific environment in the efforts to guide him toward appropriate and acceptable behavior. Discipline is basically goal-oriented; it does not exist for itself (Lee 1963b, pp. 542–579). Discipline normally has three separate, though related, roles. The *prophylactic* role consists in the establishment of classroom conditions in which the pupil is positively assisted to self-actualize by attaining the objectives of classroom activity. The *remedial* role involves that assistance to the student which helps him overcome his weaknesses and develop his strengths. The *punitive* role includes those chastening functions intended forcibly to induce the student to modify his behavior. Teachers regrettably seem to believe that discipline primarily or exclusively consists in this punitive role. Some years ago C.

R. Rogers (1939, p. 225) stated that teachers use superficial methods in attempting to help pupils with problems because their own views of the problems are superficial. Teachers tend to consider specific punitive measures rather than the amelioration of these problems. Even more fundamental is the frequent lack of awareness by teachers that constructive discipline, i.e., guidance of pupils toward appropriate and self-actualizing behavior, permeates every effective classroom moment.

Discipline exists to further learning. Lee's review (1963b, pp. 420–442, 565–566) of the research on reward and punishment as motivational factors in both constructive behavior and learning indicated that punishment usually acts either as a motivational depressant or as a negative motivational force. W. R. Butler's study (1956) of American college social fraternities revealed that those fraternities characterized by high scholastic achievement of members employed methods of controlling pledges' behavior during the latter's induction period based on the use of reward alone or on the combination of reward and judicious punishment. This policy built high morale among pledges, gave them psychological support, and, in the opinion of the investigator, was a significant factor in high scholastic achievement after the induction period. On the other hand, fraternities characterized by low scholastic achievement of members used primarily punishment and reproof of pledges during the induction period as a method of controlling behavior and also demanded that pledges follow a very rigid schedule through the week, including adherence to a specified *horarium*.

As Cutts and Moseley (1957, p. 28) have observed, punishment of itself does not teach the pupil *why* he should behave differently, nor does it instruct him on *what* new behavior pattern he should adopt. Of itself punishment is a most ineffective and in fact a useless guidance vehicle. Nor is punishment often the deterrent that it is customarily thought to be, a point illustrated in a report on a 1929 visit to European schools by Jesse B. Davis (1956, pp. 246–247). In England, Davis visited a secondary school which staged a boxing match for his entertainment. The headmaster explained that the purpose of boxing in the school's physical education program was not to teach pugilistic skills but to teach how "to take punishment without a whimper." Later, Davis noticed beside the headmaster's desk a book labeled "Floggings," next to which were a few substantial switches. The last boy flogged that day was a frequent truant. This boy had become so deeply interested in a nearby museum that he repeatedly took flogging, with a stiff upper lip and without a whimper, so that he could go to the museum rather than to school. The headmaster admitted that flogging did not deter the boy's visits to the museum. When Davis suggested that the boy be sent to the museum to prepare a report or to serve as tour guide for a class visit, the headmaster scorned this guidance-minded suggestion as absurd.

The classroom should be a learning situation characterized by the cohesion of teacher and pupils engaged in a joint search for truth, whole and entire, a positive environment which promotes teaching, learning, and guidance. Instead it quite frequently degenerates into a power situation in which the teacher exerts his will on the class by harsh punitive control. Students react by seeing how far they can escape control and how much they "can get away with." Discipline as guidance toward appropriate behavior is lost in such an atmosphere. Arbuckle (1950, pp. 156–178; 1957a, pp. 66–76) observes that teachers who discipline punitively often feel that unless they literally or figuratively hold whips over the heads of students they will lose control of the class.

In view of the Christian emphasis on love as the prime path toward encouraging self-actualization, discipline in Catholic schools should be more constructive and less punitive than in non-Catholic schools. But observation and reputation point in the opposite direction. Indeed the common conception of the woman religious teacher as a rather harsh disciplinarian was confirmed by Sister M. Agnita Spurgeon, G.N.S.H. (1959, pp. 132–135, 153–154), who investigated sister-teachers in 220 Catholic elementary and secondary schools. Sister Agnita administered the Minnesota Teacher Attitude Inventory (MTAI) to more than 1,500 sister-teachers in these schools and discovered that the lowest (i.e., most authoritarian) scores were in the area of discipline. She concluded that sister-teachers were influenced both by personal philosophy and by professional training in convent-related or other Catholic schools to believe that the teacher's role is decidedly a dominant and indeed a dominating one. Sister Agnita recommended that religious superiors and administrators work energetically with their staffs in an effort to improve this situation. Special stress needs to be given to the concept that punitive discipline is not of the essence of Catholic education. Indeed Pope Pius XII (1951, p. 4) in an address to teaching sisters observed that to try to convince or reform youths by coercion is useless.

There is some indication that convent and seminary education may be partly responsible for the undue emphasis which many religious and priests place on punitive discipline in Catholic schools. The 1959 letter of the Roman Congregation of Seminaries made it clear that the two most important and overriding elements in seminary education were complete obedience in all things and total acceptance of whatever discipline superiors impose.

Perhaps no one has more clearly fused the Christian dimension with the pedagogical and guidance functions of discipline than St. Thomas Aquinas, the Patron of Schools (*Summa Theologica*, II–II, q. 68, a. 1): "In this life there is no punishment for punishment's sake. The time of the Last Judgment has not yet come. The value of human penalties is medicinal in so far as they promote the public welfare and the cure of the offender."

MAKE EACH LESSON PUPIL-CENTERED. Unfortunately many teachers forget the centrality of the student in the learning process and focus attention on content rather than on the student. This results not only in less than adequate teaching but also in a depersonalization which hinders the teacher's classroom guidance function. Making the lesson pupil-centered does not necessitate a diminution of the *amount* of content a student learns but rather alters the *way* in which he learns it. Two studies by Koile and Treat (1961) concluded that public secondary school teachers are more pupil-oriented than are college teachers. It is probably safe to say that elementary school teachers are in turn more pupil-oriented than are secondary school teachers. One reason might be that the preservice and in-service training of teachers becomes increasingly less person- or pupil-oriented and more content-oriented with the advance in grade level for which they are preparing.

PLAN LEARNING UNITS JOINTLY WITH STUDENTS. If the student is the center of the teacher's whole effort, as Bishop Mussio (1959, p. 210) contends, he should have a voice in determining what he learns in the classroom. This not only greatly facilitates learning but also is a powerful engine for effective classroom guidance. Cooperative pupil-teacher planning gives students sufficient personality *Lebensraum* so that they have the freedom to become. It develops within them not merely a sense of responsibility but actual practice in responsible decision making. It facilitates transfer of the learning of responsibility in the classroom to responsible behavior and life planning in out-of-classroom activities. It demonstrates to the student that he is accepted by the teacher *de facto* and not merely conceptually. In Catholic schools joint teacher-pupil planning is especially crucial since these schools wish to develop active and responsive laity to assume positions of leadership in parish life.

BE ALERT TO GUIDANCE "OPENINGS" DURING THE COURSE OF THE LESSON. During a lesson, certain developments occur which provide guidance opportunities. For example, during a spirited discussion in an English class of J. D. Salinger's *Catcher in the Rye,* the teacher can utilize pupil interest and enthusiasm to encourage a particularly shy student to offer his opinion to the class. If in social studies class a student asks what function a seventeenth-century cooper performed, the teacher can integrate this information nicely into a brief discussion on the obsolescence of occupations. The guidance-aware teacher does not, however, merely wait for guidance openings to present themselves; he creates them. For example, a social studies teacher can show the film *Twelve Angry Men,* which illustrates not only the process of trial by jury but also the dynamics of personal interaction in groups. The Spanish teacher in a Catholic school can show the film *Marcellino,* a splendid vehicle for learning conversational Spanish which also incorporates sound religious attitudes. Varying teaching techniques also further guidance as well as learning. A discussion class promotes improved personal relationships, a role-playing class furthers worthwhile attitudes, and committee work fosters improved social relationships. Socialized lessons of themselves provide guidance opportunities, for as G. Marcel and Martin Buber have maintained, the human self emerges only in interaction with other selves, in a communion of selves. Hence individual guidance and counseling never supplant guidance in groups, including guidance in the classroom.

FOSTER THE DEVELOPMENT OF POSITIVE ATTITUDES.   An attitude is a relatively permanent disposition or mind-set toward a physical or mental object. Attitudes, as Allport (1935, p. 806) has noted, determine not only what a person thinks but what he sees, hears, and learns. Unfortunately many teachers think the primary goal is to teach facts; consequently they neglect to teach for the development of attitudes, which are often far better remembered and more influential in a person's life than facts. Catholic students have been learning for many, many years the fact that it is their duty to love *all* their neighbors, but it is only recently that some of these students have formed a favorable *attitude* toward the Negro, and indeed such a favorable attitude has perhaps been nurtured by national developments to a greater degree than by the Catholic school classroom. Guidance-alert teachers give prime emphasis to the development of attitudes. Role playing as a teaching device has been found particularly effective in bringing about a desirable shift in attitudes (A. Klein, 1956). The teacher's techniques in class often teach attitudes rather than the facts he presents or develops; e.g., a teacher who *de facto* gives his pupils responsibility and freedom builds these attitudes much more effectively than the teacher who talks about how valuable freedom and responsibility are but gives pupils little of either.

ASSIST EACH PUPIL TO IMPROVE HIS STUDY SKILLS.   A review of the research by Lee (1963b, pp. 343–359) concluded that students often lack definite information about efficient methods and techniques of study. Many schools still have not established how-to-study programs. The teacher must often help pupils develop study skills during class time. Even if the school has a how-to-study program, it is the responsibility of the teacher to reinforce its substance. Certainly the student should know efficient study methods to derive the greatest profit from the academic phase of his school experience. Formally supervised study in the classroom should be so conducted that study skills are easily transferred to home study and to the increasingly larger amounts of independent study within the school day urged by contemporary educators and in practice in forward-looking schools (Trump & Baynham, 1961, pp. 41–43). The student needs to know the efficient elements of studying, viz., preparation for study, studying, and following up study. He should also acquire the six basic study skills: location, comprehension, organization, integration, interpretation, and retention. In helping the pupil improve study skills, the teacher is helping him in his present tasks and is also offering further educational guidance in the sense that these skills are increasingly necessary for success at the next rung of the educational ladder, e.g., college. Teachers often cannot or will not help students in improving study skills, possibly because they know little about diagnostic and remedial procedures or about the psychology of learning. In any event, every teacher ought to be familiar with the principles of effective study (Cole, 1960; Robinson, 1961; Wrightstone, 1956).

INDIVIDUALIZE TEACHING.   Contemporary classroom teaching involves a social milieu, a group situation. As a result, not infrequently preoccupation with the class as a group causes failure to tailor teaching adequately to the developmental pattern unique to each student. Teaching becomes standardized rather than individualized. Unless the teacher so individualizes classwork that each student can operate optimally at his own ability level, however, he directly thwarts whatever instructional and guidance measures he initiates. As Williamson and Darley (1937, p. 74) have stated, "In the last analysis instructors have the greatest contact with students. Until this contact is leavened with positive attention to the individuality of each student in the group, personnel work [and guidance] will lack complete effectiveness, and instruction will miss an opportunity for more effective education." The lecture method or the "telling" method of teaching fails to individualize instruction. A developmental lesson, featuring questions, pupil reports, committee work, role-playing situations, and symposia with floor discussion, facilitates individual growth and development.

The size of the classroom group greatly affects the quality, type, amount, and dynamics of the interpersonal relationships among members. The research (cf. McKenna, 1957, p. 438) indicates that small classes are superior to large classes in quality of teaching and degree to which students learn. Unfortunately not a few Catholic educators and writers (cf. Denney, 1962, p. 146) are quite outspoken in their insistence that equal learning occurs in large classes and in smaller ones. Catholics who defend large classes may do so as an attempted justification of oversized classes in Catholic schools.

Thelen (1949, p. 142), an acute student of group process, has advocated instructional groups of the smallest operative size, i.e., of the size "in which it is possible to have represented at a functional level all the social and achievement skills required for the particular activity." He terms this "the principle of the least sized group." The theoretical and practical basis underlying this principle is that the group accomplishes its work most efficiently when its size facilitates optimal participation and contribution to group activity. Thelen notes that as the group grows larger, several changes occur which minimize the individual's role, thereby hindering group learning and activity. *First,* the group becomes less intimate and less deeply personal; members experience greater difficulty in expressing their more intimate thoughts and feelings. This results in depriving the group of such thoughts and feelings, as well as preventing the widest possible range of the needs of individual members from being met in a group situation. *Second,* the group tends to become more formal; special procedural rules must be adopted for smooth group functioning. *Third,* each person feels a lessening of sharing and hence of responsibility in meeting the demands of the group's work or task. Insufficient opportunity to participate in a group activity results in dissatisfaction. If a member is given the chance to participate and to present his ideas, even if these ideas are rejected, he is not totally dissatisfied, since he at least has the feeling of contributing. *Fourth,* each member becomes less visible; he is led to lessen participation in the group's work. *Fifth,* less time is available to each member to express his ideas as well as to test these ideas through overt participation. In a small group "each individual has sufficient latitude or space in which to behave and thus the basic abilities of each individual may be expressed, but in larger groups only the more forceful individuals are able to express their abilities and ideas since the amount of freedom in the situation is not sufficient to accommodate all group members" (L. F. Carter et al., 1951, p. 250). *Sixth,* people find it more difficult to break into discussion; so they withdraw. A study by J. Gibb (1951) showed that as the size of the group increased, a greater proportion of members reported feelings of threat or inhibition of impulses to participate. *Seventh,* the influence of each person and of his contribution to group thinking is lessened. *Eighth,* the tendency of a member is to "sit tight" because he knows someone else, particularly someone forceful, will do the job (Thelen, 1954, pp. 187–188). Studies by Bales (1953) concluded that in any group a "top" or principal participant emerges. As the group becomes larger, this person tends increasingly to speak *to* the group *as* a group rather than to specific individuals in the group. He also tends increasingly to exceed his proportionate share of group discussion. The individual members, for their part, tend to direct larger and larger proportions of communication and responsibility to the principal participant and an increasingly smaller proportion to other members. Thus the larger the group, the more centralized are both its structure and its flow of communication. From Thelen's analysis, the small group appears more conducive to effective teaching and guidance than the large group.

Catholic schools have not sufficiently individualized instruction for a variety of reasons. For many years religious believed that attention to individual needs fostered pride in students. Standardization and conformity became the watchword, particularly among women religious teachers. Even such details as eyeglass frames and the handwriting of sisters in a particular congregation were as similar as possible, so that "noxious individualism and independence" would not show themselves. Fr. Gallen, S.J. (1962, p. 60), cites the allegedly apocryphal story of a superioress who so wanted to suppress individualism in her subjects that she standardized their height by putting taller coifs on the shorter nuns. How this zealot for nonindividualization went about standardizing the weight of sisters is uncertain. This passion of women religious for conformity in externals naturally bred passion for sameness in internals. Interior thought conformity was encouraged, and creative thinking was suppressed. As Frs. Evoy, S.J., and Cristoph, S.J. (1963, p. 187), remarked, "in the minds of many [superiors], a sister is judged to be a better religious in direct proportion to her not having a single thought of her own." This overemphasis on conformity and the suppression of individualism is disappearing in more forward-looking religious congregations. Nonetheless, religious will probably always possess a somewhat greater degree of standardization of conduct and thinking than laymen because in fact and in spirit they lead a common life. Religious teachers, however, ought not to expect or demand lay students to lead a similarly regularized life. As Brother Edward L. Cashin, F.M.S. (1963), has observed, "Religious life requires more externals than do the schools. In face of this fact, it is easy to forget that each person is actually different, and furthermore he is supposed to be. Emerson said: 'He who would be a man must be a nonconformist'."

UTILIZE GROUP TECHNIQUES. Because teaching occurs in a social milieu, the teacher is perforce a group worker, but as I. J. Gordon (1956, p. 215) has noted, the class is at the outset a collection of individuals, not a group united toward purposeful and goal-directed activity. The effective teacher converts the class from a collection of individuals into a cohesive group. The formation of a well-integrated group facilitates both instructional and guidance roles in classroom activity, for it broadens the individual's horizons, teaches him cooperative behavior, permits him to explore a range of values and opinions, and leavens his individuality with the yeast of interactive experience. Several factors influence the nature of the group and its subsequent effectiveness in producing fruitful learning and guidance. The size of the group exercises considerable influence on the nature, thrust, and direction of group activity. A study by Sister M. Agnita Spurgeon, G.N.S.H. (1959, p. 136), of students in Catholic schools concluded that overcrowded classrooms cause inadequate learning opportunities, breed pupil misbehavior, and result in poor classroom guidance. Bales and associates (1957) report that as group size increases, there emerge less sensitive exploration of the point of view of other members and more direct attempts to control others. Apparently, there is greater anonymity of fellow members in a large group, resulting in less identification with self. As a group grows larger, the individual still retains his desire to participate. Hence, if the climate of a large group is reasonably permissive, such a group often fractionates into subgroups, since this is the only outlet for members' desire to participate. But fractionation thwarts coordinated group effort. An interesting and often over-looked consideration in large groups is the effect on the leader, in this case the teacher. Hemphill's investigations (1950) have shown that as the group becomes larger, the demands on the leader's role become greater and more numerous; this in turn lessens the effectiveness of the leader qua leader. Leadership function is here defined as assisting each member of the group to self-actualize in a manner consistent with his unique developmental pattern and with the goals of the group. As a result the leader first becomes inde-cisive in his attempts to continue his old functions (based on leadership patterns in a small group), then increasingly grows impatient to the extent that he begins to direct the group more and more overtly. The group becomes intolerant of the ineffectiveness of both the leader and itself. At this juncture, it begins to insist that the leader take complete control and make decisions quickly and decisively. Consequent breakdown in cooperative effort causes the teacher's instructional and guidance functions to be thwarted.

The teacher should infuse the group dynamics approach into socialized lessons. Further, he should utilize a variety of group instructional techniques, such as committee work, panels, and all-class discussions. In so doing, he not only improves instruction but also engages in effective guidance.

UTILIZE CONDUCT LESSONS AND ASSIGNMENTS.   Burton's review (1952, p. 337) of the pertinent research concluded that poor assignments are among the chief causes of pupils' failure to learn. Indeed most assignments, even so-called good assignments, are only verbal assignments. If the goal of class-room learning is both knowledge and action coequally, the lesson and the assignment should aim at developing these two objectives. The school is a learning laboratory, i.e., a workshop in which knowledge and action are learned. Since guidance involves self-actualization, manifest through overt behavior as well as through knowing, a guidance-aware teacher utilizes con-duct lessons and conduct assignments. This is particularly important for Cath-olic schools, which as Mother Therese Charles, O.S.U. (1963, p. 92), has stated, "must teach and guide the pupils to be living witnesses to Christ; and indeed formation through action is one of the essential principles of Catholic Action." The Catholic Action cell method, which utilizes small-group work based on the developmental sequence of observe, judge, act, is an excellent example of a conduct lesson (Fr. Anderl & Sister Ruth, F.S.P.A., 1945; Fr. G. P. Weber, 1952). Conduct assignments can take the form, for example, of working with a Catholic interracial council or engaging in another form of Christian social action during after-school hours.

EXEMPLIFY A HIGH LEVEL OF PERSONAL ADJUSTMENT AND SELF-ACTUALIZA-TION.   Students learn not only from what teachers say but also from what teachers are. To most students, the teacher is a living model with whom they can identify to some degree. Because of the daily contact of teacher and pupil, the teacher usually constitutes a more influential model for the student than does the counselor. A child's teacher is the leader of *his* classroom, is *his* model, even more significantly, *his* parent substitute, especially for elementary school children. If the teacher is maladjusted or lacks a high level of self-actualization, the child is often deprived of a necessary impetus toward his own satisfactory adjustment and self-actualization. Witty's review (1955) of the research on the "objective" characteristics of good teachers and the subjective characteristics of teachers perceived as good by pupils revealed that psychologically well-adjusted teachers ranked high on both counts. Teachers who are not well adjusted tend to "scream" at students, become angry easily, exaggerate minutiae, ridicule pupils, and so forth. Certainly a teacher without good mental health cannot expect to be an effective classroom guidance worker. The importance of pupil identification with the teacher as model was demonstrated in a study by Vincent (1961, pp. 99–120, 253–261), which investigated two carefully matched subgroups, viz., never-pregnant girls and unwed mothers. Results showed that the only external influence differentiating the groups was that the never-pregnant girls had been able to identify themselves with a teacher or some other adult from whom they both learned and internalized traditional sexual mores. The unwed mothers achieved no such identification and, apparently because of this lack, acquired ultrapermissive mores from a small peer group upon whose acceptance they depended.

The importance of models in self-identification and self-actualization suggests that Catholic elementary and secondary schools might profitably employ more numerous lay teachers. Religious and priests are certainly worthwhile models, but it is questionable whether they should be the sole or even the dominant models for pupils who will live in the world as laymen, who will work out their sanctification in a different religious state and in different existential circumstances. The importance of the teacher as a model also demands that Catholic schools be selective of the lay teachers they employ; elderly retirants from the public school system might be a boon to the Catholic school's hard-pressed budget, but are they adequate models for children and adolescents, to say nothing of being effective teachers?

Like all social service professions, teaching attracts to its ranks more than its share of maladjusted personalities, of those who want to work out their personality difficulties by or through their students. If classroom guidance is sometimes ineffectual, it may be that the teacher himself suffers from a personality or social deficiency (Lloyd-Jones, 1940, pp. 56–59). More discriminating selection and retention procedures can ensure that only mentally healthy and reasonably self-actualized persons become and remain teachers and guides of children and youth.

This section has dealt with minimal guidance activities which every teacher can inject into the bloodstream of the lesson. Underlying this treatment has been the thesis that while effective teaching is not automatically effective guidance, it necessitates the concomitant employment of such guidance. The lack of infusion of guidance into the lesson often results in less than total learning, in less than good education, as is poignantly demonstrated by the following story (N. J. White, 1938, pp. 151–192):

> I have taught in high school for ten years. During that time I have given assignments, among others, to a murderer, an evangelist, a pugilist, a thief, and an imbecile.
>
> The murderer was a quiet little boy who sat in the front seat and regarded me with pale blues eyes; the evangelist, easily the most popular boy in the school, had the lead in the junior play; the pugilist lounged by the window and let loose at intervals a raucous laugh that startled even the geraniums; the thief was a gay hearted Lothario with a song on his lips, and the imbecile, a soft-eyed little animal seeking the shadows.
>
> The murderer awaits death in the state penitentiary; the evangelist has lain a year now in the village churchyard; the pugilist lost an eye in a brawl in Hong Kong; the thief, by standing on tiptoe, can see the windows of my room from the county jail, and the once gentle-eyed little moron beats his head against a padded wall in the state asylum. All of these pupils once sat in my room, sat and looked at me gravely across worn brown desks. I must have been a great help to those pupils—I taught them the rhyming scheme of the Elizabethan sonnet and how to diagram a complex sentence.

The curriculum in most American schools is characterized by a subject-centered design, i.e., one which utilizes bodies of information classified into intrinsically systematic branches of knowledge as both the organizing force in and the center of learning (e.g., English, biology, history). Some alert schools have introduced the core curriculum design, which centers in broad problems of personal and eternal concern; e.g., the study of the problem of social injustice brings in such diverse subject areas as the history of the American Negro, music of the slaves, literature on man's inhumanity to man, and religious writings on the question. Because of the interdisciplinary nature of the core and because students study in large blocks of time instead of fifty-minute periods, guidance is built into the heart of the curriculum. Indeed a pure subject-centered curriculum, as intellectualists (cf. V. E. Smith, 1960) propose, makes it virtually impossible to bring guidance into the classroom lesson. In such instances the teacher can "bootleg" guidance in. Each subject can be given a guidance dimension. In social studies, citizenship is emphasized through many units. This affords the guidance-aware teacher an opportunity to integrate occupational information into the lesson, since the pupils' later occupations are a primary way in which they exercise their citizenship for the benefit of the community. A study by Gibson (1962, p. 467) indicated that subject-matter teachers were missing the chance to make their classes more meaningful and more vital to the students because of their failure to relate their subject to both occupational and educational planning.

English is another subject into which guidance can be integrated both to enrich content and to help students grow as persons. Many novels, particularly contemporary novels, discuss values of contemporary concern. A teacher in either a public or a Catholic school can forthrightly utilize these works and not "resort to teaching pallid, but safe, relics of literary history in class," to use a phrase of Brother Luke M. Grande, F.S.C. (1962, p. 2). Discussion and clarification of personal and social problems encountered by characters in literature can be of significant assistance to a pupil with personal or social difficulties. The English class can also be helpful in vocational guidance (App, 1957); for example, in a Catholic school, reading of Henry Morton Robinson's *The Cardinal* can lead to a discussion of the priestly vocation, while reading Dorothy Day's *Long Loneliness* can cause interest in a career in the lay apostolate. The composition aspect of English can also be utilized effectively. Zelma Oole's (1959) investigation disclosed that many high school students reveal problems through creative writing in English class. This transpires only if the teacher stresses permissiveness and creativity; if he rewards conformity in style, expression, and thought, he kills guidance opportunities. No school person has the right, however, to elicit self-revelation from students unless that information is to be used by the professional guidance staff for the students' benefit.

Foreign language classes contribute to the understanding of other peoples, representatives of whom might form a discriminated minority group in the community or even within the school itself. Science classes can assist the pupil develop a sense of discovery, wonder, and creative intuition, all of which are helpful in total self-actualization. Physical education can be used to develop socialization. As Pumpinatzi (1963a, p. 26) has demonstrated, participation in sports in school can give added dimensions to one's personality and serve as a basis for socially constructive leisure-time activities in later life.

In Catholic schools guidance emphasis ought always to be present in religion class. Assisting students to acquire a knowledge of their religion is the necessary first step, for as a study by Sister Maria del Carmen Bernardo, D.O.C. (1957), showed, there is a high positive correlation between moral judgment and the extent of religious knowledge, even among delinquents. Knowledge, however, is only part of the total classroom teaching goal; action, the twin goal, cannot be neglected. The German kerygmatic cathechetical theorists (cf. Fr. Hofinger, S.J., 1957; Fr. Jungmann, S.J., 1959) insistently emphasize that only through personal experiencing can the will be moved

toward action. Hence there should be conduct lessons and conduct assignments so that students have an opportunity of guided personal experiencing.
Verbalized lessons are not sufficient. In this connection a Catholic interdio-
cesan curriculum committee (Southeastern Curriculum Committee, 1956, p.
10) noted that Catholic teachers of religion "might be deceived by facile
tongues, sanctimonious apple-shining, and presence (under pressure) at daily
Mass; but photographic memories are not knowing, moralizing without deep
understanding and appreciation is not loving, and external observance alone
is not living." It is regrettable that in American Catholic schools informed
leadership for the experiential and kerygmatic approach to teaching religion
has not developed. Possibly one reason is that as late as 1963 "practically
no diocesan superintendent of schools or director of Confraternity of Christian Doctrine had special training in catechetics" (Sloyan, 1963, p. 98).
Even strong and enlightened advocates of the kerygma such as Msgr. Fuerst
(1963, pp. 380–381) still think of teaching in terms of "presentation of material." Religion classes should of necessity help students integrate the principles of religion with daily living. In this manner religion can become a
central force and a distinctive thrust in the student's self-actualization process.
All too often religion is seen as tangential to self-actualization, rather than
as its very leaven.

Guidance in homeroom activities

The homeroom is that secondary school class unit which meets with the
same teacher in a designated room once or several times a day for purposes
other than formal instruction in academic subject matter. The homeroom
is primarily a guidance vehicle. Unfortunately it has often degenerated into
an administrative unit to facilitate attendance taking, reading of announcements from the principal's office, collecting funds for school drives, and
storing pupils' clothing and books (McKown, 1946, pp. 22–47). The homeroom situation, if utilized properly, is pregnant with innumerable group guidance opportunities. Group guidance books and films can constitute an integral
part of the formal group guidance aspect of homeroom activities. Working
together as a group on problems of personal and social concern not only helps
students resolve their own difficulties but assists them to develop interpersonal
skills. The homeroom is an excellent place for providing students with relevant educational and occupational information (Fedder, 1949; Hutson,
1962b).

Guidance in student activities

Student activities, formerly called *extracurricular activities* or *cocurricular
activities,* offer unlimited guidance opportunities. Regrettably, some schools
prevent the realization of the guidance function in student activities by set-

ting eligibility requirements which exclude from participation those students who could be helped most by the program, especially in schools which make a certain level of scholastic attainment a basic eligibility criterion. This practice prevents students without success experiences in academic activities from self-actualizing in another facet of the school program. There seems to be little justification for scholastic eligibility requirements either on guidance grounds or on the assumption that preventing participation of academically poor students "motivates" them to improve their academic work. McKown (1956, pp. 600–602) has cited six studies which indicate that there is no evidence to support the supposition that participation in the activities program affects school marks adversely. Somewhat conversely, a New York State study (P. A. Cowen, 1960, p. 16) showed that high school seniors who participated with a high frequency in student activities filed a greater number of applications for college. The investigator conjectured that "students who are outstanding participants in activities tend to have superior ability" and so seek further educational opportunities. Obviously, no cause-effect sequence is implied. What this finding suggests is that academically superior students engage in activities. Involving academically inferior students in activities may subject them to certain group pressures which may result in academic improvement, but *panic* in the face of unrealistic pressures is an equally probable result.

A key guidance advantage of student activities is that they make it possible for the teacher and students to share relations at once more intimate and less formal than those which characterize the normal classroom situation, especially in schools with a subject-centered curriculum. Such close, informal relationships enable the guidance-aware teacher to know the student better on the one hand and to encourage him to take problems and concerns to the appropriate school person on the other. The student council provides opportunities for exercising mature self-direction. Unfortunately student councils are so often closely supervised by the administration that they become in actuality breeding grounds for overdocility instead of laboratories for self-responsibility. Assembly periods are effective guidance vehicles for occupational and educational information. The school newspaper provides for the exercise of initiative. It also can feature a guidance column prepared in consultation with the teacher-moderator and counselor (Sister M. Augustine, R.S.M., 1957). Every student activity teems with guidance possibilities.

Guidance in allied school activities

The teacher has an opportunity to function effectively as a guidance worker in innumerable ways other than formal classroom activities, homeroom activities, or student activities. Some of the more important avenues open to him are listed below in the form of suggestions.

1. Keep complete, guidance-oriented cumulative records. Information in these records is of significant assistance to any guidance worker wishing to obtain a succinct profile of the student's personality and achievements.

2. Compile an anecdotal record which relates significant and revealing "critical" incidents. This record is valuable when it is highly individualized and records information about the pupil's daily conduct unobtainable in any other way.

3. Utilize the report card as a guidance device, through pertinent remarks in the "teacher's comments" section. These comments should assist the parent in furthering the pupil's self-actualization.

4. Hold frequent parent-teacher conferences in the school. These conferences should be held not only at those times when the student manifests scholastic deficiency or has been charged with misbehavior but rather periodically to coordinate home-school cooperation.

5. Participate in case conferences. The case conference is a meeting of teachers, guidance staff, parents, and members of pertinent community agencies to pool information, to share insights, and to discuss collectively the development of one student. Since the teacher encounters the pupil more frequently than does any other member of the school staff, his presence at such a conference is important in the school's guidance effort.

6. Visit the pupil's home whenever possible. This demonstrates to parents that the teacher is genuinely concerned with the development of their child and so facilitates improved home-school cooperation. Visitation gives the teacher considerable insight into the nonschool existential situation and thereby places him in a better position to appreciate more fully the genesis of the pupil's behavior.

7. Always be available to students. The guidance-aware teacher is a resource person for the student. A student who needs help on problems or just has a strong desire to talk should be able to seek a teacher with whom he or she identifies, with whom he or she feels confident (Peters & Farwell, 1959, pp. 42–44).

8. Mix socially with students. The guidance-aware teacher attends student functions, e.g., dances and meetings. He visits favorite out-of-school haunts. Such practices facilitate healthy role identification for students, enhance the teacher's social acceptance by them, and enable him to observe clique groups, rejectees, and boy-girl friendships which may not be readily apparent in the school milieu.

9. Encourage pupils to see the counselor often. The alert teacher does not withhold encouragement until the student has a difficulty; he instead emphasizes that the counselor's role is to facilitate each pupil's development regardless of whether that pupil feels that he has a problem or not.

10. Make referrals to the counselor. In making referrals the teacher should not consider the counselor merely as the wastebasket in which to deposit misbehavior cases nor send the pupil to the counselor with every difficulty, however trivial. The referral is not a punitive or threatening device; e.g., "Now you behave, Joe, or I'll send you to the counselor." Procedures can

be standardized so as to provide guidelines on when and how to make referrals.

11. Participate in planning the guidance program. If the teacher is a member of the guidance committee, he participates actively in the committee meetings. If he is not a member of the committee, he can offer suggestions to committee representatives for consideration.

12. Work actively in implementing the school's guidance program. The teacher is a vital part of the school guidance team. It is incumbent upon him to do all he can to effect the realization of every aspect of the school's guidance program.

13. Assist in administering and scoring certain standardized tests given by the counselor or guidance specialist. Because of a heavy case load and lack of counselor aides, overburdened counselors must rely on teachers in certain nonprofessional mechanics of testing. Further, teachers must understand the tests administered so they can adequately interpret scores.

14. Contribute to the guidance bulletin. Every school can establish a weekly or semimonthly guidance bulletin published under the direction of the counselor. As a guidance worker, every alert teacher can make some contribution from time to time.

15. Utilize available guidance resources. Many teachers neglect to employ all guidance resources, both school and community, at their disposal.

16. Bring guidance considerations into the heart of curriculum planning. If the teacher is a member of the school or system curriculum planning committee, he can suggest that the core of the curriculum's scope, sequence, and design be permeated with guidance. Noncommittee teachers can recommend that guidance considerations be incorporated into curricular structure.

17. Initiate discussions at faculty meetings. Some meetings may concern themselves exclusively with the guidance program, but at any faculty meeting the guidance-aware teacher shows how the topic under consideration can be infused with the guidance dimension. Unfortunately many meetings are so administrator-dominated that teachers have little chance for free discussion. In such schools the staff's first step is to make the administration aware that the faculty meeting is precisely the *faculty* meeting, not an administrative meeting.

18. Engage in guidance-related action research. Every teacher can periodically embark on some research project to learn more about his students' behavior, interests, plans, etc. Such research need not be very sophisticated but rather should be aimed at learning something about the students' existential world which assists in guidance efforts. Simple questionnaires serve the purpose nicely.

In many schools it is difficult to carry out many or even any of these suggestions. Because of overscheduling, the teacher usually has little available time. Low salaries have caused a number of teachers to resort to second jobs which prevent them from engaging in guidance activities. In such circumstances, the conscientious, the guidance-minded teacher in both the public and the Catholic school does the best he can while simultaneously working vigorously to ameliorate his working conditions. Failure to fight is to perpetuate the sorry situation.

Guidance in interview activities

Frequently a student asks a teacher in whom he has confidence or with whom he has identified to see him privately after class or after school to discuss some problem or difficulty. Or it sometimes happens that a teacher requests that a student see him privately. The purpose of this private encounter or face-to-face interview may be described as, and in fact *is*, "counseling," specifically counseling within the teaching role. There is, however, considerable disagreement in professional counseling circles concerning whether the teacher *should* or indeed *can* engage in counseling. Ivey's review (1962, p. 139) of the literature reveals that *guidance* experts, whose commitment lies with both education and psychology, hold that the teacher can serve as an effective counselor, while those who claim that the teacher should not serve as a counselor usually come from the ranks of psychologists and psychotherapists not closely related to the school setting.

The arguments of those who deny the teacher a counseling role center in the contention that counseling is a highly specialized profession; teachers are not competent to engage in such professional services. Like G. A. Pierson and C. W. Grant (1959, pp. 208–209), they often make a sharp dichotomy between teaching and counseling. Still others, like Berlin (1958), hold that by suggesting that teachers engage in counseling, the school is forcing the teacher "to feel responsible for changing the personality of disturbed students."

If he is to fulfill his guidance function, however, the teacher cannot escape entering counseling relationships. One of the central arguments for this position has been tellingly stated by Arbuckle (1957a, p. 62): "The teacher *can* function as a counselor, in many modern schools he *is* functioning as a counselor, and if our children are to undergo educational experiences that should be a part of their living in a democratic society, then he *must* function as a counselor." The argument that only counselors may engage in counseling implies that the counselor is all-sufficient to the needs of students, a rather exclusive if not pompous attitude. The teacher usually knows the pupil better, for he has had more intimate contact with him than has the counselor. The teacher, unlike the counselor, has had the opportunity of observing the student day in and day out in a wide variety of class and out-of-class activities. As a result he has a more rounded picture of the student's personality contours and is in a more favorable position to see him from a vantage point which includes many life situations. Previous experiential knowledge of the client, however, can also serve to prejudice the counselor. In this connection, C. R. Rogers (1961) has cogently argued that the effective counselor must free himself from the past, both his own past and that of the client. The point applies equally well in discussing whether counselors need be trained, licensed teachers. Most counselors are unfortunately burdened with a heavy case load which often precludes their working with all but pupils with relatively serious problems. The teacher is ideally situated to act *as a guidance partner to the counselor* in interviewing students as the need arises. Also, for a variety of reasons, a pupil might prefer to talk with a particular teacher rather than with a counselor. The student should not be denied this opportunity. A wider choice of possible counselors (wider in the sense that the pupil can bring his problem to any staff member and not only to those formally designated as counselors) makes it possible for a youth to enter a counseling relationship with a staff member whose personality is most suited to his. The importance of personality matching was demonstrated in a study by Tuma and Gustad (1957), which concluded that the amount of the client's self-learning during counseling was directly related to an original (i.e., precounseling) similarity in the personalities of counselor and client.

If the view of Patterson (1962, pp. 85–105) and others that teachers should never engage in counseling were enforced in the elementary schools where there are few counselors, guidance would be dealt a harsh blow, particularly in Catholic elementary schools, where professionally trained counselors are more rare than class sizes of 25 pupils. The teacher, however, can ethically engage only in that level of "counseling" within his competence. In this connection he is to the counselor as the nurse to the physician; i.e., he takes care of minimal, first-aid situations and refers more serious cases to the professional counselor. In passing, it might be recalled that Mr. Chips never became his school's official guidance counselor. Indeed if Mr. Chips were reincarnated in an American school and set about to perform those "counseling" functions for which he was noted, it is likely that certain members of APGA would ask that APGA's professional ethics committee launch a full-scale investigation. The teacher untrained in guidance must, however, beware of identifying himself or his natural counseling skill with Mr. Chips.

There are, nonetheless, cogent factors which militate against the effectiveness of the teacher as a counselor. As Daubner (1964) has noted, perhaps the most important of these is that in the classroom situation the teacher must maintain some sort of external order, particularly if he is to please the typical "order-minded" administrator. Moreover, the teacher gives marks, which in most schools have punitive overtones. Even in forward-looking schools where marking is on a cooperative basis, marks still clearly imply judgment and authority on the part of the teacher. Counseling demands that the counselor be neither punitive nor an authority figure in the sense of having power to coerce the student. Nondirectivist theory holds that the counselor must be completely nonjudgmental, while interpretive theory maintains that the counselor must be able to suspend judgment. On the basis of role conflict, Ivey's study (1962, pp. 139–143) concluded that whether the teacher can and should counsel depends on the focus of counseling. In scholastic, further educational, or occupational "counseling" the *guidance trained* teacher can perhaps perform the function. Where personal, religious, and interpersonal pupil problems are concerned, however, students often prefer to enter a counseling relationship with someone whom they would not encounter in a classroom situation. While role conflict is always present to some degree, it can be minimized by a permissive curriculum such as the core curriculum or, even more important, by an acceptant, nonpunitive teacher personality. The personality of the teacher—or of the counselor—is far more important than his role (Lee, 1963a). The teacher's personality, while not affecting his objective status role, surely alters pupils' perception of the teacher's role. It is this very perception which is crucial.

A second cogent factor militating against the effectiveness of the teacher as a counselor is that most teachers have received no preservice or in-service training in guidance and counseling. It is morally indefensible to unleash teachers untrained in guidance into counseling with pupils. To fulfill his guidance function, every teacher might be required, for permanent certification, to have a minimum of two guidance courses designed especially for teachers, viz., in the principles and foundations of guidance and in interview and group guidance procedures, with supervised laboratory experience. This suggestion concurs with the official recommendation of the Educational Policies Commission of the National Education Association (1956, p. 92) that *all* prospective teachers take course work in guidance.

Many public and Catholic schools, particularly at the college level, have the custom of conscripting faculty members, however untrained or uninterested, to serve as "counselors" to a group of students. In actual practice these drafted faculty counselors are academic advisers; they usually concern themselves at most with advising students about course selection or with occasional remonstrances and exhortations at report-card time. The questionable practice of conscripting faculty counselors or advisers ought to be abandoned in favor of a system whereby faculty members either volunteer or are freely invited to participate in the counseling-advisement program, with the privilege of refusal. Hardee (1959, p. 73) has recommended that these faculty members be supplied with a "counseling kit" at the beginning of each term. Such a kit might not only contain information regarding the school's guidance and counseling program but also supply information on counseling methods, offer practical suggestions, outline precise procedures for referral, and present a brief introduction to the theoretical underpinnings of guidance and counseling. For maximum effect, however, these minimal procedures should be followed by a more formal, vigorous program for faculty counselors or advisers, including demonstration interviews, workshops, and formal course work. Such an in-service program profitably emphasizes that counseling constitutes "deeper" teaching and that, as Sister Marion Hosinski, S.S.M. (1963), noted, counseling facilitates learning.

The salient issue in this discussion of the teacher as counselor is that, under the circumstances described, a guidance-trained teacher can function effectively as a counselor, in addition to his broader role as the key member of the school guidance team. The teacher, however, functions in relation to the counselor much as the counselor functions in relation to the psychotherapist; each handles progressively more complex or embedded difficulties. If, as Super (1955) has observed, the counselor deals with normal problems of normal clients, then it might be said that the teacher as counselor deals with more surface or routine developmental difficulties of normal students. Some counseling theorists who claim sole dominion over the guidance enterprise for the counselor may charge this view with confounding the roles of teacher and counselor. In response, it may be noted that teacher-conducted interviews are regarded as *guidance* rather than counseling interviews. Moreover, the teacher and the counselor must each be acutely aware of his own limitations. To sin by excess in the matter of referral to the counselor or other guidance specialists seems less grievous than to sin by defect.

THE TEACHER–COUNSELOR

The teacher-counselor is a classroom teacher whose assignment includes spending one-third to one-half of his time as consultant to students, with a proportionate reduction in class load. In Catholic schools, habitually understaffed, those few teacher-counselors who exist are usually not given a reduction in class load. The position of teacher-counselor is a distinct one in the schools and should not be confused with the role of the teacher as counselor just described. In some schools the teacher-counselor is officially referred to as the *grade adviser,* since he normally is assigned to serve students at a designated grade level. Customarily teacher-counselors engage chiefly in occupational, scholastic, and further educational counseling. They are frequently part of the "inner" guidance team of which the full-time counselor is the nucleus. The teacher-counselor has more preservice and in-service training in guidance and counseling than is required of regular, full-time teachers and is usually certified as a counselor.

Teacher-counselors are often not so effective as they might be. A study by Caravello (1958) revealed that the counselor had a greater impact on pupils than the teacher-counselor; moreover, students felt that the teacher-counselor supplied little assistance in either personal guidance or in preparation for post-high school life. Loughary's study (1959) of secondary school administrators in large school systems concluded that a division of opinion exists on the relative merits of full-time counselors and teacher-counselors.

The investigator concluded that one group of administrators believed that full-time specialists might lose sight of the major educational objectives of the school, while the opposing group thought that specialized counseling skills are necessary to perform the counseling function adequately. Berdie's review (1959, p. 179) of the research bears directly on this point. It revealed that there is little support for the contention that counseling should be assigned exclusively to psychologists, there is no evidence which suggests greater effectiveness of counselors with one type of professional background, and the evidence is not clear on the relationship between the quality and specifics (i.e., particular courses such as the practicum) in professional training and counselor effectiveness.

There are several reasons for teacher-counselors' lack of optimal effectiveness. First, in some schools this position is regarded as patronage, a "plum" which an administrator "hands out" not to the most competent person but to that staff member who has proved singularly valuable to the principal, usually by conforming behavior. Second, unlike the counselor's position, there is little status attached to that of teacher-counselor. Hence, teachers often do not aspire to the position except for less than worthy motives, e.g., to have a "soft" job which takes them out of the hurly-burly of the classroom. Third, many school systems do not require that teacher-counselors have formal guidance preservice or in-service training, with the result that incompetent people are not infrequently selected. Until school administration on all levels takes seriously the position of teacher-counselor, it is dubious whether much significant progress in professionalization will be made.

6

THE ROLE OF THE GUIDANCE GENERALIST AND PERSONNEL SPECIALISTS

THE SCHOOL COUNSELOR: AN OVERVIEW

Although this book attempts to deal with the guidance role of every member of the school's professional staff, it necessarily tends to focus on the role of the counselor. Consequently, the school counselor's role in the guidance program is detailed in virtually every chapter. This chapter, in contrast, presents a broad but systematic overview of the counselor's functions. Second, it presents a brief description of the role of other commonly encountered personnel specialists.

The counselor as guidance generalist

In the relatively short history of school counseling as a distinct endeavor in the educational enterprise, there have been frequent attempts to define the counselor's role rather narrowly. He is often regarded as a specialist in counseling or testing, or both; usually such a depiction excludes from

159

his purview the school environment, the structure of the curriculum, and the quality of student-teacher relationships, despite the impact of these factors on the developing student. It is likely that these attempts at narrow ultra-professionalism have arisen as efforts to secure for the counselor a private and accepted niche in the educational establishment by emphasizing a sharp and rigid delineation between his functions and those of the teacher or ad-ministrator (McCully, 1962, p. 683). This stage in the emergence of school counseling as a profession might be compared to the struggle for autonomy in the development of the child. As the counseling function became accepted in public education, the school counselor, like the adolescent, appeared to become embroiled in the throes of an identity crisis. Counselors sought to clarify their self-identity, to structure a social role in the sense of a set of behavior prescriptions amenable to self-perception, and to test that role against reality. Such ultraprofessional writers as Weitz (1958) insisted that it is incumbent upon the counselor to educate school people to the distinctive-ness of his skills. Such distinctiveness, this view emphasized, centered, and to large measure was almost totally rooted, in the counseling phase of the counselor's role. But Schwebel (1962) and other alert counseling experts argued for a larger, more expansive role for the school counselor, viz., or-ganizing the structure of the school to facilitate optimal student development. Salinger, Tollefson, and Hudson (1960) chastised counselors and counselor educators for failing to devote attention to noncounseling implications of the counseling role in schools. They suggested that favorable development in the student depends to a a considerable extent on the structure of the educational environment. While it is generally true that a counselor is often not in a position to modify the environment directly (because of rigid ad-ministrators who "run a tight ship"), he certainly is in a strategic position to serve as a "catalyst" or motivating agent "through influencing action on others who *are* in a position to *directly* modify the educational environment." Thus, in addition to counseling, the attention of the counselor needs to be directed toward the development of new curricula, the modification of exist-ing curricula, the organization of administrative procedures, and the orienta-tion of faculty and administrators to student developmental tasks. While the allusion to the chemical process of catalysis is apt, it is not entirely appropriate. A catalytic agent chemically retains its original composition, but the counselor himself undergoes growth and change in his varied pro-fessional relationships, whether with administrators, parents, or clients.

Consultant in human development

A developmental orientation views the *school* counselor as the profession-ally trained *guidance generalist* concerned with the structure and implementa-tion of a guidance program which of its nature facilitates the negotiation of developmental tasks. Although his distinctive function, indeed that which gives him his title, is counseling, this is not his most important function. First and foremost, the counselor is a specialist in human development. His chief role in the school program is to serve as a professionally trained *consultant in human development* to students, faculty, administrators, and parents. When he acts as a consultant in human development to a particular student in a one-to-one relationship, he is engaged in counseling. To be sure, counseling is the most distinctive manner in which the counselor exercises his consultantship, but it is by no means the only way. The primary purpose of the guidance program is not counseling but rather so organizing and structuring the school environment that satisfactory student development is facilitated. It is in his role of consultant in human development that the counselor discharges his function as the nerve center of the guidance program. Counseling thus is viewed as a subrole, indeed the most important of the counselor's subroles. The totality of other counselor subroles, however, is more important that this single subrole.

The subroles through which the counselor implements the major role of developmental stimulus depend to a considerable extent on the specific circumstances which obtain in a particular setting. While the primary role of consultant in human development remains relatively constant, the subroles through which it is implemented vary in accord with such characteristics as (1) the nature of the student population, (2) the sociology of the community in which the school is located, (3) the general organization of the student personnel service, and (4) the availability of specialized guidance resources. Thus, for example, the function of the counselor is determined in one direction in a suburban high school in an upper-middle-class community where most parents expect their children to attend college and where a staff of school psychologists, remedial education specialists, and school psychiatrists is available. The counselor's function is rather different in a high school in a tenement district in "inner city" where the incidence of delinquency and narcotics addiction is high, where school dropout is the parental and student expectation, and where few specialized services are available. The counselor's concern is thus with both self and situation. In his counseling subrole he is concerned with aiding the client to organize and to actualize *self* for effective development. In his larger role, he is concerned with the organization of *situation* in such a fashion as to permit accomplishment of developmental tasks without unnecessary hindrances. In his concern with the total situation of students, the counselor needs to be aware of the characteristic structure not only of the school but of the community, the family, and the ethnic group, which all influence development. The very needs which must be met before the student can negotiate successfully the tasks of development vary as the situations vary. The needs of the bright upper-class Anglo-Saxon Protestant scion, whose family is ready to support him in Ivy League College and whose society is well adapted to his reception when he enters the world of work, are of one sort. The needs of the equally bright Negro youth living in the tenement district who will be forced to busboy his way through Concrete Campus University and who will enter the world of work as a Negro, with all considerations regarding competence, education, and experience bracketed to one side, are sharply of another sort. In the first case, the counselor will not encounter the implicit necessity of apology for the failure of the educational and social institutions which he, along with other school people, represent to the student.

Similarly, in a Catholic school context which increases for both the counselor and the student the salience of theological, moral, and philosophical convictions, counselor subroles differ from those in a school context which simply ignores such dimensions. Counselor behavior is circumscribed by one set of parameters in a school situation where human development is regarded as teleological and Christocentric, or at least directed (in R. H. Mathewson's phrase) toward an Ultimate Spiritual Ideal. Another set of parameters shapes the counselor's function in a school situation which ignores and therefore fails to accent the relevance of the student's spiritual life for human development. Consequently there is such an entity as "a Catholic counselor," i.e., a professionally trained person who regards the inner dynamism toward God as an inseparable part of every pupil's basic personality structure.

The counselor's role: empirical analyses

A number of empirical investigations have sought to determine the specific functions of the counselor through time and motion studies which detail the amount of time spent by the counselor in various activities. Hollis and Isaacson (1962) found that counselors devoted a median of 50 per cent of their time to individual counseling, followed by testing, working with teachers (only 5 per cent), and placement. No time was allotted for research, for evaluation of the counseling and guidance services, for service on the curriculum development committee, or other broad activities relative to the school's environmental structure. Gold (1962) carefully recorded the time which counselors spent in clerical and nonclerical activities. He found that 46 per cent of the time available was spent in such clerical activities as filling out transcripts, checking graduation requirements, preparing honor rolls or deficiency lists, and other purely routine clerical chores more appropriate for secretarial workers. Counseling accounted for only 25 per cent of the time, exclusive of academic advisement for immediate course selection, which accounted for the remaining 29 per cent. K. B. Hoyt (1962) has recommended that counselors spend 50 per cent of their time in contact with students, through individual counseling or group procedures; 33 per cent in contact with school people, parents, or community resources "contributing to the total complex of activities called guidance"; and the remainder in assembling, analyzing, and interpreting data required for direct contacts with students or others.

Of extreme significance is the Project Talent study (Wrenn, 1962, pp. 114–126, 194) of elementary and secondary school counselors' perceptions of counselor activity. Counselors were asked to indicate those counselor activities which in their opinion should be maintained in the future and those which they believed should be eliminated. Retaining counseling was favored by 100 per cent of the secondary school counselors but by only 71 per cent of the elementary school counselors; parent consultation by 45 and 65 per cent, respectively; teacher conferences by 37 and 63 per cent, respectively; test administration and interpretation by 41 and 33 per cent, respectively; and involvement in curriculum development by 8 and 6 per cent respectively. By way of contrast, only 50 per cent of the secondary school counselors and 24 per cent of the elementary school counselors felt that routine clerical work should be eliminated as a counselor duty. These results indicate that elementary school counselors are more firmly committed to parent consultation and far more firmly committed to teacher consultation than secondary school counselors and that neither secondary nor elementary school counselors seem to be aware of their important role in curriculum planning. This finding is brought sharply into focus when one considers that only 8 and 6 per cent, respectively, favored retaining this important function, while 50 and 76 per cent, respectively, favored retaining clerical duties. It is quite apparent that counselors in the field have not yet sufficiently defined their roles in terms of their function in a comprehensive, pervasive, all-school guidance program. Secondary school counselors especially seem unaware of their important responsibilities in serving as consultants in human development for teachers and parents, the principal "significant others" in the life of the growing student. Indeed it is precisely these significant others who influence the pupil's development far more than does even the best of counselors. Also neither secondary nor elementary school counselors apparently understand the overwhelming importance of the organization of the school environment toward a guidance thrust, as typified in their neglect of curriculum organization.

Perceptions of counselor role

Other investigations have attempted to determine how the role of counselor is perceived by students, teachers, parents, and administrators. Grant (1954a) found that the counselor was perceived as particularly concerned with the students' educational and vocational choices but not with their personal and social development. Houghton (1956), in a doctoral study directed by Grant, found parallel results. Bergstein and Grant (1961) reported that parents perceived school counselors as more helpful than either school principals or best friends of the family, although they perceived them as more helpful with educational-vocational decisions than with personal-emotional-social development. Warman (1960), in a study of college students' perception of the counseling role in an institution of higher learning, reported similar results. These investigations failed to take cognizance of the noncounseling functions of the school counselor, ignoring his role in manipulating the school and familial environment in a manner conducive to facilitating student development. Thus G. A. Pierson (1954) could legitimately complain that school counselors fail to understand that they are primarily educators who serve parents and teachers as well as students. Wrenn (1957) insisted that school counselors must be perceived as (1) educators with special professional training at the master's level and beyond; (2) generalists, i.e., competent in a number of school functions related to human development; (3) specialists in at least one type of guidance service, e.g., counseling, group work, or testing, in accord with each counselor's personal qualifications and professional preparation; (4) resource persons not only for students but also for teachers, parents, and administrators; and (5) school persons concerned primarily with normal student development rather than with pathological deviations. Tooker (1957) adds that the counselor is frequently "called upon to provide leadership in broad areas where guidance aspects may seem remote."

Little agreement emerges from empirical analyses of the counselor role. Most studies fail to detail total implementation of the school counselor's primary function as a consultant in human development. Hamburger (1962) has commented that perhaps counseling is not a profession at all but rather a cluster of related occupations. Stefflre (1964, pp. 654–659) has described the plight of the newly certified counselor who assumes a guidance position: "As he restructures his self-concept on his new job he must inevitably undergo some alienation from his teacher colleagues and some concern about which label he will wear and its influence on his self-concept and behavior. Will he think of himself as a guidance counselor, a psychological counselor, or simply a generic psychologist? What task will he feel committed to? Is he the guidance coordinator or a therapist?" If leaders in the profession cannot agree on the role of the counselor, Stefflre adds, the working school counselor's identity crisis should come as no surprise.

The counselor's role: a developmental orientation

As Stone and Shertzer (1963) have suggested, the counselor who waits for an externally supplied answer to the two-headed question "Who am I and what do I do?" does a disservice to himself and to his profession. Pallone and Grande (1964a) maintained that the counselor's role must be defined in terms of the developmental needs of each student, needs which must be met before the student can either integrate previously accomplished tasks or negotiate successfully the remaining tasks of development. They asserted that a developmentally oriented counselor role must consider the following questions: What are the developmental needs of students? How are these needs being met? What assistance is the total school program giving to the students to meet these needs? How do pupil needs vary according to community and socioethnic group? What developmental needs of the student are unmet despite the impact of the school, the family, the church, the peer group, and other agents of socialization? With what constellation of the student's developmental needs is the counselor professionally competent to deal? The counselor's role is thus a "dynamic interaction, a person-to-person interaction, an educator-to-student interaction if one prefers, but an interaction supported on the one hand by professional competence and on the other by student need."

Specifications of time and motion studies or studies of perceptions of the counselor's role often do not give proper weight to the impact and influence of various counselor behaviors on facilitating human development in students. Some of the counselor's subroles which are perceived as unimportant may in fact be far more fruitful than others which are perceived as having much more influence. Also, a mere count of the number of minutes a counselor spends in each of his subroles is not necessarily indicative of the degree to which that subrole is furthering his primary function as consultant in human development. Thus, for example, the counselor may spend only two hours a week in consulting with a curriculum revision committee, but this investment is likely to have more far-reaching guidance effects on students than twenty hours of counseling time.

An official policy statement of the American School Counselor Association (1963a, pp. 198–201) has delineated 10 distinct and minimal functions through which the counselor implements his guidance role in the educational enterprise: (1) planning and development of the guidance program, in concert with administrators, faculty, and coordinate staff; (2) individual and group counseling with students; (3) appraisal through a variety of techniques; (4) educational and occupational planning, with individual students and in terms of general vertical articulation for further education and the world of work; (5) referral to specialized resources, (6) placement, including curricular, course, educational, and occupational selection; (7) parent help, as a liaison person between home and school; (8) staff consulting and guidance teamwork with school staff members as the guidance team leader; (9) local research to determine student needs and the effectiveness of the guidance program; and (10) public relations to interpret to and to involve in the guidance program shool staff, parents, and the general community. Of particular interest is the ASCA statement that effective guidance involves cooperative effort with the entire school staff.

Minimal and implementing subroles

A developmental orientation in education and guidance regards the counselor as a generalist in human development, whose primary function is consultation about development with all those influencing and influenced by the environmental structure of the school. In this view, the counselor's *mini-*

mal subroles involve (1) consultation with administrators and faculty, (2) consultation with parents, (3) consultation with students, and (4) consultation with school and community specialists. In order to *implement* these subroles, the counselor (5) assesses developmental needs of groups and of individual students, (6) maintains a variety of types of information concerning vocational and educational resources, (7) assesses the effectiveness of guidance and counseling services, (8) provides placement services, (9) provides counseling and placement for alumni and for early school leavers, and (10) arranges for referral to competent in-school and out-of-school resources as they are needed. Since these subroles are described more fully in other parts of this book, they are only briefly identified here.

1. Perhaps the most important and often most neglected counselor activity is *consultation with administrators and faculty members* concerning the environmental structure of the school. The counselor does not seek to structure an open and permissive environment, simply one which facilitates rather than hinders development. An example of a development-hindering element in school organization is the frequently encountered division of the curriculum into college preparatory, commercial, and vocational. This sort of curriculum seems to demand that the student make certain choices prematurely. Often these choices are virtually irrevocable. The student who enters a vocational curriculum in the ninth grade (or even earlier, in some school systems), for example, rarely accumulates the requisite number of high school units needed for college entrance. A choice for which he is not ready, as the ongoing research on career development of Super et al. (1960) has demonstrated, is forced upon the student by such a curricular design. Some writers believe that if the student is unready for his choice, an answer lies in providing earlier and more frequent exposure to the world of work. Ginzberg (1960) has focused attention on the fallacy in such procedures, however, in his apt statement: "What does guidance mean for young people whose working experience will take them into the 21st century? How does one guide in an economy in which careers are the exception—in which most skills are acquired on the job and through a shifting among jobs?" The point is made in Chapter 17 that the vast majority of jobs which will be open to today's students in 1975 do not today exist. Further, Katz's important study (1963) reported data which demonstrated that differentiated high school curricula were *not* related to entry, success, or satisfaction in the labor market. The conclusion Katz reaches is that high school curricula need to be reorganized to eliminate needless crisis points, emphasizing instead training in character, flexibility, and personal maturity. The counselor needs to consult with faculty and administrators on such matters as these, so that unnecessary crisis and premature decision are both obviated. This is but one example of the type of school organization which positively accelerates the developmental process. In addition to consultation on development in general, the counselor consults with the faculty and administrators concerning the developmental progress of particular students. Here, by affecting the en-

vironment, the counselor is furthering the development of numbers of students. Unfortunately, counselors often fail to recognize their vital role in organizing the school environment for a positive guidance thrust. Indeed, perhaps because of a lingering mistrust of administrators, they often fail to develop coordinated guidance afforts, especially at the secondary and college level. The goal of consultation with administrators and faculty is to organize the school structure for optimal student development. The school is a manipulable environment. School structure organized for a positive guidance thrust necessarily involves far more than an elaborate, formal guidance service. If the school's total program is to be so organized, the counselor's active participation not only in the formal guidance effort but in the total educational effort is essential.

2. Similarly, the counselor *consults with parents* in groups and individually concerning developmental patterns and the organization of the family in such a way as to ease the accomplishment of developmental tasks. Often the counselor must seize the initiative in arranging group discussion with members of parents' organizations. For example, many parents, unaware of the labor market, insist upon having their children make airtight curricular choices. The counselor can help make groups of parents aware that such choices are premature. In helping parents to develop an understanding of human growth and to organize the family environment so as to facilitate growth, the counselor is assisting the development of numbers of students. In addition to work with groups of parents, he often needs to consult with individual parents about the developmental progress of their children. The parent consultation interview is described in Chapter 10. The counselor may also find it beneficial to organize group discussion with small groups of parents whose children are about to negotiate a common developmental task, e.g., the transition from the neighborhood school to the high school. The goal of parent consultation is to assist parents to develop realistic perceptions of their child's characteristic abilities, form realizable aspirations for him, understand the developmental tasks he faces, and lessen their own anxieties concerning his developmental progress academically, vocationally, personally, and socially. Overanxious parents are legion in an era of emphasis on high achievement evidenced by high marks. The counselor's role is to help parents form realistic expectations, not feed on excessive anxiety. Unfortunately, many counselors are maneuvered by overanxious parents into fruitless and potentially harmful exhortation sessions with students who are failing to meet unrealistic parental expectations.

3. It is likely that the major portion of the counselor's time is spent in *direct consultation with students* through individual counseling or through group procedures. Approaches, models, and techniques in counseling and group dynamics in guidance and counseling are discussed in detail in later chapters.

4. The counselor *consults with school and community personnel* concerning student development in general and in particular. These personnel include representatives of industry, business, and higher education and of the state employment services, for they are knowledgeable about present and

future vocational and educational opportunities. In individual cases, the counselor may consult with remedial education specialists, psychological service specialists, and health service specialists for information or to arrange a referral. The roles of these specialists are discussed later in this chapter. The goal of consultation with community personnel is both to interpret the guidance function as a responsibility of the community and the larger society and to enlist cooperation for its implementation.

5. The first activity carried out by the counselor in implementing these subroles is *student assessment*. The counselor seeks to develop information about student characteristics in order to assess the developmental progress typical of class groups. He also uses assessment techniques in the counseling relationship. The counselor is concerned with the maintenance of a central record of meaningful data for use by all members of the school staff as well as a confidential record of privileged data. Often he functions as director of the school testing program. He may be called upon to identify "exceptional" children, from the creative to the predelinquent. When the counselor also functions in the school's general aptitude and achievement testing program, it is his responsibility to report student performances rapidly and meaningfully to students, parents, faculty, and administrators. Electronic data-processing equipment greatly facilitates scoring and reporting.

6. In order to help students expand their phenomenal fields, the counselor *maintains an active library of information* concerning present and future educational and occupational resources. This information library contains not only the usual occupational monographs but projections for the future in an expanding industrial society. Thus, an orientation to the nature of an industrial economy is implicit in the occupational information service. The educational information service is intended to orient students both to college and to other postschool training facilities.

7. *Constant assessment of the effectiveness of guidance and counseling* is required to determine the extent to which the counselor has actually helped students meet developmental tasks adequately. The counselor conducts follow-up studies of groups of students who have graduated and entered the labor market or higher education in order to assay the particular educational, guidance, and cocurricular experiences which have been helpful in successful development. He also conducts follow-up studies of individual students who have been assisted in individual or group counseling to determine the extent to which effective self-organization has been implemented in behavior. Similarly, the construction of local norms for standardized tests is a research responsibility of the counselor. The general aim of evaluation in this context is not the production of scholarly research but rather the identification of effective and ineffective educational and guidance practices in a particular school setting.

8. In order to implement the investment of energy in the guidance effort, the counselor *provides assistance in placement* in the labor force or in educational institutions. When the student has developed realistic and realizable self-aspirations, it is the counselor's role to assist him to actualize those as-

pirations. The placement function includes assistance to students in (1) appropriate choices of courses and curricula in congruence with an emerging self-identity, (2) harmonious transition from one educational level to another, and (3) implementing occupational choices in the world of work. Effective placement also demands follow-up by the counselor to determine whether the new situation is conducive to optimal student actualization. It is apparent that placement is vitally dependent upon teamwork among counselor and both in-school and community resources.

9. The counselor *provides counseling and placement assistance for alumni* and for those who have left school early. Especially in a rapidly expanding economy which carries with it certain cultural shocks for the new worker, school alumni and early school leavers (i.e., dropouts) require counseling assistance in order to interpret their quickly unfolding self-experience meaningfully. The same is true even of the entrant into an institution of higher or further education. The school counselor represents a first recourse; often, he may refer school alumni and early school leavers to specialists in community agencies more competent to serve their needs.

10. The counselor who is aware of his limitations seeks to arrange for *referral to other specialists* competent to serve student needs. In-school specialists are discussed later in this chapter. The counselor also needs to maintain close working relationships with social service agencies outside the school. These agencies include family and child guidance clinics, mental-health service centers, psychologists and psychiatrists in private practice, and such other diverse agencies as speech and hearing centers and private remedial education facilities. Counselors in Catholic schools tend to underuse the services of the diocesan Catholic Charities psychological, psychiatric, and employment facilities. The counselor's principal function here is to motivate the student to make use of available services (Vaccaro, 1964). It is also necessary to assist clients in securing specialized services in school and in the community. According to Fr. Moynihan, S.J. (1962), referral is indicated when (1) the client's difficulty is beyond the counselor's level of competence; (2) the counselor has insufficient time to work toward an adequate solution; (3) referral services are available to meet specialized student needs, e.g., remedial education; and, of particular importance (4), certain personal factors seem to preclude a satisfactory relationship. Fr. Vaughan, S.J. (1959), has observed that Catholic counselors often fear referral to non-Catholic psychiatrists and psychologists on the basis that moral erosion is likely, but psychotherapy is predicated upon unconditional acceptance of the client or patient. No ethical psychotherapist attempts to impose a value system upon the client, though one of his goals may be to assist the client to clarify his own value structure. The referral function demands, however, that the counselor familiarize himself with available community resources and their potential role in guidance. Not infrequently, he may find it advisable to arrange referral for a client beset by theological uncertainties to astute, guidance-trained priests or religious counselors. The priest untrained in guidance may be singularly unsuited to assist clients in this sensitive area.

The issue of counselor preparation

Nowhere is the school counselor's intense identity crisis more evident or its' polarities (educator or psychologist) more pronounced than in the discussion of counselor preparation. Though opposing camps agree in general on the content of professional training programs, there is wide disparity of opinion relative to the previous background training and experience most suitable for the school counselor.

Professional Training

The content of professional training in counseling and guidance has been the object of concern for such groups as the American Personnel and Guidance Association (1961; 1964), especially such divisions as the American School Counselor Association (1963a; 1963b), the Association for Counselor Education and Supervision, and the National Vocational Guidance Association; the Division of Counseling Psychology of the American Psychological Association (1952a; 1952b; 1962); and certification boards in state departments of education. As late as 1965, many states certified counselors for school service on the basis of some eighteen to twenty-four hours of graduate course work in specified areas but without the master's degree. The most common areas required for certification include foundations of guidance, developmental psychology, counseling theory, psychometric testing, educational and occupational information, and group guidance or guidance practicum. Certainly such a program represents less than a desirable sequence of minimal preparation. By 1965, however, a number of states were in the process of revitalizing counselor certification requirements to include the possession of the master's degree based on at least 30 graduate credits. A number of states had also instituted advanced guidance certification for directors of guidance in a school or school system which required at least two years of graduate work and often the possession of an advanced professional certificate or professional diploma. The 18-credit premaster's certificate was increasingly required for the teacher-counselor. As was indicated in Chapter 1, the impact of NDEA guidance institutes had dramatically closed the gap between actual and desirable student-counselor ratios by 1964. Further, the impact of such diverse influences as the NDEA and the numerous Conant reports triggered movements to upgrade professional requirements for all educational personnel, so that, by 1965, a number of states required the master's degree for permanent certification as a teacher.

Surprisingly, the professional associations mentioned have shown general agreement concerning the content of graduate counselor training. Virtually all associations have agreed that the possession of the master's degree constitutes the minimal level of counselor preparation for school service. The following is a collation of recommended areas of competence in minimal professional training: (1) philosophical, educational, social, anthropological, and economic foundations of guidance; (2) personality organization and development, including theories of personality, developmental patterns, the characteristics of deviant personality functioning, and cultural-social determinants of personality; (3) knowledge of the social environment, including school, family, and community; (4) assessment procedures in counseling, including both standardized protocols and informal methods; (5) counseling theory and practice, including individual and group procedures; (6) knowledge of educational and occupational resources, including the economic foundations of guidance and vocational psychology; (7) professional orientation, including ethical and moral practices, consideration of the counselor's role in the educational setting, and the relationship between school and community; (8) research design and statistical methodology, for both research consumption and production; (9) the psychology of human learning, including conditions for optimal learning and teaching and the genesis of learning disorders; (10) social dynamics of family interaction; and (11) practicum experience in both counseling *and* guidance, on an individual and a group basis, specifically in a *school* setting. With regard to the last area, there is serious question whether the on-campus counseling laboratory, which deals with clients referred from schools and other sources, adequately meets the needs of future school counselors. An *externship,* similar to practice teaching in the education of teachers in the increasingly popular master of arts in teaching sequence, seems more appropriate. To be optimally beneficial, however, such an externship setting necessarily is a school guidance service, rather than a community guidance agency, a rehabilitation center, or a hospital. The APA (1952a) also recommends for some candidates (12) personal therapeutic experience. A developmental orientation to guidance necessitates also advanced study in (13) the relationship between environmental structures in school, family, and community in regard to optimal human development. Whether a single course in each of these areas is adequate depends upon the previous background of the individual counselor trainee.

By 1965, major changes were in evidence in typical patterns of counselor education. Core courses involving a number of the aforementioned areas of study were increasingly common. Proposals were advanced that minimal counselor training should involve a two-year master's sequence, with the first year devoted to basic study in the behavioral and social sciences and the second to the acquisition of professional skills. A number of universities were retailoring master's programs along these lines. It became increasingly evident that positions of responsibility and leadership demanded the possession of the Ph.D. or Ed.D. Increased professionalization had become the watchword. In some quarters, bold proposals were advanced to integrate core training in the various helping professions, e.g., school counseling, social work, clinical psychology, counseling psychology, and psychotherapy, in interdisciplinary schools or institutes of health, education, and welfare. In some universities, training in school counseling, clinical psychology, and counseling psychology had been merged in programs in mental-health psychology.

Preprofessional Preparation

Proposals to merge school counselor preparation with the training of other professions highlight the continuing debate over the most suitable preprofessional preparation for the counselor in the educational setting. While the school counselor has awesome prophylactic responsibility in mental health he is first concerned with the *educational* environment. Although most school counselors are trained in departments or schools of education, an increasing number receive a major portion of their professional training in departments of psychology. Whether this development is salutary is very much an open question. The prospective school counselor seems to have more in common with the in-service or prospective teacher or educational administrator than with the prospective experimental-physiological psychologist. Yet counselor educators, whatever their department of assignment within a university, are frequently psychologists by training or self-appointment and their interests and allegiances veer toward the "psychologist" polarity in the school counselor's identity crisis. Training programs designed by them often resemble Caliban's mirror.

Brammer and Shostrom (1960) regard counseling as a profession in which persons trained in a variety of disciplines engage. In these terms, the *counseling psychologist* is a professional counselor whose basic intellectual discipline is psychology. *Psychologist* is the substantive, indicating the basic identification; *counseling,* the modifier, indicating the professional activity. Similarly, the counselor in an educational setting may be regarded as a *counseling educator.* In the approach to guidance developed in this book, the school counselor is regarded *primarily* as an educator with a *secondary* specialization in psychological and behavioral science whose function is both counseling and guidance. In short, to fulfill his vital school role optimally, the counselor needs training in areas such as curriculum structure and school organization usually ignored by counselor training units in departments of psychology. As K. B. Hoyt (1961, p. 130) has observed, "the school has a right to expect that the services of the counselor will extend beyond the student" in the individual counseling relationship.

Some counselors and counselor educators unfortunately perceive themselves as a quasi-psychotherapeutic "new wave," a gnostic cult of specialists whose function extends only to the walls of the counseling room where they perform mystical rites. Certainly the recognition of counseling as a distinct and indispensable element of the educational experience to be conducted by specialists, at least in professionally alert and competent schools, occasions rejoicing. But extreme specialization breeds the danger of overspecializing the counselor out of the school situation, of isolating him from the combined efforts of teacher, administrator, and curriculum in the guidance enterprise. Darley (1956), a former executive secretary of the APA, has perceptively observed that overspecialization has caused a spirit of separatism in the school counselor. This spirit of separatism, behaviorally implemented, prompts a variety of misperceptions by faculty members of the counselor's role: (1) the counselor may be perceived by faculty as an administrator exercising hierarchical social power; (2) he may be perceived as the purveyor of ancillary services, by definition expendable; (3) he may be perceived as a professional leaning post for students, particularly those who teachers believe lack sufficient ability or interest and should be dropped from school; (4) he may be perceived, with justice, as a jargon addict enmeshed in the mystical rites of testing and psychotherapy, which seem nonessential in a situation stressing intellectual learning; and (5) he may be perceived as the popularizer of the myth of a confidential, existential relationship with students in order to keep his activities clandestine and esoteric. Certainly these perceptions have some basis in reality.

On the other side of the coin is the counselor who indeed waits upon an externally supplied answer for his definition of self and self-role. Typically, this counselor is neither a psychologist nor an educator; he is whatever the administrator wants him to be. Hence, he accepts without murmur routine clerical duties, such tasks as clerical scheduling of courses with or without prior student advisement, and substitute teaching at the drop of the administrator's finger. Since he has no adequate definition of self, he is nescient of his competences and limitations. He is totally situationally determined. When the administrator commands him to "treat" the neurotic or psychotic student whose pathology causes behavior problems, he undertakes to do so with gusto, though this behavior constitutes a grave moral injustice and very likely exacerbates the student's difficulties. The "good-man-can-do-anything" attitude is not infrequently encountered in Catholic schools, even though it represents the gravest offense against the virtue of humility. But Catholic education is tradition-laden with such an attitude. What difference if Father X has a bachelor's degree in philosophy and a master's in theology? He is assigned to teach algebra, biology, and physics (where he is likely to discuss the four elements of Aristotelian physics), for the sacerdotal function partakes of the magisterium. Indeed, the priest or religious untrained in guidance often does not scruple to tread with heavy boots terrain that frightens angels. In John Hersey's novel *The Child Buyer,* (1960) Mr. Cleary, the guidance director (or G, for guidance, man), is noted for his "everlasting, boondoggling snoopery." When Cleary is asked to identify and describe his duties, he replies (Hersey, 1960, p. 42):

> I give psychological tests, I.Q. tests, and so on. Then I also have to do a great deal of nursemaiding of both children and mothers.

> . . . Among students I am supposed to solve and cure insubordina-
> tion, gold bricking, dullness of mind, smoking, drinking, sexual
> promiscuity, law fracture, money madness, suicidal selfishness, aggression,
> contempt for property, want of moral anchorage, fear of failure and
> of fear.

When Cleary is asked whether he has completed adequate training in the discharge of these activities, he responds that "there hasn't been time for that as yet. Or money—the taxpayers are rather hostile to the *idea* of guidance." Cleary plans, however, to take some summer courses sometime. It is also instructive that Hersey has Cleary support the sale of Barry Rudd, a precocious ten-year-old whom he regards as a "natural resource," to a corporation engaged in the national defense effort. Cleary's "price" is a new position as guidance director in a large suburban school system.

The issue of teaching experience

Perhaps the most hotly debated issue in the preparation of school counselors is the question of whether they should be required to present prior teaching experience as a requisite for employment. Most states require that school counselors hold a permanent license to teach and present two to three years of successful classroom teaching experience. Opinion in the profession itself is sharply divided. Peters and Farwell (1959, p. 37) have urged that one of the qualifications for successful counseling in schools is understanding classroom conditions, an observation in which Stellwag (1961), a foreign visitor, heartily concurs. Many counselor educators believe that, to integrate the goals of guidance into the curriculum and total educational program, experiential knowledge gained from prior teaching experience is imperative. They also believe that such experience is necessary to work effectively with teachers, who often regard counselors without prior teaching experience as "not one of us." Similarly, some counselors seem to believe that instruction counts for little in the guidance effort. Doubtless the differential patterns of professional socialization encountered by teachers and counselors account for these unfortunate contrary notions.

Other counselor educators oppose teaching as a *necessary* requirement. The Division of Counseling Psychology of APA (1962) emphasizes the necessity of the school counselor's familiarity with the educational setting but observes that teaching experience is not the sole avenue to gain this necessary familiarity. The APGA's Wrenn Report (Wrenn, 1962, pp. 149–150) notes: "Teaching experience is not always essential, provided there is required a substantial block of supervised counseling experience in a school setting."

Such diversity of opinion, however, fails to highlight the significant realities. Counseling is, in Super's terms (1957), a late-entry profession. Successful counseling seems to demand a certain maturity and general cultural experience usually not attained before the granting of the bachelor's degree, but this is largely an assumption unbuttressed by empirical evidence. Historically, counselor preparation grew from teacher preparation; the teacher-to-counselor mode of preparation had become traditionalized and has only lately been challenged. Opponents of the tradition charge that the requirement of prior teaching experience for the counselor is analogous to requiring the physician first to prepare professionally as a nurse, a patent absurdity. If the content of the undergraduate program is necessarily teacher education, they contend, prospective counselors are burdened with first obtaining adequate preparation in the teaching of a subject-matter area in which they may lack interest. Undergraduate preparation in liberal arts or the behavioral sciences, this view holds, seems more appropriate. Further, the literature reveals no careful investigations of the effectiveness of counselors with and without prior teaching experience. Teachers' perceptions or evaluations are largely irrelevant, since it is the student whom the counselor serves. Many otherwise excellent candidates for school counseling are led, by lack of previous teacher preparation, to seek careers in such professions as social work and rehabilitation or vocational counseling, where the case load is lighter, salaries are higher, and working conditions better anyway. These counselor educators cite evidence of an apparent trend: (1) the best-known graduate schools of journalism and business in the nation refuse to accept applicants with undergraduate degrees in these fields, preferring those with liberal arts preparation; (2) several major medical schools have publicly recorded their opinion that a general rather than a specialized curriculum (e.g., liberal arts versus premedical) at the undergraduate level predicts greater professional success in medicine. They further assert that professional socialization as a teacher may actually inhibit counselor effectiveness. In C. R. Rogers's terms (1961), when the counselor's past includes a previous professional identification as a teacher, he may be bound by that past in his relationships with students. The testimony of many counselor educators suggests that the personality, psychological integration, and value structure of the counselor outweigh considerations of previous education and experience.

It is readily apparent that preparation for counseling positions in settings other than schools differs markedly from school counselor preparation, since the school represents the only social institution in which *developmental,* rather than hit-and-run, guidance is possible. What is more essential than previous teaching experience is the counselor's *commitment to education* as a total lifeway. The counselor needs to sensitize himself not merely to the needs and perceptions of faculty and administrators but particularly to those of students. Perhaps the counseling-guidance externship suggested earlier represents an adequate resolution of this element of the counselor's identity crisis.

PERSONNEL SPECIALISTS
IN GUIDANCE

In addition to teachers, counselors, and administrators, a number of student personnel specialists play significant roles in the implementation of the guidance effort. Most commonly encountered are three groups: (1) remedial education specialists, (2) psychological service specialists, and (3) health service specialists. Nearly every school and school system are seriously understaffed in guidance workers and personnel specialists. Particularly is this the case in small public school systems without sufficient funds to hire adequately trained teachers and counselors, much less personnel specialists. Catholic schools and school systems are virtually bereft of the services of professionally trained and competent specialists for at least three reasons: (1) there is a scarcity of funds even for the basic instructional services; (2) there is a serious lack of personnel to staff classrooms in anything like a reasonable teacher-pupil ratio, so that specialists cannot even be considered; and (3) most Catholic school people do not seem to recognize the necessity of specialists. Since the role of the counselor is in part shaped by the availability of specialized student personnel services in many public and most Catholic schools, the counselor has the obligation of undertaking such specialized school services other than counseling as are congruent with his professional competence.

As education becomes upgraded, it is likely that student personnel specialists will increase in number both in Catholic and in public schools. The role descriptions suggested in this section portray the function of those specialists who are currently employed in alert, guidance-minded school systems, as viewed by both specialists in the field and those professional educators who prepare specialists for their positions.

Remedial education specialists

Remedial education specialists are specially trained school people who provide professional services in the amelioration of learning disabilities. They may serve on the staff of a single school, they may service several schools, or they may be situated in a central facility to which students come. The most common remedial education specialists are the remedial reading specialist and the speech and hearing specialist.

The *remedial reading specialist* is concerned with the amelioration of reading disabilities. Reading deficiencies contribute to poor adjustment to school and therefore to dissatisfaction with the entire school program, which is verbally oriented. Hence the remedial reading specialist represents a vital need in most schools. Usually reading disability causes the student to form negative emotional reactions to the school environment as a result of his continuing experience of failure to master subject-matter content.

Consequently the amelioration of a reading disability many times involves simultaneous counseling of a supportive and integrative nature. Reading specialists frequently receive secondary training in guidance and counseling. Indeed, the recommendations of the International Reading Association call for the completion of a master's degree in remedial reading, with about half of the course work in educational psychology and guidance. Special emphasis in the professional preparation of these specialists is placed on the psychology of learning and the causes of learning disabilities. The other half of the program is devoted to the methodology of reading remediation. A. J. Harris (1956, pp. 294–296), a leading figure in remedial reading, regards the specialist-student relationship as analogous to the relationship between the counselor or psychotherapist and the client. Remedial reading may be carried on individually or in groups. In either case, the reading specialist seeks to establish a relationship that involves warmth, acceptance, security, and the communication to the student or students of a basic trust in their ability. Remedial reading is sharply differentiated from *developmental* reading, which represents an attempt to assist the student to acquire more efficient reading skills in the classroom situation. Remedial reading is concerned with students who have serious reading disorders, while developmental reading attempts to help students within the normal reading range develop more efficient reading skills. Teachers of English and others engage in developmental reading in regular classes or special *ad hoc* student groups.

The attention of the *speech and hearing specialist* is focused on those student problems related to speech and auditory discrimination. Like the remedial reading specialist, the speech and hearing specialist is trained at least at the master's level in a program which combines a psychological sequence with a remedial education function. As Zinner (1963) has indicated, these specialists seek to determine psychological as well as physical elements related to impaired speech and hearing.

Especially in well-organized counseling centers in colleges, reading and speech specialists are often members of the student personnel staff and work closely with guidance personnel. Other remedial education specialists provide ameliorative assistance in communication skills and in arithmetic deficiency.

Psychological service specialists

Psychological service specialists are student personnel workers who are trained in certain aspects of psychological service so that they can bring their unique professional skills to bear upon the school's facilitation of student development. Like remedial specialists, they may serve one school or several schools or serve a large district from the central school office.

Perhaps the counselor's closest colleague on the school staff is the *school psychologist,* trained as a specialist in the diagnosis of learning and behavior disorders. While the counselor is concerned primarily with normal development, the school psychologist seeks to discover the causes of developmental pathology which the student exhibits in the school situation. Because he is principally engaged in the administration and interpretation of clinical instruments to assess intellectual and personality functioning, the school psychologist is sometimes regarded as the clinical psychologist in the school. Gray (1963, pp. 110–118) has noted that some school psychologists engage in brief supportive psychotherapy with individual students or groups. A number of experts in school psychology, like Eiserer (1963, pp. 46–50), wish to add counseling to the functions of the school psychologist, but the influential Thayer Conference, sponsored by the Division of School Psychology of the APA, was unable to agree on the place of either counseling or psychotherapy in the practice of school psychology (Cutts, 1955). As both the quantity and quality of counselors and school psychologists increase, working relationships between these complementary professions will be established. The diversity of opinion concerning the focus of school psychology is reflective of the lack of unanimity in clinical psychology generally. Most school psychologists today function as clinicians rather than as counselors or therapists, perhaps to the detriment of the guidance effort. Present certification requirements for school psychologists tend to stress clinical assessment instead of counseling or psychotherapy and often include responsibility in remedial education. Indeed some state certification laws specifically exclude psychotherapy as a function of the school psychologist. Consequently the school psychologist usually functions only as a diagnostician. Following a diagnosis, the counselor and psychologist arrange a case conference. If counseling is indicated, the student is referred back to the counselor. If psychotherapy is recommended, he is referred to the school psychiatrist, a community agency, or a private practitioner. Most states require the equivalent of two years of graduate training for licensing as a school psychologist, and some require the possession of the doctorate.

The liaison person who maintains contact between family and school is the *school social worker*. The chief functions of the school social worker are to maintain personal contact with parents of students experiencing unusual developmental difficulties through home visits (A. Davis, 1961), family group work, and other services. A secondary function is to maintain liaison relations with community mental-health, medical, and financial resources capable of serving family needs. Far less numerous than either counselors or school psychologists (Boston, 1960, pp. 517–523), school social workers focus on the student in his existential interrelationships with the school, the home, and the community. The social worker is especially trained to work in the sensitive area of home-community relations. Interviewing and counseling are among the primary skills of the school social worker. Often he works with the student and members of the student's family simultaneously. Gray (1963, p. 268) has observed that there are considerable overlaps in school counseling, school psychology, and school social work. Social workers are trained in a two-year graduate sequence, with very heavy emphasis on fieldwork experiences, leading to the degree of master of social work (M.S.W.) or master of social service (M.S.S.). In most graduate schools of social work, the required sequence in personality and behavior is commonly taught by a psychiatrist, usually a psychoanalyst. Thus, social workers tend to be strongly psychoanalytic or neoanalytic in their approach to growth and development, a position in sharp contrast to the orientation of most school counselors and school psychologists.

The primary role of the *school psychiatrist* is differential diagnosis of mental illness of rather severe proportions. In the school setting, the psychiatrist does not generally treat cases of mental illness, though he may provide psychological first aid in cases of emotional disturbance of limited proportions. When treatment is needed, the psychiatrist usually works in the school system's child guidance clinic or in private practice. Some psychiatrists like A. R. Joyce have proposed a wider school role for the school psychiatrist. Joyce (1959), a leading Catholic psychiatrist, envisions the school psychiatrist as providing a series of consultations with school administrators, school counselors, and school psychologists. The psychiatrist is a physician with post-M.D. training, internship, and residence in selected centers or hospitals for the treatment of emotional and mental illness. An investigation by Fr. J. B. Murray, C.M. (1962), indicated that college students tend to confuse the psychiatrist with the psychologist. Central to the functions of both the school psychiatrist and the school psychologist are fostering mental health and assisting the school to structure its environment to prevent mental and emotional disorders. Unfortunately the diagnostic and treatment functions of the school psychiatrist are so emphasized as to occlude promotional and preventive aspects. Mariner and his associates (1961) and E. L. Cowen and his colleagues (1963) have reported experiments in which psychiatrists have assisted in implementing positive programs to promote mental health. This larger, preventive role for the school psychiatrist follows a trend in the mental-health professions generally, a trend anticipated by counselors when they restructured their own roles to encompass a larger service than assistance to students with problems. As an ameliorative specialist, the school psychiatrist is likely to serve as a consultant who works with students referred by the counselor, psychologist, or social worker. Following psychiatric evaluation, a case conference is often conducted to determine means of assistance. As a prophylactic specialist, the school psychiatrist serves as an occasional supervisor of counseling efforts and as an in-service educator for teachers, counselors, and other school people.

Some health service specialists

Health service specialists are members of the medical or paramedical professions who serve as school personnel workers in assessing the physical health of students, consulting with students and parents concerning health problems, and assisting in the development of positive physical health programs. The two most important school health specialists are the school nurse and the school physician.

The *school nurse* is a health specialist whose primary functions are to provide health guidance to students and to minister to their minimal health needs. In most public schools, the school nurse works in the school every day or several days a week, depending on the size of the institution. Most Catholic schools do not have a school nurse on such a full-time or regular basis. Ruth A. Klein's study (1959) of school nurses in New Jersey disclosed that home visits, health counseling, limited clinical service, and consulting with teachers and counselors concerning physical limitations in individual children comprise the principal activities of the school nurse. Klein also reported that school nurses are typically regarded as members of the team of school personnel workers. In appropriate instances, particularly in socio-economically disadvantaged communities, the school nurse assists the families of students to obtain medical treatment when necessary. Some nurses with psychiatric-nursing experience make particular contributions to the school mental-health program (Bardon & Kaplan, 1961). The nurse typically has completed the R.N. or bachelor's-degree training, with emphasis on public health nursing. The nurse's role and that of the nonmedical health educator need clarification, since there are many areas of overlap, especially in health counseling.

The *school physician* is a licensed medical practitioner whose function includes both the diagnosis and treatment of the students' ailments and leadership in the school's health program. The effective school physician frequently engages in consultation with other school people on approaches, methods, and materials for fostering and implementing preventive-medicine programs (Angers & Paulson, 1964). Since many physicians now receive at least familiarization training in psychiatry, the school physician is in numerous cases a first recourse in schools where no school psychiatrist is available. The ratio of physician to student in many public schools and in practically all Catholic schools falls far short of the desideratum.

In addition to the school nurse and the school physician, there are other medical practitioners who deal with student health needs. This group of practitioners is utilized much less frequently than the school nurse and the school physician; indeed, their role in the school health program is more problem-point-oriented and hence incidental to the total fabric of the program. Among these professional specialists are the school dentist (A. Cohen, 1964) and the school oculist (Sliepcevich, 1964).

Cooperative relationships among counselors, administrators, teachers, and personnel specialists in the school program are discussed in Chapter 7, which focuses on teamwork in the school guidance program.

7

COORDINATING GUIDANCE
THROUGH TEAMWORK

The educational enterprise is a cooperative effort of all school personnel on behalf of the student. If these constructive forces are to focus and converge for the student's maximum benefit, guidance teamwork is imperative. Without teamwork there is a fragmentation of guidance effort which reduces the potential force of the school's guidance impact on the student. Active *collaboration* in the guidance endeavor is requisite to its success. The Twenty-sixth International Conference on Public Education (1963, p. 323) formally recommended: "All guidance personnel should carry out their duties in continuous collaboration with the teachers as well as with the other members of the school staff." Organized teamwork involving guidance personnel, services, and related school activities can upgrade the quality of school guidance radically and dramatically.

TEAMWORK IN
GUIDANCE ORGANIZATION

The school system guidance program

Systematic organization and coordination of the guidance program begin at the school system level. School system coordination is carried out by various echelons of guidance personnel. The school system guidance director coordinates the efforts of all guidance personnel within the system, and school administrators at each level increase vertical articulation to harmonize and systematize guidance efforts in their schools. Catholic school systems are uniquely favored in this regard, since in many localities elementary and secondary schools—and often colleges—are conducted by the same religious order, thus providing a built-in framework for vertical teamwork. Regrettably most religious orders conducting Catholic schools have not yet taken advantage of this enormous potential for coordination; instead they run each school level in almost complete isolation. This sad fact is another testimony to the thesis that the history of Catholic schools in the United States is largely a history of untapped or wasted resources.

The school guidance program

A school can facilitate the development of an organized, systematized, coordinated guidance program which will *of itself* foster integrated teamwork in the guidance effort. For summary purposes, procedures of demonstrated effectiveness have been reduced to minimal *criteria which every school guidance program should meet:*

1. The guidance program is carefully integrated within the larger educational context of the school. The guidance effort can directly further, rather than go at parapurposes or even at cross-purposes with, broad educational goals of the particular school (Roeber, Smith, & Erickson, 1955, p. 27).

2. The guidance program has a written statement of goals which embodies the underlying philosophy of both the school and the program itself.

3. There is a clear delineation of specific functions of the guidance program in terms of the nature and extent of services offered to students.

4. The thrust of the guidance program is unambiguously student-centered.

5. The guidance program provides for comprehensive guidance in all areas of personal development and not only in those areas in which pupils customarily have problems or, what is worse, merely in a restricted number of problem areas, e.g., scholastic guidance or occupational guidance.

6. The guidance program radiates the guidance point of view to students. If students are not aware of the guidance thrust of every phase of school activity, they will not possess the sensitivity requisite for receiving maximum benefit from the program.

7. The guidance program is well organized; i.e., there is systematization, a definite overall organizational pattern, and simplicity and compactness in organizational plan and flow.

8. The guidance program is structured around the needs and exigencies of the local situation, e.g., purpose of the school, its size, financial resources, and other pertinent circumstances (Humphrey et al., 1960, p. 362). In addition, the program capitalizes on existing conditions and on potentialities inherent in these conditions (Mathewson, 1962, p. 216). It liberates guidance possibilities inherent though still dormant in the particular school.

9. The guidance program is flexible, i.e., so structured as to meet any new or unforeseen guidance situation.

10. The guidance program provides the 13 basic and distinct guidance services listed in Chapter 3.

11. The guidance program is internally unified and is not merely a collection of services.

12. The guidance program is continuous. There is no room for mere periodic or sporadic guidance in an adequate program.

13. The guidance program is pervasive, i.e., integrally infused into every facet of school life.

14. The guidance program is coordinated with students' out-of-school life.

15. The guidance program is deeply interrelated with instructional services and with school administrative services.

16. The guidance program is given adequate time in which to function. Class sizes and homeroom periods are organized for effective group guidance. Periods are set aside in which the counselor or teacher-counselor can work with students in groups. Adequate time is provided for each student to engage in satisfactory counseling with the school counselor.

17. The guidance program is such that participation by every school person in the guidance effort is positively encouraged. Guidance is restricted to counselor or guidance specialist alone.

18. The guidance program is determined cooperatively through the school guidance committee, comprised of the school guidance director, counselor or counselors, guidance specialists, and representatives of teachers, administration, and other school staff.

19. The guidance program clearly defines and delimits working relationships of all guidance workers, both vertically (i.e., echelons in the school system's guidance organization) and horizontally (i.e., guidance workers within each school).

20. The guidance program ensures that each person involved is given authority proportionate to his responsibility and task.

21. The guidance program includes guidance or personnel specialists, e.g., the school psychologist, on the ratio of 1 specialist to every 1,000 students.

22. The guidance program includes a pupil personnel services coordinator whose task is to facilitate maximum integration of the efforts of counselors, guidance specialists, personnel workers, and other staff members.

23. The guidance program includes trained and certified counselors. A ratio of 1 counselor to every 250 students is optimal.

24. The guidance program includes teacher-counselors, in the ratio of 1 teacher-counselor to every 500 pupils.

25. The guidance program includes guidance-trained teachers; i.e., each teacher has completed courses in the dynamics of human development, in the principles of guidance, and in the techniques of interviewing with supervised laboratory experience.

26. The guidance program has the active cooperation of both local school administrators and school system administrators.

27. The guidance program provides for the deep and continuous involvement of parents and other citizens in guidance efforts.

28. The guidance program provides for specialized guidance facilities, e.g., the counselor's private office and records room.

29. The guidance program provides for continuous in-service training of guidance workers. Certification is not an index of totally satisfactory guidance training; it is only minimal, not sufficient, training.

30. The guidance program provides for local research, e.g., ascertaining guidance needs of students.

31. The guidance program is constantly evaluated in terms of the achievement of its comprehensive and specialized goals.

32. The guidance program possesses inherent, built-in devices for perpetual renewal and growth. The program must never grow stale.

Teamwork among the school people

A guidance-organized school system of necessity involves school people of every echelon in the guidance effort. The nature and extent of each school person's participation depends on his school position and the degree to which it directly or indirectly bears on the guidance effort. A chart indicating the organization of personnel and guidance services in a school system is shown opposite. Public school systems typically have such an organization, while probably not one Catholic school system in the country had anything even remotely approximating it as late as 1964. This chart indicates that the guidance director in each school is subordinate to both the system guidance director and the "building" principal. In actual practice, however, the principal exercises most, if not all, control over the school guidance director. The chart also indicates organizationally no inherent guidance teamwork among counselors, teachers, health personnel, or coordinate staff. Perhaps the way to eliminate such a scattering of energies is to create, at least in larger schools, the position of *pupil personnel services coordinator,* to coordinate efforts of counselors, guidance specialists, and other personnel workers.

In public schools a vast network of school people is directly or indirectly involved in guidance. On the state level, the *state superintendent,* as the overall educational leader in the state, has among other responsibilities the energetic promotion of guidance in all school areas on all levels. In some states, the state superintendent has an *assistant superintendent for personnel services,* whose task is to facilitate administratively the development and implementation of pupil personnel services. The key personnel service, guidance, is usually administered by the *state guidance director,* whose duty is to develop, coordinate, and improve state-wide guidance assistance to local school systems. The state guidance director and the assistant state superintendent for personnel services also promote necessary guidance research, at the state and local levels. Not many states have guidance officers at the intermediate (county) level. The establishment of guidance officers at the intermediate level might improve teamwork in the state's total guidance effort (Diffenbaugh & Bowman, 1962). On the local school system level, there

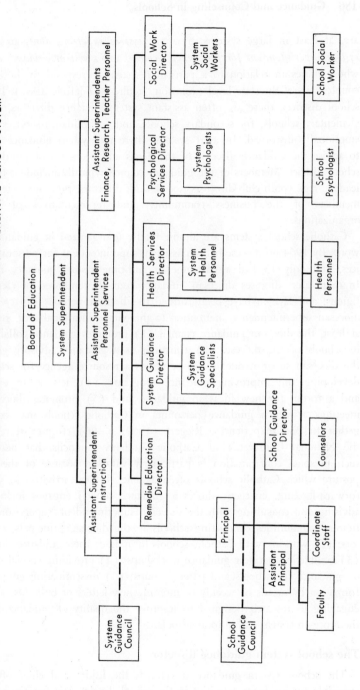

ORGANIZATION OF GUIDANCE SERVICES IN A COMPREHENSIVE SCHOOL SYSTEM are, at least in large systems, a *school system superintendent,* an *assistant system superintendent for personnel services,* and a *system guidance director,* whose duties in relation to a particular system correspond to those of his counterparts at the state level (Johnson, Stefflre, & Edelfelt, 1961). In larger school districts, there are often assistant system guidance directors, e.g., for elementary schools, for secondary schools, and for guidance services for the emotionally disturbed. In alert systems there are system guidance councils to advise the guidance director of the needs and problems of pupils in the school district. Members of the guidance council typically include community leaders, e.g., youth club directors, social work directors, prominent clergymen, members of the business community, and representatives of parents' organizations.

Catholic school systems are almost totally unorganized in guidance team-work. By 1964 no diocese had an assistant superintendent for personnel services, and only 13 had a part-time or full-time system guidance director. In more alert dioceses diocesan guidance councils composed of clerics, religious, and laymen have been formed to fill the cavernous gap created by diocesan superintendents' inattention to this vital educational area. In theory at least, the diocesan guidance council (1) promotes guidance collaboration in schools of the diocese, (2) functions as a guidance advisory group to the diocesan superintendent, (3) serves as a resource agency for schools in developing and improving guidance programs, (4) acts as an exchange and a forum for new ideas in guidance, and (5) promotes diocese-wide meetings at which guidance personnel in Catholic schools may come to-gether to pool experiences. Riegert (1959, p. 86), former secretary of the National Conference of Catholic Guidance Councils, has noted that such personal confrontation is particularly valuable because of the insular posture which Catholic schools often assume. Typical activities in which a forward-looking, energetic diocesan guidance council engages include (1) advising and consulting with the diocesan superintendent, supervisors of religious communities conducting schools in the diocese, principals, and pastors; (2) working with Catholic schools to upgrade their guidance situations; (3) conducting periodic guidance workshops; (4) providing special speakers on guidance for schools and parent groups; (5) disseminating guidance information by means of weekly or monthly newsletters or bulletins; and (6) engaging in research designed to improve the quality of guidance both in the diocesan system and in local schools.

The school system guidance director

The school system guidance director is the leader and chief officer responsible for guidance activities in the school district. His functions include interpreting the guidance situation and needs to the assistant superintendent for personnel services, developing guidance services in the district, improving and coordinating existing services, and working with the community to encourage guidance teamwork between the system's guidance program and non-school agencies. Typical activities of the system guidance director include (1) forming system-wide committees (e.g., a vocational information committee) to research and report findings on methods of improving particular aspects of the system's guidance efforts; (2) arranging in-service activities for guidance workers (e.g., courses, institutes, and workshops); (3) preparing special guidance programs (e.g., a traveling lecture series on mental health in the schools); (4) serving as a clearinghouse for information and for innovational guidance practices; (5) issuing a periodic newsletter to inform school personnel of research in the field, reports by guidance committees, and so forth; (6) providing guidance assistance to schools which evince a need for or request assistance; and (7) supervising and working with the individual school's guidance director. Brother Philip Harris, O.S.F. (1956, p. 281; 1958), an expert in guidance organization, has recommended that the system guidance director work with community vocational agencies in a common job survey, a placement program, and a pool of employment openings in the community.

The system guidance director, while insisting on high minimal guidance standards in schools within his district, nevertheless is careful not to impose uniformity. A cardinal organizational principle is that each school must be free to develop certain guidance aspects unique to its situation and to its student clientele. For example, sound occupational guidance in a culturally deprived area may not be sound in a school located in a socioeconomically advantaged neighborhood, and the guidance program in an elementary school in which administrator and teachers are apathetic toward guidance is quite unlike that in another elementary school in which administrator and teachers are more forward-looking.

Personnel specialists

Most guidance or personnel specialists, such as the school psychologist and psychiatrist, serve several schools. Administratively they report to the school system rather than the building principal. Budgetary considerations normally make it impossible for a single elementary or secondary school to have a guidance specialist assigned exclusively to it. In addition, the guidance specialist's work is so psychologically technical that the normal building principal could not reasonably be expected to supervise his activities. Some specialists, such as the child guidance clinician, operate in a centralized school system setting. These considerations foster the organizational pattern by which specialists report to the school system directly.

Because guidance specialists do not report administratively to the building principal, it may happen that their work is only loosely coordinated in the local school's integrated guidance effort. The principal and, particularly, the school guidance director have responsibility for integrating the specialist as a member of the school guidance team. As a guidance team worker, the specialist should be a member of the guidance committee, contribute to the guidance bulletin, work with teachers to become more aware of psychological processes involved in the teaching-learning situations, speak to school and parent groups, work closely with counselors, be involved in the school's guidance in-service program, and participate in case conferences.

School administrators and teachers may regard the guidance specialist as a useless frill to the educational enterprise. In fact, the specialist provides invaluable assistance to students. Thus, for example, a federally supported experiment (Pallone, 1960) at St. Francis College (New York) utilizing the services of a visiting psychologically trained social worker resulted in (1) a high rate of school retention of moderately and seriously disturbed students treated by this specialist, (2) improved mental health for students treated, and in some instances, (3) referral to a consulting psychologist or psychiatrist. Unfortunately there are too few personnel specialists in public school systems and hardly any in Catholic school systems.

The local school guidance director or coordinator

The guidance director or coordinator is a member of the school staff, sometimes called the head counselor, who is charged with responsibility for coordinating and administering the guidance program within his particular school and with certain administrative responsibilities with respect to other counselors. Only large public secondary schools normally have a sufficient number of counselors to warrant a school guidance director; elementary and small high schools usually have too limited a counseling staff to justify this position. Catholic schools consider themselves fortunate if they have a single certified counselor. Larger public and private non-Catholic universities and alert smaller public and non-Catholic colleges often have a college guidance or personnel director. But Brother John J. Jansen, S.M. (1955), and Helen B. McMurray (1958, p. 143) concluded that guidance and personnel services in Catholic colleges are usually not coordinated under a single director particularly trained for the job. Alert school systems might consider appointing a pupil personnel services coordinator for each school. Such a coordinator performs all the functions now discharged by the school guidance director or head counselor, plus further integrating the efforts of personnel specialists.

The school guidance director has many roles which facilitate teamwork. His roles require him to:

1. Supervise the entire guidance program in the school. This necessitates working closely with the assistant principal in schools which formally designate an assistant principal in charge of guidance.

2. Coordinate guidance efforts of school personnel, i.e., administrators, teachers, counselors, and other staff.

3. Synchronize guidance efforts of the school staff with efforts of school system personnel workers, e.g., school psychologist and school nurse.

4. Promote guidance-mindedness not only in administrators and teachers but in students as well.

5. Serve as the leader of the counseling staff, including teacher-counselors.

6. Supervise the work of counselors and teacher-counselors.

7. Maintain a centrally located cumulative record file for exclusive use by the counseling staff.

8. Develop standardized referral procedures.

9. Direct the standardized testing program.

10. Establish a library of educational and occupational information (either in a separate office or in a designated section in the regular school library).

11. Supervise the professional use of guidance bulletin boards placed in strategic locations in the school.

12. Serve as editor of the weekly guidance bulletin.

13. Assist teachers to improve their skill in guidance, e.g., by providing suggestions on the use of anecdotal records, helping them improve interview techniques, and providing information concerning the meaning and interpretation of standardized test scores.

14. Work with school administrators in planning and implementing group guidance activities in assemblies, classrooms, homerooms, field trips, and the like.

15. Be chief energizer and director of the guidance in-service program.

16. Coordinate his school's guidance efforts with those of other schools through meetings with his counterparts from other schools and with the system guidance director to facilitate vertical and horizontal articulation among the various schools. The school guidance director also works closely with the system's child guidance clinic.

17. Establish cooperation in the guidance enterprise between home and school.

18. Establish a standard operational procedure for case conferences.

19. Participate in case conferences.

20. Establish cooperation in the guidance effort between the school and nonschool social service agencies, e.g., employment agencies and psychological clinics maintained by Catholic Charities in many cities.

21. Develop procedures for continuous evaluation of the guidance program.

Few of these functions are more neglected than the establishment of a weekly guidance bulletin. Such a bulletin serves to remind pupils and schoolmen of the existence and thrust of the guidance program. Brother Alois, C.F.X. (1959), has noted that a guidance bulletin includes information on mental health, social life opportunities, career opportunities, further educational data, and the like.

The school counselor

The work of the school counselor was treated in Chapter 6. As was indicated there, much confusion exists in professional circles on the delineation of the counselor's role. For example, L. D. Schmidt's review (1962, p. 600) of the research has concluded that counselors themselves are not always clear as to their role and indeed often feel that they are performing tasks contrary to the counselor's distinctive role. Frequently they are not aware of their responsibility as a member of the school guidance team; they too often operate as "loners" rather than as a central part of the team guidance effort. A study of elementary and secondary school counselors conducted by the American School Counselors Association (Wrenn, 1962, p. 194) revealed that the counselors surveyed failed adequately to grasp their role in the total educational context. While 71 per cent of the surveyed counselors listed counseling as one of their basic functions, only slightly more than one-third listed conferences with parents and teachers, group guidance, and test administration as basic activities of the counselor. Further, only 12 per cent listed the collection and dissemination of vocational information as a basic counselor function, and only 8 per cent mentioned involvement in curriculum development as a basic activity. It is quite possible that these counselors were insufficiently oriented to school teamwork because of the ultraprofessionalism advocated by certain counseling theorists. Such an ultraprofessionalism fails to grasp how crucial to the success of the guidance program are the relationships between the counselor and other school personnel. If the counselor wishes to make guidance an integral part of school life, to permeate every school experience, he works with teachers, administrators, and coordinate staff in all the phases of guidance planning, development, and operation. Ultraprofessionalism, which is tantamount to false professionalism, would have the counselor operate in a separate world, with his office walls forming a moat between school life and interviews in the counseling office. G. E. Hill's review (1961, p. 356) of the pertinent literature, however, concluded that there has been a strong increase in emphasis on the counselor as a member of the school team working toward achievement of defined educational goals. The American Personnel and Guidance Association's 1961 official statement of policy titled *Standards for the Preparation of School Counselors* states that a major responsibility of the counselor is to work cooperatively with teachers, staff, administrators, and community people. In fulfilling his team guidance role, the counselor works with teachers and administrators informally and formally (e.g., through an in-service course) to upgrade the quality of the guidance effort. He shares with staff members appropriate data, with due regard to confidentiality. He assists the staff in identifying pupils with special needs or problems, participates in staff meetings and in case conferences, assists the teachers in providing group guidance to their pupils, works on the curriculum committee, and is the spark plug for the school guidance committee. These activities constitute minimal teamwork roles for the counselor.

The teacher-counselor

The teacher-counselor is a regular teacher whose assignment includes duties as a consultant to students. In this capacity, he can serve as an effective liaison person between teachers and the counselor or counselors. The teacher-counselor has a definite role to play in fostering school guidance teamwork. He is a member of the school guidance committee, contributes to the school's weekly guidance bulletin, participates in the school's guidance in-service program, works with teachers and counselors in coordinating and improving educational and occupational information, and participates in case conferences.

Strang and her associates (1953) in the New York State Association of Deans and Guidance Personnel have recommended the establishment in the school of small guidance units, each under the direction of a teacher-counselor. Periodically, at least once a week, a certain number of subject-matter or problem-area teachers who instruct the same pupils meet together and work out guidance approaches for use with students. The establishment of such small guidance units exemplifies effective guidance teamwork.

The teacher

Chapter 5 emphasized the teacher's function as a guidance worker and as an integral member of the school guidance team. The teacher, like the counselor, is a member of a guidance team. He cannot attempt to shirk his guidance responsibility, on the one hand, or to assume that he is the only really effective guidance worker, on the other. The specific methods by which the teacher can play his optimum role in effective guidance team-work were discussed in Chapter 5.

The principal and other school administrators

Perhaps no one in the school creates more numerous blocks to or more easily facilitates effective guidance teamwork than does the building principal. A study by R. W. Hopkins and Sarah W. McDaniel (1961) of problems encountered by school system personnel administrators in efforts to upgrade local school guidance programs concluded that these administrators experienced greater difficulty in working with building principals than with any other school functionaries, including counselors, teachers, and superintendents. "Interference" in school guidance teamwork possibly originates in basic value differences between principals as a group and counselors as a group. Peters (1963) cited a study which showed statistically significant differences between the two groups in several preference areas. Counselors demonstrated preferences for exhibition, affiliation, and intraception, while principals displayed manifest needs in deference, order, aggression, achievement, and endurance.

To ensure the implementation of an effective and integrated guidance program, guidance-aware principals typically perform the following functions:

1. The principal "must believe in, understand, and want a program of guidance services" (Zeran & Riccio, 1962, p. 205). He must see that the guidance program directly furthers the school's total educational effort. In this connection, Rothney and Farwell's review (1960, p. 168) of the pertinent research concluded that counseling and guidance services indeed assist in accomplishing the totality of objectives of the American secondary school. If the administrator favors guidance, he soon involves teachers and other staff workers in cooperative guidance teamwork. If nothing else, the need to conform tends to sway some of the guidance-resistant staff to cooperation in the guidance effort.

2. He works out cooperatively with the guidance committee and the school's guidance coordinator the pattern of guidance organization and administration. He requests the school system guidance director to assist in initiating the school's guidance organization and administration. While there are certain broad guidelines which can be followed, many of them are based more firmly on theoretical considerations than on empirical research. A review of the research by Reed and Stefflre (1963, p. 152) concluded that there are disproportionately few experimental investigations on the organization and administration of guidance services.

3. He ensures that guidance-mindedness permeates every activity and operation of the school. There can be no divorce between guidance and other aspects of the school program. Because the school is a manipulatable environment, effective teamwork between guidance and other school programs can coalesce to further student self-actualization. Guidance orientation is easily thwarted by negative policies in guidance-related areas. Class sizes of less than 25 pupils are essential for effective classroom guidance. An NEA research study (1956, p. 67) concluded that "when the class size moves from thirty to forty, problems with pupils tend to at least double." (Many elementary class sizes in Catholic schools number more than 50 pupils.) The principal cannot allow the homeroom period to become a time for transacting administrative business. Catholic school administrators especially need to foster a guidance viewpoint. What one Catholic school administrator wrote to Fr. (later Msgr.) Sheehy (1929, p. 207) seems still generally true of Catholic schools today, viz., that the governing principle is that religious operate the school and hence any student group fits into the organization only in the manner and to the extent that the religious administrators, not students or counselors, desire.

4. He recruits and retains the best possible counselors and guidance-minded school staff. The administrator regards the counselor's job

not as a "plum," a reward for subservience or even for general good service to the school. Nor does he award the post to an elderly faculty member on the ground either of seniority or that the member is too old to keep up with the hectic pace of classroom teaching. Rather, he selects the counselors and school guidance director solely on the basis of competence. The alert principal also ensures a sufficient number of teacher-counselors.

5. He orients the staff to the guidance program and provides continuous guidance in-service opportunities. His faculty handbook not only has a section on guidance but is saturated with the guidance emphasis. He also provides a guidance materials resource center for counselors and all members of the guidance team.

6. He does not assign to the counselor functions not in keeping with the counseling role. C. C. Stewart's summary (1959) of pertinent research concluded that public school administrators tend to assign to counselors such extraneous duties as preparing the master class schedule, taking care of attendance records, assigning students to class, recording marks on transcripts, handling punitive discipline, and engaging in clerical duties easily handled by a clerk. Indeed it sometimes happens that the principal presses the counselor into service as a substitute teacher. As a result of administrative mistreatment, the counselor has too little time to perform his central function, counseling, or indeed his basic counseling-related tasks. Alert principals work toward hiring counselor aides who file tests, distribute occupational and educational information, and perform other nonprofessional tasks so that the counselor can be freed to perform his proper role. Such a counselor aide should be hired if for no other reason than the poor economics of employing a $9,000-per-year person for a $4,000-per-year job. Reed and Stefflre's review (1963, p. 154) of school practices notes that electronic data-processing equipment has significantly increased the efficiency of gathering, recording, and distributing essential pupil information in guidance work. Similarly, the function of punitive discipline is incompatible with counseling (Lee, 1963a). Cortale's study (1961) of selected public secondary school principals in Nassau County, New York, however, revealed that 50 per cent of the respondents believed that counselors should handle punitive discipline to a slight degree, usually in the capacity of follow-up after punishment meted out by the administrator. Only 2 per cent of the principals felt the counselor should handle punitive discipline to any great degree. A pupil who misbehaves should be referred to the counselor not for punishment but for assistance (Marian R. Brown, 1950, p. 180).

7. He performs appropriate guidance functions. One of these is punitive discipline (although the principal often delegates this function to an assistant principal). Punitive discipline is carried out in the context of rehabilitating the offender, for only then can it have a positive guidance thrust. Certainly there is no cause for punishment for punishment's sake or for punishment as a deterrent. Kate H. Mueller (1958, p. 302) has noted that the knowledgeable school administrator in his treatment of a student offender "is gradually turning away from the humanities, philosophy, and religion as the source of his principles and theories, and borrowing from the social sciences

newer conceptions: mental health, modal behavior, student mores, subculture patterns, the reinforcement and extinguishing of motives." She goes on to say that the administrator as punitive disciplinarian is substituting relative standards for absolute ones and recognizing individual needs and group demands; thus he attacks discipline with a posteriori empirical methods, with little apology to the a priori emphases of history, philosophy, or religion. Although this position of situational ethics is limited from a Catholic point of view, Catholic theology does teach that guilt in any moral act is contingent, among other things, on circumstances surrounding and affecting the act. Too much cold, inhuman punishment has been meted out in the name of upholding absolute unwavering Catholic principle; psychologically enlightened Catholics see the offense in the context of the offender, his perceptions, and his world. The aware principal refrains from performing guidance functions not within his proper pale; for example, he does not assume a counseling role. Kemp (1962a) found that principals were more evaluative than counselors, while counselors tended to be more understanding than principals. Principals had a greater personal need than counselors for pupils' overt achievement and orderliness. Hence by role and sometimes by personality, the principal is not suited to counseling; if he desires to help students personally, he confines his activities to advisement. This applies also to college administrators. McMurray's study (1958, pp. 33–34) of more than 100 Catholic women's colleges revealed that in most instances the dean, an administrator, served as *the* academic "counselor"; indeed in many instances the dean also was the college's director of guidance, resident hall supervisor, and coordinator of other functions.

8. He ensures the counselor and other guidance workers freedom to function effectively. His administrative policies aim at giving the counselor the greatest latitude in which to operate, rather than at restricting his activities. As Fr. Shurr, S.J. (1963, p. 401), has observed, laws which bind men rather than free them are poor laws. Fr. P. E. Campbell (1940, p. 660) noted that "there is . . . something repulsive in the enforcement of restrictions that aim merely to repress and not to motivate. The system of autocratic control deserves the ill-repute into which it has fallen. It has only the doubtful merit of convenience for those in authority." The unenlightened principal places the counselor in a dilemma. Is the counselor's primary allegiance to the student he is supposed to serve or to the school, i.e., the administrator, he is supposed to serve? Does student self-actualization mean freedom from student noise, disturbances, outbreaks, and in general tight control, or does self-actualization mean assisting the student to achieve his potential? The answer is easily the second alternative if one reads the literature written by counselors; according to Correll (1962), however, the answer is easily the first if one goes into any school, particularly a college or a university. Thus the administrator is in effect telling the counselor to be kind and benevolent to students so that he can more successfully exercise control over them. Unfortunately Catholic schools even more than public schools have succumbed to autocratic, undemocratic pressure from administrators. Sister M. Bernard McGrath (1948) concluded that Catholic education and student

freedom are compatible; Catholic school administrators should utilize democratic principles to the fullest, although the reverse is usually true. Even in Catholic schools where both administrator and counselor are religious, a spirit of democracy and freedom of counselor operation should prevail. As Fr. Gallen, S.J. (1962, p. 59), has written, "A superioress whose principal instrument of government is implacable vigilance is simply eating her spiritual daughters; and make no mistake, they feel her teeth. She is stunting and stabilizing their human and spiritual growth in a confused, weak, and immature adolescence."

9. He works *with,* rather than *on* counselors and other guidance workers to improve the guidance program. Etymologically, the word "administrator" means "to minister unto," but the reverse is usually the pattern. An interesting study by Chenault and Seegars (1962) disclosed that principals wished counselors to play a decision-making, leadership role vis-à-vis their clients, while counselors favored impartial observation and understanding. Principals desired counselors to be firm and assertive, while counselors preferred to be acceptant and helpful. This study emphasizes that the administrator often projects his "commanding" functions onto other school personnel. If he began to work with and not on these personnel, possibly this projection would diminish.

10. He works with the guidance committee and school guidance coordinator in determining a budget for guidance, in allocating physical facilities for guidance and particularly for counseling, and in assembling and storing guidance materials. Insofar as the first task is concerned, the guidance program needs at least 5 per cent of the total allotment of school funds. With regard to the second, the ASCA (1963b, p. 197) recommended: "The school counselor should have physical facilities appropriate to his work, including a private counseling room, a storage facility for student records and environmental information, and a student waiting area." New school buildings should allocate sufficient space for the counselor's office. In new Catholic school plants this provision is sometimes not included, so that guidance-oriented principals have had to convert oversized broom closets into counseling offices. One energetic sister-counselor (Sister Xavier Rosaire, 1944, p. 42) solved the problem of lack of funds for furniture for the counseling office by resorting to the nonprofessional tactic of sending appeals to furniture companies for donations. Often the principal is reluctant to provide a separate counseling suite. K. H. Parker (1957, p. 254) found that principals preferred to situate the counselor's office within the main administrative unit of the building, while counselors wanted offices as far away from the administrative unit as possible. The principals' preference may have resulted from a desire for the counselor to be readily accessible to assist in administrative duties. Most guidance experts suggest that the counselor's suite be located away from the administrative unit, not only to obviate administrative duties but also so that the students do not perceive the counselor as part of the administration. Adequate space in the teachers' library or in another accessible location for pertinent guidance materials is essential.

11. Alert principals of Catholic schools involve the layman integrally and

completely in the guidance program. Studies (cf. Dawson, 1962) of Catholic schools usually reveal that the lay teacher or counselor is not even regularly apprised of administrative decisions, much less has a role to play in their formulation. Many Catholic schools have separate teachers' associations for laymen and religious, a sort of apartheid. Laymen rewarded in Catholic schools are often those whose characteristic external virtue is total conformity to the wishes of the clerical or religious administrator. What Callahan (1963, p. 176) has noted in the larger Catholic context can be applied to the Catholic school milieu: "The layman is urged to be a free man in society; but if he observes how reliant some bishops and priests are upon docile laymen, how alarmed they become when faced with even a respectful challenge to their wisdom, then it is difficult for the layman to believe much store is set by freedom." The position of the celebrated European theologian Fr. Karl Rahner, S.J. (1959, pp. 9–50), that healthy clerical-lay tension is necessary for the Church's growth, is certainly not espoused by the vast majority of Catholic school administrators. But if the guidance program in Catholic schools is to grow and develop, not only lay involvement but also free expression of lay opinion are necessary.

12. The principal enlists parent and community cooperation in guidance. The principal, like the teacher, stands *in loco parentis* and hence must involve parents in the development and realization of the guidance program. Since the school is an agency of the community, citizens should become in some way involved in guidance.

13. He works with the school guidance coordinator in developing a process of continuous evaluation of guidance services. Systematic and scientific evaluation is vital if the program is to grow. Evaluation is not instinctive in the minds of administrators. Sister Anne Frances Hoey's study (1957) of problems of girls in selected Catholic women's colleges revealed that while administrators (with characteristic optimism) thought that they had provided guidance services in almost 90 per cent of the identified problem areas, students reported they used guidance facilities less than 50 per cent of the time. Perhaps students were unaware of the existence of the guidance facilities, or perhaps these guidance services existed only in the minds of the administration and on paper, a not uncommon phenomenon. In any event, adequate evaluation of the program would have quickly brought the disparity to light.

Coordinate staff members

Coordinate staff members are school people who are not teachers, administrators, or counselors. Coordinate staff members, like every other member of the school team, have a guidance responsibility. For example, the *school librarian,* a coordinate staff member, can give considerable guidance impetus to his work. He can recommend guidance-oriented books to students, display prominently books with a guidance viewpoint, and set aside a place for educational and occupational materials and for books which deal with personal and social maturation. In a Catholic school, the librarian can feature books of solid spirituality and de-emphasize works which savor of saccharine piety, other-worldliness, or Jansenism. Every coordinate staff member should be alert to make referrals to the counselor. Self-referral by the student is superior to referral by others since psychologically a person cannot be helped unless he wants to be helped. But it often happens that an individual is not aware that assistance is available in a particular difficulty; in such cases referral is in order.

SCHOOL–COMMUNITY
COOPERATION IN GUIDANCE

Parents

American schools, both public and Catholic, stand *in loco parentis*. The counselor and other school guidance workers represent the parent, are merely substitutes for the parent, and therefore must involve the parent as deeply as possible in their work. This has been affirmed for public schools in a famous decision by the United States Supreme Court, viz., 268 U.S. 510, 45 Sup. Ct. 571 (Oregon decision). In Catholic schools, canon law clearly states that school people are simply parental substitutes. The essential parent-child relationship is a bond which no cleric, no religious, no lay person of whatever authority has the power to usurp (Fr. Boffa, 1939, pp. 87–88). Both by natural right and by efficient functioning, parents are partners with the school in guidance. Pope Pius XII (1942, p. 12) stressed the necessity of cooperation between parents and school personnel, noting that school personnel, however skilled, can have little success without parents' active collaboration or coworking as a team. Such collaboration is blocked by the school which involves parents only when their offspring manifest some immediate and more or less urgent problem; when the problem disappears, so also vanishes active collaboration. A study by Wilkow (1962, p. 85) suggests that parents seem to perceive the counselor as a threat to parental authority vis-à-vis the child. Wilkow conjectured that if parent-school contacts are regular rather than sporadic, parent-counselor tension can be significantly reduced.

Home-school cooperation in guidance is crucial at every level. The elementary school child is beginning to cope with problems of the nonhome world, and he needs the combined assistance of parent and school to meet this developmental task effectively. The adolescent is maturing to and for independence. Crucial factors in achieving independence are child-parent confidences in which the child can reveal his deepest concerns, anxieties, joys, and sorrows. The school encourages healthy parent-child relationships within the positive developmental context of the young person's growing thrust toward independence. Eugenie A. Leonard's investigation (1930, p. 180) of confidential relationships of high school girls and their mothers determined that many possible blocks can impede the development of such a relationship, e.g., maternal lack of complete giving of her being to the child manifested by ridicule, indication of lack of interest, a sense of hurry, misunderstanding of the child's attitudes, and emotional outbreaks such as weeping or nagging. When parent-child relationships break down, the child sometimes seeks the counselor as a parent substitute. One counselor task is to attempt to restore a confidential relationship between parent and child, without stunting the child's developmental task of acquiring independence. Apparently some religious counselors are only belatedly beginning to understand the parental role qua parental role. To speak of the parent as a "guidance counselor" to his own children (cf. P. Harris, 1960a) is a patent absurdity. *The primary parental role is the rearing of children;* it is more accurate to speak of the guidance worker as a "school parent" or even as a "parental agent." It is the counselor and teacher who must cooperate with the parent. The parent, qua parent, has primary rights; whatever authority the school or school functionary has issues *from* and *through* the parent. Doubtless the lack of experiential knowledge of the parental role occasions the not infrequent attempt to deny or ignore the crucial importance of the parent in the child's life.

It behooves the guidance worker to cooperate fully with parents. Berdie (1960, pp. 461–462) reported that high school seniors who wished to continue formal schooling regarded the attitude of their parents as important as any other reason for this decision. Apparently, parents talk about college or other postschool plans when the child is still very young. Interestingly, the level of education of the mother seemed in this study a more potent factor than that of the father. The types of organizations and recreational activities in which families participate are directly related to the incidence of college attendance of offspring. A study by the Brookings Institution (Baer, 1961, p. 441) concluded that values are distributed in an hierarchical pattern with respect to one's occupational and educational level. At the bottom of the occupational-educational ladder there is heavy concern with such values as income, security, physical working conditions, and so forth, a finding reminiscent of A. H. Maslow's need hierarchy. As one moves up the ladder, there emerges concern with such values as a sense of achievement, challenge, service to others, independence, self-expression, and creativity. These attitudes are in turn passed on to one's children and form a powerful directional thrust on the young person's life goals. The research review by McClelland and his associates (1953, pp. 275–333), together with their own investigation, concluded that the greatest source of achievement motivation is parental emphasis on the child's independence. The more the parents stress individual development and self-expression, the greater the motivation.

Catholic schools are particularly remiss with regard to involving the parent in the guidance effort—or in any school function, for that matter. Clerics or religious conducting schools seem unaware of several factors: (1) natural law, canon law, and the encyclicals hold that education is primarily a right of the family, not of priests and religious; (2) the Catholic school is operated by the Church, and the lay person is as much or more a part of the Church as the priest or religious, for, as Pius XII stated at the Second World Congress of the Lay Apostolate, "you [laymen] *are* the Church!"; (3) as an integral member of the Mystical Body, the Catholic layman has a priestly function, a royal function, a prophetic function (Fr. Congar, O.P., 1957), all of which entitle him to full participation in the Church's activities, including the Church's schools; and (4) the Catholic parent bears the financial burden of supporting the Catholic school and hence has a right to involvement in school activities. The role of the laity is so pivotal to the life of the Church itself that Cardinal Newman (1961) taught that the Catholic laity should be consulted before a dogma is defined. If laity are to be consulted in the definition of Church doctrine, then surely they should be consulted in matters of school policy and operation. In recent years a vocal and educated Catholic laity has sought its rights in regard to Catholic schools. As Callahan (1963, p. 109) has noted, "It is hardly surprising that the layman should on occasion seek within the Church some of the same rights he has within society." Certainly no Catholic parent should come to the teaching sister, brother, or priest with an attitude of servility or inferiority, a condition far too prevalent in contemporary American Catholic schools.

Sister M. Roswitha Englehardt, I.H.M. (1957, p. 132), found that "slowness on the part of religious teachers [and guidance workers] to include parents in school life results in part from the teacher training program [of the religious] which has not given enough attention to the objectives and purposes of parent-teachers' associations" or to the role of the layman in the Catholic school. The investigator (p. 113) also reported that parents are more than willing to engage in effective cooperation with the school if religious authorities afford them an opportunity. Sister Roswitha (p. 115) also discovered that very "ancient" nuns in the schools studied were unwilling to cooperate with the home, thus hindering cooperation by younger sisters.

There are two levels on which the counselor and other guidance workers can cooperate with parents in school guidance efforts. One level, primarily informational, involves little depth of cooperation. Some useful activities at this level include informing parents about guidance facilities available to their children and sending guidance bulletins to provide information about recent guidance activities, testing programs and results, high school and college entrance, and treatment of special problems. Teacher comments on report cards can be guidance-oriented, particularly since printed trait ratings on standard report cards almost invariably tend to appraise docility and indeed overdocility, as witness such items as "listens to and follows directions," "neatness," and "care of materials," with no mention of such crucial traits as "intellectual curiosity," "originality," "creativity," and "willingness to explore ideas opposed to his own." Parents can be encouraged to supply experiences which satisfy some of the child's needs. For example, it might be wise to purchase a pet for a shy, unsocial elementary school child. In an address before the American Psychological Association, Levinson (1962) advanced the thesis of the dog as "cotherapist," observing that a dog satisfies a need for dominance, complete acceptance, and a warm relationship. Levinson indeed called for research on dog-supportive therapy. M. L. Hoffman's review (1962, p. S-20) of pertinent research concluded that frequent parental expression of warmth and affection toward the child, together with appeals to the child's needs for affection and self-esteem, appears to foster development of an internalized moral code. On the other hand, use of techniques which are physical or otherwise directly assert the parents' power over the child favor the development of a moral orientation based on fear of external detection and of punishment. Some parents and school people are so exacting or reproachful of a child's behavior, for example, in sexual spheres, that he is reduced to helplessness in meeting inner needs in nonsexual spheres.

The second level of parent-worker interaction calls for deeper cooperation. Four distinct activities lie within this layer, viz., parent-teacher conferences, case conferences, parent-teacher association activities, and the school guidance council.

The conference between the parent and teacher or counselor is a learning experience which provides growth opportunities for both parent and worker. A study by Wall (1962) indicated that when parents had personal conferences with the guidance worker concerning themselves, their offspring, the nature of test results, and other matters, there was a significant positive change in the behavior of their offspring, indicating that parents not only "learned" guidance orientation but applied this new learning when dealing with their offspring. The conference helps the worker confirm or deny his observation of a pupil's behavior. To be optimally fruitful, parents should be prepared beforehand to engage profitably in such a conference. I. J. Gordon (1958) reported action research in which four guidance-oriented teachers wrote a script of a "model" parent-teacher conference, secured fifteen minutes of air time from the local television station, and, after writing parents to inform them of the program, acted out the script the morning of the conference day. The result was a superior conference.

The case conference, in which the counselor, head counselor, appropriate teachers, administrators, school staff, and the parents are involved to discuss the development of the child, has proved an effective manner of assisting the student and involving the parents in the guidance effort.

Parent-teacher associations offer splendid opportunities for parental involvement in the school. Too often in public and particularly in Catholic schools, however, the administration transforms the PTA into a social organization, devoted to cake sales, fashion shows, and perfunctory meetings in which parents have no opportunity to discuss, much less to formulate, basic school or guidance policy. Occasionally the counselor may address the PTA. The conscientious counselor attempts to involve the PTA in formulation of guidance policy and in day-by-day workings of the program. PTA groups in public schools usually are affiliated with the National Congress of Parents and Teachers (founded in 1897), a parent organization which advises local organizations on how to become more deeply involved in school policy and practice. PTAs in Catholic schools may join both the NCPT and the National Home and School Service (founded in 1960). The NHSS, the national body for PTAs in Catholic schools, is far less dynamic than its public school counterpart. For example, NHSS literature clearly indicates that the prime interest of this association is not in shaping school policy in any way. Nevertheless the NHSS represents a positive effort. Not national affiliation but individual school action is the crucial factor in increasing parental involvement. Sister M. Roswitha Englehardt's investigation (1957) disclosed that religious principals perceive the role of the PTA as fostering spiritual development of its members through lectures on family Communion and the like.

The school guidance council, composed of the head counselor or pupil personnel services coordinator, other counselors, representatives of the administration, teachers, parents, and community leaders is the primary policymaking body with respect to the school guidance program. In performing this function, it works closely with representatives of the PTA and other school-parent-community committees, such as a "youth needs committee." The council might sponsor periodic "unmet guidance needs" conferences, organized gatherings in which parents and other citizens have the opportunity to discuss those student needs which they believe the school, family, and community are currently failing to meet adequately. A catalogue of unmet needs forms the springboard for later action by the guidance committee.

The community

The pupil's out-of-school life undeniably has a greater impact on his development than his in-school life. If guidance efforts are to be successful, the school of necessity deeply involves the community and family in its guidance program. Every school needs a citizens' advisory council to coordinate school-community efforts. A representative of this council should be a member of the school guidance council. Alert counselors work closely with nonschool youth agencies to extend guidance cooperation beyond the referral service to active, continuous collaboration for a community-wide guidance thrust. Mass media such as the local newspaper, the radio and television station, and the motion-picture theater can cooperate in promoting positive child and youth guidance in their respective fields. Local government and industry similarly have guidance roles.

The parish

Catholic elementary schools are customarily parish agencies, but little school-parish guidance teamwork actually occurs. The same seems true of Catholic high schools and the group of parishes from which their student bodies are drawn. Yet one of the purposes of a Catholic school is to assist students to take an active part in parish life both during their school careers and after. To foster such cooperation, parishes must make organizations meaningful to students. Fr. P. J. Sullivan, C.S.C. (1959, pp. 88–91), found that the greater a person's interest and liking for the work of a given parish organization, the greater his or her activity. He also found that the majority of parishioners are not interested in parish organizations. An important reason for apathy is that parish organizations rarely afford the layman an opportunity to participate fully in the life of the Church. Such organizations are often overdominated by priests, and the layman, whether student or adult, has little to say on matters of importance.

In the failure of adequate parish-school teamwork, the Catholic school is often as much at fault as the parish. A nationwide study by Fr. Cassidy, O.S.F.S. (1962), revealed that in Catholic high schools little emphasis is placed on the layman's role in the life of the Church. Only 55 per cent of the schools mentioned the lay apostolate as an aim in religious guidance, only 48 per cent gave any sort of preparation for parish leadership, and only 34 per cent had Catholic Action groups in even the loosest sense of the term. Many priests and religious still have a concept of the laity which is out of date by contemporary Catholic theological teaching. Thus, for example, a priest (Fr. Hogan, 1963, pp. 324–325) could recently write: "To be sure, it is better to have religious [teaching] theology, philosophy, history and some of the sciences because of the problems which arise with religious bearings," as if theologically informed Catholic laymen could not deal with these problems just as well. From Pope Piux XI onward, every Pontiff has stressed the importance of Catholic Action, the participation of the laity in the apostolate of the hierarchy through an official mandate of the local bishop (Fr. Civardi, 1936; Fr. Ferree, S.M., n.d.). Indeed in his first message after his election to the papacy, Pope Paul VI explicitly mentioned the importance of Catholic Action, the layman's role in the life of the Church. Certainly every school in cooperation with a nearby parish could establish militant Young Christian Student (YCS) cells (Fr. Anderl & Sister M. Ruth, F.S.P.A., 1945). Channeling a student's religious desires into making rosaries, sewing alter linens, and other pedestrian tasks only serves to extinguish his zeal. Catton's study (1957, p. 563) of an ultraevangelical cult whose leader was regarded as Christ concluded that people (including some Catholics) seeking God by attending prayer meetings of this "far-out" cult "tended to be those who had strong religious interests that were not being satisfied through normal [church] institutional channels."

To begin effective school-parish teamwork, (1) there should be coordination between school and parish on such matters as pre-Cana conferences; (2) guidance-mindedness should pervade the invitation of children and youth to participate in joint school-parish activities, since unfortunately only "good children" take part in these activities while those students who could profit most from the experience are neglected; (3) schools should cooperate with parishes in Catholic Action groups or dynamic lay Catholic activities such as the Papal Volunteers for Latin America (Fr. McAuliffe, O.P., 1962); and (4) schools should involve students more actively in liturgical life.

COORDINATING GUIDANCE
AND CURRICULUM

The curriculum either positively promotes or dissipates the effectiveness of a guidance program. Indeed any adequate curriculum, judged solely from the curriculum standpoint, has a guidance thrust (Kelley, 1955). Certainly the goals of curriculum and guidance are deeply related. G. E. Hill and R. O. Morrow (1957) concluded that the quality of guidance services and curricular offerings was rated by a jury of experts as more closely related to a low dropout rate than any other factors. Yet despite the relationship between guidance and curriculum, most of curricular literature misunderstands, bypasses, and is ignorant of a guidance thrust. The same is doubly true of the attention given to curriculum in professional guidance literature. Convention programs at APGA, NCGC, or APA rarely deal with curricular matters in any knowledgeable way. On the local school level, guidance operates as an almost isolated program, with little teamwork attempted with the curriculum specialists. The curricula of small private liberal arts colleges have a particular mystique about them in the United States, but where are the personnel and guidance services in these colleges, hoary with age, to say nothing of the integration of antiquated or nonexistent guidance programs? Alert colleges (Brunson, 1959) attempt some sort of curriculum-guidance integration, but these are exceptions rather than the rule. How many teachers at every school level like to boast that they "cover the ground," but how few actually touch it? Some writers like Rudin (1958) have considered a key reason for school failure to be academic anti-intellectualism, defined as the active or passive resistance of a student to involve himself in the intellectual activities of class or school. The question, however, is whether a nonmeaningful curriculum actually fosters such a pupil attitude.

How often do schools or school systems experiment with curricula to make them more meaningful, more guidance-oriented? A formal recommendation by the NEA Project on Instruction (1963, p. 22) suggests that a school system allot not less than 1 per cent of its annual budget for curriculum research, experimentation, and innovation.

Low (1953, p. 38), a curriculum expert, has noted that "the typical [i.e., common] needs of youth provide a sound starting point for establishing curriculum content." But how often is curriculum content determined by educational authorities with little attention to what the child or youth needs to learn in order to mature? Fr. Schneider's doctoral dissertation (1943) concluded that curricula in rural Catholic secondary schools are based on urban models and on college entrance goals, both of which fail to meet the educational or life needs of their pupils. This observation is probably valid today. Certainly any rural or urban high school which is a terminal institution must tailor its curriculum content so that learning experiences are eminently functional in the life of each pupil (Sister Aimee Ely, F.C.S.P., 1940). A study of presidents of Catholic women's colleges by Sister M. Leonita Smith, O.P. (1961), cited a definite need for reappraisal of current curricula in women's education, with more emphasis placed on family studies. Fr. Roesch, S.M. (1954, pp. 340–370), found that the major factor causing dropouts from urban Catholic schools was failure of the school to tailor curriculum content or academic standards to the needs and abilities of students. Many students expressed a desire for a Catholic education but not under existing conditions, i.e., a strict academic curriculum geared to the very intelligent. Of dropouts who transferred to public schools, only 19 per cent judged the curriculum of the Catholic school superior to that of the public school. These findings are consistent with data from earlier studies on Catholic schools, notably those of Mitchell (1940) and Fr. (later Msgr.) Stuardi (1947).

A first step toward a sweeping revision of curriculum content in a guidance-oriented direction is the instructional adaptation of current traditional course content to the needs and concerns of students. Even the traditionalist American Council on Education (1948, p. 11) has noted that the teacher is more effective if he attempts to apply his subject matter to student needs. Borow's review (1959) concluded that experiments in which teachers used instructional methods based on human relations skills, personality adjustment behaviors, and so forth produced relatively fertile results in both academic learning and personal self-actualization. Of interest in this connection is an experiment (Seeley, 1959) carried on in a Canadian secondary school. Some classes at different grade levels were told they would have one hour a week to discuss whatever they wanted to with the teacher, in the classroom, during a regular subject-matter period. Regardless of what the children said, the teacher neither approved nor disapproved, but in nondirective fashion merely reflected feeling, and only rarely intervened to keep discussion running smoothly. These experimental classes were called "human relations classes." Feelings expressed by students gained momentum. By the end of the term the experimental students, despite substantial time "lost" for participation in human relations classes, made significant gains in marks for all school subjects, including English, the subject in which the experimental group sacrificed half of its time for human relations classes. Three years after the conclusion of the experiment five students of the entire grade 10 group, i.e., both experimental and control, were awarded major scholarships to the University of Toronto on the basis of competitive subject-matter examinations. Four came from the experimental group, one was a new arrival from outside the school system, and one was a member of the four-times-as-numerous control group. While one experiment is not conclusive, the results are worth noting, particularly when taken with evidence (Lee, 1963b, pp. 204–205) about superior scholastic attainments of core curriculum classes as compared with matched traditional, subject-centered curriculum classes. Unfortunately many contemporary American schools are unwilling to attempt curricular experimentation in this post-Sputnik, post-Conant day of emphasis on college preparation, which now extends into elementary school. Catholic schools have always had a deep tradition of ultraconservatism and antiexperimentation. Lack of guidance-oriented curricular experimentation regrettably prevents exploration of new and perhaps more fruitful curricular-guidance approaches.

The second step toward a sweeping revision of curriculum content in a guidance-oriented direction is a fundamental re-examination by the school of its present curriculum design. Curricular design is "the pattern or framework or structural organization used in selecting, planning and carrying forward educational experiences in the school. Design is thus the plan that teachers follow in providing learning activities" (Saylor & Alexander, 1954, p. 245). The curriculum design in most public and Catholic schools is the subject-centered approach which utilizes bodies of information classified into intrinsically systematic branches of knowledge as both the organizing force and the center of learning; e.g., the subject of English literature is learned in chronological fashion. On the rare occasions when curriculum is discussed in guidance journals, it seldom occurs to the writers that there might be other types of curricular designs, some of which are better suited to guidance than the subject-centered approach. One such guidance-oriented curriculum design is core. The core curriculum centers on interdisciplinary problems of both "eternal" and personal concern to the student. Subject material is brought into the learning situation as needed to solve the problem under consideration, without respect for precise subject-matter boundaries. Thus, for example, a study of the problem of social injustice might involve such diverse subject areas as history of the American Negro, music of the slaves, literature on man's inhumanity to man, religious writings on the question, and so forth. What Msgr. George Johnson (1941) said of the total student-centered curriculum design applies with equal cogency to the core curriculum; viz., the new design does not dispense with traditional subject matter but rather reorganizes subject matter in order to accomplish real learning. Certainly there is nothing sacrosanct about the subject-centered design or any other curriculum structure for that matter; the important thing is that pupils learn. Carefully conducted research investigations (Lee, 1963b, pp. 204–205) clearly indicate not only that pupils in a core curriculum learn social leadership and other behaviors more effectively than matched pupils in traditional curriculum but also that core pupils score higher in standardized achievement tests measuring subject-matter learnings. Core is psychologically a sounder curriculum design than the subject-centered approach because it makes learning experiences meaningful and relevant (Hennis, 1962). Teachers who have utilized the core design testify that core has made guidance more effective and more pronounced in the classroom (cf. Curriculum Guidance Conference, Board of Education, New York City, 1955, p. 17). Core is guidance-oriented to such an extent that structurally guidance is an integral, inseparable part of the curriculum itself (V. E. Anderson, 1964; Faunce & Bossing, 1958; Willey & Strong, 1957, pp. 393–540).

In Catholic schools it is imperative to integrate religious guidance into curriculum structure if such schools are to attain their distinctive purpose. In a subject-centered approach, neither religious guidance nor religious subject matter is integrated into the curriculum. Hence, Catholic schools seem superfluous; it would be far less expensive and just as profitable in terms of religious learning outcomes to erect catechism centers next to public schools so that Catholic children could attend public school and receive separate religious instruction in another building. Public schools can teach algebra, history, and Latin just as well as or better than Catholic schools. When Catholic schools isolate religion in a separate course, as indeed they must to follow a subject-centered curriculum, they teach students that religion is separated from the rest of knowledge, from the rest of life. Msgr. Kevane (1963, p. 219), speaking of such concentration, remarked: "In this approach, first of all, religion tends to become a thing apart; it exists in a hermetically sealed capsule, a Cinderella among the offerings of the curriculum, without credit, without intellectual standing, often without administrative consideration, and lacking a real living contact with the academic structure and intellectual content of the school." A subject-centered curriculum is not a unified but a fractionated curriculum in which each subject area is considered separately and in which guidance lies outside the classroom. Such a disintegrated curriculum in a Catholic school promotes what Fr. Twomey, S.J. (1961, p. 9), has termed "compartmentalized Catholicism," i.e., the concept of Catholicism as being one segment of life rather than related of its very necessity to every area of study and of living.

A core curriculum or even a core-type curriculum in a Catholic school attempts to integrate religious content and guidance into the entire school program, without doing violence to content or transforming the curriculum into a disguised religion course. One attempt toward effective integration is the Guiding Growth in Christian Social Living syllabus series (Sister Mary Joan, O.P., & Sister Mary Nona, O.P., 1944–1946) for Catholic elementary schools. Another example is the experimental curriculum (Sister M. R. Carter, 1946) introduced into a Catholic school by a group of Ursuline sisters. This innovation, one of the few attempted by Catholic schools, aimed at fostering curricular integration and was rated as successful. Fr. O'Kane (1962) reported that the relationship between religion and American life in the period from 1865 to 1914 was ignored or neglected in American history texts commonly used in public schools at the beginning of the 1960s. Yet Catholic educators like Sister M. Jacqueline Grennan, S.L. (1963), and Sister Virginia Maureen, S.S.N.D. (1964), feel that any treatment of religion or philosophy is totally out of place in a nonreligion textbook in a Catholic school; indeed they maintain that there should be no special Catholic textbooks at all, except for religion class. Doubtless, they are motivated by exposure to the sorry excuses for adequate textbooks which have been published for the Catholic market. Integrating the Christian dimension into the curriculum demands far more than pietistic clichés or "baptism" of sound secular texts.

But why should Catholic schools, which as Fr. Koob, O. Praem (1964, p. 659), has observed "tend to mirror the public schools," exist as a separate entity? Certainly the very *raison d'être* of the Catholic school is so to integrate religious content and guidance into all areas of school life that the student more deeply understands the relevance of religion to daily life and learns to live that religion in out-of-school and postschool life. Indeed Mary Perkins Ryan (1964), a well-known Catholic writer, has carried Sister Jacqueline's argument to its logical conclusion and questioned the existence of Catholic schools, utilizing many of the points Sister Jacqueline advanced. That Mrs. Ryan was pilloried by the Catholic press after her bold and arresting proposals is itself testimony to the quasi-paranoid suspicion many Catholics hold of the innovational or experimental. Indeed, emotion colors perception, and most of her critics misread Mrs. Ryan's invitation to debate whether Catholic schools *as presently organized* adequately serve the needs of all members of the Church as radically and irresponsibly advocating the sudden and violent overthrow of the Catholic school system.

The third step toward a sweeping revision of curriculum content in a guidance-oriented direction is a basic overhaul in the structure of the school itself. An example of such a drastic reorganization is elimination of the lockstep graded system which characterizes America's schools. Most public school systems (Goodlad & Anderson, 1963; Msgr. Hoflich, 1960) and a few alert Catholic school systems already have ungraded the first three years of elementary schools with excellent results. The dynamic Pittsburgh diocese has ungraded the entire elementary school, and there are a few ungraded experimental high schools (Kauth & Brown, 1962). The chief advantage is that the ungraded system permits every student to work at his own rate, thus tailoring the school program to each student's unique developmental pattern and effecting a merger between guidance and curriculum.

GUIDANCE COORDINATION THROUGH IN-SERVICE EDUCATION

In-service education consists in those learnings, whether organized by the system, by the school, or by the individual guidance worker, intended to improve the worker professionally. The purpose of in-service education is to continue the professional preparation of workers so that they can perform their functions more effectively. To be even minimally effective, guidance workers need continual in-service education. Archer's comprehensive review (1960) concluded that many staff members felt the need for in-service course work. A guidance worker who received his master's or doctor's degree in 1941 and failed to keep abreast of the field would be unfamiliar with non-directive counseling and its pervasive influence, with many commonly used tests, with the revolution in vocational guidance theory, and so forth. In-service education is crucial for the religious teaching in Catholic schools. A vocation survey (Sister M. Judith, 1956) by the Sister Formation Conference of 14,000 secondary school students taught by women religious disclosed that only 20 per cent thought religious life broadening, only 22 per cent rated nuns as professionals, and less than 50 per cent thought sisters were "cultured." Students with these perceptions are not likely to benefit from counseling or guidance offered by sister-counselors or sister-teachers. A vigorous in-service program could go far in eliminating some factors which gave rise to these students' realistic impressions. For the priest-teacher who, without benefit of previous course work in the subject area, undertakes to instruct pupils in any course to which he is assigned on the "good-man-can-do-anything" hypothesis, in-service education usually amounts to basic preservice training.

The most common types of in-service education are (1) formal courses, (2) faculty meetings, (3) professional reading, (4) membership in professional associations, (5) workshops, and (6) institutes. Formal course work may be given by a board of education or by a university graduate school. Normally formal courses offered by a university are of a higher caliber than those offered by the board of education. Perhaps the greatest impetus to high-level in-service courses was provided by the guidance institutes established through the National Defense Education Act of 1958.

A faculty meeting is, or at least should be, a cooperative enterprise whereby teachers, staff members, and administrators pool ideas to further the school program. Unfortunately many administrators subvert the valuable in-service nature of the meeting. In-service growth cannot take place in a meeting in which the role of the faculty and the guidance staff is to listen passively to the principal or one of his assistants. Effective faculty meetings for in-service growth in guidance feature cooperative planning and management. A certain number of meetings each school year can be given over to a consideration of guidance. During such meetings, counselors and guidance supervisors may discuss various aspects of the program; the school guidance director may offer suggestions on effective use of the classroom as a guidance vehicle; the librarian may initiate discussions on use of the library for guidance purposes; the counselor may give a demonstration interview; members of the guidance and psychology departments of a nearby college or university may speak on new emphases in guidance; and a teacher can prepare a research report on some guidance topic of interest to the group, take ten minutes of the meeting to summarize his findings, and then open discussion to the entire faculty.

A study by Sister M. Ursula Grimes, S.S.J. (1961, p. 257), is consistent with the finding of other research that parochial school teachers feel professional reading offers valuable in-service education while faculty meetings and workshops are of little value. This finding indicts lifeless Catholic school faculty meetings and emphasizes the value of in-service reading in professional growth. It is regrettable that not all guidance workers fulfill the obligation of improving competence through professional reading. The Holy See realized the necessity of continuous professional reading when it stated that every religious house shall have a library containing books on the entire field of pedagogy. Non-Catholic books should be included in the professional library of the school or religious house.

Professional reading for guidance workers includes not only books but particularly periodical literature. The most important guidance periodical is undoubtedly the APGA's *Personnel and Guidance Journal* (1958, p. 589), a monthly publication whose purpose is to deal "with significant practices in personnel and guidance work, current problems in the field, trends in training personnel and guidance workers, and theory and research that give practical application." Each of the six divisions of APGA publishes a quarterly journal of especial interest to the members of that division. Division I, American College Personnel Association (ACPA), issues the *Journal of College Student Personnel;* Division II, Association for Counselor Education and Supervision (ACES), *Counselor Education and Supervision;* Division

III, National Vocational Guidance Association (NVGA), *Vocational Guidance Quarterly;* Division IV, Student Personnel Association for Teacher Education (SPATE), *Student Personnel Association for Teacher Education Quarterly;* Division V, American School Counselor Association (ASCA), *The School Counselor;* and Division VI, American Rehabilitation Counseling Association (ARCA), *Rehabilitation Counseling Bulletin.*

The most important Catholic journal for guidance workers, the *National Catholic Guidance Conference Journal,* is the successor to the *Catholic Counselor.* According to its masthead, this journal "is a professional quarterly of theory, research, and informed opinion about problems and issues in guidance, counseling, student personnel administration, and supporting psychological services in Catholic educational institutions and school-related agencies." Similarly, the masthead states that "the *Journal* seeks to center its attention upon the contributions of a Judaeo-Christian heritage to the evolving theory and practice of personnel services and upon problems and developments related specifically to Catholic schools and colleges or to Catholic students in other institutions." Unfortunately, this journal typically publishes little empirical research, a fact which reflects that Catholic education's normal resistance to experimentation has probably been introjected by guidance specialists in Catholic education.

Other guidance-related journals which school counselors and professionally alert school guidance workers read include *American Psychologist, Child, Child Development, Childhood Education, Education, Educational and Psychological Measurement, Harvard Educational Review, High School Journal, Human Relations, Journal of Abnormal and Social Psychology, Journal of Clinical Psychology, Journal of Consulting Psychology, Journal of Counseling Psychology, Journal of Educational Psychology, Journal of Educational Research, Journal of Elementary Education, Journal of Experimental Education, Journal of Higher Education, Journal of Personality, Journal of Psychology, Journal of Social Psychology, Mental Hygiene, School Review,* and *Teachers College Record.*

Some professional journals for a Catholic audience which occasionally or regularly carry articles on guidance include *Bulletin of the National Catholic Educational Association, Catholic Educational Review, Catholic Educator, Catholic High School Quarterly Bulletin, Catholic Psychological Record, Catholic School Journal, Insight,* and *Lumen Vitae.*

Reviews of educational and psychological research, as well as indices to educational and psychological literature, are invaluable tools to the research-minded school guidance worker. Perhaps the five most comprehensive such works are *Annual Review of Psychology, Education Index, Encyclopedia of Educational Research, Psychological Abstracts,* and *Review of Educational Research.* For Catholic journals, probably the best single index is the *Catholic Periodical Index.*

To promote his own continuous and fruitful in-service growth, every school guidance worker should be a member of professional associations. Certainly every guidance worker in a public or a Catholic school should belong to the American Personnel and Guidance Association. Founded in 1952 as a result of a merger of several guidance organizations, APGA has for its chief purposes to advance personnel work and guidance as a science and a profession, to promote sound personnel and guidance practices, and to provide leadership and cooperation for the various groups in guidance and personnel work. As was mentioned earlier, APGA has six divisions. Division I, American College Personnel Association, for workers in college student personnel services, including administration and teaching; Division II, Association for Counselor Education and Supervision, for supervisors, administrators, and counselor educators on state or local levels and in colleges and universities; Division III, National Vocational Guidance Association, for counselors in schools, government, industry, and public and private agencies; Division IV, Student Personnel Association for Teacher Education, for workers in personnel and guidance in a teacher preparing institution; Division V, American School Counselor Association, for guidance directors, personnel service directors, school counselors, and teacher-counselors on the elementary and secondary levels; and Division VI, American Rehabilitation Counseling Association, for rehabilitation counselors in hospitals and guidance agencies. The American Board on Counseling Services, Inc., is an arm of APGA which biennially reviews the quality of services rendered in guidance agencies and publishes a directory of approved agencies. Membership requirements vary from division to division, but school counselors with the requisite educational and experiential background can qualify for professional membership in Division III, NVGA. Many counselors belong to several divisions. Most states have state-wide branches affiliated with APGA, and there are also many regional and local branches. There are also state, regional, and local associations affiliated with divisions of APGA, especially Divisions III (NVGA), V (ASCA), and VI (ARCA). Many school counselors also belong to Division 17 (Counseling Psychology) of the American Psychological Association. Graduate students in guidance and counseling are eligible for student membership in APGA and APA.

The National Catholic Guidance Conference is a national association of guidance workers in Catholic schools and Catholic guidance workers in other schools and agencies. As indicated in Chapter 1, NCGC was incorporated in 1962 as a merger of three parent groups. Regular membership is restricted to members of APGA; associate membership in NCGC is virtually unrestricted. NCGC has as its aims improvement of guidance services in Catholic schools, sharing of emerging practices, and infusion of a religious dimension into guidance theory and practice. In forward-looking dioceses, there are diocesan guidance councils affiliated with NCGC. Local diocesan councils, largely as a result of unwarranted opposition or nonsupport by diocesan authorities who regard the priest or school chaplain untrained in guidance as the only legitimate counselor, have not yet demonstrated the vigorous leadership that is their potential; nevertheless their existence represents a needed step in the direction of professionalism. Catholic school guidance workers should be members of local councils. The American Catholic Psychological Association is an organization of Catholic psychologists, but without interest divisions.

Workshops are important vehicles for in-service growth. A guidance workshop is a gathering of workers, supervisors, and consultants to discuss cooperatively some professional problem, e.g., procedures in counseling the emotionally disturbed. Guidance workshops can feature panel discussions by workers followed by open discussion from the floor, intensive discussion groups by school system guidance leaders and by professors of guidance, development of experimental curricula integrating guidance, and closed-circuit televised lectures by state or regional guidance experts. Many alert school systems operate their own closed-circuit television stations. The archdiocese of Boston operates educational television station WIHS. Though primarily intended for instructional use for students, it can be used for workshop purposes as well. As a culminating activity, the workshop can incorporate field trips to referral agencies.

Institutes are periodic lectures or demonstrations by experts for large groups of school staff to provide an opportunity to improve the quality of their work. Guidance in-service institutes can have speakers from APGA, NCGC, NEA, and the school system personnel and guidance office or professors from nearby colleges and universities. Commercial guidance motion pictures and filmstrips produced by such groups as the McGraw-Hill Text-Film Library, the National Education Association, and *Encyclopedia Britannica* can be shown. Demonstration master counseling interviews can be held with subsequent explanation and discussion. A model role-playing situation can be enacted.

A vigorous spiritual life is essential for the Catholic teacher in both public and Catholic high schools. Unless a guidance worker is soaked in solid spirituality, he runs the danger of becoming blind to the intimately spiritual relationship between his guidance function and the workings of God in the world. A healthy piety, which sees the world as joyous and good because it is of God, rather than a Jansenistic interpretation of the world as a prison house and a source of evil, will do much to give the Catholic guidance worker the *élan* necessary to an effective apostolate.

Special difficulties seem to confront Catholic schools in developing effective in-service programs. A nationwide study of women religious conducted by Sister Mary Ralph Fahey, S.N.D. (1960), concluded that there are scattered efforts rather than well-developed in-service programs in the congregations studied. Most of the sisters are thrown more or less haphazardly into summer courses, workshops, and conventions with the confident hope of their superiors that somehow God's grace will supply requisite knowledge and skill. Sister Ralph also reported that undergraduate work was pursued by sisters usually in colleges or novitiates conducted by their own congregations, thus fostering inbreeding. Graduate work was almost exclusively restricted to the summer session, although in larger cities this was augmented by late-afternoon and Saturday classes. Hence graduate training was sporadic and sandwiched in on the side, so to speak. Sister Ralph's investigation disclosed that it is customary for religious communities to assign all sisters first to elementary teaching, after which some of them "work their way up." This unfortunate practice channels the young sister's interests, aptitudes, attitudes, and skills into elementary education, all of which she is quite likely to import wholesale into secondary school or college. The investigator believed the practice of assigning all young sisters to the elementary grades is based on a false, theologically outmoded concept of humility. Another difficulty is that in-service education for Catholic school staffs is not usually attached to certification requirements, as is customary in the public school system. As late as 1963 half of the dioceses permitted individual schools to certify their own staff members, with the other half being certified by the diocesan superintendent (Catholic Property Administration, 1964, p. 28). Certainly no sound professionalization, much less a vigorous in-service program, is possible under such conditions. Many small Catholic women's colleges are now opening graduate divisions, the prime purpose of which often is to award the master's degree to sisters of the congregation operating the institution. This promotes and reinforces inbreeding and stifles in-service growth. A brighter note is the effort of the Sister Formation Conference to provide thoroughgoing professionalization for sisters before they enter school service. The hope is that such an endeavor will have beneficial effects on subsequent in-service programs.

EVALUATING THE EFFECTS OF
TEAM GUIDANCE EFFORTS

Evaluation of the school's program of guidance services consists in the accurate, comprehensive appraisal of these services in terms of their goals. Evaluation of the guidance program is a team effort, involving the school guidance director, counselors, the assistant superintendent for personnel services, the system guidance director, school system guidance specialists, teachers, school administrators, coordinate staff, parents, citizens, members of community social service agencies which work with the school, and students (Stoops & Wahlquist, 1958, pp. 308–336). Unfortunately students are often left out of the evaluation process altogether.

In systematically evaluating the effectiveness of school guidance services, there are six steps. (1) The objectives and goals of the guidance program and each of its services are defined. (The 13 guidance services in a minimally comprehensive school guidance program were delineated in Chapter 3.) (2) Criteria which adequately measure the degree of attainment of the objectives of the school guidance program are selected. (3) Instruments which measure the defined criteria are chosen or constructed. Perhaps the best-developed and most comprehensive instrument is "Section G, Guidance Services" of the *Evaluative Criteria,* 1960 edition, published by the National Study of Secondary School Evaluation (1960, pp. 273–288). While intended for use in the accreditation of secondary schools, this instrument can be adapted for appraisal of the guidance program in elementary schools and in colleges. (4) The evaluation is made under rigorously controlled conditions, particularly when it is carried on through an experiment. (5) Data are statistically analyzed with an optimal degree of sophistication to ascertain the extent to which criteria measured are in fact realized in the school guidance program. (6) Results are interpreted so as to pinpoint the strengths to be solidified and the weaknesses to be ameliorated. Evaluation of the program should not be conducted solely through instruments but should also include informal procedures, such as conferences involving school staff, parents, and community citizens. Evaluation must be continuous throughout the school year, not restricted to certain predetermined times. Evaluation of the school's guidance services is an empty exercise unless results are implemented by a subsequent program of action on the part of the counselor, principal, teachers, and school staff.

part **3**

GUIDANCE AS PROCESS:
PROCEDURES AND TECHNIQUES

8

THE ASSESSMENT FUNCTION
IN SCHOOL GUIDANCE

Nature of assessment and data-gathering

The assessment of student characteristics is the most important initial step in organizing the school guidance effort for a positive developmental thrust. Guidance which effectively assists students in readying themselves for and in meeting their developmental tasks is anchored in an accurate description both of the history of the developmental progress of each student and of the manner in which the student is currently organizing his personality. The function of assessment and data gathering is *descriptive* rather than diagnostic or evaluative. *Diagnosis* implies the detection of deviations from normal developmental patterns, especially in terms of behavior and learning disorders. *Evaluation* suggests the weighing of probabilities for success in such life endeavors as school and work. Both diagnosis and evaluation are subsumed in the assessment function. *Assessment* implies a considerably broader description of the student in his total life situation. As Sundberg and Tyler (1962, pp. 80–81) have noted, assessment implies the "systematic collection, organization, and interpretation of information about a person and his situations." The result of the assessment process is the development of "a working image or model of the person-situation." Guidance assessment is concerned with the description of both (1) the general characteristics of members of the student body and (2) the specific characteristics of individual students seeking counseling assistance.

The description of the general characteristics of the student body is essential in structuring the school environment to facilitate growth. From this use of assessment and data-gathering procedures, the guidance staff, administrators, and faculty infer the fashion in which the school should be structured for a positive guidance thrust. An effective guidance program, including its counseling service, must be organized to meet the developmental needs of a particular student body. The guidance staff may learn through assessment and data-gathering procedures that most students in a particular high school seem to experience an unusual amount of difficulty in forming satisfactory boy-girl relationships, a normal developmental task of adolescence. The staff then arranges for discussion with administrators, classroom teachers, and advisers of extracurricular activities to ascertain whether certain school practices or regulations inhibit satisfactory developmental progress. As a result of these discussions, steps may be taken to reorganize the school environment so as to eliminate obstacles to total student development.

In another case, the guidance staff may learn that a majority of students in a senior high school aspire to attend college and have the necessary scholastic ability. The families of these students, however, are financially unable to support them while they pursue higher education. It therefore becomes incumbent upon the staff to marshal and to make available information concerning college loans, assistantships, earn-learn programs, scholarships based on economic need, and other sources of financial aid. The college information library, career days, and the guidance bulletin board can highlight detailed information on the solution of this student concern, e.g., those urban universities in which part-time study and full-time employment are possible and in which academic standards prevail. To focus on the totally residential (and usually prestigious) campus environment in this situation is to reinforce or inject unrealistic and unrealizable aspirations for many students.

Similarly, the Catholic high school which accents the high-tuition Catholic college or university as against the low- or free-tuition public institution decidedly does a disservice by creating needless conflicts in students whose families are unable to meet the costs involved. Indeed, such families may be unable to supply a Catholic higher education precisely because they have demonstrated (at least in the mind of much of the diocesan press) their Catholicity in unusually large families. This fact is often ignored or considered irrelevant by not a few clergy, religious, and laymen. As late as 1963, one ordinary made it necessary for Catholic parents and students to receive formal, explicit permission of the chancery office to attend non-Catholic schools and colleges. This situation obtained *despite* the fact that (1) the high schools of the diocese could accommodate only 20 per cent of the Catholics of high school age and (2) there was but one Catholic college within the diocese, which enrolled only women, had a capacity of only 400 students, and was not regionally accredited. In contrast, there were a great many public high schools whose faculties and student bodies comprised a sizable number of Catholics; further, in the same diocese there existed five non-Catholic colleges or universities, three of them tax-supported. About 25 per cent of the population within the geographic boundaries of the diocese was Catholic, indicating that Catholic parents were contributing heavily through taxation to the support of the public institutions. Whether the chancery readily granted permission is not the issue; rather this anachronistic policy served to create needless guilt feelings in parents and students. As Fr. Haas, O.P. (1964), has observed, an unrelenting emphasis on the necessity of attending a Catholic institution of higher learning must be abandoned as unrealistic for many or perhaps for most Catholic students in the face of rising tuition costs. This situation is aggravated by the fact that the learning experiences available at many Catholic colleges are academically inferior to those obtainable on the nearby non-Catholic campus. Instead, Fr. Haas suggests, the attention of teachers and counselors must be directed toward preparing the Catholic student to succeed on the secular campus.

Ascertaining the specific personality characteristics of each student is the necessary starting point for the counseling relationship. Before undertaking to establish a counseling relationship, the developmentally oriented interpretive counselor seeks to discover as much as he can about the client. He wishes to know the client's characteristic patterns of behavior, the degree of consolidation of self-identity, and the chief self-aspirations of the client. The counselor's purpose is not evaluative; he is seeking to *understand* the client from the client's frame of reference. The inspection of assessment information prior to the first counseling contact helps the counselor prepare himself to be maximally receptive to the client. The counseling interview itself is, of course, a very valuable assessment vehicle. During the interview, the counselor has the opportunity to verify the observations made by other school people and students about the behavior, attitudes, and values of the client. He also learns how the client is capable of functioning under optimal conditions of unconditional acceptance and the absence of threat. During the counseling process, the client or the counselor may wish to employ additional assessment devices, especially psychometric instruments, to corroborate, to evaluate, or to diagnose. The use of precontact and during-contact assessment data assists the counselor in developing and revising a "working image" of the client and his situations. Client-counselor interaction in the interview serves to strengthen, modify, or elucidate the working image suggested by precontact assessment data.

SOURCES OF ASSESSMENT DATA

Guidance workers employ a variety of techniques and sources of assessment data. As Cottle and Downie (1960) have emphasized, the use of longitudinal information (e.g., the cumulative record) presents a developmental picture of the student in a variety of life situations. On the other hand, cross-sectional information (e.g., guidance tests) freezes the student in a particular, perhaps atypical, moment in his developmental history. Cottle and Downie (1960, pp. 3–7) regard multisource longitudinal information, recorded by a number of observers, as more stable and reliable. They suggest indeed that longitudinal information is necessary to the teacher and the counselor in order to interpret cross-sectional data meaningfully. While psychometric instruments are an important source of cross-sectional information, they should be incorporated into the longitudinal picture of student development through cumulative school records.

In addition to psychometric instruments, the principal sources of assessment data are cumulative school and guidance records, anecdotal records, trait ratings by teachers, student autobiographies, guidance questionnaires, parent conferences, case conferences, and sociometric devices.

The cumulative record

The purpose of the cumulative record is to present an overall longitudinal view of the student's development in a compact, unified summary. There are three principal types of cumulative records, viz., the cumulative school record, the cumulative guidance record, and the cumulative counseling record.

The Cumulative School Record

Since the school is vitally concerned with all areas of student development, especially as they impinge on the "teachable moment," the cumulative school record contains far more than an account of academic achievement. Though this record is now recognized as an indispensable part of the educational operation, it is a relative newcomer to the educational scene. It received great impetus in the early 1930s, when the American Council on Education developed its "Cumulative Record Form." The cumulative school record was subject to extensive experimentation during the Eight-year Study conducted by the Progressive Education Association (Aiken, 1942). Traxler (1947, pp. 13–16) clearly regards this record as a guidance vehicle. Listing its "'general uses,'" he feels the cumulative school record is valuable in (1) enabling teachers to become acquainted with new students quickly, (2) organizing students of similar interests into small discussion groups, (3) identifying students who may need assistance, (4) planning special programs for academically talented students, (5) identifying gifted and talented students, (6) furnishing some indication as to possible causes of poor school adjustment,

(7) providing information for conferences with students about school achievement, (8) affording data for conferences about misbehavior problems, (9) supplying background information for parent conferences, (10) furnishing information for teacher conferences, (11) permitting greater selectivity in choosing courses, (12) providing data for educational and vocational planning, (13) supplying information concerning case studies of students, and (14) forming a basis for recommendations to colleges and prospective employers. Elsewhere, Traxler (1957, pp. 297–298) has recommended that records should be as reliable, valid, and objective as possible; that they should be continuous throughout the student's educational career; and that a system of cumulative record keeping must be accompanied by in-service education of teachers in their use (see also F. S. Brown, 1961, pp. 76–87).

An efficiently organized cumulative school record contains the following kinds of information about the student: (1) personal data, e.g., date and place of birth, and sex; (2) home and family background, e.g., mother's and father's occupations and educational level, number and ages of siblings, and names and ages of others living in the family home; (3) record of health and physical growth, including physical limitations; (4) pertinent personal characteristics; (5) summary of records in previous schools; (6) scores on psychometric devices, with name of test, date administered, source of norms used, and performance, e.g., Sequential Tests of Educational Progress (STEP) Reading, April 18, 1965, 58th percentile for high school sophomores in spring testing; (7) special aptitudes, e.g., musical; (8) scholarship ratings, e.g., marks and rank in class; (9) participation in student activities (sometimes called "extracurricular activities"); (10) out-of-school community or leisure activities; (11) work experience; (12) interests and hobbies; (13) educational aspirations; (14) vocational aspirations; (15) personal and social adjustment; (16) outstanding in-school or out-of-school achievements; (17) particular needs, e.g., medical; (18) anecdotal records; (19) educational or vocational placement, or both, e.g., college and occupation entered; (20) absence information; (21) disciplinary action if applicable, e.g., suspension; and (22) pertinent miscellaneous information. Lee (1963b, pp. 494–495) has suggested that the cumulative record, to be maximally helpful to guidance workers and teachers, should possess certain characteristics: The cumulative record should be (1) based on the school's avowed educational philosophy; (2) so constructed that it aids guidance and instruction in the most effective manner; (3) comprehensive, i.e., inclusive of more than the student's scholastic attainments; (4) cooperatively formulated by guidance workers, teachers, and administrators; (5) longitudinal, i.e., continuous throughout the student's entire school career; (6) readily accessible to guidance workers and teachers; (7) available to inquiring parents; (8) decentralized and centralized, i.e., one copy for the homeroom teacher's possession, another in the central administrative office, another for the guidance department's files;

(9) well organized, e.g., nonrepetitive; (10) concentrated, i.e., compressed into consolidated form; (11) visible and legible; (12) easy to prepare, i.e., not requiring burdensome clerical activity by the school person; (13) cooperatively filled in by school people and students in appropriate places; (14) contain the keys necessary to its interpretation, e.g., the meaning of scholastic marks; (15) admissible of easy and repeated handling, e.g., of card stock rather than paper; and (16) durable.

The Cumulative Guidance Record

Unlike the cumulative school record, which is intended for use by both teachers and guidance workers, the cumulative guidance record is intended for use by the professional guidance staff only. Information of a more confidential nature is recorded on the cumulative guidance record. Ideally, guidance records constitute an addendum to the guidance department's copy of the cumulative school record. In addition to the information contained in the record, the cumulative guidance record contains, according to Cottle and Downie (1960, pp. 15–16), the following data: (1) a personal data form, i.e., guidance questionnaire, completed by the student; (2) the student's autobiography; (3) other personal documents, such as written school-work, letters, and diaries; (4) case histories supplied by social service agencies, if applicable; (5) ratings and reports of employers; (6) reports of in-school specialists, e.g., school psychologist, social worker, and psychiatrist; (7) summaries of counselor-parent or specialist-parent consultations; and (8) a brief account of counseling or group work contacts. In the cumulative guidance record, the account of the interview with the client is presented in brief, summary form. Specifically, the record contains the date, the name of the counselor, the source of the contact (i.e., client- or counselor-initiated), the purpose of the interview, type of contact (i.e., interview or multiple counseling), the general focus of attention (e.g., personal, social, further educational, vocational, religious, or scholastic), and notation of referral to another personnel or guidance worker, if a referral is made. Because of its inherently confidential nature, the cumulative guidance record is intended for use only by members of the guidance staff and in-school pupil personnel specialists. It is particularly valuable should the counselor leave the school, so that the client's contact with the new counselor can be integrated with his relationship with the old counselor. The cumulative guidance record is also indispensable in the guidance, counseling, and placement of alumni.

The Cumulative Counseling Record

Of an extremely confidential nature is the cumulative counseling record maintained by each counselor for his personal use. This record contains a detailed summary of the content of the interview, as well as the identifying data contained in the cumulative guidance record. The counselor writes his summary of each interview as soon as possible after its termination. He seeks to identify, for his own benefit, the shifting perceptual concern, the client's self-feelings, feelings toward the counselor, teachers, parents, and others, the degree to which rapport has been established, the client's readiness to accept responsibility, his efforts at consolidating self-structure, and the degree to which he is attaining integrative self-actualization. Finally, there are a summary of the case to date and a broad plan for the next interview or group session. Since the counselor or group worker must include in the cumulative counseling record data of a highly confidential nature, this document constitutes privileged information, i.e., a professional secret. As such, the contents of the record may not be communicated to others, even to pupil personnel specialists, to the client's parents, and, in Catholic schools, to the school chaplain, without the client's express permission. The only exception to this principle occurs when the client is so emotionally disturbed as to be unable to manage his own affairs. Such a decision, however, will be made only after consultation with the school psychologist and psychiatrist. On this point, the ethical code of the American Personnel and Guidance Association (1958) is quite clear. The question of confidentiality is discussed briefly later in this chapter.

The anecdotal record

The anecdotal record is a series of short statements by teachers or staff members stating, as objectively as possible, incidents regarded as critical or significant in the development of the student. The ability to observe behavior while suspending evaluation or judgment of the behaver is a skill not well developed in most people, including teachers, counselors, and other guidance workers. The most useful anecdotal record simply states the behavior observed, avoiding either evaluation or interpretation. Anecdotal records, if evaluative, often reveal far more about the observer than the observed. Consider the following statement, recorded by a homeroom teacher in a Catholic school: "John committed a sacrilege today during homeroom. I was forced to use physical discipline to correct his evil statements. May God forgive him." When the school counselor (in this case, a priest) inquired about the statement, he was told that John had questioned whether religious really take the vow of poverty seriously. He commented that his pastor drove a Lincoln automobile and was often seen in the rather elegant restaurant where John worked evenings as a busboy. The sister-teacher, chagrined at his comments, slapped him. It was evident to the priest-counselor that the sister-teacher's behavior, especially when related to her typical pattern of acting, was rooted in her own personality difficulties (specifically, the defense mechanism of *reaction formation*). These personality difficulties caused this sister-teacher to have a continually deleterious effect on the class and on the entire homeroom program. Indeed her personality problems probably rendered her psychologically unfit as a school person. When she was questioned by the counselor about her behavior, the sister-teacher defended herself on the basis that John had verbally abused a religious, which constitutes sacrilege. In the hands of a skilled homeroom guidance worker who had come to accept herself and others, John's comments might have become the spur to helping every member of the class learn the distinctions between diocesan clergy and members of religious communities and thereby form a more realistic, more positive perception of both.

The anecdotal record should be submitted by the observer especially after critical incidents. Periodic anecdotal records, of a summary nature, should also be made during each school unit, e.g., each semester. Strang (1949, pp. 49–50) has suggested that guidance workers concentrate on the following student characteristics when writing anecdotal records: (1) learning abilities, e.g., eagerness in class, vocabulary range, types of questions asked; (2) study habits, e.g., persistence and frustration tolerance; (3) personal characteristics, e.g., physical defects, posture, malnutrition, and fatigue; (4) skill in social relations, e.g., emotional control, aggressiveness or submissiveness, withdrawal, and daydreaming; (5) speech difficulties; (6) impaired performance in motor skills; and (7) "nervous" habits or other particularities. In the report of the American Council on Education's Commission on Teacher Education (1945, pp. 33–51) project on the observing and reporting of student behavior, four types of anecdotal records were identified: judgmental, i.e., the teacher's evaluation of the behavior as appropriate or inappropriate, good or bad; interpretive, i.e., the teacher's or observer's explanation of student behavior from his (the teacher's) frame of reference; generalized description; and specific description. As teachers and other guidance workers were trained in observation, they became more descriptive, records became more detailed, and fewer interpretive conclusions were drawn. The most useful anecdote report, of course, would be that which explains behavior from the student's frame of reference. Since the ability to share the perceptual world of the student is a skill normally acquired only after considerable reflection and training and since an empathic relationship is stunted in a subject-centered (as contrasted to a core) curriculum, it is unlikely that many teachers are able to write such records. Consequently the specific, nonevaluative description of behavior is to be preferred in anecdotal reports.

The following guidelines are essential in the preparation of a useful anecdotal record: (1) The purpose of the anecdotal record is guidance-oriented, not administration-oriented. (2) The observer records only those events which he believes are pertinent to understanding the student's development. (3) The record comprises a representative sampling of student behavior. (4) The anecdotal record is a developmental history, not an indictment. (5) The report is embedded in the social context in which the behavior was observed, e.g., a socially disruptive class. (6) The report is short and specific. (7) The form of the report permits easy understanding by all guidance workers and school people. (8) The record is essentially an objective, factual description of the student's particular behavior. (9) Interpretive comments, if offered, are clearly labeled as such and are recorded separately from the observation.

The anecdotal report is completed on a special form included in the student's cumulative record folder. The form contains such minimal information as the name of the student, date of observations, name of the observer or recorder, specification of milieu and antecedent events, objective description of behavior, and comments relative to the typical or atypical character of the observed behavior. Traxler (1949, pp. 17–22) has suggested that the observer make a brief note of the behavior during the observation, indicating simply the student's name and a one- or two-word associative comment. As soon as possible thereafter, the observer completes an anecdotal record.

It is vital for the guidance worker or counselor who uses anecdotal records and observations to have experiential knowledge of the school person who made the observation, so that the worker can give appropriate weight to the observer's description and comments. If he lacks direct knowledge of the observer and his state of personal integration, the guidance worker should approach anecdotal records cautiously and prudently.

The trait rating scale

The trait rating scale is commonly used to elicit the rater's perception of the student on a number of characteristics, such as persistence, quality of class participation, concentration, eagerness to learn, and the like. The observer is asked to rate the student from high to low, to characterize him in terms of certain descriptive terms (e.g., "always" to "never"), to characterize him on a scale from 1 for "high" to 7 for "low," or vice versa, or to place him within the top 25 per cent, the lowest 25 per cent, and so on.

It is open to serious question whether the traits which the observer is asked to rate exist as functional psychological unities. Although the determination of the reliability of ratings, i.e., interrater reliability, is not a difficult statistic to calculate, most rating scales used by schools (and employers) tend to be haphazardly organized. Too few scales include specific instructions as to the meaning of the characteristic to be rated or the meaning of the various points on the scale. Thus as Lee (1963b, p. 496) has observed, the trait rating scale has the following disadvantages: (1) it is interpretive rather than factual; (2) lack of training or specific instructions causes the rater to project himself into the rating; (3) most raters tend to assign median points chiefly because they lack information about either the trait or the scale points; and (4) the "halo" effect is quite prevalent (i.e., observers tend to rate a student similarly for all traits on the basis of their concrete knowledge of him relative to a single trait). Three steps can be taken to overcome these disadvantages. First, a thorough description of the trait to be rated may be reproduced in clear, unmistakable fashion so that all raters receive the same denotative and connotative meanings. Second, the precise nature of the scale points can be carefully explained; e.g., the teacher or counselor may be asked to rate this student in terms of the top-to-bottom quartiles of the students *of whom he has personal knowledge*. Third, inter-rater reliability coefficients should be calculated to determine whether the instructions have been sufficiently well explained to produce dependable, not chance, ratings.

Since the student's behavior is partly a function of his social situation, it is quite likely that the teacher of English may rate Johnny as significantly more eager to learn than does the mathematics teacher. As a global or general index to teacher impressions, the trait rating scale may provide some information on the way in which the student's behavior *varies* as a function of self-in-situation.

The autobiography, the diary, and other personal documents

Autobiographies are either structured or unstructured. The structured autobiography requires the student to follow an organized outline, e.g., school history, home life, principal interests, and the like. This format resembles an expanded or enlarged questionnaire. The unstructured autobiography permits the student to tell his life story in his own way. While both types are representative of projective devices, it is readily apparent that the unstructured autobiography is more likely to elicit meaningful information about the client's perceptual field. A. C. Riccio (1958) regards the following as the chief disadvantages of the autobiography: (1) there are questions of validity, reliability, and confidentiality in the autobiography; (2) many students are not able to be candid and so produce a distorted picture of themselves; (3) the material often is quite complex; and (4) there are innumerable problems of interpretation, often rooted in a poor or infelicitous choice of words by students. On the other hand, the autobiography is useful because (1) it provides an opportunity for students to reveal themselves and their perceptual concerns, (2) it affords much psychological and social information from the student's frame of reference, (3) it furnishes a rough gauge to the student's attitudinal orientation and value system, and (4) it represents a relatively nonthreatening mode of data gathering. The same considerations apply to student diaries or to open-ended themes (e.g., on such topics as "my ambition").

When the autobiography, the diary, and other personal documents are to become part of the student's guidance record, their use and disposition must be clearly understood by the student. He must be assured that these materials are to be used for guidance purposes, not to satisfy the worker's desire to pry or to exercise vain curiosity. Of course if the personal document is to lie unread in the guidance file, it is a wiser practice to eliminate it altogether as a data-gathering and assessment technique. *No school has the right to elicit information from the student which will not be used with due rapidity for his direct or indirect benefit.* Further, from the phenomenological point of view, the personal document must be used with reasonable speed if it is to present an accurate picture of the student's self-concept. A characteristic of childhood and of adolescence is that the parameters of the self-concept change constantly in response to shifting self-projections. While the autobiography of a well-motivated student may accurately represent his phenomenal self at the time of its writing, it may become in weeks a relic of a frozen moment. Guidance should never degenerate into an archaeology of useless relics.

The guidance questionnaire

"The questionnaire is a printed device which asks the pupil to indicate specific information which the school regards as important for the guidance of students, e.g., home study conditions, work experience, further educational plans" (Lee, 1963b, p. 499). The information obtained from the questionnaire permits the guidance staff to modify the guidance program to ensure that the needs of the students are met. It also supplies counselors with background data on clients.

While the nature of the questionnaire implies that it is a structured device, it may vary in the degree to which it is structured, depending on its purpose. Skillfully devised questionnaires are reproduced by Tyler (1961, pp. 297–300) and by Cottle and Downie (1960, pp. 19–26, 93–97). The guidance questionnaire is sometimes used by school counselors when the student seeks counseling assistance, so that information contained on the cumulative guidance record may be brought up to date. The direction of the counseling relationship might, however, be unduly influenced by the client's responses to a counselor-structured questionnaire. The use of a questionnaire in such cases seems justified only when the counselor has learned the client's immediate perceptual concerns prior to the first interview and when the questionnaire can be helpful in elucidating that concern. The phenomenologically oriented counselor seeks to establish the counseling relationship at the point of the client's perceptual concern, not at the point of concern imposed by the counselor.

The parent conference

Conferences between parents and the guidance worker can be helpful in gaining insight into the background of the student's present developmental status. W. J. Mueller and J. W. M. Rothney (1960) found considerable inconsistency between the description and the prediction of personality and behavior traits of students made by teachers, by parents, and by students through self-reports. They concluded that an increased number of conferences between parents and teachers (and other guidance workers) would shed much light on the context of student behavior.

In their role of guidance workers, teachers can utilize parent conferences with great effectiveness. An NEA (1959) study showed that 99.2 per cent of the public school teachers surveyed believed parent-teacher conferences to be important guidance vehicles but only 40 per cent made use of this practice. In Catholic high schools, the proportion may even be lower because of time limitations placed on many religious. Sister M. Gabrieline, I.H.M. (1955), has advocated that teachers employ the techniques of the counseling interview in the parent conference. Parent conferences held by teachers during home visitation are an important function of the teacher's dual role of instructional leader and guidance worker. Communities of women religious teachers whose constitutions forbid home visitation during the day, or after dark, or without a sister-companion might make appropriate modifications in order to render their educational apostolate more fruitful.

Conferences between counselors and parents, while similar to teacher-parent conferences, evince some important differences. Parent-counselor consultations are discussed in Chapter 11.

The case conference

The case conference is a meeting of guidance workers, teachers, administrators, and school personnel specialists who have worked with a particular student. Parents are frequently invited to attend. The purpose of the conference is to pool information, share understanding, and collectively discuss the developmental status of an individual student. A number of investigations have demonstrated that teachers, counselors, guidance specialists, clergymen, and others do not understand the student or client as well as they believe. Often they have an erroneous or one-sided impression of the client, through no fault of their own. They observe the student typically in but one, relatively restricted, social situation. This type of observation often can cause a distorted image, since behavior is a function of self in the totality of life situations, not merely in one situation. A composite and hence more accurate picture of the student can usually be gained only from a pooling of information and of understanding. In the case conference each person's restricted perception of the student broadens into a total portrayal of the self in the total life situation, a portrayal which not only amplifies but many times radically alters a personal observation. For example, the history teacher alleges that a student presents overt misbehavior problems, while the art teacher says he is extremely creative, the counselor notes his emotional sensitivity, the social worker reports that the boy has been working to augment the family income during his father's unemployment, his employer considers him dependable, and the school nurse notes a residual anemia which foreshortens physical activity. Margolin and Williamson (1961, p. 11) have commented that, despite the fact that the case conference has long been recognized as a sound data-gathering and assessment technique, it has only recently been introduced into the school program.

Sociometric devices

Sociometry is a general technique which attempts to ascertain the dynamic interpersonal relationships among members of a group (Moreno, 1953, pp. 140–175). It is valuable in guidance assessment in identifying students whose peer relationships are hindering or assisting their self-actualization. In recording the interpersonal relationship or social interaction a "sociogram" is drawn as a graph of this social interaction. Arrows are used to indicate communication pathways or choices of working-group partners, dotted lines to indicate rejections, and double-headed arrows to indicate reciprocated choices. Persons receiving many communications or choices are called *stars,* while those receiving few communications or choices are termed *isolates.* Guidance workers tend to be more deeply concerned with isolates than with stars since the former often represent students who have failed to self-actualize in some developmental area. Gronlund (1959, pp. 289–291) has identified five types of isolates, viz., the self-sufficient, the withdrawn, the aggressive, the cultural, and the emotionally disturbed.

There are two basic types of sociometric devices, the unstructured and the structured. The *unstructured sociometric device* consists in carefully observing and recording social communication and other social interaction among members of a group or of an aggregate. For example, Krech et al. (1962, pp. 390–392) present detailed tables delineating the social interaction among world political leaders during the 1960 United Nations General Assembly. In this situation, Premier Nikita S. Khrushchev appeared to be the star, i.e., the center of social interaction. President Dwight D. Eisenhower received social communication through personal visits from a number of world political leaders, but he did not reciprocate. Prime Minister Harold Macmillan acted as his emissary in one-way communications with Khrushchev. Social psychologists have developed the unstructured sociometric device into a sophisticated observational procedure and have produced elaborate mathematical formulas to determine group and individual expansiveness, cohesiveness, and integration.

Since few teachers or guidance workers have developed acute social observational skill, *structured sociometric devices* are typically employed in the school setting. These devices ask the student to indicate his choices among his peers or classmates relative to a school activity, a class activity, or a leisure-time activity. Such questions as "With whom would you like to work on a class project?" represent *task-oriented* sociometric devices. Such questions as "With whom would you like to spend a leisure afternoon?" represent *person-oriented* devices. There are inherent weaknesses in both types as far as the school situation is concerned. The task-oriented question is likely to indicate that the academically able or socioeconomically advantaged students are stars. The person-oriented question imposes the limitation of confining the respondent's choices to members of his class; in fact, the student's closest friends may be persons attending other schools. Thus it is virtually impossible to conclude that a student is a social isolate on the basis of a sociometric device alone. Further, the sociometric choice might possibly be a momentary and fleeting phenomenon. Only when certain students are consistently rejected by their peers in a variety of types of social situations (e.g., different classes) is there need for concern by the counselor and other guidance workers. Even then, this information must be integrated with other sources of data. The unconsidered haste of some teachers and guidance people to shove the presumed isolate into social activity (e.g., by pairing him with a star as with a "big brother") *may* actually hinder rather than accelerate his own unique developmental progress. Unless and until the guidance worker has the opportunity to observe all variations in self-behavior as a function of situational variation, extreme caution is in order. The purpose in collecting sociometric data is to assess a student's social development, not to inaugurate drastic social reorganization.

PSYCHOMETRIC INSTRUMENTS
IN GUIDANCE ASSESSMENT

Psychometric instruments, i.e., psychological tests, constitute perhaps the most sophisticated and well-developed assessment techniques used in guidance. It is therefore an imperative obligation for all guidance workers, including teachers (Noll, 1961) and counselors, to develop a thorough, functional understanding of the underlying theory, statistical framework, developmental availability, and applicability of psychometric instruments in the guidance process. Indeed, professional competence in guidance testing and test interpretation is a categorical moral imperative for the guidance worker. Adequate counselor training of necessity includes course work in psychometrics and supervised practice in the use of tests in counseling. Every school person needs a basic understanding of test construction. Since it is assumed that both prospective counselors and teachers will take rigorous courses in testing, this chapter presents a brief overview of salient issues in the use of tests in guidance assessment. Detailed information about educational, psychological, and guidance tests has been presented by Anastasi (1962), Berdie et al. (1963), Cronbach (1960), Super and Crites (1962), and R. L. Thorndike and Elizabeth Hagen (1961). Especially valuable is Goldman's work (1962), which focuses on the use of tests in counseling.

Steimel (1960) urges that all test users need an adequate understanding of (1) psychometric statistics, especially of such concepts as mean, median, standard deviation, standard error of measurement, regression and prediction, and percentile; (2) reliability; (3) validity; and (4) the construction and use of appropriate norms, since this information is essential for accurate test interpretation. Seashore (1958) has suggested that psychometric instruments serve such interrelated purposes as administration and counseling, prediction and description. Goldman (1962) has identified four principal non-counseling uses of psychological tests: (1) selection of candidates for the school, (2) placement of individuals within the school, (3) adaptation of institutional practices to meet the needs and characteristics of particular individuals, and (4) development and revision of school practices to meet the needs and characteristics of students in general. Hence it can be seen that psychological tests are essential in a comprehensive school guidance program.

Some common misunderstandings about psychological tests

A number of misunderstandings impair the efficiency of both school-wide testing and individual testing for counseling purposes. *First,* teachers and counselors frequently misunderstand what can be predicted from the results of psychological tests. If the XYZ Test of Archaeological Aptitude is reported by the test publisher to have high correlation with success in an archaeological career, guidance workers commonly assume that the results of an XYZ test administered to a high school senior are capable of predicting success in such a career. When one examines the XYZ test manual more closely, however, one finds that the test has been standardized on a sample of archaeologists whose mean age is forty-two. From this information, it is impossible to determine what these successful archaeologists were like when they were eighteen; even more important, it is impossible to ascertain how they might have performed on the XYZ test had they taken it at the age of eighteen. Thus it is not absolute success which can be predicted, but only *similarity*. In other words, the results of the XYZ test might be used to find out whether a high school senior bears resemblance to a forty-two-year-old archaeologist. Whether such resemblance is sufficient to indicate probable success in the field is a most unsettled question. The same observations apply to values inventories and personality measures. For a test to claim true predictability, it is necessary to execute a longitudinal study. Such an investigation would minimally involve the following steps: (1) A large number (preferably in tens of thousands) of high school seniors are tested in 1970 on a particular battery. (2) At five-year intervals until the year 2000, each subject is retested on the same battery. (3) After the year 2000, statistical calculations are computed to determine the fashion in which the 1970 scores relate to the subjects' occupational status in 2000. (4) It is now possible to use the 1970 results to predict success. Great caution must still be exercised, however, since the social factors influencing development of high school students in the years 2000–2010 may be quite different from those acting on the original subjects in the years 1960–1970. Very few such longitudinal studies have been carried out. An approach was made by R. L. Thorndike and Elizabeth Hagen (1959, pp. 22–50), who studied a group of 10,000 officer candidates tested in 1943 by the United States Army Air Force. Super's Career Pattern Study (1961) is a longitudinal investigation of vocational development, and Flanagan's Project Talent (Flanagan & Dailey, 1960) is a long-range study of academically able students.

Second, there is widespread belief that the aptitude, interests, values, or personality characteristics measured by tests constitute psychological realities. This belief points up what is essentially a methodological problem in test construction. For example, a group of research workers wishes to construct a test which will indicate similarity between test subjects and chronic alcoholics. A vast number of items, relating to family background, behavior patterns, religious beliefs, political attitudes, and even reading comprehension and school achievement, are included in the first or experimental form of the test. The test is administered to a sample of chronic alcoholics and nonalcoholics. Items which fail to discriminate significantly between the two groups are discarded from the instrument. It is administered again, and norm groups are established. By the process of what Townsend (1953, pp. 20–23) has called "the word magic game," the researchers dub the instrument the "Alcoholism Proneness Scale." This appellation seems justified, since the instrument adequately discriminates between alcoholics and nonalcoholics. A mass of statistical computation adequately demonstrates the instrument's discriminatory power, but essentially a number of test items have been related to *one* sort of behavior only. Sometime later, another researcher in an altogether different context attempts to find the correlates of creativity. Unfortunately, he is a believer in the "scattershot" technique; so he uses a wide variety of instruments, whether or not he believes that the trait these devices allege to measure is related to creativity. The introduction of computer technology makes his scattershot technique feasible. To his surprise and to the chagrin of the first researchers, the Alcoholism Proneness Scale shows a high relationship to creativity. Alcoholism proneness as defined in this instrument becomes an invalid construct or concept. What the instrument now appears to measure is social deviation. Since the first group of researchers had investigated but one sort of behavior, the relationship or predictive efficiency of the instrument to other types of behavior was unknown to them. In the meantime, of course, it is likely that a number of potentially creative children in the schools had been identified as potential alcoholics on the basis of the Alcoholism Proneness Scale and had been given special guidance services to prevent their falling victim to John Barleycorn (see Bernardoni, 1964). The statistical technique of factor analysis (Cattell, 1958) is likely to obviate the word magic game in psychometric construction.

Third, there is the more basic assumption that "correct" responses to objective test items (e.g., multiple-choice items) display *additive* properties. This assumption is rooted in the notions that an *absolute* zero exists, that there are *equal units* between raw score points, and that items are necessarily *homogeneous* as long as they vary in common statistically. In other words, raw scores of 85 on an instrument whose maximum score is 130 are regarded as equivalent, despite the fact that there are literally thousands of possible combinations of 130 items taken 85 at a time capable of producing identical raw scores (Nordberg, 1955a; 1955b; 1955c). The larger relevant issue seems to be the *cognitive style* of subjects who use vastly different thought processes to arrive at identical scores (Gardner et al., 1959, pp. 137–146). Until further research is reported, there is little justification for assuming that those who make identical scores on tests have identical cognitive styles and thus are equal in whatever item or manner of solving the item on the instrument is tested.

Fourth, there is the more familiar confusion of testing with counseling. M. J. Byrne (1958) charged that counselors have the responsibility to see that students learn as early as possible that the counseling process does not consist in taking a battery of tests and learning the test results. Steimel (1961b) accurately and acutely characterized the situation:

> Somehow as soon as testing is mentioned, the whole [attitudinal] set of the counseling relationship is changed. In the first place, there is the tendency of the client to look to these instruments for answers to his problems. It is almost as though testing process becomes a substitute for counseling process. The onerous task of systematically working through each step . . . in an attempt to reach an acceptable solution is ignored and in its place the student looks to a test to do what he himself is unwilling or unable to do. Instead of seeking a psychological sound solution which results from a careful consideration of one's strengths and weaknesses, one's likes and dislikes, and one's preferences and prejudices, the client is led to settle for a few unrelated findings about his ability, achievement, and interests. The counselor, too, is often tempted to use the test as a crutch. It is so easy to assign a battery of tests, interpret the results, and assume that the findings will resolve any difficulties the client may have. In either of these cases, the psychological test actually constitutes a hindrance to the counseling relationship. Chances are that had the individual been left to work through his own problems in the absence of both the tests and the counselor, he would be better off.

Categories of psychological tests

Psychological tests may be classified in two ways, viz., according to the internal structure of items and according to their purpose. The items in a psychometric instrument are miniature stimulus situations to which subjects are asked to respond. Stimulus situations of *high internal structure* limit the subject's ways of responding. For example, there are only two ways of responding in a yes-no or true-false examination. Multiple-choice examinations may increase the ways of responding to four or five by presenting four or five different possible selections. These exemplify items of high internal-stimulus structure. On an arithmetic achievement test or a classroom test, the subject may be given a problem and told to record only the answer. His ways of behaving in solving the problem are not limited by the internal structure of the test item. This type of item represents *relatively moderate internal structure;* nonetheless the subject's attention is focused on an internally structured field, in this case mathematical ways of behaving. An essay question which requires the subject to write about the causes of the French Revolution increases the possible ways of behaving. The same is true, for example, in a personality inventory which uses the incomplete-sentence technique. These illustrate items of *markedly low internal structure.* When the examination directs the student to write an essay on a topic of his choice or when he is asked to react to an inkblot, the opportunities for behaving are vastly increased. These are items of *very low internal structure.* Some students respond considerably more freely when they are confronted with test situations which seem to define a particular role for them, while others respond more freely and more efficiently when they are allowed to structure their own ways of behaving. The interpretive counselor is especially interested in the client's free response, but he also needs to know about the client's ways of behaving in more structured situations. Thus, the counselor needs information both from standardized objective instruments, from less highly structured devices, and from projective instruments in developing an accurate working image of the client.

Psychometric instruments may be categorized according to the characteristics they attempt to measure. The more common instruments are those which attempt to measure intelligence, academic aptitude, scholastic achievement, special aptitudes, specific aptitudes, interests, and personality.

Intelligence tests measure what Wechsler (1958, p. 7) has called "the aggregate or global capacity of the individual to act purposefully, to think rationally and to deal effectively with the environment." Operationally, intelligence seems to indicate the individual's capacity to profit from experience. This reinforces the standard concept that intelligence is a measure of a person's ability to make associations. Intelligence tests of high internal structure include such instruments as the California Short-form Test of Mental Maturity, the Concept Mastery Test, the Henmon-Nelson Tests of Mental Ability, the Ohio State University Psychological Test, the Otis Quick-scoring Mental Ability Test, and the Pintner General Ability Tests. Intelligence tests of low structure, e.g., the Revised Stanford-Binet Scale and the Wechsler Intelligence Scales, are clinical instruments, administered and interpreted only by those with special training in clinical psychological examination. In general, intelligence tests with high internal structure tend to be group intelligence tests, while those with low internal structure are usually individual intelligence tests.

Academic aptitude tests attempt to assess the student's ability to profit from a particular type of academic experience, e.g., continued education. The Cooperative School and College Ability Tests (SCAT), the Science Research Associates' Tests of Educational Ability, and the Psychological Corporation's College Qualifying Test are examples of scholastic aptitude tests available to the counselor and guidance staff. The Scholastic Aptitude Test of the College Entrance Examination Board is restricted in its sale and use. Most scholastic aptitude tests report both verbal ability and nonverbal or mathematical ability scores.

Scholastic achievement tests evaluate the development of educational skills and measure specific learnings. In this category are the Sequential Tests of Educational Progress (STEP), the Stanford Achievement Tests, and the Iowa Tests of Educational Development (ITED). These tests usually present a multiscore profile. The STEP series, for example, reports scores in reading, writing, mathematics, science, social studies, listening, and essay composition.

Special aptitude batteries measure the student's ability in a number of discrete fields. This category includes the Differential Aptitude Test Battery (DAT), the Flanagan Aptitude Classification Tests (FACT), and the California Multiple Aptitude Tests. These tests usually report a number of scores on discrete aptitude instruments. The DAT, for example, reports scores in verbal reasoning, numerical ability, abstract reasoning, space relations, mechanical reasoning, clerical speed and accuracy, spelling, and sentence usage. The National Merit Scholarship Qualifying Test is a multifactor scholastic aptitude battery with restricted use.

Specific aptitude tests attempt to assess ability in specific areas. Examples of this kind of instrument include the Bennett Test of Mechanical Reasoning and the Seashore Test of Musical Ability.

Interest inventories endeavor to appraise the student's interests, usually educational and occupational. In this category are the Kuder Vocational and Occupational Preferences Records, the California Occupational and Vocational Interest Inventories, the Thurstone Interest Schedule, and the Strong Vocational Interest Blanks for men and for women. While these instruments are of markedly to moderately high stimulus structure, the Ammons Vocational Apperception Test is of markedly low structure.

Personality and adjustment inventories attempt to assess personality traits, structure, and functioning. Of particular importance in school guidance and counseling are such instruments as the Science Research Associates' Youth Inventory and the Mooney Problem Check Lists, high school form and college form, which present global impressions of student perceptual concerns useful in counseling and in group guidance. Other tests in this category are the Bernreuter Personality Inventory, the California Psychological Inventory, the Minnesota Counseling Inventory, and the Edwards Personal Preference Schedule. A personality measure of high internal structure which has proved extremely valuable in the differential diagnosis of emotional disturbance is the Minnesota Multiphasic Personality Inventory. This instrument, however, is restricted in sale and use to properly qualified psychologists who are members of the American Psychological Association. This restriction also applies to such low-structure personality measures as the Rorschach Psychodiagnostic Plates, the Thematic Apperception Test, the Children's Apperception Test, and the Blacky Pictures. Personality measures of low internal structure available to properly qualified counselors are the Rotter Incomplete Sentences Blank and the Rohde Incomplete Sentences Test. The chief source of information about, and informed critical evaluation of, psychological tests is the *Mental Measurements Yearbook,* edited by Oscar Krisen Buros of Rutgers University and published by the Gryphon Press, Highland Park, N.J. It is imperative that each school guidance office contain at least one copy of the current edition for use by counselors, other guidance workers, and interested teachers and administrators.

Integration of assessment data in counseling

The role of the counselor in preparing for the counseling relationship consists primarily in integrating assessment data into an initial working image of the client. This image of the client, derived as it is from data rather than from a personal encounter, must of necessity be elaborated, modified, and altered as the relationship unfolds. The process of integrating assessment data into a valid picture is largely an exercise in *internal consistency.* Thus, for example, the available precounseling data reveal that a male client lives with his grandmother, a maiden aunt, three sisters, and a mother and father. This information might lead the counselor to infer that the client is possibly subject to excessive female domination. Such an hypothesis must be held tentatively, however, until its tenability is checked through reference to other information gained from cumulative records, from psychometric instruments, and, most important, from the counseling interview itself (Bonney & McGenearty, 1962). Indeed, it is imperative that the counselor regard *all* assessment data, even though gleaned from the interview, as tentative. His purpose is not to diagnose, evaluate, or judge the client but to assist him to understand himself better and thereby to self-actualize optimally. The phenomenologically oriented school counselor answers affirmatively C. R. Rogers' trenchant question (1961, p. 55): "Can I meet this other individual [i.e., the client] as a person who is in process of *becoming,* or will I be bound by his past and by my past?" Rogers goes on to assert that "If, in my encounter with him, I am dealing with him as an immature child, an ignorant student, a neurotic personality, or a psychopath, each of these concepts of mine limits what he can be in the relationship." Tyler (1961) expressed the same comment in different language when she insisted that assessment data in counseling are intended for the benefit of and use by the client. In counseling, as opposed to other educational and instructional services, assessment data are used for description rather than evaluation or diagnosis.

A Paradigm for Assessment and Data Gathering in Counseling

Sundberg and Tyler (1962, pp. 86–88) have elaborated an "information-processing" model or paradigm for the work of the clinical psychologist. Adapted for assessment in school counseling, the paradigm consists of four distinct but related stages—preparation, input, processing, and output—which constitute steps in which the data are gathered, collated, and utilized for guidance purposes.

In the *preparation* stage, before the client comes into the office for the first interview, the counselor's role is to receive data from three sources: (1) information from the referring source or from the client himself as to the purpose for seeking counseling; (2) precontact data from cumulative records, psychometric records, and other sources; and (3) the counselor's own relevant speculative knowledge, e.g., of personality theory, developmental patterns, vocational development theory, labor-market information, and the like.

In the *input* stage, which usually occurs as a result of the counselor-client encounter, there are six steps: (1) The counselor utilizes the data gathered in the preparation stage, supplementing these with further intake information, e.g., a guidance questionnaire. (2) The counselor develops a working model of the client, viz., a picture of his personality structure and perceptual concern as revealed from the data. (3) The counselor may make initial decisions in cooperation with the client for further assessment (in an interpretive counseling situation, this decision is frequently made by the client after the counselor has expansively reflected his feelings). (4) Contact information is obtained from the counselor's observations and from statements made by the client during the interviews. (5) This contact information interacts with the goals of this particular counseling relationship as seen by the client and to an important, though lesser, extent by the counselor. (6) Decisions are jointly made by the client and the counselor relative to the need for further assessment information, e.g., to confirm a certain self-aspiration.

In the *processing* stage four principal steps occur: (1) Mechanical procedures are used to organize assessment data; e.g., tests are scored. (2) In relevant instances (e.g., psychometric devices) statistical procedures are employed to organize data; i.e., prediction equations are applied to test results. (3) These procedures interact with the counselor's inferential processing and organizing of data in terms of the client's life history and, more important, in terms of how life history currently affects self-organization. (4) Statistical and clinical inferences interact to produce the counselor's professional interpretation of the self-situation of the client; i.e., a working model of the client is elaborated more fully.

In the final or *output* stage, (1) the counselor and the client *jointly* interpret assessment data, with the counselor offering confirmation and support as needed or assisting the client to expand his phenomenal field; (2) other sources of information about the client *may* be tapped (e.g., a case conference may ensue); and (3) these additional data, intersecting and meshing with the now reasonably well-developed working image of the client, allow the client and counselor to consider the course of action to be followed (e.g., continuation in counseling, referral to a remedial education specialist, referral to psychological service specialists, or a decision to seek placement in the labor market or an institution of higher learning).

This model involves both "clinical" and "statistical" processing of assessment information (Meehl, 1954, pp. 83–127). Constant interaction between assessment information, counselor observation, and client response ensures that assessment data are interpreted *ipsatively*, as well as normatively, i.e., within the client's frame of reference. It must be emphasized that in an interpretive counseling relationship it is the client whose working image of himself is the important factor; i.e., these four stages have as one of their purposes to assist the client to develop an accurate working image. An indispensable purpose is to give the counselor a tentative working image of the client.

Ethical and moral use of guidance data

One overriding principle governs the use of assessment data and techniques in a developmental guidance program. In its simplest form, this principle holds that *the school ethically and morally has no right to elicit information from students unless that information will be used with reasonable speed to the direct or indirect benefit of the student.* The structuring of the school environment or any aspect of it for the purpose of facilitating pupil development contributes directly to the student's welfare. Similarly, research and data gathering about student development promote the welfare of the individual student. The mere collection of information with no intention of relating that information to the student or helping him integrate it into the self-structure, however, cannot be justified. Msgr. Goebel (1941b, p. 74) observed that mere record keeping in no wise constitutes guidance. At worst, record keeping and test scoring become busy work for an emasculated guidance staff. At best, they highlight a lack of consideration for the student's self-actualization.

The principle enunciated in the previous paragraph has far-reaching impli-

cations, some of which are perhaps not immediately evident. One such implication is that all standard tests, of whatever type and for whatever purpose,
must be interpreted individually to the student in such fashion that he is
able to utilize them in a meaningful manner to promote self-actualization.
Even achievement batteries administered for purposes of placement or grouping within the school should be interpreted to the student. The tests exist
for the student, not the student for the tests. Indeed, Fr. Paul, O.S.F.S.
(1961), has advocated making the student the custodian of his own cumulative record. Such a responsibility-centered suggestion implies that the counselor-student ratio is low enough to permit personal, confidential contact between the individual student and the counselor following any school-wide or
class-wide testing program. The time needed for the test interpretation interview varies in accord with the student's present level of self-actualization and
his ability to incorporate into his self-structure new or even threatening perceptions. Frequently the client may wish to establish a counseling relationship
for purposes of self-exploration after a test-interpretation interview.

A second implication concerns the use of assessment and formal data-
gathering techniques during the counseling process itself. Since the interpretive counselor enters the counseling relationship with a wide array of cumulative records, anecdotal reports, psychometric results, and other relevant data,
the use of tests and other formal data-gathering devices during counseling
occurs only when there is real need for information beyond what is already
available. The counselor's function is to help the client integrate, order, and
find meaning in his developmental history. What is of primary importance
in the counseling relationship is the client's own perception of his self-organization and level of self-actualization. The client's developmental history is
valuable only insofar as it illumines his *present* behavior and his
self-organization.

Confidentiality

All pupil assessment data, including questionnaires, autobiographies, and
psychometric results constitute privileged information, i.e., entrusted professional secrets. This is also true of information revealed by the client *during*
the counseling interview. As entrusted secrets, such information *must* be kept
confidential by the counselor and guidance worker. The only exception occurs
when the professional judgments of the counselor, psychologist, and psychiatrist concur that the client is incapable of managing his own affairs. Since
it is most unlikely that a student with such a tenuous grasp on reality would
be able to maintain himself well enough to function in a school setting,
this case is more hypothetical than real.

The question of the precise limits of confidentiality, however, needs clarification. Tennyson, Blocher, and Johnson (1964) have reported three situations. In the first instance, a group of parents in one large metropolitan

suburb demanded that the school drop a personality inventory from its testing program. In the second case, the executive council of a state school board association resolved that student personnel records are the joint property of school and parent and that parental consent must be obtained before any information is released to an agency or individual outside the school. In the third situation, a parent in a populous New York City suburb demanded to see certain information in his child's cumulative record. When this parent was denied permission, he carried his case to the New York State Supreme Court, which ruled in favor of the parent. The state commissioner of education subsequently ruled that the state must respect the wishes of parents to review school records. As a result of the notoriety and publicity given to this case, when the new local school board was elected, it promptly installed a regulation that no tests might be administered without the prior consent of parents. Less well known is a 1961 court ruling in a suburb of Washington, D.C., concerning anecdotal records. During a parent-teacher conference, a mother happened to notice what she regarded as a derogatory comment about her son on his cumulative record. The mother charged defamation of character and subsequently won a court ruling in her favor. In the early 1960s a popular book accused school counselors who administer personality inventories of practicing medicine without a license. Gross (1962) contended that emotional development is a proper concern only for the psychiatrist, a licensed physician. Hence, he charged, school counselors who administer personality tests are guilty of practicing psychiatry without a license. Strangely, some segments of the Catholic press supported this position, though it betrays a lack of familiarity either with human developmental needs or with the goals of guidance.

A number of commentators have urged that confidentiality in the counseling relationship is relative rather than absolute. Notwithstanding, the present writers strongly assert that no guidance worker may ethically or morally release information about the client to *anyone,* including his parents, administrators, or school specialists without the formal, express permission of the client. In actual practice, few students refuse permission. Nevertheless, the ethical dilemma remains. Parents, as the prime educators, have primary rights and responsibilities for their children. Yet parents are bound to respect the inviolability, integrity, and privacy of their children. Most parents typically lack a sophisticated understanding of the meaning of psychometric results. Thus, for example, to reveal the intelligence quotient, expecially in view of the lack of comparability of IQ scores on different standardized tests, is to invite confusion and perhaps resentment, not to mention odious neighborhood comparisons. Indeed, information revealed during an interview may focus precisely on the issue of domineering parental control over the student as he attempts to fulfill the normal developmental task of emancipation from the home. To convey such information to his parents invites recrimination against the student and may destroy the counseling relationship. The growth-facilitating relationship in counseling must be kept absolutely, not relatively, free of the threat of evaluation.

An analogy between the counseling and the medical professions may cast clearer light on this brambly question of confidentiality. When the parent gives his family physician permission to treat his child, he relinquishes control over the physician's *choice* of assessment techniques or manner of treatment. Much, or even most, of the physician's concern is directed toward charting normal progress in physical development. To do so accurately, he chooses such techniques of assessment as he believes best suited to his purpose. The parent is equipped by neither professional competence nor experience to dispute his choice of methods, but the *parent reserves absolutely the right to discontinue* treatment at any time he wishes. In the school situation, the parent entrusts the education of his child to school authorities. School people alone have the professional competence and experience, for example, to determine the content of the curriculum. Only members of the English faculty have the competence and experience to select appropriate teaching tools and methods in that area of knowledge. The guidance function is implicit in education. Thus it seems to follow that only those with professional competence and experience in guidance are enabled to determine the choice of assessment techniques or "treatment" method. It must be emphasized, however, that the parent who disagrees with such procedures reserves absolutely the right to remove his child from the school setting as well as to institute either legal or political action directed at changing school policy. All analogies limp, as does this one. The counseling relationship may even involve a person's inviolability and integrity more than does the disease-treating relationship with a physician. Hence this analogy does not fully highlight the confidentiality which must undergird and pervade the counseling relationship.

In the practical situation, the counselor will probably find it easy to communicate to parents or other school people general comments on developmental difficulties which the client is undergoing without revealing confidences. The counselor may make statements to the effect that "John seems to be having some difficulty in social adjustment," rather than "John told me that he wants to crawl a wall whenever he's near a girl." It is essential that the counselor never *presume* the permission of the client to reveal confidences. Permission must always be formal and explicit, much like the permission a priest needs to reveal to another what was said under the seal of confession. Tennyson and his associates (1964) have offered the following as tentative guidelines to counselor confidentiality. First, in collecting information, the guidance worker can justify an invasion of another's privacy only if the information is to be used in the *school* in a way which is beneficial and helpful to students. Second, when the counselor either elicits, or allows the client or parent to divulge, personal information in the course of interviewing, testing, or other contact, the client or parent must be aware of the purpose for which the information is desired and the way in which it will be used. Third, the counselor must distinguish between appraisal data which describe the student's academic performance and those which describe his behavior and personality. Fourth, when a student specifically requests that certain information be held in confidence or *when such intent is reasonably interpreted from the content* of the counseling interview or the context of the relationship, the counselor may reveal such information only if a psychiatrist and a psychologist testify that the client is not capable of managing his own affairs. Fifth, in the case of other information, e.g., scores on psychometric tests, the counselor may reveal these data only if it is necessary to do so and when the purpose clearly is to help the student. The counselor must exercise his professional judgment in determining the extent to which he is able to communicate "a feeling for the student" without revealing specifics. This information should be conveyed in general, rather than in specific, terms. Until such a set of guidelines is accepted generally by parents and administrators, it is likely that the counselor will need to assert his position somewhat aggressively. Indeed, as S. C. Stone and B. Shertzer (1963, p. 45) have observed, "The behavior demanded in a counseling situation is frequently directly opposed to that required in a situation where the counselor interprets to nonclients that which he does with his clients. If the individual is not willing to defend and fight for what he knows and believes to be his appropriate, professional role, he should seek employment in a situation where this struggle has already been won for him. It should be noted that few, if any, such school situations exist."

9

SCHOOL COUNSELING:
APPROACHES AND MODELS

Nature of counseling

Counseling is commonly regarded as the heart or core of the guidance program. Not atypically, Moser and Moser (1963, p. 12) have written: "Within the guidance services, counseling may be thought of as the core of the helping process, essential for the proper administration of assistance to students as they attempt to solve their problems." According to this view, other guidance services are perhaps lures, overt or covert, through which to entice students into the counselor's office. Similarly, the teacher's discharge of guidance responsibilities is regarded as effective only when he is able to motivate the student for referral to the skilled professional counselor. This view seems typical of the counselor who seeks a secure niche in the educational enterprise. Implied in this position are the unwarranted assumptions that (1) every student needs counseling, apparently because he has "problems" of some nature which demand professional attention, and (2) the school guidance program exclusive of the counseling service is ineffective in fostering optimal student development.

243

A developmental orientation to guidance, however, regards the counseling function quite differently. Counseling is, to be sure, an important aspect of the guidance program. But of paramount importance, both in the guidance program and indeed in the work of the school counselor, is the entire *environmental structure* of the school (Salinger et al., 1960). In short, the incidence of serious personality or other disturbances varies in proportion to the degree to which the educational, family, and community structures have become guidance-saturated. It bears repetition that the school counselor is a specialist in human development, not in psychopathology or educational-vocational choice alone.

As was indicated in Chapter 3, *guidance* encompasses the totality of what is done in and by the school to assist the student to negotiate the tasks of development. Guidance thus implies the *organization of the total school environment* so as to facilitate positive development. The emphasis is on situational organization in relation to self-actualization. *Counseling* encompasses a more limited service, involving a relationship between a competent counselor who is particularly knowledgeable about human development and skilled in interview techniques and one or more students called clients. Through the counseling relationship, the counselor attempts to assist the client minimally so to *organize himself* as to facilitate the satisfactory accomplishment of developmental tasks. The emphasis in counseling is on self-organization in relation to both (1) consolidation of previously accomplished tasks and (2) readiness to accomplish remaining tasks. This notion of counseling does not presume the existence of problems embedded in the self or of obstacles to development insurmountable by the client, whether arising from self or from situation. Rather, it suggests that the specific function of the *school* counselor is to attempt to help the *student* organize his internal self-structure in order to maximize opportunities for self-actualization.

Disease and Crises Approaches

Regrettably, few counseling theorists have yet freed themselves from what Walker and Peiffer (1957) have called the "disease orientation." Most writers still emphasize the notion of the client as a person with a problem, as one who needs help, or as one who is racked by indecision. Thus Mortensen and Schmuller (1959, p. 301) state that counseling at bottom helps the client to meet his problems. According to Cottle and Downie (1960, p. 1), "The first task of the counselor is to identify those who need help." Similarly, Tolbert (1959, p. 6) comments that " . . . perhaps the meaning of counseling becomes a little clearer. It seems primarily to be helping people with problems." Fr. Curran (1952, p. 1) regards counseling as a relationship in which "*a person objectively surveys the past and present factors which enter into his personal confusions and conflicts.*" Each of these theorists emphasizes to a greater or lesser extent a disease orientation. More saliently for the work of the school counselor, each makes an unwarranted assumption that clients are experiencing disturbances, conflicts, problems, or even pathologies which demand professional intervention. Williamson (1961a, p. 181), whose earlier work had championed what might be considered a disease orientation, has commented: "Perhaps we may soon discover that developmental problems are normal in adolescents of varying social and cultural backgrounds, and that counseling is an educational service for all youth, not only those encountering unusual difficulties in their development."

Often counseling is viewed as the process of making decisions *with* or *for* the student relative to his education, career, or marriage. These are typically regarded as "critical life decisions." The aim of this approach to counseling is to resolve the present decision, rather than to build the capacity for independence in present and future decisions. Brother Philip Harris, O.S.F. (1960b, p. 18), has suggested that the major role of the counselor is "that of an objective listener who gently guides the counselee to . . . decisions." G. E. Smith (1955, p. 156) sees counseling as "essentially a process in which the counselor assists the counselee to make interpretations of facts relating to a choice, plan, or adjustment he needs to make." In the same vein, R. H. Byrne (1963, p. 61) speaks of counseling as *"a service of assistance . . . in which the intention is to influence the behavior of another person who seeks help in matters of plans and decisions, and in matters of satisfying interpersonal relationships."*

Although there has been virtually universal agreement that school counselors deal with essentially normal rather than pathological clients, the disease orientation persists, perpetuating an emphasis upon pathological rather than normal developmental problems (Sinick, 1961). Trout (1954) believes that such an orientation perdures because counselors have attempted to adapt the terminology of medicine and psychiatry in their efforts to become professionalized, "instead of developing new concepts to identify the new insights and discoveries of counseling." Although a body of evidence has suggested the lack of readiness for mature vocational choices in secondary school students, a decision-making orientation persists, perpetuating hit-and-run guidance (Pallone, 1961d). Since vacillation is characteristic of *normal* adolescence and in fact is essential to the process of exploration preparatory to the consolidation of secure self-identity, counseling which aims at making premature educational or vocational decisions may in the long run create more serious problems than it solves. Barry and Wolf's trenchant comment (1962, p. 188) applies here: *"The most widely used guidance practices defeat rather than implement the aim of helping the student."*

The Developmental Approach

To limit the process of counseling in schools to dealing with pathologies or, worse, to fostering premature life decisions is seriously to hinder a developmental thrust. Some alert guidance experts, such as Mathewson (1954; 1962, pp. 311–312), have urged that counseling needs to be seen as developmental, cumulative, oriented to long-range personal, social, and cultural development rather than to the solution of immediate difficulties, and open to all students rather than restricted to problem cases. Tyler (1958, p. 8), attuned to both a phenomenological personality theory and a developmental view, limits "the meaning of counseling to one kind of process—that of helping a person attain a clear sense of self-identity." Elsewhere, Tyler (1961, p. 17) suggests: "We can sum up by saying that the psychological purpose of counseling is to facilitate *development*." She considers counseling part of the process of education. As a person becomes more aware of his internal self-structure built up through previous development, the better able he will be to influence his subsequent development. "The main purposes of counseling are to promote this kind of awareness" (Tyler, 1961, p. 17). Arbuckle (1961, p. 139) emphasizes a phenomenological view when he says of counseling: "It is in the uniqueness of this relationship that the individual called the client begins to see things that he never saw before, begins to realize strengths he never knew he had, so that he can see and accept the unpleasant [i.e., open himself fully to his self-experience], and begins gradually to see a new and brighter world." Brother John M. Egan, F.S.C.H. (1961b), has provided an excellent summary along phenomenological-developmental lines:

> The desired outcomes of counseling would involve greater insight into self, an increased confidence in one's own problem-solving capacity, a newer and more adequate method of handling future problems, a reordered self-expectancy, a reorganization of one's perceptual field with regard to oneself and others, an incorporation into the self-structure of previously denied experiences . . . a greater degree of self-acceptance and self-approval.

C. R. Rogers' early definition (1942, p. 18) avoided either a disease or a choice-point orientation, but it failed to distinguish counseling from psychotherapy: "*Effective counseling consists of a definitely structured, permissive relationship which allows the client to gain an understanding of himself to a degree which enables him to take positive steps in the light of his new orientation.*"

These approaches view counseling as a process aimed at assisting the student or client in the organization of the self-system in order to assure facility in coping with remaining tasks of development. This organization of the self-system represents the consolidation of the elements of self-identity accruing from the successful accomplishment of earlier developmental tasks. Self-acceptance and the formation of a secure self-identity emerge as dominant themes. Focus is placed on normal developmental processes in normal clients. Developmental approaches seem more appropriate than disease orientations to the work of the school counselor, whose primary responsibility lies in fostering optimal self-actualization for all students. Since the developmental approach emphasizes readying the self for further developmental experiences, it is more appropriate than crisis-point or decision-making orientations. The developmental approach suggests that the primary role of the school counselor is to assist the client in the task of achieving integration of self-experience with self-perception and of helping him open the self-system to the expanding influence of his unfolding self-experience. Organization of the self for optimal personal development implies that the client has achieved the capacity to reflect integratively upon the meaning of his experience of himself and to order his self-experience integratively into the core of the self-concept. It is this phenomenon which Rudikoff and Kirk (1961) have called "mobilizing" the client toward self-actualization and which they regard as the goal of counseling.

Counseling versus Psychotherapy

An unfortunate legacy of the disease orientation has been widespread confusion between the scope and function of counseling and that of psychotherapy. Blum and Balinsky (1951, pp. 15–17), for example, make the unwarranted assumption that persons who seek counseling would actually prefer psychotherapeutic treatment but fear that a stigma may be attached. Hence, they conclude, counseling is synonymous with psychotherapy. It has already been mentioned that Rogers (1942; 1951) identifies counseling with psychotherapy. Arbuckle (1961, p. 145), a school counseling theorist who has attempted to adopt the Rogerian model without modification, has chastised school counselors who he believes "are still not aware that the Client-centered [i.e., Rogerian] counselor considers counseling and psychotherapy to be synonymous." Such an identification, however, seems possible only if one assumes that clients for school counseling are in fact diseased, seriously abnormal, or pathological personalities.

On the other hand, Tyler, among others, believes that psychotherapy is concerned with changes in deviant personality structures: "The aim of therapy is generally considered to be personality *change* of some sort. Let us use *counseling* to refer to a helping process the aim of which is *not to change the person but to enable him to utilize the resources he now has* for coping with life" (Tyler, 1961, p. 12). Brammer and Shostrom (1960, p. 6) characterize counseling as educational in nature, supportive to the client, and emphasizing service to normal persons. They regard psychotherapy as primarily reconstructive, focusing on conflicts and tensions of an embedded (rather than a developmental or situational) nature and emphasizing service to persons with severe or incapacitating emotional disorders. Sechrest (1958, pp. 2–10) reflects a widely held view when she suggests that the job of the counselor is to educate or re-educate, not treat, the student. In these approaches, counseling is not a synonym or even a euphemism for psychotherapy. Indeed, Super (1963a, p. 238) has charged: "Psychotherapists have misappropriated the term 'counseling' in order to make their work palatable to a larger public, and in so doing have done counseling a real disservice." Counseling, he continues, deals with students "who are facing the normal developmental tasks." In Super's view, training as a psychotherapist may actually disqualify one for the practice of counseling.

Lack of precision in distinguishing counseling from psychotherapy seems partially a semantic problem. Rogerians, for example, believe that any sort of encounter between a counselor following Rogerian methods and a client constitutes psychotherapy. But *therapy* designates a process of healing. Hence, the term implies a condition of pathology within the person who needs to be healed. The material object (to use Scholastic terminology) of psychotherapy is a pathology or an abnormality of the personality. Its formal object is the basic and fundamental reconstruction of the personality or the self to alleviate the pathological condition. In contrast, the material object of school counseling is a relatively normal self in the process of becoming. The formal object of school counseling is the organization or reorganization (i.e., the consolidation of past developmental experiences) of the self-structure in such a way that the self can undertake most fruitfully the remaining tasks of development. Changes in the basic structure of the personality are not implied in the counseling process, while they are central to the psychotherapeutic process. Nonetheless, both counseling and psychotherapy are essentially communicative acts which seek to assist the person. Thus the particular "tools" or techniques of communication used in one process *may* have implications for the other. A further consideration is that the school counselor works in a paternalistic setting with clients in the process of becoming, so that even highly self-defeating behaviors usually represent developmental difficulties rather than embedded pathological personality features. The treatment of a problem in lack of self-control in a high school freshman is vastly different from the treatment of the same problem in a middle-aged adult whose lack of self-control has had a history of a dozen years. Further, though most psychotherapy theorists insist that the successful therapist of necessity must be perceived as an equal by the patient, school counseling is indeed a student-educator interaction. The question is whether the school counselor can turn the student's inevitable perception of him to the student's benefit by becoming a truly "significant" other in the client's developmental process. The school counselor's role in mental health and personality integration is prophylactic and organizational, while that of the therapist is ameliorative and reconstructive.

Scope of Counseling

As an important guidance service and as the distinctive (though not necessarily the most important) function of the school counselor, counseling is an integral part of the entire guidance effort. Like that of other guidance services, the scope of counseling is not narrowed to the particular needs of those students who present recurrent problems. Unlike many other guidance services (e.g., the information or homeroom program), however, counseling is voluntary from the client's point of view. The *client* must seek to establish a relationship with the counselor if the relationship is to be fruitful. The counseling service is open to all students. This position does not imply that all students need counseling, even of a developmental nature. Indeed, a well-organized, comprehensive, developmentally oriented guidance program achieves success precisely by facilitating the accomplishment of developmental tasks. It is likely, however, that most pupils may benefit from consultation with the counselor concerning the degree to which their past developmental experiences have become consolidated in the elements of self-identity. The counseling service can often be of significant assistance to the student as he attempts to negotiate developmental tasks within the framework of his own unique developmental history. Counseling is available, for example, to the student making satisfactory developmental progress who wishes confirmation of a particular self-aspiration no less than to the student who is experiencing difficulty in the task of emancipation from the home. In Shoben's apt phrase (1962b) the aim of counseling is to facilitate "the examined life."

COUNSELING MODELS

The function of a theory of counseling is to make "'articulate a set of ideas by which the counselor can discover or create a necessary order out of the buzzing confusion of the counseling relationship" (Shoben, 1962a, p. 621). Whatever the field, *theory* represents an attempt to order the cumulative experiences of persons knowledgeable in the field (e.g., counselors) into valid general laws of behavior. A counseling theory thus represents a set of guidelines, or a *model,* for the behavior of the counselor in his professional relationship with clients.

If theories operate as models for counselor behavior, then it seems to follow that counselor behavior varies as theories vary. This hypothesis has been subjected to several investigations, which have produced the general finding that there are few differences in the actual behavior of counselors, regardless of their theoretical position, provided other conditions are met. Wrenn (1960) found that one's actual *experience* in counseling is a more important factor than theoretical orientation. There were no significant differences in the behavior of experienced counselors, irrespective of the theories they held. Hopke (1955) discovered that neither the attitudes of counselors nor their principal theoretical positions are evident in their actual counseling behavior. These findings seem to imply that the situational factors in school counseling tend to outweigh theoretical orientation. In a carefully constructed analysis of relationships considered ideal by psychotherapists of varying theoretical orientations, Fiedler (1953) found that psychoanalytic, Rogerian, Adlerian, and eclectic psychotherapists largely agree on notions of the ideal relationship. He concluded (1) the nature of the ideal therapeutic relationship is essentially similar among professionals who employ different methods of treatment founded on varying theoretical bases; (2) though they come from varying schools, therapists attempt to create essentially the same relationship with clients; and (3) the effective therapeutic relationship appears to be a function of "'expertness" rather than of theoretical position. Perhaps the major implication of the Fiedler study is that neither theory nor technique but the *quality of the relationship* between counselor and client is the principal dimension in the counseling process. Thus Patterson (1962, p. 110) contends, "Counseling is a *relationship;* it is not a bundle of techniques or a bag of tricks."

If the essence of counseling is *relationship,* then theories or models of counseling are blueprints offered the working school counselor which attempt to indicate how best to go about establishing meaningful relationships. Hence it is correct to assume that overlaps will be found. Indeed, Hahn and Mac-Lean (1955, p. 28) regard the difference between theories of counseling as virtually wholly semantic, "such as the once-heated battles between the 'directivists' and the 'non-directivists.' " Following a careful review of the literature, Brammer and Shostrom (1960, p. 25) suggest that "all approaches stress the significance of adequate rapport, acceptance of the client, need for support, professional status of the counselor, and some type of limits." Thorne (1962a) believes that the usual dichotomy between directive or counselor-centered models and nondirective or client-centered models is more artificial than real. He urges counselors to abandon their so-called theories and concentrate on elaborating operational descriptions for the dynamics of creating and maintaining a counseling relationship. Fr. Vander-Veldt, O.F.M., and Odenwald (1957, p. 277) comment:

> Any good counseling must naturally be client-centered in the sense that the problems, interests, and needs of the client are of primary importance; obviously the counselor cannot learn or decide for the counselee; neither should he try . . . to force his thoughts, opinions and feelings upon the client. It is questionable whether any efficient counselor [regardless of the theory he presumably espouses] has ever overlooked this rule.

Arbuckle (1961, p. 148) indeed contends that no counselor could deny that he is client-centered, unless he were engaged in a dialogue with himself.

"The question is not, 'Are you client-centered?' but rather, 'Just how client-centered are you?' If the answer is 'Not at all,' then it is difficult to see how such a person could be a successful counselor."

Mythical Directivism

There exists a popular misconception concerning "directive" or counselor-centered counseling. It is often thought that this model regards the client as a person in a state of dependence who needs the technical assistance of a professional helper; consequently it is the task of the counselor to assume an active role in initiating, shaping, and structuring the counseling relationship. He makes plans for the client and exhorts him to follow them. Indeed the student or client is usually termed a *counselee*. The passive form of the noun indicates that the student is perceived as one *to whom* something is done. This erroneous view of directivism insists that the counselee stands at a critical choice point and urgently needs direction from the counselor. The principal counselor behaviors involve advisement, the prescription of behavior, test giving, and exhortations to do good and avoid evil. Sister Mary Xavier, O.S.U. (1960, p. 35), supplied an almost classic index to the basic rationale of this view of the directive model when she commented: "The insufficiency of man in himself impels the counselor to advise others." The sketch of the mythical directivist portrays him as one who feels he, and only he, knows what is best for this client—or perhaps for any client. Indeed, only such a feeling could "impel" him to advise others.

This ultradirective point of view has been ascribed, doubtless by detractors, to E. G. Williamson. Yet this version of directivism begins to look like a straw man once one reads the Williamson works. The present writers do not contend that there are no school counselors who behave in the ways described. Indeed, ultradirectivist guidance workers are all too frequent, especially in Catholic schools where piety and obedience to a superior's unreasonable command to function as a counselor (without training, but to satisfy the demands of an accrediting agency) often substitute for competence. Similarly, Catholic tradition is often construed by religious counselors to mean lack of complete acceptance of the client, followed by the necessity of giving this son of Adam heavy-handed advisement. But the present writers do maintain that these workers are *not* directivists in the mold of Williamson or any other theorist; rather they are simply poor counselors. It is not the directivist model but rather the lack of the worker's competence and trust in the client which accounts for such behavior.

The primary issue in the directive versus nondirective controversy does not revolve around the question of the direction or nondirection of the client's life, value system, or plans by the counselor. Rather, the primary issue is the *control of communication* in the counseling process. In the Rogerian position, the counselor is *less* directive in controlling communication; in other models, the counselor is more active in communication control.

Client control: Rogerian nondirective model

Carl R. Rogers and his associates have elaborated a model for psychothera-peutic patients which has gained wide following among school counseling theorists. Rogers' nondirective model is firmly rooted in phenomenological personality theory and is quite compatible with a developmental-task orienta-tion. Nonetheless, it is a model derived from observation and experimenta-with clients facing major problems of psychopathology. Such school counsel-ing experts as Arbuckle and Patterson have adopted the model virtually with-out qualification. Indeed, Fr. VanderVeldt, O.F.M., and Odenwald (1957, p. 277) count Williamson as a convert to nondirectivism.

Nondirective counseling is essentially an unstructured process whereby the client gains insight into the dynamics of his personality or self-structure. With this insight, he is able to function more effectively. Ideally, the content, the course, and the direction of the interview are determined by the client. The counselor's role is to attempt to communicate an empathic understanding of the client's perceptual world. *Empathy,* an outgrowth of rapport, is the term used to designate the counselor's ability to experience the client's phe-nomenal self as it is experienced by the client, while still retaining his own identity (Rogers, 1951, pp. 29–30). Empathy develops only when the counse-lor experiences and communicates what Rogers (1942, pp. 126–128) calls "'unconditional positive regard" for the client. Unconditional positive regard implies that the counselor sees the client as a person of dignity and worth, with an unassailable right to self-direction. Indeed, the client has within him an urge toward self-direction, self-regulation, and positive health; the task of the counselor, Rogers maintains (1959a, p. 25), is to help him liber-ate this urge. Rogers (1957b) has suggested that there are six conditions necessary to effective counseling: (1) two persons are in psychological con-tact; (2) the first, called the client, "is in a state of incongruence, being vulnerable or anxious"; (3) the second, the counselor, is congruent or inte-grated in the relationship; (4) the counselor experiences unconditional posi-tive regard for the client; (5) the counselor experiences an empathic under-standing of the client's internal frame of reference and endeavors to com-municate this experience to him; and (6) the communication to the client of the counselor's emphatic understanding and unconditional positive re-gard is achieved to a minimal degree. According to Rogers, no other condi-tions are necessary. Significantly, Rogers indicates that neither special pro-fessional knowledge on the part of the counselor nor psychometric evaluation of the client is necessary to effective counseling. This emphasis on the lack of necessity for special professional knowledge is more pronounced in Rogers' later writings.

In order to create the kind of relationship which permits maximum growth in the client, Rogers (1961, pp. 50–55) believes that the counselor must be able to answer the following questions affirmatively: (1) Can I *be* in some way which can be perceived by the other person as trustworthy, as dependable and consistent? (2) Can I be expressive enough as a person so that what I am will be communicated unambiguously? (3) Can I let myself experience positive attitudes toward this other person, attitudes of warmth, caring, liking, interest, respect? (4) Can I be strong enough as a person to remain separate and distinct from the other; i.e., can I experience my own feelings and needs as well as his? (5) Am I secure enough within myself to permit him his separateness and distinctiveness; i.e., can I give him the freedom to *be?* (6) Can I let myself enter fully into his perceptual world, seeing things as he does, without judging or evaluating? (7) Can I receive him as he is and communicate this attitude? (8) Can I act with sufficient sensitivity in the relationship so that my behavior will not be perceived as a threat? (9) Can I free him from the threat of external evaluation? (10) Can I meet this other individual as a person who is in process of *becoming,* or will I be bound by his past and by my past? The foregoing treatment underscores the Rogerian stress on the total acceptance of the client and on the communicating of a warm, giving relationship in which the client feels free. For Rogers, however, such an atmosphere is only the means toward the end. This climate generates the client's release of negative and hostile feelings, which is followed in turn by a faint, initial expression by the client or patient of positive feelings. Gradually the client develops insights into his concerns, insights based on intellectual values and goals. Then he begins to initiate totally self-concerned and self-directed activities, after which he evaluates these activities.

Once a "helping" relationship has been established, it becomes the task of the counselor to assist the client to liberate his internal forces. In this existential encounter, counseling is "essentially a process of making free," to use Fr. van Kaam's phrase (1962, p. 403). When the internal forces driving the person toward positive health have been liberated, the client is able to achieve progressively higher levels of self-integration.

The principal modes of counselor *verbal* behavior in the nondirective interview flow correspond to his empathic, acceptant understanding of the client's perceptual world. Counselor verbal behavior is *reflective* of the intellectual and emotional content of the client's communication (Rogers, 1961, pp. 338–346). Never is judgment of the client, his feeling, his value system expressed or implied. Since the counselor simply reflects the client's communication back to him, it is assumed that the client is controlling the content of communication. If the counselor does not verbally reflect, he attempts to express his understanding of the client's communication through such nonverbal communicative signals or vocalizations as "Uh-huh" or "Mm-hmm." Originally, Rogers felt that counselor reflection of client content ought to be phrased in the form of a declarative statement. Later, however, he commented (Rogers, 1951, p. 28) that "when the counselor statement is declarative, it becomes an evaluation, a judgment made by the counselor, who is now telling the client what his feelings are." Since evaluative verbal behavior is antagonistic to nondirective principles, declarative statements are to be avoided.

Rogers early focused on the question of communication control as the distinctive characteristic of nondirectivism. If the counselor is responsive to the client's feelings and reflects his empathic understanding, the interview is client-centered, for "the material which comes forth is the material which is emotionally relevant to the client's problem." On the other hand (Rogers, 1942, p. 138), if the counselor responds to the intellectual content of the client's statements, "the direction of the interview follows the pattern of the counselor's interest." Elsewhere, Rogers (1951, p. 150) has suggested that the counselor avoid evaluative comments in order to underscore his total acceptance of the client as the locus of evaluation of his own feelings:

> In client-centered therapy, however, one description of the counselor's behavior is that he consistently keeps the locus of evaluation with the client. Some of this is evident in the way he phrases his responses. "You're angry at ———"; "You're confused by ———"; "It seems to you that ———"; "You feel that ———"; "You think you're bad because you ———." In each of these responses the attitude as well as the phrasing is such as to indicate that it is the *client's* evaluation of the situation which is being accepted.

It is evident that Rogers' basic orientation lies in the psychotherapeutic process. Whether his model is the *most* effective for school counselors is a question which needs serious rethinking. Certainly the Rogerian emphasis on the individual and his responsibility has had a salutary effect on the practice of school counseling, but the assumption that the client contains within himself sufficient resources to resolve the issue which has led him to seek counseling is perhaps less appropriate for school counseling than for psychotherapy. It has already been noted that one of the positive functions of the school counselor is to assist the client to expand his self-experience; the nondirective method, however, tends to make him a prisoner of his own perception, for the counselor merely reflects the client's feelings. The client-centered resistance to psychometric evaluation is also more appropriate for psychotherapy than for counseling.

The major issue which seems to give nondirective counseling its distinctiveness needs further exploration. The question as to whether a nondirectivist does indeed direct and control an interview as efficiently as a counselor of another persuasion may be legitimately raised. It is true that he does not question, probe, provide insights, or give advisement, but *in choosing client statements to which to respond, he is in effect both evaluating and focusing.*

He *evaluates* by responding to *this* but not to *that* statement. He *focuses* by the very response itself, indicating his own feeling that the content or mode of feeling of the statement *to which he responds* does indeed have significance. Counselor control of communication flow might be minimal in nondirective interviews, but it can hardly escape being both present and operative. The only sort of interview in which counselor influence does not control, modify, focus, or direct communication is one in which the invariable counselor behavior is *silence*. Empathic counselor responses probably tend to reinforce the communication of content similar to client statements which they follow, whatever the intent of the counselor. Indeed, one of the foundations of the interpretive model for school counselors is this principle of verbal reinforcement.

Counselor control models

Control of communication is assigned by other theorists to counselor rather than client. Generally, other models suggest variable counselor behavior during the course of the interview. The degree of direction and lead offered by the counselor varies in accord with the precise parameters of the counseling relationship he is attempting to establish with a particular client. As Thorne (1962a, p. 345) has suggested, the method of selecting appropriate techniques of counseling to fit "'the indications and contraindications of each individual case has long been the standard procedure in the older clinical sciences." Williamson (1950, p. 232) has urged that *"the effective counselor is one who adapts his techniques . . . to the personality of the student. . . . The essence of counseling is to do that which needs to be done to assist the student."*

Case Study Model

E. G. Williamson is the foremost exponent of the case study model, which emphasizes the ability of the counselor to synthesize relevant data about the client into a coherent picture. Clinical procedures suggested by the model (Williamson, 1950, pp. 101–102) include (1) analysis of the student through collection of data about him (e.g., from cumulative records); (2) synthesis of data to reveal significant trends in the student's strengths and weaknesses; (3) diagnosis, or drawing conclusions about the characteristics of the student and possible causative factors; (4) prognosis, or the prediction of likely future developments in the student's adjustments; (5) counseling, or "the steps taken by the student and the counselor to bring about adjustment and readjustment"; and (6) follow-up, including assistance with new problems or the recurrence of old problems and evaluation of the effectiveness of counseling. Thus Williamson's *"modus operandi . . .* is to collect as much data as possible before the student sees the counselor for his first interview" (1939, p. 64).

Counseling, the fifth step in the clinical procedure, is characterized as a relationship "in which the client takes full responsibility for participating in *learning about himself* with the counselor performing the secondary role of a 'teaching assistant' who aids in the learning process of the client-pupil" (Williamson, 1950, p. 109). Counseling includes *personalized assistance* to students "concerning a wide variety of *transitional, situational,* and *developmental* problems and assistance" (Williamson, 1950, p. 219). Thus counseling services are organized around student needs. Once the counseling relationship has been engaged following the collection and analysis of case data, the techniques of counseling include (1) *establishing rapport,* or the inspiration in the student of the feeling of personal understanding; (2) *cultivating self-understanding,* by motivating the student to utilize his assets optimally; (3) *advising or planning* a program of action through reaching cooperatively with the student an interpretation of data about self; (4) *carrying out* the plan thus initiated; and (5) if necessary *referring* the student to other personnel workers or specialists, for example, a remedial reading specialist (Williamson, 1939, pp. 131–138; 1950, pp. 225–239). Williamson and Darley (1937, p. 117) early warned counselors against dictatorial advising or persuading. Their conception of the student in a *normal, developmental* state of dependence upon adults is reflected in their comment: "He seems to want the counselor to be sympathetic in attitude yet positive in the suggestions [he makes]." Specific behaviors in the interview are only sketched lightly by Williamson (1950, p. 110; 1962). Both counselor and client participate in (1) the definition of the problem; (2) identification of associated self-attitudes; (3) identification and acceptance of the integrated roles of counselor and client as a *working team of learners;* (4) collection, refinement, and verification of relevant facts; (5) interpretation of the relevant facts and their implications; and (6) learning new ways of adjustment by the client with the encouragement of the counselor. Counselor verbal behaviors, typically include questioning, leading the client, explaining test results, and giving information.

Emphasis in Williamson's model is placed squarely on the expertness of the counselor. The counselor is not seen essentially as an expert in human development; rather, there is implicit in this model a problem-decision orientation. Williamson's case study model is not founded on a specific theory of personality function and development. Its roots seem to lie in a trait-and factor-prediction approach to vocational guidance, even though Williamson (1965) regards many problems as developmental in nature. This model avoids the disease orientation implicit in the client-centered model. That Williamson's model should have been pilloried as a directivist management of the client's affairs hardly squares with what he has written about counseling during more than a quarter of a century. It is true, however, that the counselor directs communication in this model more actively than in the

Rogerian model. Hence, Williamson's model contends that the counselor should seek to control the interview so that only data pertinent to the client's concern are discussed. Rogers, on the other hand, holds that whatever the client feels he has a need to discuss directly assists him. Williamson's model relies heavily on case history and psychometric data, while Rogers holds these to be irrelevant. However, the differences between the positions of Rogers and Williamson are becoming less noticeable. While Williamson (1962) regards "the counselor as technique" and admonishes the counselor to "be himself" in the interview, Rogers (1961) has urged that the counselor needs to be "dependably real," congruent, or genuine in the relationship.

Eclectic Model

Thorne (1959; 1962b) has offered a *directive-eclectic model* which attempts a reconciliation between the use of skillful diagnostic techniques and client-centered counseling in clinical psychology. In this model, the counselor assumes responsibility for the direction of the relationship while following nondirective communication patterns in the interview. Thorne's cardinal principle is that *the need for direction is inversely correlated with the person's potentialities for effective self-regulation.* The need for direction is determined by the counselor in his analysis of psychometric and other data on the client. The basic responsibility for the direction of the relationship rests on the counselor, even though he may choose to delegate some responsibility to the client himself. Thorne's model probably approaches the needs of the school counselor more closely than those of either Williamson or Rogers.

Cyclical Model

Super (1957, pp. 307–309) has sketched in germinal form a cyclical model for vocational counseling which seems well suited to school counseling. The principal orientations of Super, a counseling psychologist specializing in vocational development, are toward phenomenological personality theory and a developmental-tasks approach. Indeed, as is indicated in Chapter 15, he has applied both orientations to the investigation of vocational development. Though Super has not developed the model fully, it represents a sound current approach. Steps in the cyclical model include (1) nondirective *problem exploration* and self-concept portrayal; (2) directive topic setting for further exploration; (3) nondirective *reflection and clarification* of feeling for self-acceptance and insight; (4) directive *exploration of factual data* obtained from tests, occupational pamphlets, extracurricular experiences, and so forth, for reality testing; (5) nondirective *exploration* and *working through of attitudes* and feelings aroused by *reality testing;* and (6) nondirective consideration of possible lines of *action,* for help in decision making. This final step gives a decision orientation to Super's model. Nonetheless, it approximates a viable set of guidelines for the school counselor.

Self-in-situation Model

Mathewson (1962, pp. 317–318) has also sketched in germinal form a self-in-situation model along developmental lines. Like Super's, his model has not been elaborated fully. The tasks which Mathewson identifies for the school counselor are the following: (1) The counselor develops a *harmonious psychological relationship* with the client. (2) He then *draws the client out* through skillful questions, leading remarks, and encouraging comments to reveal how he is looking at things and how he is feeling about them. (3) As the counselor begins to move with the client in his "meanings," he *attempts to perceive* things in the way the client perceives them, the better to understand the client. (4) As he seeks to understand the client, he also *"sizes up" the client's situation* and his relation to it in its various aspects, i.e., what the client feels about himself, how he thinks others feel about him, his reactions to other people, his goals, his directions, and his values. (5) Through further questioning, leading, evaluating, and interpreting, the counselor *attempts to help the client utilize* the counseling experience as a means of rearranging and re-evaluating his perceptions of himself, of his situation, and of his relationships within that situation. Mathewson's model seems to be rooted in phenomenological personality theory, but his counselor behaviors exert far more communication control than is the case in the Rogerian model. Further, Mathewson does not indicate the role of the counselor in assisting the client to self-expansion by opening the self to new experiences.

Noncoercive Model

Nordbeg (1958), a Catholic counseling theorist, has offered a "noncoercive" model which attempts to correct what he believes are certain tendencies in nondirectivism unacceptable to Catholicism. His primary concern lies in the responsibility of the counselor in the area of material sin (to use Scholastic terminology). "A Catholic counselor cannot in conscience encourage a client who decides that the solution to his problems lies in committing adultery, abandoning the sacraments, practicing artificial birth control, or the like" (Nordberg, 1958, p. 43). Nordberg (1963c, p. 5) further objects: "A premise that 'anything goes' if it pleases the client is not compatible with Catholic thought, although we must remember that the counselor's concern with objective norms should be more strategic than tactical." Nordberg's basic assumption seems to be that the nondirective counselor, refraining from evaluative statements and placing the locus of evaluation totally within the client, might encourage material sin by reflecting feeling or remaining silent

Other Catholics have also examined this question, and they do not concur. Fr. J. T. Byrne (1960) concluded that the Rogerian notion which contends that man possesses strong tendencies toward the good within himself is not contrary to Catholic theology. Fr. Moynihan, S.J. (1958, p. 328), found no necessary conflict between nondirectivism and Catholicism. Pallone (1964) suggested that to be more expansive for Christian fulfillment of the person nondirective methodology needs to substitute a Christian philosophy of *person* for a Neo-Rousseauvian point of view. The *sui juris* character of person seems a sounder philosophic ballast for the person's inalienable right to self-direction. To correct this situation, Nordberg (1958) suggests the adoption of a noncoercive approach. Presumably, the noncoercive counselor indicates to the client that a contemplated plan of action involves material sin, but he does not prevent the client from implementing the plan beyond this admonition. Nordberg retains basic Rogerian procedures, while rejecting the phenomenological bases thereof. He (1963b) finds the roots of empathy, for example, not in the psychological reality of the counseling relationship but in what the Scholastics call "connatural knowledge." According to Nordberg (1958, p. 42), the noncoercive approach "retains such client-centered techniques as reflection of responses, supportiveness, and gentle probing, but we reject the assumption that any solution that serves to integrate the client is *therefore* satisfactory. We correct the 'authoritarian' by saying 'Lead, but lead gently.' We correct the non-directivist by saying, 'Lead gently, but lead.' " The noncoercive "model" has some relevance for the work of the school counselor, quite apart from its author's concern with material sin. A noncoercive approach to decision making in general, for example, might prove useful for the introduction of new elements of experience into the client's phenomenal field.

The self-interpretive model: synthesis for learning self

Earlier in this chapter, both disease and choice-point orientations were eschewed in favor of developmental approaches to the counseling function in schools. It has been emphasized that the client in school counseling is a person in the process of becoming, in the process of development. Such commonly encountered characteristics as dependence and alienation from one's family of origin usually represent for the student normal, even necessary, developmental realities rather than embedded pathologies. Hence, effective school counseling necessarily aims at assisting students to gain a firm sense of self-identity, to self-actualize, by consolidating the elements of self-identity which have accrued from the accomplishment of prior developmental tasks, by integrating these tentative and partial self-definitions into the organization of self-structure so that the remaining tasks may be negotiated satisfactorily. Effective counseling, indeed the effectiveness of all guidance services, is gauged by the extent to which the client is assisted to incorporate the totality of his self-experience, to reflect upon the meaning and implications of his experience of himself for his perception of himself, to open himself to the meaning for self of new experience, to formulate a realistic and realizable self-aspiration. In short, the ultimate goal of guidance, and perhaps of education, is self-knowledge; the process which characterizes education and guidance is the process of *learning self.*

The *self-interpretive model* is a dynamic synthesis of dynamic concepts about human development and about the process of communication intended to serve as a guide to behavior for the school counselor. Control of communication is lodged primarily in the counselor, who uses his communicative skills to assist the client to explore himself and ultimately to *learn himself.* The counselor's relevant knowledge about human development, especially of the developmental tasks characteristic of each life stage, alerts him to the probability that certain perceptual concerns are likely to arise. His knowledge of the effectively functioning personality alerts him to the necessity of attempting to enter the perceptual world of the client. The counselor's basic respect for the client's right to self-determination issues from his orientation toward a humanistic metaphysics of man and of value (and for Catholic interpretivists, toward a Judeo-Christian orientation). Hence the counselor believes that no one has a right to tamper with the internal person of another, that each person is essentially free in his human condition. Yet the counselor also recognizes that the individual experience of any single person is but a slit in the world of experience, and thus he may introduce percepts previously unavailable into the client's phenomenal field in order to assist the client toward the expansion of self. The school counselor following the self-interpretive model shares with the Rogerian therapist (though perhaps for different reasons) a firm belief in the basically positive thrust of each person.

The self-interpretive counselor seeks to help the client to interpret his self-experience, especially the experience of reception by the counselor as an object of value. When self is able to interpret the meaning of self-experience accurately, then self is ready to consolidate both a realistic perception of self in the here and now and a realizable self-aspiration. Then and only then is the self ready for the expansion of experience, for an existential overflow from self, for a "process of making free."

The self-interpretive school counselor, attuned to the developmental approach, has no need of hit-and-run counseling techniques. His client is almost invariably a student, whose life situation is largely a supportive school environment structured to facilitate development. The school counselor is in a position to attempt to create a relationship which extends not over days or months (as is the case in counseling in such settings as community agencies, rehabilitation centers, and hospitals) but over years. Under these circumstances, the counselor is enabled to contribute positively as a "catalyst" in the process of becoming. The interpretive counselor functions, in Perry and Estes' apt phrase (1953), as a ""collaborative consultant" in the process of development.

Communication Control: Mutual Contingency

The question of communication control largely distinguishes nondirective from directive counseling models, with other models occupying points on the continuum between the polarities of absolute client control and absolute counselor control. Self-interpretive school counseling falls at a point on this continuum closer to the nondirective polarity.

A more useful distinction, however, can be made in terms of the contingency of communication between the self-interpretive school counselor and his client. It has already been mentioned that the goal of this model is to help the client interpret the forces within his self-structure *for* and *by* himself. Through communication flow in the counseling relationship, the counselor attempts both to assist the client to discover the nature of self-forces and to act as an element of social reality against which the client can test his tentative interpretation of himself.

Sociologists who have applied Bales's procedures (1950) for interaction process analysis to the process of communication have distinguished three primary communication patterns. In the mutually independent (or mutually noncontingent) pattern, the verbal communication of one communicator has no measurable effect on the verbal communication of the second communicator. This pattern is typical of a conversation in which each speaker in fact is merely talking aloud to himself, not really communicating. In the partially contingent pattern, the verbal communication of the first communicator modifies to some degree the verbal communication of the second, but the second is also attentive to forces within himself which shape his own communication. A common example is an interview which follows a predetermined schedule, as in an employment situation. The employer or interviewer seeks to elicit certain kinds of information from the applicant. When the applicant responds (e.g., with information about a certain kind of previous experience), the interviewer deviates from his schedule of questions long enough to engage in conversation about this experience, but he soon returns to his schedule. In the mutually contingent communication pattern, the verbal communication of each communicator deeply affects the behavior of the other. In this situation, both attend to common objects of conversation, sharing perceptions in common and, in short, truly communicating.

In a larger context, counseling which adheres rigidly to any *single* type of verbal behavior, as does nondirective counseling with its emphasis upon the reflection of feeling, represents an only *partially* contingent communication pattern. The counseling model itself is the counselor's behavior "schedule." In self-interpretive counseling, the communication pattern is *mutually* contingent, since the counselor selects his verbal behaviors from a wide repertoire of such behaviors. Hence, the self-interpretive counselor employs not only a wide variety of verbal techniques in the course of the counseling relationship but even within the course of a single interview. As Williamson noted, the essence of counseling is to do that which assists the client. Thus, an adequate model for school counseling necessarily is not constricted to single modes of counselor verbal behavior. Counselors whose allegiance to a theoretical counseling model prevents true communication within the counseling process cannot create a mutually contingent relationship. To that extent, the counseling model may actually interfere with the counselor's goal of assistance to the student.

In a study of verbal behavior in school counseling supported by the U.S. Office of Education, Pallone and Grande (1964a) analyzed counseling interviews with psychologically normal secondary school students experiencing normal developmental concerns. The dimensions they investigated were the relationship between modes of counselor verbal behavior and the focus of the client's developmental concern. Their investigation showed that (1) the focus of the client's concern has no significant effect upon communication patterns in school counseling; (2) primary modes of counselor verbal behavior affect communication patterns; i.e., interpretive and confrontative verbal behavior, as single modes, produce significantly greater results than reflective or interrogative behavior; and (3) communication patterns in counseling are very significantly affected by the *interaction* of counselor verbal modes and the focus of the client's concern. Hence, Pallone and Grande (1964a, p. 13) concluded: "Were it assumed that the counselor's repertoire of verbal behavior is to be limited to a single mode, interpretive verbal behavior emerges as the modal verbal behavior most effective . . . when focus centers on normal developmental needs." The strongest finding, however, was: "These conclusions suggest that the school counselor needs to adopt a flexible repertoire of variable verbal behaviors from which to select that mode of communication best suited to the elicitation of content as . . . focus varies." In other words, the most effective counseling interviews are those characterized by mutually contingent communication patterns.

Shaping the Process

The starting point for the interpretive counseling process is the perceptual concern presented by the client. It is not, however, this immediate concern, difficulty, or problem which needs attention. Rather, the relationship of this particular concern to the client's perceptual field is the vital matter. In the *initial stages* of the relationship, the counselor commonly employs nondirective reflection of feeling in order to assist the client to generalize his perceptual attention by such communicative behaviors as expansive reflection, which tends to help the client connect his immediate concern with the phenomenal field. This subsequently prepares the client to explore the phenomenal field and to become ready to make the shift from the immediate perceptual concern to the parameters of self-structure. For example, the client who comes to the counselor's office with the lament that he has failed to meet the deadline for filing a scholarship application will perhaps be hindered in his development as a person if the counselor takes emergency steps in his behalf. The role of the counselor in this case is to broaden the client's concern from the immediate to the usual or habitual behavior pattern which may have been incorporated into the structure of the self. "Bailing the student out" is not a helping process in this case.

In the *middle stages* of the process, the counselor attempts to assist the client to relate his immediate perceptual concern to his wider personality structure. Thus, in the case of the student mentioned above, is the failure to meet the deadline an outcome of a passive-aggressive behavior pattern? To assist the client in exploring his phenomenal field, the counselor may employ sensitive probing by use of the focusing remark as well as interpretive refraction of self-experience by means of the interpretive comment as methods to stimulate the client to make self-corrections in his ways of perceiving himself and the manifestations of himself (e.g., his aspirations and accomplishments). The interpretive comment is a short, tentative analysis by the counselor of what the client has said, perhaps to suggest a new line of explanation of client behavior. Both the focusing remark and the interpretive comment are distinctive characteristics of the interpretive model. The *raison d'être* of sensitive probing derives from the counselor's speculative knowledge of human development plus his experiential knowledge of this particular client's developmental pattern. Other counseling behaviors come into play during this second stage. The aim of this critical second stage of the counseling relationship is to ready the client to develop more effective integration between self-perception, self-experience, and self-aspiration. The task for the counselor is to assist the client to explore and examine the vectors of the self-structure. During this second stage the counselor may introduce new percepts into the client's field for the client's consideration; indeed such percepts (e.g., a compromise vocational choice which combines the characteristics of two other choices over which the client is conflicted) may provide a base upon which effective integration can be built.

The *final stage* is begun by a gradual narrowing of focus. The perceptual-experiential field has been examined and explored; it is ready to be integrated and to converge with reality. This narrowing of focus reaches its fruition in the final figure-field consolidation, in the culminating integration which harmonizes self-experience and objective reality into a psychologically sound self-structure. Now the client increasingly initiates self-directed measures to see his perceptual concern in the context of an examined self-structure. The counselor who has been successful in this relationship has made himself dispensable and has aided the client to achieve a higher degree of self-reliance in integrating or organizing the self for optimal development.

Counselors following the self-interpretive model employ a variety of verbal behaviors, varying in accordance with the exigencies of a particular counseling relationship. Factors influencing the counselor's selection of verbal behaviors are the focus of the client's concern, the stage to which the counseling relationship has progressed, the level of self-integration displayed by the client, and the counselor's judgment relative to the client's readiness to develop insight into self-organization. Self-interpretive counselors employ primarily, but not exclusively, declarative statements. In the first stage, declarative statements which reflect or mildly interpret the client's statement content, such as "You feel that . . . ," are generally utilized. Such statements tend to help the client objectify cognitive and emotional content. At least for clients in the normal range of psychological functioning, *objectification seems to facilitate more orderly, cognitive approaches to perceptual concerns.* In the middle stages of the relationship, interpretive comments are employed with deftness and professional skill. In the final stage, integrative and recapitulating remarks, coupled with verbal support as needed, are employed. Specific verbal behaviors implied in the "shaping" of the interpretive counseling processes are exemplified in Chapter 10.

Empirical Foundations

The self-interpretive model for school counselors is rooted in a phenomenological personality theory and a developmental-tasks approach to human growth. Empirical foundations for counselor verbal behaviors in the self-interpretive model, however, are found in research on the social psychology of communication. However else it is conceived, counseling is regarded as "reciprocal verbal behavior, usually between two people" (Strong, 1964, p. 660). While the study of the communication process in general has relevance for counseling, of more direct interest are investigations of communication patterns in "helping" relationships, especially in "helping" dyadic (or two-person) relationships.

Robinson (1955) complained that the social psychology of the counseling interview had not yet been thoroughly investigated. Super (1963a) charged that he knows of "no specific study of the methods or processes of counseling as done in schools," asserting that many published studies which claim to have investigated the counseling process actually analyzed psychotherapeutic rather than counseling interviews. Indeed, Super disclaimed the assumption that the same processes are involved in counseling and in psychotherapy.

Nonetheless, Vance and Volsky (1962) contend that counseling and psychotherapy have common underpinnings in the dynamics of verbal communication, and Strong (1964) asserts that "any research dealing with the nature of verbal behavior is of vital importance to counselors." No licit assumption can be made, however, that principles of effective communication observed in conversational or psychotherapeutic dyads are unilaterally generalizable to the counseling interview. Rather, studies of communications systems in these settings are suggestive of lines of approach for empirical verification in counseling.

The self-interpretive model accepts the Rogerian notion that the client himself is the best, and perhaps the only adequate, source of information about his internal self-structure and self-organization. A number of studies, of which Bugental's (1952) is typical, have shown that increases in communication about self, or self-relevant content, are characteristic of successful counseling. Todd and Ewing (1961) demonstrated that positive self-reference increases in successful counseling. Rosalind D. Cartwright (1957) concluded that successful counseling increases the consistency of the self-concept. In view of Cartwright's finding, the relationship between increased self-integration and client production of meaningful self-statements is apparent. Thus successful counseling seems to be predicated on the counselor's ability to emit dexterously verbal behaviors which tend to increase the utterance of meaningful self-relevant statements by the client, specifically, self-relevant statements which assist him to examine the elements of self-organization.

A basic model for the analysis of the facilitation of self-relevant content in counseling emerges not from counseling or clinical research but from social psychology. Verplanck's classic study (1958) of the reinforcement of opinion statements is significant for the provision of experimental data on the acceleration of one class of verbal communicative behavior. But its major impact lies in demonstrating that complex verbal behavior is subject to research investigation and to conditioning or learning procedures. Verplanck concluded that both agreeing and paraphrasing tend to accelerate, and silence to extinguish, opinion utterance in conversational dyads. Though both agreeing and paraphrasing increase opinion utterance, there is a slight difference in favor of paraphrasing. The paraphrase in conversation is analogous to the nondirective response in counseling. Similarly, Hildum and Brown (1956), investigating verbal interaction between interviewer and interviewee in an opinion poll, reported that the verbal stimulus "Good" (but not the participatory signal "Mm-hmm") served to bias or reinforce interviewee communication content. This verbal comment is analogous to the counselor's deft employment of supportive statements at judicious points in the counseling process. Additional evidence regarding the effect of conditioning procedures upon verbal content was provided in demonstrations of the "Greenspoon effect." Greenspoon (1955) reported success in using nonverbal communication to accelerate the rate of production of certain types of words by subjects. Krasner (1958), Frank (1961), Kimble (1961), Wimsatt and Vestre (1963), and Strong (1964) have provided detailed reviews of research on verbal conditioning procedures. The major findings reported in these reviews are the following: (1) The social prestige of the "persuader" or communicator very significantly affects verbal production in subjects. (2) Subjects who "typically" comply, i.e., in whom compliance has become a personality pattern, more readily respond to a verbal cue emitted by the communicator. (3) Little evidence is available that verbal reinforcement procedures (regardless of the counseling or psychotherapeutic models in which these procedures inhere) are related to basic personality change. (4) Simple participatory comments (e.g., "Mm-hmm") are as effective as complex verbalizations by the communicator in accelerating the communication of emotionally laden content. (5) The psychological, social, or other dependence of the subject on the communicator accelerates the conditioning of certain classes of verbal content.

Studies of communication in the psychotherapeutic dyad yield some interesting results. In the psychiatric setting, Weiss, Krasner, and Ullman (1963) studied the effect of praise and reproof on the incidence of emotionally toned statements among patients. Minimal social reinforcement (e.g., "Good") served as a sufficient stimulus to increase the patients' rate of emotionally toned statements. Reynolds, Schwartz, Pavlik, and Carlock (1963), studying the effect of verbal reinforcement on subjects of high and low anxiety, found that two-thirds of their subjects increased in rate of verbal production after minimal reinforcement. An interesting study of the specificity of the therapist's statements in relation to client productivity was reported by Seigman and Pope (1962). Specificity related negatively to meaningful productivity in psychiatric interviews. Therapist communications of high specificity (i.e., those least effective) included using a single word to indicate attention or acceptance, a brief remark telling the client to proceed, or a request that the client speak about broad, unexplored areas. Communications of low specificity (i.e., those most effective) included posing challenging questions and asking for specific factual information. High-specificity items in this study seem analogous to nondirective behaviors, while low-specificity items seem to correspond to gently probing behaviors in counseling. Speisman (1959) conducted an important study of client resistance in relation to therapist interpretation. Superficial interpretation (e.g., restatement of the content of the client's communication) and "deep" interpretation (e.g., therapist statements which alluded to content at the "unconscious" level) both increased the client's resistance and inhibited his communication. Moderate interpretation, however, effectively maintained communication. Similar results were reported by Rickard and Dinoff (1962). Moderate interpretation as a mode of communication is analogous to the interpretive refraction of self-experience in the interpretive counseling model. Here, the school counselor reflects the meaning of the client's communication as he understands it, widening the essential meaning, however, to include a broader range of self-feelings. Similarly, Frank and Sweetland (1962) reported that therapist interpretation is associated with an increase in client understanding and insight, while interrogation is associated with parallel decreases. On the other hand, Snyder's early investigation (1945) suggested that therapist interpretation inhibits client insights. When psychiatric patients were contrasted with normal subjects, Slechta, Gwynn, and Peoples (1963) found that the latter responded more readily to verbal conditioning in a situation simulating psychotherapy. This conclusion seems to hold particular significance for developmental counseling with normal clients.

As Super (1963a) has testified, research on the dynamics of communication in the counseling dyad is sketchy at best. Nearly all such research has focused upon the analysis of transcribed counseling interviews in order to classify counselor verbal behaviors, and this in itself is a monumental task. Certainly Berdie's study (1958) is the most important attempt at taxonomy. Over a seventeen-year period, Berdie analyzed several thousand counselor statements from interview transcriptions in order to classify counselor verbal behaviors according to purpose and technique. Muthard (1953) in a similar attempt at taxonomy formulated the construct "counselor subrole behavior." Subsequently, Danskin (1955) and A. E. Hoffman (1959) employed this construct to describe counselor behavior. The "roles" played by counselors include giving and asking for information, supporting, clarifying, explaining, and the like.

Early efforts at exploring the dynamics of communication in counseling, as distinct from the taxonomy of counselor verbal behaviors, were concerned primarily with the description of the effect of single counselor utterances upon immediate client responses. Muthard (1953) observed that both counselor and client verbalizations were determined by the topic under discussion. Carnes and Robinson (1948) studied the relationship between "client talk ratio" and counseling effectiveness, concluding that the topic, or presenting problem, exerts an influence upon the relationship between the amount of client talk and growth. Grigg and Goodstein (1957) reported that client satisfaction with counseling varies directly with counselor interview activity and directiveness.

Silence as a technique in counseling has been investigated by Cook (1964), who found that the counselor's ability to tolerate silence was predictive of counseling success. Brams (1961) reported that effective communication in counseling is related to the counselor's ability to tolerate ambiguity and open-endedness. Schwebel (1960) has commented that the counselor's ability to educate and to re-educate the client is a factor in the duration of counseling (and presumably in the sequence of events), since it may speed the process and avoid unnecessary plateaus.

The general direction in these findings seems to support the broad notion on which communication in interpretive counseling is based. A declarative statement of agreement or paraphrase or a one-word utterance, such as

"Good," appears to serve the purpose of conditioning the production of opinion statements. The ability to tolerate silence and ambiguity and the characteristics of the learning situation tend to speed the counseling process. Since counseling is verbal behavior between two people, the question for the counselor is how to increase the client's production of one kind of verbal behavior, i.e., statements about the client's perception of his self-organization. The available research evidence tends to support the counselor verbal behaviors suggested in the self-interpretive model.

Counseling as Communication

The interpretive model regards counseling as a communicative process, demanding a variety of verbal and nonverbal behaviors on the part of the counselor. The ability of the counselor to employ varying verbal and non-verbal behaviors at appropriate stages of the counseling process largely determines his effectiveness. Some other models tend to limit counselor verbal behavior to a single mode, e.g., the Rogerian emphasis on the reflection of the client's statements.

Communicative behavior is both verbal and nonverbal. Buehler and Richmond (1963) have organized a taxonomy of communicative behaviors. Their categories are (1) biochemical communication, i.e., body contact; (2) motor movement, i.e., posture, facial expression, and gesture; (3) speech, i.e., word and nonword sounds; and (4) impersonal or technological communication through such communicative tools as charts or diagrams. Routh (1958) has suggested that voice tone and inflection, the counselor's posture, his gestures, and other nonverbal cues constitute effective communicative signals received by the client. The counselor who verbalizes statements which are intended to convey warmth and acceptance while at the same time expressing preoccupation through an emotionless voice tone is likely to communicate only disinterest. Similarly, the counselor must be perceptive and sensitive to nonverbal communication from the client. Indeed, according to Loughary (1961, pp. 26–28), the most important of the counselor's communication skills is the ability to listen perceptively. Listening, however, constitutes only one aspect of the process of receiving the client's communication. To understand the client's message, the counselor decodes both verbal and nonverbal communication, assesses conflicting meanings, and integrates the meaning and the content of the client's communication (Ruesch, 1961, pp. 21–26). His response to the client must be coded in both verbal and nonverbal communicative behaviors which converge to present one unambiguous, clearly decipherable message to the client.

The range of nonverbal communicative behaviors is both protean and global. Peculiarities in facial expressions, the way one holds his hands while speaking, and the like exhibit such great diversity as to be virtually unclassifiable. On the other hand, such practices as the location of the counselors' offices in an abandoned coal locker next to the furnace room (as was the case in one small Catholic college, until city building inspectors ordered this college building torn down) appear to constitute a global communication, which conveys a certain evaluation of the worth of the counseling service.

Pohlman and Robinson (1960) constructed a novel investigation to determine the aspects of the counseling situation which students found to be disconcerting. Results indicated that the following were among the *nonverbal* behaviors identified as disconcerting: counselor acts superior, aloof, or insincere, has halitosis, seems in a hurry, winds his watch, yawns, arrives late, rearranges his clothes, glances at papers on desk, looks out of the window, paces the floor, clears his throat or coughs repeatedly, pulls his ear, does not look at client, cleans his pipe, puts his feet on desk, slouches, holds interview in nonconfidential surroundings, and shifts his position often. Among the *verbal* behaviors identified as disconcerting were the following: counselor simply repeats client statement, interrupts, uses poor grammar, talks rapidly, uses unusual words, always agrees with client, swears, does little talking, shows lack of understanding of client's religious background, and tells the client what to do. If these behaviors appear troublesome to clients, it is likely that they inhibit the flow of communication and ultimately affect the success of the counseling process. Because of its emphasis on refractive communication whether by the focusing comment, the interpretive remark, or simply the reflection of feeling, the interpretive model demands the optimal flow of communication.

Nonverbal communication should be proportioned to the verbal behavior of the counselor and should act in concert with the content of his verbal communication. Extraneous nonverbal communications should be eliminated from the counseling situation, since they tend to distract the client's perceptual attention and impede his communication. Verbal communication and nonverbal communication should be of such a unified fabric that neither by itself is obvious to the client. Verbal communication content is reinforced or extinguished by corresponding nonverbal signals; hence, nonverbal communication ought not to speak more emphatically than the corresponding verbal content. In view of the multiplicity of possible specific and global nonverbal communications, these few principles must suffice.

Hence, attention is focused on the counselor's repertoire of variable verbal behaviors. The interpretive model specifies a range of communications, varying according to the stage of the counseling process and the exigencies of the particular moment of the interview. There is much evidence that indicates that variable behavior is more effective in the school counseling situation than adherence to one particular mode. Sonne and Goldman (1957), for example, found that high school students in general preferred an eclectic counseling approach to a nondirective approach. While the

Rogerian technique employed chiefly one mode of verbal behavior (reflection of feeling), the approach called *eclectic* was characterized by such varying behaviors as questioning, interpreting, and offering to intervene in immediate problems. Mink and Sgan (1963) reported that students found both non-directive and authoritarian (i.e., advisement) orientations unsatisfactory. Grigg and Goodstein (1957) reported that clients were better satisfied with their counseling experiences when the counselor played a more active, directive role than when the counselor was a reflective listener. Indeed, Hopke's investigation (1964) determined that the most common verbal behaviors for experienced school counselors are questioning (50 per cent), supportive remarks which recast or interpret the client's statement (22 per cent), supportive comments (13 per cent), comments which communicate understanding (11 per cent), and evaluative comments (3 per cent). On the other hand, Grigg's investigation (1961) found that more experienced counselors tend to be less active, to exhibit less control over the interview, to make fewer direct suggestions, to give less advice, and to wait for the client to develop topics for communication. Results of the investigation by Pallone and Grande (1964a), summarized earlier, underscore the necessity for a wide variety of communicative behaviors in the school counselor's repertoire.

The self-interpretive model seeks to increase the incidence of client statements relevant to self-structure and the present organization of personal resources. Communication is thus directed toward eliciting from the client a particular class of verbal statements, i.e., those which convey the client's perception of his present level of self-organization preparatory to undertaking more effective organization. Results of investigations of the process of communication in conversational, therapeutic, and counseling dyads provide the conceptual and empirical foundations for the self-interpretive model for school counselors.

Toward a Definition

Counseling is conceived in the interpretive model neither as a process of decision making nor as a thinly veiled psychotherapy. A definition of counseling as conceived by the interpretivist runs along these lines: *Self-interpretive counseling is a process of communication, primarily verbal in nature, through which a client is assisted to organize himself maximally for the successful negotiation of developmental tasks. This assistance is supplied at the client's request by a skilled counselor who serves as a collaborative counsultant as the client examines the structure of his self-perception and self-aspiration in relation to his self-experience and achieves sound consolidation and integration in the self-system.* It is assumed that the client is a person in the process of becoming (e.g., a student) and that the setting for counseling is a supportive environment (e.g., a school).

Initially the counselor employs nondirective reflection of feeling in order to immerse the client in an atmosphere of acceptance and confidence. Once this atmosphere has been firmly established, the counselor employs the broad technique of interpretive refraction of self-experience. Here the focusing remark and the interpretive comment are utilized. Finally, the client narrows the focus to his concern, in congruence with reality.

Unlike Rogerian nondirectivism, interpretivism is a counseling framework eminently relevant to the school milieu. It recognizes the school's role in broadening the student's horizon and it faces the problem that many clients do not possess sufficient ego strength to develop insights by themselves. It utilizes case history materials and psychometric data in order to gain a valid longitudinal and cross-sectional portrait of the client's developmental history, to interpret self in many situations.

In contrast to directivism, interpretivism does not render the client passive but keeps him active by reflection of feeling, by the focusing question. Its approach is relatively unstructured so that the client is not in a psychological vise or clamp: he can freely express and release. Interpretivism promotes independence and self-direction in the client. It does not encourage a situation in which the counselor has an overly facile solution prepared once the client has been psychologically "categorized."

Philosophical Rationale

Self-interpretive counseling is anchored in phenomenological personality theory and a developmental-tasks orientation to human growth. Philosophically, its anchorages lie in a Judeo-Christian metaphysics of man-as-value. Its basic rationale can be summarized as follows (Pallone, 1962b):

> There is a short passage by an anonymous author which could serve as an appropriate prologue for the remarks that follow: "The dean declared that young people were seriously deprived of self-reliance and initiative by being guided out of their difficulties or being counseled over their frustrations; that there was a danger of graduating them into the hands of the social worker, the marriage counselor, and the psychiatrist. The dean feared that the result would be a race of leaners, who, at the first intimation of frustration, would betake themselves to a professional helper."
>
> We who are charged with providing counseling services decline the role of the professional leaning post.
>
> We see ourselves instead as neutral "catalysts" in the process of becoming whereby the student becomes a self-sustaining, psychologically integrated person (in the Thomistic sense), relying upon the direction of no one but himself and his own highest good in making the major decisions of his life. The degree of our activity in the "catalytic" function is directly proportioned to the student's need *and* desire for assistance in seeking his own personal life style. Once that style is set, we relinquish our roles without regret.

In playing our roles, we operate under certain assumptions concerning the nature of man and his freedom and the wellsprings of human behavior:

(1) We do not believe that every student is hopelessly maladjusted or confused and thus in need of direction from subtle external influencers [*sic*].

(2) We do believe that students face a series of developmental tasks inherent in the nature of childhood and adolescence and in the nature of the school experience.

(3) We do not believe that students are incapable of making sound choices regarding their futures without the sage advice of an all-knowing trained professional counselor.

(4) We do believe that the professional counselor is equipped through training and experience to make a substantial contribution to the student's process of self-definition by providing relatively objective appraisal and information to the student concerning both himself and the world of reality.

(5) We do not believe that it is our function to serve as prying inquisitors who question the motives and emotional health of every student who marches to the beat of a different drummer.

(6) We do believe that it is basic to the principles of humanistic education to assist students to mobilize their personal strengths in such fashion as to minimize obstacles between themselves and their own optimum development as persons.

(7) We do not believed in "programmed" or automated development through hidden manipulation of the psychological environment so that the student's life style falls into line with some goal we have predetermined for him.

(8) We do believe in making available such resources as will foster self-exploration, with view to no goal other than stimulating knowledge of oneself—an ancient and worthy end.

10

SELF–INTERPRETIVE COUNSELING: DYNAMICS OF COMMUNICATION

In the preceding chapter a number of models for counseling were reviewed briefly, and the self-interpretive model was introduced. Following a general statement of the principal features of the self-interpretive model, (1) its usefulness as a viable synthesis in the school counseling situation with essentially normal clients was suggested; (2) its emphasis on variability in counselor verbal behavior in relation to client and situation parameters was indicated; (3) the general shape of the self-interpretive counseling process was outlined; (4) empirical support for the model was suggested; and, finally (5), the basic rationale for the model, anchored in developmental psychology, perceptual theory, and a philosophy of man-as-value, was summarized. Self-interpretive counseling was characterized as a model for assisting the student to *learn himself,* to experience himself in the counseling relationship as an object of value to the counselor, to consolidate the elements of self-identity formed from the completion of prior developmental tasks, and to organize or mobilize these elements of self-identity for the negotiation of future tasks.

273

This chapter presents an overview of the implementation of this model in the *school* counseling interview, focusing on the dynamics of communication between client and counselor. This presentation is not intended as a do-it-yourself manual for the prospective counselor or the teacher or even less as a bag of tricks. Rather its purpose is to familiarize the reader with the self-interpretive model in operation in counseling interviews with secondary school clients who exhibit a range of perceptual concerns.

The counselor's repertoire of communicative behaviors

In self-interpretive counseling, the counselor needs a repertoire of communicative behaviors from which to select the precise means of communication which seems best suited to the particular stage of the counseling process. The success of the self-interpretive counselor depends upon his ability to help the client examine his present self-organization, to assess the need for more effective integration, to achieve a maximal level of self-integration, and to generalize from maximal self-integration to the tasks of development.

Nonverbal communication, it was suggested in Chapter 9, must be proportioned to the counselor's verbal communication in such fashion that the client receives a single clear message. In no case should the nonverbal communication speak louder than the counselor's verbal content. Global nonverbal communication (e.g., the location of the office, arrangement of furniture, lighting, and confidentiality) must be directed toward creating within the client a sense of security in the counseling situation. In view of the multiplicity of individual idiosyncracies in nonverbal communication, these principles must suffice. Hence attention is focused primarily on the self-interpretive counselor's *repertoire of verbal behaviors*. Few investigators have attempted to classify the counselor's communicative behaviors. Certainly Berdie's study (1958) at the University of Minnesota Student Counseling Bureau is the most important attempt at taxonomy. Over a seventeen-year period, Berdie analyzed several thousand counselor statements from phonographic recordings and typescripts of actual counseling interviews. The resulting taxonomy categorized counselor statements according to purpose and according to technique. Four purposes identified were (1) eliciting attitudes or information; (2) introduction of counselor's feelings, attitudes, or information; (3) facilitating the client's perception of relationships between facts or ideas; and (4) establishing an interpersonal relationship. Among the techniques identified were leading and direct questions, requests for repetition, generalization from the counselor's experiences, interpretation, restatement, clarification, summarization, advising, stating alternatives, challenges, approval and disapproval, reassurance, expressions of sympathy, test description, social amenites, and simple participation (e.g., "Uh-huh"). In a similar vein, A. E. Hoffman (1959) identified 14 counselor verbal behaviors, which he termed "counselor subroles." These included friendly discussion, information gathering, diagnosing, information giving, supporting, structuring, listening, asking for elaboration, reflecting, participating, advising, rejecting, and tutoring (see also Patterson, 1963).

Communicative signals are *verbal stimuli* to which clients respond. Stimuli of high internal structure present little opportunity for the client to project much of self into his response. "Tell me your name," "Do you like to fish?" "Where did you go to high school?" are verbal stimuli of high internal structure. Stimuli of low internal structure (often called ambiguous or indefinite stimuli) provide the opportunity for the client to project himself into his response. "Tell me about yourself," "How do you feel about yourself?" and sentence fragments or one-word communicative signals are verbal stimuli of low internal structure. The shape of the interpretivist counseling process moves from statements of relatively low to somewhat higher internal structure.

Chief among the verbal behaviors included in the self-interpretivist's repertoire (in addition to those used for social amenities) are the exploration of the client's phenomenal field, the expansive reflection of client statements, sensitive probing, the constructive use of silence, the interpretive refraction of the client's self-experience, expansion of the client's perceptual field, integrative recapitulation, and, occasionally, mild confrontation.

Exploring the phenomenal field

In order to establish a meaningful relationship with the client, the interpretive counselor seeks to understand him in terms of the range of perceptions found in his phenomenal field. For optimal understanding, the counselor needs to know how the client perceives himself and others, what objects have positive or negative valence, what aspirations the client holds, what his principal motivations and values are, and what level of organization or integration obtains within the self-system. In short, the counselor needs to understand *who the client believes himself to be* or who he believes himself to be becoming, to sensitize himself to the client's world. This seems an essential step whether counseling is to focus on confirming or on organizing self-structure.

The process of self-interpretive counseling essentially seeks to assist the client to develop realistic perceptions of himself in relation to the tasks of development. The first step in testing the realism of the client's perceptions is to determine the nature of those perceptions. In this process, analogous to the step Super's model (1957) regards as self-concept portrayal, the counselor is seeking information about the client's self-structure. The procedure is largely that of asking open-ended questions, which function as miniature projective devices. In view of the *internally evaluative* nature of a question, however, the interpretivist prefers to state declaratively situations to which the client responds. Instead of emitting such questions as "What do you think are your principal interests?" or such commands as "Tell me about yourself," the interpretivist states open-ended problems. Through the observation of the client's responses, the counselor *infers* the client's perceptions. Later, he checks the accuracy of his inferences through declarative statements to which the client responds.

The following excerpt is taken from a transcription of an initial interview with a junior in high school. She has come to the counselor to seek information relative to preparing herself for entry into the labor market or into a college. The client's cumulative records indicate that she is virtually multi-potential. Her grades have been generally above average, her standardized test scores indicate above-average performance, and there seem to be no areas of interest or extracurricular activity which predominate. The counselor's role is to elicit from the client a portrayal of the phenomenal field.

Client: Sometimes I lean this way, sometimes I lean that way. . . . I just don't really know which way to go . . . or even whether to go to college at all. . . .

Counselor: Uh-huh . . . Suppose you projected yourself ten years into the future, when you're twenty-seven. Just daydream about it out loud. Tell me what you see yourself doing. . . .

Client: I don't know. . . . Sometimes I'd like to be an engineer, sometimes an artist, sometimes just selling dresses at the ———— Shoppe. . . . I'd like to be a lot of things . . . (pause) . . . I suppose I'll be living here. . . . I'll probably be married and have three kids and be just miserable *(laughs)*. . . . But I'll be a good mother. . . . I'll probably have gone to college because I got nothing better to do. . . . But I really probably. . . . I don't see myself doing anything with my education . . . with *an* education . . . and I'll have arguments with my mother-in-law, if I have one. . . . But if I really had my way, I'd be an architect, or an engineer, or an artist. . . . But that's why I came to see you, to tell me what to do. . . .

Counselor: . . . Mm-hmm. . . . So you have so many ways of . . . so many different ways of seeing yourself that it's hard to put them together . . . and you think that you want someone to tell you what to do. . . .

Client: Yes . . . because they've *got* to fit together, so I can know.

The developmentally oriented counselor sees in the client's description of herself the problem of identity diffusion, a situation typically encountered in normal adolescent development. The client seems to be demanding a pre-mature definition of self, evident in her statement that her ways of perceiving herself have "*got* to fit together." Her final statement probably ought to read "so I can know who I am." The counselor begins to perceive fleeting and diverse self-perceptions, some of them negative, some of them rejected by the client. He begins to infer the outline of the self-concept. In this case, he makes the decision that the most appropriate focus of concern is the client's diffuse identity and the urgency of her premature attempt at self-closure.

The kind of open-ended statement made by the counselor in this exchange has admittedly limited applicability. Another technique which has occasionally proved useful is phrased in the following manner:

Counselor: Remember the television show "The Millionaire"? Let's suppose that Michael Anthony came to call on you, to deliver a check for a million dollars. But there's a condition attached. Even though you don't need the money, you have to spend your time in some worthwhile way, in a job or doing something else. You can't just sit home and do nothing. Just daydream out loud about what you see yourself doing.

Other verbal behaviors, less broad in scope, which may be used include such statements as "Tell me something about how you see yourself." Regardless of the wording, the intent of this sort of counselor verbal behavior is to offer a broad stimulus field into which the client may project himself. From these client projections, the counselor infers the structure of the phenomenal field. Questions or statements of low specificity are preferable, since the extent to which the client may project his internal perceptions varies negatively with the specificity of the verbal stimulus. The less structured the stimulus (i.e., the counselor statement), the greater the degree of client self introjected into the response.

Reflecting and expanding the client's perceptions

The self-interpretive school counselor employs reflection of the statement of the client's feelings or perceptual concerns to communicate his own efforts at empathic understanding and to synthesize the content of the client's communications. The counselor's reflection attempts to broaden the underlying cognitive content or feeling tone to a *wider area of the client's self-experience* than was implied in the client's communication. He thus seeks to *broaden the client's perception of the meaning of his statements and perceptions to the issue of self-organization.* The simple restatement of the client's content is insufficient to clarify for him its implications.

The following excerpt is taken from a transcription of an initial interview with a high school senior. He has come to the counselor to ask what reassurances might be offered to his parents concerning the probability of his admission to college. The contact was initiated by the client, who wants apparently a quick way of dealing with his parents' uncertainty and anxiety. It is readily recognizable that this perceptual concern is often encountered in normal development.

Client: I just wish I could find some way to put some sort of . . . ah . . . I guess reassurance to my parents. I try to explain to them I have one main plan and try to stick to it, to go to ———— [name of a college].

And they'll agree. But we'll be talking about it later, and they—my
Mom, mostly—will begin to say but what if you don't make it. . . . I
mean, they want something with no loopholes. . . .

Counselor: . . . So, in a way, you feel that they don't have faith in
you . . . that they're unsure of you . . . that you can't feel they're backing you.

Client: . . . Yeah, my parents—they expect something that is perfect. They
expect me to do something that is perfect or flawless. I tell them that's
impossible. . . . But when I do something, it's got to be perfect. They
expect that when I do something it's gotta be *holy* . . . (pause). . . .

Counselor: . . . You get the feeling that you're kind of on trial. . . .

Client: All the time, no matter what it is. Do everything perfect or don't
do it at all. They want me to do the exact thing—grades, girl friend,
when I go out, you name it. . . . And it's hard for me to . . . satisfy
them . . . no matter how hard I try. . . .

Initially, the client spoke of wanting some sort of reassurance to offer his
parents concerning his probability of college admission. At the end of this
exchange, his perceptual attention has been broadened to include a wider
area of parent-child relationship. Offering the client some quick way to allay
his parents' concern might have resolved an immediate trouble, but it would
not have permitted the client to explore the meaning of his immediate self-
experience (i.e., his parents' need for "no loopholes") in the broader context
of his self-organization. As later excerpts indicate, the need of his parents
for reassurance in this instance is related to a broader area of his own behavior. Similarly, the mere reflection of the content of the client's initial
statement (e.g., "You're concerned about finding some way to assure them
you'll be admitted to college") would not have served to move the focus
to a broader and ultimately more meaningful plane. Counselor behaviors of
this sort are likely to be employed as the principal means of communication
in the initial stages of the counseling process.

Sensitive probing

The self-interpretivist employs probing sensitively when he feels that the
client is capable of dealing with perceptual awareness of material only hinted
at in earlier communication. The counselor's relevant knowledge (of this
client and of the normal tasks of development) serves as an indicator directing his attention to broad areas of possible concern. When probing is successful, the counselor is actually *shifting the focus of the client's concern* to
elements or percepts in the phenomenal field previously not related by the
client to his immediate perceptual concern. In general, sensitive probing is
related to implicit rather than explicit content in the client's communication.
Declarative statements are usually more satisfactory than questions, though
skillfully constructed questions, phrased tentatively, are occasionally effective.

The following exchange occurred immediately after the exchange cited above. The counselor feels that the client is ready to make the connection between his parents' insistence upon perfection and the client's academic performance. School cumulative records indicate that while this client demonstrates above-average intelligence, his academic performance has usually been in the average to below-average range.

Counselor: . . . Like you should be the straight-A student. . . .

Client: That's what she—they—want all right. When I tell them I'm not a person that can do this all that easily, they say that's not what the tests show. . . . They make me feel like . . . like I've got to live up to the standards. . . . I mean, I really try to live up to what they want. I'll sit there and study for two hours—but if I take a break . . . or . . . well, I feel guilty about it . . . trying to do the exact thing, the perfect thing. . . . And what they don't realize is I can't really hack it. . . .

Counselor: The pressure is there for you to live up their standards . . . like studying is something you've got to do for them, isn't it, not for yourself?

Client: . . . That's really about it. . . . The standards are so high . . . it's like you keep reaching for them and you can't make it. . . . I can't seem to satisfy them. . . . You can't have any . . . *joy* in studying just for yourself. It's always are you doing what the teacher wants? How are you going to succeed unless you keep . . . reaching for the As. . . .

The effect of sensitive probing in this illustration has been to focus the client's perception on the relationship between the underlying theme of his immediate concern (i.e., his parents' attitude toward standards of perfection) and his experience of himself as a student of average achievement. The counselor has controlled communication to the extent that, by probing sensitively, he has focused the content of the client's concern. On the other hand, it is likely that an awkwardly worded question (e.g., "What does this attitude of theirs mean to you as far as studies are concerned?") would have elicited a denial from the client of any connection. The counselor must be able to judge *the client's readiness* for a shift of focus in communication, and the shift must be accomplished dexterously and imperceptibly.

Interpretive refraction of self-experience

The verbal behavior called interpretive refraction of the client's self-experience is employed by the counselor to offer *tentative hypotheses* to the client *about the meaning of his self-experience*. Here, the counselor is offering his own tentative analysis as the prism through which the client's self-experience is refracted. The school counselor is an adult member of the staff of a school, an organized agency of society. Regardless of his ability to create a feeling of acceptance in the client, he functions as and is likely to be perceived as a surrogate of society. In these circumstances, he often becomes the "social reality" against which the client tests the realism of his own perceptions and interpretations. In using interpretive refraction, the counselor is inviting the client to consider the meaning of his self-experience through the prism of the counselor's perception of its meaning. Again, the preferred mode of communication is the declarative statement, though an open-ended question may be employed with beneficial results.

This exchange occurred following the exchange just cited. The counselor is offering the client a tentative hypothesis concerning the meaning of his experience of himself as an average student in relation to his parents' attitudes toward excellence.

Counselor: . . . So you get to feeling that, if you can't do it, if you can't do it for yourself . . . set your own standards, can't study for the joy of it, but just to please them . . . then what's the use of trying at all.

Client: (Very long pause) . . . I think I see . . . (pause). . . . That's. . . . That must be it about my grades. . . . If everything I do is gonna be wrong, no matter how I do it, because they want perfection—then if the goal is so high that you're gonna fall short—then why shoot for the top 10 in the class and fall down below what they want anyway. You get the same results. You're there, no matter how—no matter what effort means. You're there, so why knock yourself out and they're still dissatisfied (*speaking rapidly*). . . .

Counselor: . . . So you just settle for—

Client: (*Interrupting*) Yeah, that's what I guess I've been doing, now that I think about it. Settling for what I can get—without too much effort, because I can never make their standards. . . .

Counselor: But if you began to set your own standards. . . .

Client: Then I guess I wouldn't be so—feel so guilty about disappointing them. . . . Or about disappointing myself either. . . . Now that I think about it, I guess I'm afraid to set my own standards. . . . Now that I think about it, why would I want somebody else to set my standards for me? I could set my own standards, I wouldn't have to be. . . . I mean I know I'm not dumb . . . but I know I'm not perfect either, so I wouldn't have to be in the top 10. . . .

Interpretive refraction has been successful in this case, since the client has been able to understand more clearly the meaning of his academic self-experience. A process of reintegration of the self-system, incorporating this new understanding, is already beginning to take shape. The client's academic self-experience seems to have been largely self-created, issuing from his expectation that he would fail to satisfy his parents' expectations. Once he has introjected the counselor's perception of the meaning of this experience, he can begin to organize himself in such fashion that he need not anticipate frustration in attempting to fulfill unreasonable expectations. An open-ended question might have served reasonably well as the first counselor behavior in this exchange. The counselor's statement might have been worded, "You begin to feel that there's not much use in trying, don't you?" Whatever the wording, the interpretation must be offered as tentative.

Interpretive refraction essentially consists of an offer to the client to use the counselor's perception of the client's self-experience as a closer "approximation to reality" or as a correction for inaccurate perception. For interpretive refraction to succeed, the counselor must be very sure that the client is ready to receive a novel perception of the meaning of self-experience. The client needs to be in a position to consider the implications of the tentative interpretation offered by the counselor for the organization or reorganization of self-perception and self-aspiration. In the example cited, the client is ready to recognize his self-expectations when he can perceive that his present academic behavior represents a retreat from imposed standards issuing from fear of failure. He is ready to organize his self-aspiration in such fashion that he develops his own standards of academic performance. He can expect himself to succeed, not fail.

This is a difficult mode of verbal behavior to master. The counselor needs to be prepared for the client's rejection of his interpretation. He needs to be able to accept the reality of the client's rejection and yet continue the counseling process in a positive direction. One of the surest ways of rejecting the client and of demolishing the counseling relationship is to force an interpretation on the client for which he is not ready, e.g., through repetition, insistence, or some other means of verbal bombardment.

Confirmation and support

The tasks of adolescence are directed toward the formation of an independent, secure self-identity. One of the important developmental tasks of adolescence is emancipation from the home. As a result of this normal, inevitable process, the adolescent is likely to feel alienated from the home and family environment. The adolescent group provides some security and support to the adolescent in his search for self-identity, functioning as the first testing ground against which the adolescent validates his self-perceptions. The counseling relationship represents another testing ground against which the adolescent tests the realism of his perceptions. Unlike the patient in Rogerian psychotherapy, the school counseling client is in a state of normal dependency. Far from refusing to validate the client's perceptions, the self-interpretivist seeks to confirm realistic perceptions and support the client in self-advancing attitudes and behaviors.

When the client "tries out" a realistic self-perception on the counselor, the interpretivist reinforces the perception by confirmation. When the client expresses favorable attitudes toward self or toward other objects or persons in the phenomenal field, the counselor supports these expressions. The counselor's role is *not* to dispense reassurance. For example, the counselor never makes the client feel that his principal perceptual concern is after all not very serious, that it is common for adolescents to feel this way or that way, and the like. To do so is ultimately to reject the client. No matter how ordinary or how temporary, the client's perceptual concerns are of great importance *to him.*

If the client is able to confirm, in the security of the counseling relationship, realistic perceptions, he is ready to project his perceptions into self-experience. The school counselor who attempts to maintain an attitude of neutrality at this crucial point in the counseling relationship ultimately does his client a disservice. Through confirmation, the counselor offers cognitive assent to the client's statement, judgment, perception, or tentative self-organization. Through support, he offers emotional cushioning. The counselor verbal behaviors used in confirmation and support are quite similar. Both supportive behaviors resemble *evaluative* reflections by the counselor, through which the counselor offers his evaluation of the client's self-organization when and only when such evaluation is necessary for more integrative self-organization.

The exchange below is taken from the transcript of the fourth interview with the male student identified in earlier examples. In previous interviews, the client has examined his self-structure and has initiated more cohesive self-integration. Immediately prior to this exchange, the client and the counselor had been discussing the client's desire for a greater degree of independence of his parents in making decisions.

Client: I mean . . . I'm an *individual.* I can't—ah—always do what someone else tells me, even if . . . even if it's my parents—because in later life I may not have my parents, and I'm going to have to make my own decisions . . . for myself.

Counselor: And this is the only way to get training for making your own decisions, isn't it?

Client: It's the *only* way. . . . Sometimes I may make a wrong decision about something, but—ah—it's the only way you're going to learn. And usually I don't want to make a very big decision without consulting my parents anyway . . . so the things I want to make my own decisions in, if something goes wrong, it couldn't mean that much . . . just chalk it up to experience. . . .

Counselor: So, since these decisions would not be major ones, the only one who is likely to be hurt if you make a wrong decision—

Client: (*Interrupting*) In effect, it would only hurt me . . . but I mean, it wouldn't be something that terrible. . . .

Counselor: And you learn.

Client: That's right. And you know the *next* time you have to do something like that, go about it a different way . . . that's the way you've got to learn. . . .

Counselor: . . . It seems to me that you've got a pretty realistic grasp on this thing. . . .

Client: Well, I hope so. . . . I hope it's a good grasp on the right thing. . . .

Counselor: You have some doubts about that? . . .

Client: When I think them over, I don't . . . 'cause I know that some of the things I might do—ah—don't please my parents . . . but we can work it out. . . . I mean, both my parents are pretty near forty-five, each one of them, they're pretty set in their ways, and the odds of my changing them . . . are pretty slim. . . . The only thing I can do is try to be myself and follow what I believe to be right. . . . If I believe it's right, I think I should do it . . . and my parents—I love them and I need them and I believe they only want what's best for me . . . my parents and I will have to just try to work it out. . . .

Counselor: It seems to me that what you've said is . . . that . . . a lot more than I'm just going to live with it. It seems to me that you've said I'm going to be *me,* and I'm going to kind of reconcile what my parents want and what I want, and still be *me.* . . . And I think that's pretty important.

The counselor has attempted to communicate to the client confirmation of the client's perceptions of parent-child relationships and of the need for training in independence. He has attempted to convey to the client the feeling that the counselor supports him in his efforts to operationalize a perception of himself as a person in the process of *becoming* independent.

Other situations also demand confirmation and support by the counselor. The client who is well integrated and has made a tentative choice of college or career may seek counseling for confirmation of his perceptions about himself. Especially when this sort of interview occurs after a series of contacts between client and counselor (perhaps spaced over the entire span of the client's stay in a particular school), little purpose seems to be served by the failure of the counselor to respond to the client's inquiries. In essence, the client is asking: "Can you give me some indication as to whether this choice is realistic?" Here, counselor verbal behavior might appropriately be worded, "From what I can tell, on the basis of your performance here, on results of aptitude tests, on the basis of what I personally know of you as an individual, your choice seems to be (or seems not to be) appropriate." The simple reflection of feeling as a response to such a request [e.g., "You want to know whether this choice is realistic." "Yes (*growing angry*), that's what I said. Are you going to say something or not?" "You're getting a little disturbed because I refuse to answer"] constitutes a common caricature of the nondirective model.

It must be noted that the counselor ought to avoid giving the client the feeling that he and the client are united against the world. Such behavior is likely only to engender an abnormal dependency upon the counselor. The creation of dependency constitutes what Lawton (1958) has called neurotic interaction between the client and the counselor. Confirmation and support are used to assist the client in reality-testing his perceptions, not in wooing him away from other significant adults.

Constructive use of silence

This counselor behavior is virtually self-explanatory. Very often the beginning counselor feels acute discomfort during an interval of silence in the interview because he believes that nothing constructive is happening, but the contrary is often the case. A number of studies reviewed in Chapter 9 have indicated that the counselor's ability to tolerate silence is related to counseling success. A period of silence is often precisely what the client needs, as he reflects and attempts to integrate material discussed in the preceding interval. It is the client who must ultimately organize the self-structure efficaciously. Much of what is most constructive in the counseling process occurs outside the counseling room, between visits, as the client integrates and consolidates perceptions which successively approximate reality. Inside the counseling room, much of what is most constructive occurs during periods of silence.

On the other hand, the counselor must be able to judge whether a particular interval represents constructive silence or simply awkward and unnecessary silence. Once a relatively close relationship has been established, the counselor may know the client well enough to read nonverbal cues to determine whether consolidation and reflection are occurring within him. Certainly he must make such a determination before he intervenes with verbal behavior too rapidly and thus distracts the client from constructive internal processes.

In the following exchange, the internal processes at play during the interval of silence may be inferred from the client's later statements. This excerpt is taken from the fourth interview with the male client identified in earlier examples.

Counselor: You feel that you can wait until this works itself out . . . in time when you finish your schooling. . . .

Client: I can put up with it. . . . It may require—it may require a couple of arguments or something, but—ah—every family has their arguments. . . . The only thing I can try to do is show my parents I am capable of making my own decisions . . . and try to make each decision correctly. And when my parents see that—ah—I am successful, I guess that will lessen the . . . the . . . cord . . . between us. . . .

Counselor: The cord? . . .

Client: The cord, I mean, will loosen the tie. . . .

Silence: *The interval of silence lasts for a period of two minutes and fourteen seconds. During this period, the client exhibits no signs of uneasiness or impatience. Rather, he seems to be preoccupied with inner thoughts. Neither he nor the counselor shifts his position. The counselor infers* *from these nonverbal cues that the client is reflecting upon the meaning of the term* cord, *apparently in reference to the umbilical cord. It is the counselor's supposition that the client is facing the reality of his biological and economic dependence upon his parents, factors which he, in his striving for independence, sometimes minimizes. Thus the counselor judges the silence to be able to serve a constructive purpose, and he allows it to continue as long as the client wishes. The reflection and consolidation which occurred during this period may be inferred from the client's statement which broke the silence.*

Client: (*Without changing posture*) The thing is I gotta remember my parents are my parents . . . and we . . . we weren't put on earth to—ah—to fight with each other. We have to work with each other—but as we go through life, it's . . . you have to learn more and more to make your own decisions. And you learn to make them correctly. You just have to make sure that you don't hurt them as you do. . . .

Silence: *Another interval of silence, this time lasting seventy-two seconds, intervenes. The counselor judges that the client's most recent statement is now being integrated internally.*

Client: . . . No, it's more than that . . . than not hurting them. . . . It's respecting them . . . even . . . because, after all, they're your *teachers* as much as anything else . . . and they're trying to do their best to teach you the best way they know how . . . and for that you've got to love them. . . .

Had the counselor intervened, even if he had intervened precisely to say the very things which the client ultimately said, an internal process of learning and organization would not have occurred. The most significant learnings are internal, in counseling as well as in teaching. To be able to use silence constructively, the counselor needs a sensitivity to the internal processes of his client which is the product both of rapport with the client and of experienced clinical judgment.

Some periods of silence, on the other hand, are not constructive and indeed may well serve to disrupt the relationship. The client may feel that the counselor simply is not interested enough in him to continue the discussion. This experience is not uncommon when the counselor attempts to adhere to a Rogerian model when dealing with normal persons. For example, to fail to respond in some way to a client's statement or request for information at a point when no constructive internal process is likely to occur will usually communicate a lack of interest to the client.

A final use of the technique of silence is aimed at the nonreinforcement of statements, attitudes, or behaviors which are injurious to the self or to other persons or those statements or behaviors which may involve material sin. Ample illustration of this use of silence is given later in this chapter. Of interest in this connection is the important theological principle *qui tacit, tacit.* Indeed, failure to remain silent in the face of the expression, for example, of unfavorable attitudes toward dogmas of faith may disrupt the counseling process to the extent that it may become impossible to help the client regain an appropriate perception of himself and of the body of the faith (see Fr. Grau, S.J., 1958).

Expanding the phenomenal field

The self-interpretivist shares with the Rogerian the position that the client has within himself strong forces striving toward health, indeed, striving toward the good. But the notion that the client has within himself all resources necessary for the most effective self-perception and self-aspiration is less certain. Often the student is caught in the throes of normal developmental conflicts over figures in the field when consideration of factors presently outside his perception may resolve conflicts quite satisfactorily. For example, a college sophomore may be conflicted over the declaration of sociology or business administration as a field of concentration. At his developmental stage and educational level, satisfactory development seems to require preliminary vocational self-definition. When the percept of personnel management or human engineering as a career is introduced into the field, reorganization in the valence system is enabled to occur. Positive valences formerly attached to business administration and to sociology may now be attached to the newly introduced percepts. The conflict is resolved through *creative synthesis* of forces within the field. But the creative synthesis hinges upon the *expansion of the phenomenal field* to include percepts beyond the client's immediate sphere of experience. Rousseve (1962) has made the point well in regard to expanding the phenomenal field of minority students. The Negro student who develops an aspiration for himself as a Negro teacher in a predominantly Negro college, for example, needs the expanding influence of information about the career of such a distinguished university professor as Dr. Kenneth Clark of the City University of New York. Thus Rousseve suggests that "what we must do is attack more vigorously the Negro's image of himself so that he might aspire."

The immediate experience of any single individual is but a slit in the universe of experience. One of the goals of counseling for the interpretivist is to help the client develop openness to his own self-experience. The point has been made that in the integrated person a permeable membrane lies between self-perception (both the self-as-perceived here and now and self-aspiration) and the self-as-experienced. But another important goal in school counseling is to help the client develop an openness to the *expansion of self-experience,* an *openness of self to new experience.* Counseling which aims at effective self-organization has as a positive obligation introduction into the phenomenal field of expanding influences.

Another positive obligation, as has been noted elsewhere, is to help the student learn to tolerate ambiguity and to avoid premature closure in order to ensure openness to self-experience. Premature self-definition hinders the process of development. The counselor seeks to assist the client understand the reality of an unfolding universe of self-expanding influences. The role for the counselor is considerably different from that of simple information giving. He seeks to introduce dexterously new percepts into the client's field which grow out of and are related to present perceptions of self. His role is not that of advisement, or simply telling the student that such and such is best for him. His role is essentially that of the collaborative consultant, who draws upon an accumulation of his own professional experiences to offer tentatively percepts for the client's consideration.

The most common examples of field-expanding percepts are the skillful introduction of information about educational and occupational resources and about self through the use of psychometric devices. Both topics are discussed elsewhere in this book. For the present, the focus is on counselor verbal behavior in the counseling interview when the counselor's task is expanding the client's phenomenal field.

The following excerpt is taken from a transcript of an interview between a college sophomore and a counselor in the college guidance center. The client has come with the request that the counselor "give me some tests so that I can know which way to go." Cumulative records indicate generally satisfactory grades. Extracurricular activities include an art club and a biology club. Prior to this excerpt, the counselor and the client had discussed the client's perception of the artist and the biologist. The client's interests and inclinations do not seem to be related either to medicine or to biological research; teaching biology appears to be a last resort.

Client: So there it is. . . . And I have to declare a major by the end of the semester. . . .

Counselor: . . . And you feel that some type of test is going to be able to tell you what to do. . . .

Client: (*Pause*) . . . Actually no, but . . . they may help. I really know what I want to do. I want to be an artist or something along that line . . . but then there's this biology thing . . . my highest grades . . . so I really don't know which way to go. . . . I think I'd probably be happiest as an artist . . . but I don't buy the whole Greenwich Village kick . . . so I can at least back into teaching and make a decent living as a biology teacher someplace . . . but . . . (*pause*). . . .

Counselor: Mm-hmm. . . . I wonder if you've ever thought about a new field, one that's just now beginning to open up—medical illustration. . . . It might be one way to put some of these things together. . . .

Client: *Medical illustration?* . . . Tell me more. . . .

The counselor's tone is tentative; he is offering an hypothesis for the client to consider. The burden of accepting this new percept, elaborating its dimensions, and integrating it into the field belongs to the client. This mode of counselor behavior affects the client quite differently than direct advising, e.g., "I think that your problem is quite easily resolved. Enter the field of medical illustration." Similarly, a tentative declaration in which the counselor expresses his own concern is more effective than a direct question, e.g., "Why don't you go read some occupational pamphlets about medical illustration and come back to see me?" The phrase "some other time—when I'm not so busy" seems implied in the counselor's statement. In the excerpt cited, however, the percept introduced by the counselor is related to the client's present self-organization and is likely to be assimilated into the self-system. In order to use effectively the technique of expanding the field, the counselor must be able to judge the client's readiness to open himself to experiences and perceptions previously unavailable to him, else the technique becomes authoritarian verbal bombardment. When the client accepts such expanding influences, especially in matters of educational or vocational self-definition, subsequent counselor roles often include providing meaningful, objective information through occupational-educational literature and through planned or casual client observation. Similarly, a further counselor role is to assist the client to incorporate new percepts into the organization of the self-system, especially within the aspirational self.

Integrative recapitulation

During the course of successful counseling, the client clarifies his perceptions of himself, develops new perceptions, integrates self-experience meaningfully, and optimally organizes the self-structure. When counseling is maximally successful, these developments occur so imperceptibly that the client is scarcely aware of the process. To assist the client in consolidating these developments and integrating them into the self-system, the self-interpretivist uses the technique of integrative recapitulation at judicious points in the counseling process. He offers the client a broad summary of his level of self-organization at that moment. Implicitly, but not explicitly, he is inviting the client to introject favorable perceptions arising from counselor-client interaction. The element of confirmation is present in this technique, but the counselor is confirming not a single perception or a set of related perceptions but a broad spectrum. In essence, the counselor is *offering confirmation of the present integration of the client's self-system*. In so doing, he is reinforcing both the elements of the self-system and the relationship of the elements to each other.

Integrative recapitulation is used less often than other behaviors in the interpretivist's repertoire. It is employed sparingly, when needed to help the client consolidate the newly developed patterns of perception or behavior. It is also employed in the closing or terminal stages of the counseling relationship. Often integrative recapitulation by the counselor precedes focusing the client's attention upon the initial perceptual concern he brought to the counseling relationship, in order to bring to bear upon that initial concern the client's present self-organization.

This excerpt is taken from the eighth and final interview with the male high school senior who initially presented concern about his parents' ambivalence toward his admission to college. Although the relationship was terminated at the end of this interview, it was likely that there would be future contacts as the client projected his newly organized self into reality. (In actuality, there were two additional interviews, which focused on the selection of a college.) Immediately before this exchange, the client had related that he had come to feel a new perspective not only on the issue of his relationship to his parents but even to himself. During this exchange, the client gives what is virtually a classic description of the integrated or mentally healthy person.

Client: The way I feel about it is . . . well, if a person is basically honest with . . . society and himself, there can't be anything wrong with him. He may not be smart, he may not have a college diploma, but he's—ah—still . . . still all right. . . . It's the person who does things dishonestly who . . . isn't all right. . . . Not honest with himself—what is that again—true to himself—and true to other people . . . like me being true to my mother and dad. . . . And the thing is . . . you *can* be true to yourself and true to other people too if you just . . . if you just don't expect too much from them, don't expect perfection. . . . That's the way I feel *now*. . . .

Counselor: (*Pause*) . . . It seems to me that you're not saying that my parents are overbearing, I can't stand it around them, I've got to get away to college. . . . That would be one extreme. . . . And you're not saying at the other extreme well, I don't know, I can't do anything without checking with the folks. It seems to me that what you're saying is I am *me*. I'm going to have to be independent later on in life. I'm learning to be independent now. I try to do things. . . . I'm learning to be honest with myself and honest with other people . . . and the surprising part of the way you feel is that there really aren't *necessarily* any conflicts about being honest, being true, to yourself and being honest with other people, so long as you can accept them . . . that you feel that you can have your own standards, be yourself, and still not have to disappoint anybody . . . if you don't expect perfection of them, just as you don't expect perfection of yourself. . . .

Client: (*Pause*) . . . That's just about the way I feel . . . that's the way things ought to be. . . . I guess that's just about the way things are . . . and y'know, I'm not mouthing, I really believe it, I really feel it. . . .

Often integrative recapitulation is followed by a period of constructive silence. In this case, the silence was rather brief. Again readiness is the key to the effective use of this technique. The client must be ready to consolidate previous changes in perception. He must similarly be ready to integrate the resulting consolidation into the self-system. Counselor verbal behavior is again declarative rather than imperative or interrogative. Interrogation (e.g., "Can you tell me what exactly you have learned about yourself in counseling?") seems most inappropriate to serve the purpose of consolidative reflection. Indeed interrogation of this sort very likely satisfies a need of the counselor for reassurance, rather than a need of the client for integrative organization. The integrative recapitulation is a particular kind of hypothesis offered to the client, since it concerns self-organization rather than single percepts or sets of percepts. But the principles suggested earlier in connection with the offering of hypotheses by the counselor apply equally here.

Mild confrontation

The final behavior in the self-interpretive counselor's repertoire is mild confrontation, an emergency measure used sparingly, if at all. The purpose of confrontation is to place the client squarely in view of reality at a time when he is unready or unable to achieve realistic perception by more integrative means or when realistic perceptions lie outside his range of self-experience. Counselor judgment is an important element in the decision to employ confrontation. The counselor must first be convinced that unless he intervenes rather directively, the client will persist in a series of self-defeating behaviors or in behaviors which are harmful to others. Further, shortness of time must preclude other counselor behaviors. The effect of confrontation with reality is to apply mild "shock" to the client, in an effort to jolt him into realistic perception. Often, when the counselor perceives that the client is about to make a self-defeating decision, mild confrontation remains the only technique at his disposal. In using mild confrontation, the counselor seeks to forestall such a self-defeating decision until the client has had time to consider its ramifications more thoughtfully. The desired outcome of confrontative counselor behavior is the creation of a counseling relationship in which the client is free to examine and perhaps reorganize self-structure.

The purpose of confrontation, however, is not to frighten the client. The person's unassailable right to self-determination *includes the right to self-defeat*. The counselor must be prepared to meet frustration even as he envisages the client's future frustrations. The counselor's desire to help the client avoid needless frustration must never conflict with his conviction of the client's right to self-determination.

The following excerpt is taken from a transcript of an interview with a college sophomore. This represents the first contact with the counselor. It occurs two days before the end of the second semester of the sophomore year, which is the college's deadline for declaration of a field of concentration. The client has come to the guidance office "to see what the tests showed," i.e., those aptitude tests which were administered at admission and during the college-wide sophomore testing program. He states his intention to declare engineering as a major field of concentration, despite two previous failures in mathematics and one in physics. His out-of-school activities and interests, however, seem to incline him away from engineering. His information about the fields of engineering is quite vague and nonspecific. Indeed, the principal piece of information about engineering on which he has based his choice is the average starting salary of graduate engineers. High school records indicate similarly below-average grades in mathematics and the sciences. The client has structured an unrealistic and probably unrealizable self-aspiration precisely because he has closed his perception of himself to the meaning of his self-experience. Immediately prior to this exchange, the counselor has interpreted to the client the results of a number of previously taken tests, which prognosticate little or no success in the study of engineering, though they indicate above-average language ability.

Client: Yeah . . . so what the tests say is that I'll really have to give it some going. . . . But, what the heck . . . I don't know of any other occupation where I can make as much money so quickly. . . . So I guess it will be engineering . . . (*pause*) . . . is that it?

Counselor: . . . (*Pause*) . . . Mm-hmm. . . . Well, let's look at it this way. . . . You told me you were interested in football. Suppose you—you probably know more about it than I do—suppose you were the coach, and you had—ah—a big tough line and a . . . a couple of good running backs, but you didn't really have a passer on your team. . . . What kind of strategy do you think you'd use? Would you pass or run? Think up a lot of plays involving passing?

Client: Well, heck no. I'd run.

Counselor: You'd run. . . . Isn't it the same kind of thing here? Capitalize on your strengths? Pick up your abilities and run with them? . . .

Client: (*Constructive silence*) . . . Okay. . . . Okay, I think I get the message . . . but where do I run *to?*

The client's last statement is an indication that the counselor's confrontative behavior has produced an admission that examination of self-structure is in order. Confrontative behavior is difficult to master, for this mode of communication lends itself very readily to authoritarian evaluation and prescription, e.g., "But you don't stand a chance for success in engineering. You'd better find some other field." The aim in mild confrontation is not to frighten the client out of a decision, a perception, or a behavior pattern. Rather, it is intended to demonstrate to him the advisability of undertaking a counseling relationship. Confrontative behavior, it must be remembered, is an emergency measure and should be regarded as a last resort. When the client fails to respond, the counselor does not reiterate or intensify the shock effect of confrontation. He respects the client's wishes in this as in other matters.

Varying behavior according to interview purpose

Self-interpretive school counselors vary their verbal behavior in accord with the characteristics of the client, his level of self-integration, and the point to which the counseling relationship has progressed. An important factor in the selection of appropriate communicative behaviors is the purpose of the interview. Among the categories into which school counseling interviews can be classified are the client-initiated, the familiarization, the informational, the test-interpretive, the referred, the parent-consultative, and the referral.

Client-initiated interviews are those arranged at the request of the client because he wishes to discuss a particular perceptual concern with the counselor. In the initial interview, the counselor's behaviors are primarily exploratory and reflective. Occasionally sensitive probing is useful to determine the extent to which the client's immediate perceptual concern has colored his self-organization. The first client-initiated interview is regarded as the beginning of a counseling relationship which may extend over a period of several interviews, during which the client consolidates and reorganizes the self-structure. Subsequent interviews in the counseling process once the relationship has been established are customarily scheduled once or twice a week. In school counseling, each interview generally is scheduled for thirty minutes, though more time is desirable. At the conclusion of a particular series of interviews, i.e., when the client's self-structure has been sufficiently well integrated, the client may seek additional contacts for informational, supportive, or other purposes. It is interesting to note that studies by Kirk (1955) and Dement (1957) have indicated that it is usually the academically superior students who seek to establish a counseling relationship. Their typical perceptual concerns are assistance in self-assessment, assistance in vocational orientation, and difficulties in social development.

The *familiarization interview* may be either client-initiated or counselor-initiated. Its purpose is to familiarize the student with the facilities of the counseling service. Such interviews are typically arranged shortly after a student enters a new school. The aim is to inform the student of the services available to him when he feels it necessary to seek counseling. Occasionally the familiarization interview itself will serve as sufficient stimulus to focus for the client a recurrent perceptual concern. But usually the familiarization interview is a relatively isolated contact. Counselor verbal behaviors which are most appropriate are exploratory and informational, i.e., factual statements relative to the scope and range of the counseling service. The second purpose of the familiarization interview is to allow the counselor to meet, even briefly, as many students as possible. When the client later seeks counseling assistance, he will not be approaching a stranger.

Informational interviews are usually client-initiated. The client is seeking specific factual information which he feels is relevant to the perceptual self.

Such interviews may occur in relative isolation. When this is the case, appropriate counselor behaviors generally include exploring the client's phenomenal field, confirming and supporting appropriate perceptions, and expanding the client's phenomenal field. Indeed, expansion is often what the client is seeking. Other informational interviews may be follow-ups from a previous counseling relationship; e.g., the client who has developed through the counseling relationship an appropriate vocational self-aspiration now seeks information concerning its implementation. When this is the case, counselor behaviors are typically those which expand the client's field and which confirm and support his appropriate perceptions. It is likely that the skillful information interview is the most common and most neglected in school counseling.

The *test-interpretation interview* is related to the interpretation to the client of results of school-wide standardized testing programs. Such an interview may be either client-initiated or counselor-initiated. The important issue is that it be conducted, for the client has a right to be informed of his performance on these evaluative instruments, even though they are intended to serve primarily an administrative rather than a guidance purpose. Here the counselor seeks to integrate the resulting information meaningfully into the client's self-structure. Telling the client test results without interpreting their significance for him at his particular stage of development and self-organization does not suffice. At best, it is ineffective; at worst, it constitutes verbal bombardment. Indeed, as Olsen (1963) has indicated, the brand-new counselor often welcomes the opportunity to strut his armamentarium of newly learned technical terms before the client, to his and the client's ultimate detriment. In order to expand the client's field through the introduction of new percepts or the confirmation of established percepts, the counselor needs first to explore the client's perceptual field. When test results are incongruent with self-perception, dexterous employment of support is indicated.

An *interview with a referred client* is usually arranged by the client or by the school administrator or teacher who has referred him. Typically, the client enters the counseling situation with a fairly well-defined topic. Often, however, this topic may be only marginally related to the client's principal perceptual concerns. The first interview with a referred client thus may be akin to a client-initiated or an informational interview, depending upon the reasons underlying the referral. One of the principal counselor tasks here is the assessment of *client readiness* to undertake a counseling relationship. Underlying reasons for referral to the counselor may range from the referrer's feeling that the counselor is better equipped to answer certain questions to the expectation that the counselor will be able to exhort a classroom discipline case to avoid aggravating the teacher. When reasons such as the latter underlie the referral, the counselor must anticipate hostility and resentment on the part of the client. In these circumstances, it is extremely important to communicate the feeling of acceptance to the client. If a comfortable relationship is established in the first interview with the referred client, he may seek to establish a client-initiated counseling process. Appropriate counselor behaviors include exploration, expansive reflection, and confirmation and support.

The *parent consultation interview* may be either parent-initiated or counselor-initiated. When the interview is initiated by the client's or student's parents, it is typically informational in nature. The parent seeks objective information about his child, clarification concerning educational and vocational orientation, and objective information relative to the implementation of the student's self-aspiration in view of the family's circumstances. As in informational interviews with students, the counselor needs to know something of the realities of family interaction (e.g., financial resources) in order to introduce percepts constructively. As Schneiders (1963a) noted, however, confidentiality concerning the content of counseling interviews with the student does not cease to operate in parent consultation. The parent has a right to information about educational and occupational resources and perhaps even to the results of standardized tests. But the communication between counselor and client remains privileged. When the counselor initiates consultation with the parent, he first secures the consent of the client. Counselor-initiated parent consultation often is arranged to inform the parents of the desirability of referral to a specialized agency capable of dealing effectively with special problems.

The *interview for referral* to another personnel service worker or to an out-of-school agency is usually initiated by the counselor. Typically, this interview constitutes one in a series of interviews in the counseling process. Referral may be made, for example, to a developmental or remedial reading clinic, an employment service, a health facility, or a mental-health agency. In any case, the counselor needs to prepare the client appropriately for referral. This process includes assisting the client to develop motivation to seek specialized assistance. In suggesting contact with another agency, the counselor is cautioned not to present to the client a picture of problems so embedded as not to be amenable to resolution. Rather, the counselor needs to state frankly the limits of his competence and suggest tentatively that the client consider contact with a specialized service more competent to assist him. The most efficacious procedure is for the counselor to arrange a first appointment with the client's and parents' permission. Similarly, the limits of confidentiality demand that the counselor seek the client's permission to reveal information to the specialized practitioner or agency. The only instance in which this principle is held in abeyance occurs when the client had been diagnosed by a competent psychologist or psychiatrist as psychotic and therefore unable to manage his own affairs. Indeed, it is only under these circumstances that the counselor is justified in revealing the client's confidences even to his parents. Since the cooperation and support of the parents for referral to specialized agencies (especially mental-health facilities) is ethically and legally necessary, the counselor needs the client's permission to discuss the matter with his parents. In making the referral, the counselor should offer the client and his family as much support as he is able to give during the course of their contacts with specialists. Motivating the client for referral is likely to involve the use of interpretive refraction and occasionally mild confrontation.

Preparing for the interview, for whatever purpose, involves the effort of the counselor to learn as much as he can about the client. Cumulative records, anecdotal records, psychometric records, information about the client's concern from the referring agent (if any), and the counselor's relevant knowledge of human development are the principal sources the counselor consults. The aim is to describe, not to evaluate, the client. The counselor also consults the student's cumulative counseling record, which lists briefly the date of each previous interview, the name of the counselor, and a one- or two-word description of the focus of the interview. If the counselor has had previous interviews with the student (e.g., prior contacts in a continuing counseling relationship), he consults his private records, which contain fairly detailed notes of those interviews. These private records are intended for use only by the counselor or by the counselor and supervisor; they are not made part of the cumulative record. The counselor's readiness for the interview consists in his ability to sensitize himself to anticipate the client and thus prepare to receive him warmly.

Establishing psychological contact

The counselor's first task in a counseling relationship is to attempt to establish psychological contact with the client. The counselor must be prepared to receive the client warmly and to communicate to him the feeling of what the Rogerians call warm positive regard. Psychological contact with the client implies that the counselor is willing to accept him as he is, to attempt to understand behavior and motivation from the client's internal frame of reference, and to communicate his unconditional acceptance of the client as a person of worth, dignity, and self-directive capacity (Lifton, 1958). Videbeck's important sociological study (1960) demonstrated that normal subjects introject readily evaluative reactions of persons introduced to them as specialists in various areas. The evaluative reaction becomes a learned perception of self incorporated into the self-concept. The school counselor is an adult member of the school staff, perceived as a surrogate of society. He functions as the "generalized" adult world for the individual client. It is likely that the essence of constructive self-organization in counseling lies in the client's experience of himself as an object of value to the counselor. The counselor communicates this evaluation to the client in a range of global and particular nonverbal behaviors. The seating arrangement in the counseling room, for example, easily lends itself to interpretation by the client. When the counselor is seated behind a large desk topped with innumerable papers and journals and the client is seated directly in front of him in a straight chair, he is unlikely to feel that the counselor is interested in him as a person. On the other hand, a seating arrangement which tends to minimize the counselor's position of authority seems to put the client more at ease and to communicate acceptance of him as an individual in whom the counselor has deep interest.

Client Readiness

A major factor in establishing psychological contact is the client's readiness. The client's immediate perceptual concern is the major dimension in his readiness for counseling, but as Grant (1954a) indicated, clients seek the counselor's assistance in areas in which they perceive him as capable of making positive contributions. Empirically, Grant found that secondary school students perceive the school counselor as helpful in educational and vocational orientation but not in broad areas of personal and social development. In a similar study in a college setting, Warman (1960) found that students and faculty members perceived the role of the counseling center as concerned primarily with vocational choice and adjustment to college routine, while counselors considered self-development as their primary concern. After counseling experience, however, students shifted their perceptions to approximate those of the professional counselors. One issue which emerges in client readiness is thus the image of the role of the school counselor. Another is the image of the counselor or the counselors in a particular school. McQuary (1964) found that clients prefer counselors who exhibit such personality characteristics as understanding, competence, personal interest, confidentiality, acceptance, experience, warmth, lack of bias, sincerity, and a good reputation.

The perception of the counseling role and the image of the counselors within a particular school function as global communications which color the student's feeling relative to the amount and type of assistance available. His readiness for counseling is thus related both to his need and to the perception that helpful assistance will be available from the counselor. These considerations argue for the necessity of familiarizing both the students and faculty with the full range of developmental counseling which the school counselor is prepared to render. Favorable impressions of the counseling service initiate the process of establishing psychological contact even before the client arranges the first interview.

Developing Rapport

Effective psychological contact eventuates in a comfortable relationship between client and counselor in which the counselor is able to anticipate the thoughts and even the feelings of the client. Through continued interaction, the counselor learns to read even minuscule postural movements as client nonverbal communications (Pittenger, 1963). The extent to which psychological contact has been established can be gauged, as Pepinsky and Karst (1964) suggest, by the rapidity with which client and counselor converge on common meanings and understandings.

Rapport is the term usually employed to designate psychological contact in the counseling situation. Perhaps its essential meaning is best exemplified in Fr. van Kaam's pregnant phrase (1959), "the experience of 'really feeling understood.'" As Buchheimer and Balogh (1961, pp. 4–6) have indicated, rapport develops from the mutuality of understanding through communication in the counseling relationship. Rapport is thus a property of the client (R. P. Anderson & G. V. Anderson, 1962), i.e., the experience of really feeling understood, which arises from social interaction with the counselor. Schwebel, Karr, and Slotkin (1957) regard "counselor relationship competence" as the cornerstone of effective psychological contact.

Fr. McIntyre, S.J. (1958), has suggested that rapport is predicated on the counselor's unqualified acceptance of the client. According to Fr. McIntyre, sincerity toward the client demands sincerity toward self. The counselor must be attuned to the reality of his own needs and personality and must have accepted himself. Most important, Fr. McIntyre contends, the counselor must accept unconditionally man's capacity for self-direction. Sheerer's study (1949) empirically demonstrated the relationship between the counselor's acceptance of himself and his acceptance of the client. Streitfeld (1959) also demonstrated the relationship between self-acceptance and other-acceptance, but he found no relationship between counseling success and acceptance of others or of self. Of interest also is the finding by Mendelsohn and Geller (1963) that similarity in personality and interests between client and counselor tend to have positive effects in establishing and maintaining rapport.

Counseling theorists as diverse as Rogers (1942) and Williamson (1939) stress the necessity of establishing adequate rapport as the first, essential step in successful counseling. Moreover, their viewpoints are surprisingly similar when Rogers (1960) urges counselors to be themselves, to be dependably real, in the relationship, while Williamson (1962) regards the counselor himself, his very person, "as technique." Thus, it appears that rapport is a property of the client arising in response to his experience of the counselor's person as warm, acceptant, nonthreatening, and nonpunitive.

In an effort to determine whether certain personality characteristics of the counselor were uniformly and dependably related to the client's experience of rapport, Grande and Pallone (1965) reported significant positive relationships between client rapport, as measured by the Anderson and Anderson Rapport Rating Scale (1962), and such counselor characteristics as ego strength, spontaneity in human relationships, and divergent instead of conforming patterns of thought. Similarly, they found that client rapport was negatively related to counselor authoritarianism and rigidity in regard to moral issues. In a second aspect of their study, Grande and Pallone found that Catholic students counseled by priests, brothers, or sisters typically experienced a lower degree of rapport than otherwise similar clients counseled by laymen or laywomen. Further, client rapport was significantly related to such personality characteristics as an orientation toward people rather than things, tendermindedness, and sensitivity only when the counselor was a lay person, although lay and religious counselors did not differ in the extent to which they possessed these characteristics. The investigators conjectured that perhaps the religious garb acts as a barrier which inhibits communication to the client of the personality characteristics of the religious counselor and hence inhibits rapport. Apparently Catholic students *no not expect* the religious counselor to exhibit such characteristics as warmth, spontaneity, sensitivity, and deep personal interest and hence do not respond to these characteristics even when the religious counselor possesses them as fully as does the lay counselor.

Although empirical evidence on the dimensions and correlates of rapport in counseling are not definitive, the essential factors in establishing and maintaining psychological contact with the client seem to be (1) certain counselor personality characteristics inclining the counselor toward warmth and sensitivity, (2) the counselor's openness to the client as a person as to an object of value, (3) the creation of an atmosphere of acceptance, (4) the suspension of judgment or moral evaluation of the client, and (5) the ability to convey to the client the feeling that he is understood and valued.

Dependence and Termination

Any human relationship which exists over a period of time is likely to cause certain feelings of dependency in both parties. It has already been suggested that adolescents are in a state of normal dependence relative to their developmental stage. The development of rapport between the school counselor and the client may intensify the student's normal dependent tendencies. The client may come to feel that *only* the counselor *really* understands him. When the counselor is a prescriptive advice giver, he may create abnormal dependence in the client. It is also normal for counselors to derive some satisfaction from the knowledge that they have been able to implement in the counseling relationship their percepts of themselves as "helping" persons. Indeed, their desires or needs to help others are strong motivating factors in their own process of occupational choice. But abnormal dependence upon any other person, including the counselor, hinders normal developmental processes. The interpretivist follows the principle that *the prime obligation of the counselor is to make himself as dispensable as possible as soon as possible.* The interpretivist rejects the role of the professional leaning post. Underlying many of his behaviors, this principle informs his practice. It is for this reason that his verbal behavior focuses on the internal self-organization of the client, not upon his own expertness. It is indeed an earmark of his expertness that he places, along with the Rogerian, the locus of decision and action within the client. His obligation lies in helping the client develop mature *self*-reliance anchored in a secure self-identity.

The question of the appropriate point at which to terminate the counseling relationship poses special problems. Ideally, the relationship is terminated when the client has effected maximal self-integration. Given the circumstances of the school setting and the dangers of abnormal dependence, however, the interpretivist usually terminates the relationship when the client has achieved the *minimal* level of self-integration sufficient to negotiate developmental tasks without great difficulty. McCall (1963) has observed that the principal human motive is to maximize self, but that man is often driven by his existential situation to concretize his urge toward self-maximization into what is practicable and achievable. The supportive environment of the school and the possibility of further client-initiated contacts allow the interpretivist to terminate the relationship earlier than a similar relationship with an adult client might be terminated in a mental-health facility or community guidance agency. Earlier termination may be resisted by the client, but it forestalls abnormal dependence.

Suspension of judgment: an illustrative case

Counselor acceptance of the client and the suspension of counselor evaluation or judgment are essential to establishing and maintaining psychological contact. Counselor acceptance must occur, Brother John M. Egan, F.S.C.H. (1958), has suggested, even in the face of material sin. Though the values of the counselor intrude into the relationship, Schneiders (1963a) believes that the counselor's responsibility is to "manipulate this intrusion in such a way as to maintain respect for the integrity of the client." Patterson (1958a) has suggested pointedly that the counseling relationship is not an ethics classroom. Nor, according to Fr. Rupp, S.M. (1957), is it a confessional where guilt is evaluated and penances are assigned. Counselor acceptance lies at the root of the client's feeling of really being understood and of the growth-facilitating experience of himself as an object of value.

The following case material is taken from the transcript of the initial interview with a male high school junior. He has been referred to the guidance laboratory of a nearby university by the principal of his high school. It is apparent in the first exchange that the client has been poorly prepared for referral. He enters the counseling room with evident hostility. The counselor endeavors to communicate to the client that he understands the client's hostility and accepts him *with* the hostility, not in spite of it. Prior to the initial interview, the counselor had received some information concerning the client. His high school record displayed primarily grades of C and D. Otis IQ scores ranged from 94 to 97.

Client: Damn if I know why I'm here. . . . I'm here because they sent me. . . .

Counselor: Somebody over there just wanted you to come over here. . . .

Client: Yeah, it must be grades or attitudes, one of the two. . . . But I don't understand—how many students they got over there they had to pick me. . . .

Counselor: Mm-hmm. . . .

Client: Grades, that must be it. . . . They wanted to find out why I wasn't doing better. . . . The way I understand it, my IQ's all right and everything's all right, but my grades. . . . So they told me to come out and find out what my problem was. . . .

Counselor: Uh-huh . . . grades and attitudes. . . .

Client: Well, I guess I give 'em the impression I just don't care or something like that . . . to that effect. . . .

Counselor: . . . And you kind of resented being told to come here. . . .

Client: Well, it's not that, I just thought. . . . Well, the way I look at it, they got me . . . five hours. . . . I mean they got me from nine to three, and when I get out of there—if and when—I don't see what it is to them what I do, y'know what I mean? . . . They're over me and everything, and when I graduate, I'm never going back, y'know what I mean? . . . So in that sense, it . . . it doesn't matter what I do, y'know what I mean? . . .

Counselor: (*Pause*) . . . So you feel why the devil should they single me out. . . .

Client: Yeah, that's what I was wondering . . . (*pause*). . . . Well, my grades . . . they're lousy. . . .

Counselor: . . . And I guess they're always after you over there to do better . . . keep telling you you can do better. . . .

Client: . . . Everybody's always getting their digs in me, always telling me I got the wrong outlook on everything, y'know what I mean? . . . The way I look at it, everybody's got their opinion. . . . I mean, I'm . . . indifferent, that's what they all tell me. . . . My dad and I get along real well, except on that, he—he'd let anybody do anything they wanted to, anything, anytime . . . he's the first one to help 'em and the first one they walk over . . . go out of his way for them and everything. . . . I can see doing something and not expecting anything in return, y'know what I mean?—but to get walked over, that's another thing. . . .

Counselor: (*Pause*) . . . and you and your dad get along well except—

Client: (*Interrupting*) In his words, I don't give a damn for anybody or anything but my own. . . . He tells me my outlook is wrong and that in some way he's failed me . . . or failed himself more'n me . . . failed to show me the light. . . .

The client's hostility and resentment were evident in his initial statements. The counselor interpreted his resentment and endeavored to convey acceptance of the client and his feelings. By accepting the client, the counselor made it *unnecessary* for the client to continue his hostility. The focus of discussion moved quickly from the client's resentment over referral to conflict with his father. The counselor's relevant knowledge of personality development and function now allows him to infer that the client's initial resentment against school authority was actually displaced resentment against his father. Objective statements of fact, to the effect that the client had been referred precisely because of the interest of his teacher in him, would have reflected reality but not the client's perceptual world. Such statements would have been tantamount to rejection of the client's feelings. The client's appeal for understanding is underscored in his often-repeated statement, "y'know what I mean?" Shortly after this exchange, the client becomes perceptually aware of the counselor's acceptance and focuses on the counseling process itself.

Client: I'd rather have a few friends than a lot, y'know what I mean? . . . (*pause*) . . . I keep expecting you to tell me something. . . . I don't know what. . . .

Counselor: What do you figure? . . .

Client: Well, you're going to tell me that I'm wrong or something like that. . . . I told this all before. . . . I'm just waiting for it. . . . I told this before to other people, and they come out with these earth-shaking answers, y'know, that're going to settle all my problems like a godsend . . . (*pause*) . . . but all I got so far is a shake of the head, so I'm kinda curious. . . .

Counselor: Maybe disappointed. . . .

Client: No, not disappointed . . . maybe . . . well, if you began with the earth-shaking answers, it'd be like . . . like everyone else. . . .

The effect of the counselor's second statement ("Maybe disappointed") was to focus the client's attention on his expectation of exhortation and his readiness to reject the counseling relationship. The client begins to understand that the counseling process is not "like everyone else." In this exchange, the client no longer needs to appeal for understanding; he simply says "y'know." This expression may indicate that the client is beginning to experience that he and the counselor are rapidly converging on meanings and understanding; he has experienced acceptance to the extent that he anticipates that the counselor is "reading" the meaning of his communications.

About ten minutes after this exchange, the client begins progressively to test the limits of counselor acceptance. He is still seeking to determine whether the judgmental, earth-shaking answers will be forthcoming.

Client: The only thing I really get a charge out of studying is religion and the more you go into it, the more I find personally it's hard to believe . . . y'know. . . . I'm not a good Catholic, but I'm not the worst, but some of that stuff I just can't go along with, y'know. . . .

Counselor: Uh-huh. . . .

Client: . . . I don't see how some guy can sit down and say no meat today, but then today we'll give you a dispensation and you can eat all you want. . . . I just don't see that myself . . . I . . . (*pause*). . . .

Counselor: . . . It's a little hard for you to take. . . .

Client: Well, I mean . . . the guy's the same as I am and they give him a beanie and a prayer book and the first thing you know he's making laws for me and I don't understand that. . . . Like they said, the first they come out with twenty-four-hour fast, the next day it's ten hours or three hours for this and that. . . . I don't see how they can. . . . I'm not saying they do it to their own fancy, y'understand, but. . . . And if they came out with no meat on Thursday, we'd have to go along with that, y'know what I mean? . . .

The client here has attacked at the least the magisterium of the local ordinary and at the worst the supremacy of the Pope, depending upon the referrent of the phrase "they give him a beanie and a prayer book." Certainly the client seems in error. To many, it would appear unthinkable to let him persist in error, confusion, or ignorance. *But the counseling process is not a religion class.* The theological principle *qui tacit, tacit* applies. The only appropriate role for the counselor is *unconditional acceptance and lack of support for erroneous client beliefs.* Fr. Curran (1959; 1960) asserts the tendency to contradict or chastise must be held in check even in a pastoral counseling situation. In view of the earlier reference to conflict between father and son, the counselor has formed the hypothesis that the client is actually attacking symbols of authority, thus indirectly underscoring the severity of father-son conflict. The client's reintroduction of an appeal for understanding ("y'know what I mean") is evidence that this behavior consists in testing the limits of counselor acceptance. A few minutes after this exchange, the client begins to utter heretical statements. In both cases, contradiction or chastisement would serve to disrupt the counseling process, place the counselor in the prescriptive position of "everyone else," and make him rejectable by the client.

Client: One of the. . . . Now I've gone into a little thought about it. One of the biggest—ah—ah . . . what am I trying to say? . . . Well, when they say Mary's the Mother of God, I don't understand that at all. God's God, right? God had no beginning, God had no end. So when Christ became man, in a sense, God was Christ, but Christ wasn't God, right? . . . Christ was man, man couldn't be God, but God could be man. So when Christ died, God didn't die, man died . . . and Mary was the Mother of man, not God . . . so when He died, so did her—ah—ah . . . what am I trying to say? . . . her—ah—ah. . . .

Counselor: Son? . . .

Client: Yeah, her son died, God didn't die, y'know what I mean? So Mary was the mother of God, I don't understand that at all. . . .

Counselor: And this causes you a great deal of confusion. . . .

Client: (*Somewhat angrily*) It don't. . . . I mean I don't lose any sleep on it or anything, but . . . I don't understand how they come right out with . . . (*speaking rapidly*). . . . Surely somebody's got to have gone to some length to think it out. I mean, I'm no quiz kid and I figured it out . . . in my own mind I figured it out. . . . I—ah—all these great—ah—theologians, seems like somebody should've figured it out. And I don't see where, they found a place in there where they say there's a purgatory, where there's a hell. They always speak about—ah—something like that. I think personally, now I may be off track, but I think personally hell's a state of the mind. I don't think there has to be any physical pains, do you? They always say in the next life you're going to serve God and this and that. . . . Well, wouldn't that be the hell itself, or is it? . . . (*very long pause*). . . .

Counselor: . . . . I've heard that hell is precisely the knowledge that one will never see God. . . .

Client: Yeah, yeah. . . . Another thing I thought out about this little job is this apple bit and this Adam and Eve. Now what I think about it is there never was. . . . I don't believe that there ever was a garden; I don't believe there ever was anybody banished. . . . What I think it was, was when he said I will not obey, and that was all there was to it. . . . Don't you think so? . . .

Counselor: . . . That certainly would seem to be the essence of it, wouldn't it? . . .

Client: . . . And when they go off on Jonah in the belly of the whale, now that's something else altogether. . . . Any . . . any imbecile knows that over a period of—how long was he supposed to be in there?

Counselor: I think it was three days.

Client: Well any imbecile knows that digestion takes place in—what is it, five to eight hours or something like that . . . (*pause*). . . .

Counselor: I don't know what it is for a whale. . . .

Client: (*Pause, but short of constructive silence*). . . . Yeah, I guess, I guess the more you go into it . . . the harder it gets. . . .

The counselor's role here is unconditional acceptance. He supports (i.e., reinforces) favorable positions. He suspends judgment of the meaning of the client's attacks on religious authority until he can enter fully the client's perceptual world and determine their meaning *for him*. The client has progressively tested the limits of counselor acceptance. When the counselor continued to suspend judgment on major issues (e.g., the Divine maternity of Mary), the client was disarmed. Then he resorted to a rather fruitless discussion of the length of time needed for digestion by whales. The effect of the final counselor statement in this exchange is to focus the client's attention on the probable meaning of these concerns, i.e., their value as a network of defenses against self-experience. The counselor has learned that the client is much disturbed about parental relationships, from the client's difficulty in selecting the word "son" in relation to Christ. Thus the counselor believes that, in questioning the relationship between Christ and Mary, the client is actually questioning his relationship to his own mother. The counselor is now convinced that the client is neither essentially in error nor in heresy. His beliefs seem to have a root in the dynamics of family interaction. Were the counselor not convinced that the client's beliefs were anchored in failure to develop healthy parent-child relationships, however, he might consider this a case which could be more appropriately handled by a pastoral counselor. The following exchange, which occurs after forty-five minutes of the initial interview, serves to organize the meaning of the client's perceptual concerns and behaviors earlier in the interview. The counselor had probed the area of parental relationships sensitively subsequent to the exchange just cited.

Counselor: . . . And your mother. . . .
Client: Well, my mother . . . she isn't . . . (*long pause*) . . . and they—ah. . . . I guess I might as well tell you . . . what it amounted to was . . . (*speaking softly, emotionless, flat*). . . when my father got back from the war, he was decorated . . . a glory hound and all that . . . and—ah—he was on the juice for quite a while, he just couldn't—ah . . . and my mother got so fed up, she left . . . and I was staying with a baby-sitter at the time . . . and he took off and never came back . . . so I was just . . . *left,* y'know . . . with the baby-sitter, which she eventually got married . . . and that's who I've stayed with ever since . . . not adopted or anything, y'understand . . . (*pause*). . . .
Counselor: . . . I see. . . .
Client: . . . I was about three years old at the time. . . . I see him from time to time. I usually say hello, don't have much else to. . . . I saw her once; I see the guy quite a bit . . . usually find him around one of the bars, something like that . . . (*pause*) . . . I don't know. . . .
Counselor: . . . So your father. . . .
Client: He's the guy I'm living with. . . . Yeah, I like to call him that . . . but . . . (*pause*) . . . in return for what he's done, I've done nothing . . . and I don't see any solution to it either. . . .

Here the ultimate thematic concerns are suggested: Who am I? How do I behave? The client's statement, after indicating that his natural father could usually be found in one of the bars, might be amended to read "I don't know my self-identity." The task of forming a secure self-identity is a normal developmental task. Here it has been exacerbated, hindered, and impeded by the factors which the client has just related. Counselor behavior throughout this interview has consisted essentially in verbal statements of low internal structure to permit maximum self-projection in client response. Though the counselor anticipated an underlying father-son tension, he did not expect the obstacles to self-identity which ultimately appeared. Earlier cues had suggested the presence of paternal pressure toward school success which the client rejected, a common cause of poor academic performance. At these revelations, the counselor himself is shocked and must control his tendency to *sympathize.* Rather, he seeks to *empathize by responding at a feeling tone which approximates that of the client,* in the same sort of disconnected statements which the client has used. The counselor's behavior here is intended to communicate to the client the counselor's efforts to understand the world as it appears to the client. Near the end of the interview, the client appeals for reassurance that he is not just another case to the counselor to be dealt with in a pat way.

Client: . . . One thing I was curious about . . . every individual falls into a certain classification, don't they? . . .

Counselor: No, I wouldn't say that. . . .

Client: Well, all right, not classification, but group of some sort. . . . I mean you put them into categories . . . (*pause*). . . .

Counselor: . . . I don't like to put people into pigeonholes. . . .

Client: . . . What I was getting at is, y'know . . . do you ever get anything that's *really* interesting, y'know what I mean? . . . (pause) . . .

Counselor: I think this is a pretty interesting young man we have right here. . . .

Client: (*Constructive silence*) . . . Yeah? . . . You really think so? . . . And no earth-shaking answers. . . . (*pause*) . . . Well, this is going to be different anyway. . . .

The counselor has conveyed to the client an experience of himself *as an object of value* to the counselor, the essence of the growth-facilitating counseling process. The recurrence of the statement "y'know what I mean" indicates the client's quest for such assurance. The counselor has communicated to the client that he is regarded as an individual and as an object of value, not as a "case" to be pigeonholed. The client has internalized the feeling that counseling is a "different" kind of relationship. The case material presented in this section suggests the necessity for suspension of judgment and unconditional acceptance on the part of the counselor. Only under such circumstances can the counselor learn how the client perceives himself. Since behavior is a function of the field as perceived, it is essential that the counselor be able to enter the client's field before he can judge the relevance and meaning of the client's behavior. Thus the evaluation or judgment, the tendency to contradict or chastise, and the inclination to sympathize need to be extirpated from the counselor's repertoire of behavior. In this case, the client entered the counseling relationship with hostility. His perceptual concern was not poor academic performance, the cause for referral, but rather the manner of referral itself. Through the course of the interview, the client expressed sentiments of hostility toward his teachers, the Church, and even against traditional Church teaching. It was only under conditions of total counselor acceptance and suspension of judgment that the client was able to express his abiding perceptual concerns over self-identity. At this point, growth facilitation through the counseling process is ready to begin.

To review, the major dynamics which were illustrated in this interview included the client's attempts to direct hostility transferred from the school situation toward the counselor, his appeal for understanding, his general sense of futility and the need for self-assertion, a focus on the novel experience of acceptance in the counseling relationship, testing the limits of counselor acceptance through progressive attacks upon religious authority, major self-revelations concerning lack of identity and the origin of hostile reactions to authority through communication of his abandonment as a child, and appeals for reassurance. In the counseling relationship which ensued, these dynamics were explored in relation to the development of a secure self-identity and to academic adjustment. When the Wechsler Adult Intelligence Scale was administered to the client, his full-scale intelligence quotient on this clinical instrument measured 132, strongly at variance with previous scores. Counseling ultimately resulted in greater self-integration.

Evaluating counseling effectiveness

Counseling remains the most difficult guidance service to evaluate. Varying perceptions of the role of the counselor tend further to obfuscate already complex issues. The insensitive school administrator may wish to judge the effectiveness of counseling solely on the basis of the number of students who entered the "right" school or were placed in the "right" jobs. Insensitive administrators often value counselors more highly for the number of clients they "handle" than for the degree of self-integration these clients attain.

Surely the outcome of the counseling relationship must be evaluated in terms of the goals of counseling. Disease-oriented counseling models thus regard amelioration of pathologies as the criterion of success. Sufficiently sensitive instruments exist to compare pretreatment and posttreatment conditions of the clients served. Decision-oriented models regard the "right" choice of education or career as the criterion for success. Follow-up studies of counseled and noncounseled students may provide data on success and satisfaction in educational or vocational endeavors. But the self-interpretive model regards effective self-integration as the criterion for success. The first question the interpretivist asks is: "Has the client become more effectively integrated?" The second is: "Does his postcounseling level of integration demonstrate itself in more effective personal functioning, e.g., in the satisfactory accomplishment of remaining developmental tasks?"

The second question is easier to answer than the first. Instruments exist to measure functioning in the various areas of living, and precounseling and postcounseling measurement may produce indications of change. But the first question is harder to answer. The phenomenal field is a vastly difficult area for measurement with any sort of precision. Yet, to evaluate the effectiveness of interpretivist counseling, it is necessary both to determine change in levels of integration and to relate change to more effective functioning.

Clients tend to regard counseling as more successful than counselors, as Pohlman (1964) has demonstrated. Perhaps an explanation can be found in the differential expectations of client and counselor. It is unlikely that the opinions of either clients or counselor, however, will serve as adequate demonstrations of increasingly more effective self-integration. Of the instruments presently available, devices based on "Q technique," used to evaluate the effectiveness of client-centered psychotherapy, seem best suited to the goals of self-interpretive counseling (see Mowrer, 1953). Clients are asked to "sort" a series of self-referent statements of neutral social desirability into categories along a continuum from "most like me" to "most unlike me." Q sorts may be made for the perceived self, the ideal self, and the self-as-experienced. Changes in relationships can be determined by increasingly greater congruences, but as Patterson (1964) has argued, there is some evidence that certain placebo effects tend to contaminate Q-sort studies. Yet psychometric devices of markedly low internal-stimulus structure (e.g., projective tests), while global in nature, do not lend themselves to precise statistical analysis.

The dynamics of the counseling process, especially the effect of counselor verbal behavior on growth facilitation, is another challenge to scientific evaluation. While cataloguing the number of counselor statements into the various modes of communication and relating these to change in the client may provide some interesting statistical designs, it is not the bald *number* of reflective, interpretive, etc., statements which forms the prime issue. Rather, it is the *sequence, timing,* and *organization* of varying communicative behaviors which form the central issue for the interpretivist.

Counseling is a process which involves client growth in internal self-organization, an internal process which does not lend itself to precise measurement. Evaluation of the counseling process involves design of controlled experimental conditions which are difficult to obtain in a process as unpredictably flowing as counseling. Indeed, more than one writer has charged that using counselors as experimenters who structure their interviews on the basis of a design for an evaluative study is injurious to confidentiality and therefore unethical. D. H. Ford (1959) has denied the charge, contending that every counselor and therapist has an obligation to attempt to discover the type of counseling relationship and method most effective for counseling assistance.

Several procedures are commonly used to evaluate the effectiveness of school counseling. Although the interpretivist recognizes them as not entirely suited to the goal of counseling as he perceives it, he may be forced to use such procedures in view of the lack of more appropriate methods. *First,* external criteria such as job success and satisfaction or educational success are utilized. The inference may be made that more effective functioning issues from more cohesive self-integration. *Second,* precounseling and postcounseling comparisons are made on tests of personality organization, value orientation, occupational information, and the like. Such comparisons are uncertain because of the network of tangled, intertwining variables in the counseling process. Further, to isolate (and therefore demonstrate) that change is attributable to counseling, control groups with identical properties are necessary. *Third,* opinions on the effectiveness of counseling are solicited from the client, his teachers, friends, and parents and from the counselor and counselor-supervisor. But this procedure may precisely highlight the placebo effect. Further, a client with a dependency need may tend to regard counseling aimed at helping him achieve self-reliance as ineffective. *Fourth,* counseling effectiveness can be assessed by attempting to measure the extent to which the client "really felt understood." The rapport scale developed by R. P. Anderson and G. V. Anderson (1962) may be used for this purpose. This procedure is more compatible with the goals of self-interpretive counseling, which places great stress on establishing and maintaining growth-facilitating psychological contact. Counselors who have not completed rigorous course work in statistical method and research design owe it to themselves to become intimately familiar with Kerlinger's manual (1964) on behavioral research.

11

GROUP PROCEDURES
IN GUIDANCE

Rationale for group procedures

Efficiently organized school guidance programs do not rely solely on the one-to-one counseling relationship in assisting students to self-organize optimally for successful development. Integrated into the total guidance program are a variety of group experiences on a one-to-several or a one-to-many basis. The utilization of group procedures in guidance is anchored in the commonality of the developmental tasks characteristically encountered in certain periods of life. Indeed, the mutual support arising from group interaction among students facing common tasks is an important element in the achievement of self-integration by each group member. Many essential guidance functions, particularly those related to expansion of the phenomenal field, lend themselves more readily to group procedures than to individual procedures. In recognition of this fact, Wrenn (1961, p. 15) urged counselors and other guidance workers to "use planned group situations as carefully as the interview is utilized in the development of improved student self-understanding and the facing of psychological realities."

Several inaccurate notions persist about the nature and function of group procedures in guidance. Some public and particularly Catholic school people regard group guidance as an inexpensive substitute for individual counseling. This notion is conveyed in the frequently encountered assertion that the counselor or guidance worker can multiply himself by conducting group activities. Implicit in this assertion is the supposition that the chief concern of counseling is the dispensation of bits of information about educational and occupational resources, perhaps combined with some test giving, services which can just as well be proffered in groups as in one-to-one relationships. Another common approach has regarded as the operational definition of group guidance whatever goes on during the homeroom period.

Among the misconceptions about the nature of group guidance procedures which Bennett (1963, pp. 20–24) has identified are the following: (1) group guidance is an information-giving process, (2) group guidance is an alternative to the counseling program, and (3) any member of the school staff is adequately prepared to conduct group guidance "classes." A more accurate perception, according to Bennett, views the relationship between group procedures and individual counseling as reciprocal and complementary. Some guidance functions are best implemented in the individual counseling situation, while others are best implemented in group situations. The focus is not on economy of counselor time or teacher personnel but on student need. Special skills and training are necessary to engage effectively in group procedures, and often neither counselors nor teachers are well equipped in these areas. Counselor preparation programs in universities usually train students more thoroughly to conduct the individual interview than to conduct group sessions. A study by Harmon and Arnold (1960) revealed that most working school counselors surveyed were dissatisfied with their sketchy preparation for group guidance but were satisfied with other aspects of their training. Even when adequate course work is available, there is rarely an opportunity for practicum experiences in group guidance. Teacher training tends to remain directed toward the production of subject-matter specialists who emphasize content rather than student need. Classroom activities and the communication skills of the subject-matter specialist are usually teacher-centered or subject-centered, not student-centered. Notable exceptions to this pattern have developed, however, especially in training programs for prospective teachers in the core curriculum design (Lee, 1963b, pp. 286–342; Willy & Strong, 1957, pp. 393–474).

Regardless of the cognitive object of learning, learning essentially is a property of the student. "Good" teaching is thus as necessarily student-centered as either group guidance or individual counseling. Emphasis belongs in both functions on the idiographic rather than on the nomothetic plane. Group guidance procedures represent one avenue through which the student is assisted to learn himself, to learn the important sectors of self, and to expand self. The role of the group worker is to help the student actualize his internal drive toward self-knowledge and self-expansion by and through a *group* situation. The effective implementation of this role requires competence in stimulating growth in groups of students. Hence, Wrenn (1962, pp. 130–131) has suggested that leadership for what he has termed planned group experiences "calls for an understanding of the dynamics of group interaction that makes it quite different from the supervision of homeroom situations or occupational information classes." In view of the intrinsic values of the group experience as a human relations laboratory for students, the range and variety of group procedures, and the types of situations in which group procedures are more appropriate than individual counseling, the graduate preparation of prospective counselors and teacher-counselors needs to be strengthened. Cognitive course content and supervised practicum experiences in group guidance need to be provided or improved. The focus of the training program in group guidance should be aimed at producing a *functional understanding of the dynamics of group process and their relevance for guidance.*

Group guidance is not individual counseling dispensed to a group instead of to an individual. Rather it is guidance which depends on group interaction for its fruition. Thus counseling and group guidance are far more distinct than the mere number of students at a session. The distinction is precisely that the student's growth from counseling comes from his dynamic encounter with one counselor, while his growth from group guidance arises from his encounter with both group and group worker.

Elements of group process: a sketch

A considerable body of knowledge about the dynamics of group formation and interaction has been developed at both the conceptual and the empirical levels. Sociologists such as Bales (1950) and Olmstead (1959) and social psychologists such as Thibaut and Kelley (1959) and Sherif and Sherif (1956, pp. 119–361) have summarized the fundamental principles of group behavior. Guidance experts like Strang (1958) and Lifton (1961, pp. 130–163) have sought to apply these principles to the guidance situation. Research has been stimulated since World War II by the rapid development of the field of *group dynamics* as an interdisciplinary specialty (D. Cartwright & A. Zander, 1960, pp. 3–32) involving researchers in the allied social and behavioral sciences of sociology, psychology, and education. Group workers in guidance need an adequate understanding of group behavior in order to function successfully. If they are to perform their tasks effectively, they need an understanding of the principles of group formation and cohesion, social reality, pluralistic ignorance, group size, and leadership style.

Group Formation and Cohesion

On psychological grounds, Sherif and Sherif (1963) have distinguished between the group and the collection of individuals in the "togetherness situation." A group is composed of a number of individual members who have established *reciprocal relationships* with each other. These relationships do not exist in the togetherness situation, except in the most general way. C. A. Gibb (1964) points out that persons who are grouped together in the mind of an observer are often mistaken for a "real" group. For example, a guidance worker may regard all tenth-grade boys as a group, though no reciprocal relationships have been established among them. Gibb prefers to designate these individuals an aggregate or a collection. Nor does the possession of a common characteristic among individuals in an aggregate (e.g., eleventh-grade girls who have expressed a desire to enter the profession of veterinary medicine) constitute the essential quality of a group. The fundamental and distinguishing characteristic of the group is the *interdependence* of its members on each other in the achieving either of a common goal or of mutually shared goals. Hence, according to Gibb, "*The term functional group refers to two or more organisms interacting, in the pursuit of a common goal, in such a way that the existence of many is utilized for the satisfaction of some needs of each.*" In these terms, a collection of students previously identified as socially reserved or withdrawn who attend a homeroom class during which the counselor or teacher lectures them about ways to overcome shyness constitute a *togetherness situation*. Of course, there is a minimum interdependence of students even in this situation; e.g., they must observe appropriate classroom decorum so as not to interfere with other students or with the authoritarian group leader. But this is essentially a togetherness situation, since the students depend on the "group" worker, not upon each other, in gaining whatever benefits may accrue. The same students interacting in a discussion or a role-playing situation, however, focused on the same concern, are interdependent on each other and less dependent on the direction of the teacher or the counselor. Under these circumstances, they constitute a functional group.

Groups are formed because members believe that group interaction will be beneficial to them. Members remain in groups, as Festinger, Schachter, and Back (1960) have demonstrated, as long as they continue to believe that group interaction is beneficial. Weiss and Pasamanick (1962) determined that alienation from the group results when the member no longer shares a common goal. The *cohesiveness* of the group depends on the extent to which each member feels that his purpose in joining the group is being satisfied. Lipton and Feiner (1956) have described the stages of growth in a group of students who were receiving remedial reading assistance. These stages include (1) disorganization, or the togetherness situation; (2) individual competition among students; (3) team competition among students; (4) group solidarity or cohesiveness; (5) socially adaptive verbal interaction relative to planning group activity; and (6) group-initiated and group-directed learning activity. These stages indicate that the togetherness situation may evolve over time into a group situation. Thus, for example, students invited by the guidance worker to join a discussion concerned with dating behavior may initially exhibit reluctance to engage in free interchange. If this "collection" of students persists over time, reciprocal relationships will eventually be established among members and between members and the guidance worker. As Sherif and Sherif (1963, p. 84) have indicated, "If togetherness situations continue, with individuals facing some common problem, or some common circumstance of significance to them, *in time* their interactions take on distinctive properties characteristic of human groups. At the least such distinctive properties include some degree of organization of function and position in the group and some standards or norms regulating relationships among individuals." Shure and his associates (1962) demonstrated that newly formed groups are typically unable to concentrate on goals so long as the group roles remain unspecified. Thus, group members detour from their perceptual concerns (i.e., purpose in joining the group) long enough to develop appropriate group roles.

One of the principal tasks of the guidance worker in facilitating the formation of a group is to convey to potential members the notion that their roles will likely be quite different from those in the traditional, subject-centered classroom situation. The role of the student in the traditional classroom is typically and unfortunately either passive or merely reactive, while that of the group member is active, participative, and involved. Newer curriculum designs, however, view the class as a group and not as an aggregate. When problem solving, discussion, and other group methods are used in teaching, indeed the class *becomes* a group. Similarly and equally unfortunately, the typical teacher is active and controlling, while the effective group leader is less a director than a stimulator. In many group guidance situations, the leader also conveys to the prospective group members that in time they will assume leadership roles themselves, often on a rotating or quasi-leaderless basis.

Social Reality

At the root of group formation and cohesion lies a set of common perceptions about objects of central importance to the group. Group membership is predicated on the persistence of common perceptions central to group purpose. Catholics, for example, hold the common perception that the Pontiff is indeed the Vicar of Christ on earth. Should a member of the Church change his belief on this important matter, he detaches himself from the Church. Either he rejects the group or the group rejects him.

On the other hand, lack of common perception of objects not of central importance to the group does not disrupt group cohesion. As long as there is common perception on essential issues, a variety of divergent perceptions may be tolerated or actually encouraged by the group. Hence there is no unanimity of belief among Catholics on the desirability of water fluoridation, and there is no "Catholic position" on the San Francisco Giants; there is, however, a Catholic position on the divinity of Christ. Nonetheless, members of a group interacting closely may come to hold common perceptions of objects not central to the group. In a student group, John, Harvey, and Mark each aspire to become physicians. They agree that a basic liberal arts preparation in college is to be preferred to a strictly premedical program. In the course of securing further information, John happens to espouse the candidacy of Tom for the student council presidency. Harvey and Mark are relatively uncommitted on this issue, but because of the cohesion they have developed with John, they are favorably disposed to John's arguments in favor of Tom. Soon they too espouse Tom's candidacy.

Turk, Hartley, and Shaw (1962) have demonstrated that common group membership and high cohesion vary with social influence and social influence-ability. The more an individual perceives commonality between himself and another, the more receptive he becomes to social influence and the more he anticipates influencing the other. Similarly, Bass (1959) found that common motivation creates consistency in group attitudes and performance. Mc-Cleary (1956) has commented that classroom groups usually fail to perceive their roles in common and suggests that teachers must create groups with common perceptions in place of the usual classroom aggregates.

Many areas of human behavior preclude the perception of cognitive objects on the basis of the structural properties of objects alone. In such cases, *social reality* becomes the testing ground for the validation of one's perceptions. Schachter (1960, p. 269) suggested: "On any issue for which there is no empirical referent, the reality of one's own opinion is established by the fact that other people hold similar opinions. Forces exist [within the group] to establish uniformity and thus to create 'reality' for the opinion." In his pioneering studies in 1935–37, Sherif (1953) demonstrated that groups act as social frames of reference through which members perceive and judge the relevance of objects, persons, ideas, and so forth. Established reciprocities and group interaction tend to produce lines of social influence which urge group members toward consensus on many issues other than those central to group purpose.

Pallone's investigation (1965) of religious authority and social perception has particular implications for the question of social reality and also for leadership style in a Catholic educational setting. This study demonstrated that social authority rooted in the clerical role in the religious membership group is capable of being extended to influence even members' perceptions of nonambiguous visual stimuli, an issue clearly not central to the purpose of the group, i.e., the Catholic Church. In this experiment, randomly selected Catholic college students of normal visual acuity were asked to estimate the magnitude of a series of geometric objects (squares) projected on a screen. On the second and third trials, they again were asked for size estimates, but now they were exposed to the experimenter's confederate, who attempted to influence the subjects to alter their initial estimates drastically, although no rewards or punishments were threatened or imposed. Groups A and B received influence attempts applied by a confederate wearing clerical garb, i.e., a black suit and a Roman collar; group C, by a confederate wearing normal business clothing. On the second trial, subjects in groups A and C were required to report their estimates aloud while in the presence of the confederate and on the third trial in writing. This procedure was called *severe-mild conformity pressure sequence.* Group B was accorded the reverse treatment, i.e., *mild-severe conformity pressure sequence.* The clerical and neutral confederates attempted to influence the subjects to perceive the stimulus objects as grossly larger or smaller than the sizes reported by subjects in their initial estimates. On the fourth trial, subjects estimated the sizes again but not in the presence of the confederate. Subjects in group C, exposed to the neutral confederate, were relatively unaffected in their perceptions either in his presence or afterward. Subjects in group A, exposed to the clerical confederate in the severe-mild sequence, not only agreed with his estimates while in his presence but also in the final trial, indicating that they had interiorized his obviously distorted perceptions. Subjects in group B, exposed to the clerical confederate in the mild-severe sequence, rejected his estimates while in his presence but surprisingly agreed with those estimates in the final trial, apparently because they were unable to withstand the experience of "rebellion" against clerical authority, even in an area far removed from the clerical role. These results held true uniformly, regardless of personality factors within subjects predisposing them to conforming patterns of behavior. Apparently Catholic students perceive the occupant of the religious role as a decisive testing ground for their own perceptions, as social reality, even when the objects to be perceived are neither ambiguous nor central to group purpose. The authoritarian, prescriptive religious who wishes to use the role of counselor or guidance worker to impose his own views on students can take comfort in these findings. On the other hand, the religious teacher or counselor who perceives both education and guidance as joint searches for truth needs to de-emphasize dramatically the authority which students expect to accompany the religious role.

The adolescent in an aggregate classroom situation amply illustrates the points discussed above. The adolescent exists in what might be termed a state of "developmental" alienation; i.e., he no longer feels such close ties to the family that the family group serves as a reference group. The counselor very often in the one-to-one interview relationship becomes social reality for the client, but his peers constitute his primary social testing ground. It is among peers that the adolescent typically projects self into adult roles; the reactions of his peers form the reactions of social reality. In the controlled group guidance situation, the supportive effect of the group assists the individual member in testing the reality of his perceptions of himself and others. For example, the issue of emancipation from parental control may become the focus of group concern. The individual member perceives that his struggles toward greater independence are shared by other group members. In their reactions to his own feelings and striving, he comes to perceive common elements of this developmental task. He may learn more appropriate ways of behaving and may assist other members of the group to more appropriate behavior. The supportive tendency of the group situation, as Hicks (1962) discovered, assists the individual member toward positive evaluations of himself. Similarly, after reciprocal relationships have been established by groups, difficulties encountered by the individual member tend to become the concern of the group, even though they may not be related directly to group purpose. For example, group interest may have initially focused on the question of academic underachievement, but the difficulties related by one member in the area of social relations may occupy group attention. The group comes to feel the individual member's concerns as its own.

Pluralistic Ignorance

The question of pluralistic ignorance is closely related to social reality. Everyone has had the experience of leaving the classroom after a lecture during which no student questioned the teacher for clarification of content or terminology. After the lecture, however, each student discovers that none of the others had dared raise a question, having assumed that everyone else understood the lecture thoroughly and that raising a question would be a public display of ignorance on his part. This example illustrates pluralistic ignorance, also evident in attitude formation.

Mary, Monica, Helen, and Margaret are the members of a high school guidance group focusing on the improvement of study habits. Relatively early in the development of group interaction, Monica makes the statement that she feels that studying is a waste of time, since she intends to marry immediately after graduation. Mary internally, not vocally, disagrees with this position; she believes that each student has a personal obligation to develop her maximum academic potential, regardless of the future choice of lifework or lifeway. Neither Helen nor Margaret voices disagreement. Thus Mary assumes that she constitutes the minority of one. At the same time, Helen and Margaret each silently disagrees with Monica, but because no one has expressed disagreement, Helen and Margaret each also feel that she is the minority of one. None of the three yet feels secure enough in the group situation to withstand the minority-of-one position. Kerlinger (1962) thus identifies pluralistic ignorance as "the condition when each member of a group assumes that all other members of the group, except himself, accept a group norm or some belief or attitude uncritically."

In the guidance group, the role of the counselor or group worker is to assist group members to evolve openness in their ability to accept freely each other's opinions and beliefs. The group member needs to feel that he may express himself without threat of reprisal or rejection, even though he may engage the minority-of-one position, a position which tends to increase the pull toward conformity to group norms. The security of the group is analogous to the security of the individual counseling relationship. The acceptant attitude which characterizes the counselor in the one-to-one relationship needs to be shared by all group members. Total group acceptance of each member in large measure dictates the roles played by group members. Acceptance and the support of the group for openness of expression prevent the occurrence of instances of pluralistic ignorance.

Group Size

Both the quality and the quantity of interaction among group members is affected by group size. E. J. Thomas and C. F. Fink (1963), after a careful review of the research literature, concluded that group size is related to (1) group and individual performance, (2) distribution of participation, (3) the nature of members' interaction, (4) group organization, and (5) the satisfaction of members with the group experience. Pruitt (1960) observed that a group session of one hour permits a rectangular distribution of ten minutes per member of participation time when the group contains six members, but that that time is halved when the group contains twelve members. Pruitt also commented that a group session in the homeroom period (usually thirty minutes or less) in which some 25 or more students are involved may allow less than one minute of participation time per student. Such situations invite dominance of the group by more verbally facile or vocal students. A congruent finding was reported by Fitzgerald (1963), who determined that the willingness to discuss self-relevant topics in a population of Catholic girls was related to the "social distance" the subjects perceived between themselves and other members of a group. Social distances (e.g., differences in parental socioeconomic status or ethnic background) are likely to be accented in large groups where the opportunity to develop meaningful member interaction is reduced. The large-group situation very likely favors students of higher socioeconomic status by supporting their efforts to achieve leadership roles. Maccoby's study (1962) of class differences in choices of authority roles revealed that boys of upper-class families tend to select roles which involve training, supervising, or controlling others.

A number of experiments have adduced evidence that frequency of interaction increases the opportunity for significant personal interrelationships to develop among members of a group, persons in a togetherness situation, or members of different races. Indeed Raab and Lipset (1959), in their lucid, nontechnical work on the nature of prejudice, suggest that increased frequency of interaction among members of different races provides psychologically the soundest solution to the problem of racial prejudice, for only in increased interaction can one person encounter another as a person, rather than as a stereotypic representative of a particular race. Goslin (1962), in his sociological analysis of the accuracy of self-perception in relation to social acceptance, observed that greater acceptance both of self and of others follows increased interaction. Group size is the prime factor controlling the opportunity for effective member interaction. To be effective, guidance groups must permit direct, unhindered communication pathways between and among members. The channels of communication should be open directly within all vectors of group interaction. In large groups, communication pathways are necessarily routed through the group leader. The communications network system in large groups prevents rapid feedback from the member to the group.

Leadership Style

The role behavior of the leader can serve to accelerate or to stifle group process. The classic studies of Lewin, Lippitt, and White in the late 1930s, reported by Lippitt and White (1958), identified three leadership styles. The authoritarian leader was characterized as dominating the group situation by command and prescription. The democratic leader, on the other hand, encouraged and assisted in group discussion but abided by the wishes of the majority of the group. The laissez-faire leader played a passive role in social participation; his passivity and inaction indirectly resulted in the group members' attaining freedom for decisions. On the basis of locus of evaluation, Kemp (1964) has distinguished authoritarian, democratic, and group-centered leadership. The authoritarian leader places the locus of evaluation within himself, the democratic leader within the organization (i.e., structural process) of the group, and the group-centered leader within the group members. Kemp's research discovered, surprisingly, that both authoritarian and democratic leaders typically implement their roles in the group through questioning, analysis, suggestion, approval, shared decision making, clarification, and group self-evaluation. Group-centered leaders, however, attempt to understand the behavior and statements of members from the members' own frames of reference. The verbal behaviors of these leaders typically involve acceptance, clarification, and reflection. Central in this contrast of leadership styles is the *extent* to which the *leader controls the group.*

Carl R. Rogers (1951, pp. 401–402) has supplied a paradigm for group leadership in teaching which is quite consistent with the aims of group procedures in a developmental guidance program. The stages of evolution of the group leader are (with some slight modifications) basically the following: (1) Initially the leader has much to do with setting the mood or climate of the group experience by his own basic commitment to trust in the group, which is communicated in many subtle ways. (2) The leader helps to elicit and clarify the purposes or goals of group members. (3) He relies on the members' desire to implement these purposes as their motivational force. (4) He endeavors to organize and make easily available all resources which he anticipates group members may wish to use. (5) Most important, the *group leader regards himself as a flexible resource to be utilized by the group* in the ways which seem most meaningful to them. (6) In responding to expressions from the group, he accepts both intellectual content and emotionalized attitudes. He endeavors to give each aspect the approximate degree of emphasis which it has in the perception of both the individual and the group. (7) *As the acceptant group climate is established, the leader is able to change his role and become essentially a member-participant.* (8) The leader, as member-participant, remains alert to expressions of feeling. He endeavors to understand and to help the group understand these from the speaker's frame of reference. (9) When group interaction is charged with emotions, even conflicting emotions, he attempts to maintain a neutral and understanding role, in order to give acceptance to the feelings expressed. (10) Finally, he recognizes that the extent to which he can behave in these ways is limited by certain parameters of his own attitudes and those of group members. He does not pretend acceptance or understanding when he cannot feel it internally.

T. Gordon's investigation (1955, pp. 166–169) of group-centered leadership disclosed that the most characteristic qualities of the group leader were his belief in the capacity of the group for self-direction, his willingness to surrender leadership to the group, and his desire to reduce the dependency of the group on himself. The qualities which least characterized the group-centered leader were a belief that the leader has inherently greater stature or ability than members, the conviction that the unmotivated need constant prodding, and the seizure of initiative for topic setting and goal setting. Strang (1961), reporting data from an experiment with high school students, observed that students felt that the group leader should not dominate, that he should make sure everyone has a chance to participate, and that he himself should take an active interest in group activity or discussion.

A number of studies have relevance for leadership style in group guidance. Ostlund (1956) found that the imposition of threat via evaluation on an integrated group produced increased cohesiveness but deteriorated actual performance, since the group's energies seemed to be marshaled toward the maintenance of cohesion. The implication for group procedures in guidance highlights the necessity of the removal of the threat of evaluation. Pryer,

Flint, and Bass (1962) reported that groups are more likely to become more effective if the leadership role is consistent, and Hamblin, Miller, and Wiggins (1961) found that the perceived competence of the leader controls the morale of the group. M. E. Shaw and W. T. Penrod, Jr. (1962), determined that the effect of the introduction of new information on the performance of the group was related to the group's attitude toward the trustworthiness of the source of information.

The picture of the effective group guidance leader which emerges is that of a group-centered member-participant who allows students to interact freely without the threat of evaluation, who is perceived as competent and interested by group members, and who is consistent in his attitudes and behavior. Perhaps his most important characteristic is his willingness to allow the group to use him as a flexible resource. This role implements the larger role of the counselor as a collaborative consultant in human development. As a member-participant in the group situation, he becomes a consultant on developmental tasks on a one-to-several basis.

Guidance in togetherness situations

There are many occasions on which the counselor or group guidance worker deals with students on a one-to-many basis, especially when it is useful and necessary to supply certain kinds of information which *the professional person believes* students need. He may deal with only one particular class, with all the classes in a given year, or even with the entire student body. This type of guidance service constitutes guidance in the togetherness situation. It is distinguished from group guidance insofar as (1) it is based on the *professional worker's* rather than on the *student's perception* of what the student needs to maintain or to achieve satisfactory development; and (2) it is the kind of one-to-several situation which does not permit interaction and feedback, since it is almost completely controlled by the counselor or guidance worker. Guidance in the togetherness situation is primarily an *informational* service. Goldman (1962) has usefully distinguished process and content in group guidance. Much of what passes for group guidance, he rightly charges, is distinguished from teaching only by content, not by process. Guidance in the togetherness situation correctly employs the methods of sound teaching.

Orientation Information

Togetherness guidance situations are best employed to orient students to certain developmental, situational, or transitional circumstances. The career conference and the college day are perhaps the prototypes of orientation services. The aim is to present information to students about vocational and occupational realities or about educational resources. The same procedures are often helpful in orienting parents. The administrative organization of such orientation services may center in assembly programs for an entire class or for the whole school. As is indicated in Chapter 15, the most appropriate type of career conference is one which orients students realistically to the nature of the labor market, rather than one which attempts to lure them into premature vocational decisions. A series of guidance assemblies planned during the course of a semester or the school year which focuses on a number of dimensions, e.g., educational and vocational opportunities or even the developmental tasks characteristic of particular periods of student development, constitutes a very effective type of togetherness guidance. By stimulating student consideration of topics for discussion in guidance groups or in individual counseling, ongoing togetherness guidance services can be integrated into the total guidance effort.

Orientation to a transitional period in a new school setting is an important guidance function. Ackerman (1962) has described a program of vertical integration guidance to ease the transition of sixth graders into the junior high school environment. Counselors from the junior high school visit the sixth-grade classrooms, present pertinent and essential information, conduct question-and-answer sessions, and invite students to seek individual counseling. The visitation aspect of the program is discontinued once the student enrolls in the new school. The orientation program described by Mennes (1956) for high school freshmen involved the issuance of a student handbook, the introduction of an orientation-to-high-school unit in the social studies class, conferences with student council members, class-wide assemblies, the availability of individual counseling interviews (familiarization), and a variety of social activities. In organizing and administering this program of vertical integration, members of the guidance staff were assisted by other school people and students. An interesting feature of such an omnibus program as that described by Mennes is the inclusion of an opportunity for feedback through individual counseling and through participation in the social studies class, a rebirth of Jesse Davis' concept in the pioneer days of school guidance. Among the varieties of orientation programs encountered on the college level are the rather loosely structured series of lectures by the academic dean, detailing the history of the college, academic and disciplinary regulations, and the like. More highly structured is the program of pre-entrance togetherness and group meetings described by Seymour and Guthrie (1962). An orientation program at the college level which makes use of both togetherness and group situations has been implemented by Glanz, Hayes, and Penney (1959) at Boston University. Freshmen enroll in a course in the dynamics of personal adjustment. Group guidance is provided by the instructor in small-sized groups of students selected from his classes. In addition, larger assemblies and lectures are used to introduce topics for discussion in guidance groups. This plan appears to hold considerable promise for secondary schools.

Togetherness guidance situations are sometimes useful in familiarizing large numbers of students with the services available in the school's guidance division. Richardson and Borow (1952) successfully utilized an orientation assembly to explain the aims and procedures of the vocational counseling service. Siegel (1960) similarly utilized an orientation assembly preparatory to placement counseling. He made the salient point that the purpose of the assembly was essentially educational and was not considered an aspect of the counseling process.

Test Orientation

A variety of educational and psychological tests are administered on a school-wide or a class-wide basis. An appropriate use of togetherness guidance is a pretesting meeting to explain the nature and purpose of the instruments to be used. The relevance of these instruments for students can be suggested in a nonthreatening manner, so that they may be motivated properly for test administration and hence forego fear responses. Large-scale assemblies are unsuitable for this purpose, however, since they prevent meaningful feedback between the students and the guidance worker. Homeroom periods, which provide greater opportunity for questions and discussion, are more satisfactory.

A number of guidance workers have attempted to use togetherness situations for test interpretation. Brother Austin, F.S.C. (1959), reported an experiment in which test results were made available to large numbers of fathers and their sons in a Catholic high school. Interpretive material was distributed, and a lecture on the implications of test results for educational and vocational planning ensued. Brother Austin frankly regarded the procedure as a drastic measure undertaken only because of a student-counselor ratio of 1,000:1. Herman and Ziegler (1961) described a meeting of parents of university freshmen during which an interpretation of their children's performance on pre-entrance guidance tests was presented. D. H. Ford (1962) described an unusual procedure in which three contacts were made between students and counselors. First, test results were presented in a togetherness situation. Then a second, large-scale meeting was held. During this meeting the counselor presented certain vocational predictions based on test results, circulating among students to answer questions. These contacts were followed by individual interviews. Ford claims that this procedure precludes variations in counselor interpretations and predictions, since standard explanations are presented in the togetherness situations. He has apparently ignored the issue of the student's self-involvement or indeed of the very real factors of client history which even permit meaningful test interpretation or meaningful learning. Ford's method is apparently rooted in an authoritarian-prescriptive approach to guidance, an absolute rather than a relative faith in trait and factor prediction, and an administrator's typical view to economy of counselor time. It is quite probable that counselors of every persuasion from Williamson to Rogers would find exclusive use of this procedure abhorrent. Hancock (1962) has suggested the use of visual aids (e.g., charts showing means, standard deviations, and the like) in test interpretation in togetherness situations. Needham, Stodola, and Brown (1963–1964) have experimented with motion pictures to explain test results to large numbers of students.

Orientation to testing programs represents effective investment of counselor time; certainly the togetherness situation can be used with some profit for this purpose. But the interpretation of test results, even of school-wide batteries administered for the convenience of school officials rather than for the benefit of the students, is wholly inappropriate in a togetherness situation. When students have formed functional groups, tests may be interpreted in the group setting, which of its nature provides both mutual support and a suitable atmosphere for the discussion of the particular dimensions of the individual student's developmental pattern that give test results *ipsative* meaning. It is the integration of these results with the student's self-perception which makes them meaningful to him. The presentation of test results in togetherness situations eventuates in verbal bombardment, whatever the intentions of the counselor.

Guidance in classroom groups

The basic elements for group formation are present in the classroom, from a limited point of view. All members of the class share a mutual goal, viz., passing the course or, more hopefully, learning something from the complex of their common classroom experience. Their basic motivations, however, may vary widely. Some students show genuine interest in the learning experiences; others regard the class as a necessary step to promotion and eventual graduation. There is also a certain interdependence of members relative to orderly teacher-student interaction which learning in a social situation (the classroom) involves. In this fashion, the classroom group stands somewhere between the togetherness situation and the functional group. One factor customarily inhibiting the development of effective group cohesion in the classroom group is class size. It is not uncommon to find that the members of a class form a number of relatively autonomous functional subgroups. The use of group procedures in classroom groups is circumscribed not only by the size of the group but also by the level of cohesion which has been or can be developed and the commonality of perceptions and developmental tasks.

Group procedures have typically been applied in two types of groups, the homeroom and "guidance classes." It is unfortunate that these kinds of experiences are often regarded as the totality of group guidance or even the sum total of guidance.

The Homeroom Group

Bennett (1963) has described the early view of homeroom as "the home base of the pupil, with a teacher who served as his school parent in helping him to adjust in the new environment and make the most of his new opportunities." The homeroom, staffed by teachers without training in group guidance procedures, became the first historical locus for group guidance efforts. In addition to serving as the center for administrative detail, as a political unit in student government organizations, and often as an extracurricular activity center, the homeroom has been given certain guidance functions, primarily related to the dispensing of information. More recently, guided group discussion, led by the homeroom teacher, has become a standard feature. Assignment to one or another homeroom is typically made on a relatively random basis. For group formation, the interests, needs, developmental patterns, and perceptual concerns of members must be similar. Lack of similarity in the homeroom setting inhibits group process. Thus, topics chosen for group discussion arise from the lowest common denominator binding students into the homeroom group. In actual practice, topics are usually chosen by the teacher with or without consultation with a few verbal student leaders. Group discussion, in this situation, is not an organic product of group interaction. Still, the homeroom has sometimes proved useful, especially in relation to such transitional tasks as adjustment to new school settings.

Generally, however, experience with homerooms as the primary vehicle for group guidance has proved unsatisfactory. After reviewing the available research, Lifton (1961, p. 139) cited the following reasons for the failure of homeroom guidance: (1) lack of time for group members to explore areas of concern and define mutual purposes, (2) infringement of administrative detail on the homeroom period, (3) lack of training and indifference of teachers or homeroom sponsors, (4) shortage of group leaders trained in group procedures, and (5) inadequate program planning. In addition, Lee (1963b, p. 503) has suggested that the high teacher-pupil ratio in some public and most Catholic schools inhibits group activities.

Pry (1961) conducted an interesting and informative investigation of the opinions of teachers and students on the value and organization of the homeroom guidance program. The school in which the study was conducted had recently increased the length of the homeroom period from nineteen to thirty minutes. When the period was nineteen minutes long, Pry found that 36 per cent of the students and 48 per cent of the faculty favored abandoning the homeroom period altogether, 74 per cent of the faculty felt group discussion was dominated consistently by a few students, and 76 per cent of the students preferred a student group leader to a teacher. After the period was lengthened, 25 per cent of the students and 43 per cent of the faculty still favored abandoning the homeroom period, only 66 per cent of the faculty reported domination of discussion by a few students, and 88 per cent of the students preferred a student leader. The interplay between class size, length of time allotted, and teacher interest is abundantly evident here. Group guidance cannot be carried out effectively by teachers untrained in group process in large classes with minimum opportunity for member participation. To improve the effectiveness of the homeroom program, even in its minimal function as a vehicle for the dispensing of relevant information and the provision of an opportunity for guided group discussion, it is imperative that (1) homeroom sponsors be selected from among teachers and counselors with adequate preparation in *group procedures* in guidance and human developmental psychology (many core teachers have such training); (2) adequate time be devoted to the homeroom period; (3) the size of the homeroom group be held to 12 students per worker per hour to allow for effective group interaction; (4) homeroom assignments be made in cognizance of the specific developmental histories of students, not on a random basis; and (5) opportunities be provided for adequate consultation and supervision with group work specialists. These suggestions indicate that the basic purpose of the homeroom is guidance, not administration. As long as the homeroom is regarded as an administrative vehicle and organized accordingly, little can be done to improve its guidance role.

Specialized Guidance Classes

In view of the widespread dissatisfaction with the results of homeroom guidance, special "classes" were created in many schools to focus on certain guidance needs. The most common of these specialized guidance classes is perhaps the course in occupational information, of which Hoppock (1963, pp. 165–201) is the champion. Other courses have focused on how-to-study programs, personal adjustment, social living, senior problems, and the like. These courses tend to be frankly informational in approach. Many of the issues mentioned in connection with homeroom guidance apply here, though there are notable differences. While the homeroom is a continuing feature of the student's yearly schedule, these specialized guidance classes are generally available at specific points in his educational career. Their effectiveness could be improved if they were made available as electives to the student at any point at which he felt that his goals could be best satisfied by enrolling. If these courses were to be electives, enrollment could be limited to a small enough number of students to allow group interaction to develop freely. Finally, the completely informational approach, often relying on textbooks, should be abandoned in favor of such group procedures as sociodrama and group discussion. Process as well as content distinguishes group guidance programs. Organic group structure could then replace classroom structure.

The most effective use of specialized guidance classes is primarily the supplying of sound, adequate information to students about to negotiate a common developmental task. For example, to high school seniors who are about to enter college might be offered a "guidance course" in adjustment to college routine, coping with greater freedom from parental and faculty control, and specialized study skills. Optimal effect can be realized, however, only when group size permits the development of an organic group structure.

Guidance and counseling in functional groups

Group procedures in guidance are most fruitfully utilized in functional groups of four to eight students who exhibit common characteristics and are facing common developmental tasks. It is in this situation, the one-to-several relationship, that reciprocities are established, cohesion develops, the properties of group structure begin to emerge, and the maximum supportiveness for the individual is realized (Bany & Johnson, 1964, pp. 33–37). In the togetherness situation, the group guidance worker is necessarily a leader, often an expert; in the classroom group, he plays the role of leader-stimulator. It is in the functional group that he becomes most readily the member-participant, the flexible resource, the collaborative consultant in development.

Organizing the Group

On the basis of the commonality of perceptual concerns, students are invited to join a group which has already been formed or to organize a new group. Students may be referred to the counselor by teachers or by administrators either for group guidance or for individual counseling. In practice, it is common that after one or two individual interviews counselor and client may come to feel that the most appropriate service to assist the client in readying himself for remaining developmental tasks is group work rather than individual counseling.

In small guidance groups, concerns common to the group or the group-to-be arise from the internal self-structure of members in relation to their particular developmental patterns. Sometimes students with common concerns, e.g., students interested in a particular career field, those readying themselves for transition into the world of work, or those experiencing a particular type of developmental difficulty, are known in advance to the counselor or group guidance coordinator. The important issue is the commonality of concerns among group members, as Tauber and Isaacson (1961) have emphasized. Group meetings must be scheduled at convenient times, and they should ordinarily occupy from forty-five minutes to an hour. During the first meeting, the group guidance worker is likely to be more active than in later contacts as he assists the group to define its central concerns and to set limits for itself.

Emerging Roles

As with the counselor, the group guidance worker's principal function is to make himself dispensable rapidly, so that group interaction can begin to shape the group experience. Cohn, Ohlsen, and Proff (1960) have identified the roles which typically emerge in the small guidance group. Their first category is *information* roles, which include the information seeker, the opinion seeker, the information giver, the opinion giver, the structurer, and the role player. Second, there are *positive* roles, embracing initiator, clarifier, interpreter, reflector, evaluator, expediter, and supporter. Finally, there are *negative* roles, including the passive resister, the nonparticipant, the blocker, the aggressor, the recognition seeker, the help seeker, the follower, and the dominator. Group members typically play a series of roles, especially in the early stages of group interaction. One of the important functions of the group guidance worker is to help the group analyze and interpret the types of roles which emerge. It remains the responsibility of the group, however, to channel negative roles into more constructive behaviors.

The specific procedures or techniques employed in guidance in functional groups depend upon the emergent roles in the group structure, the major perceptual concerns in the group, and the level of group integration and self-integration among members. The most common techniques utilized in guidance with functional groups are organic group discussion, role playing, role taking, and multiple counseling.

Organic Group Discussion

Analogous to what Bonner (1959, pp. 199–231) calls "collective problem solving," this group procedure emphasizes verbal interaction among group members in an atmosphere free of the threat of evaluation. Responsibility for directing the flow and content of the communication interaction among members is placed in the group itself. Since the group worker does not attempt to control or limit communication flow, discussion is organic to the group. This important characteristic distinguishes organic discussion in the functional group from guided discussion (whether guided by the group guidance worker or by student leaders) in the classroom group. The extent to which discussion veers away from the selected topic is also a matter for group control. The members of the group are not simply students with common interests or concerns; they are students who the group guidance worker believes can benefit specifically from *group* experience. Thus, the relatively "freewheeling" atmosphere of organic group discussion of itself has beneficial characteristics, for the member learns that he can express peculiar, deviant, or simply outlandish ideas without fear of group rejection or counselor rejection. The expression of such ideas may be neither productive to group welfare nor constructive. The salient feature, however, is the feeling of belonging, of group acceptance, which accompanies the expression. Indeed, the counselor himself, as a member-participant, may express outlandish ideas in order to test group solidarity and assess the group's capacity for self-direction.

It is evident that organic group discussion embodies what has been termed, in the Armed Forces and later in corporate executive circles, *brainstorming.* This technique is especially useful when the members of the group have evinced satisfactory development and consolidation of elements of self-identity, i.e., when counseling (individual or multiple) is not indicated and what seems to be necessary is precisely *group* experience. Whether organic group discussion produces group decision is relatively unimportant in terms of the larger relevant goal. It is the quality of group experience which ultimately produces greater self-integration in each of the group members.

Role Playing

Role playing is a relatively common technique in both teaching and guidance in classroom groups. In role *playing,* students attempt to behave in the way they feel certain persons in social situations would behave. For example, the adolescent boy who experiences difficulty in gaining permission to use the family car is asked to play the role of his father, while another plays the role of the petitioning adolescent. It is anticipated that role playing will assist the student to clarify his own attitudes and to understand more clearly the attitudes of others. Role playing is an effective technique for this purpose. H. H. Mann and Carola H. Mann (1959) reported a study which contrasted role playing with leaderless group discussion in relation to interpersonal adjustment. They found that role playing tended to increase one's desirability as a friend, diligence in attending to group goals, and cooperation considerably more than did group discussion. This finding is typical of other similar studies. Role playing may often be integrated into larger groups to focus on a number of personal, social, and vocational-educational areas. Even in classroom groups, students might role-play, for example, an interview between a job applicant and an employer. Lee (1963b, pp. 314–315) has suggested a number of ways in which role playing may be used by subject-matter teachers in a regular classroom situation.

Role Taking

Role *taking* involves a considerably more profound social experience than does role playing. As Moreno (1960, p. 84), the noted architect of the techniques of psychodrama and sociodrama, has suggested, role playing *"may be considered as an experimental procedure, a method of learning how to perform roles more adequately."* The roles one "plays" involve projection of self either into the roles of "generalized" others (e.g., *a* teacher, *a* storekeeper) or into "significant" others in terms of one's own life. When the role player projects himself into the role of a significant other in his own life (e.g., the student's own father), he is perceiving his father's role as *he,* himself, *has experienced* it, not as his father experienced it. In role taking, however, one *becomes* the other—not a generalized other, but *this* other. The role taker assumes the self of the other in all its concrete existential reality.

Role taking implies that the attitudes and behavior of the other are "frozen"and thus must be assimilated by the role taker after he has learned the contours and vectors of the other's self-system. Thus, as Moreno (1953, pp. 73–89; 1960, pp. 85–86) indicates, role playing is a *playing* at being another, while role taking is a striving to *become* the other.

Role taking becomes possible only in a small-group situation in which members have interacted freely with each other, so that the contours of self become visible. When one member invests himself in the role of the other, he strives to perceive the world as the other perceives it, to react to and to evaluate perceptual objects (including himself) through the prism of the other's self-concept. Role taking implies that the role taker *perceives the role of the other precisely as the other himself experiences it*. It is clear that role taking is an exercise in empathy. The empathic relationship between members is rooted in the acceptant climate of free group interchange.

Prior to the introduction of role taking, the group must have interacted over time, so that the selves of members have been explored. In the initial stage of role taking, one member takes another's role in a specific situation; later, role taking broadens into a spectrum of situations. The chief value in role taking is to help each other explore the implications of the self-structure as it is experienced by the member himself. The more the role taker experiences what the other experiences through an empathic relationship, the more acceptant he becomes of the other. The more acceptant he becomes of the other, the more he begins to accept himself. The role of the group guidance worker here is essentially that of the member-participant. When he is asked to do so by the group, he himself takes the roles of others. Often this procedure is helpful in introducing the technique of role taking in the group situation. Role taking is indicated in situations in which group members appear to have made satisfactory developmental progress but lack sufficient group experience.

Multiple Counseling

Multiple or group counseling is a relationship between a skilled counselor and two or more clients who exhibit similar perceptual concerns or developmental difficulties. It is distinguished from group psychotherapy in somewhat the same fashion as individual counseling and psychotherapy are distinguished from each other.

Multiple counseling offers the individual student the supportive group structure as he attempts integrative self-actualization. Cohn and his associates (1963) feel that group counseling is useful because (1) it provides an opportunity to test reality in an accepting atmosphere, (2) group cohesiveness allows the member to experience helping others, and (3) group members can orient themselves to resources outside the group. Rossberg and Jacques (1961) cite as the chief value of the multiple counseling relationship the easing of communication flow from individual group members through the social support of the group. On the other hand, Boy, Isaksen, and Pine (1963) believe that fear of reactions of group members may tend to inhibit free expression. They see multiple counseling primarily as a process of developing readiness for individual counseling. Driver (1954, pp. 19–34), one of the champions of multiple counseling, also hopes that individual counseling will result from multiple counseling. Surely this has been one of the common functions of group counseling, but it represents a misuse of group experience. If group counseling is to be used (and there are certain ethical questions concerning the extent to which self-revelation by group members is to be encouraged in a group situation in schools), then its justification is precisely that *group* experience is likely to be more beneficial to the client than individual counseling. Gazda (1963) has made a thorough review of the literature relative to group counseling in schools.

The role of the counselor is essentially that of collaborative developmental consultant *to the group.* The behaviors described in the preceding chapter relative to the individual are emitted by the interpretivist in relation to the group. He assists the group in exploring its image of itself, he helps the group focus on relevant topics, he assists in facilitating the group to interpret its own experience of itself, he helps the group expand its perception of itself, and the like. He relies upon member interaction to control the process of communication. Members themselves reflect, expand, and explore each other's perceptual selves; focus and sensitively probe each other's phenomenal fields; interpretively refract each other's self-experience; confirm and support each other; occasionally confront each other in a mild fashion; and assist in integratively recapitulating both individual and group experiences. For these procedures to be effective, or even tolerated, an acceptant, permissive group climate needs to be established. The counselor becomes progressively less active as the group structure emerges, until he becomes a member-participant. Group projects are often initiated and undertaken by the group. Multiple counseling is not a shortcut or an emergency measure. It is indicated only when group support and experience are likely to hold maximum benefit for the client and to accelerate most rapidly maximal self-integration.

Group psychotherapy and *multiple psychotherapy* are often unfortunately confused with group or multiple counseling. While the terms *group counseling* and *multiple counseling* in general are used interchangeably among counselors, the parallel terms in psychotherapy have quite distinct meanings. Group psychotherapy is a one-to-several relationship between a psychotherapist and several clients or patients (Klapman, 1959), the purpose of which is therapeutic personality change in each group member. Ginott's work (1961) on group psychotherapy with children is of special interest to school counselors. Group psychoanalysis is a one-to-several relationship between a psychoanalyst and several patients (Wassell, 1959), the purpose of which is the reorganization of each member's behavior pattern based on the analytic restructuring of the personality. Just as group guidance and counseling should not be undertaken by guidance workers untrained in group procedures, so group psychotherapy and group psychoanalysis represent further specializations for trained psychotherapists. On the other hand, multiple psychotherapy generally designates a relationship of one *patient* to several *professional workers* (e.g., psychiatrists, psychotherapists, psychologists, social workers, and rehabilitation counselors) operating as members of a single therapeutic team. Responsibility for case management, hence for therapy, is assigned to the team jointly, rather than to individual members. Thus, an outpatient may be seen by a social worker, a psychologist, and a psychiatrist on a ratio of 3:2:1.

part 4

GUIDANCE: FACILITATING
HUMAN DEVELOPMENT

12

PERSONAL DEVELOPMENT
AS A GUIDANCE FOCUS

Holism: an emerging dimension in guidance

Traditionally, guidance theory and practice have tended to identify "types" of guidance as educational, vocational, social, and personal guidance (cf. Moser & Moser, 1963, pp. 220–247). There may be some value in such distinctions on a logical or conceptual basis, *if* each type is considered the formal object of a particular regimen of guidance activities and *if* the material object of each is the optimal personal development or self-actualization of the student. Unfortunately, however, classification of guidance into types often has the effect of obscuring both the philosophical and the psychological approaches to the fundamental unity of the human person. The familiar Scholastic maxim which holds that *all acts are attributable to the person* is supported by the contemporary research of behavioral scientists. Indeed, Allport (1955, p. 46) has observed that modern psychological research has bolstered the Thomistic position of *homo integer,* of man as a behavioral unity. Both philosophy and psychology thus argue toward a framework in guidance theory and practice which views the human person as indivisible

335

and nonfragmentizable, i.e., as holistic rather than atomistic. Hence guidance workers need to "surrender the models that would compress human personality" into airtight, sealed compartments (Allport, 1962, p. 380). Person, personality, or behavior cannot be fragmentized. What the person thinks, feels, or does in one area of life has profound implications for his behavior in all other areas. Psychologists (cf. Bugental, 1963; Nordberg, 1960a) have come to recognize the fundamental unity of the person and his behavior. Philosophers (cf. Msgr. Hart, 1956, pp. 194–202; O. S. Walters, 1958) have proposed that psychological theory and practice demand a philosophical substratum capable of providing adequate conceptual foundations and ballasts for the interpretation of this fundamental unity. Regrettably, guidance theory and practice have been slow to reorganize the "need-areas" approach to account for this important conceptual position. As Nordberg (1960b) noted in a memorable indictment of Catholic writers on guidance and psychology, the most important advances in stabilizing a holistic view of man's nature and behavior capable of serving as a conceptual underpinning for guidance practice have been made by non-Catholics unfamiliar with the Thomistic philosophy of human nature; their holistic position has been arrived at by empirical evidence. In guidance practice, such writers as Barry and Wolf (1962, pp. 17–22), Cribbin (1955), Pallone (1964), and Fr. Curran (1952, pp. 13–15) have urged counselors to perceive the client as a singular, unique, unitary person, not as the aggregation of atoms of behavior. Indeed, Barry and Wolf (1962) have written an epitaph to one atomistically perceived need area, vocational guidance. These authors favor instead the adoption of a vantage point which perceives the focus of guidance as the *person* in a *total* developmental matrix.

Trends toward the holistic view in guidance are in evidence both in counselor preparation programs in leading universities and in the organization of guidance and counseling services in some alert schools and colleges. Graduate schools at one time trained specialists in vocational or educational or social or personal guidance. The present trend is toward a broad program of preparation to fit the counselor to work holistically with his clients, whatever their particular needs at the moment when counseling is desired and offered. Formerly guidance and personnel services, particularly in colleges, were organized in such a way that the guidance staff consisted of a collection of specialists in each need area. Thus, a student might be directed to one student personnel worker for educational guidance, to another for vocational guidance, to a third for spiritual counseling, and so forth. Sometimes counselors were assigned to work exclusively with one grade level and perhaps with one grade level in one need area, e.g., the vocational counselor for the ninth grade. Currently the trend in forward-looking guidance installations is toward the provision of comprehensive guidance and counseling services to each client by a single, broadly trained, developmentally oriented counselor.

Emphasis is placed on the holistic nature of the client, not on the atoms of his behavior. A single counselor may work with a client from the time of his entry into the school setting until he leaves. The counselor provides services in all areas of educational, vocational, social, and personal development throughout the student's career in the school and in his postschool placement in the world of work or in an institution of further education. Service to graduates is further facilitated when the alumnus returns to the counselor whom he has come to know over a span of time and who has direct experiential knowledge of the client and his unique developmental pattern.

Holism vs. Atomism

Counselors whose focus of service is limited to one need area lack direct personal experience with the nuances of singularity which define the client as a holistic person with a singular developmental pattern. Indeed, the very process of counseling in the initial stages, especially in the establishment of rapport with the client as a person, is accelerated by a holistic strategy and impeded by an atomistic strategy. An atomistic strategy partitions and fragments the client according either to need sectors or to such purely contingent considerations as grade placement. However important particular needs (e.g., for information about occupations) might seem to be for the *immediate* life situation of the client, it is with the holistic person in his *total* life situation, in his particular *Dasein,* that the counselor must ultimately deal.

Contrast the holistic, developmental approach to guidance suggested in the preceding paragraphs with the fragmented, compartmentalized "organizational patterns" advocated by F. W. Miller (1961, pp. 59–60):

> 1. The counselor may be given responsibility for the counseling of all pupils at a certain grade level—for example, the tenth grade counselor.
> 2. He may be given responsibility for the counseling of all pupils of one sex at a certain grade level. . . .
> 4. Division of responsibilities may be in terms of guidance services rather than groups of students. One counselor may be in charge of vocational guidance (the occupational files, the career conference, job placement), another counselor in charge of college planning (college entrance examinations, college catalogue file, scholarship applications), and another in charge of the testing program. Under this arrangement, students often have the oppotunity to choose their own counselor.

The student who encounters such organizational patterns as these is likely to be unable to develop a meaningful relationship with *any,* let alone with all, counselors. Especially if the student is experiencing a developmental difficulty is he likely to develop the "volleyball" syndrome, and with good reason.

Environmental consistency, no less in the school (and thus in the guidance office) than in the home, is essential to favorable developmental processes.

An index to the acceptance, encouragement, and implementation of the holistic approach in guidance practice among leaders in the profession is provided in the 1961 decision of the American Personnel and Guidance Association (APGA) relative to its evaluative agency. In that year, APGA shifted the focus of interest of its agency which evaluates guidance centers from an emphasis on vocational guidance and job adjustment to an emphasis on generic counseling functions. Thus the American Board on Professional Standards in Vocational Counseling was renamed the American Board on Counseling Services, Inc.

Ultimately it is always the singular, holistic person who behaves, experiences satisfaction or dissatisfaction, and makes decisions relative to educational, vocational, social, or personal affairs. Inevitably, then, every kind of guidance service is at bottom *personal* guidance, in the sense of the assisting of the person to effective behavior and optimal development. Nonetheless, the focus of guidance efforts may at one time be directed toward his vocational development, at another toward his social development, and so on. Even these distinctions, however, are more artificial and symbolic than real. The client's progress in vocational development, for example, is inextricably bound to his social and educational development; conversely these flow into the totality of his personal development. The Scholastic principle, demonstrated in psychiatric and psychological research, which holds that *"Actiones sunt suppositorum"* (All acts are to be attributed to the person, not to any atom of his being) bears repetition.

Persons vs. Problems

Some counselors and counselor educators have entered demurrers to the holistic approach, citing their diffidence to consider personal counseling as the principal focus of their efforts. Hoppock (1953, p. 124), for example, has long maintained that a need exists for the specialized vocational guidance function, quite apart from developmental guidance directed at self-actualization. According to Hoppock (1963, p. 106), "The client whose emotional needs are not met in his job can often correct this situation more readily by changing his job than by changing himself." Yet the very language employed indicates that vocational adjustment constitutes one aspect of self-realization. Counselors who insist on fragmentizing and compartmentalizing guidance functions blind themselves to the experiential evidence of their own guidance practice. Counselors deal precisely with *persons* who may have problems, for example, of school adjustment, and *not* with *problems* per se. The observation has been made in Chapter 7 that one of the salutary effects of a student-oriented philosophy and of such curricular designs as core has been to make teachers, once attuned to a fragmented, subject-oriented view of the student, again aware of the student as a singular human person. Even some of those educators who hold the intellectualist position on the goal of the school but who simultaneously recognize the substantial unity of person, personality, and behavior argue that the teacher and counselor deal specifically with the student qua person and not with atoms. Such a view is based on the concept that intellectual development cannot proceed fruitfully until there is apt disposition of the *persona* of the student qua learner. Until the student has fulfilled the appropriate prior tasks of personal development, be they emotionally, physiologically, socially, or vocationally oriented, he cannot fulfill the task of intellectual development. The actualization of intellectual capacity, considered by intellectualists to be the only appropriate aim of the school, occurs only when the "teachable moment" has arrived, i.e., when the student is aptly disposed psychosocially (Pallone, 1962a).

Other guidance experts tend to adopt a distorted view of the holistic approach to guidance services. They state either that (1) counselors are not trained as psychotherapists and thus are unfit to engage in personal development counseling or that (2) the job of the counselor is to meet the *expressed* needs of the client, whatever they may be (Peters & Mueller, 1960). The first of these contentions fails to distinguish between the treatment of serious mental disorders (psychotherapy) and assistance with developmental problems within the normal range (developmental counseling). The developmental counselor approaches the client as a person in an attempt to foster optimal development in his singularity qua person. The second contention partakes of the character of "hit-and-run" or problem-point guidance which centers on assisting clients at certain choice points. Both of these unbalanced viewpoints fail to recognize that the client is not fragmentizable and that the effective school counselor, regardless of his orientation (or of what he believes to be his orientation), interacts with a *person in the process of becoming,* within the parameters of a unique developmental pattern and a life situation which is uniquely the client's own. The only possible focus for guidance, as Mathewson (1962) has noted, is the *self-in-situation.* Effective guidance, therefore, concentrates on the singular individuality of the holistic client qua person, within a particular *Dasein* or singular life situation.

Client needs for assistance in some areas of life may assume greater perceptual importance for him at given times. Thus, for example, high school seniors may experience such acute anxiety concerning admission into college or into the labor market that they virtually ignore other life areas. A *perceptually dominant need* tends to overorganize the person with regard to the satisfaction of that need but to underorganize him with regard to the satisfaction of other needs (Shaffer & Shoben, 1956, pp. 37–38, 134–135). While certain needs of the client tend to be dominant in specific developmental stages of his life, these particular needs can be met only within the context of total personal development. Effective guidance never loses sight of this capital point. These developmentally dominant client needs constitute *focal points* for guidance services, rather than distinct, separate, compartmentalized types of guidance.

Personal development: primary guidance focus

Personal development is the principal, encompassing guidance focus which concentrates on the holistic person and his development in his concrete existential situation. Personal development guidance, concerned with fostering the student's capacity for self-actualization, aims at assisting him in the effective integration of forces within the self and within the world of reality. More precisely, personal development guidance concentrates on helping the student to grow optimally in his capacity for coping rationally and prudently with the tasks of human development and life. It will be recalled from Chapter 2 that personality is regarded as the pattern of adjustment or habits of dealing with the problems of living. Young (1952, p. 5) regards personality as the "body of ideas, attitudes, traits, values, and responses (habits) which an individual has built into roles and statuses for dealing with others and with himself." Consequently, effective personal development implies integrated personality function. Many behavioral scientists consider positive personality integration synonymous with *mental health*. This contention suggests that the self-system is integrated in such fashion that self-experience, realistically perceived and evaluated, is melded into realistic self-perception and self-aspiration. Thus Symonds (1946, pp. 569–571) advances the following *characteristics of the integrated personality:* (1) freedom from conflict within the self, (2) reconciliation of freedom and discipline, (3) resolution of conflicts between selfish motives and social good, (4) holding of conscious ideals, and (5) ability to concentrate one's energies on sound goals. To these might be added another prime characteristic, viz., *the ability to integrate one's self-experience without the need for distortion.*

Effective guidance toward personal development and personality integration requires counselor familiarity both with the process of human development and with a knowledge of the psychodynamics of the integrated personality. The counselor needs to become aware of those developmental processes which seem to produce mature, integrated, fully functioning, self-reliant adults. He needs to gain an understanding of why some persons are effective and others ineffective in dealing with life situations. Hence training for effective school guidance workers (including teachers who seek to discharge their guidance responsibilities adequately) counts among its positive obligations affording the worker (1) a functional understanding of the dynamics of sound personality development and mental health; (2) an acquaintance with the varied forms and expressions of personality dysfunction, especially in relation to the social structure of the school; and (3) an awareness of environmental influences arising in the school which can shape and promote positive personality integration. In short, the worker must know the personality dynamics of the developing self in the changing existential situation.

The integrated person: a sketch

Psychological literature is replete with clinical case studies of personality dysfunction, since it is usually the poorly functioning person who comes to the attention of psychological service centers. As Sawrey and Telford (1963, p. 393) observe, effectively functioning persons cause relatively few social problems: "Thus it is not surprising that the problems of behavioral maladjustment and mental illness have had a priority over the question of how the normal and above-normal individuals attain and maintain these functional levels." Although comparatively few longitudinal studies detailing favorable processes of development leading to healthy integration have appeared, some psychologists have studied animal development in an effort to reason by analogy to human development. Seitz (1959), for example, reached the conclusion after studying developmental processes in the cat that "early infantile traumata have persistent effects upon adult behavior." Whether such findings are generalizable from adult cats to adult human beings is at best a moot question. Travers (1961) and Allport (1962) do not seem to think so. Allport regards generalizations drawn from animal learning, for example, to be restricted in applicability to learning in animals. He has cited the need for "normative standards for the maturity of personality" derived from longitudinal study of *human* development rather than from animal development. Seitz's finding, of course, is in full accord with a Freudian approach to personality theory. But the Freudian approach is based largely on generalizations from the clinical study of a single case to a general law of behavior, a procedure hardly defensible as representative of scientific vigor. For example, Sigmund Freud based his theory of castration anxiety on a clinical study of the now-famous "Little Hans." Clinical case studies, while instructive and perhaps suggestive of directions for empirical research, are never conclusive, in view of the multiplicity of case-specific variables. One of the current challenges to mental-health psychology is the design and execution of longitudinal empirical research upon which to base a science of mental hygiene. In view of the limited research to date, it is necessary to describe the integrated personality in terms extrapolated from *clinical* observation of poorly functioning persons. Data and theories *derived* from these data are thus restricted in generalizability (Schneiders, 1955, pp. 33–38; R. W. White, 1964, pp. 94–143).

Within these limitations, it is possible to offer, at some risk, a few broad generalizations about the favorable processes of personal development or, more accurately, about the functioning of the sort of person in whom such processes find fruition. A touchstone in this regard might well be the 1931 definition of mental health suggested by the National Committee for Mental Hygiene (1962, p. 381): mental health is "the adjustment of individuals to themselves and the world at large with a maximum of effectiveness, satisfactions, cheerfulness, and socially considerate behavior, and the ability to face and accept the realities of life."

The mentally healthy, or effectively integrated, person usually displays the following seven characteristics (Bernard, 1957, pp. 171–191; Jahoda, 1958, pp. 23–29):

THE EFFECTIVELY INTEGRATED PERSON TENDS TO EXHIBIT AN ACTIVE, EXPLORATORY POSTURE TOWARD LIFE. He displays a variety of interests as well as the capacity to sustain these interests. In general he is relatively eager to respond to unfamiliar situations. Experimental psychologists interested in operant conditioning procedures have observed that a fundamental feature of living organisms appears to be an active, exploratory response to the environment. Thus, for example, the initial response to frustration or to any obstacles encountered in the pursuit of goals is exploratory behavior. Such explorations may be viewed as attempts to overcome obstacles through repeated adjustive trials, until a solution is found. Successful solutions are reinforced precisely because they are successful in allowing the organism to pursue its goals. In the face of frustration, even such organisms as laboratory rats actively seek to control the environment and its challenges by repeated efforts to master obstacles. J. S. Brown (1961, pp. 207–220), an experimentalist, thus regards frustration as a "general energizer" which evokes repeated exploratory behaviors. The active, exploratory posture toward life implies that the effectively integrated person displays *confidence in his ability to master the environment*. When obstacles present themselves, the effectively integrated person circumvents impediments through exploratory activity. The growth of confidence in one's ability to master the environment is the product of social interaction in which one has experienced success in attempts to control the environment. The overall guidance function of the school in providing developmental opportunities which allow the student to experience success in attempts at mastery readily becomes evident. It is not here suggested that a student be exposed to the opportunity for overly simple (and thus meaningless) success experiences. Rather, his efforts effectively to master his environment should not be thwarted by school practices which stifle student initiative, since such initiative represents the attempts of the self to explore the environment in search of personal satisfaction. Such procedures as meaningful student government and student-centered (not teacher-centered) classroom pedagogical techniques provide useful developmental opportunities. The product of such practices will be a maturing person who relies upon his own initiative in overcoming obstacles, who seeks actively and independently to find new solutions to problems. In such behaviors is the active rather than the passive posture toward life displayed.

THE INTEGRATED PERSON TENDS TO ACCEPT HIMSELF. The integrated person perceives himself realistically. He has established an optimal discrepancy between self-perception and self-aspiration in relation to self-experience. His experience of himself, inferred from the behavior of others, is relatively congruent with self-as-perceived in the here and now and in the future (self-ideal or aspirational self). His aspirational self is realizable in terms of his personal strengths and capacities. Thus he has little need for illusion regarding himself now or in the future. The very achieving of self-acceptance means that the integrated person evaluates his positive and negative characteristics objectively and is able to accept even negative or threatening perceptions of himself (McKinney, 1960, pp. 130–131; C. R. Rogers, 1951, pp. 40–41). Self-acceptance suggests that *all* self-experience is open to perceptual awareness: the "permeable membrane" of the self-concept is not closed even to negative percepts of self. Just as an active, exploratory posture toward life implies an openness of *self to experience,* so acceptance of self implies the openness of *self-awareness to self-experience.* Permeability, or the openness to self-experience, indicates the lack of the psychological necessity to distort the meaning of one's self-experience through the use of defense mechanisms. It must be noted that self-acceptance implies satisfaction with oneself but *not* complacency, smugness, or resignation. Rather, it implies the ability to face reality without flinching and without the need for gross distortion. Positively, it implies the capacity to live comfortably with oneself and with the world of reality.

THE INTEGRATED PERSON TENDS TO APPRAISE REALITY ACCURATELY. Since he has little need to distort his self-experience, the integrated person has little need to project his feelings of insecurity or anxiety upon the environment. He is able to assess reality and to behave in accord with this realistic appraisal. Indeed, the integrated person perceives some realities as *malleable* and subject to his control. Consequently he feels capable to some extent of mastering his environment. He perceives other realities as relatively non-malleable. He thus adjusts his self-aspiration, his self-perception, and his self-experience accordingly. In appraising reality accurately, the integrated person responds to the properties of the environment. He sees the environment as capable of modification, not as an immutable context in which he must submerge his attempts at mastery. Joyce (1960, p. 122), a Catholic psychiatrist, seems not to share this view: "The mature person has to accept the stubborn reality of things as they are without retreating from them or being overwhelmed by them. . . . The mature person does not try to transform reality. . . ." In sharp contrast to this position, Symonds (1946, p.

6) points out that for the integrated person, "environment can be conceived as something to be molded, manipulated, and mastered. On the other hand, it may be thought of as something to which to submit and to conform." Applicable here are the views of St. Vincent de Paul, and in modern times, Dorothy Day and Catherine de Hueck, who felt that the duty of the Catholic included not only almsgiving but a direct assault upon the social system which makes almsgiving necessary. The notions of autoplastic and alioplastic change are important in this connection. Autoplastic change implies reorganization of the self to accommodate the needs of the situation. Alioplastic change implies reorganization of the situation to accommodate the needs of self. Personal adjustment counseling carried on by psychologically oriented workers tends to focus almost exclusively on autoplastic change, i.e., adaptation of self to a nonmalleable environment. Personal adjustment counseling by sociologically oriented workers (e.g., social workers) has traditionally focused on alioplastic change, i.e., adaptation of the environment to a nonmalleable self. Developmental personal counseling regards both self and situation as malleable. Structuring the school environment to facilitate favorable development is not coddling in disguise. Rather it implies providing progressive developmental experiences in modifying and in being modified by the environment.

THE INTEGRATED PERSON ACCEPTS RESPONSIBILTY FOR HIS OWN BEHAVIOR. Since he feels capable of assessing reality and of controlling the environment, the integrated person is able to accept responsibility for his behavior without distorting his motives. As Fr. VanderVeldt, O.F.M. and Odenwald (1957, p. 397) have pointed out, a responsible person is one who is able and willing to face reality, who no longer looks for escape mechanisms to "solve" his problems, who has outgrown his childish attitudes and is willing to meet his obligations and duties as a mature person. Because the integrated person accepts himself, he has developed some insight into his own motivation, and therefore he can face even negative or unpleasant facts about himself. Hence, he is able to face the *consequences* of his behavior without the need to project its causes on persons or situations beyond his control (Fr. T. V. Moore, O.S.B., 1950, pp. 329–330).

THE INTEGRATED PERSON HAS THE CAPACITY TO POSTPONE GRATIFICATION OF HIS DESIRES, NEEDS, AND WISHES. The integrated person understands the motivation of, and accepts responsibility for, his behavior. Once these conditions are met, he is able so to order his behavior that it is not necessary for him to gratify immediately every need, impulse, or want. The person who is unable to delay gratification often behaves in ways which inhibit the achievement of more appropriate, long-range, or even ultimate goals. If circumstances prevent the integrated person from satisfying a desire, he is able to find some gratifying substitute (Redl & Wattenberg, 1959, pp. 198–201). This characteristic of the integrated person has sometimes led guidance workers to adopt an excessively otherworldly point of view. Though every behavior ultimately has some relevance to man's last end, it is not necessary to refer each behavior to God for its justification. Rather, the ability to postpone gratification implies the *ordering* of behaviors in terms of the relative importance of one's goals. For example, a high school student may be studying for an important examination when a friend invites him for a ride in a new sports car. The well-integrated student is able to postpone gratification in view of the relevant larger goal.

THE INTEGRATED PERSON DISPLAYS AN EFFECTIVE BALANCE IN HIS BEHAVIOR. The integrated person accepts himself, understands his motivations, appraises reality correctly, and exercises control over himself. Hence he is capable of effecting an optimal balance between intellectual, emotional, volitional, and physical needs in planning his behavior. He neither overintellectualizes nor fails to recognize cognitive needs; similarly, he accounts his emotional and physical needs in planning his behavior. Prudent decisions relative to the planning and implementing of courses of action are evidenced in the behavior of the integrated person. His behavior is designed both to assist himself in the fulfillment of his needs and at least occasionally to assist others in the achievement of appropriate goals.

THE INTEGRATED PERSON HAS THE CAPACITY FOR LOVE, IN THE SENSE OF THE WILLINGNESS TO PRIZE THE PSYCHOLOGICAL, SOCIAL, OR PHYSICAL WELFARE OF ANOTHER (ESPECIALLY OF A "SIGNIFICANT OTHER") ABOVE HIS OWN WELFARE. The integrated person has the capacity to postpone the immediate gratification of his own needs and to order these needs according to a prudent hierarchy. Hence he is able to assess the needs and wishes, the desires and welfare, of others realistically. He is sensitive to the needs of others and is able to account these needs into a hierarchy of goals. In this fashion, the integrated person opens himself to the welfare of those around him. In the ability to open oneself sensitively and to give of oneself to others, Fr. Nuttin (1962, p. 244) finds the epitome of self-actualization: "There is, on the other hand, the 'rich' form of self-preservation and development, which consists in *being open* to others as to a source of riches. . . . This 'openness' is the channel by which man 'gives himself' and by which he 'receives,' i.e., his channel of self-realization. It is *life itself*." It is in the moral gift of self, Fr. Nuttin concludes, that man reaches the full development of his personality. In the same vein, Fr. Lepp (1963, pp. 30–32) regards the inability to love as the most serious indication of emotional disorder. He regards persons unable to love as "emotional cripples." The personality unfolds most humanly and most fully when it is able to perfect itself by giving itself to the well-being of others. Conversely, persons insensitive to the needs of others and unable to give themselves in a "love of benevolence" (in Scholastic terminology) regard others as objects for the gratification of their own needs.

It is apparent that civilized society could not exist unless the majority of its members were reasonably well-integrated persons. Indeed, psychological literature is replete with evidence which suggests that those persons who overtly violate society's norms are specifically those who have failed to develop at least minimal personal integration (see Kisker, 1964, pp. 8–15).

In the school milieu, effective personal integration is geared toward the achievement of the primary goal of the school, viz., assisting the student to develop in truth. The guidance worker who is attuned to a developmental orientation regards the student as a person in transition, a person in the process of becoming. He does not anticipate that his clients will exhibit the level of personal integration typical of fully functioning adults. Rather, it is precisely this goal toward which education and guidance are aimed. The guidance worker's concern in personal development is directed primarily to the structuring of an environment which fosters effective integration. Secondarily, he is concerned with significant deviations from favorable patterns of personal development which may impede or halt the process short of that goal. These obstacles to optimal personal development often form the focal points of his assistance to students. Guidance workers attuned to a holistic approach to their tasks, moreover, perceive satisfactory progress in a favorable course of personal development as antecedent to (and indeed indispensable to) satisfactory development in social, vocational, or religious areas. In this vein, Fr. Stafford, C.S.V. (1961, pp. 3–10), has commented that the holistic approach implies that the counselor is aware of the psychological dimension of all problems presented by students, much as the teacher is aware of the Christian dimension in a class in mathematics or woodworking. A holistic approach further demands that the guidance worker approach every pupil need with the total spectral view of the "purely physical to the truly spiritual." As W. H. Sharp (1960, p. 54) has observed, "If one removes the adjectives, such as educational, before the noun counseling, a clearer perception may evolve. The counselor has to be able to consider and deal with the whole individual, the total aggregate of the behavior presented by the client." Even those educators who would limit the involvement of the school in the life of the student to strictly intellectual learnings admit the relevance of personal development guidance for the execution of the function they assign the school. For example, the student who attempts to convince his fellow students of the condition contrary to fact that he exhibits adequate leadership qualities and should be treated as a leader is unable to spend the requisite effort in intellectual learning. Instead, he directs his energies toward distorting his perceptions of those classmates who resist his attempts to exercise leadership. The holistic approach to man thus obligates the guidance worker to adopt the position that the first responsibility in the school guidance effort must be directed toward the enhancement of favorable developmental experiences leading to effective personal integration.

Self-defense, adjustment, and integration

In executing this function, guidance workers need to be alert not so much to the presence of gross, fully developed psychological disturbances in students as to indications of persistent difficulties in satisfactory personal development. They should be alert both to rigid efforts by a student to defend the consistency of faulty self-perception and to his inability to accept self-experience. A developmentally oriented worker sees the student as a person in the state of becoming, in the process of attempting to forge a self-identity. Nonintegrative behaviors often are "tried out" by students. But such behaviors rarely have been reinforced sufficiently to jell into fully developed personality dysfunctions. Thus guidance workers must be able to distinguish student behaviors which are indicative of faulty patterns of development (Biber, 1961).

Psychologists concerned with effective personal development have employed a number of concepts and distinctions which have proved useful to guidance workers (cf. O'Kelly & Muckler, 1955; Shaffer & Shoben, 1956). Among the most important of these are the concepts of *adjustive* and *integrative behaviors*. Those responses from the psychosocial environment which lead the person to make inferences about self-experience threatening to the consistency of the self-concept tend to evoke anxiety. To cope with the anxiety arising from such threats to consistent self-perception, the person attempts to defend himself through behaviors which preserve the consistency of the self-picture (Moffit & Stagner, 1956). When these defensive behaviors are successful in reducing the anxiety occasioned by the threat to self-consistency, they are called *adjustive* behavior mechanisms; when they fail to reduce anxiety, they are called *nonadjustive*. Whenever threat is experienced by the self, the self "tries on" a number of behaviors to reduce anxiety, in a relatively random exploration. Those behaviors which succeed in reducing anxiety are reinforced and are likely to be repeated in response to any future threats to self-consistency. The *pattern of such behaviors* (whether adjustive or nonadjustive) *adopted for habitual use by the self in coping with the problems of living constitutes personality.* Adjustive behaviors are regarded as *integrative* when they are self-advancing, i.e., when they permit the person not only to respond realistically to threat but also permit him to make future self-advancing adjustments. Adjustive behaviors are regarded as *nonintegrative* when they either do not permit such an advance or are actually self-defeating. Although nonintegrative behaviors may reduce immediate anxiety, they impede future integrative adjustment. Nonadjustive behaviors are always nonintegrative, since they fail to reduce anxiety arising from threat to self-consistency. Adjustive behaviors succeed in reducing the immediate threat. When adjustive behaviors foster the ability to make future self-advancing adjustments, they are integrative. Adjustive behaviors are nonintegrative when they hinder future self-advancing adjustments.

The degree to which a person exhibits adjustive and integrative characteristics of behavior in coping with problems or threatening perceptions is largely determined by the level of self-acceptance and the flexibility in self-perception at the moment when the threatening perception enters the phenomenal field. As was suggested in Chapter 2, the quality of adjustive behavior is increased when the self is flexible and open enough to incorporate even highly threatening perceptions. The flexible, open, integrated person is able to modify the self-concept while still maintaining its internal consistency and security.

Mechanisms of Defense

The behaviors by which the nonintegrated person maintains the consistency of a faulty self-picture, i.e., by which he denies or distorts the meaning of his self-experience, are regarded as the mechanisms of defense (see Fenichel, 1945, pp. 141–167; Anna Freud, 1946, pp. 3–72, 149–190). Even the reasonably well-integrated, self-actualized person makes occasional or frequent use of the mechanisms of defense when self-experience threatens the central core of "what is really me." These mechanisms are relatively "normal" ways to handle frustration or threat, but their exaggerated, habitual, or excessive use breeds serious emotional disturbances which may mature into neuroses or psychoses. Defense mechanisms serve as a means of allaying the anxiety aroused as one perceives ambiguity or disparity between self-concept and self-experience. In particular cases, the mechanisms may be adjustive or nonadjustive, integrative or nonintegrative.

A hypothetical class in freshmen English might contain, among others, seven students who aspire to become professional writers. This perception of self-as-writer has been developed through interaction with parents, teachers, and friends and has been reinforced by past self-experiences of success. Each of the seven has developed a relatively high level of facility in language usage. Central to the self-concept of each is the self-aspiration to become a highly skilled writer who will compose *the* great American novel. The teacher of English, a demanding person of high scholastic standards, assigns a theme on a specific topic. Each of the seven diligently composes his most polished prose, submits the paper at the appointed time, and anticipates an A. When the teacher returns the papers, each has received a C. The C mark constitutes, for each of the seven, a highly threatening preception of self. Anxiety is engendered as self-consistency is threatened. Each responds by defending himself from threat to the self-picture according to a pattern of adjustive behaviors reinforced in the past and adopted for their value in reducing anxiety.

Denial, Rationalization, Projection

The first student visibly displays shock beyond belief when his C paper is returned. His self-system is rigid and inflexible, admitting of no modification in self-perception. The C mark is highly threatening. He is unable to sustain threat to self-consistency or to reorganize his self-concept in cognizance of threat. Before he leaves the classroom, he crumples the paper and deposits it (perhaps ostentatiously) in the wastebasket. He has thus effectively destroyed the evidence of the threatening perception. He has *denied* the perception. The denial has reduced immediate anxiety and is thus adjustive, but it is nonintegrative because the student will have learned nothing from the experience, since his theme-writing behavior will not be modified. In addition, a nonintegrative behavior has been reinforced once again. Denial is thus "a mechanism of defense against anxiety or guilt in which the facts or logical implications of external reality are refused recognition" (Nurnberger et al., 1963, p. 352).

The second student also displays shock when his C paper is returned. His self-system is similarly inflexible; so the mark is highly threatening. But a gleam of understanding creeps into his eyes when he remembers that the teacher is of Italian extraction and he of Scotch-English and that the teacher once mentioned he dislikes students who wear Army shoes and duck-tail haircuts. Now the student undergoes the "Aha!" experience. Suddenly he understands that his low mark has nothing to do with the quality of his paper. Rather, the low mark issued from the teacher's ethnic prejudice. This student has *rationalized* the threatening self-experience. The rationalization has reduced immediate anxiety, serving an adjustive need, but it is a nonintegrative, self-defeating adjustment. Thus, "Rationalization refers to the process of presenting more ego-inflating reasons in place of ego-deflating 'true' reasons to account for one's practices or beliefs" (Sawrey & Telford, 1963, p. 48). A further distinction might be made between the "sour-grapes" and the "sweet-lemon" forms of rationalization. In the former, the person convinces himself that an unattainable goal is not worth having anyway. In the latter, the person convinces himself that a substitute goal is superior to the unattainable one (J. C. Coleman, 1956, pp. 91–92).

The third student is equally dismayed. His rigid self-system remains consistent, however, when he begins to ponder the possible motivations of the teacher. The teacher, after all, is much interested in creative writing. He has read to the class some of his original poetry. Why, the student wonders, would a really talented writer be engaged in an occupation so obviously uncreative as teaching high school English? Then it becomes abundantly clear that this teacher had once aspired to become a professional writer (just as the student now does). But the teacher has failed in his ambition. Bitterly disappointed, he turned in desperation to teaching. Now he seeks revenge by assigning low, discouraging marks to other aspiring writers more talented than he. This student has *projected* his own insecurity and lack of confidence onto the teacher. Projection serves him in the reduction of the immediate threat, but it is nonintegrative and self-defeating. Thus, "Projection is a defensive reaction by means of which we (1) transfer the blame for our own shortcomings, mistakes, and misdeeds to others" or (2) "attribute to others our own unacceptable impulses, thoughts, and desires" (J. C. Coleman, 1956, p. 90). The situation in which the person denies responsibility for his own behavior and insists that his deeds were caused by the influence of "bad companions" or of satanic temptation is an example of projection frequently encountered in schools.

Compensation, Withdrawal, Identification

The fourth student seeks to assuage his anxiety with the quick decision that, all things considered, becoming a creative writer is not so important as he had imagined. Thereafter he loses interest in English and in creative writing. He transfers his attention and aspirations to mathematics and experiences success in mathematics classes. As a result, he envisions a career as a mathematician. His self-aspiration begins to center around self-as-mathematician, and the ambition of self-as-writer is forgotten. His adjustive behavior has involved both *compensation* and *withdrawal*. He has compensated for a real or imagined deficiency by withdrawing from the situation in which threat is potentially lodged. He has transferred his energies elsewhere. At first glance, this appears a reasonably healthy adjustment. But the behavior is nonintegrative. First, the student has failed to benefit from the immediate experience by modifying his theme-writing behavior. Second, a self-defeating adjustment has been reinforced which bodes ill for the time when he may meet a source of frustration in mathematics. "The term *compensation* is used to describe . . . adoption of a substitute function or role which provides or tends to provide some tension-reducing satisfaction" (Young, 1952, p. 115). In this case, the student has compensated by entering another field. To the extent that his interest is not temporary and his ability is adequate, the compensating mechanism may be relatively effective. "The person who moves away from threat as his dominant way of meeting stressful situations is described as being timid and withdrawn" (Sawrey & Telford, 1963, p. 69). In other cases, withdrawal may provoke more severe disturbance, while in still other instances (e.g., when situations are nonmalleable) it may possibly be integrative and self-advancing. Habitual withdrawal from threat may eventually provoke escape from the responsibilities of life through what is termed the *flight from reality,* typical of the psychotic personality who escapes into a private world.

The fifth student, much threatened, happens to be a dilettante of literary biography. The teacher's mark is to be expected by the prospective writer; was not this the experience of a Heywood Broun and an F. Scott Fitzgerald? "They," i.e., teachers, for whatever reason, are never friendly to "us," i.e., Broun, Fitzgerald, and "me"—so his reasoning goes. And this, alas, is part of life, he contends. This student has *identified* with well-known figures. Identification comforts him and reduces the immediate anxiety, but it is equally nonintegrative. Identification is thus "a process in which the individual experiences a particular form of close involvement with another person or group and in which the self is experienced as if encompassing the other individual, yet still separate and distinct from the other" (Nurnberger et al., 1963, p. 358). A common behavioral mechanism, identification is often encouraged among students. Teachers and parents urge them to pattern their lives after a person distinguished in some field of endeavor. In Catholic schools the models with whom students are encouraged to identify are the saints. Thus identification can be integrative when it is founded on a realistic self-perception and when the behavior of the model for identification is worthy of imitation, but the use of identification as a means of maintaining *inaccurate* self-perception or an unrealizable self-aspiration constitutes a gross distortion of reality.

Reaction Formation, Integration

The sixth student evinces a more complex set of behaviors. It is immediately apparent to him that the teacher lacks all sense of literary taste, is incapable of distinguishing an exceptional student theme (i.e., his own) from a mediocre one. Obviously, the teacher needs help in this task; so the student resolves immediately to obtain for and present to the teacher several standard handbooks on literary criticism and on the evaluation of student themes. In most high schools such a move would hardly win friends among the faculty. This complex adjustive behavior constitutes *reaction formation,* which involves (1) the projection of one's own inadequacies onto another and (2) the formation on the part of self of a desire to help the other rid himself of the "fault" which self has projected onto other. The example of reaction formation customarily cited is that of the Puritan preacher, like Nathaniel Hawthorne's hero in *The Scarlet Letter,* who warns and chides his congregation about their preoccupation with the sins of the flesh. Thus, "Reaction-formation consists of the adoption of a behavior pattern which is directly the opposite of the reaction-tendency the person is trying to deny or refute. In other words, reaction-formation consists of the functioning of a pattern of behavior that is directly opposed to an anxiety-arousing impulse or act" (Sawrey & Telford, 1963, p. 130). Certain practices in Catholic schools relative to outmoded notions of appropriate dress, presumably motivated by the faculty's desire to protect students from sexual temptation, suggests a morbid preoccupation on the part of these schools with certain features of the human body and indeed with the body itself. To be sure, these practices bear a strong resemblance to the mechanism of reaction formation.

The seventh student is dismayed mightily by what he considers a low mark. His first reaction is shocked disbelief. Shortly, he inspects the teacher's comments, here a split infinitive, there faulty subject-verb agreement. He recalls that the teacher had announced that the principal dimension of interest on this theme assignment was to be structural clarity and grammatical precision. This student, a prospective writer, feels stupid and foolish for ignoring the teacher's admonitions. His self-concept is still threatened, but he is able to recognize and admit to glaring errors. On the instant, however, he resolves that he will henceforth become more attentive to structural clarity. He recalls the teacher's advice that clarity of usage is essential to the conveying of one's message. There are one or two notes made by the teacher pertaining to the student's poor paragraph transitions. These he does not fully comprehend. But by the end of class, he is able to summon enough courage to approach the teacher, paper in hand. The teacher spends ten minutes with him after class on the broad reference of the pronoun, and the student goes his way, armed with new skills. His self-concept has been threatened, but he has responded positively, flexibly, and integratively to the threat. He may no longer be able to think of himself as the naturally gifted molder of words who need not concern himself with the harsh discipline of grammar in order to achieve his self-aspiration, but, in the process, he has come to appraise himself more realistically. Both self-concept and immediate behavior have been modified. His self-advancing adjustment has served toward more effective personal integration. Of the seven students, the first six by their nonintegrative adjustive behavior have reduced the immediate anxiety over self-consistency by attributing the source of threat to a situation or person extrinsic to themselves. Only the seventh has demonstrated the self-acceptance and permeability of self-perception necessary to incorporate the threatening perception or self-experience into the phenomenal field. Subsequently, he has been able to reorganize his self-concept in the light of this new self-perception.

Quality of Adjustment

The adjustive behaviors employed by the first six students in the hypothetical class—denial, rationalization, projection, compensation, withdrawal, identification, and reaction formation—constitute the principal *defense mechanisms* used by the psychological self. The adjustive behavior employed by the seventh student represents effective integration of self-experience into self-perception. It is rare that a person utilizes exclusively a single self-defense mechanism to preserve self-consistency. Rather, adjustive behavior tends to be only conceptually analyzable into component mechanisms, though one mechanism typically predominates in a person's adjustive pattern. In the final analysis, the extent to which excessive use of the self-defense devices separates self-perception from reality determines the quality of one's adjustive behavior. As Bonner (1961, p. 476) has observed:

> This struggle for self-maintenance is an effort to maintain one's self-image, one's perception of oneself as an enduring person. This may be either normal or neurotic. Normal self-defense is the desire to maintain one's integrity and self-esteem without utilizing crippling mechanisms. Neurotic self defense . . . consists in the use of self-deceptive techniques which serve to hide from the person, and presumably from others, his real or imagined defects and weaknesses. Defense mechanisms are self-impairing only when they lead to false perceptions of oneself and others and when they distort and damage interpersonal relationships. They are normal and inescapable techniques of adjustment which, if their employment is not abused, contribute to personal equilibrium.

Hence, the use of the various mechanisms of defense to maintain self-consistency represents a normal psychological dynamism. This point cannot be overemphasized. The *protracted or excessive use* of these mechanisms to maintain inaccurate, distorted self-pictures, however, may eventually produce serious emotional disorders. Thus, for example, a healthy use of compensation may, by immoderate use, degenerate into unhealthy *overcompensation.* At the least, protracted or excessive use represents the avoidance of responsibility; at worst, the continued shielding of self from the meaning of self-experience gives rise to the fantasies and delusions encountered in the major psychoses.

Environmental Adaptation

It has already been stressed that the proper use of defense mechanisms constitutes a normal psychological process. The quality of the mechanism is determined by its value in anxiety reduction and its effect on self-integration. Some mechanisms, e.g., identification and compensation, may provide the person more positive assistance in coping with life's challenges. Similarly, the pattern of adjustive behaviors must be evaluated in terms of the concrete life situation. Mental health is a relative, not an absolute, characteristic. Indeed, mental health characterizes a number of divergent patterns of adjustive behavior. What is psychologically normal in one environment or situation may be quite abnormal in another. J. E. Gordon (1963, p. 566) states it aptly: "Suppose that a person were perfectly 'normal' in competitiveness, compared to his society, but that he emigrates to another society which is more competitive than his former one. Compared to his new society, he is now abnormally noncompetitive, and he is urged to do something about it, even though he has not changed his way of behaving one bit." The point may well be taken with regard to certain occupational groups as well as societies. A highly creative person, given to flights of ideas, would be considered abnormal among accountants, whose work activity demands a considerable compulsive attention to detail. In other words, a behavior which among men in general might be considered abnormal or pathological is, in a particular concrete situation, self-advancing rather than self-defeating. Fr. E. F. O'Doherty has suggested that a predisposition toward psychotic delusion might help to explain a readiness for certain types of religious mystical experiences. Thus Fr. O'Doherty (1964, p. 173) comments that "in a given case, a vision, for example, might be the same kind of phenomena as an hallucination—in other words, a very natural and almost normal event in psychopathology, but used by God, as he might use any other phenomena of the natural order, for a purpose of his own."

Certain abnormal or pathological needs of the person may become a predominant feature of the personality but remain under the relative control of the self and indeed help the self advance. This process might be illustrated by the selection of accountancy as a profession by a person who has an abnormal need for orderliness and a compulsive attention to detail. Such a process is called, by Freudians, placing *pathology in the service of the ego* or the self. The salient point about this process is that it highlights the role of *environmental adaptation* in determining mental health. For example, a study by Bateman and Jensen (1958) discovered that persons with extensive religious training tend to turn inward their anger resulting from frustration. They show less hostility toward the environment and toward others, but they tend to blame themselves excessively. It is likely that their level of self-confidence is weakened as a result of this tendency. Thus counselors working in Catholic and other church-related schools should not be surprised by a generally low level of self-confidence in students. While Bateman and Jensen's finding might be cause for concern among men in general, low self-confidence is currently considered the norm for persons with extensive religious training. Mental health must be assessed not only in terms of the inner dynamics of the person but also in terms of his environmental adaptation. Hence, according to norms for the general population, an adolescent boy who is extremely self-effacing, excessively deferrent to his elders, and exceedingly uninterested in members of the opposite sex is likely to be regarded as relatively poorly adjusted or at least as not having resolved important developmental realities. But among candidates for the religious life, the same person is regarded as very well adjusted or even as mentally healthy. What is abnormal or undesirable or even self-defeating relative to one sociocultural context may actually be normal, desirable, and self-advancing in another. The issue of environmental adaptation is intimately related to the issues of adjustive and integrative behaviors.

Guidance and effective integration

The goal of the school guidance program is to promote optimal personal development or self-actualization in each student. In view of this primary goal, effective personal integration constitutes the major focus for guidance efforts in the school. School counseling aims at assisting the student-client not only toward more effective integration in the particular decision, concern, or problem at hand but also toward developing and enlarging the *capacity* for self-expansion though openness to self-experience.

Guidance efforts within the school milieu make provision both for positive promotion of effective personal integration and for the detection and amelioration of faulty developmental patterns likely to impede effective personal integration (A. D. Miller, 1958). Principal emphasis is placed on the enhancement of favorable developmental patterns and on the capacity for self-acceptance. In the holistic approach, each so-called need area, e.g., vocational, scholastic, social, and religious, is considered an avenue through which the student finds an opportunity for self-actualization. Counselors following a developmental approach place chief emphasis on promoting effective integrative development. The principal function of guidance, according to Shoben (1962b), is to implement the role of the school as an agency of healthful development. Guidance workers, however, also recognize the secondary obligation to assist students who have difficulty in opening themselves to the world of experience and who consequently feel obliged to defend themselves rigidly against threat.

Several positive obligations appear incumbent upon *all* school personnel actively to promote personal development as the major guidance focus.

1. The first positive obligation for administrators, teachers, and every type of guidance worker in promoting effective personal integration is the *recognition of the unity and singularity of the person of the student* and of his unique developmental history. Holding the student in "warm, positive regard" is a mandate for the administrator and teacher no less than for the counselor. It is too easy for the administrator of the large comprehensive school and for teachers burdened with large classes to ignore the student as an individual, denying at least implicitly his substantial unity. Many who affirm philosophically a holistic view of man tend in practice to ignore that view (e.g., the efficiency-oriented [not person-oriented] religious administrator). Administrators are prone to be far more concerned with programming, scheduling, and the manipulation of classes or groups than with the needs of individual students. Teachers are inclined to be concerned with the progress of the class as a class rather than with the development of each student as a person. Even counselors tend to deal with test scores or with

problems rather than with persons. Each of these conditions represents not only a fragmentizing of the human person but also a denial that a growth of the "part" is contingent on the growth of the whole.

2. A second obligation of school personnel in the promotion of positive personal integration is the *communication to the student of the recognition of his individuality.* Carl R. Rogers (1958, p. 14) has phrased this as a question: "Can I receive him [the client] as he is? Can I communicate this attitude?" When the school environment is so rigidly structured as to preclude the individualization of teaching, discipline, or student activity, the student can only draw the inference that his individuality is not valued by school personnel. The integration of this perception in the self-system is likely to impede the student in his quest for a feeling of intrinsic worth.

3. A third obligation is the *provision of experiences conducive to effective integration.* These experiences are both casual and formal, ranging from the attitude of the teacher toward the student as an individual to an open-door policy for ready accessibility in the counselor's office. Such experiences aim at assisting the student to fulfill the specific tasks inherent in his unique developmental pattern and to provide him with the opportunity to draw inferences which increase his sense of self-worth. Lee (1963b, pp. 423–424) has suggested that the school needs to consider teachers as role models of the well-functioning adult for students to identify with and emulate (see also Farnsworth, 1961). It is primarily through the provision of experiences which accelerate favorable personal development that the school communicates to the student its recognition of his singularity and the uniqueness of his developmental pattern.

4. Another obligation of school personnel in furthering positive integration is the *organization of the environment* in such fashion that the accomplishment of the student's developmental tasks is accelerated, not hindered (Hollister, 1959). The school must develop a tolerance for student attempts to fulfill developmental tasks commonly faced at certain periods (e.g., the common adolescent task of identity exploration). The school is by nature a supportive, paternalistic environment. While it has an obligation to fit the student for the competitive world of adult life, the school must also perceive the student as a person in the process of becoming. It is thus necessary for the school to encourage students to follow what Morris (1959) has called the ultimate imperatives to know who one is, to know what one is choosing in life and from life, and to take final responsibility for his choices. Values are inevitably taught and learned in schools despite disclaimers by traditionalists and intellectualists. Thus, for example, the fierce, hostile competition among eighth graders in Catholic elementary schools for entrance into Catholic high schools represents a value-learning experience. The value taught and the value learned seem to be that failure is unacceptable and that hostile, and indeed cutthroat, competition is acceptable to achieve one's ends. Nor is the case limited either to Catholic or to elementary schools. Through education and through American society is emblazoned one shining value: *do not fail.* What one succeeds *at* is largely a matter of filling in

a blank, no matter how vainglorious or ignoble the object. Hence, according to McGovern (1964), among the factors which hinder the development of a positive mental-health program in schools is "the unconscious need on the part of the school and community for scapegoats, i.e., those persons who are visible examples of failure." Further, McGovern charges, "Children who succeed are regarded as good, bright, conscientious," while those who fail are "regarded as bad, i.e., lazy, obstinate, devilish." These values seem to undercut the reality of the Mystical Body, whose members Christ enjoined to love one another. Charity, growing only *through* love of one's fellowman, seems a more important goal of the Catholic elementary school than successful admission into a Catholic high school. Growth in love represents the acme of personal development. School environments which support or reinforce behaviors laden with values which are not related to growth in charity tend ultimately to impede the full personal development of the student. In the cases mentioned above, it is the capacity for love and the ability to postpone gratification of one's own needs which are impeded.

5. A fifth obligation is the *cultivation of a holistic developmental orientation* among school people, students, and parents. It has been observed that environmental consistency is essential in favorable personal development. Hence a holistic, developmental orientation which recognizes and prizes the student as a unique person must permeate the school milieu. It is equally necessary that the family environment be open and flexible enough to encourage and tolerate the attempts of the developing student to fulfill his tasks. Similarly, it is important that students themselves understand something of the nature of the tasks inherent in development. Guidance efforts are directed, for example, at easing the trials of puberty and relieving undue anxiety over sexual function among students. In order to do so, it is necessary to provide information and communicate a developmental view to school people, students, and parents, so that each group might be better prepared to deal effectively with this developmental task. Similarly, information about the dynamics of the religious crisis often encountered in middle and late adolescence will serve to reduce anxiety among parents, students, and teachers (Mother M. McCollough, 1963). Schneiders (1964b) has noted that "some conflict in adolescence is unavoidable *and even necessary* for adequate maturation"; he thus regards adolescent emotional conflict as essentially developmental rather than pathological. School people and parents, as well as students, who are informed relative to the tasks and crises attendant upon the process of becoming can the more readily contribute positively to favorable development.

6. Finally, there is the obligation to *recognize disturbances in personal development* among students and to arrange for appropriate school or community resources capable of dealing effectively with such disturbances. Counselors, trained to work with essentially normal persons, are usually prepared to deal effectively only with developmental difficulties, not with major abnormalities. Teachers and other school people trained in personality dynamics are often able to recognize incipient and burgeoning psychological aberra-

tions in students. Such identification by guidance workers constitutes *gross diagnosis*, in which the worker detects certain rather blatant and recurrent nonintegrative or nonadjustive behaviors in the student that seem continually to impede his satisfactory developmental progress. *Differential diagnosis* (i.e., the identification of the particular malfunction) is a matter only for the specialist with training in clinical psychological procedures. Ignorance of the dynamics of mental health often leads the teacher or counselor to attribute nonintegrative behavior to malice or caprice. In this connection, a little learning is a dangerous thing. Thus, for example, students experiencing *school phobia* (e.g., minor illnesses which prevent school attendance) are quite often regarded as malingerers by psychologically uninformed teachers and counselors. Instead of referring these students for competent help, they cajole, threaten, or exhort them to fulfill their moral obligations. As a last resort they remand such students to the administration or any other handy Torquemada. It is also important that counselors and other school people refrain from perceiving each student who marches to the beat of a different drummer as hopelessly maladjusted. Indeed, those who so perceive students are typically projecting their own inadequacies. On the other hand, it is probably preferable to err by excess in the matter of referring for differential diagnosis pupils whose nonintegrative behaviors are really only transitory, rather than to err by neglect in not referring some students whose later lives may be marred by major disturbances. Major disturbances in later life might well have been ameliorated had they been observed and treated as they developed in childhood or adolescence. In much the same fashion that the physician does not scruple to set the broken arm of a terminal cancer patient, so guidance workers should not refuse the *normal* range of guidance services to seriously disturbed students who are unwilling or unable to undertake intensive psychological or psychiatric treatment (Pallone, 1963c). As Super (1955) noted, counseling deals with the normal concerns of normal personalities or even with the normal concerns of abnormal personalities.

The role of the school counselor

Just as the common cold may mature into lethal pneumonia if not properly treated at its inception, so nonintegrative behavior patterns may mature into neuroses, psychoses, or serious character disorders. The school counselor deals primarily with normal students in the process of becoming, many of whom respond to frustration, conflict, or threat through nonintegrative behavior. Hence he is in a crucial position both to identify and to help ameliorate developmental difficulties *before* such problems are reinforced, *before* they become firmly entrenched in the structure of the personality and mature into major disturbances.

It is only relatively recently (cf. Wrenn, 1962, pp. 127–128) that the vital role of the school counselor in positive mental-hygiene efforts has been widely recognized. Indeed, many counseling theorists and practitioners are still reluctant to emphasize this role. Research into the incidence of severe mental disorders in the American population (cf. Kisker, 1964, pp. 8–15), however, has engendered recognition of the need for preventive measures and for early diagnosis and treatment. In many nonmetropolitan areas of the nation, as Redl and Wattenberg (1959, pp. 427–428) point out, school counselors may be the best-trained persons in the community to deal with disturbed children. In the emerging strategy for the promotion of positive mental health, a major emphasis has been placed on the school and its effect on the process of development (cf. Bower, 1961).

Along with other school people, the counselor has a primary obligation in the *structuring of an environment* conducive to favorable processes of personal integration. As a person with at least minimal skill in psychometrics, developmental psychology, mental hygiene, and the techniques of counseling, he is in a strategic position for early detection and assistance. He is able to offer assistance to students whose early nonintegrative behavior patterns may still be channeled into more favorable developmental processes. He is called on to offer adjustive developmental counseling to these students. The aim of his counseling efforts will be to help them rid themselves of the need for crippling defense mechanisms by assisting them to develop insight into their motives and to attain flexibility, openness to self-experience, and more meaningful integration in the self-system. Interpretive counseling, the model for which has been outlined earlier, has as its aim the amelioration of an impinging developmental difficulty and the development of the capacity to resolve future difficulties without assistance.

With good reason, the beginning counselor is likely to feel diffident about focusing his counseling activities on matters of personality disturbance. It is to prepare him to undertake counseling concerned with the holistic student that an intensive, supervised laboratory experience in counseling is essential in counselor preparation. Further, the bases for undertaking developmental counseling lie in a meaningful, *functional* understanding of the dynamics of human development and mental health. This knowledge must regenerate itself continually after formal course work has been completed, through in-service activities which familiarize counselors with both contemporary empirical research and theoretical formulations. Regardless of the level of experience of the counselor, the awareness of the limits of his professional competence demands that he seek *ongoing, responsible supervision* in his efforts at personal development counseling. Specialists in mental hygiene (e.g., psychologists, social workers, and psychiatrists) are available within the more alert school systems to serve in a consultative capacity (Caplan, 1959; Lytton, Knobel, & MacNeven, 1960). Such in-service supervision gives the counselor focus in adjustive counseling, helps him evaluate his own behavior in the counseling relationship, and assists him in reflecting on the satisfaction of *his own needs* in the counseling encounter.

13

SOCIAL DEVELOPMENT
AS A GUIDANCE FOCUS

DEVELOPMENTAL TASKS AND SOCIAL INSTITUTIONS

Personality is generally regarded as a person's pattern of responses or habitual ways of behaving. It is apparent that man's social context is implied in the notion of personality. Indeed, personality may be regarded as *learned habitual responses reinforced by social situations*. But in any social situation, an organized society makes known its demands on the individual person; that is, in any social situation there are *cues to acceptable behavioral alternatives*. Similarly, formal social institutions organize themselves in such fashion that the individual person perceives the cues to available behavioral alternatives. Thus, for example, the business community quite easily makes it known that wearing a Hawaiian sport shirt, lavender Bermuda shorts, and sandals constitutes an unacceptable behavioral alternative for its members, its prospective members, and those who wish to make transactions within its confines. In this sense, personality is constituted by learned habitual responses to cues to acceptable behavioral alternatives inhering in social institutions. When the person has become socialized, he regards behavioral alternatives

360

not accepted or approved by society as a generic term as unavailable to him.

From the point of view of developmental tasks, the function of a major social institution—family, school, church, peer group—may be regarded as so organizing itself as to ease successful negotiation of developmental tasks. The avenues or pathways through which the individual negotiates his tasks represent behaviors, however, and these behaviors similarly are circumscribed by cues to acceptable behavioral alternatives inhering in social institutions. Mention has already been made of school structures which, by demanding premature vocational choices and concomitant self-closure, make open-endedness an unacceptable alternative behavior, even though the ability to tolerate ambiguity is essential to adolescent exploration. Examples of a similarly constricted range of behavioral alternatives inhering in the family as a social institution are legion. Many Catholic parents, for instance, insist upon taking their young infants and children to Mass with them, even though the Church as a social institution does not require Mass attendance before seven, the "age of reason." When these children are unable to concentrate upon the Mass, or at least sit quietly, because they are not yet developmentally ready to do so, the parents impose further behavior restrictions and indeed create needless conflicts. Clearly the relationship between successful resolution of developmental tasks and the structure of social institutions, in which inhere cues to available behavioral alternatives in the resolution of tasks, is an interpenetrating one.

The nature of social development

Save for those rare exceptions who seek a Walden even more remote and asocial than Henry David Thoreau's, man both theoretically and operationally lives his existence within the context of society. Man lives in a series of societies: family, peer group, classroom group, ethnic group, professional or occupational group, civic community, national community, Mystical Body. To do so satisfactorily, it is necessary for him to bring his personal life-style at least minimally into accord with the structure of the society in which he lives; i.e., he must fit his needs to the avenues of need satisfaction deemed acceptable within his society. As Sherif and Sherif (1956, pp. 369–372) have observed, most human motives are sociogenic, arising from social influences and norms. The ways in which these motives can be satisfied are circumscribed by the avenues of need satisfaction tolerated or supported by the norms of the group or groups which have salience for the individual person. Even biogenic motives are socially circumscribed and adapted. For example, even though all societies recognize hunger as a basic human motive, few societies approbate cannibalism as a means of hunger reduction. Similarly, though some societies do not uphold the moral prescription which discountenances the coveting of one's neighbor's wife, no modern society approves the murder of the husband as an acceptable behavior.

From birth onward, man lives in a series of societies, including the family, the church, the school, informal societies such as the play group and the adolescent interest group, and finally the broader adult society. Each of these groups makes its particular demands upon the developing person. It was observed in Chapter 2 that fulfillment of the major developmental task of childhood, socialization, leads the developing person to the perception that his needs can properly be met only when the demands of the society are fulfilled. For example, the right of the individual to life can be guaranteed only when society's proscriptions against aggressive violence directed against another's person are observed by the majority of citizens. In precise terms, the needs of the individual can be satisfied only when group norms are operable.

Social psychologists and sociologists call those societies in which the person experiences maximum interaction with other members and in which the majority of his needs are met (such as the family) *primary societies,* or primary social groups (cf. Krech et al., 1962, pp. 394–402). Many believe that it is the primary social group experience which shapes the direction of the person's adjustment to later social groups (Redl & Wattenberg, 1959, pp. 89–93). As M. Deutsch (1949) has suggested, each society makes special demands upon the person to adapt himself to its structure, so that the needs of all members may appropriately be achieved. In his study of the fashion in which individual motivation or need is related to the satisfaction of the needs of the group as a group, E. J. Thomas (1957, p. 366) concluded that "members facilitate one another regarding goals to the degree that the efforts of each actually serve to move others toward their respective goals." An athletic team or an industrial production group aptly illustrates this point.

Capacity for adult socialization

Thus, the social context in which man exists exercises certain controls over his behavior. Viewed positively, membership in a society demands that the person have the capacity to postpone the immediate gratification of certain of his own desires so that the welfare of others is not impaired and that he develop the capacity to love in the broad general sense of the willingness to consider the well-being of another as important or as more important than his own. The ability to postpone gratification and the capacity for love represent characteristics of effectively integrated persons.

An avowed purpose of American education and of guidance as its sub-process is to facilitate the development of mature, fully functioning adults capable of prudent living (in Scholastic terminology) in a free society. Since the accomplishment of this developmental task implies, for each student, appropriate social development in each of the groups or societies in which he holds membership prior to and preparatory to the assumption of adult social roles, social development emerges as a major guidance focus. It is important to bring a proper perspective to bear upon social development as a guidance focus: development within and adjustment to social groups prior to entry into adult society hold especial significance since they prepare the individual for an effective role in that society. C. H. Miller (1961, p. 182) has suggested that guidance services have a twofold task in social development: (1) "to assist the individual with the process of development while *temporarily* living in his world of youth society and culture, and (2) to help him to understand, accept, and plan for a realistic role in the adult world." Indeed, many developmental psychologists regard a modicum of social *mal*adjustment as necessary and efficacious in each developmental stage. Perhaps it is more useful to perceive certain types of social tensions and conflicts as constituting necessary elements in the process of normal development. As Chapter 2 indicated, for example, the seemingly maladaptive oscillatory behaviors of adolescence constitute essential steps in the process of self-exploration. In regard to college students, Sanford (1962) has proposed that open-endedness and ambiguity in social relationships are essential to facilitate the process of becoming. Similarly, Ausubel (1954, pp. 48–50) regards adolescence as a state of *developmental disequilibrium,* in which social relationships are disturbed. Accordingly, guidance efforts are not focused exclusively on the immediate problems of social adjustment experienced by the child or adolescent within his immediate social context, for to do so would be to turn attention exclusively to transitory situations. Rather, effective social development guidance focuses upon the immediate social adjustments of the student as they relate to the development of the capacity for effective social living in the adult world and to the capacity for contributing creatively to the welfare of the adult society. Thus social development guidance encompasses the range of interpersonal relationships in the developmental pattern of the student as they bear upon the capacity for adult socialization.

Social group relationships

Specialists in the area of social development agree that the quality of primary group experience bears important implications for the progress of normal socialization. Since the process of socialization, in common with other aspects of the person's total developmental pattern, is teleological and epigenetic, appropriate or satisfactory socialization at any stage of development is accelerated or impeded by the level of prior social adjustment. Social groups of special interest in guidance efforts in the educational setting are the family and the peer group, for these societies bear dramatically upon the total personal development of the student in his life situation.

The Family

Family relationships provide the first models for social living, both chronologically and in order of psychological importance (Hurlock, 1959, pp. 214,

319). From family interaction, the developing person derives his basic value orientation, his perception of social roles, the good life, acceptable behaviors, and appropriate goals. Bronfenbrenner's conceptual integration (1958) of a quarter century of research on parent-child relationships suggested that a generally more permissive quality in the family group relationship very likely is mirrored in greater flexibility and self-reliance in children in the process of development. Mathewson (1962, p. 46), a guidance expert, has observed that "a school pupil's conception of appropriate behavior, the value of continued education, and the level and type of occupation that he may follow" is likely to arise primarily from family norms shared through family interaction throughout his life. It has already been observed that the child's perception of the world as supportive or nonsupportive and his primordial orientation toward it arise from family interaction. Developmental difficulties inhering in family interaction typically express themselves in the school setting in insecurity, hostility, aggression, or egocentricity. As behaviors, however, their etiology may be mistaken by teachers and counselors not alert to the roots of such disturbances and socially disruptive modes of behaving. For example, a negativistic, hostile attitude toward teachers, who represent authority to the student, might well be the expression in behavior of a poor relationship between the child and his father, who first represented social authority in his life. Indeed, the hostile, aggressive child in the Catholic school may be perceived by teachers and administrators as willfully obstinate, the captive of Satan, sinful, rather than as one suffering from a serious pathological disturbance in interpersonal relationships. Consequently, such a child may become the object of moral recriminations and exhortations, which tend to increase his insecurity in the face of authority and thus to reinforce his negative and hostile feelings. Or he may become the object of expulsion guidance, which effectively removes from the school situation a problem too difficult or time-consuming for it to solve. The shy, timid, insecure student, who seems fearful of contributing to class discussion, who appears constricted in interpersonal relationships with his classmates, who is overly attentive to the "demands" of the teacher, or who is simply overly dependent upon the direction supplied by the teacher, probably is projecting into the classroom a series of attitudes and behaviors acquired in the family milieu. In Catholic schools, the religious role of teachers serves to increase their salience as authority surrogates for the child, thus preventing effective assistance in improving responses to authority. Guidance efforts in such cases may be directed immediately toward assisting the student to achieve effective *stimulus discrimination* between home and school situations. Through effective stimulus discrimination, he may be enabled to distinguish the stimulus field of the home situation from that of the school situation and to respond differentially to each, rather than to continue to generalize his response from one to the other.

Effective stimulus discrimination in such cases is accomplished through (1) the manipulation of the school environment in such fashion that the demands placed on students are distinguished from the use of authority of discipline reminiscent of the home situation; (2) so structuring the school environment that the child is challenged in the school setting to fulfill his developmental potentialities, i.e., through positive rather than proscriptive or punitive motivational procedures; and (3) counseling with the student experiencing such developmental disturbances to help him develop insight into the differential dimensions of the two situations so that his responses may be differentiated. In a more remote fashion, guidance efforts, through the provision of information to parent groups and through parent consultation, may be directed toward improving intrafamily relationships. In cases in which the quality of primary group experience in the family has deteriorated markedly, the counselor may be called upon to suggest that the family seek therapeutic assistance at a family service agency, such as those maintained by Catholic Charities in more alert dioceses.

Consistency, Relationship, Conflict

The quality of social development within the family and thus the roots of developmental difficulty seem to be determined principally by three factors in intrafamily relationships: (1) *the degree of consistency* in the family environment, (2) *the quality of relationships between parents,* and (3) the generating of *conflict* between the norms of the family and those of other social groups.

It has been indicated in Chapter 2 that the developing person needs consistency in the psychosocial environment in order to progress toward effective personal integration. Studies of authoritarian and permissive family environments in relation to the later personal and social adjustment of children indicate that the major contributing factor in the ratio of severe emotional disturbance is the degree of consistency in authoritarian or permissive family structure. Indeed there seem to be few significant differences in the incidence of severe maladjustment in later life arising from one or the other atmosphere, but poor mental health is predicted by inconsistency among parents. Maccoby, Gibbs, and associates (1964) found that upper-middle-class and upper-class parents tend to be more permissive in child rearing, while lower-middle-class parents tend to favor authoritarian or prescriptive regimens. Even though not productive of increased mental disturbance of a serious nature, authoritarian home environments are regarded by Frenkel-Brunswik (1958) as impeding openness to experience and thus constituting an obstacle to optimal self-actualization. Though his study did not employ "permissive" and "authoritarian" as categories for family interaction, Andry (1960, pp. 117–119) concluded that delinquency is related to family environments marked by rigid discipline and constricted, nonspontaneous relationships between parents (especially fathers) and children. Even more interesting was his finding that socially disruptive behavior or delinquency is likely to result from a lack of consistency in *patterns of affection* toward the child.

An inconsistent family environment presents conflicting values to the child, who is psychologically pulled apart by the variant expectations and demands of his parents and siblings toward him (Sears, Maccoby, & Levin, 1957). The predictable result is insecurity and constriction. Presented with conflicting values and avenues of behavior, the child, driven by the desire to protect himself from recriminations on either side, chooses either not to act or to act out his conflicts aggressively. In later life, he is likely to assume a passive, anxious posture toward social involvement, presenting a fearful, constricted approach toward coping with the problems of living. Or he may erupt into aggressive, violent, or delinquent behavior. The inconsistent environment, with alternate demands, introduces varying figures into the child's perceptual field. Each of these figures is charged with a positive and a negative valence: the pleasure of one parent, the displeasure of the other. In such a conflict situation, there are two avenues of response: (1) the immobility of the organism, or (2) the active rejection of the demands of each parent. In the latter case, by rejecting the conflicting orientations toward life presented by his parents, the child makes aggressive assaults upon the structure and authority of organized society, which his parents have represented to him. In the first case, immobilized, the developing person is likely to be impeded as he generalizes his anxiety over conflict to other situations, with the consequent trammeling of the developmental process. In the latter instance, the developmental process is arrested, and serious social pathology results.

Common observation, as well as considerable empirical research, suggests that the relationships between parents and between parents and siblings profoundly affect the social development of the child and the adolescent. Positive relationships, marked by harmony and a sense of family belonging, tend to generate security, warmth, and spontaneity in interpersonal relationships. Negative relationships, marked by dissension and recrimination, tend to generate mistrust and aggressiveness. W. C. Becker and his associates (1959) concluded that children who are unable to control aggression tend to come from families in which both parents are maladjusted emotionally, quarrel with each other, and deal arbitrarily with the child. Children who exhibit shyness and insecurity tend to come from families in which the father is indecisive, maladjusted, or openly hostile toward the child. In the accompanying factor analysis of empirical results, these researchers identified a factor which they called parent-child harmony as contributory to the emotional health of the children. As Bonner (1961, p. 171) has observed, "There probably is no child who can daily witness his parents' resentments toward each other without suffering intense emotional insecurity." Locke (1951), among others, has demonstrated the strong relationship between the marital adjustment of spouses and that of their parents. Some investigators (cf. Nye, 1957) have suggested that separation or divorce is preferable, from the point of view of the personal and social adjustment of the child, to continued exposure to a family situation marked by emotional stress. Poor relationships within the family tend to focus the inconsistency in the family environment.

Family and School Values

The norms of family life are likely to reflect the sociocultural context in which the family lives. Thus, the goals, values, and behaviors approbated in the white Anglo-Saxon Protestant family living in "exurbia" tend to differ significantly from those of the Negro or Puerto Rican family housed in a tenement in "inner city." Each may be appropriate to the family's immediate social context, but such norms are likely to conflict with each other (Korbin, 1951); each is likely to be somewhat variant with regard to middle-class urban values considered typical of American schools and teachers (Bandura, 1962). The resolution of such norm conflict influences (1) the salient dimensions in the student's social development, (2) the ease with which he can adapt himself to the variant norms represented by the sociocultural contexts of his fellow students, and (3) the extent to which he is capable of modifying those behaviors based on norms which are in conflict. Norms arising within the family, embedded in their socioeconomic class (i.e., membership group), may conflict in the student with norms he perceives as arising from the socioeconomic class to which he aspires (i.e., reference group). Studies such as those of Seigel and Seigel (1953) and Charters and Newcomb (1958) suggest that there are situational cues which tend to increase the salience of one group and determine the person's feelings and behavior. In any comprehensive high school there are a variety of subcultures, ethnic groups, and socioeconomic classes, each with a class-specific set of social norms. Since the geographical area served by the elementary school is usually smaller, the range of norms represented is likely to be narrower. Positive social development requires that the student be capable, first, of prudently resolving norm conflicts while simultaneously recognizing the individuality of other students and, second, of tolerating and encouraging norms, values, and behaviors which differ from those of his own family.

Conflicts are also likely to arise between the behavior expectations of parents and those of school personnel, e.g., relative to independence or emancipation from the home. Cohesive, harmonious families may become chagrined when the eldest child, upon entering high school, begins gradually to focus his attention and interest on the peer group rather than on the family group. Such refocusing must inevitably occur if he is to fulfill the developmental tasks of adolescence. The "social distance" between parent and child tends to increase as the child matures, as he begins to associate more closely with his peers, and as he starts to reject parental attitudes and values (Alice Anderson & Beatrice Dvorak, 1963).

Through the provision of information to parents relative to normal progress in social development, guidance workers can do much to ease for students these and similar transitions and to allay the anxiety of parents. Bauer (1962, p. 137) has observed that many parents seem to wish to "jet-propel" their children into adulthood, regarding the young person's social popularity as a vital index of their own success as parents. In so doing, such parents wish to circumvent the evolutionary, epigenetic progress of normal development and burden the child with social responsibility beyond his capacity to handle it prudently. They regard social development in childhood and adolescence as an end in itself rather than a transition. Here is another source of conflict between parental norms and the norms of the developmentally oriented school.

Similarly, achievement motivation in the school setting seems to be related to certain family characteristics. Rosen (1961) found that family size, birth order, and mother's age, interacting with the family's socioeconomic status, are related to the deveopment of achievement motivation in boys from eight to fourteen years of age. Parental income level also affects school motivation and success. Coster's investigation (1959) disclosed that high school students from families of higher socioeconomic status are more likely to participate in extracurricular activities, hold student office, achieve high marks, attain the honor roll, and remain in school. The goal of the school, optimal development for each pupil in terms of a unique developmental pattern, may run counter to the expectations of the family in regard to both in-class and extraclass achievement, as well as to level and quality of educational achievement.

The peer group

The next group the child encounters chronologically, and probably in order of importance for psychosocial development, is the preschool play group of age mates, in which reciprocal relationships arise spontaneously from interaction, without a pre-extant social structure (Hurlock, 1959, pp. 145–148). Later peer groups generally arise within and center in the school. In middle and late childhood, these groups tend to exert little compelling behavior control over the individual student, possibly because his behavior is largely controlled by family norms. Yet such play groups eventually come to mirror the dynamics of social interaction and develop institutionalized or traditionalized norms, values, and relationships among members (Merei, 1949). A sense of acceptance more than a sense of belonging characterizes normal social development during this period of late childhood. Horrocks and Buker (1951) demonstrated that though friendships tend to fluctuate markedly in late childhood, the degree of social acceptance expressed by the group for the individual is not dependent upon the stability of his own friendships or group membership. Stability of friendship, however, and therefore the opportunity for the emergence of cohesively operating groups, tends to increase with age. Some guidance workers and even guidance experts (cf. Strang, 1958, pp. 262–264) are overly enamored of such devices as the sociogram, through which teachers or counselors identify "stars" and "isolates" within classroom groups. These workers hope to integrate the isolate into the social life of the classroom, a goal which betrays both a middle-class emphasis on social popularity and the failure to regard childhood and adolescence as essentially developmental and transitional stages. While the sociogram and other sociometric devices may be useful in the hands of a school person skilled in group dynamics, little stock can be placed in sociometric ratings in the classroom as indices of social development. The classroom is not a free, unhampered play group social situation; rather, definite work outcomes are expected by both students and teachers. Indeed, most teachers employ the more traditional pedagogical techniques which tend to stress individual achievement rather than social feeling and concern for the welfare of others, a condition which, paradoxically, is in sharp contrast to classroom procedures in the Soviet Union (Bronfenbrenner, 1962). In such a highly charged, work-oriented milieu, social relationships may not arise easily. The school, no less than the family, must learn to tolerate both the asocial intellectual recluse who prefers to spend time alone with his books and the child who is slow to develop socially, provided that neither behaves out of fear of rejection by the peer group. The slow, gradual process of development cannot be jet-propelled by parental cajolings and teacher exhortations to wallflowers. Even though Gronlund and Whitney (1956) found that the pupil's classroom sociometric status is a fairly reliable index of his general social acceptability among his peers in the school and in the neighborhood, they cautioned teachers and counselors against overgeneralizing. In cases of low social acceptability in the classroom, they suggested it is beneficial to check sociometric results in other situations before scheduling the student for special assistance with social development problems. It must be emphasized that the *developing person's perception* of the quality of his social interaction, combined with his developmental history, constitutes the salient feature activating guidance assistance.

Group Control of Behavior

Common experience suggests the reality of the adolescent peer group as a cohesive, dynamic sociocultural unit which exercises behavior control in matters of speech, dress, and taste, of which rock 'n' roll and the ducktail haircut are some artifacts. But scientific evidence is far from unanimous on this point. In his classic study of the influence of the "gang" upon adolescent boys, Thrasher (1936, p. 37) proposed that the gang, or cohesive peer group, arises as the "spontaneous effort of boys to create a society for themselves where none adequate to their needs exists." Ausubel (1954, p. 384) regards the adolescent peer groups as "*the* major training institution for adolescents in our society" and suggested that the school's capacity for influencing the adolescent lies in its capacity to provide occasions for the inculcation of the peer culture. Yablonsky (1959) has introduced the notion of the "near-group" as a taxonomic category for the delinquent gang. Near-groups, in his view, are marked by such characteristics as diffuse role definition, impermanence, shifting membership, and self-appointed, disturbed leadership. It is likely that Yablonsky's near-group construct, in contrast to highly cohesive and efficiently organized groups (e.g., the Church) at one end of the continuum and simple aggregates or mobs at the other, might be generalized to adolescent peer culture groups in a broader context. Yet the research of Elkin and Westley (1955) on early adolescents led them to conclude that the primary behavior controls were direction and approval of adolescent activities by adults; further, the power of the adolescent group over the behavior of the individual appeared to be in a large sense a mythical artifact of psychologists. Thus, they regard the peer group among adolescents as largely mythical.

A number of researches by group dynamicists have elaborated leadership and followership roles in childhood and adolescent peer groups. Lippitt and his associates (1958), for example, have detailed the influence of the adolescent peer group (or the near-group) leader both in establishing and enforcing group norms and in providing a model for imitative social behavior. Harvey and Rutherford (1960) found that status positions and leadership roles correlate highly with popularity in elementary, junior high, and senior high school students, and that high-status students exert measurable influence on the perceptions of low-status students. The origins of group cohesion have been outlined in such studies as those of Sherif and Sherif (1953), in which intragroup and intergroup conflict, generated experimentally, accelerated the emergence of group cohesion. In a fifteen-year follow-up study of student leaders and nonleaders in high school, Mary C. Jones (1958) found considerable shifting in patterns of social interaction. Many students who were inactive and unpopular in high school had found appropriate avenues of social interaction in later life, while many active and popular students had become socially inactive. Jones (p. 110) suggested that apparently "opportunities to lead and to influence of the kind available in high school are relatively lacking to these individuals as young adults." Thus it is possible that early success in leadership roles in a relatively constricted student population may actually tend to produce frustration as the individual in later life faces greater competition for comparable roles. Merei's previously mentioned investigation (1949) of children's play groups concluded that power relationships eventually tend to become institutionalized and to reflect social power relationships in adult social organization.

Empirical evidence relating to the adolescent peer group or near-group, though not yet definitive, permits certain tentative conclusions about the origin and strength of the age group as an operable sociocultural unit: (1) adolescent near-groups appear to arise during or immediately after the emancipation of the adolescent from parental control, at the very time when adult society, particularly the school, fails to provide adequate role models for the developing person; (2) adolescent peer groups represent the attempt of adolescents to induct new members into the transitional life stage between childhood and adulthood by establishing conduct norms and role models in which exploratory behavior is tolerated and encouraged; and (3) adolescent peer groups exhibit internally structural properties similar to those of other social organizations.

Adolescent Vocabulary

In supplying a microsociety with reciprocal relationships, the adolescent group serves a valuable function in social development. In the casual interaction characteristic of the near-group and in the formal interaction of designed association, the loosely traditionalized norms of the adolescent microsociety (its culture) exercise a certain control over behavior and serve a function in adolescent exploration. There are few adolescents, for example, who eschew the adolescent vocabulary, even though they may resist the habits of dress. Adolescent speech patterns themselves suggest that the adolescent feels suspended between two worlds, childhood and adulthood. In the adolescent vocabulary, words typically have two meanings: a "public" meaning, shared with adults, and a "private" meaning, shared only with members of the adolescent microsociety. Such planned ambiguity represents a bending of the world of reality to fit the disposition of the adolescent's perceptual field, and it resembles, though in more mature and controlled fashion, the fantasy of childhood. Guidance workers should not attempt to squeeze such ambiguity into a univocal pattern, for by so doing they choke off a vital facet of the youth's social growth and exploration.

The lower limits of adolescence, as a period of enculturation, seem to be descending in modern society. Behaviors once considered appropriate in middle or late adolescence are now approbated in upper elementary grades by parents and teachers. The sixth-grade prom is no longer rare. Concurrently, the upper limits of adolescence as a period of at least economic dependence on the family appear to be ascending as the trend toward post-high school educational and vocational training finds a wide following (Mead, 1960). Thus it appears likely that the salience of the adolescent microsociety and its culture will be underscored. Perhaps because of the sheer duration of its ascendancy, the adolescent culture is likely to become an even more important testing and training ground in social development. Conflicts are likely to be generated with greater celerity between adult society, represented by parents and teachers, and the adolescent microsociety, as a near-group in which the adolescent feels understood and accepted and which he perceives as capable of satisfying his immediate needs for security and a sense of belonging. A developmental orientation dictates that parents and school people perceive the adolescent group, though important as a training ground for adult social roles, primarily as a long but temporary social encasement epigenetically subsumed into the primary goal of social development, viz., the generation of persons who in adult life will make creative contributions to their society.

Social Behavior and Delinquency

Most sociologists and psychologists agree that the most serious human disturbances arise from a failure in interpersonal relations. Sociological and psychological research on crime, delinquency, and other socially disruptive behaviors seems to support this position. Cases of serious failure in the process of social development constitute a category of emotional disturbances termed "sociopathic personality disturbances" by the American Psychiatric Association (1956, p. 46). Characteristic of such disturbances are chronic conflicts with the norms of adult society as institutionalized in law and chronic counterconformity to the prevailing cultural milieu. Thus Kvaraceus (1957, p. 99) has noted that clinically (as distinguished from legally) "a delinquent is a juvenile . . . who habitually resolves his personal-social problems through overt-aggressive behavior which dominant society finds bothersome and contrary to its value identifications." The delinquent perceives his own behavior as purposeful and adjustive, while society views it as counterconformist. Although persons who exhibit such disturbances may at root be suffering from severe psychopathological conditions, the predominating feature in their behavior is an aggressive acting out of their hostilities against the established social structure. Because of their socially destructive character, behaviors expressive of hostility or aggression in social situations are of particular concern in education and guidance (Patricia Jones, 1964).

Though psychologists tend to regard delinquency as primarily psychogenic, most sociologists regard it as arising from failure in social interaction or in the socialization process. Sellin (1962), a sociologist specializing in research on crime and delinquency, regards present research on causation as still largely in the "impressionistic, speculative stage of development." But he also clearly regards delinquent behavior as arising primarily from conflicting social norms, and he prefers as a descriptive term "abnormal conduct" to "crime" or "delinquency." Scarpitti and associates (1960) demonstrated that adolescent boys who develop and internalize a favorable self-image and socialized attitudes toward parents, friends, school, and the law resist delinquent behavior despite the fact that they may reside in a high-delinquency area. By analogy, the delinquent is seen as the person who has failed to develop both favorably socialized attitudes and a favorable self-concept. In the same vein, A. K. Cohen (1955, pp. 28–32) distinguished sharply between crime and delinquency. He characterized delinquency as nonutilitarian, malicious, and negativistic, useful chiefly as an avenue of expression of antisocial feeling by members of what he termed the "delinquent subculture." Crime, on the other hand, is a utilitarian lifeway in that those who practice it do so in order to acquire money. Redl and Wineman (1957, pp. 194–195) view the behavior mechanisms of the delinquent ego as pathological exaggerations of the normal mechanisms of defense found in psychosocially normal persons. Reviewing the literature on theories of causes of delinquency, Travers (1964) concluded that while social and psychological factors interact in each case of delinquency, one set of factors tends to predominate in any given case. Glueck and Glueck (1959) have done much research in the prediction of juvenile delinquency.

Utilizing a multiple-factor approach, Kvaraceus (1954) found that delinquents are distinguished from nondelinquents on the basis of personality factors, physical and economic factors, family composition and relationships, and school factors. Summarizing the research relating delinquency and the school situation, V. M. Murphy (1946b) concluded that the delinquent has often been truant, has frequently been a classroom discipline problem, has been a grade repeater, has usually been placed in a grade inappropriate for his mental age, holds hostile attitudes toward school and teachers, is limited in his academic ambitions, has only vague vocational aims, has a relatively low IQ, and does not fear failure or defeat.

Failure of the schools

Only in recent times has the school been regarded as an appropriate agency through which to attempt to prevent or to control delinquency. Indeed some school people argue that too large a role has been assigned to the school. Gnagey (1956), for example, declared that it is fallacious to accuse the schools of contributing to any major extent to delinquency. Monahan (1957) suggested that, in view of the strong relationship between the quality of family group experience and the incidence of delinquent behavior, the single most effective means of allaying and preventing such behavior would be to inaugurate a program of strengthening and preserving family life. Fine's review (1955, p. 151) of the research concluded that "almost 90 per cent of those traits which characterize a delinquent appear in children before they are eleven." The most important single factor was home conditions.

Yet Goodwin Watson (1963), the renowned social psychologist, has given dramatic testimony to the failure of the schools to effect favorable socialization processes, a failure he believes not unrelated to school dropout and antisocial behavior. He cites a 1962 *New York Times* story of four dropouts from a Southern school. These youths, who pleaded guilty to charges of breaking and entering, were given the choice by the presiding judge of returning to school or of serving sentences as members of a chain gang; *all four chose the chain gang*. It is obvious that the school as a social institution had failed to reach these four young men, to motivate them toward healthy self-actualization, to socialize them. Such failures on the part of the school and of its guidance efforts tend to accelerate the stream of socially maladapted adults, often ill prepared for the world of work, who generalize the malicious and negativistic behavior of the delinquent into crime as a productive lifeway. Indeed one investigation (A. C. Johnson, Jr., 1942) based on twenty years of prison work concluded that schools play a substantial role in the making of criminals. If adolescents are to eschew socially disruptive modes of behavior and develop new goals, McClelland (1963, p. 60) has suggested, "they need the contagious enthusiasm of someone who cares and the opportunity to change their self-images, to dream up new possibilities for themselves, and to choose and try out new courses of action." The problem facing society, McClelland continues, is how to institutionalize such enthusiasm and how to keep it operable.

V. M. Murphy (1964b) has outlined a broad role for the school guidance effort in relation to delinquency. Eschewing expulsion guidance, his plan embodies the provision of remedial services, flexible curricular offerings, a program of identification, family consultation, developmental guidance, provision of healthful group experience, and personal counseling. Further, Murphy charges, each of these services is necessary in any efficient school guidance program. Hence, "A well-run guidance program, operating for the optimal development of all youngsters in the school, provides the personnel and facilities to assist the pre-delinquent."

The counselor and social development

The counselor is in a strategic position to identify and ameliorate difficulties in social development in students before they develop into social pathologies, which may later be reinforced into permanent and crippling features of the personality. Students who exhibit difficulties in socialization have been impeded in the development of healthy interpersonal relationships. They tend to be hostile, aggressive, or excessively withdrawn in social interaction, as a result of unfavorable developmental experience in primary groups or in peer groups. Counseling designed to assist the student to gain insight into the dynamics of his asocial, antisocial, or disruptive behavior is best supplemented by group experiences planned to give him the opportunity to encounter satisfying social developmental processes. Group techniques in guidance and counseling, discussed in Chapter 12, may be utilized to advantage in providing such experiences. Additionally, socialized lessons in the classrooms as well as the activities program (formerly called "extracurricular activities") should be utilized to serve this function.

It has already been observed that the counselor or other guidance workers may have occasion to consult with members of the family, especially when family and school norms conflict. From such an encounter may come plans to manipulate the family environment in order to remove obstacles to favorable processes of social development (Redl & Wattenberg, 1959, pp. 508–509). As Peixotto (1960) has suggested, a visit to the family home may be quite informative both for the counselor and for the child's teachers, since "knowing the reason for the person's behavior often makes it easier to accept the behavior and thus the person, in this case, the child." When a school social worker is available, such a family visit would usually be undertaken by this specialist. Similarly, the counselor may find it profitable to consult with other persons with whom the client has regularized social interaction, such as athletic coaches, the parish priest, and youth leaders.

As in other aspects of development on which guidance service is focused, however, the *first* obligation of the counselor or guidance worker, in cooperation with other school people, is to structure a social environment within the school setting which accelerates positively healthy social development. Implicit in the discharge of this first obligation is the provision of information to parents, teachers, and students relative to the favorable processes of development and to typical causes of impairment of that process. Implied also is the facilitation of the positive developmental process through orientational, informational, and other guidance contacts with students, teachers, and parents. Programs of in-service training for teachers and group meetings with parents represent excellent vehicles for affecting modification in both school and family social environments.

A *secondary* obligation in the school guidance effort is the provision of adequate counseling services. Conducted individually and in groups, counseling may be designed, through the enrichment of primary group experience, to ameliorate and thus to modify and socialize the client's hostile, aggressive, or withdrawing social behavior. Since the counselor and the guidance worker rarely escape their roles as members of the educational establishment, they represent organized society to the client. In social development counseling, at least in the initial stages of the counseling encounter, the worker stands in a favorable position to help the client turn his perception of the worker as a social representative to advantage, i.e., within the warmth of the counseling relationship to ameliorate previous unfavorable social experiences.

Pervading all such efforts, however, in a developmentally oriented program is a recognition of the epigenetic character of social development. To this recognition is coupled a high tolerance level for the unique developmental patterns of individual students. The guidance worker needs to allay the fears of parents and students concerned about popularity or searching for "pat formulas" of social adjustment. In offering a mature, sophisticated view of the "dangers" of social "adjustment," R. W. White (1961, p. 296) advanced three propositions which developmentally oriented school people will do well to adopt and to circulate among parents and students:

> (1) Social growth can easily be injured by adult pressure to participate— for two basic reasons: (a) Adult pressure disregards the child's anxieties and thus encourages a purely defensive adjustment; (b) it also disregards the natural rate of social growth and thus makes demands for which the child is not ready. (2) Social growth does not take place exclusively in social situations; much of it occurs necessarily in imagination. (3) Social growth is promoted by having strong interests, not necessarily social in character, which can be shared with those similarly interested.

SOCIOSEXUAL DEVELOPMENT
AS A GUIDANCE FOCUS

One of the most important aspects of social growth is sociosexual develop- ment, or personal growth which results from encounters with members of the opposite sex. If total maturation of the self is to take place, every boy and every girl needs contact with the opposite sex to fulfill his or her per- sonality, to bring his or her personality to the fullness of masculine or femi- nine selfhood. Students from schools which have a vibrant social life typically appear more poised, relaxed, and mature than do young people from schools which neglect the sociosexual aspects of the educational program. Sociosexual development is a prime guidance focus, an essential part of any school's program of education, as not a few educational associations have officially noted (American Council on Education, 1940, p. 6).

Numerous unfortunate consequences arise from a neglect of sociosexual development. Many students fail to acquire social assurance when dealing with members of the opposite sex or to acquire grooming skills or social etiquette. Indeed some youths, particularly males in single-gender schools and colleges, may develop socially unacceptable personal and social habits. Such behavior partially represents an attempt to sublimate the frustrations of not having the opportunity to mingle with girls; it also reflects the fact that the softening and refining influence of the opposite sex is absent during this critical time of development. Many psychologists believe that one of the causes of the almost universal practice of masturbation among adolescents of both sexes is the attempt to compensate for inadequate or infrequent or unsatisfactory social relationships with members of the opposite sex.

In Catholic schools the faculty and administration verbally caution the students against mixed marriages; yet in practice they often foster such mar- riages by so restricting social life contacts that students are driven to non-

Catholic places of amusement in order to find a wide range of contacts—out of which marriage partners frequently are selected.

The need to focus on sociosexual development

The Public School

While there is considerable socializing among the sexes in public schools, there is usually not a planned program of guided sociosexual development. Public school men seem to labor under the impression that if boys and girls are thrown together indiscriminately, a vibrant sociosexual development will ensue. If there is sexual laxity among public school students, some share of the blame must be borne by administrators and guidance officials who have failed to include an organized sociosexual guidance emphasis in the school's overall program.

The Catholic School

Numerous studies (cf. Sister Mary M. Walsh, R.S.M., 1955) have indicated that a poor social life constitutes one of the major problem areas for youths in *Catholic high schools.* A study by Sister Mary A. Signorelli, M.Z.S.H. (1956), reported that students in a Catholic girls' high school felt they lacked self-confidence and a sense of security in social situations. Similarly, Mary E. Smith's study (1950) disclosed that freshman girls in Catholic colleges tended to feel ill at ease at social affairs. Fr. Roesch, S.M. (1954), determined that Catholic girls who had transferred to public secondary schools offered the common complaint that Catholic school officials prohibited the use of cosmetics and beauty aids. These studies seem to indicate that Catholic schools fail to promote social life opportunities. Perhaps this failure arises because most officials in Catholic secondary schools are priests or religious and hence are celibate. Consequently they not infrequently fail to grasp the crucial importance which sociosexual life plays in human development. These studies also indicate an attitude of prudery and Jansenism in many Catholic schools, which blind school officials to the importance of providing social life opportunities. For example, one religious educator, writing her master's thesis under the direction of a prominent Catholic educational philosopher, castigated Catholic high school girls for choosing a pleasant personality, health, and courtesy as essential to social success on the ground that these ideals represented materialistic and secular values inconsistent with the Christian way of life (Sister M. A. Signorelli, 1956, p. 116).

The research evidence also points to weakness in social life and sociosexual guidance in *Catholic colleges.* This problem is more acute in women's than in men's institutions; a man has more opportunity to seek a suitable marriage partner. In the case of a girl, however, the college years frequently represent one of the last opportunities for meeting, on a large scale at least, a wide selection of suitable prospective mates. By the time she graduates from college, a girl in American society is well on the way to becoming too old to interest many men looking for wives.

Girls in such institutions often perceive their most serious problems to center in inadequate social life and inadequate guidance for sociosexual development. A comprehensive national study (Havemann & West, 1952, pp. 55–56) revealed that almost one-half of all Catholic women college graduates remain spinsters, as compared with one-third of all Protestant college women graduates and one-fourth of the Jews. While some local studies tend to modify this startling figure, nevertheless the nationwide investigation remains the most reliable to date. Shinn's nationwide study (1959) of Catholic women's colleges concluded that social life opportunities available in many of these institutions are too restricted and too few in number to meet adequately the personal-social objectives which these colleges claim are their goals. Indeed college administrators seemed to be somewhat reluctant to encourage social life. Lee's review (1961b) of research concluded that sociosexual and social life programs in Catholic women's colleges are weak and in dire need of upgrading.

There is some indication that Catholic women's colleges confuse the social life program with the social program. Certainly social life is far richer, more diverse, and indeed more exciting than holding frequent teas. Yet Shinn's study (1959) revealed that 24 per cent of the responding Catholic women's colleges had from one to five closed dances per year, while a resounding 37 per cent held from one to five closed teas annually. Further, 73 per cent of the colleges sponsored three or fewer informal dances per year, and 50 per cent scheduled two or fewer annually. Nearly half of the colleges reported they did not plan social events with neighboring colleges. Shinn remarked, "Little opportunity is provided [by Catholic women's colleges] for cooperative social planning between the boys and girls of other colleges."

Catholic women's college administrators probably restrict social life opportunities for students in order to reduce the number of sexual problems. Quite predictably, however, just the opposite happens. Sister Anne Frances Hoey's nationwide comparative study (1957) determined that Catholic girls in Catholic women's colleges reported more numerous sexual problems than otherwise similar Catholic girls who were Newman Club members in secular universities. A frequently cited problem of Catholic women's college students was lack of opportunity to meet members of the opposite sex. It seems incumbent upon Catholic women's colleges to re-examine unduly restrictive rules, e.g., the number of times per week a resident student may leave the campus in the early evening or the time at which a girl must return to the residence hall after a night date.

There seems to be an inverse relation between quality of social life in Catholic colleges and attitudes of sister-administrators. Sister-administrators who assert that the social life program needs no improvement tend to have poor programs, while sister-administrators who believe that much could be done to make the program better usually sponsor a fairly good program (Lee, 1961b).

The inadequacy of sociosexual development and social life programs in Catholic schools probably arises from an unhealthy and unwarranted fear of sex. Catholic schools are customarily operated by celibates; they often fail to realize that sexual desires and marriage-oriented aspirations of lay students are both legitimate and indeed requisite if they are to develop and mature properly. Not a few priests and religious have attitudes toward chastity motivated by what Fr. A. Leonard, O.P. (1963), has identified as hidden disgust of sex, the inability to face one's own sexual nature. It is the mature person who neither negates sex nor overemphasizes it but rather treats it as a natural, satisfying aspect of life (Bowman, 1960, p. 94).

All too many Catholics, including teachers, guidance workers, and students, have a distorted view of sex. In Catholic circles, sex is usually repressed or suppressed. Among more "progressive" spheres of Catholicism, such repression is condemned as inhuman, but even in these circles sex is usually viewed as a force to be contained. Not many Catholics grasp the concept that sex is to be utilized for personal development. It is an odd fact that the Blessed Mother has become in Catholic education almost totally the symbol of virginity, while theologically it is her Divine motherhood, a sex-laden fact, which is the source of Mary's glory.

Sociosexual development guidance in Catholic schools is in drastic need of revision. Young people are frequently told that sexual drive is animal-like and represents brute and irrational elements. Indeed not a few Catholic teachers derisively refer to the emotional attraction of youths to members of the opposite sex. Often these attitudes cause guilt feelings which lead to less than adequate sexual adjustment in marriage. Perhaps most destructive of all attitudes is the persistence of the fallacious theological notion that every sexual transgression is a mortal sin. Thus a nationwide study (Brother B. Leanman, S.C., 1956) of eighth-grade boys in a Catholic elementary school revealed that nearly 75 per cent believed all sins against sexual purity were mortal. The origin of this mistaken belief is the so-called doctrine of the *parvitas materiae,* which states that in cases of sexual sins there is no light matter; i.e., everything is a grave offense. Fr. Adam's careful analysis (1958) of the question shows that the doctrine of *parvitas materiae* is contrary to the traditional theological teaching of the Church.

While there is undeniably a definite moral danger in the sexual sphere, there are also dangers in other areas involving growth. Sexual dangers should be neither overlooked nor magnified. Risks are inevitable if growth is to take place.

Unfortunately many Catholic and public schools regulate all conduct, including sexual conduct, by external control imposed by the administration rather than by helping to develop within the student inner personal ideals and restraint. As a result, when the young person leaves the sphere of external control, he either rebels against the imposed system or reverts to that standard of conduct he has set for himself. Effective guidance endeavors to assist young people develop a code of conduct consistent with their basic value system. Schools and particularly churches are still resorting to outmoded and ineffectual methods of external control, with a predictable lack of success. A careful study by Ehrmann (1959) of students in a large university concluded that the heterosexual behavior of male students was only slightly affected by religion and church attendance.

The vast majority of non-Catholic high schools and colleges are coeducational and hence provide students the opportunity to interact and thereby develop sociosexually. Most American Catholic high schools and colleges, however, are single-gender schools. Indeed a strong condemnation of coeducation of youth was enunciated by Pope Pius XI in his encyclical *Christian Education of Youth* (1936, pp. 26–27). This proscription was reinforced in an instruction by the Sacred Congregation of Religious (1958) which holds that coeducation in Catholic high schools is permissible only in localities in which the bishop deems this evil gravely necessary. In such instances the Sacred Congregation has listed specific precautions which must be taken; e.g., boys and girls must sit on opposite sides of the classroom and must enter and leave the school at different times. Religious (*religiosi*) are not permitted to conduct coeducational secondary schools. Religious who teach in these schools must be men or women whose virtue and maturity have been proved by experience—a provision which probably excludes young religious from teaching in such schools (see Fr. Connell, C.Ss.R., 1958; Fr. Frison, C.M.F., 1959).

The instruction of the Sacred Congregation recommended that *coinstitutional secondary schools* be established. A coinstitutional school is one which has chiefly separate facilities for students of each sex, with a few common facilities shared by both groups. In practice, a coinstitutional high school usually consists of one building with two separate, sealed-off wings. The two most commonly shared facilities are the library and the school cafeteria. Thus to all intents and purposes a coinstitutional school is an administrative fiction; there are two separate schools under one roof, often quite isolated from each other in everything except physical proximity.

In view of a well-founded science of behavior, Catholic educators would do well to rethink their entire position on coeducation. Certainly on the college level, coeducation is conducive to the students' sociosexual development and to the fostering of intraconfessional marriage (as distinct from mixed marriage). The old argument that a single-gender Catholic college promotes distinctive education for that sex is dubious at best. Indeed, a study by Wessel and Sister M. Rita Flaherty (1964) revealed that after one year in a Catholic women's college girls were significantly less feminine than when they entered the college. The 1958 instruction by the Sacred Congregation does not include colleges in its prohibition of coeducation (Fr. Frison, C.M.F., 1959, pp. 44–46). Indeed, Fr. McKeough, O. Praem (1954, p. 295), has noted, "Since many archbishops and bishops in the United States have explicitly and implicitly given their blessing to coeducation [on the college level], the question of its compatability with the specific or traditional teaching of the Church is not open for discussion."

Perhaps Catholic bishops and educators should likewise rethink their position on coeducation on the secondary level. At this important developmental period in a person's life, adequate sociosexual growth is crucial both to healthy personal development and to orientation to the heterosexual world in which he will live, work, and find his fulfillment. As American Catholicism sheds its cloak of Jansenism, more and more numerous Catholic youths need to be educated in schools where they may have opportunities for sociosexual development. A study by Sister M. Assunta Highbaugh, O.S.B. (1960), showed that a high percentage of students who resigned from Catholic single-gender high schools gave as their reason a desire for coeducation. Although the 1958 instruction condemned coeducation as an evil, it noted that the greater evil is for Catholic youths not to receive a Catholic education; hence to avoid the greater evil, it might be well for bishops and diocesan superintendents to establish Catholic coeducational secondary schools. In those subject or problem areas in which coeducation seems unwise, e.g., physical education, *coinstruction* can be initiated, through sexually segregated classes within a coeducational school. While a coeducational high school does not guarantee adequate sociosexual development, it can eliminate some of the barriers which now exist.

Personality development through sociosexual relationships

A person achieves his or her natural and supernatural perfection not as a human being but as a *male* human being or as a *female* human being. In other words, a person can attain fulfillment only through his masculinity or through her femininity. Any attempt to live as if one were neuter gender is a denial of a basic, concrete fact of one's existence.

As indicated in Chapter 2, perhaps no developmental period in a person's life is more highly characterized by an intense search for one's masculine or feminine role than is adolescence. It is one of the tasks of the school to assist the youth in his or in her search. In adolescence for the first time a boy is aware that he is a male human being; the girl, that she is a female human being. But this awareness is vague, and youth is beset with fears and doubts. The boy and the girl are propelled to find out what the limits and contours of their personalities are really like. They need to explore, and they will gratify this need no matter what. If the school does not assist young people in this exploration, they will explore unaided.

Association with members of the opposite sex is the natural and most liberative type of sexual exploration. During adolescence, youths begin to find that companionship with members of the opposite sex brings forth not only new physical dimensions but also personality traits they never realized they possessed.

Regrettably many Catholic educators still view sociosexual companionship as primarily or exclusively preparatory to choosing a marriage partner. On the contrary, sociosexual companionship has for its primary purpose the development of each person, the bringing out in the boy of his masculine self and in the girl of her feminine self through interaction with another human being whose personality complements his or her own. Undoubtedly Catholic de-emphasis of sociosexual relationships within the context of the development of each person is based on a concept of marriage which regards as its primary and exclusive purpose the procreation of children. Consequently for centuries the Catholic concept of the aim and glory of marriage tended to center not in the spiritual goal of mutual perfection of partners but rather in the ideal of breeding and begetting. Catholic theologians and educators (cf. Fr. Häring, 1963) are now reassessing the primary purpose of marriage in terms of a developmental axis. Marriage is now being viewed in its natural-supernatural dimension as a state which has as its primary goal the optimum development of the man and woman through conjugal love. This new awareness has profound implications for school guidance, because now the fostering of sociosexual development is seen as *in se* not only facilitating personal development but also furnishing the most realistic preparation for the marriage relationship.

To assist young people to develop the sociosexual dimensions of their personality, the school must help them to come to an accurate perception and understanding of their sexual roles. Research investigations have indicated that such a perception and awareness have proved more difficult for girls than for boys in contemporary American society. M. C. Shaw and associates (1960, p. 195) reported that girls are often confused regarding the feminine role. Such confusion is doubtless due to overstress on masculine culture and ideals in American society (see Helene Deutsch, 1944). As Sister Ernest Marie, C.S.J. (1960), has suggested, many girls have rejected femininity as second best to masculinity. D. Pumpinatzi (1963b, pp. 15–27) has stated that a woman's fullness, the perfecting of her being, lies in her wifehood-motherhood; all her activities, ranging from companionship to career, flow from and into this enriching wellspring of wifehood-motherhood. A womans' primary role does not preclude simultaneously a host of social and occupational endeavors; rather, these other activities are pivotally related to and extended from her wifehood-motherhood orientation. Warren's study (1959) of graduates of a private nondenominational women's college concluded that married alumnae whose marital satisfaction scores were high (on an adapted Hoppock scale) tended to have higher scores on the housewife scale (as measured by the Strong blank for women) than did alumnae whose marital satisfaction scores were low. Married alumnae who rejected the housewife role tended to have a lower marital satisfaction score than did those who accepted the housewife role.

School guidance which aims at preparing women to live fruitfully in modern society cannot be based on a pre-World War I concept of woman's role in society. For a variety of reasons, not only contemporary single women but also contemporary married women with children are in the labor force on a full-time basis. In former days the almost exclusive career for a married woman was that of housewife-homemaker. Occupations in which spinster ladies were permitted to engage were limited. Today's open society has made the situation more complex. Super (1957, pp. 77–78) has identified seven distinct career patterns for women: stable homemaking career, conventional career, stable working career, double-track career, interrupted career, unstable career, and multiple-trial career. While many mothers from low socioeconomic levels enter the labor force to augment the family income, many mothers who are college graduates have full-time nonhome careers; for personal fulfillment they need the growth opportunities which such careers can provide. Warren (1959) noted that married alumnae with occupations other than housewife have higher marital satisfaction scores than alumnae with no other occupation. Joel's investigation (1963, p. 78) of girls in the senior class of a socially exclusive nondenominational women's college found that almost as many planned to work before they married as after; nearly 85 per cent planned "to enter or re-enter the world of work after the birth of children, when children are between 3 and 5 (17.8%), 5 and 10 (23.4%), 10 and 15 (19.8%), or over 15 years old (13.2%)."

To integrate successfully the two roles of wife-mother and career woman is necessary if working mothers are to avoid dualistic perception and behavior. Wifehood-motherhood remains the perfective element. Without this integrating principle, the condition which Pallone (1963b, p. 74) has described as "absentee motherhood" can develop, with the result that the woman fails to perfect herself, her husband, and her children. The school can assist students to see in the here and now the concrete relationship which studies, interests, and activities have with the role of wife and mother.

Dating

Dating refers to social relationship activity for other than a matrimonial commitment (see Burgess & Wallin, 1953, pp. 63–109) and is clearly distinguished from courtship. Dating provides "sexual" pleasure, sociosexual companionship, and marital potentiality. On any given date, any one or combination may predominate.

Sexual pleasure is not merely an inducement to marriage but, even more important, a principal path through which an individual attains personal (and therefore spiritual) fulfillment. Venereal pleasure is merely one type of sexual pleasure. Further, much sexual and venereal pleasure is not sinful. Only "unlawful" sexual pleasure is sinful. Sexual pleasure lawful to one's state in life is crucial to attaining physical, mental, emotional, and spiritual maturity. Hence a school which tells youths that they should not seek sexual pleasure from the dating relationship will cause unnecessary and unnatural neurotic guilt. Indeed such poor advice will likely result in inducing the promiscuous behavior which the school had hoped to prevent. The school should concentrate on helping youths attain mentally healthy and morally licit pleasure from the dating encounter. This is no easy task in the modern world. Today's girl believes that she must make her body increasingly provocative to boys, while at the same time she objects to their reaching for it. She fears that she will not attract her share of boys, and, paradoxically, she fears the very boys she attracts so skillfully. Many regard adolescence as skiing gracefully in and out among the trees on the slippery snows of adolescent sexual purity while still having a "good time." Personal and spiritual development through legitimate and necessary sexual pleasure is forgotten amid the network of schemes and intrigues involved in "the dating game."

The second reason for dating, viz., sociosexual companionship with a view to personal enjoyment and development, has already been discussed. This should be simultaneously a latent purpose and a cardinal outcome. One controversial and frequently discussed aspect of dating for sociosexual companionship is "going steady." Going steady refers to that social relationship in which both partners refrain from company keeping with a peer of the opposite sex, although matrimony may or may not be the goal of the two partners. Going steady is not "going steadily," which refers to that social relationship between a boy and a girl in which each of the partners engages in company keeping with the other regularly but not exclusively. From a developmental point of view, steady dating is unwise because it restricts sociosexual exploration from the contact of one youth with many members of the opposite sex. Further, most adolescents are not developmentally ready to sustain an intense sociosexual relationship. But, *in individual cases,* such a steady relationship may provide a therapeutic life experience for youths who have been deprived in the family of healthy primary group relationships.

In Catholic circles, there is a great concern about the moral aspect of steady dating. A number of theologians maintain that steady dating, whether by matrimonially uncommitted youths or by engaged couples, constitutes a proximate occasion of sin (Some aspects, 1958, p. 137). Every moral theologian agrees that anyone who freely and without sufficient reason places himself in a proximate occasion of sin commits a sin by that very fact. St. Alphonsus Liguori (m. 462) believed that it is the rare individual who escapes mortal sin in company keeping with any frequency. But if company keeping is a proximate occasion of sin, then why are engaged persons morally permitted to see each other, whereas steady dating without the intention of marrying is forbidden? St. Alphonsus holds that engaged couples should be permitted to visit each other only once or twice before the marriage because of the grave likelihood that more frequent visitation would constitute a proximate occasion of sin. Other theologians believe that frequent company keeping is morally permitted for engaged couples because this type of activity constitutes a "necessary" proximate occasion, i.e., a proximate occasion for which there is grave and sufficient reason, since courtship is an essential preparation for marriage.

Many contemporary American Catholic theologians, such as Fr. Connell, C.Ss.R. (1955, p. 186), and many priest and religious guidance workers in Catholic schools (Girls' Academy Chaplain, 1957) believe that steady dating is *generally* a proximate occasion of serious sin and quite possibly serves as a source of morally culpable scandal to other students. Other moral theologians (Fr. Connery, S.J., 1958; Fr. Connors, C.S.Sp., 1957), however, do not concur that steady dating constitutes a proximate occasion of serious sin. The number of these benign theologians is increasing. Fr. Connery, S.J. (1958), has suggested that this entire dispute has failed to focus on the real issue. The real issue, he maintains, is not steady dating but whether the partners are committing serious sins either during the date or as a result of it. Certainly steady dating does not inevitably lead to sin. Such a morbid view is based on a Jansenistic and Neo-Manichaean conception of human nature. It might be noted that teen-agers have the moral right to go steady in view of their right in canon law to marry (Fr. Connors, C.S.Sp., 1957; Fr. Springer, S.J., 1959). Indeed, many marry as soon as they finish high school or shortly thereafter, and not a few college students marry while still in school. Statistics show that earlier marriages are becoming more frequent in the United States. Such legalistic emphases, of course, fail to consider the *natural,* i.e., the tasks of adolescence embedded in society and cultural norms. Surely the spirit of Vatican II runs counter to such legalistic emphases.

Some public and many Catholic high schools have taken strong administrative positions on steady dating. Hardly a year goes by but that some priest or religious does not make national or even international headlines for resorting to expulsion guidance on a steady dater. Steady dating, however, is conducted outside school hours in such a fashion that it is not directly related to the school's educative function. Hence if steady dating neither interferes with the pupil's development in truth, whole and entire, insofar as the school has responsibility over this development, nor causes scandal, school people, whether public or Catholic, have no authority to regulate it. *Such regulation is the province of parents.* Both the Church and the state recognize parental primacy in the responsibility for the development and education of their offspring. Certainly if parents approve the practice of steady dating, the school may not prohibit it.

Fr. Connors, C.S.Sp. (1957, p. 252), has observed that pastors have no lawmaking power. Hence on their own authority they have no moral power to forbid steady dating. Consequently priests and pastors who are principals of *parochial* elementary or secondary high schools lack moral power to command their students to refrain from steady dating. Further, no pastor or bishop can legislate against canon law. Since canon law states that boys and girls may marry at sixteen and fourteen years of age, respectively, the bishop cannot forbid steady dating unless for some important accidental reason, for example, if such a practice is causing widespread scandal. As Fr. Connors stated, however, "it is hardly possible that he [the bishop] could make exclusive association with a member of the opposite sex a general disability for attendance at the high schools and/or colleges of his diocese. This conclusion is based not on a consideration of the motive in making such regulations, but on a consideration of the limits of the Ordinary's power."

School people such as Fr. Werling, O.Carm. (1959, p. 324), feel that the school should establish a policy excluding steady daters from membership in activities or at least from any election, award, or honor. This practice is unsound and discriminatory. From an educational standpoint, the school has no right to deprive a student of equal opportunity solely on the basis of a school person's moral judgment. This is particularly true if parents approve the student's conduct. By excluding a student from the opportunity for full participation in its activities, the school will reinforce rather than discourage the practice of steady dating. The lack of affection and support from parents and school is often a prime reason why the youths decided to go steady in the first place.

Fr. Connors, C.S.Sp. (1957, p. 251), has stated that no confessor can legitimately withhold absolution from a young penitent solely on the ground that he or she is steady-dating or that he or she has refused the confessor's command to discontinue. The confessor can merely suggest that the pentitent abandon this practice. Chaplains and school priests should take this admonition to heart.

Steady dating does present a developmental and a moral problem with which school people must cope. A guidance-oriented administrator or teacher faces the problem realistically in terms of promoting optimum pupil growth naturally-supernaturally. The principal reason why a boy or a girl decides to go steady is not solely or even usually physical attraction. Important psychological factors are operative. Often a youth finds in a steady date the fulfillment of some psychosocial need which the school or the home has left unfulfilled, e.g., assurance of love, ego support, a sense of security, guidance, and so forth. Abandoned by home and school, the youth quite naturally has recourse to a steady companion. It might well be that for some youths steady dating is necessary for sound psychological development. Thus, for example, an insecure student who is made to feel inferior by the home and the school quite possibly needs a "steady" to counteract such inferiority feelings. If the school sincerely wishes to reduce the incidence of steady dating, then it should, through its guidance program, ensure every student the opportunity of having his or her psychosocial needs met, at least on a minimally adequate level. Such an emphasis seems in accord with the spirit of Vatican II.

Of course, not all, or even the majority, of students who "go steady" do so to fulfill psychosocial needs of an abnormal nature. Rather, there are strong forces in the adolescent culture which approbate going steady, and there are strong needs in *normal social development* which propel youths to going steady. For the majority of American teen-agers, it is safe to say, going steady represents an avenue—and for many, the only available avenue—of *learning how to sustain a relationship* with members of the opposite sex in something akin to a primary group experience. Since many informed Catholic behavioral scientists believe that, in view of social and cultural norms interacting with tasks of development, going steady is a normal and natural adolescent behavior, it behooves Catholic school people to bear in mind that the supernatural builds on the natural.

Orientation to Marriage

American youths in general are marrying at a younger age than did their parents and grandparents. In 1890 the median age for an American woman at first marriage was 22.0; by 1958 it had dropped to 20.2. Reliable estimates predict that by 1980 the median age will drop to between 19.9 and 20.2. One out of every four girls is married by the age of eighteen, and one out of every two at just a little over twenty. A 1960 study (Baer, 1962, p. 760) of more than 40,000 graduates from about twelve hundred degree-granting institutions of higher learning revealed that the majority of students had married within two years after graduation; in fact, most marriages had taken place before graduation or shortly thereafter. Because an increasing number of youths are marrying earlier and because high school is the terminal institution for most young people, orientation-to-marriage activities are necessary on this level as well as on the college level. Students usually become oriented one way or another, and it seems preferable that such orientation come from the school in concert with the family.

But very few public or Catholic school people have adequately met this need. One Catholic psychiatrist (Cavanagh, 1962, p. 11) has observed tartly that "marriage is the only vocation for which no previous training is usually considered necessary." This is incomprehensible in view of the adjustive and developmental difficulties which each partner experiences in marriage, particularly during the first years. Catholic schools are perhaps more derelict in their duty to provide marriage orientation activities than public schools. Often marriage orientation in Catholic schools concentrates on morality and chastity and neglects such aspects as psychological and physical satisfaction, childbearing, financial management, and so on. Fr. Saalfield (1958, p. 54) has noted that proper orientation to marriage is a responsibility which weighs heavily on Catholic secondary schools, and one which in conscience they cannot shirk.

On the college level little had been done until the end of World War II. Since that time most large and some small secular colleges and universities have begun to offer courses in marriage and family living. A great deal of effort is still needed to coordinate, upgrade, and popularize these courses. Very few institutions make even one course in marriage and family living compulsory for all students, with the result that such courses are usually taken chiefly by those majoring in sociology, child study, and home economics. There is even a great deal of uncertainty as to where such courses belong in the academic spectrum. A study by J. T. Landis (1959) indicated that while 52 per cent of the courses in marriage and family living were offered in the department of sociology, 18 per cent were listed under the department of home economics, with the remaining 30 per cent of the courses being given by a variety of other departments, ranging from business administration to architecture. Glover (1950) found that of professors of marriage and family living courses investigated, 44 per cent had no counselor preparation, 33 per cent had taken one or two courses in counseling, and only 11 per cent had more than four courses in counseling. The extent of counselor preparation is important since professors of marriage and family living become involved in counseling whether they wish to or not; indeed, counseling has become accepted as an important part of every marriage and family living course (Luckey, 1963). Very few Catholic colleges or universities have special undergraduate or graduate courses in marriage and family living. This lacuna is paradoxical both in view of the Church's strong stand on marriage and the family and in view of the claim made in most Catholic college catalogues that the particular institution provides "distinctive emphasis" for the preparation of women (or men) qua women (or men), a preparation which hopefully includes marriage and family living. That the latter emphasis is not always appreciated can be inferred from the remark made by the dean of a Midwestern Catholic women's college to a group of her students who wished to cooperate with a nearby Catholic men's university which was sponsoring a marriage orientation workshop: "We train ladies; we don't breed mothers!"

Every public and Catholic secondary school and college needs a course, or at least a workshop, in marriage and family living, which includes a consideration of attaining one's masculine or feminine role, the exploratory nature of dating, purposes of courtship, characteristics of a desirable mate, economic preparation for marriage, male and female anatomy, sexual hygiene, and philosophical and spiritual principles underlying and suffusing conjugal love and sexual relationships. In Catholic schools the Catholic dimension of sociosexual relationships and of marriage should occupy a prominent place. Some parts of the marriage and family living course or workshop may be given to a coeducational group; other parts, to a sexually segregated group. For maximum benefit to the students, these courses need to be closely coordinated with the school's organized guidance program, particularly with its counseling service. A vigorous program of social life should complement the course and the guidance program.

Adequate orientation for the sexual aspects of marriage should be a cardinal aim. The degree of sexual orientation and adjustment which husband and wife bring to marriage constitutes the greatest difference between partners in terms of background, knowledge, attitude, and training (Foster & Wilson, 1942, p. 78). Adequate marriage orientation has two pivotal elements. *First,* accurate and complete sexual knowledge is essential if the young person is to fulfill his sex role and to utilize marriage for optimal personal development. Cavanagh and Fr. McGoldrick, S.J. (1958), have noted that sexual misinformation, usually on the side of prudishness, causes sexual neurosis and severe psychic invalidism. Effective orientation begins before puberty. Young boys need accurate information about nocturnal emissions, and young girls about menstruation, *before* they undergo these natural phenomena. Nor should information referring to sexual anatomy or hygiene be taught alongside erroneous moral, health, or biological beliefs. *Second,* healthy attitudes toward sex must pervade the school's instructional and guidance efforts. There are numerous causes of impotency in the male and frigidity in the female: (1) revulsion for sex acquired by rejection of one's sex role and identity, brought about by parents, clergymen, and school people who may have inculcated the attitude that sex is dirty, animalistic, or at best an extremely low form of human activity; and (2) neurotic guilt feelings. A review of pertinent research by Reiss (1962, p. 265) concluded that restrictive sexual backgrounds hinder rapid sexual adjustment in marriage. Hence, schools should attempt to foster more healthy and more natural-supernatural attitudes of sex as a profound aspect of human fulfillment, as a participation in and sharing of a human and a Divine endeavor of supreme importance. The school should be realistic in admitting that it is no easy task to educate pupils to exercise great restraint and absolute control of sexual desires during the first twenty or more years of their lives and then expect them suddenly to achieve sexual fulfillment upon marriage.

No marriage orientation program can be adequate or complete without attention to the spiritual dimension. The pivotal Christian emphasis was stated by St. Paul (Ephesians 5:21–32): the marriage between husband and wife is a symbol of the mystical union between Christ and the Church. Fr. Kothen (1947, pp. 11–15) has stated that just as mutual love is the primary meaning and first principle of Christ's relationship with His Church, so also is love the primary meaning and first principle in the husband's relationship with his wife. Dietrich von Hildebrand (1961, p. 83) has observed that love between man and woman is the deepest source of love in human life. In another place, he (1942, p. 13) has stated: "Being in love is so far from being contemptible, so far from being the consequence of the fall of man [as some theologians have stated] that it constitutes the only animate state in which we can break all the fetters of indolence and phlegmatic everyday life." Students need to become eminently aware of this axial concept of love as the center and nucleus of marriage. Marriage should not be treated as a matter of law, of rights and duties, but rather, as Fr. Oraison (1958, p. 58) has stated, as a question of loving and of constantly being loved.

Catholics have traditionally held that the primary and indeed almost exclusive purpose of marriage is the procreation of children, together with certain minor secondary ends such as "allaying concupiscence." Consequently, as Fr. Dantec (1963, p. 83) has observed, "far too many preachers, far too many [Catholic] introductory books for young people on the subject of marriage pay almost no attention to anything but their duty to have and educate children." More forward-looking theologians and educators are reassessing marriage as a state of love in which each of the partners grows naturally-supernaturally and perfects the other partner through conjugal love. Such a view sees marriage primarily as a sacrament of love, not as a legal permission to breed. Certainly if the procreation of children by sexual intercourse were the primary or exclusive end of marriage, many childless couples could be said to have failed to attain the primary end of their state in life. This view of marriage does not deny or conflict with the tremendous importance of the propagation of children but instead places such propagation within the broader, more meaningful, and more perfective context of mutual conjugal love. If students are to exercise that total giving of themselves which marriage demands, however, the school, particularly through its guidance program, should assist them to eradicate narcissistic strains which impede such giving.

To improve guidance for sociosexual development, schools can profitably:

1. Provide healthy outlets for sociosexual exploration, outlets which are neither overly restrictive nor overly permissive. Sociosexual exploration is crucial to development. A policy of segregation by sex creates sexual frustrations which seek release in mentally, emotionally, and spiritually unhealthy

channels. On the other hand, the school needs parental cooperation in discouraging use of the home for premature sexual exploration through promiscuous party games. Simple prohibition, however, is ineffective; rather, healthier, more integrative activities need to be inaugurated.

2. Organize a well-developed social life program. In his socioanthropological studies of courtship and marriage, Malinowski (1927, pp. 126–127) concluded that primitive cultures do not merely exercise a negative impulse; they also afford societal inducements to courtship and amorous interests, e.g., establishment of certain festive seasons. Public and Catholic schools in general have not attained the level of primitive cultures in this regard, since these agencies of civilization often thwart the introduction of social life.

3. Appoint a counselor as the person in charge of social activities. In large colleges and universities, the position of social director has been created and filled by a trained guidance person interested and knowledgeable in the furtherance of sociosexual development among the students.

4. Furnish some suitable place within the school plant where boys and girls can mingle socially. This is particularly important in a boarding high school and college. If the school does not provide such a place, young people supply their own spots, many not of an optimum developmental variety, e.g., a parked car.

5. Sponsor informal get-togethers in which boys and girls can meet, play records, or just relax in each other's company without the pressures attendant at many of the more highly organized events.

6. Hold frequent school dances. To some school people a few of the more "lively" teen-age dances seem like mating season on Seal Island or the puberty rites in some remote jungle thicket. Notwithstanding, these dances provide a healthy outlet at once vigorous and sociosexual, hence meaningful to youth in *their* terms. Many youths hesitant to approach a member of the opposite sex in a cafeteria or at a social are not at all hesitant to assume a bolder posture in a dance situation. The school might even sponsor dance clinics to help students whose dancing skills need improvement.

7. Promote social life programs within the school and among schools in the surrounding area, especially in a single-gender school. The social director can utilize the school bus for transporting pupils to nearby schools. Some schools have found a student-operated "date bureau" useful.

8. Establish high school and college weekends consisting in a series of planned, sociocultural activities, e.g., jazz concerts, dances, folk sings, and the like.

9. Maintain adequate telephone ratios in resident institutions.

10. Hold marriage conferences and workshops for high school and college seniors to implement, not supplant, regular marriage orientation provided throughout the year.

14

VOCATIONAL DEVELOPMENT
AS A GUIDANCE FOCUS

The nature of vocational development

Vocational development designates the aspect of personal development which is concerned with broad preparation for entry into, as well as successful, satisfying performance within, the world of work, *leading to economic and emotional self-sufficiency*. As a guidance focus it concentrates upon (1) the student's general orientation to the demands and realities of the world of work; (2) his understanding of the nature of the labor market and his role in it within the context of a rapidly changing economic structure; and (3) his capacity accurately to assess his abilities, needs, motivations, and interests in relation to work. *Vocational adjustment* is characterized by the capacity to integrate one's developing self into the labor force and the ability to find satisfaction in an occupational role or series of roles which the individual assumes.

The student with whom the counselor works has an occupational life expectancy which extends into the twenty-first century. Many of the jobs which will become available to him in middle life do not exist today (Barry & Wolf, 1962, pp. 85–89). According to the U.S. Department of Labor (Wolf-

392

bein, 1964, p. 168), nearly 2 million jobs (of a total labor force of some 70 million) are being affected yearly by the impact of automation. Though this fact does not suggest that all the holders of these jobs are becoming unemployed, it indicates that many workers need to acquire greater flexibility in terms of both occupational skills and psychological adaptability. The accelerating rate of technological innovation, G. Watson (1963, p. 4) has observed, requires "flexibility, adaptability, and skill in tackling new projects." The number of workers in the labor force by 1970 will increase to more than 100 million, a figure equivalent to the total national population in 1920 (U.S. Department of Labor, 1960, p. 13). Paradigms for vocational development derived from analyses of workers whose careers began in 1920 may thus prove unusable for counseling with students who will enter the work force during the coming decades. The labor market in the United States, implicitly or explicitly, has been based on the economic supremacy of members of a socially favored race. The abolition of discriminatory practices against Negroes and members of other minority groups in both education and employment will soon topple economic supremacy of the whites and will doubtless bring about greater competition for jobs at all levels of occupational skill (Ginzberg et al., 1956, pp. 119–124).

It therefore becomes evident that the primary emphasis in vocational development guidance can no longer be placed upon the selection or choice of an occupation which the student expects to enter and in which he expects to remain. Some occupations and even whole industries may disappear as others arise. Indeed, some alarmists believe that even the teaching profession is threatened by automated learning devices. It is not likely that this profession will disappear, but it is probable that the instructional tasks of the teacher in the programmed learning situation will change and that the training of teachers will perforce be modified. It is quite possible that personal characteristics of teachers who function effectively in pedagogical situations utilizing traditional instructional methods will differ in many respects from those of teachers who function satisfactorily in situations involving automated learning or programmed instruction.

Emphasis in vocational development guidance must center in a broad orientation to the world of work in its developing realities and in the development of flexibility and a secure self-identity in relation to work. Flexibility, adaptability, and a secure self-identity will be particularly important because of anticipated economic change. These characteristics, it will be remembered, mark the mature, self-reliant adult. Thus, the relationship between vocational development and personal development is clearly an intimate one.

Lifework and lifeway

Some confusion may be engendered by a failure to distinguish *vocation* in the religious or theological sense and *vocation* in the psychological sense.

In the religious sense, vocation refers to the way of life or to the "state in life," i.e., the canonical states or divisions of religious, clerical, and lay. More popularly, though less accurately, distinctions are sometimes made between the married, single, and religious states. The present writers employ the term *lifeway* to designate these canonical states or divisions. In the psychological sense, vocation refers to the work of life, to one's occupation, or, more specifically, to that series of occupations which constitutes one's "career." Thus the term *lifework* designates occupation or career.

Vocational development guidance assists students in formulating for themselves both a lifeway and a lifework. Often guidance tends to emphasize one at the expense of the other. Even students considering a religious lifeway must give attention to a lifework within that lifeway. For many students, the selection of a religious lifeway (e.g., the teaching brotherhood or the nursing sisterhood) implies the simultaneous selection of a lifework.

Conversely, the religious lifeway in many orders, congregations, and communities encompasses a number of different sorts of lifework, e.g., the pastoral ministry, teaching, research, medical missionary activity, and the like. Similarly, the selection of a lay lifeway by a Catholic student precludes certain aspects of the pastoral ministry as a lifework, e.g., preaching in a church. A comprehensive program of vocational development guidance provides opportunities for fostering exploration of (1) the lifeway, (2) the lifework, and (3) the lifework within the lifeway. Of especial importance is the student's ability to distinguish the attractiveness of the lifework from the attractiveness of the lifeway. The lifework most intimately associated with the sacerdotal lifeway, for example, is the sacramental ministry. The student who feels attracted to both the priestly lifeway and the professional lifework needs to determine whether he might fulfill this lifework as adequately or perhaps even more adequately in another lifeway. Occupational exploration and the clarification of the self-concept are thus of prime importance in planning for both the lifework and the lifeway. A broad orientation to the changing character of the world of work is needed even by those who enter the religious lifeway, for the specific function within the Church performed by a particular community is also subject to change in response to the changing needs of the Church. If the plan for the reorganization of Catholic educational efforts in the United States advanced by Mary Perkins Ryan (1964, pp. 137–160) were widely adopted, the lifework of the science teacher, for example, would largely disappear within the religious lifeway. In such a situation, members of teaching brotherhoods and sisterhoods as well as many priests would have to adapt themselves to apostolic lifeworks other than teaching. The reverse of this situation arose at various times in Europe when semicloistered communities of sisters were forced by the exigencies of the times to enter the active life of teaching. It is interesting that there are still some communities which have clung to this lifework even though the exigencies which made it a necessary evil (in terms of their lifeway) have disappeared.

Lifework and self-identity

Vocational development constitutes an aspect of personal development which is intimately linked to the formulation and consolidation of a mature self-identity. MacArthur (1961, p. 58) has observed that "two special issues are seized upon as foci" in the developing person's "diffuse agitation over who on earth he may be." One of these issues is his occupational identity, or identification with a chosen or preferred lifework; the other is his psychosexual identity.

Ausubel (1954, pp. 437–438) has suggested that lifework plays a crucial role in the process whereby the adolescent becomes a person in his own right and acquires intrinsic feelings of adequacy and worth. For Wheelis (1958, p. 124) the lifework contributes to the individual's sense of "durable identity." The process of identity formation, Erikson (1956) has commented, evolves from "significant identifications" with members of an occupational group and from the expectation of "consistent roles" in the world of work. Practicing school guidance workers have also noted the relationship between lifework and self-identity. Bachrach (1959, p. 4) contends that counselors frequently encounter students who declare that they lack clear vocational goals but who have actually failed to develop a clear self-image. In such cases, he continues, "there is frequently some awareness on the student's part of the real nature of his difficulties," and "a vocational-educational approach engenders feelings in the student that his problem is not really understood."

The world of work in an era of economic restructuring seems to demand that sort of flexibility and adaptability which characterize what Combs and Snygg (1959, p. 45) regard as "the adequate self—a self capable of dealing effectively and efficiently with the exigencies of life, both now and in the future." In contemporary American society, lifework may thus be regarded as an avenue through which the self demonstrates its adequacy.

The principal task in personal development, viz., the development of a secure sense of self-identity, coincides with the development of self vis-à-vis the world of work. In this vein, Wrenn (1962, p. 109) declared that "primary emphasis in counseling students should be placed on [their] developmental needs." Since the tasks of vocational development form one aspect of healthy personal development, guidance in schools should focus on the *total* development of the person. Barry and Wolf (1962, pp. 184, 195) were rather more explicit in their contention that *"there is no justification for the separate practice of vocational guidance,"* since *"a man's work is an integral part of his self-concept."* Vocational development guidance is therefore a conceptualization of personal development guidance in terms of a personality thrust toward broad orientation to the world of work (Pallone, 1963c, p. 92).

Approaches to vocational development

Historically, vocational development formed the first focus for guidance efforts in schools. As indicated in Chapter 1, Frank Parsons and other early guidance workers conceived occupational choice as a single, discrete event in the life of the person. With the introduction of psychological testing, an actuarial approach to the prediction of vocational success developed. Guidance workers sought, in Bell's famous phrase (1940), to "match men and jobs." Both men and jobs were perceived statically. The client for vocational counseling was regarded as having reached a terminus in his development. The job was perceived as uniform and nonmalleable. The counselor might test an eighteen-year-old high school senior in an attempt to match his abilities with those of a specific occupational group, even though the members of the group on which the tests had been standardized had an average age of thirty-five. Little, if any, consideration was given to the process of development in the client *or* to the developmental status of the members of the standardization sample. Rather, it was somewhat naïvely assumed that the interests, aptitudes, and so forth of neither the client nor the members of the sample had undergone or would undergo change. Only such bald and patently questionable assumptions governed the static model in vocational guidance.

More recently, vocational psychologists have proposed *developmental models*. Vocational development has been described by Super and his associates (1957, p. 52) as an "ongoing, continuous, generally irreversible, orderly, patterned and dynamic process" through which self implements self-concept in the world of work. The choice of an occupation is the attempt of the developing self to select a work activity and a setting appropriate to the self-concept. Since one's life-style depends largely upon one's occupation and its financial rewards (Super, 1957, pp. 17–35), the student's occupational choice is regarded as a critical life decision. From the lifework will stem not merely the necessities and luxuries of life but also socioeconomic status, leisure-time activities, seasonal schedules, social associates, and the like. Even within the religious lifeway, the lifework has an important bearing upon the person's life-style. The priest whose lifework involves university teaching lives quite a different life from his confrere who is engaged in pastoral duties in the slums of "inner city."

Contemporary vocational psychologists regard vocational development as a "lifelong process . . . never dependent upon one choice alone," not as a discrete event in the life of the person (Roe, 1964, p. 212). The specific course of vocational development and the determinants of the process vary in the theories which have been advanced by the principal researchers in the field.

Self-concept Model

Super and his associates (1957, p. 43) at the Career Pattern Study at Teachers College, Columbia University, have offered a vocational development model which emphasizes *life stages in the elaboration and crystallization of a vocational self-concept.* Havighurst's notion of developmental tasks and Buehler's identification of life stages, both mentioned in Chapter 2, have been utilized in this model. Vocational developmental tasks are "those which relate directly or indirectly to the world of work." Super's initial formulation (1957, pp. 71–79) of vocational life stages has been modified in the light of research data at the Career Pattern Study to include the following: (1) the *exploratory* stage, involving tentative exploration, transitional exploration, and trial exploration with little vocational commitment; and (2) the *establishment* stage, involving trial, stabilization, and advancement (Super, 1963b, pp. 80–81). Corresponding to these stages and substages are five developmental tasks: (1) crystallizing a vocational preference, (2) specifying a vocational preference, (3) implementing a vocational preference, (4) stabilizing in a vocation or occupation, and (5) consolidating status and advancing in an occupation. Super and Overstreet (1960, pp. 7–8) suggested the following postulates as the foundations for a vocational development model:

1. Vocational behavior develops through a process of growth or learning to provide the person a behavioral repertoire.
2. Vocational behavior develops from less complex and effective to more complex and effective behavior from childhood to maturity and beyond, becoming increasingly reality-oriented and more specific.
3. As the person develops increasingly complex behavior, he progresses from one life stage to another, each of which makes characteristic demands upon him. Acquisition of the behavioral repertoire to cope with the characteristic demands of the next life stage or to negotiate the vocational development tasks of that stage is requisite to success in handling the demands of the next stage; progression from one stage to another depends upon readiness for more complex vocational behavior and the ability to cope with the tasks of the next stage.
4. Vocational behavior indicates vocational development maturity, through determination of the tasks characteristic of each stage, determination of typical behaviors of others facing the same tasks, and qualitative evaluation of the effectiveness of the individual's behavior.
5. When behavior is highly developed, it becomes highly effective; hence, vocational maturity is a predictor of vocational adjustment.

6. Vocational behavior results from a number of intersecting determinants, some of which (e.g., intelligence, aptitude, socioeconomic status) are more important than others and which vary in importance from one stage to another.

7. Vocational behavior also includes a variety of situationally determined task- or job-specific behaviors as well as vocational developmental tasks.

"In choosing an occupation one is, in effect, choosing a means of implementing a self-concept" (Super, 1957, p. 196). Super (1963b, pp. 11–15) identified the following processes as the elements of a phenomenological or self-concept theory of vocational development: self-concept formation, exploration of both self and environment, self-differentiation, identification with key figures in the psychosocial and occupational environment, role playing in fantasy, reality testing to confirm or contradict the occupational self-concept, translation of self-concepts into occupational terms, and implementation of the occupational self-concept in the world of work. In general, the developing person's vocational choices or preferences narrow from fantasy in early life to reality as he approaches adulthood. In this process, *exploration* plays a key role. Jordaan (1963, p. 59) has stated: "Vocational exploratory behavior refers to activities, mental or physical, undertaken with the more or less conscious purpose or hope of eliciting information about oneself or one's environment, or of verifying or arriving at a basis for a conclusion or hypothesis which will aid one in choosing, preparing for, entering, adjusting to, or progressing in, an occupation." Principal among the factors which facilitate vocational exploration are the ability to tolerate tension, uncertainty, ambiguity, frustration, and internal feelings of adequacy (Jordaan, 1963, p. 73).

Exploration must be distinguished from *reality testing*. Super (1957, pp. 84–85) has suggested the following relationship between exploration and reality testing: "Adolescent exploration is not so much a process of developing a new picture of one's self as of putting it into words and thus developing a basis for finding out what sort of outlets there are in society for a person who seeks to assume a given kind of role, and then of making modifications in the self-concept to bring it in line with reality. Adolescent exploration then may be viewed as a process of ascertaining and testing reality." Super and Overstreet (1960, pp. 141–142) summarized the phenomenological or self-concept theory of vocational development:

> Vocational choice is seen as a process, extending over a period of time. It is a sequence of lesser decisions, some of them decisions as to the level toward which to strive, some of them decisions as to the field in which to work which bring about a progressive reduction of the number of alternatives open to the chooser. The vocational behavior of the indi-

vidual is a function of his personal resources and of the demands which society makes upon him. Vocational behaviors and vocational developmental tasks can be classified according to life stages, each life stage confronting the individual with some new developmental tasks peculiar to that stage. . . . Vocational adjustment is judged by the extent to which vocational behavior results in the accomplishment of a developmental task with long-term satisfaction to the individual in meeting socialized objectives.

Choice Stages Model

The economist Ginzberg and his associates (1951) at the Project on the Conservation of Human Resources at the Columbia Graduate School of Business offered a vocational development model based on *stages in the choice process*. Eschewing the "theory of occupational choice [which] holds that individuals make decisions about the future accidentally," these researchers identified three stages in occupational choice. The *fantasy period* begins in early childhood and is largely concerned with nonfulfillable wishes. The *tentative period*, corresponding to adolescence, is characterized by recognition of the problem of occupational selection; tentative choices are made on the basis of probable future satisfactions. During the *realistic period*, in late adolescence and early adulthood, the characteristic dimensions of the world of work impinge upon subjective factors within the person until an adjustive compromise has been effected.

Life Needs Model

Roe (1956) proposed a *need-oriented* theory of occupational development. Thus she regards the job as a principal source of need satisfaction, often of an unconscious need. Needs arise in early life and derive their strength primarily from parent-child interaction. Broadly psychoanalytically based, Roe's model (1964, p. 203) was founded on studies of personality differences between occupational groups and upon studies which suggested that such differences were rooted in childhood experiences. Interpersonal relations emerged as a major dimension in Roe's classification (1957) of occupation according to field and enterprise. She proposed a paradigm for types of parent-child relationships which eventuate in person orientation or non-person orientation and suggested that occupational choice is predicated upon differences in orientation. Thus parents who vacillated between warm and cold, concentrated emotionally on the child, and appeared overprotective, overdemanding, and defensive tended to produce children whose major orientation was toward persons. Tests of hypotheses about family influences on career development derived from Roe's paradigm, however, have not been confirmed by subsequent empirical research (cf. Utton, 1962), leading her to call for new models for research in parent-child relations (Roe, 1964, p. 210).

Social Affiliation Model

In research sponsored by the National Merit Scholarship Corporation, Holland (1963, p. 548) has offered what might be described as a *social affiliation* model in vocational choice. The person making a vocational choice "in a sense 'searches' for those environments which are congruent with his personal orientations." Holland identified six types of personal orientation: realistic, intellectual, social, conventional, enterprising, and artistic. The choice of a field of occupational endeavor is explained by the "birds-of-a-feather" hypothesis: "Every person, other things being equal, is impelled toward those *groups* (occupational classes) whose members have personal orientations similar to his own. (This might be called the 'birds of a feather' hypothesis.) In one sense, choosing a vocation means finding people who are like one's self" (Holland, 1962, p. 2). In Holland's model (1962, p. 3; 1963–1964) the choice of level of occupational endeavor within the chosen field "is a function of a person's intelligence and self-evaluation, which can be defined as the relative worth that the person attributes to himself." Occupational classes designate types of people, while vocational interest is regarded as a drive toward social affiliation. "By regarding a person's interest, occupation, and vocational knowledge as information about his personality, we can integrate a broad range of human behavior in a single theory of personality and thus avoid the need for separate theories of 'interest' and 'personality' " (Holland, 1964, p. 273).

Developmental Tasks Model

Havighurst (1964) presented a vocational development model based on his scheme of *developmental tasks,* in which he attempted to integrate Erik Erikson's concept of psychosocial developmental crises and Super's outline of vocational life stages. Six stages with corresponding developmental tasks were postulated by Havighurst: (1) age five to ten—identifying with a worker, e.g., parents, during which time the concept of work becomes part of the ego ideal; (2) age ten to fifteen—acquiring the habits of industry, during which time the individual learns to organize both time and energy in order to satisfy work needs, e.g., schoolwork, and also to give work priority over play in some situations; (3) age fifteen to twenty—acquiring an identity as a worker, during which time the individual chooses and prepares for an occupation and gains work experience to ensure economic independence; (4) age twenty-five to forty—becoming a productive person, during which time the individual masters occupational skills and advances; (5) age forty to seventy—maintaining a productive society, during which time the individual perceives the social significance of his occupation and pays attention to the induction of young workers in stages 3 and 4; and (6) age seventy and older—completing a productive and responsible life, during which time the individual withdraws from a satisfying work role.

Self-in-situation Model

Tiedeman and O'Hara (1963) have adapted the *self-in-situation model* to the area of vocational development. This model integrates and focuses Erikson's notion of psychosocial developmental crises on the evolving self-in-vocational-situation. Vocational development is only conceptually distinct from personal development. "Career development then is self-development viewed in relation with choice, entry, and progress in educational and vocational pursuits. It is an evolving conception of self-in-situation which is occurring over *time* in man who is capable of anticipation, experience, evaluation, and memory" (Tiedeman & O'Hara, 1963, p. 46). Vocational development may be analyzed according to the two principal periods of (1) anticipation and (2) implementation and adjustment. The stage of anticipation involves the substages of exploration, in which fantasy choice is narrowed to patterned alternatives; crystallization, in which additional exploration is focused and subsequently recrystallized; choice, in which a relevant goal is selected; and specification, in which the choice is made fit for implementation. The implementation and adjustment stage involves three substages: induction, i.e., socialization into the selected occupation through training or work experience; transition, i.e., the modification of occupational requirements to harmonize with the assertive needs of the person; and maintenance, i.e., a condition of dynamic equilibrium alterable either by the choice of the worker or by the exigencies of the world of work (Tiedeman, 1961). Such exigencies, indeed, are given due consideration by Tiedeman and O'Hara (1963) who seem to agree with Caplow (1954) that error and accident play an important role in vocational adjustment. A person's work history is likely to include periods of unemployment, layoff, retraining, dual employment, or intermittent withdrawal from the labor force for vacations, leisure, retraining, and the like. "A complex theory of career development must relate career to work with allowance for all of these contingencies" (Tiedeman & O'Hara, 1963, p. 68). In an era which promises to hold major economic reorganization and redistribution of the labor force, such an approach seems most appropriate. Both the worker and the job are multidimensional. A worker with given characteristics, abilities, and interests might find success in a number of different occupations. Similarly, "as long as an employee continues to satisfy the work demands of his employer, the employee or his supervisor may redefine the employee's position from time to time without changing the employee's job" (Tiedeman & O'Hara, 1963, p. 72). This approach, proceeding along an idiographic dimension, seems far removed from the nomothetic or matching-men-and-jobs orientation of classical vocational guidance (see O'Hara & Tiedeman, 1959).

Hoppock's Synthetic Model

After reviewing the pertinent research and theory on lifework development, Hoppock (1963, p. 114) was led to ask: "What can a counselor extract from the conflicting theories now available? Must these theories only add to his confusion?" To provide a working model for counselors in schools and community agencies offering vocational development guidance, Hoppock synthesized the elements of a composite theory, presented not as paradigms for research workers but as a series of speculations about vocational behavior useful to the counselor and guidance worker in the guidance relationship. Hoppocks' synthetic model or composite theory (1963, pp. 114–115) includes the elements listed below:

1. An occupation is chosen to meet an individual's needs.

2. The occupation that an individual chooses is the one which he believes will best meet the needs which are of most concern to him.

3. Needs may be intellectually perceived, or they may be only vaguely felt as attractions which draw an individual in certain directions. In either case, needs influence choices.

4. Vocational development begins when an individual first becomes aware that an occupation can help him to meet his needs.

5. Vocational development progresses and occupational choice improves as an individual becomes better able to anticipate how well a prospective occupation will meet his needs. Thus his capacity for anticipation depends upon his knowledge of himself, his knowledge of occupations, and his ability to think clearly.

6. Information about an individual affects occupational choice by helping him to recognize what he wants and by assisting him to anticipate whether or not he will be successful in collecting what the contemplated occupation offers him.

7. Information about occupations affects an individual's occupational choice by helping him to discover the occupations that may meet his needs and by aiding him to anticipate how well satisfied he may hope to be in one occupation as compared with another.

8. Job satisfaction depends upon the extent to which the job that an individual holds does indeed meet those needs which he feels it should meet. The degree of satisfaction is determined by the ratio between what he has and what he wants.

9. Satisfaction can result from a job which meets an individual's present needs or from a job which promises to meet such needs at some future time.

10. Occupational choice is always subject to change when an individual believes that a change will better meet his needs.

Career development in women

According to the U.S. Department of Labor (1960, p. 7), by 1970 one of every three workers will be a woman. Buckley (1963), a Labor Department specialist in employment trends, predicts that more and more women will be prepared to enter dual careers as homemaker and labor-market worker. Some commentators (cf. Useem, 1960) on the role of women in the modern world actively discourage girls and young women from making a commitment to marriage and homemaking alone. In her summary of the pertinent research, Bott (1963) noted that junior high school girls center their planning on occupation and education rather than on marriage, that the multiple or dual role becomes more popular during high school, and that university freshman women expect college to prepare them for fuller personal development in both marriage and occupation. When formal education succeeds in preparing women adequately for marriage, however, it does so virtually by accident. "Catholic as well as secular and public schools and colleges tend to devote more time and attention to the preparation of the [female] student to wade through mazes of Victorian poetry or matrix theory than they do the building an attitude of mind concerning the roles of man and woman in the begetting and socializing of the next generation" (Pallone, 1963b, p. 75).

Though guidance authorities (cf. Wrenn, 1962, pp. 131–132) have underscored the need for realistic vocational development guidance for girls and women, Bott (1963) questions whether existing vocational development theories are capable of illuminating the process of lifework development in women. Among vocational theorists, Super is virtually alone in devoting some attention to the variations of career patterns observable in the working lives of women. Super (1957, pp. 77–78) has classified women's career patterns into the following categories: (1) stable homemaking pattern, in which women marry shortly after leaving school and never enter the labor market; (2) conventional pattern, in which women enter the labor force after school, marry, leave the labor force, and do not re-enter it; (3) stable working pattern, in which women enter the labor force to remain and do not marry; (4) dual-track pattern, in which women enter the labor force after school, marry, but continue in the labor force; (5) interrupted pattern, in which women enter the labor force after school, marry, leave the labor force, then re-enter it after their children start school; (6) unstable pattern, in which women sporadically alternate between the labor force and homemaking; and (7) multiple-trial pattern, in which women enter a succession of unrelated jobs and develop no occupational identity.

Though extremely useful as a conceptual schematization for categorizing the work histories of women in the labor force, Super's system of classification does not address itself to the dynamics of the vocational choice process in relation to *feminine* interests, needs, motivations, and satisfactions. Does an occupation *or* homemaking offer woman in the modern world the greater opportunity for optimal self-development? How does the initial expectation of marriage and a family, i.e., of a state of economic dependency, shape the girl's vocational behavior? Does the prospect of economic dependency through marriage free the girl in her schooling to select areas for nonutilitarian values? What may be said of the personal adjustment difficulties of women who enter occupational fields customarily filled by men? To answer these and similar questions demands the integration and conceptualization of a considerable body of information not presently provided in vocational development theories. Much investigation remains to be done in the elaboration of the dynamics of vocational identity development among women. A number of research studies on career development in women have been undertaken, but these typically have concentrated on isolated aspects of development, with no attempt to integrate empirical studies and theoretical models into a cohesive framework. Thus, for example, Bott (1962) investigated the effect of mother-daughter interaction in relation to educational and vocational choices of Catholic high school girls. Sister Marion Hosinski, S.S.M. (1964), delineated the relationship between nursing students in a vocationally oriented curriculum and these girls' self-perceptions, self-ideal perceptions, and perceptions of the occupational role of the ideal nurse. Since Sister Marion's subjects were student nurses, the investigation focused on vocational development among girls in an occupational role culturally associated with feminine interests. Until vocational psychologists and occupational sociologists elaborate an adequate theory of vocational development in women, counselors in schools must exercise caution in attempting to understand the dynamics of occupational selection, marriage-career conflicts, and the differential psychology of the sexes. Freidan (1963, pp. 322–364), a female psychologist, has excoriated American educational practice and the social structure for the "progressive dehumanization" of the woman, which she contends leads to "forfeiture of self." Thus she believes that wholesale revisions are necessary in education and in the fabric of society to prepare women adequately to fulfill their "own unique possibilities as separate human beings."

Lifework and value orientation

Modern theories of vocational development quite appropriately emphasize lifework as a specific opportunity for self-actualization and personal fulfillment. Work is thus presented as a value in itself, an axiological dimension through which the developing person assumes or expresses his inherent "personness." Work is a value-laden aspect of personal striving, both in the natural and the supernatural orders.

Empirical studies of value orientation in relation to work have tended to follow Super's concept (1957, pp. 298–300) of intrinsic and extrinsic work values. Intrinsic values are those inherent in the work activity, e.g., rewards for work arising from essential aspects of work. Extrinsic values are those associated with factors external to the work activity itself, such as monetary rewards. Super and his associates (1960, pp. 100–103) developed a "work values inventory" for use in the Career Pattern Study. This inventory and adaptations of it have been employed in several studies (Kinnane & Pable, 1962; Kinnane & Suziedelis, 1962) which have attempted to delineate value orientation along extrinsic versus intrinsic dimensions. In general, it has been found that persons engaged in occupations which require creativity, independence of behavior, spontaneity, and similar worker characteristics (e.g., the professions) are motivated by intrinsic work values.

What is disturbing is the converse finding, viz., that workers in the so-called routine occupations fail to discover significant values intrinsic to the work activity. Such a finding suggests a failure on the part of the worker to attain personal development, social significance, existential meaning, or supernatural dimensionality in his lifework. A misconception of religion which places stress on otherworldly values rather than on the worth of this world has unfortunately reinforced this devaluation of work. Thus, for example, Lenski's study (1961, p. 248) discovered: "Of the . . . Catholic males who both had a Catholic education and attended Mass regularly, *not one* reported a real liking for work, and fully one-third said they would quit tomorrow if their financial situation permitted." Lenski argues that Catholic schools appear not to be developing attitudes, beliefs, values, and intellectual orientations which make it possible for persons to enjoy their work. His investigation also disclosed that those Catholics who held positive attitudes toward work no longer attended Mass regularly.

This perception of work as a valueless entity in effect denies the sacramentality of *all* reality. Such a denial is doubtless related to the failure of Catholic theologians and guidance experts to develop (or simply to insist that there be developed) a theology of the meaning of work adequate to serve as a ballast and an inspiration to the modern person in the contemporary world of work. This failure might be regarded, to use the phrase of a Hebrew theologian (Sandmel, 1961, p. 379), as an evasion of modern theology, which more and more bears "startlingly little substance or relevancy" to the existential situation of modern man.

In Catholic schools at least, "vocational guidance should emphasize the temporal and spiritual realities of the sense of dedication in any and every field of endeavor," even in the ordinary, humdrum, monotonous, hard, routine (O'Sullivan-Barra, 1955, p. 28). Stancioff (1955, pp. 8–9) aptly portrayed the requisite approach to work as a value-laden activity: "There are so many dull things to be done in the world, even through the eyes of grace. That is one of the things that many unrealistic Catholics—as well as all romanticists—forget. They tend to assume that every child is a budding artist, that every man, were he not denied self-expression by a harsh system, would fill his days with beauty-bearing labor. But . . . man loves to tinker as well as to create. And even in the middle ages there were quite as many people making chains and pikes and cooking pots as statues for cathedrals."

Since Newman, there has been no serious Catholic attempt to develop a mature theology of work based on the integration of religion, vocational theory, and the modern world of work. Cardinal Newman's views, indeed, were bound by time and space and have relevance primarily in an agrarian, preindustrial society. Lee (1963b, p. 526) has observed: "Catholics in general do not think of work as a divinely impregnated act, something which of itself joins the person to God. Rather, it is conceived of as something which is done when one is not praying, or at best something which may be offered up to God, sanctified by a religious intention." A germ of a theology of work was suggested by Fr. Teilhard de Chardin (1960, p. 31), who observed that each labor *of itself* fulfills Christ Himself. Surely the priest-workers of France demonstrated and lived a theology of work applicable to the monotonous, humdrum, routine existence of the factory laborer. But such seedlings have not as yet borne fruit and indeed have been suppressed by official Church circles.

J. O. Nelson (1963, p. 166), a Yale theologian, approximated a mature theology of work when he argued that the spiritual meaning and dimensionality in lifework have relevance to guidance practice in all settings, not simply in religious schools. An adequate theology of work must "make real the vast cosmic assertion that the living God exists, and has a direct I-Thou content for each person he has brought into life and set to work on this tiny, amazing planet." Until such a theology appears, lifework will not be perceived as intrinsically valuable in either the natural or the supernatural order.

FACILITATING LIFEWORK
DEVELOPMENT

Guidance efforts which are focused on lifework development have as their ultimate objective the facilitation of the pupil's readiness to enter the world of work. It has been suggested earlier in this chapter that the world of work will exhibit far different parameters in the future than it does at present. Thus the basic need of the student in lifework development is a *broad orientation to the realities of the world of work in a changing, shifting economic structure, coupled with a secure self-identity and a sense of self-adequacy.* In order to effect this orientation, guidance for lifework development aims at widening occupational horizons, fostering vocational maturity, and promoting self-exploration.

A number of studies have indicated the influence of various "significant others" in the student's phenomenal field as they bear upon occupational choice. Uzzell (1961) found that the principal influencers of occupational choice, in order of impact, were persons within the occupation, information gathered from mass media, personal contact with persons in other occupations, books about the occupation, experience or course work related to the occupation, and hobby interests. Steinke and Kaczkowski (1960–1961) reported that ninth-grade girls were influenced in their occupational preferences by the following factors, arranged in order of impact: parents, ability and personal factors, relatives or friends, personal contact with persons in the occupation, articles in books and magazines, school subjects, and courses in which highest grades were earned. Investigating the influencers of *educational* choice among junior high school students, H. J. Parker (1963) found that boys were affected (in order) by their father, their mother, a teacher, an older brother or sister, another adult, or a peer. Among girls, the rank orders of mother and father were reversed. Among college freshmen, Carlin (1960) found that vocational choices were influenced by past academic achievements, the personal influence of teachers, extracurricular success, and the study of occupational information materials. As an incidental finding, Gribbons (1964) reported that many high school students make decisions which are based on inaccurate or irrelevant information about occupations and the world of work.

From these and similar studies it becomes clear that students in the process of development tend to base their decisions largely upon the example, advice, or urging of parents, other adults, teachers, and friends. Only rarely is contact with the counselor or even with occupational information materials indicated as a principal source of influence upon lifework choice. It is likely that the advice or urging of parents, teachers, and other adults is rooted in a perception of a static, relatively stable, economically secure labor market. Students internalize these perceptions and thus are resistant to a perception of a dynamic economic structure, with consequent reorganization and reorientation in the labor force. Thus a positive obligation of the counselor and guidance worker in lifework development is to provide a broad orientation to the realities of work not only to students but especially to teachers and parents, since the last two emerge as significant influencers of occupational choice. The guidance worker fulfills this obligation through programs of parent education and through consultation and in-service education for teachers and school administrators. In order to keep himself informed of changes in the labor market so that he can present valid and current information, the counselor needs to maintain contact both with the U.S. Department of Labor and with the division of youth services of the state employment service. It is necessary for him to become acquainted with such publications as the Department of Labor's periodic *Occupational Outlook* and other manpower reviews. Many counselors both in preparation and in service are unaware of the program of vocational testing, counseling, and placement available to all youths through the local offices of the state employment service. Service to Catholic schools in this respect has never been questioned on constitutional or any other grounds. To receive U.S. Department of Labor bulletins and publications, counselors should get in touch with the nearest regional office of the Bureau of Employment Security of the Department of Labor or write directly to Department headquarters in Washington, D.C. Especially valuable is the publication *Counseling and Employment Service for Youth,* U.S. Government Printing Office Document 1963 0-661320, available at a nominal cost from the Superintendent of Documents, U.S. Government Printing Office, Washington, D.C.

Widening occupational horizons

Virtually every conceptual model for vocational development reviewed in the preceding pages has emphasized the centrality of extensive *occupational exploration* in preparation for entry into the world of work. To accomplish this task, the student needs to become acquainted both with a variety of occupational fields and with the general nature of the economic structure. In this task, he needs exposure to occupations in the form of published occupational information materials, career conferences featuring knowledgeable persons, and *planned* vocational exploration through part-time work experience.

It seems likely that orientation to the world of work in a realistic rather than a fanciful or capricious manner should be encouraged relatively early in the life of the student. Kaye (1960) suggested the fourth grade as an appropriate initial point for occupational orientation. Arbuckle (1963–1964) indicated the necessity for avoiding distortion of reality in occupational daydreaming even in childhood through the presentation of valid, accurate occupational information. Tennyson and Monnens (1963–1964) indeed have observed that elementary school reading and social studies materials tend to distort the world of work. D. A. Green (1960–1961) has suggested that early vocational orientation may assist in reducing the ratio of dropouts.

Occupational information materials are available in abundance from the U.S. Department of Labor, professional and trade associations, and commercial publishers. The counselor will find the *Dictionary of Occupational Titles* of the Labor Department particularly useful, especially Part IV, which focuses on worker trait requirements. It is unfortunate that most of the available materials are geared to a nomothetic rather than an idiographic approach. Yet the existent materials may be of some assistance in stimulating the student's curiosity. It is also regrettable that the high readability level of much available occupational information impedes its usefulness to students in the exploratory process. R. A. Ruth examined the readability level of commercially published occupational information materials presumably aimed at a secondary school population. Although these materials included information about such occupations as waiter and waitress, baker, and apprentice, Ruth (1962) discovered that the mean readability grade level (according to the Flesch formula) was 14.7, or roughly equivalent to material ordinarily encountered in college texts and in professional journals. A similar finding, utilizing the Dale-Chall scale of readability, was reported by Watson, Rundquist, and Cottle (1959). The use of fiction as a source of occupational information has been questioned, since fiction frequently contains distortions. Notwithstanding, Sacopulos (1961) has suggested that fiction may arouse the curiosity of the student and motivate him to seek more definitive occupational information. It also seems clear that the readability level of fiction will be more appropriate than that of other types of occupational information.

In addition to information about occupational fields, the guidance office's library of informational materials must include information about *avenues* of preparation. College bulletins, entrance requirements, announcements of technical and professional schools, and information on other types of posthigh school training are needed. Vocational choice implies the selection of an educational level and usually a relatively specific course of preparation. Implicit in such information too is information about means of financing further education, whether through scholarships, loans, or part-time work. In view of the intimate relationship between educational level and occupational choice, guidance toward realistic educational goals is a function of vocational development guidance. As early as the junior high school, choices are made which profoundly affect the parameters of the student's occupational horizons. Diamond (1962, p. 11) has observed that the "eighth grade may be viewed as a crossroads, a point at which the student plans his high school program according to whether he will get a job after leaving high school or go on to higher education." Perhaps, however, the ninth grade might be more accurately regarded as the critical juncture for divergent vocational paths. Pallone (1961d) has questioned the wisdom of a curriculum structure which requires such premature choices, especially in light of the research of Super and others on the vocational maturity of secondary school students.

Experiential information about occupations has been fostered in students in a number of ways. Kaczkowski, George, and Gallagher (1963) reported that an exploratory school course in shopwork had an appreciable and measurable impact on vocational planning and on the clarification of goals. Hoppock has long championed a group guidance approach to occupational information and was instrumental in the formation of the Academy of Teachers of Occupations as an interest group in the National Vocational Guidance Association. Rubinfeld and Hoppock (1961) reported that 80 per cent of both graduates and dropouts, eight years after the completion of such a course, recommended its retention and indeed suggested that it be made a requirement. Borow (1960–1961) has suggested the adoption of courses in vocational planning at even the college level.

Promoting self-exploration

Information about the world of work merges into the student's perceptual field not as an isolated figure but as a figure charged with a potential personal valence. It is never the occupation of teaching that is considered in vocational thinking, for example, but rather self-as-teacher. Pritchard (1962) thus has suggested that "self-at-work" exploration constitutes the essence of occupational exploration. To integrate meaningfully the perception of occupations and occupational roles, it is necessary that the student first have developed a relatively stable self-identity. It is also apparent that meaningful self-at-work exploration demands an openness to experience and a permeable membrane between the phenomenal field and the world of reality. Hence it is readily apparent that vocational development is an aspect of personal development.

Additional figures in the phenomenal field which are important in vocational development include perceptions of one's characteristic abilities, aptitudes, motivations, orientations, and interest. Some of these perceptions and characteristics may be measured through psychometric devices. This information should be integrated into the client's perceptual field by means of successful guidance practices. Williamson (1964, p. 857) has declared: "I conclude that man's recently won freedom of choice of vocation is relatively meaningless, if not downright precarious, when he makes his choices without some *valid* knowledge of his own capabilities and potentialities." Adequate self-knowledge thus constitutes a prerequisite for the initiation of the process of projecting oneself meaningfully into the world of work. Clarification of self-identity, modification of the phenomenal field, the perception of one's life choices, and the meaningful integration of these figures into a vocationally mature self constitute the aims of lifework development guidance. As Cox (1961) has observed, the focus is upon the meaning of lifework choice for the individual, not merely upon the fact of choice.

Fostering occupational maturity

The essence of occupational maturity is the readiness to assume responsibility for oneself through psychological and economic self-support. The occupationally mature person knows himself reasonably well, is realistically oriented to the world of work, and faces the prospects of an expanding and shifting economy with a sense of self-adequacy. Specificity of occupational choice is *not* essential to occupational maturity and indeed may possibly even impede a realistic orientation to work. Both occupational exploration and self-exploration are lifelong processes and require flexibility and adaptability.

Guidance workers tend to be "security-oriented" and to value specific occupational choices, frequently at the cost of trammeling student vocational exploration. Often such security orientation arises from the fact that these guidance workers are commonly drawn from the ranks of the middle and lower-middle class, with the emphasis on economic security built right in. But change and uncertainty are realities in the present-day world of work. Thus Dole (1963) contends: "One of the counselor's important tasks is often to teach clients, professional colleagues, and parents the facts of uncertainty. If we live in an ambiguous world, the counselor can prepare young people for it. He can teach his clients how to capitalize on their anxieties about the future; how to predict trends; anticipate the unexpected; and plan trial experiences to serve as the bases for later decisions." In a similar vein, Wolfbein (1964, p. 171) suggested that it is a positive obligation of the counselor *"to help the individual withstand the onslaughts and, in fact, take advantage of the inevitable changes which will occur in the world of work."* In the modern world of work, counselors need to emphasize (1) fluidity and adaptability at changing jobs and patterns of jobs; (2) maximum skill development; and (3) optimum self-realization within a total picture of family, job, and avocational pursuits (Nelson, 1962). Personal maturity, especially self-adequacy, and vocational maturity are thus identical.

Placement: injecting self into work

The placement function, often neglected as an aspect of vocational development guidance, serves the purpose of implementing the vocational self in the world of work. A readiness for self-support, emerging as the product of the investment of the school's guidance efforts, remains a readiness only until it is actualized in the placement function. Thus the counselor has a positive obligation to assist in the placement of the student, whether in a position in the world of work or in a program of further education. Vocational maturity finds fruition in entry into work as a self-sufficient member of society. Placement readiness is, then, a developmental concept, indicating an apex in orientation to the world of work and in personal development (Stevens, 1962). Like vocational maturity, placement readiness seems to involve an orientation to the realities of change and uncertainty in the world of work (Shulim, 1962).

In the face of an expanding economic structure and an educational framework which is slow to adapt itself to a shifting occupational context (L. Thomas, 1956, pp. 9–18), placement services are likely to be necessary for alumni as well as for graduating students. During the trial work period, i.e., immediately after leaving school and entering the labor market on a full-time basis, the worker is likely to experience both massive cultural shocks and a number of job changes. Both placement and counseling services are necessary to assist alumni in integrating their vocational experiences into meaningful and usable patterns. Such patterns, following involvement in the world of work, may be fashioned in a more realistic and idiographic manner. For the worker will have learned that each job setting has idiographic dimensions which make even the world of work malleable. Most occupations are capable of absorbing a number of different types of personalities and of satisfying a number of types of interests. Role behaviors involved in jobs may thus be adapted to fit the needs of the individual. Thus, for example, an interesting finding reported by Sister Marion Hosinski's investigation (1964) of student nurses was that the nursing role was wide enough to permit many types of personalities to feel fulfilled within the nursing profession, *even though* there was little commonality of occupational role perception among nurses. Job descriptions and work activities are subject to reorganization to meet individual needs. Young entrants into the labor force need to feel that it is acceptable for them to seek work situations, in the same occupation or across occupations, which are more conducive to their optimal self-actualization.

A lifework development guidance program

An effective lifework development guidance program minimally provides the following services:

1. A broad orientation to economic realities in the world of work. This activity can effectively be carried out by integrated guidance teamwork between counselors and teachers of social studies, especially of economics. Not only students, but parents and teachers as well, need to be apprised of the dynamic flux of a rapidly changing labor market in which careers may become the exception rather than the rule.

2. General information about the world of work, presented realistically and meaningfully from elementary school onward. This information concerns the nature of work, varieties of work roles, broad interest areas, information about major industries and services, and receptivity to obsolescent and burgeoning work activities.

3. Relatively specific information about particular roles in the world of work or occupational demands, requirements, and satisfaction. The execution of this function demands the maintenance of a comprehensive library of occupational information materials of relevance to students in a particular school setting.

4. Familiarity with avenues of preparation for specific roles in the world of work. This function demands the maintenance of a comprehensive library of educational information materials, including announcements of colleges, universities, technical schools, and other institutions of further education, as well as on-the-job training programs.

5. Opportunity for casual work observation and exploration of self-at-work. This function is executed through informal contacts with a variety of work roles.

6. Opportunity for planned, systematic work observation and exploration of self-at-work. This function is executed through formal industrial visitations, "career" conferences related to students' expressed interests, part-time paid or volunteer employment, summer employment, and vocational interest clubs. Employment is particularly important, since this provides some index, through contact with workers in the chosen field, to the realism of tentative vocational choices. To execute this function, it is necessary for counselors to maintain a placement service focusing on employment opportunities as an avenue to vocational exploration rather than as a means of gaining monetary return. A developmentally oriented placement service, for example, makes it possible for the prospective journalist to spend the summer as an office boy in a newspaper plant rather than as a soda jerk or hod carrier.

7. Normative and ipsative appraisal of vocational potentialities, through administration and meaningful interpretation of aptitude and interest inventories, when and as needed and desired by the client. The purpose here is not to direct the student's vocational exploration from outside the self but rather to assist self to confirm self-at-work exploration.

8. Opportunities for group guidance and counseling for students facing common vocational development tasks and for their parents to understand the tentative nature of adolescent vocational choices.

9. Opportunities for individual counseling to further exploration, to provide creative synthesis, or to confirm tentative self-at-work exploratory choices.

10. Placement in institutions for further education or in positions in the world of work to implement the result of vocational exploration.

11. Alumni placement and counseling services to assist students to interpret the meaning of their work and educational experiences.

12. A final obligation is the discouraging of premature vocational choices so as to prevent or decelerate premature self-closure. In this connection, it may become incumbent on the counselor *to counsel so as to create vocational confusion* in order to hinder the trammeling of the process of exploration. As Sanford (1962) noted, it is the obligation of the school to help students learn to wait until their self-experience begins to unfold into a meaningful pattern before attempting self-definition, both personally and vocationally. Such an exercise can become for the student a lesson in the ability to tolerate ambiguity which will serve him in good stead in the world of work of the twenty-first century.

15

SCHOLASTIC DEVELOPMENT
AS A GUIDANCE FOCUS

Scholastic development guidance is assistance to the student so that he can progress optimally in his present school situation and solve any special academic problems. It is *not* educational development guidance, which may be defined as assistance to the student with respect to opportunities and placement in a higher school level, e.g., information concerning colleges or technical schools open to secondary school youths.

Unfortunately many teachers and counselors conceive scholastic development guidance as helping the student obtain higher marks. Consequently this guidance focus in the main has degenerated into counselor exhortation to do better or to try harder. Some guidance workers of a less narrow orientation view scholastic development guidance as the implementation of such exhortations by means of administering achievement tests and keeping records. The core of scholastic development guidance, however, is centered far deeper than exhortation, the administration of tests, or the keeping of records. Rather, it consists in attempting to build the type of school program which optimally fulfills the student's unique developmental pattern. Emphasis

414

is placed not so much on demands made by the school program on the student as on how the student can derive maximum benefit from the program.

Failure to self-actualize scholastically is often due to causes other than lack of academic aptitude, including social, vocational, religious, and, particularly, psychological maladjustments or difficulties. In former times, when a student manifested a scholastic difficulty, the teacher or "guidance" worker merely told him that he was not trying hard enough, that he was lazy or indolent. Modern guidance workers realize that this view is simplistic. A student, for example, may not be "trying hard enough" because a personality disorder prevents him from trying harder. Before he can try harder, the personality dysfunction must be removed. Hence at bottom, scholastic development guidance, like all other guidance foci, is a form of personal development guidance.

Scholastic development guidance is not an isolated focus but rather is intertwined with other guidance foci. This interrelationship was brought out by the experience of the Study Skills Office at Yale University (Fedde & Kover, 1960). Originally set up to instruct undergraduates in basic reading speed and comprehension and in fundamental mathematical operations, the office soon found itself performing other unanticipated functions, e.g., serving as an informal screen and referral center for students with personal problems. Such problems often come to the surface in counseling with students experiencing academic difficulties. Some investigations (cf. Tennyson, 1956) on utilization of time by school counselors reveal that up to one-third is spent in scholastic development counseling, a fact deplored by many counselors and counselor educators, who fail to understand that scholastic development guidance is not simply scholastic advisement but is linked with other areas of student development. Unfortunately many educators who set an intellectualist goal for the school and see guidance solely in terms of improving student scholastic success do not grasp the interrelatedness of this area and other zones of human development.

Scholastic Development and Personal Development

A student's scholastic development, interests, and performance must be seen as part of and a result of his maturation as a person. He is exploring the contours of his personality, seeking new independence, and striving to accomplish the developmental tasks appropriate for his level of growth. His body is maturing and becoming more restless, active, and other-thrusted. It is within this texture that adequate scholastic development or dysfunction occurs. Thus V. M. Murphy (1964a) has noted that underachievement or overachievement in scholastic matters can rarely be separated from a student's personality development and need pattern. Empirical investigations have demonstrated that personality exerts a definite and marked influence on scholastic achievement. Jensen's review (1958) of research, together with his own study, revealed that nonintellective personality factors are related to achievement. A review of research by M. C. Shaw and associates (1960, p. 193) indicated there is usually some specific personal maladjustment in scholastic underachievers. Studies by Kirk (1952) and by M. C. Shaw and J. Grubb (1958) have concluded that hostility plays a role in the personality matrix of the academic underachiever. An interesting study by Chambers (1957, p. 183) revealed that empathy is significantly related to scholastic success.

Numerous investigations have related profiles on the Minnesota Multiphasic Personality Inventory (MMPI) to scholastic achievement. While the findings have sometimes conflicted with each other, most investigations indicate a strong relationship between adjustment and achievement. D. P. Hoyt's and W. T. Norman's study (1954) of maladjusted and normal students (as measured by MMPI) revealed that maladjustment affects scholastic achievement by producing *both* "underachievement" and "overachievement," depending on the nature of the student's particular maladjustment. To illustrate: one student may defensively overcompensate for feelings of deficiency by intensive studying and so become an overachiever while another may dwell on deficiency feelings to such an extent that he is either paralyzed in his attitude toward study or spends too much time on introspection and too little on studying, thereby becoming an underachiever. Maladaptive personality traits are easily transferred to maladaptive patterns in scholastic development. Scholastic underachievement may be a manifestation of personal underachievement. An interesting converse to the principle that scholastic growth is an extension of personal development came from a study by J. E. Williams (1962), which concluded that concentration on scholastic improvement during counseling interviews had a marked effect on facilitating the client's personal adjustment and restoring a healthy self-concept. Man's personality, like man himself, is not an island. On the other hand, as Murphy (1964a) observed, the very terms *over* and *under* in relation to school achievement are open to serious doubt. While counselors and school people who lack vigorous training in psychometrics bandy these terms about with aplomb, those school people who understand psychometrics are far more cautious. Presumably the student is an *underachiever* if his school performance is "lower" than what scores on intelligence or aptitude tests predict. But tests represent a *single* sample of behavior, perhaps atypical in terms of "test-wise" school populations. Marks, however, represent *typical* or usual behavior. Even more uncertain in its connotation is the term *overachiever*. Whether one has rigorous psychometric knowledge or simply recalls the Scholastic axiom *"Nemo dat quod non habet,"* this term is a patent absurdity. The psychometrically aware counselor will immediately recognize that a student in an overachiever simply because the usual intelligence or aptitude test is insensitive to shadings in differential ability, achievement motivation, and cognitive style. Yet the terms are used in the literature and hence are employed in this discussion because they have become customary, even though they probably are invalid both empirically and conceptually.

Sex differences are marked in school achievement. A study of high school graduates by the U.S. Office of Education reiterated what other studies had discovered, viz., when compared with boys of similar academic ability, girls are more likely to earn superior marks (Baer, 1963, p. 501), probably because they are generally more docile and conforming than boys. Erb's study (1961, p. 361) of college students revealed that conformity is highly correlated with academic achievement for females but not for males. The investigator hypothesized that female conformity includes academic achievemment as a culturally desirable symbol, whereas male conformity to his male peer group precludes scholastic achievement. A study by M. C. Shaw and associates (1960, p. 195) revealed that male underachievers in high school had more negative self-feelings than did male achievers. This did not occur in the case of female underachievers. The investigators hypothesized that this finding might explain why academic underachievement is predominantly a male rather than a female problem. There was no great difference between the self-concept scores of female achievers and female underachievers, whereas there was a significant difference in self-concept scores between male achievers and male underachievers.

Roth and Meyersburg (1963) described the characteristics of what they termed the "nonachievement syndrome." Their investigation demonstrated that the student who fails to achieve scholastically at a level commensurate with his ability typically exhibits depression, self-disparagement, anxiety, functional disability in relation to study, and a sense of hopelessness and frustration. The relationship between self-disparagement, i.e., the feeling "I can't do it," and functional study disability is apparently circular. I. D. Harris (1961), one of the few psychiatrists involved in research on learning disability, reported from his research that such disability is related to family disorganization, unrealistic parental ambition for school success, and birth-order position, since parents expect firstborn children to mature rapidly. The most resistant cases of school underachievement or nonachievement, however, seem to result from the "passive-aggressive" syndrome. The child is exposed to unreasonable demands of parents and teachers. Unable to reject these demands for high marks directly, he turns his frustration and aggression inward. He "aggresses" against parents and teachers by "passivity" in the learning situation. Bettelheim (1955) has described a treatment protocol for severe cases of learning disorders which was developed at the University of Chicago's Orthogenic School.

Scholastic Development and Social Development

It has been shown throughout this book that scholastic development is intimately bound up with social development. Studies which demonstrate that interpersonal relationships, milieu, and socioeconomic status affect academic achievement have been cited. No program of scholastic development guidance can be effective without adequate consideration of the social matrix of academic growth.

Scholastic Development and Religious Development

There is abundant evidence that religious development and religious milieu affect scholastic development. A study by Koos (1931) and another by R. E. Hill, Jr. (1961), indicated that graduates of church-related high schools failed to perform as well scholastically in college as graduates of public high schools, despite the fact that the former had higher scholastic aptitude. Hill opined that there are a number of elements in Catholic high school life, e.g., conformity and dependence, which are not conducive to optimal scholastic performance in the relatively unstructured non-Catholic college setting. Lenski's study (1961, p. 270) revealed that 81 per cent of Catholic clergy investigated ranked obedience as far more important than intellectual autonomy as a key learning outcome in the school. Hill's hypothesis and Lenski's finding perhaps explain results of a study by Knapp and Goodrich (1952), which indicated that Catholic colleges and universities produce far less than their proportionate share of scientists. J. D. Donovan's investigation (1964, pp. 151–168) concluded that Catholic college and university professors "have a relatively poor record of professional achievement" measured in terms of publication; professors who did not publish came from more religious families than those who did publish. Professors holding a doctorate from non-Catholic universities published more frequently than those with a doctorate from a Catholic university. Poor scholastic development by Catholics is apparently due more generally to religious misorientation than to ethnic factors. Strodbeck's study (1958) of the achievement drive in third-generation Italian Catholic and Jewish high school students in New Haven indicated that Catholic students did not have as high an achievement need as Jewish students; the investigator hypothesized that this was largely a result of the view of Catholicism as emphasizing the imperfectibility of man. (It must be noted that the "new theology" in Catholicism stresses the perfectibility of the human person through the salvific efforts of the Divine encounter.) On the conceptual level, Msgr. Ellis (1955), Fr. Weigel, S.J. (1957), and O'Dea (1958) have trenchantly noted that Catholic emphasis on overdocility, a false concept of humility, excessive otherworldliness, and a Jansenistic conception of man has resulted in a crippling of a full, well-rounded intellectual development in Catholics. A massive, nationwide study financed by *Time* and *Life* magazines and conducted by the Bureau of Applied Social Research at Columbia University (Havemann & West, 1952) provided a considerable body of evidence on Catholic graduates of both Catholic and nondenominational colleges. Catholic graduates, both male and female, as a group tended to have a lower average salary than their Protestant and

Jewish counterparts, were more politically isolationist, were far more prejudiced than Jews but somewhat less than Protestants, and tended far more strongly toward a conservative belief system than Jews but somewhat less strongly than Protestants. Yet the academic records of the three groups were almost identical.

Scholastic Development and Vocational Development

Vocational development and scholastic development are intertwined. Rezler's review (1960, p. 137) of research on the effect of definiteness of vocational choice on scholastic achievement concluded that the majority of investigations indicated a direct relation; if a student had a fairly definite vocational choice, he achieved better scholastically than a student of the same ability who had not made a definite vocational choice. A study of over-achieving Catholic high school girls by Sister Emerentia Herlihy, B.V.M. (1962), concluded that they usually had a definite plan for the future and had perceived a significant relationship between success in high school, effectiveness in an occupation or in higher education, and productivity as a member of society. The pressures favoring premature vocational choices, as Sanford (1962) suggested, however, very often short-circuit the process of self-exploration and personal development. Hence, although definite vocational choice may be related to school success, no *causal* relationship can be inferred. The counselor who dangles a vocational choice before his client, much as a driver dangles a carrot before his donkey, in the vain hope thereby to motivate the client to achieve the highest marks, ultimately does a disservice. Rather, the task of the counselor is to help structure a school curriculum which does not thrust upon students choice for which they are not developmentally ready (Pallone, 1961d).

Prediction of scholastic success

As was pointed out in Chapter 9, the prediction of *individual* behavior is mathematically possible but not causally adequate. It is extremely difficult, even impossible, to predict individual behavior on the basis of tests or of past performance. Nowhere is this more nearly true than in attempts to predict an individual's future scholastic development. The dynamic and complex nature of the human organism, the varied chance and planned influences to which it is subjected, and the force of a host of environmental factors, as well as the broad matrix of need shifts, need-motivational successes, emotional encounters, and perdurance or persistence, make the prediction of scholastic success by means of any instrument, past performance, or combination of these a manifest risk at best. A study by J. N. Jacobs (1957) revealed that girls represent a more predictable *group* than boys in regard to scholastic success. Similarly, Seashore's review (1962) of discussions with counselors and his own research led him to conclude that marks of female students are more predictable from aptitude tests than marks of male students.

It is generally agreed that the best predictor of scholastic success is a combination of four factors, viz., previous academic marks in various courses, reading score, intelligence quotient, and verbal ability (see Bloom & Peters, 1961). Even more important than a student's record, however, are his drive level, need structure, family and cultural milieu, and, as Schneiders (1957) has noted, emotional stability. These nonintellective factors powerfully affect intellectual performance and can never be overlooked by the guidance worker.

Prediction must always be utilized as an indicator of *some* of the pupil's potentialities; it should never be used to close the doors on a student's growth by categorizing him or by classifying him into a type mold.

Preadmittance guidance

Preadmittance guidance is assistance to the student from the time when he applies for admission to the moment when he begins formal activities under the school's auspices. In alert schools, these activities start with pre-admittance services. Usually the initial steps in a preadmittance program are directed toward ascertaining whether or not the educational goals of the school are suitable to a particular student's developmental need pattern. In all too many schools students are merely shipped to the school at the next higher level with little attention as to whether or not it is appropriate for them. Colleges, notably private colleges, tend to be more circumspect in pre-admission guidance. Most private institutions require students to take College Entrance Examination Board tests, as well as aptitude tests and similar instruments. Some colleges also request of each applicant a brief autobiography. The director of admissions at the University of Chicago has found that this autobiographical sketch is the most important document which the applicant submits, since it gives the college personnel worker indispensable nonintellective data.

Testing is only one phase of preadmittance guidance. It should be preceded by "open-school" days, in which applicants (and prospective applicants) can visit the school to talk with teachers, administrators, and, especially, counselors to ascertain whether the school is suitable for their personal fulfillment. The practice of open-school days applies not only to the college level but to the high school level as well. Each applicant should be interviewed by a guidance worker in the receiving school so that applicant and school can appraise each other in terms of mutual acceptability. McMurray's investigation (1958) of Catholic women's colleges discovered that preadmittance guidance was confined chiefly to group guidance, with few or no interviews with trained personnel workers; nor did these colleges indicate signs of organized planning to assist individual high school students to determine whether or not to go to college or to learn which college was best suited to their needs. Non-Catholic colleges are also remiss in not providing adequate personal interviews with applicants. High schools as well as colleges should have special "admissions" personnel and conduct research to improve preadmittance guidance services (Humphreys et al., 1960, pp. 241–248).

For a preadmittance guidance program to be successful, vertical articulation among the various school levels is necessary. Trained personnel workers from each of the lower- and higher-level schools should visit each other, confer with students in lower-level schools to ascertain their aspirations, and interview students already in the "receiving" school to discover whether its program is appropriate for them. Attempts should be made to put vertical articulation on an institutional basis rather than allow it to remain contingent on a personnel worker's initiative. In Catholic education there is little organized vertical articulation even among schools conducted by the same religious congregation. Each school seems to be operated as a single, isolated empire. This lack of organized vertical articulation is another illustration that the history of American Catholic education is largely a chronicle of wasted resources.

The director of admissions, as well as his assistants in the admissions office, should be trained in personnel work. Their graduate studies should include courses in the interpretation of test data, interview skills, principles of guidance and personnel work, occupational and educational resources, and fundamentals of human development.

A well-organized, guidance-oriented program of preadmittance services operated by trained personnel workers might prevent the results detailed in the rather well-known story:

> The headmaster in a private New England preparatory school presented to his institution's admissions committee the record of a boy who was described as "ranking 12th in a class of 14, having a stubborn streak, and being sometimes rebellious but usually conforming." The committee voted unanimously to reject the applicant. The headmaster then revealed that these data were taken from the Harrow school record of Winston Churchill.

Orientation

Orientation is assistance to a student to help both him and the institution attain greater perceptual congruence concerning the goals and procedures by which the school can optimally further his self-actualization. Orientation is necessary so that the school can better serve the student, not so that he can learn how to conform more compliantly to its rules and regulations. Sister Mary Estelle, S.S.N.D. (1957, p. 28), has noted that orientation is a developmental process; a day or even a week is not long enough for an adequate orientation program. An effective program should perdure minimally for the first term of the school year.

Many types of activities characterize an effective orientation program. Lecture-discussions by admissions personnel, faculty members, upperclassmen, and, particularly, guidance workers constitute one important phase of orientation. How-to-study courses may be offered. Each student should receive a handbook which stresses not primarily school rules and regulations but, more important, how the school can assist him, e.g., the availability of its counseling service, its remedial service, and its activities program. In larger institutions, tours can be conducted to acquaint students with the resources of both institution and community. Some schools use an "older-brother" or "older-sister" plan whereby, on the basis of an interest profile, intelligence, and personality traits, an incoming student is "assigned" a closely matched upperclassman who serves as his school brother or her school sister for the academic year. The orientation program should include group guidance and individual counseling on scholastic matters, personal development, social adjustment, vocational exploration, and religious fulfillment.

Selection of appropriate educational goals

Appropriate educational goals are those which further self-actualization. It is not enough that they be objectively appropriate for the student's self-actualization; the student must both perceive and value his school experience as appropriate. Rezler (1960) conducted a study of a group of students with matched scholastic aptitude subdivided according to college marks into three subgroups, viz., high achievers, average achievers, and low achievers. The investigation concluded that a major factor causing variation in scholastic achievement was the student's value of and attitude toward college education. Many members of minority groups and children of immigrants tend to prize education highly and hence to overachieve scholastically.

Students frequently select institutions for reasons other than appropriate educational goals. Often they choose to attend prestigious Eastern preparatory schools primarily because there they can meet the type of person who will facilitate their rise up the socioeconomic ladder. Similarly, more and more numerous students are clamoring to enter college not so much for an education but because the college degree is viewed as a passkey to social and economic success.

The concept of a liberal education as freeing oneself from the superficial and tasting of the deep draughts of the richness of reality is true enough in the objective order. In the concrete situation, however, a heavy concentration in the liberal arts is required of all high school students, and many drop out prior to graduation because they see no practicality in these areas of study as far as their own career objectives are concerned. College students customarily regard liberal arts courses as vocational subjects, i.e., courses which fit them for such careers as teaching or give them interesting material to inject into business conversations over a martini. Students vocationally committed to such careers as medicine, engineering, and agriculture usually take their liberal arts courses because these courses are required rather than because they help them self-actualize. The relation between college curriculum and vocational choice is borne out in a study by Forrest (1961), which disclosed that change in a college student's major field was closely related to change in vocational choice. In 80 per cent of changes of major field there was also a shift in vocational choice. Rezler's study (1960) of overachieving, achieving, and underachieving college students of matched scholastic ability found that the parents of all three groups seemed to have no clear-cut value system to pass on to their offspring; indeed, they viewed the purpose of college as providing a salable degree to assist students to obtain jobs which would pay enough to raise a family according to the "American standard of living." Parents expected their offspring to be industrious and disciplined in college, to "give primary attention to their studies, and to have vocational goals sufficiently compelling to attempt the drudgery involved in much learning." Significantly, underachievers tended to introject these parental attitudes, while overachievers tended to modify or go counter to these values.

The regard for education as an economic vehicle rather than an avenue for self-fulfillment is paradoxically characteristic of Catholic students. T. N. McCarthy (1960b), an experienced Catholic college counselor, has remarked: "One fact clear to anyone dealing with Catholic college students is that the vast majority come from families that value education as the number one vehicle of upward status mobility but are almost totally ignorant of education as a way of life." A study by Malnig and Cristantiello (1956) of freshman student interests in a Catholic men's college revealed that while the academic subject area students liked best in high school was history, fewer freshmen elected to major in history in college than in any other subject area. The investigators hypothesized that perhaps these students believed that history had little practical value for a direct, economically profitable vocational goal. O'Dea (1958, p. 118) has observed that Catholic students enter the lucrative professions of law, medicine, and politics in far greater proportions than they embark on intellectual careers. These studies give rise to speculation about the altruism and spirituality of the motives of Catholic students and of the schools which helped shape these motives.

Berdie's review (1960, p. 461) of research concluded that, of all groups (including religious, racial, and national), the one which consistently fails to send its proportionate share of members of high scholastic ability to college is the female sex. While this conclusion is in one sense regrettable, the guidance-oriented educator must be careful to express sound reasons for his regret. It is undeniable that for most girls college is one or all of the following: (1) a transitory stage between high school and marriage, a stage a bit more pleasant than entering the labor force after graduation from high school; (2) an environment in which a girl can advance socially if she goes to the "right" college and meets the "right" people; (3) a milieu which presents numerous opportunities to meet a wide range of boys with promising socioeconomic futures; and (4) an opportunity to obtain a salable skill (e.g., teaching) which will be useful whether she remains single or marries. As a result of inappropriate educational goals, many girls who attend college spend four wasted years from the viewpoint of optimal self-actualization. Inappropriate goals cannot eventuate in a commitment to reflective thinking or in self-activity requisite for full scholastic development; instead, many girls become scholastic underachievers not in the sense of attaining poor marks but in the more profound sense of failing to become truly educated.

Guidance workers on the high school level can help students understand that college attendance is only one form of continuing education after graduation. A youth should attend an institution of higher learning only if this type of post-high school education is adequate and appropriate for the furtherance of his own self-actualization (Lee, 1959).

Inappropriate educational goals may originate within the student or his family, but they are also frequently induced by the school. Schools often have inflexible curricular offerings or a narrow range of courses within a given curriculum, both of which make their educational programs unsuitable for many students. Most Catholic high schools are college preparatory in their educational thrust, even though many students do not intend higher education. Usually the curriculum is composed of watertight, isolated, fragmented segments called subjects rather than broad, meaningful, life-related problem areas. Little wonder that such narrow curricula are perceived as inappropriate by many young people. The counselor should be one of the school people who take the lead in working to effect an evolution toward a meaningful curricular design such as the core curriculum (see Faunce & Bossing, 1958; Lee, 1963b, pp. 201–208; B. O. Smith, W. O. Stanley, & J. H. Shores, 1957, pp. 311–386).

Selection of a suitable curricular track

American secondary schools and colleges commonly offer two types of curricular track, viz., the course-cluster and the ability-group tracks. The *course-cluster track* consists of several basic and distinct groupings of broad subject-matter areas, each being aimed at a radically different educational or vocational objective. There are customarily six broad groupings, viz., college preparatory, general (or modern), commercial, industrial arts, home economics, and agriculture. The first two are lumped together under the term *academic;* the last four, under the category *vocational.* The *ability-group track* comprises several distinct classifications of students based on learning aptitude. Usually there are three echelons, viz., high, middle, and low.

The American school system is so structured that the secondary school, specifically the junior high school, is normally the first unit of the educational system in which the student can make a choice of courses. Super has coined the term "the critical ninth grade" to indicate the time when the course-cluster track becomes in a sense a prevocational choice from which the pupil in succeeding years moves to the point of irreversibility of vocational choice (Super et al., 1960). This selection of course-cluster track, initially made in the ninth grade, has deeper ramifications than merely the choice of course or subtrack. The adolescent, considering choices open to him, is standing on the threshold of awareness of self-identity and of responsibility to self. His course-track decision, as he well knows, represents one of the first chances in his life in which he himself can determine what he will become. Thus what is important is not merely the decision per se but also the developmental process which occurred within him as he made the decision. Such a process development may become the archetypal development style after which much of his later behavior will be consciously or unconsciously patterned. Yet he is not ready, vocationally or emotionally, for airtight, irrevocable choices.

Adolescence is a period of exploration of self and the interaction of self with milieu, including course work. Opportunities must always remain open even through college for a student to switch course-cluster tracks; e.g., a student who in the ninth grade wishes to become a mechanic may discover in the twelfth grade that he can become an engineer. Wolfle (1954, pp. 24–74) has noted that only 38 per cent of employed college graduates, including lawyers and physicians, work in the field of their major study. The comprehensive high school and the university which provide for work in all course-cluster tracks facilitate track switches in appropriate cases.

Placement of a student in the ability-group track most appropriate for optimal self-actualization is not merely a matter of assignment based on test scores to a high, middle, or low group. Placement, if it is to achieve success, is contingent upon pupil and parental perception and acceptance of pupil ability. Wrenn (1958) concluded that students habitually overemphasize their scholastic ability. An investigation by Herman and Ziegler (1961) showed that parents rate both the academic abilities and the personality characteristics of their children higher than results of a standardized academic aptitude test and personality inventory. From the guidance point of view, both pupil or parental overestimation and what the counselor does in the light of this overestimation are important.

It is one of the basic tasks of the counselor to assist the student to self-actualize through the selection of an appropriate course-cluster track, an ability-group track, and specific courses within each track. A pupil should choose a course-cluster track only after consultation with counselor, parents, and appropriate teachers; educational and vocational aptitude tests should be used to ascertain possible directions of choice. The choice of a course-cluster track should be periodically evaluated by the student as he proceeds through secondary school and college. On the high school level, effective ability grouping does not extend to every subject or curricular problem area but rather is determined separately for each individual subject or area. For example, a sophomore student whose verbal aptitude is low but whose quantitative ability is high can be placed in a low-ability sophomore class in English but in a high-ability sophomore class in mathematics. More alert colleges are beginning to introduce honors courses and even honors programs for scholastically gifted students. The counselor can help the client assess the wisdom of enrolling in a course simply because it does not require much work. A study by C. Brown (1961) of college students who selected majors on the basis of what degree program would afford the highest marks disclosed that such a selection neither challenged students' abilities nor gave them companions of similar ability, personality, or interests. In short, this selection hampered self-actualization. The counselor can also assist the student in the selection of appropriate school activities (Dunn, 1959, p. 25).

Improving study and work habits

It is the obligation of every teacher and guidance worker to assist students to improve study and work habits. The key factor in studying is not how much time and effort are expended but rather how much learning takes place.

Students often need assistance in improving their habits. Di Michael's investigation (1943) of freshmen in a Catholic high school revealed that most of them lacked definite information about efficient methods and techniques of studying. A survey by Danskin and Burnett (1952) of university students of *superior* scholastic achievement discovered that their habits were mediocre in the light of optimum study habits recommended by educational psychologists and by experts in study methodology. Lee (1963b, p. 350) concluded that study habits and techniques were acquired by the overwhelming majority of students in an accidental, haphazard manner of trial and error; poor habits and techniques were learned early in pupils' careers and remained relatively fixed unless the school made definite efforts to correct them. Such corrective efforts involve a simultaneous three-prong effort, viz., a how-to-study course, continuous individual help from teachers in improving student study skills, and maintenance of a study clinic within the school where students experiencing above-average scholastic difficulty can be given special attention.

At the beginning of a student's elementary, junior high, senior high, and college experience, the school may offer him a how-to-study course, in reality a group situation which concentrates on adjustment to the new learning situation through the improvement of study skills and work habits. Such a course, taught by a counselor or a trained teacher-counselor, continues for a full semester. The research has indicated that a how-to-study course is beneficial in helping students learn about and acquire efficient habits. Often it is advisable to utilize one of the better how-to-study books now on the market as a textbook for the course.

Excluding study work in the classroom itself, there are three basic types of study, viz., formally supervised study, independent study, and home study. Formally supervised study is customarily conducted in a study hall. The guidance-oriented study hall supervisor converts the hall from an administrative dumping ground into a situation is which students either independently or as a group are helped to improve study habits. Independent study is coming into greater and greater prominence as a definite feature of the regular school day. The Trump Report (1960, pp. 40–43) recommends that senior high school pupils spend, on the average, twelve hours each week in independent study. The research has shown that independent study is particularly effective for intellectually superior students (see Burton, 1950, pp. 234–235). Home study enables teachers and parents to cooperate in helping the student to improve his learning habits. These contacts between home and school can subsequently be broadened to include other pupil concerns and developmental tasks.

Alert teachers have long since abandoned the type of classroom instruction which relied exclusively on the textbook. If the student is to derive optimum benefit from collateral readings and supplemental materials, he needs the following minimal skills: how to use the library, how to take efficient notes, how to evaluate what he has read, and how to relate what he has read to his everyday life. Teachers and guidance workers should assist students to develop these important skills, as well as to apply the general principles of studying. How-to-study courses and study clinics are not sufficient; individual attention to the improvement of study methods is imperative.

Working with exceptional children

An exceptional child is one who deviates from the normal range of students. In the usual comprehensive school or college there are four main groups of exceptional children, viz., the intellectually gifted, the intellectually slow, the creatively gifted, and the emotionally disturbed and the physically or mentally handicapped.

The Intellectually Gifted

Guidance for the intellectually gifted student is often conceived as merely helping him attain maximum achievement in academic matters. The school is frequently bedazzled by his intellect and is thus blinded to the necessity of assisting him to develop *all* the dimensions of his personality.

Intellectually gifted pupils often face developmental tasks and problems somewhat different from those of "normal" pupils: (1) They frequently become aware of their developmental tasks before they have the psychophysical resources to meet them optimally. (2) They are talented in so many areas that their very embarrassment of riches presents problems in educational and vocational choice. (3) They are frequently so intellectually perceptive that the school's religious program seems puerile to them, and doubts of faith naturally arise. (4) Their intellectual needs and interests are such that the school's normal curriculum and program cannot effectively challenge them, especially in elementary schools and in small high schools and colleges. (5) They are often subjected to unusual pressures by parents, teachers, and peers. (6) They are frequently more sensitive and more compulsive than normal pupils. For example, Gladys H. Watson's study (1960, p. 104) of college students revealed that "the honors students [referred for counseling] tended to be compulsive, driven people with few or no satisfactory interpersonal relationships."

As Kohlbrenner (1964) has observed, it is only since World War II that the schools began giving attention to *all* gifted students below the college level. Some of the guidance-oriented activities in which schools are currently engaging to assist the gifted student to develop optimally include (1) introduction of organized methods of identification of intellectually gifted students as early in their school careers as possible; (2) provision of specialized curricula adequate to their interests and level of development; (3) introduction of enrichment or acceleration programs, or both; (4) encouragement of a greater use of independent study; (5) greater employment of supplemental teaching materials, collateral readings, and educational field trips; (6) curricular reorganization so that the students can grasp the unity and wholeness of reality, e.g., introduction of the core curriculum; (7) particular attention to the hitherto nonachieving student of superior intelligence, especially the female student and the youth from a socioeconomically disadvantaged neighborhood; (8) organization of divisions within the superintendent's office for special attention to education and guidance of the intellectually gifted; and (9) the training of counselors and teachers to work more effectively with intellectually gifted students (see Drews, 1961; E. Joseph, 1963; National Society for the Study of Education, 1958; Passow et al., 1955).

The Intellectually Slow

Only with the advent of progressive education was the intellectually slow pupil regarded as worthy of school. Unfortunately many school people stopped at this insight, with the result that educational and guidance programs for the intellectually slow are often not distinctive in terms of the uniqueness of this group.

The intellectually slow often have a developmental need pattern somewhat different from those of normal pupils: (1) They often have difficulty in concentration and in fixing their attention for any period of time. (2) They feel frustrated because they do not succeed in schoolwork, a goal highly prized by both peers and adults. (3) Their concerns and interests are in the concrete, practical, here-and-now order rather than in more abstract, un-meaningful learning ideals proposed in traditional textbooks and curriculum guides. (4) They are not oriented toward the verbal symbolism quite preva-lent in most classroom teaching. (5) They often tend to act without thinking through the purpose or consequence of their actions.

Most schools issue pious platitudes about assisting the intellectually slow students, but few do more than rudimentary work in this area. Among more effective guidance-oriented devices are (1) inauguration of a work-study pro-gram, in which the senior high school student spends part of his day in school and part in working for a salary with an employer in the community; (2) establishing remedial clinics, especially in reading, writing, and speech; (3) utilizing teaching methodologies which feature nonverbal learning mate-rials, e.g., audiovisual materials; (4) reorganizing the curriculum, deleting nonmeaningful elements and inserting practical learnings within a curricular design such as core; and (5) providing for special guidance facilities and guidance workers specially trained to work with the intellectually slow.

The Creatively Gifted

Creativity is the process by which a person takes particular elements in reality and from them fashions a new element. While the new element is not completely different from its constituent elements, it is nonetheless a fresh, new form of reality. Creative thinking is the process of filling in gaps or of rearranging reality into new and unique patterns. Every person creates, according to his talent for creativity. Some psychologists have asserted that creativity exists only when what is produced is objectively valuable or meritorious, but objectively, "in every creative act there is absolute gain, something added," as Berdyaev (1955, p. 129) has observed. Subjectively, this view ignores the worth of the creative act to the student, ignores the fact that the production may be valuable as far as his capacities are concerned. While all students are creative to some degree, not all are creatively gifted. The term *creative child* is not synonymous with the phrase "child with artistic talent," since artistic creativity is only one facet of creativity.

Intellectually gifted students are not necessarily creatively gifted, and vice versa. A study by Getzels and Jackson (1962) found that the top 20 per cent of creatively gifted students did not rank in the top 20 per cent on intelligence tests. Hence creativity is not dependent on intelligence. Compara-tive studies by Torrance (1962b) on the elementary school level and by Getzels and Jackson (1958) on the high school level of a group of creatively gifted pupils and a group of intellectually gifted pupils revealed that while both groups received the same score on standardized achievement tests, the creatively gifted scored considerably lower on intelligence tests. Certainly fascination with high IQ *scores* should not blind guidance workers to other forms of talent.

Creatively gifted students have many distinctive personality characteristics of which Torrance (1961, p. 12) has listed some of the more important: " . . . always baffled by something, attracted to the mysterious, attempts difficult jobs (sometimes too difficult), constructive in criticism, courageous, energetic, full of curiosity, independent in judgment, independent in thinking, intuitive, perceptive, becomes preoccupied with a problem, questioning, regresses occasionally, unwilling to accept anything on mere say-so. . ." A review (Drews, 1961, p. 34) of the research on creative people has revealed that they have a high degree of tolerance for uncertainty, asymmetry, and ambiguity. Creative pupils tend to be flexible rather than rigid in personality, since as Sister Adrienne Carmena, C.S.J. (1962), has observed, the creative act is of its nature the giving of new form by transcending the old order; hence the strict formalist is never free to create. Getzels and Jackson's investigation (1958) revealed that the intellectually gifted pupils studied held a self-ideal consonant with the one they believed the teachers would most readily approve, while the self-ideal of the creatively gifted was not consonant with what they perceived to be the teacher-approved model. Creative students are usually nonconformists, and question authority; as a result, the school usually represses rather than releases their talents.

The creatively gifted student faces many unique problems: (1) His parents, peers, and school people often regard him as "different," odd, or somehow queer. (2) Parents and school people make premature attempts to eliminate fantasy at the elementary level, instead of attempting to fuse it with intellective elements of the child's personality. (3) Adults place many restrictions on the creatively gifted child's curiosity. (4) Adults tend to be suspicious of the child because of his nonconformist tendencies. (5) The school does not afford him the opportunity of making mistakes. (6) The school overemphasizes verbal skills and forces his creative thrust to be channeled in this direction.

Guidance-oriented activities to assist the creatively gifted to develop optimally include (1) allowing more freedom for individual exploration and bringing less pressure to bear for group conformity, (2) restructuring the curriculum so that formal learning opportunities are available to the creatively gifted, (3) utilizing group work in the classroom in such a way that it releases rather than represses creativity (Fiedler's study, 1960, concluded that task- and efficiency-oriented groups may breed social conditions which inhibit creative behavior), and (4) working with local universities in studying the phenomenon of creative thinking. In the last connection it is interesting to note that in Torrance's discussion (1959) of leaders in studying creative thinking, not a single American Catholic institution of higher learning is mentioned.

The Emotionally Disturbed and the Physically or Mentally Handicapped

The emotionally disturbed student, in this context, is not simply one who has experienced occasional developmental difficulties but rather one who is suffering an embedded pathological personality disorder. In larger school systems, there are usually special schools organized with specially trained teachers, counselors, and psychologists on their staffs. In smaller school systems, the emotionally disturbed student is often part of a regular class. If he is not receiving psychotherapeutic assistance, one important role for the counselor is to help him and his parents find appropriate school and psychiatric treatment. Special education programs for the emotionally disturbed have been described by Bettelheim (1955) and by Redl and Wineman (1957). Similarly, physically and mentally handicapped students (e.g., the trainable mentally retarded) are accorded special education conducted by specialists in larger school systems but may be integrated into regular classes in smaller systems. In view of Federal, state, and private support for special education, however, only backward school systems have failed to provide at least minimally adequate programs. Counseling and guidance for these students with atypical needs demand a specialized type of preparation akin to rehabilitation counseling. More alert programs to prepare special education teachers include professional guidance training. When the counselor encounters these special needs, his role is appropriate referral; in addition, within the limits of his competence, he offers what assistance he can to students and their parents, focusing on common tasks of development.

Scholastic deficiency

The term *scholastic deficiency* refers to pupils who fail courses and to all students whose academic achievement is not commensurate with their ability. The research evidence has indicated that scholastic deficiency is fairly continuous throughout any one person's school career. B. L. Sharp's review (1962, p. 247) reported in general significant relationships between marks in high school and in college. A study by M. C. Shaw and D. J. Brown (1957) of scholastic underachievement of bright college students revealed that the college underachiever had usually been an underachiever in high school. Six major factors contribute to scholastic deficiency or success: personality, socioeconomic milieu, the teacher-pupil relationship, school policy, curriculum, and residence.

A review of research by Goldburgh and Penney (1962, p. 133) concluded that personality characteristics, particularly hostility and anxiety, are significantly related to academic underachievement. A study by Murphy (in Merrill & Murphy, 1959) of two groups of low-scholastic-ability students, one of overachievers and the other of low achievers, revealed that low achievers were less achievement-oriented and less aggressive than their overachieving counterparts. Tiebout's research (1943) indicated that whereas candidness about their abilities characterized overachievers, defensiveness, rationalization, ignoring of failures, and exaggeration of successes characterized underachievers. Kirk (1952) has conjectured that academic failure has meaning in terms of unconscious satisfaction derived from hostility usually directed toward some member of the family who demands scholastic success (see also I. D. Harris, 1961). Goldburgh and Penney's study (1962, p. 136) discovered that the underachieving student tends to have difficulty in his relationship with his parents and to feel hostility toward teachers, who represent to him parental substitutes. Kimball's investigation (1952) concluded that scholastic underachievers have an essentially negative relationship with their fathers. Certainly the body of research hinted at in this paragraph indicates that scholastic deficiency is far more complicated than is apparent from the charges of "laziness," "obstinacy," or "lack of cooperation" with which uninformed school people often confront pupils.

There is little doubt that socioeconomic milieu has definite effects on scholastic deficiency. Academic values are usually not prized in a socioeconomically disadvantaged area, with the consequence that many students deliberately counterconform to the school's educative efforts. Although little has been done to correct this situation, the most dramatic example of the pooling of the school's guidance, instructional, and administrative resources occurred in the early 1960s in the famed Higher Horizons program in the New York City public schools (see Reissman, 1962; Wrightstone, 1958). The results of this program were so encouraging that other forward-looking school systems began to initiate similar programs in their areas.

A review of the pertinent research by D. A. Davis (1962, p. 799) concluded that one of the two major reasons for school dropouts is an unsatisfactory teacher-pupil relationship. A study Rocchio and Kearney (1956) concluded that a high school teacher who creates a classroom atmosphere of fear and tension and thinks primarily of subject matter to be covered rather than in terms of what pupils need to learn is more likely to give failing marks than a teacher who is warm and is interested in his pupils as persons. A nationwide study (Brother B. Leanman, S.C., 1956) of 10,000 eighth-grade boys in Catholic elementary schools found that 25 per cent reported that their greatest problems came from school sources, particularly from excessive strictness of teachers. The suggestions given in Chapter 5 for improving teacher-pupil relations should be followed by every teacher who wishes to discharge his obligation as a guidance worker.

School policy is not infrequently a cause of scholastic deficiency and dropouts. In his study of Catholic elementary schools Brother Bernadine Leanman, S.C. (1956, pp. 471–472), found that one boy received corporal punishment because of a misplaced dollar sign. Some schools practice suspension or expulsion guidance. Many have such strict rules and prohibitions that any sort of exploration is choked and personal development necessary for scholastic achievement is asphyxiated.

It is almost universally acknowledged that an inadequate and inappropriate curriculum is a primary cause of scholastic deficiency and dropout. If the curriculum is not meaningful to the student, he is not interested, does not learn, or even want to learn. Often a curriculum in a school remains fixed simply because it is "traditional" or is deemed best for college preparation. Lee's review (1963b, pp. 201–208) as well as the results of the Eight Year Study (Aiken, 1942) have shown that the traditional curriculum is not more effective in terms of college preparation than the core curriculum, which gives focal attention to *both* pupil interests and needs and to those learnings which the school believes every pupil should acquire. Indeed one of the features of the core curriculum is that the guidance function is built into its very structure. The activities program should provide an opportunity for students to express their interests. Yet students who could profit most from this program are denied participation on the ground of scholastic deficiency. McKown (1956, pp. 600–602) has cited six studies, all of which indicate that there is no evidence that participation in activities affects marks adversely.

While the evidence is conflicting, the majority of the studies seem to indicate that, in general, residence in a fraternity or sorority house tends to have an adverse effect on scholastic achievement (Crookston, 1961; Diener, 1960; Willingham, 1962). A few private New England colleges are attempting to eliminate residential fraternity houses on or near their campuses. Few Catholic institutions of higher learning permit residential fraternity or sorority houses.

Early School Leavers

One of the greatest problems confronting education is the early school leaver or dropout. The dropout problem is severe; 40 per cent of all American youths do not complete high school. Early school leavers, already disadvantaged because they are young and inexperienced, find employment opportunities increasingly more difficult since employers require a high school diploma for all but the most menial occupations.

Research indicates that the majority of dropouts display personal problems and an expressed dissatisfaction with the school program. It may be that the second of these factors constitutes a major cause of the first. A study by Lichter and associates (1962, p. 246) discovered that dropouts reported unhappy school experiences. Studies by the U.S. Department of Labor (Wolfbein, 1959) found that most early school leavers expressed dissatisfaction with the school program; this was the most homogeneous factor among dropouts. R. H. Byrne's review (1958) of research on dropouts concluded that the majority reported school held no interest for them. A study by

Fr. Roesch, S.M. (1954, pp. 340–370), discovered that prominent among the reasons for transfer from Catholic to public schools were that the Catholic school curriculum was too narrow, punishment was excessive, discipline was too strict, and school regulations were overly detailed and unrealistic in terms of youths' developmental needs. The study by Lichter and associates (1962, pp. 248–249) revealed that many of the early school leavers investigated had severe emotional problems, and a study by Drasgow and McKenzie (1958) disclosed that college dropouts were significantly more maladjusted than were graduates. An investigation by F. G. Brown (1960) of male and female dropouts during the first semester of college found that the males tended to be irresponsible and nonconforming, and the females withdrawn and depressed.

Guidance workers dealing with potential dropouts should remember that in many instances it is better for the student's self-actualization that he leave school, particularly when the school program is neither adequate nor appropriate for his developmental fulfillment. If the curriculum is not interesting, meaningful, or valuable to him or does not offer him a broad range of educational choices and opportunities, it is unethical to suggest that he remain in that particular school. The guidance worker should cooperate with the administration to effect a broader, more meaningful curriculum. He should also articulate with guidance personnel at the elementary school level, where scholastic malfunction usually begins. In any event the counselor should help the dropout leave school without injured pride or a wrecked self-concept due to overenthusiastic stay-in-school campaigns. He should aid the client to make his school-leaving experience and his subsequent employment self-actualizing, since most dropouts do not leave school to effect constructive plans (Lichter et al., 1962, p. 247).

Promoting optimal scholastic development

There are ten broad or general methods which might profitably be used for optimal scholastic development.

First, organize schoolwide efforts to stimulate scholastic development in every student. Both public and Catholic schools are failing in this regard. Fr. Stack (1958) reported a paucity of guidance services for scholastic development in Catholic institutions. A study by Wehmeyer (1959) of scholastic achievement of first-semester freshmen at a large Midwestern Catholic university concluded that the availability of formal high school guidance programs to high- and low-achieving freshmen was not a significant factor in the differences between the two groups. He surmised that high school guidance programs do not adequately assist students in optimal scholastic development. Nor are schools and colleges properly stimulating students of high intellectual or creative ability. Waggoner (1957) found that little special effort was made by state universities to stimulate or challenge the intellectually superior student. This finding could probably be validly generalized to other types of secondary and collegiate institutions. A study of 1958 high school graduates conducted by the U.S. Office of Education (Baer, 1963) showed that one-fourth of high-scholastic-ability students ranked below the upper third of their class in terms of school marks. A study by Lurie, Goldfein, and Baxt (1960) of counseling and guidance with underachieving ninth-grade students revealed that within a year they showed more improvement in appropriateness of occupational plans and had a lower dropout rate than a matched control group which received no formal guidance assistance. Boarding schools and colleges can make residence hall living an educational experience instead of merely offering a place to sleep. Certainly the school should at all times eschew suspension and expulsion guidance. Such procedures force the student away from the hopefully beneficent influence of the school.

Second, suffuse the student in an atmosphere of positive encouragement for learning and for scholastic development (see Campanelle, 1960). Unfortunately schools often create a climate of fear in the area of scholastic development. Such fear prevents mature academic growth. The nationwide study by Brother Bernadine Leanman, S.C. (1956, p. 475), of eighth-grade boys in Catholic elementary schools disclosed that nearly half were afraid of failing. Brother Elmo Bransby, C.S.C. (1949, p. 127), reported that nearly 50 per cent of Catholic high school boys also were afraid of failing. Fr. J. T. Byrne's study (1957) of problems of students in Catholic men's colleges revealed that by far the major problem was in the area of scholastic development. Fear leads to rote memory and possibly even to partial academic paralysis, certainly not to that scholastic development which love of truth can bring.

Third, identify students in terms of the optimal scholastic development unique to each. Not only the gifted but *every* pupil should be appraised so that a school program may be planned in terms of *his* development. The guidance office cannot rely totally on intelligence scores or on marks. Low intelligence scores may reflect reading retardation to a greater degree than a basic lack of aptitude. Marks, particularly in elementary school, may be due to conformism, overdocility, halo effect, or sheer rote memory rather than to intellective or creative factors. Nationwide programs of pupil identification, such as Project Talent, can serve as models for school systems. Tests which examine creative intelligence need to be devised.

Fourth, help students develop a sense of the value of education, of culture, of the intellectual life. T. N. McCarthy (1960b, p. 114) has remarked that unless Beethoven's Fifth Symphony were 90 proof and obtainable in a package store, fathers of many youths would be totally indifferent to it. A study (Sister M. A. Signorelli, M.Z.S.H., 1956, p. 97) of students in a private Catholic girls' high school, where a premium is placed on culture, revealed that the overwhelming majority of the students lacked appreciation for classical music as well as for classical and modern art. In the same school, the section of the daily newspaper most frequently read by students was the comics, indeed, by a more than 2:1 ratio over the next most frequently read section, sports. Sister Rose Matthew Mangini, I.H.M. (1958, p. 253), has argued that the present low estate of American Catholic contributions to culture and scholarship "rests largely with the Catholic teacher [in the Catholic school] and hence to a considerable extent with the Sister teacher." Catholics need to acquire the vision which regards thinking and participation in culture as directly Divine acts, as Divine as praying. Unfortunately too many Catholic schools have regarded intellectual knowledge primarily as an apologetical device, a method of "refuting enemies of the faith." For their part, public school people need to see intellect and culture as gateways to a new, more profound *engagement* with reality, rather than as avenues to financial profit. Schoolwork is not an unproductive occupation, as some people imagine, but rather one of the most fruitful endeavors in which an individual can participate.

Fifth, arrange special administrative provisions for promoting scholastic development. There are several types of such administrative provisions: (1) In the *enrichment* type, the student remains for the same period of time at a given school level but is provided deeper learning opportunities than are available in a regular class. Honors programs in high schools and colleges exemplify enrichment (see Fr. Grollmes, S.J., 1964). Another enrichment plan is the year of foreign study sponsored by some colleges and universities. (2) In the *acceleration* type, a student skips one or more grades during his school career. Acceleration is especially important for intellectually and creatively gifted students. The real progress of such students comes not from formal schooling but from independent work. The longer a person remains a student, the longer he is subordinate, relatively passive, and looking to others instead of to himself as the source of ideas and new frontiers. H. C. Lehman's research (1953) disclosed that the most outstanding creative work tended to come early in the careers of famous scientists, inventors, artists, and musicians, usually when these men were under thirty years of age. Reviews of the research by Pressey (1962, p. 12) and by Faries and Perry (1960, p. 565) concluded there is overwhelming proof that academic acceleration of students promotes favorable scholastic development. An important study subsidized by the Fund for the Advancement of Education of the Ford Foundation (1957) which investigated students who skipped the last year of high school (42 per cent had only ten years of schooling) discovered that these students did better scholastically than matched students who did not accelerate. A modified form of acceleration is the Advanced Placement program, in which students take certain college courses for college credit while they are still in high school. (3) In *nongraded schools,* students are not forced to progress scholastically according to a lockstep plan which fails to account for individual developmental differences; rather, advancement to the next level of learning is determined by actual scholastic accomplishment and growth. Some public and Catholic school systems have inaugurated nongraded primaries, and a few forward-looking upper elementary and high schools are also nongraded (see Goodlad & Anderson, 1963; Msgr. Hoflich, 1960; Kauth & Brown, 1962).

Sixth, make special curricular provisions for promoting optimum scholastic development of every student. Since only 60 per cent of American youths graduate from high school, a college preparatory curriculum, or even a modification of it, is inappropriate for many high school students. For intellectually slower students, work-study programs could be introduced (E. Murray, 1962). Only curricula meaningful to students here and now can prevent dropouts. In 1962 the Federal government allocated $250,000 to public school systems to encourage dropouts to return to high school. Some school systems used rock 'n' roll songs in an attempt to lure early school leavers back to school, with the songstress belting out lyrics such as "Play it cool and stay in school." But for the most part this crash program proved a failure, chiefly because of the fact that the school program was not geared to handle returning dropouts.

Seventh, provide remedial clinics in such areas as reading, quantitative thinking, and speech. Not only elementary and secondary schools need remedial clinics, but colleges and universities as well. As Centi (1957) has noted, institutions of higher learning, both non-Catholic and Catholic, are becoming less intellectually heterogeneous; remedial clinics and programs become necessary. Reading disabilities, sometimes masked, often lie near the root of scholastic deficiency (Pallone, 1961b). A study by Seegars and Rose (1963) concluded that the student with an average IQ and a high level of verbal understanding is more likely to earn high marks in college than a student with above-average intellectual capacity and poor reading comprehension. Brother Harold Bluhm, S.C. (1961), reported that a developmental reading program is of significance is raising the students' achievement level. Pallone's investigation (1961a) disclosed that among students of average intelligence with reading retardation, thirty-six hours of intensive reading instruction not only raised their reading ability but also had the effect of improving their College Board verbal scores, raising their level of self-confidence, improving their self-concept, and fostering feelings of self-adequacy.

Eighth, encourage scholastic development within the classroom (see Kolesnik, 1963). Scholastic development occurs only when there is freedom to learn and to explore. Teachers are prone to talk about encouraging the open mind, but in reality it is the mind closed firmly like an enraged clam on the textbook or outline book which scores the highest mark in a course. Lecturing, rote memorization, and other activities which invite pupil passivity are inappropriate. A wide variety of teaching devices, such as role playing, cell technique, independent study, team teaching, audiovisual instruction, and field trips, should be utilized. Intelligent, creative, and imaginative teachers must be recruited if scholastic development of students is to take place.

Ninth, provide formal group guidance opportunities, both during homeroom periods and in specially scheduled group periods. The counselor should conduct the latter. A study by Spielberger, Weitz, and Denney (1962) discovered that students with high levels of anxiety who regularly attended group guidance sessions achieved greater success in academic performance than did a matched group of students who did not attend the sessions.

Tenth, provide a counseling service to assist in scholastic development. Unhappily most of the work masquerading as scholastic development counseling is merely advisement, in which the counselor exhorts students to do better in the next marking period. Scholastic development counseling promotes academic growth through the medium of personality growth. As Motto (1959, p. 247) has observed, the development of insight by the client into the personal factors underlying underachievement should be one of the key goals in counseling focused on scholastic development difficulties. Many research investigations have disclosed that directive counseling has a limited effect on the academic performance of students with scholastic development difficulties (see Callis, 1963, pp. 180–181; Klingerhofer, 1954; Searles, 1962). Nor should it be assumed that every teacher is automatically a fit counselor on scholastic development problems merely because he has responsibility for scholastic development in the classroom (see Daubner, 1964, pp. 93–94). In view of the multiplicity of psychosocial disorders which may underlie scholastic difficulties, the counselor working in this sensitive area needs a firm grounding in the dynamics of personality dysfunction, especially as related to the school situation.

16

RELIGIOUS DEVELOPMENT
AS A GUIDANCE FOCUS

The nature of religious development

Religious development is personal growth seen in the deepening of the bond between man and God and between man and the God who is in every man. The primary emphasis in religious guidance is to assist the student as far as possible to grow in grace so that he may give maximum glory to God and in so doing self-actualize. Only by giving glory to God through the medium of fruitful everyday living can an individual self-actualize in the fullest and deepest sense. Because of the divinized context of human life and indeed of the sacramentality of the entire sweep of creation, the religious dimension is intertwined in man's every action, whether he realizes this primal fact or not (Fr. Teilhard de Chardin, S.J., 1960). Hence it is not wholly accurate to speak of religious development as a distinct guidance focus, implying that it is set apart from other foci. Instead, religious development is a focus for personal development, intertwined with other foci. Religious development guidance is sometimes salient, sometimes latent in guidance. It aims primarily at personal development rather than at the solution of religious problems. This is not to say that religious development guidance does not assist in eliminating religiolife difficulties, but instead to emphasize that elimination of these problems is seen within the total context of facilitating positive personal development and religious growth. Religious development as a guidance focus does not transmit religious values but rather assists students to self-organize optimally so that they may be aptly disposed for the reception of grace.

The goal of religious development guidance is to effect a bold transformation in the student's life and development, as Abbé Michonneau (1948, p. 16) has observed. According to von Hildebrand (1948, pp. 1–23), such a transformation must be preceded by a readiness to be transformed. It is here that the cumulative effect of the school's total guidance effort has a major role to play. The school can assist in the religious development of a student only to the degree to which he is ready for assistance. The "bold transformation" can be effected not by teaching the student religious and spiritual principles but only by helping him to fall deeply in love with God. Man needs not only to love God but to be in love with Him. Since human love needs as its object a concrete rather than an abstract reality, his love naturally is directed to Christ, the God made flesh. Only by being in love with God can the student respond to God with his whole being; only then can he attain that spiritual enthusiasm necessary for deep human living. In so loving God, the supreme good, the individual optimally self-actualizes. St. Thomas (*De Veritate,* q. 21, a. 1) has observed that a reality as good perfects another reality according to both its nature and its existence. Since God's nature and existence constitute the plenitude of goodness, the human being is perfected to the degree to which he is in love with God. Commenting on this passage of St. Thomas, Diggs (1947, p. 19) remarked:

> And it is to such goods perfective both according to their natures and existences that love is directed. Love seeks the perfection which the good affords. Love moves to the seizure and possession of goods if they are regarded as goods for the lover, or moves to the transformation of the lover into the loved if the goods are regarded as goods in themselves. In either case it seeks union with the good in order that it may be perfected by the good. For the good being good in virtue both of its nature and its existence can perfect the lover, can give the lover its goodness *only by being joined to the lover in its existence.* Love thus seeks union with the good which it seeks. [See also Aquinas, *Summa Theologica,* I, q. 78, a. 1; *Summa Theologica,* I–II, q. 28, a. 1; *De Veritate,* q. 22, a. 1.]

Guidance for effective religious development is guidance for *today,* for the here and now, for the present concrete existential circumstances in which the student is situated. Religious development guidance which is excessively otherworldly, which is always heaven-bound, does not help the student live fruitfully in this world; if the student does not live fruitfully in this world, he does not attain bliss in the next. As Johann von Goethe remarked, the present is a mighty divinity. Unfortunately many school people look upon education primarily as a preparation for postschool life rather than as comprising life itself. They forget to consider that the best preparation for later life of any sort is self-actualization in the present, in the here and now.

Some educators, particularly Catholic educators, have used the terms *moral development* and *religious development* synonymously. Such a usage is both incorrect and confusing, since moral development constitutes only one aspect of religious development and is not the highest form of guidance for such development, as it is directed usually at fortification against temptation. In its fullness guidance for religious development aims at optimal personal growth through the improvement of the level and pervasiveness of religious experience. A student could be quite moral and yet not have optimally self-actualized the religious dimensions of his personality; e.g., in a Northern city it is not normally immoral for a Catholic student to be silent on *de facto* racial segregation, but if he fought such segregation, he would be developing religiously. Moral "guidance" aims only at the minimum, while religious guidance seeks the maximum in personal fulfillment. Growth in theological virtues and in the life of grace is the goal; the aim is not merely to discourage immorality.

Of capital importance is John Dewey's distinction (1939, p. 1010) between religion and religious. *Religion* "signifies a special body of beliefs and practices having some kind of institutional organization, loose or tight," while *religious* denotes value attitudes "that may be taken toward every object and every proposed end or ideal." For Dewey, all experiences, whether aesthetic, scientific, moral, or political, are intertwined with the religious; indeed religious experiences cannot exist by themselves, apart from a meshing with some other experiences. All men are basically religious, whether or not they adhere to a specific formal religion. Consequently every student, in a public or a church-related school, can improve the quality of his experiences in order to self-actualize optimally. Catholic educators who deny the distinction between religion and religious are at a loss to explain how an atheist who has no religion and may overtly detest all religions can be charitable and even more charitable than, for example, a Catholic who possesses religion. The banners of humanitarian advances (in the ultimate analysis, the banners of Christ) have been carried more vigorously in the last 200 years by nonreligionists than by Catholics. The Catholic explanation for the fact that every person is value-oriented regardless of his religious affiliation or lack of it is that God is present in every man, in every reality, whether that particular man, atheist or religionist, recognizes this presence or not. To equate religious guidance with religion destroys the possibility of a program of religious development guidance in the public schools of a pluralist society.

A host of empirical studies, such as those of Friederichs (1960), Hart-shorne and May (1928), Hightower (1930), Kirkpatrick (1949), Kvaraceus (1944), and Mursell (1930), have found that religionism (membership in a particular religion) has no pivotal relationship with ethical behavior, humanitarianism, altruism, and nondelinquency. A study by Middleton and Putney (1962) of normative standards and behavior patterns of religionist and skeptic (nonreligionist) college students concluded that, first, religionists were more likely to believe in traditional ascetic standards than were skeptics but the two groups did not differ in the degree to which they believed in elements of common social morality; second, religionists and skeptics did not differ in the degree to which they lived up to the norms which they professed; and, third, the two groups reported the same degree of violations of conventional social morality. The study concluded that there was no evidence to support the assumption that sanctions imposed by religion are essential to the preservation of basic social morality.

The present writers do not cite the aforementioned investigations in order to support a thesis of religious relativism but rather to demonstrate that God is so infinite that no one religion or, indeed, all religions combined have a monopoly of His presence. Catholicism possesses the plenitude of God's penetration in the world, but this fact does not negate God's dwelling in the overtly labeled non-Catholic aspects of earthly reality. Indeed Catholic theologians have begun to rethink in an expansionist direction the concepts of God's indwelling in the world and the doctrine of baptism of desire.

The awareness of such pivotal concepts as a merciful God, a realization of the difference between normal guilt and neurotic guilt and between sorrow and guilt, assists the religiously committed guidance worker to deal with troubled students so as to utilize the salvific qualities of religion. Actually, from a therapeutic point of view, the sublimation of one's problems into religion is quite advantageous, even if the religion is objectively false or is merely a mental projection of the client.

Religious development guidance regards a student's religiolife problems not so much as difficulties in themselves but as obstacles impeding the full development of the pervasive religious dimension of personal growth. Every religious problem is not an atomistic difficulty nor one which admits of a facile or even a simplistic solution. For example, a priest-psychologist told of a fellow cleric who was appointed chaplain of a girl's summer camp. Whenever a girl brought a religious problem to him, the cleric summoned his pocket edition of the *Summa Theologica* to show that St. Thomas not only provided the answer to her problem but had in fact anticipated her very difficulty nearly 700 years ago. Religious problems arise not only from holding false values but from possessing correct values and right knowledge yet failing to implement both in one's daily life.

Because of the particular sensitivity of the whole realm of religious development, the counselor or adviser, even a directivist, should avoid prying into this area unless the student expressly invites him to do so. Unfortunately this is not always realized, as witness the statement of one priest–guidance director (Fr. Saalfield, 1958, p. 80) :

> The priest or religious who is counseling an adolescent will be intensely concerned with the religious development of the counsellee. . . . A counseling session should never be completed without some discussion of spiritual affairs, or some encouragement of a finer religious life, or some indication about the pre-eminent importance of this phase of student growth. . . . As a result of discussion and by arrangement of the counsellee, provision should be made to supply any lack in the fundamentals of spiritual development. This work should take priority over all other work. . . . The Catholic counselor should ask the pupil "How often do you go to Mass and confession?" Catholic counselors must create right attitudes.

Perhaps the three most flagrant faults in this passage are the following: (1) Many counseling sessions would be entirely useless in terms of the benefit to the client if strictly spiritual affairs were dragged by the heels into the interview. (2) Overtly spiritual affairs in many instances cannot take priority, since the difficulty manifested by a particular student at a certain time may, in terms of furthering optimum growth, call for other then manifest religious development guidance. Indeed, all guidance is religious guidance in the sense that personal self-actualization is *in itself* religious development. (3) No counselor, whether priest, religious, or layman, has the right to delve into a student's spiritual life by asking on his own initiative such personal questions as whether or not the student attends Mass; to be sure, such counselor indiscretion will doubtless serve only to intensify a student's religious problem, should he even have one.

There is a tendency among Catholic guidance workers to regard religion as a panacea for all problems, for all failures to self-actualize optimally. Such an overly pietistic view tends to disregard the fact that while man was made for God and not God for man, nevertheless religion was created for man and not man for religion. The introduction of religious considerations into the interview might seriously hinder or obstruct the client from self-actualizing or solving a problem; e.g., a client whose obsessive-compulsive tendencies have caused problems with religious scrupulosity should not be reminded of his obligation to strive for spiritual perfection.

Man is not only *homo sapiens* but also *homo credens*. Because he is a believing animal, every person has within his very personality structure the "need" to believe. Jacob's study (1957) of youth in non-Catholic colleges reported that nearly 80 per cent stated they personally felt a need to believe in some religious faith or philosophy. Case histories given by Ostow and

Scharfstein (1954) indicate that disavowal of religion or formal worship does not cancel a person's need to believe in basic values. Certainly education and guidance for life in this world only are not even education and guidance for life in this world.

Religious development guidance in public schools

From both a constitutional and a professional viewpoint, is religious guidance permissible or desirable in a public school setting? Some groups such as the Protestants and Other Americans United for the Separation of Church and State (POAU) would doubtless contend that such activities have no place in an American public school and must constitutionally be left to the home and church. From a professional point of view, however, guidance workers in a public school of necessity deal with religious values since such values are a part of the student's personality and are often embedded deeply in his developmental process. Particularly in the counseling interview is appropriate consideration of a client's religious values important. If counseling is to explore *all* the client's feelings relevant to his self-actualization, then it is difficult to imagine how religion can be excluded from the counseling encounter. Since many of a client's difficulties in attaining optimal personal development are connected with values, his total value orientation (which usually includes religious values) must be considered. Certainly if the student introduces religious considerations or overtly religious problems into the interview, the counselor is obliged to consider them. As one non-Catholic psychotherapist (Meehl, 1959, p. 255) has noted, religious material in this sense is like any other material which comes up during the course of an interview.

Segal has observed that the counselor must do nothing to impede the client from honestly looking at his own developmental pattern; to the extent that a client's values help or hinder optimal self-actualization, to that extent should values be considered in the interview. Segal (1959) underscores the capital point that the counselor's personal religious convictions and indeed his attitude toward religion must not interfere with a client's self-actualizing. For example, if a student explains that he is having guilt feelings about masturbation, attributing such feelings to conflicts between physiopsychological needs and his Roman Catholic religion, an atheist counselor should not seize this opportunity to show the client how religious beliefs are impeding normal needs. Rather the counselor should assist the student to discover whether more is involved than the client's surface explanation, e.g., masturbation as a method of releasing tension caused by fear of the opposite sex or by scholastic underachievement, which he has rationalized by casting blame for his tension on religious prohibitions. C. R. Rogers (1958) has noted that the counselor must permit the client to be what he is, to receive the client unconditionally as he is. To accept the client in all but his religious dimension, to exclude religious concerns from the counseling interview, is to accept him conditionally. But by the same token total acceptance demands that the counselor assist the client exclusively on the client's own terms and not treat him as an object upon whom to unleash the force of the counselor's missionary zeal, however laudable this may be in itself. The counselor's chair is not a pulpit. The religiously committed counselor should under no circumstances violate the integrity or God-given freedom of his client by overtly or covertly insisting that he accept or otherwise incorporate into his ego structure religious beliefs or even belief in religion. Rather, as K. W. Mann (1959, p. 262) has pointed out, the professional and indeed more effective course is to help the client become aware of the availability of religious beliefs for possible incorporation into his self-system as he sees fit. While the counselor cannot ethically attempt to change his client's religiovalue structure, he can legitimately assist him to become aware of veerings inside this structure, incongruities which may be causing difficulty since they are operating at cross-purposes within the context of the structure.

Psychologically, the counselor's religiovalue orientation *de facto* influences his client. A deep value commitment of any kind affects one's entire being and makes an outward thrust no matter how hard a person attempts to hide it. Gestures, voice intonations, in fact, the very way the counselor has organized his personality, all those ooze his value orientation. For example, if a Christian client tells an agnostic counselor that the devil is causing his problem by means of temptation to sin, the counselor will not believe this causal explanation but will instead encourage the client to investigate some psychological factor which the counselor believes is the real cause. Like counselors, clients listen to reality with a third ear. The phenomena of identification and transference occur in the counseling relationship (Schrier, 1953). Such identification is not necessarily harmful to the client's progress in self-actualizing, for as Chapter 3 indicated, clients' problems tend to lessen as their values become more congruent with those of the counselor. Because of this very fact, however, the counselor must be particularly careful not to impose his own religiovalue system subtly on the client by unconsciously inducing him to believe that the counselor's insights, proposed solution, or indeed his very religiovalue orientation is most appropriate for the client.

Thus far, mention has been made only of Christian clients and non-Christian counselors. The same considerations apply with additional force to Christian counselors dealing with non-Christian clients or simply to Catholic counselors dealing with Catholic *or* non-Catholic clients. The history of Catholicism is largely the history of proselytizing, and it is likely that every Catholic has been imbued to some extent with missionary zeal. Certainly the counseling room is *not* the place to win converts from among either non-Christian or non-Catholic Christian students. It is often difficult for Catholics to be as objective relative to their own subtly persuasive efforts as they are vigilant to proselytizing by others. For example, a non-Catholic may reveal to a Catholic counselor intense guilt feelings about dancing and smoking, which the client's religion forbids. The Catholic counselor of integrity does not seize this opportunity to launch an offensive to win a soul for Christ; his moral obligation in counseling is to the client, not to his own crown in heaven.

Church authorities attempt to supplement religious guidance in the public school by religious activities clubs. Catholic students are urged to join Newman clubs, Jewish students Hillel clubs, and Protestant students religious clubs geared either along demoninational lines or on the broad orientation of Protestantism. While such clubs serve some religious needs, they do not generally enroll in active membership anything near a bare minimum of students. Since most students professing a religion attend public or non-denominational private schools, leaders of the respective churches might give more attention to this important phase of the pastoral ministry. Nor can Catholic church leaders be apathetic in this regard. For example, it is reliably estimated (J. A. O'Brien, 1961) that by 1990 about 90 per cent of all Catholic students in higher education will be enrolled in non-Catholic colleges. Happily some alert Catholic churchmen (Fr. R.. Butler, O.P., 1963; Fr. Haas, O.P., 1964) are striving to make the Newman Club apostolate more pulsating and meaningful in the lives of Catholic students in non-Catholic schools.

Religious development guidance in Catholic schools

The fullness of religious guidance occurs only in a church-related school. A formal religious program comprising a host of developed, coordinated activities and services is one of the prime reasons why Catholic ecclesiastical leaders established the Catholic school system in America. Yet, as study after study reveals, the religious development program in Catholic schools is quite weak.

Canon 682 of the Code of Canon Law states that lay persons have the right to receive from the clergy, in accordance with the provisions of ecclesiastical law, spiritual benefits, especially the necessary means for salvation. As two canon lawyers, Msgr. Abbo and Bishop Hannan (1952, p. 689), observe, this canon "thus definitely states that in the Church the laity do not exist for the benefit of the clergy, but rather the contrary." Fr. Woywod, O.F.M. (1957, p. 341), another canon lawyer, notes that corresponding to the right of the layman under Canon 682 there is an *obligation* on the part of the clergy to make available to the laity spiritual benefits. The term *spiritual benefits* used in Canon 689 includes "the sacramentals, Christian doctrine, indulgences, blessings, dispensations, remembrance in prayer, and the performance of liturgical functions" (Abbo & Hannan, 1952, p. 689). By extension an adequate religious development program in Catholic schools is an obligation of the clergy under the provision of Canon 682, whether or not clergy conduct the school.

Why, in the light of canonical, theological, and existential obligations to provide students with a vigorous program of religious development, are Catholic schools remiss in this regard? Perhaps one answer can be found in the fact that Catholic school people seem to regard religious development as automatic if an institution is under Catholic auspices. A Catholic school atmosphere is certainly conducive to religious development, but there is a vast difference between such an atmosphere and the provision of actual services. For all their religious atmosphere, Catholic schools have not demonstrably proved themselves as producing more fervent Catholics than have non-Catholic institutions of learning. A summary of pertinent research by Brother Edward L. Cashin, F.M.S. (1963), revealed no appreciable differences in standards of conduct between Catholics who graduated from Catholic high schools and Catholics who graduated from non-Catholic high schools. A study by Fr. Morocco (1957) showed that only 62 per cent of students in Catholic secondary schools chose as their primary personal ideal a religious personage. It is interesting that the most frequently mentioned names were Bishop Fulton Sheen and the Blessed Virgin Mary—Christ was named by only nine students. An investigation by Mother Marie Edmund Harvey, R.S.H.M. (1954, pp. 46–49), concluded that in Catholic women's colleges there was no significant change in the religious attitude of students from freshman to senior year. These studies seem to lend support to the contention that a religious atmosphere by itself is not enough.

Father Dunne, S.J. (1961), has noted that Catholic colleges and universities increasingly "shy away" from discussing, much less emphasizing, their religious nature. Deferrari (1963, p. 273) has stated: "Entirely too many Catholics, including Catholics who should know better, believe that a college becomes Catholic in the best sense through its chapel, religious exercises, and general Catholic atmosphere." He notes that little thought is given to integrating religious development into classroom teaching.

The promotion of religious activities, a basic part of the Catholic school's religious development program, seems quite weak. Investigations of Catholic women's and men's colleges made respectively by McMurray (1958, pp. 130–140) and Brother John J. Jansen, S.M. (1955, pp. 194–203), found that these institutions frequently neglected to provide for renewal and intensification of the spiritual life of their students. For the majority of Catholic women's colleges, Mass was the only scheduled religious activity of the orientation program; only 28 per cent of these colleges reported a daily opportunity for students to confess. Less than half of the Catholic women's and men's colleges provided suggested spiritual reading. In both women's and men's colleges religious development guidance practices tended to be of a group nature rather than the ideal of personal counseling. Findings such as these indicate that Catholic schools must begin to inaugurate a pervasive, continuing, and comprehensive program of religious activities services. Is the school chaplain precisely that, the chaplain, or is he a priest whose primary duty is teaching and who is a chaplain "on the side"?

Correlative to religious development, and indeed one of its suppositions, is a vigorous and effective program of religious instruction. As Allers (1940, p. 147) has noted, God-oriented behavior depends not only on the willingness of a person to do the good but also on his knowledge of what is good. There is considerable evidence that Catholic schools are not effective in assisting students to acquire either a deep knowledge of the truths of religion or the ramification of these truths in everyday life. A study of Catholic high school pupils by Fr. J. A. Francis, S.V.D. (1962), revealed that students performed quite poorly on a test appraising knowledge of the sacraments. Diaz's study (1952) of a matched group of Catholic students in Catholic and in public high schools showed no differences in ability to apply selected principles of moral law to actual and hypothetical life situations. Indeed religious training and religious education had no significant effect on the performance of these students; the only significant variable was intelligence. Callahan's review (1963, p. 156) of research concluded that "the Catholic educational system has by no means decisively proved its value in producing stronger, better-informed or more effective Catholics. . . . Instead, it is apparent that when compared with the Catholic graduates of public and secular colleges, it is difficult to find any significant evidence that the graduates of Catholic institutions are notably stronger or more faithful or more apostolic Catholics." This research evidence indicates that Sheed's pointed question (1952) is as pertinent now as it was originally: Are Catholic schools *really* teaching religion? How alive are they to the kerygmatic approach to teaching religion? With what frequency do these schools utilize diverse pedagogical methods? How often do they carry out curricular innovations or experiments designed to ascertain whether there may be superior structural procedures for effective teaching of religion? Is all religion learning factual or cognitive? Does the school consciously and overtly set up learning situations which offer opportunities for the student to act charitably, to express consideration for others, to exhibit selflessness? A program of religious development cannot hope to be effective without the support of a satisfactory and indeed a vigorous program of religious instruction.

One of the key tasks of the religious development program is to assist the student attain a rich spiritual life so that he may deeply Christianize both himself and his environment. But the religious development guidance in most Catholic schools does not significantly help the student do either. A sociological study by Fr. Fichter, S.J. (1954, p. 22), revealed that in an American parish identified as typical only 6 per cent of the congregation were "nuclear" Catholics. A nuclear Catholic was described as one who not only makes the annual Easter duty and attends Sunday Mass but who also receives Holy Communion weekly or oftener and participates to some degree in parish organizations or functions. How well are products of Catholic schools Christianizing their milieus? A key difficulty in this regard is that Catholic schools are often run not as schools but as ivory towers, unrelated to the very environment which the students are to Christianize. Fr. Stanton, S.J. (1962, p. 434), has observed that students in Catholic schools are carefully taught to ". . . know the books they should not read, the movies they should not see, the TV ads and shows they find offensive, the magazines they want removed from drug stores, and the Communists they want to see deported or imprisoned." He continued: "How many of our young high-school and college graduates envision taking positions where they radically affect the very structure of society," impregnating it with the spirit and the work of Christ? Fr. Twomey, S.J. (1961, p. 8), has noted that alumni of Catholic schools are "ill-equipped to fill the role of the Catholic layman as outlined by Pius X." How many laymen integrate Christianity into all areas of their lives? How many Catholic school administrators view as successful products of their institutions graduates who contribute to the alumni fund? A distinguished English Catholic (St. John-Stevas, 1963) who visited the United States in the early 1960s was able to remark: "Never has a branch of Catholicism so rich in numbers and material resources made a smaller contribution to the world of ideas than the Church in America." Catholic schools have failed to develop scholars who have made an impact on the American cultural and intellectual scene. Do Catholic schools, particularly if they are of the socially "exclusive" variety, base their programs on vibrantly Catholic principles or upon the bourgeois ethic? Certainly Catholic schools should primarily turn out better and more dynamic Catholics, not graduates with a middle-class mentality.

One area in which the failure of Catholic schools to provide an effective and penetrating program of religious development yields to relatively simple empirical research data is that of racial discrimination and ethnic prejudice. A vibrant religious development program would significantly raise the religious ideals, attitudes, and actions of students and graduates above the observance of elementary laws of the Church. If the instructional and guidance programs in the Catholic school were effective, its students should have a higher social morality and consciousness than the students in a non-Catholic school. Yet study after study points to the fact that products of Catholic schools share the same racial and ethnic prejudices as non-Catholics from non-Catholic schools. As Fr. Fichter, S.J. (1960, p. 124), has remarked, "Catholics share in the anti-Semitism of the Northeast, in the isolationism of the Midwest, in the prejudices against the Mexican in the Southwest." Nor have Catholic school instructional and guidance programs improved this situation over the years. A 1945 investigation by Fr. Morrison, O.S.B. (1946), revealed that in Southern Catholic schools the learning experiences available did not significantly affect or change racial prejudices of Catholic students. Thus 75 per cent of the Catholic high school students believed in the maintenance of social barriers between whites and Negroes, only 15 per cent believed that Negroes were equal to whites in intelligence, and 4 per cent regarded Negroes as little better than animals. A careful investigation by Fr. Fichter, S.J. (1951, pp. 265–266), of a typical Southern parish concluded that only 12 per cent of Catholic respondents favored a racially integrated parish. In 1962 Lawler (1962, p. 595) was able to remark that "recent surveys have indicated that students in Catholic schools in the South have much the same attitude as other [non-Catholic] students" in non-Catholic schools. Brother Edward L. Cashin, F.M.S. (1963), concluded that in matters involving social justice awareness public school graduates have shown themselves more alert and sensitive than have products of Catholic schools. Perhaps those clergy and religious responsible for the administrative leadership of the instructional and guidance programs in Catholic schools are remiss in this entire matter. Loretta M. Butler's study (1963) of one Southern diocese concluded that efforts of clergy and religious to educate Negro Catholics have been too little and too late. Fr. Schuyler, S.J. (1962, p. 441), has stated that "religion has supplied *relatively* little force to the movements for social reform." It is one of the tasks of a church-related school to assist every student to become aware of the social justice dimension of religion so that he can effectively transform his milieu in a totally Christ-oriented direction.

This section has underscored the fact that religious development programs in Catholic institutions are quite weak, scattered, ineffective, and nonpervasive. The situation is not, however, completely bleak.

Yet in many cases positive accomplishments are not without qualifications. A study by Msgr. Novicky (1959) of matched (including religiously matched) students concluded that Catholic school students possessed more fraternal charity than public school students possessed, as measured by the Fraternal Charity Index developed by the investigator. The greatest differences were found at the twelfth-grade level. Unfortunately this was a conceptual assessment of the pupils' fraternal charity, rather than an operational evaluation of how charitable they were in their everyday lives. Catholics have been known to talk more loftily than any other group about fraternal charity and yet to practice it less. Fr. G. B. Barrett, S.M. (1958), conducted an investigation of Catholic high school boys who were offered four choices on each of 80 questions. Each choice represented one of four identified ideals, viz., religious value, altruistic value, self-interest value, and social approval value. The religious value items accounted for 32 per cent of the selections; the altruistic, for 23 per cent; the self-interest, for 29 per cent; and the social approval, for 16 per cent. No comparison was made with Catholic students in Catholic and public high schools so as to ascertain the effectiveness of the Catholic school program. A study by Sister M. Eugenia Ziegler,

C.S.A.C. (1958, p. 308), of the values of Catholic adolescent girls attending a Catholic girls' academy and a central diocesan high school revealed that in both cases the students' two highest values, as measured by the Allport-Vernon Study of Values, were religious and social. But studies such as those of Burgmeister (1940, p. 15) have demonstrated that women in general have these two ideals as their highest values.

McMurray's study (1958, p. 139) found that in Catholic women's colleges there is an increasing trend away from obligatory attendance at such spiritual exercises as May devotions, Benediction, and night prayers. This trend represents a maturing view that the function of a religious development program is not to command or require the student but to assist her to see for herself the important place which religion and religious exercises play in the total process of her optimal self-actualization.

If Catholic schools are committed, at least verbally, to a strong program of religious development, why is it that their programs are relatively weak and ineffectual? There are at least two prominent reasons. First, Catholic schools are run more generally as shelters than as educational institutions which have as their goal the development within the student of truth, whole and entire. All too often Catholic school authorities view the primary goal of the institution as preventing students from succumbing to moral (almost always interpreted as sexual) temptation and keeping them away from experiences which could lead to questioning or doubting the Faith. Forrest's study (1960) of National Merit Scholarship winners who withdrew from church-related colleges to enter secular campuses reported as typical comments of the transferring students: "The college administration assumes a degree of immaturity which I can't bring myself to concede," and "I've come to think college should be a place where you learn to take the responsibility of making your own decisions. Here well-meaning clerics want to solve every problem for me." Of interest is the fact that nearly three times as many National Merit Scholarship winners withdrew from church-related colleges to go to secular campuses as transferred in the other direction. In an effort to prevent students from yielding to temptation of every sort, the Catholic school tends not only to insulate them from life and its hurly-burly but also to coddle and spoon-feed them. As Bishop Gerald E. Carter (1959, pp. 25–40) has observed, in far too many Catholic schools students are not permitted to fail in life situations. Indeed there is implicit in the operation of these schools the suggestion that students are denied the right to fail not only because the priest or religious thinks that by sheltering them he or she is thereby automatically promoting virtue but also because the priest or religious is more interested in the "virtuous" performance of his or her own duties than in the total mature development of those students under his or her charge.

A second reason for the relative weakness and ineffectuality of guidance programs is that, in more than 90 per cent of the cases, priests and religious are the school's counselors. Religious and even diocesan priests to a large extent were trained to renounce the world and must live in the world in a state of perpetual renunciation. Such a total commitment to renunciation cannot prove optimally effective in guidance work with students who as lay-men must seek perfection by embracing that world which the religious has renounced. Many priests and religious have never attended an educational institution in which there was a well-developed guidance program. Studies of personnel services in Catholic men's and women's colleges by Jansen (1955) and McMurray (1958) came to a similar conclusion concerning the attitude of priests and religious toward the guidance program in a Catholic school.

> The training in the novitiate, scholasticate, or seminary of a particular group of religious teachers can, and sometimes does, militate against the development of an adequate personnel point of view in the organization and administration of personnel services. . . . [Catholic] colleges in which the [religious] administration and teachers have had little or no training in counseling, guidance, and psychology are apt to ignore important psychological methods of assisting students to develop com-plete personalities. In some cases personnel services were superimposed upon the academic structure of the college with teachers and administra-tors assuming additional responsibility for personnel services because the accrediting agencies required the availability of a minimum number of personnel services (McMurray, 1958, p. 28).

The concept of religion

The form and thrust of a Catholic school's program of religious develop-ment are largely shaped by the concept of religion held by its administrators and faculty. Fr. Tanquerey, S.S. (1937, pp. 67, 69), makes a distinction between religion objectively and subjectively considered. Objectively consid-ered, "religion is the totality of truths and obligations by which a person's entire life is ordered to God as his final end." Subjectively considered, it is a person's "voluntary inclination and indeed virtue by which through both acceptance of suitable truths and fulfillment of appropriate precepts he pays to God due worship and respect." Many intelligent modern thinkers deny God and religion. Feigl (1953, pp. 8–18), integrating Auguste Comte's posi-tivistic theory with the position of scientific humanists, lumps theology with magic, animism, mythology as remnants of and regressions to prescientific thought patterns. Jung (1952, p. 134) remarked that "the alleged colloquy with the divine is only a soliloquy." The Catholic concept of religion is that of an intelligible teleological lifeway which pervades every thought and action of the person who embraces it. The goal of religion is not blind observance or the exercise of formal ritualism but an assistance by which man lives in the most fruitful manner possible and thus glorifies God. Catholicism contains a certain small core of doctrines which has remained unchanged and a large outer layer of customs and teachings intended to make this inner nucleus relevant for living in a particular society and time. The tendency is to equate the outer nonessential and adaptable layer with the inner fundamental kernel, so that Catholicism loses its temporal and situational universality and becomes rigidly fixed to a particular time and to a particular place. With the impetus provided by the Second Vatican Council, many encrusted outer-layer patterns of Catholic thought, behavior, and feelings are no longer stoutly defended within Church circles but instead are being eliminated. Forward-looking Catholic educators no longer attempt to promote religious observance by instilling a fear of God's wrath. The emphasis is now upon love of God in Himself and in His creatures. Intelligent Catholics have abandoned the idea of equating the millennium with a return to medieval life and have stopped thinking the thirteenth the greatest of all centuries. The millenium is now, and the greatest of all centuries was the first. Priests like Fr. Küng (1962) and Fr. Lepp (1962) maintain the "natural law" is very vague and slippery to discern; they stress instead re-emphasis of Scripture as the wellspring of Christian commitment. Notwithstanding these advances in Catholic thought and attitude, many or even most Catholics cling to outmoded ideas concerning religion. One of the most influential and destructive of these decadent beliefs is Jansenism (E. W. Lehman, 1959, p. 84).

If by creation all things participate in God, they do so all the more because of the Incarnation and the Redemption. Jansenistic overstress of original sin and its consequences has resulted in a neglect of these two pivotal mysteries. Cardinal Suhard (1950) contends there is nothing which escapes the Redemption, there is no reality not washed in its blood. Fr. Teilhard de Chardin, S.J., dedicated his spiritual classic, *The Divine Milieu* (1960), thus: "For those who love the world." All creation is a hymn of praise to its Creator, Who dwells within it. Religious development should lead each student to make his own life a love song to all reality.

There are four basic attitudes contemporary Catholics have toward the world. Some view the world primarily as an object of ascetic exercises, an evil to be avoided. Others perceive it as of no spiritual importance in itself but useful only for purposes of ecclesiastical propaganda. Still others hold that the world is spiritually irrelevant, that fulfillment as a human being is only accidentally related to man's religious destiny. These attitudes are among the first fruits of Jansenism. The fourth attitude, that of love for the world, authentically characterizes the authentic Christian. Pope Paul VI (1963b) stated: "We shall not forget the fundamental attitude of those who want to convert the world is loving it."

Partly as a result of Jansenistic influence, Catholics are prone to attempt to go to God by means of otherworldly actions; they either neglect mankind's welfare or actually oppose it in the name of going more swiftly to God (Lee, 1962). In this connection A. C. Riccio's study (1962b) confirms similar investigations. His study of responses to the Ten Commandments by Catholic, Protestant, Jewish, and religiously nonaffiliated students revealed that Catholics placed greater emphasis on the man-to-God commandments, while all other groups placed greater emphasis on the man-to-man commandments. This emphasis is correct when it is coupled with an emphasis on man-to-man relationships. It is one of the tasks of the Catholic school's religious development program to assist students toward the realization that the swiftest way to God is by charity to one's neighbor, to become aware that charity does not consist merely in wishing him well. Generally the most effective way to become a saint is to become a better "natural man."

The concept of the Church

One of the prime goals of religious development in Catholic schools is so to assist the student that he self-actualizes by means of full and active membership in the Church. For such self-actualization he needs an accurate concept of the Church. It is not a far-off entity, something to be regarded as "other"; rather, as Pope Pius XII remarked to the Second World Congress of the Lay Apostolate, every Catholic, lay and religious, *is* the Church. The Church lives *through* its members, not separated and apart from them.

The mistaken notion of the Church as an entity apart from its members has led many Catholic educators to develop the notion of the Church as a cold, impersonal, and perfect entity. This notion should be replaced with the more accurate concept of a warm, tender, living organism which can and indeed has made mistakes. As Fr. Küng (1962, pp. 56–57) has observed, the Church is at once spotless and spotted. Pope Paul VI (1963a, p. 1) has remarked: "The Church also recites the *Confiteor.*" Fr. Karl Rahner, S.J. (1948, p. 15), has written: "The Church is a sinful Church: that is a truth of faith, not just a fact of her primitive experience. And it is a shattering truth." To credit the Church's positive accomplishments to the eternal Church and its misdeeds to churchmen is obviously simplistic. Msgr. Cuardini (1952, p. 150) observed that Christ is always with His Church, because who can separate Christ from His cross? Catholic educators should not be reluctant when students become aware of the dark side of the Church. Youths can warm to the Church as a human as well as a Divine reality far more than to a Church perceived as a cold, impersonal force.

Lay spirituality

For the Catholic school's program of religious development significantly to assist the pupil to self-actualize spiritually and personally, it must be geared to him in his present existential situation. Since Catholic school students are lay persons, religious development guidance must be centered on this pivotal fact. Most of contemporary Catholic spirituality originated in the medieval monasteries, geared to the spiritual growth of a monk in a monastic setting. What is needed today is a new spirituality for the layman, to help him glorify God and sanctify himself because of his lay state, not despite it, because he lives in the world, not despite that fact. In the absence of a developed theology and spirituality of the layman, each Catholic school must endeavor to produce a lay-oriented spirituality appropriate for the religious growth of students. For the lay student living in a world characterized by temporality, the Catholic school must develop the awareness that Catholicism is pertinent to his here-and-now concrete situation.

Catholic schools should strive to assist the student fulfill that tremendous thrust for idealistic living and self-sacrifice characteristic of the developmental dynamics of youth. One study (Sister M. de L. McMahon, 1955, p. 385) of Catholic high school girls showed that the desire to lead a more nearly perfect life is more active in youth than is commonly believed. Catholic youths wish to give of themselves for the love of Christ as He is in Himself and in His creatures; guidance should assist them to self-actualize in this dimension. These young persons agree wholeheartedly with Peter Maurin (1961): "We can only imitate the sacrifice on Calvary by trying to give all we can."

Pope Pius XII noted that the consecration of the world is in its essence the task of laymen, who are intimately involved in economic and social life and who participate in government policy making. Thus active participation in the apostolate is the duty of every Christian layman as well as of every priest and religious. Many Catholic school persons fail to grasp this pivotal point; many discourage apostolically minded students from fruitful work in the apostolate by conveying the impression that lay apostles are almost exclusively minions of the clergy and religious. One Catholic religious school person (Sister M. Leonella, 1963, p. 10) believes that the student council in a Catholic elementary school best exercises its apostolate by learning the name of the local bishop, praying for vocations to the religious and clerical life, and interviewing missionaries. No mention is made of lay missionary activities, participation in Catholic Action, or the ideal of the lay apostolate as a total commitment.

Religious development must take into account papal statements of the twentieth century which delineate the apostolate of the layman as an independent lifeway, related to and extended from the apostolate of the bishop. Religious guidance in Catholic schools must be geared not to prospective priests and religious but to intelligent laymen of tomorrow's world. Catholic Action groups should be established in every Catholic school. The classic definition of Catholic Action given by Pope Pius XI is "the participation of the laity in the apostolate of the hierarchy." Catholic Action is a concrete proper term defining a specific organization; it is not a synonym for any religiously related activity carried on by Catholics or of writing to congressmen petitioning for Federal funds for Catholic schools. Because Catholic Action is a participation in the mission and graces of the hierarchy by means of an official episcopal mandate, it is higher than and different from Catholic activities. Catholic Action is the highest form of apostolic activity in which a layman can engage. The Young Christian Students and the Grail are examples of groups specializing in student Catholic Action. Fathers Bouscaren, S.J., and Ellis, S.J (1951, p. 216), two prominent canon lawyers, state that "according to repeated declarations of His Holiness, Pius XI, the energetic promotion of Catholic Action is one of the duties of pastors" under canon law. Catholic schools seem to be remiss in this regard. Donnellon's investigation (1954) revealed that despite repeated papal pronouncements and exhortations on Catholic Action, most deans in Catholic men's colleges had no accurate concept of the nature of Catholic Action; moreover, they listed as Catholic Action any religiously related activity in which students participated, ranging from a Pan-American club to a dramatic club. Only 16 per cent of schools surveyed had a Young Christian Student (YCS) section.

The Catholic school should help develop the awareness that adequate lay spirituality is characterized by both an active interior life and a vibrant exterior life. In this regard the lay Catholic seeking perfection would do well to imitate Pope John XXIII, who, as Pope Paul VI tellingly stated, "personified and expressed that essential mark of the Church in releasing its latent energies in a double direction, interior and exterior." To lead a vibrant Catholic life in the world is to be neither a recluse nor an activist but a happy balance between both. Youths have a tendency to become victims of what Dom Chautard (1945) has termed "the heresy of activism," i.e., the performance of a host of externals without taking commensurate time to nourish them by a developed internal life. Indeed, for some the orientation to external activity may well be a means of flight from confrontation with their inner selves.

A program of religious development is incomplete if it neglects to cultivate the proper spirit of asceticism. Paramount in Christianity is the doctrine of the cross. While the cross is unchanging in its nature, it is ever changing in its existential dimension. That is to say, everyone must always help Christ carry His cross but in the manner appropriate to his own concrete sociotemporal condition. Catholic schools should not seek to develop within students a type of asceticism based on bygone days when wealth and good times were regarded as evil or at least as not the path to perfection (perhaps as an unconscious projected rationalization or reaction formation). Asceticism must be consonant with the times. An asceticism not delicately poised and carefully balanced can easily lead to sadomasochism. The greatest mortifications a layman may be called on to practice are commonly charity and justice toward his neighbor, and these constitute asceticism in the finest sense of the term. Those who by their concrete condition are called to more intense suffering must be mindful that martyrdom is of a slow and unspectacular type but is indeed a grace. The theology of spiritual victimhood might be suited to the psychodynamic needs of some students.

The purpose of religious development is to help the student grow into a vibrant, virile Catholic. Unfortunately piety is often substituted for wholesome holiness so that the "model" products of Catholic schools are more likely "holy Joes" than vigorous saints. But as Pascal (1908, p. 136) wrote, "experience makes us see an enormous difference between piety and goodness." Red-blooded students strive toward saintliness but are repelled by "holy Joeism." Fr. Koob, O. Praem (1963, p. 1), of the Secondary School Department of the NCEA, has remarked that Catholic schools are confusing "a certain pietistic holiness with honest-to-goodness teaching of Christianity" and that many Catholic teachers are "rushing madly into the Victorian era." The plaster-art statues of saints in the corridors of many Catholic schools operate at cross-purposes with a vigorous religious development program; so also do hymns of the saccharine variety commonly sung at religious devotions. Such overpietism serves to repel the normal child and youth from developing religiously. Thus James Baldwin (1963, p. 19), the celebrated American Negro writer, could state: "Every artist is fundamentally religious. But I haven't been to Church in twenty years. . . . I was raised in the Church but I have abandoned Christianity as an organized religion. The Church is the worst place to learn about Christianity. I have rejected it because the Christians have rejected Christianity. It is too pious, too hypocritical."

The school chaplain, the priest-counselor, and the school priest

The *school chaplain* in a Catholic school is the priest officially attached to the educational institution and charged with chief responsibility for the religious development of the students and faculty. He is distinct from the priest-counselor and the school priest. The *priest-counselor* is that clergyman engaged in part- or full-time work in the school interviewing students to assist them self-actualize their religious dimension. The *school priest* is a clergyman whose main responsibility is to an agency other than the school but who performs certain functions in connection with the school's program of religious activities or religious development, e.g., a parish priest who comes to the school on Thursday afternoons to hear the students' confessions.

There are 10 basic functions which a school chaplain performs if he minimally fulfills his role: (1) He assumes responsibility for the school's program of religious development and religious activities. (2) He integrates the programs of religious counseling, religious development, and religious activities with the total school program. (3) He coordinates the religious development program with the religious activities program. (4) He counsels students on religious concerns or problems related to religious development. (5) He encourages participation by every student in the broad range of experiences available through the school's religious activities program. (6) He directs, implements, and improves the quality and quantity of the religious activities program; e.g., he inaugurates a Young Christian Student section. (7) He leads the school's program of religious services in a manner meaningful to each student. (8) He institutes new religious services helpful to students in their religious development; e.g., he starts evening Masses in resident schools. (9) He engages in the pastoral ministry in the school milieu. (10) He initiate or improves cooperation between school and non-school religious agencies, particularly the nearby parish.

The unique nature of the chaplain's role as religious leader demands that he be a resource person totally at the disposal of the students. In this sense the term *minister* is quite accurate. The priesthood is not a commanding function but a ministerial one; it is a service profession. The successful chaplain exercises his ministry with students, not on them. In so doing he spares no effort to serve the flock committed to his care. What de Hueck (1950, p. 41) wrote to seminarians can apply with equal relevance to the chaplain in his school apostolate: "Surely Christ Crucified is worth more than the minimum. Or is He?"

The chaplaincy is a distinct form of the priestly ministry; hence for its fruitful exercise it demands special preparation and training. It cannot be assumed that a priest successful in parochial life will also be maximally effective in the school setting. Coordination of religious development and religious activities necessitates that he be well grounded in education; counseling with students demands that he have a knowledge of psychology, guidance, and counseling; leading group discussions and seminars on religious affairs requires that he know the principles and methods of group dynamics and effective teaching. Only priests trained in these areas should be assigned as school chaplains. Such a situation calls for career chaplains, priests who spend their lives as school chaplains. The current practice of sending any priest to fill the post of chaplain, with ordination as his only special training, is professionally unsound from almost any standpoint. This situation is compounded by the fact that most chaplains are full-time religion teachers. Such a dual role often prevents the chaplain from projecting that totally nonpunitive image necessary for free and open counseling on serious religious concerns. From the point of view both of role conflict and of total absorption in one task, the school chaplain should be a full-time chaplain, with no teaching duties.

The role of chaplain is more in keeping with the priestly ministry, objectively and subjectively considered, than is classroom teaching of mathematics,

Latin, history, and so forth or administering a school. A study of Fr. Fichter, S.J. (1962), concluded that the role which priests prefer is that of spiritual father, confessor, and counselor. Yet despite this preference and the fact that the uniqueness of the priesthood can only be exercised through sacramental and sacerdotal functions, many priests spend a disproportionate amount of time in classroom teaching or in school administration, so that the priesthood becomes a sideline occupation. They might be said to be "moonlighting" when they engage in sacramental and sacerdotal functions. Awareness that the roles of chaplain and priest-counselor constitute fundamental sacerdotal concerns in a Catholic school might do much to offset this regrettable situation.

Every priest-counselor should be competent and qualified. Professional training in counseling is one of the requisites for competence, but unfortunately all too many Catholic school people think that valid ordination and good intentions automatically provide competence in the area of counseling and guidance. Most priests receive no professionally oriented psychological training in the seminary and so are lulled into the feeling that their theological background and course or courses in pastoral theology are all-sufficient to counseling needs. Cavanagh & Fr. McGoldrick, S.J. (1958, p. 30), noted: "Sooner or later [psychologically untrained] priests will learn about these things the hard way, by making mistakes, causing pain, and intensifying the problems of people by misdirection. Some never learn, and in this respect become and remain a definite social liability." As grace is dependent on nature for its actualization, so the sacerdotal ministry as counselor demands professional knowledge and technical skill. Finally, priest-counselors must be adaptive and flexible. For example, it may well be that clerical garb of itself connotes such an authoritative relationship that it inhibits the free relationship necessary for effective counseling. The heroic priest-workers in France laid down their cassocks and plunged into the social milieu in overalls so that clerical regalia would not set up a barrier to a spiritual relationship. Some American and French priest-psychologists do not wear cassocks or clerical trappings when engaged in counseling or therapy.

The school priest is generally not integrated into the overall school program. As a result his potential impact is considerably weakened. The school and the chaplain should exert every effort to make the school priest a definite, actively cooperating member of the school team.

The greatest obstacles confronting priests in their work with students are strained relations between clergy and laity. While this strain is not so severe in the United States as in certain European countries, it is present as a barrier to totally free communication and rapport. Certainly the past lies like a shadow hindering working harmony and mutual understanding of clergy and laity. For too many centuries the clergy have regarded the laity as second-class members of the Mystical Body. Santopolo's investigation (1956, p. 92) concluded that both Catholic lay students in college and seminarians do not believe that clerical-lay relations are nearly as harmonious as priests and religious think they are. By isolated training and by comparatively separatist lifeways after ordination, many priests live in a ghetto of what Abbé Michonneau (1948, p. 136) has termed "clerical culture." Moreover, as Fr. C. F. Donovan, S.J. (1960, p. 90), has noted, "Many Catholic personnel workers are themselves vowed to obedience, or they work in a milieu where obedience is the primary virtue. It is all too easy to transfer the superior-subject relationship of the religious community to the school situation, and covertly assume the role of superior to whom unquestioning submission is owed by the students." A possible solution to this dilemma is re-emphasis of the ministerial role of the priest and de-emphasis of his authoritative function. Moreover, an implementation of the idea of Fr. Karl Rahner, S.J. (1959, pp. 9–50), of promoting healthy clerical-lay tensions might provide a continual fresh and free atmosphere for meaningful and uninhibited encounters between the priest and the lay student.

Spiritual Direction

Spiritual direction may be defined as assistance which one person, usually a priest, gives to another to assist him to self-actualize religiously. Effective direction has been hampered by erroneous concepts of the nature of this function. Certain spiritual writers have stated that the spiritual director is the directed's superior in religious authority; hence he has the right to prescribe even in minute detail the person's course of action or his selection of a state of life. In this view, submission to a director becomes an obligation of obedience. Some spiritual writers have identified the commands of the spiritual director with the will of God, so that he who resists the director's commands thereby resists God's will. The spiritual director becomes the arbiter and controller of conscience. Many modern theologians (cf. de St. Joseph, 1958; Leclerq, 1946, pp. 248–249) have noted that such a view has no foundation either in tradition or in ecclesiastical teaching. Countering this outmoded conception, Frs. Hagmaier, C.S.P., and Gleason, S.J., have noted that over a century ago the Venerable Liebermann (1959, pp. 39–40), a prominent and celebrated spiritual director, wrote: "The spiritual director having once ascertained God's action in a soul, has nothing else to do but to guide it, that it may obey the promptings of grace. He must never attempt to inspire a soul with his personal tastes and individual attractions, nor lead it after his own way of acting or his own peculiar point of view. A director that would act thus would often turn souls from God's own guidance and oppose the action of divine grace in them." In the same vein, Fr. Dalton, S.J. (1962), has stated that with the advances and new knowledge from counseling psychology spiritual direction should be abandoned in favor of *spiritual nondirection.* Unlike spiritual direction, spiritual nondirection centers on the person rather than on the problem.

The spiritual director may perform several functions, e.g., counseling, advisement, and teaching. Fr. Breedlove (1962) concluded that in the case of sinful actions the spiritual director, even if he is employing nondirectivism, is obliged to give fraternal correction. Frs. Hagmaier and Gleason (1959, pp. 43–44) also maintain that in such instances the spiritual director is compelled to give advice. Even in cases of this kind the obligation of fraternal correction is not necessarily to give advice or commands but rather to help the person to self-actualize maximally. In other words, fraternal correction can be equated not only with advisement or commanding but rather with *any* general help efficacious to spiritual development. Frs. Hagmaier and Gleason (1959, pp. 32, 36) remarked: "Recent research has confirmed the long suspected theory that the imparting of information is likely to be the least important and least effective of the counsellor's techniques"; they also commented, "Often, unfortunately, advice is neither what the individual wants nor what he needs or can use at the moment." Williamson (1959, p. 9) wrote that the counselor should "not use the method of 'arguing' for the adoption of a set of values, nor does he 'expound' the virtues and advantages of particular values which may seem to us appropriate to the individual student. Rather should [the counselor] help the individual become fully perceptive of his current value orientations, of the several alternatives open to him for consideration, and of the role his values play in development and adjustments."

A psychologically trained, knowledgeable spiritual director can do much to assist pupils to grow and develop religiously. Conversely, a well-intentioned but psychologically untrained or nonknowledgeable director can cause untold damage. The trials and tribulations of Teresa of Ávila at the hands of pious but inept and unintelligent spiritual directors is well known. It is a serious moral obligation on the part of the bishop, pastor, and Catholic school authorities to make sure that the school spiritual directors are psychologically well trained and knowledgeable. In the case of a spiritual director, training and knowledge are more important than personal holiness, as St. Teresa herself maintained.

The Retreat

A retreat is a period during which a person withdraws from his normal milieu to pray and meditate. Closed retreats are those in which the participant completely withdraws from his customary milieu, usually to a special retreat house designated for this purpose. Open retreats are those in which the participant partially withdraws from his usual environment, returning to it in the afternoon or evening. Because of the exigencies of modern school life, the open retreat is more usual, but at transitions in students' lives, e.g., graduation, closed retreats are generally provided by the Catholic school. Most retreats for lay students are three-day retreats, although some closed retreats may perdure a week.

The annual retreat in the Catholic school is a vehicle for religious development in a group context. Pope John XXIII (1959, p. 406) called the retreat "a blessed oasis of prayer" where the retreatants "may attain peace, serenity, comfort and spiritual refreshment, renewal and pardon, and holy resolutions to persevere in faithfulness to the Divine law."

A cardinal purpose of the school retreat is to effect permanent rather than temporary change in spiritual lifeway. In this connection, Fr. Hennessy, S.J. (1962, pp. 266–278), investigated an experimental group of Catholic high school youths in a closed three-day retreat and of a control group in an open three-day retreat. He found pronounced improvement in the former group as compared with the latter in expressed religious ideals at the conclusion of the respective retreats. Five months later, however, there were no statistical differences between the groups in the area of religious ideals; indeed, religious attitudes of students were much as they had been before the retreat. Religious practices of the experimental group (Mass attendance and the like) had improved. For students who lack theological sophistication, *cursillos* might well serve as the retreat vehicle.

The Religious Bulletin

The religious bulletin serves to stimulate students and can provide source material for group guidance periods. The *bulletin apostolate,* to use Fr. F. J. Weber's term (1964), can be fruitful if material is written urbanely, wittily, and in the idiom of those for whom it is intended. Each issue of the bulletin could center on one theme. Generally the chaplain serves as editor of the religious guidance bulletin.

The Religious Question Box

The religious question box is for the use of students who may wish to raise anonymous inquiries on particular problems or issues. Its purpose is to bring into the open difficulties which for one reason or another the student is reluctant to discuss with the chaplain, priest-counselor, school priest, or other school guidance worker. On the basis of these questions, the chaplain and his clerical coworkers can obtain a better insight into less apparent problems. Such knowledge helps these priests in planning the content of sermons and the material to be posted on the religious bulletin board and inserted in the religious bulletin. A box should be located in a prominent place on each floor of the school building, not just in the chaplain's suite.

RELIGIOUS PROBLEMS

Religious doubts are interwoven in almost everyone's daily existence. The strangest thing about doubts and temptations is that students (and guidance workers) should find them strange. Tempests make many plants take deeper roots. The school's role is not to shield and shelter students against religious problems but rather to help them develop strong religious and personal roots.

Evil and moral guilt

Not all wrongdoing is blameworthy. Many people commit acts of evil either because they fail to realize what they are doing is wrong or because for one reason or another they are not morally responsible for their acts. From a religious point of view, blameworthy wrongdoing constitutes sin. Modern developments in psychology, psychiatry, and philosophy have pointed to the necessity of a re-examination of both the nature and the concrete conditions of sin.

Sin implies that the sinner is free to commit the sin. But how free is a person? Certainly he is basically free, but his freedom is limited by a host of exterior circumstantial forces and also by his inner psychological configuration in both its essential and its developmental aspects. Is there not a welter of hidden forces operating, the totality of which exercises considerable weight? Environment plays a large role in conditioning thought or behavior; e.g., a child raised by an extremely selfish mother is likely to introject the same value system unconsciously. Numerous studies (G. J. W. Smith, D. E. Spence, & G. S. Klein, 1959) have shown the conditioning effect of subliminal stimuli on perception and judgment.

For Catholic guidance workers and priests, mortal sin remains the basic substrate of negative elements in religious problems, but the entire concept of mortal sin in the concrete order is itself a problem. As Fr. Rondet, S.J. (1956), has noted, mortal sin involves a deliberate turning away from God as one's source of life and final end. Yet it would seem manifestly impossible for anyone to make such a self-destructive choice except out of ignorance, excessive fear, or emotional disturbance, each of which removes wrongdoing from the category of mortal sin. Various solutions have been proposed in an attempt to solve this dilemma. Some theologians, following Cardinal Billot, have asserted that it is *impossible for a person to commit a mortal sin,* even with sufficient intellectual reflection and full consent of the will, unless he had express and antecedent knowledge of God. Others have argued that the soul makes the choice between heaven and hell at the moment it is released from the body in death. Still other theologians make a distinction between sins deserving hell and those that merely deprive the soul of sanctifying grace. Each of these three proposed solutions is, however, rejected by the majority of contemporary theologians.

Probably the most common existing solution to the problem of mortal sin is the Thomistic distinction between material and formal sin. This distinction is the familiar duality of objectivity and subjectivity in theological clothing. Thus an act objectively (materially) can be grievously sinful, but the person, through ignorance, fear, or seriously excusing circumstances, may not be responsible or blameworthy for the wrongdoing; hence such a person does not sin mortally. Since sin is a free act of the will involving sufficient intellectual awareness of the serious anti-God nature of the deed, it is only in this subjective relationship that real or formal sin is possible. But as Fr. Rondet (1956, p. 175) observes, it is possible for a person to be in mortal sin and still somehow remain joined to the Church. He wants both the created good (his sinful object) and the Uncreated Good. "Though cut off from the life-giving milieu of the Church he remains somehow under her influence. Grace no longer dwells within his soul, but it still surrounds him on every side. And this causes him uneasiness and sickness of spirit—signs that show he is still in contact with God." A prior question is whether the combination of psychological factors and environmental conditions so affect a person's judgment and his freedom that in fact it is difficult for anyone to commit a mortal sin at all. Discussions of this question usually center in the issue of man's freedom, but more consideration needs to be given to the clarity of man's judgment, which may be clouded both by inner psychic factors and by environmental conditions. Certainly what is needed is a new inquiry into the theology of sin in the light of contemporary developments in psychology, psychoanalysis, phenomenological philosophy, and the "new theology." A satisfactory theology of hell must be considered in the light not only of these factors but also of the concept of God's mercy. Perhaps far fewer students commit mortal sins and go to hell than Catholic school people believe.

It cannot be overemphasized that Catholicism recognizes that the final form of judgment (and hence of guilt) resides in the individual's own perception of the morality of his act, regardless of whether the act is objectively right or wrong. Both classical Catholic theology and modern psychology hold that the crucial thing is how a person perceives and judges reality to be, rather than how reality actually is. Hence one can never be certain that another has sinned even through he has committed an objectively evil act. Consequently, Catholic school people should never judge a student in the moral sphere and should indeed be very hesitant to punish him for alleged moral transgressions. What Valverde said in another context is cogent in this matter, viz., that some persons "take the easy course of proscribing what they are incapable of judging." Even if a student's sinfulness seems "obvious," he should not be judged, because there may be a host of circumstances which render the "obviously sinful" act not sinful at all. Guidance workers must be especially sensitive in this area, since their basic role demands that they be nonjudgmental.

Moral guilt is culpability for a transgression. Because by nature man both tends to God and participates in Divine goodness, he suffers remorse for wrongdoing. Such remorse can be of three types: (1) necessary and healthy (sorrow), (2) necessary but *in se* neither healthy nor unhealthy (sense of guilt), and (3) unnecessary and unhealthy (neurotic guilt feelings). The sense of guilt refers to the necessary internal awareness of the immorality of one's wrongdoings, while neurotic guilt feelings are the complex of psychologically warped emotional reactions to misdeeds or their consequences. Hence there are from both a theological and a psychological point of view healthy and unhealthy guilt (Aden, 1964). It is quite easy for a student, particularly if he has neurotic tendencies, to become excessively burdened with neurotic guilt feelings. Zilboorg (1964), a Catholic psychiatrist, has stated that guilt feelings can stem from and be a form of masochism, a psychopathology. It is the responsibility of guidance workers not to heighten neurotic guilt feelings by reminding the student of the horror of sin but rather to eliminate any vestiges of unhealthy guilt feelings. Rabbi Kagan (1959, p. 264) tells of the Hasidic (Jewish) explanation for the liturgical listing of sins in alphabetical order on Yom Kippur (Day of Atonement): "If it were not otherwise, these Rabbis said, we should not know when to stop beating our breasts, for there is no end to sin and no end to being aware of sin, but there *is* an end to the alphabet." Such a view represents a mentally healthy attitude toward guilt and wrongdoing in general.

Catholic school people should concentrate on encouraging students to be more deeply in love with God, rather than berating them for sins. Besides being destructive, the latter practice helps to induce neurotic guilt feelings in the students. Youths will sin anyway, and castigating them only hinders their approach to God. Christ's basic message was love for all men, Redemption. The first person to whom Christ appeared after His Resurrection was Mary Magdalen. The Scripture recounts that Christ was often in the company of the sinners rather than with the pious religious leaders of the age. Indeed He made as His vicar a man who denied Him not once but three times in succession. *"Ubi caritas et amor, deus ibi est"* (Where love and charity dwell, there also God abides).

Doubts of faith

In later childhood and particularly adolescence, many Catholic students experience doubts concerning religion. These doubts are part of the natural process of growing up, since an individual's concept of his religion must increase proportionately with the expansion of his self-concept and his concepts of reality. The Catholic religion is not closed to questioning or doubts, for then it would cease to require faith for membership. As Fr. Küng (1963, p. 146) has noted, "Doubt is the shadow cast by faith." The truths of religion are absolute, but human understanding of these truths is not absolute. Maturity demands the shedding of a childish form of Catholicism and the elimination of marginal elements of religion, particularly superstitious and magical appendages. If an adult has never experienced doubts of faith during late childhood or adolescence, it is problematical whether he has ever shed the baby skin of a childish religion and grown to the fullness of a vibrant, mature religious commitment.

A study by Prouty (1955, p. 34) of university women with varying levels of intelligence revealed that the higher the mental ability, the greater the religious skepticism. Skeptical girls, however, generally possessed higher ethical principles, greater tolerance, fewer worries, and more self-confidence than girls of lower intelligence with less religious skepticism. This investigation suggests that more religious questioning and doubting can be expected of students of higher intelligence. It also reveals that religious skepticism does not result in lower moral principles or in personality disintegration, as some simplistic Catholic school people maintain.

Although doubts of faith are almost inevitably necessary for the development of mature religious belief, they are nonetheless painful and anguishing to the youths undergoing them. Instead of grinding out the same old answers to the pressing doubts of a youth, the Catholic school person should re-examine his answers with a view to their relevance to the youth's predicament; further, he should re-examine his own concept of the problems. Perhaps the problems are different now than when the "answers" were formulated, and hence the answers are no longer valid, if indeed they ever were. Youths want religious doctrines, like all other data of reality, to stand tests. Theologians (Tanquerey, 1937, pp. 180–207) assert that miracles constitute most convincing arguments for the validity of Catholic faith, and what else is a miracle but an empirically verifiable datum?

If religious development is to be effective in faith, it is necessary that the other activities in the Catholic school not operate at cross-purposes with it. For example, Fr. A. Godin, S.J. (1963), has noted that the school should never view religion as a means, e.g., invoking the fear of God to maintain order in the classroom. Superstition should not be fostered, e.g., telling children that Christ was the only person ever exactly six feet tall. From the very beginning, students even in the elementary school must be helped to view the faith as a living, vibrant encounter with the God Who dwells immanently on earth.

Scrupulosity

Etymologically, "scruple" is derived from the Latin *scrupulus,* a pebble which slipped into the shoe of a person while walking and thereby caused annoyance and irritation out of all proportion to its diminutiveness. Fr. Barbaste, S.J. (1953), has defined *scrupulosity* as a species of obsessive-compulsive neurosis characterized by inordinate preoccupation with the moral and religious order. He has delineated four symptoms of this form of neurosis: (1) habitual abulia, or inability to make decisions; (2) anguishing doubts characterized by anxious, painstaking checks and rechecks of each action; (3) obsessions, i.e., compulsive images or ideas which "impose themselves" on the individual despite efforts to eliminate them; and (4) phobias, or intense foolish and irrational fears out of proportion to the object or cause.

According to Fr. Barbaste, there are two schools of thought about the causes and symptoms of scrupulosity. The first holds that the dominant symptom is a hypersensitive fear response to situations involving conscience. Treatment consists in both helping the client realize that his guilt is minimal or nonexistent and assisting him to plunge himself into other tasks. The second school of thought regards the dominant symptom of scrupulosity as the sense of personal inadequacy springing from a habit of inattention and vague preoccupation. Treatment consists in encouraging the client to fix his attention and wholehearted efforts on the task of the moment, thus checking his tendency to obsess or daydream.

Most psychologists, who regard scrupulosity as an obsessive-compulsive neurosis coupled with and focused on religious authority as a defense against a weak ego (or inadequate self), use both methods of treatment in actual practice. Schneiders (1964a, p. 82) observed that psychologists and psychiatrists such as Rudolf Allers and Frs. Thomas Verner Moore, O.S.B., John W. Stafford, C.S.V., and Joseph Nuttin view pride as the basic quality and dominant feature of scrupulosity. Nolan (1963, p. 96) has called attention to a little-observed phenomenon: scrupulous persons are not normally sorry for their alleged transgressions; rather they merely have neurotic guilt feelings about them, which is quite a different matter. Fr. VanderVeldt, O.F.M., and Odenwald (1957, p. 377) have noted that an overprotective education induces in a child a feeling of insecurity, the basic trait of scrupulosity. Also they have observed that rigid moral and religious training is conducive to scrupulosity, especially when coupled with exaggerated moral instruction. Both Catholic parents and Jansenistically influenced Catholic schools of the shelter type should reassess themselves on this matter.

Scrupulosity is a fairly common phenomenon. Fr. Mullen's study (1927) of 400 girls in a private high school whose student body was representative of American-born students of varying national extractions revealed that one-fourth of the girls admitted feeling habitually scrupulous and 50 per cent stated that they suffered from passing attacks of scrupulosity. An investigation by Fr. Riffel, S.J. (1958), produced results almost identical with those of Fr. Mullen's earlier study.

Most psychotherapists believe that scrupulosity is an embedded psychopathology and a specific form of obsessive-compulsive neurosis and regard its treatment as a matter for the professional psychotherapist. Yet such cases often come to the attention of the priest in his pastoral role, and the scrupulous person is often highly resistant to forgoing reliance on the priest in order to seek professional treatment. Since the prognosis is generally not good, certainly the alert pastoral counselor resists allowing himself to be maneuvered into a situation in which he must become involved in a role

difficult even for the most effective psychotherapist. Pastoral psychology training centers, such as those at the Catholic University of America, Iona College,
and the Menninger Foundation and Clinic, have focused special attention
on this delicate problem.

The classical authors of spiritual life agreed that advisement was the best
course of action in dealing with scrupulosity (see Fr. Casey, S.J., 1948, pp.
38–47). Priests were told to issue short, simple, precise rules and commands
to the client. These rules were never to be altered in the slightest. Further,
the commands should be obeyed without question. Notwithstanding these
suggestions by the spiritual masters, modern psychology regards scrupulosity
as a psychological difficulty rather than a moral problem. Hence the recommendations of these classical authors can only be regarded as "first-aid" devices. Such first aid is appropriate for (1) use by the psychologically naïve
spiritual director rather than the psychologist and (2) aid to the client in
coping with the onset of a short attack of scrupulosity so that he will not
be temporarily immobilized.

Yet even these first-aid ministrations may heighten the problem rather
than help it, for such devices tend to build an abnormal or neurotic dependence on the priest and abnormal dependence is the heart of the scrupulosity syndrome. That is, the scrupulous person has not learned to differentiate
the magnitude of his supposed wrongdoing (and, to this extent, his inability
to appraise reality correctly resembles a psychotic break with reality). Hence,
he relies abnormally on the commandments and precepts but cannot apply
them correctly. Unable to judge reality, he relies upon the commandments
and precepts to function as his very self or ego in defining reality. When the
priest uses advisement or pastoral command, he is actually feeding the neurosis, for the scrupulous person is now invited to substitute neurotic dependence
upon a misinterpretation of the commandments and precepts for a neurotic
dependence upon the priest. Such heavy-handed pastoral management of scrupulosity is likely only to expedite the acceleration of this neurosis into an
active psychosis.

As Fr. Tanquerey, S.S. (1930, pp. 443–456), has noted, confession is
a torture for the scrupulous and hence should be simplified for them. In
any event, the priest should refer the scrupulous to a psychologist or a
psychiatrist (Fr. Riffel, S.J., 1963).

Alcoholic difficulties

Since temperance is a cardinal virtue, its practice is religiously meritorious
and intemperance is *objectively* sinful. Even conservative theologians (cf.
Jone, 1951, p. 57), however, believe drinking is a mortal sin only (1) when
the person becomes so intoxicated that he suffers complete loss of reason
or (2) when he becomes intoxicated without "sufficient reason." Complete
loss of reason is defined as total inability to distinguish between right and

wrong. But usually by the time this stage has set in, the alcoholic content in the blood is so high that the person has fallen into sleep or stupor. Hence it is doubtful whether anyone commits a mortal sin by imbibing alcohol or even by the intention to "get drunk," since the person's intention is rarely to lose reason but rather to lose mental or physical anguish. Some Catholics fail to grasp the addictive nature of alcoholism. For example, Fr. Prümmer, O.P. (1957, p. 288), states that drunkenness is immoral if it involves gratifying an inordinate desire for alcohol. Most medical and psychological authorities, however, regard alcoholism as a serious disease.

In the prevention of difficulties with alcohol, the school utilizes both instructional and guidance services. Every state has a law that alcohol education must be provided in schools. Unfortunately this legislation is not taken seriously by many schools. In an adequate program of alcohol education, spiritual principles as well as scientific facts should be emphasized. Fr. J. C. Ford, S.J. (1961, p. 42), has observed that educators should avoid exaggerations about the effects of alcohol, e.g., "alcohol is poison" or "drinking shortens life." R. G. McCarthy and E. M. Douglas (1949, pp. 141–278) have found that discussion situations utilizing problem-solving techniques are excellent vehicles for alcohol education. They can be supplemented with filmstrips and motion pictures, assembly programs featuring special speakers on alcohol, role-playing situations, and other socialized lessons.

The school can work with the family in improving alcohol education. In Italy, the *bambini* have a few drops of wine in their water; over the years the ratio is increased. In this way the child's tolerance to alcohol is built up; perhaps more important, alcohol consumption is regarded as a normal activity rather than as an abnormal and special phenomenon. It is not surprising that Italians have one of the lowest rates of alcoholism in the world. Ireland, however, has a disturbingly high rate. Most state laws restrict alcoholic consumption in public places to those over twenty-one years of age. This practice has probably created a greater number of problems than it has solved. Youths will drink before they are twenty-one; prohibiting such activities in a respectable group atmosphere causes many to drink surreptitiously, a habit which they often retain throughout life, much to their detriment. States and schools which directly or indirectly regard alcohol as an *ipso facto* evil not only neglect its positive benefits but also create problems where none should exist.

Much research on the problem of alcohol remains to be done. Perhaps the outstanding work in this field has been carried on at the Yale Center of Alcoholic Studies. The *Quarterly Journal of Studies on Alcohol* contains research data on the question. The National Council on Alcoholism has done valiant work in promoting alcohol education. Societies such as Alcoholics Anonymous, the Salvation Army, the Total Temperance League, and the Sons of Matt Talbot have helped to salvage many alcoholics who might have been originally prevented from falling into the clutches of "demon rum" by a realistic program of alcohol education in schools.

Sexual problems

One major cause of heterosexual problems is that man's physiological structure has not grown as rapidly as his civilization. A person's body after the onset of puberty is geared to marriage, while society demands that he or she remain in school for some years after puberty. This problem is particularly serious for the male. A review of research by Berelson and Steiner (1964, p. 303) concluded: "In the United States, at least, the general pattern of sexual behavior is pretty well established in men by age sixteen (later for women), and by the time of marriage most men have already passed the peak of their sexual capacity, which occurs in late adolescence."

How promiscuous are present-day students in sexual conduct? The evidence indicates that promiscuous conduct is not so common as many popular writers lead the public to believe. Grater's confidential-questionnaire study (1960) of sophomore and junior female students in a large Midwestern state university revealed that 92 per cent stated that they had never engaged in sexual intercourse and 100 per cent believed that intercourse was morally wrong if the participants were not engaged (if engaged, the percentages were 75 and 90, respectively), 76 per cent stated that they had never engaged in heavy petting, and 98 per cent believed heavy petting was morally wrong. Some behavioral scientists and investigators (cf. Kinsey, Pomeroy, & Martin, 1948, p. 397) contend there is little difference in the rate of premarital sexual activity from one generation to the next and that the older generation tends to make exaggerations in their comparisons. P. H. Landis' review (1960, p. 267) of research concluded that an overwhelming majority of high school and college boys and girls believed that petting was not essential to dating popularity. Those who did pet on dates usually felt guilty afterward. While many skeptics, including both young men about town and priests who hear confessions, may doubt these contentions, they appear reasonably accurate. The chief difference between sexual behavior today and that of a generation or more ago probably lies not in the behavior itself but rather in the fact that such activities are conducted more openly in modern society than was dared in "the good old days."

School people seldom strike a proper balance in the sexual attitudes and beliefs they convey to students. All too many are either overpermissive on the one hand or rigid on the other. Kirkendall (1960), perhaps the most celebrated champion of the overpermissive approach, has remarked that to achieve a better sexual morality it is necessary for parents and educators to abandon negative and authoritarian proscriptions on premarital sexual activity and promote a positively oriented sexual ethic based on the importance of achieving optimally satisfying personal relationships. He contends that what is important is not the alleged goodness of the acts in terms of conventional mores, taboos, and abstract logic but rather the role of sexual activities in promoting a self-satisfying, deep relationship between partners. Another overpermissive viewpoint (Stokes, 1962) is contained in the following quotation:

> By the time Freudian psychology offered its challenge, our culture had amassed a truly weird array of irrational attitudes about sex. Most of them seem to have stemmed from the Judaeo-Christian doctrine of sex as original sin. [sic]. Specific examples of the irrationalities produced by this mystical concept are: (1) a generally guilty feeling about all erotic emotion; (2) a violent fear of autoerotic enjoyment, especially masturbation (3) repression or denial of childhood sexuality; (3) restriction of teen-age sexuality to an unreal, romantic, de-sexualized idealism that ignores the erotic emotions and physical realities of sex; (5) establishment of monogamous marriage as the sole permissible setting for the expression of sex; (6) creation of a pattern of weak, stereotyped sexual behavior within the marital framework. . . .

Poffenberger (1960) has legitimately criticized Kirkendall's views, observing that mores are not antithetical to good human relationships and that the establishment of fulfilling interpersonal relationships does not constitute the totality of moral behavior or of fruitful living. For his part, Stokes seems to base his plea for overpermissiveness on the fact that Puritanical views (e.g., that all sexual pleasure is somehow sinful) must be discarded. Indeed thoughtful Catholics and non-Catholics are equally vehement in denouncing Puritanism and Jansenism. While some educators are overpermissive on sexual problems, most Catholic school people are excessively strict, narrow-minded, rigid, and prudish. Fr. Adam (1958, p. 52) has defined prudery as "an unbending moral attitude which regards everything sexual as impure and, therefore, seeks to ignore it—an inflated sense of shame behind which, by the law of extremes, private lust may quite frequently lurk." Prudery has generated the fig-leaf mentality as regards sex and has made one of God's greatest and most noble creations shameful and guilt-laden.

Fr. Adam has observed that Manichaeanism is the root of the sexual question in the Catholic Church. Manichaeanism was a third-century heresy which regarded all physical matter including the human body as evil in itself; hence marriage and sexual pleasure constituted crimes against God. Jansenism is a variation of Manichaeanism. In the ancient Church, before the onset of Manichaeanism, there existed a healthy attitude and theology of sex and chastity. Fr. Adam (1958, pp. 23–62) has noted that despite the official and emphatic stand which the Church has repeatedly taken, there are still many Catholics who maintain the Manichaean attitude and condemn lawful sexuality as against nature and grace, as not fully "spiritual." The mainstream of Christian teaching has always prized sex as one of God's greatest treasures and means of participation in Divine life.

Fr. Adam (1958, p. 13) has commented that sexual rigidity has done more harm to the Church than the actual sinning which such rigidity intended to combat. Fr. J. L. Thomas, S.J. (1958, p. 32), an authority on family sociology, has stated: "Doubtless well-intentioned people have initiated a 'smear campaign' against sex in the hope that they could dissuade people from sinning against chastity and in order to strengthen personal self-control. Paradoxically, experience shows they have accomplished neither of these purposes, for their approach deprives the sexual drive of none of its force while destroying its human significance. We do not eliminate reality by denying its existence or by giving it a dirty name."

The emphasis placed on sexual transgressions in Catholic schools sometimes leads pupils to believe that Christianity is merely a sexual moral code. The word "immoral" has become synonymous with sexual misdeeds; "purity" is equivalent to sexual innocence. The beatitude "Blessed are the pure of heart" is customarily interpreted as the "sexually pure of heart," an interpretation rejected by contemporary Catholic theologians. Indeed many students receive the impression that if a person is sexually pure, he is *ipso facto* a good Catholic. The fact that the chief concern of Catholic morality is love for God through one's fellowman is often forgotten not only in theory but in practice.

Is sex as big a problem in Catholic schools as the treatment of the question by priests and religious seems to indicate? The research evidence answers this question in the negative. Fr. J. T. Byrne's nationwide investigation (1957) of student problems in selected Catholic men's colleges revealed that moral problems comprised only 14 per cent of all student difficulties. Of the moral problems, 67 per cent were concerned with sex. Thus sex accounted for only 9 per cent of all problems experienced by Catholic college men.

Masturbation

A Catholic psychiatrist (Cavanagh & Fr. McGoldrick, S.J., 1958, p. 548) has written that masturbation "is probably the most common disturbance in the sexual field. No other practice has been so widely discussed and so poorly understood." Doniger's review (1961) of research concluded that 95 per cent of adolescent boys and a large proportion of adolescent girls practice masturbation. A psychiatrist specializing in the relationship between religion and mental health (Booth, 1961) has observed that what he terms "normal masturbation" seeks a sexual outlet because for one or another reason a person is prevented from engaging in legitimate sexual intercourse. This type of masturbation is occasional rather than habitual. "Masturbation as a means of relieving sexual tension in a socially harmless way has no [medically] bad consequences. It is not habit-forming." Habitual or compulsive masturbation has little to do with sexual desires as such and is indeed traceable to deep personality problems, often resulting from inadequate performance in some sphere, e.g., poor social life or failing school marks, or from guilt feelings (Booth, 1961, pp. 54–56).

Catholic theologians have held that, objectively speaking, masturbation constitutes a grievous sin. But compulsive masturbation which is strongly habitual diminishes both clarity of the intellective judgment and free exercise of the will; hence it may be no sin at all and certainly not a mortal sin (Fr. Hagmaier, C.S.P., and Fr. Gleason, S.J., 1959, p. 216). Compulsive masturbation is more a psychological problem than a moral one. Even occasional masturbation may not be mortally sinful, since the sexual drive which surges strongly in adolescence may, because of a variety of contributing circumstances, temporarily overcome the youth. Psychologically speaking, masturbation is debilitating in that it represents a person's attempts to attain satisfaction without the experience and risk of going out of himself. Thus masturbation chokes personality growth. Psychologists regard masturbation as immature sexual behavior, of the autoerotic type. Fixation at this level of sexual behavior prevents the development of mature heterosexual interest and activity.

In dealing with students who masturbate, the guidance worker should not attempt to effect a solution on the basis of false information, since misinformation reinforces the student's fears and neurotic preoccupation with guilt closely bound up with masturbation. One investigator (Pullias, 1937) found that 83 per cent of the boys in his study believed that masturbation has seriously damaging consequences, including physical defects, insanity, or mental damage. Often Catholic manuals on chastity intended for youth perpetuate such misinformation (Kirsch, 1930, p. 258). Truth and morality never come about by the use of untruth, however, no matter how praiseworthy the purpose. The fact of the matter is clarified in the summarization of the overwhelming research evidence gathered by Cavanagh and Fr. McGoldrick, S.J. (1958, p. 549), who stated: "No harmful physical effects directly attributable to masturbation have ever been observed."

Merely telling (or commanding) the student to refrain from masturbation does not facilitate a solution. Nor should the guidance worker attempt to have the student concentrate on breaking the habit or practice itself. Above all, he should never resort to harsh measures or threats when counseling with a student with masturbation problems. Such measures or threats only entrench the practice more firmly, since that very practice is usually caused by a need to compensate for insecurity, neurotic guilt feelings, an inferiority concept, poor performance in some activity, or lack of a legitimate outlet for sexual drive.

One efficacious way to deal with a student who has masturbation problems is to assist him to concentrate on other and perhaps stronger needs. In this manner the youth can sublimate and rebuild his attitudes around another self-satisfying but healthy core.

A Catholic Theology of Sex

There is much confusion in Catholic theology in regard to sex, for there is still a heavy Manichaean and Jansenistic tendency in certain Catholic circles. Thus, for example, theology books (Jone, 1951, p. 154) refer to breasts and genitalia as the "indecent parts" of the anatomy. Most of the theologizing is done by celibates, who are often prone to exaggerate dangers in the sexual sphere. Fr. Adam's extensive review (1958) of the literature reveals many Catholic theologians and preachers have declared that sexual transgressions constitute the most serious kinds of sin. Most theologians of the last two centuries have maintained that in the sexual sphere all sins are mortal. Thus Fr. Prümmer, O.P. (1957, p. 230), wrote that "direct voluntary sexual pleasure outside of marriage is grievously sinful and never admits of slight matter" because all venereal pleasure is in a direct way related to the act of procreation, which God has reserved to the state of marriage. Fr. Adam's careful analysis (1958) has shown that this doctrine of no "slight matter" (*parvitas materiae*) is both grossly incorrect and counter to the teachings of traditional Catholic theologians. Yet how often are Catholic schoolchildren led to believe that all sexual transgressions are automatically mortal sins? How many unnecessary guilt feelings are thereby induced?

A sound Catholic theology of sex can be stated in two basic assertions: (1) A few intrinsically evil acts (e.g., fornication, adultery, and sodomy) are always *objectively* seriously sinful. (2) All other actions are sinful *only* if they incite thoughts, desires, or actions which lead to *voluntary* delectation in *unlawful* venereal pleasure outside the married state. Thus, for example, "necking" or attending particular types of films are *in themselves* not sinful but may be if they incite participants to voluntary delectation in unlawful venereal pleasure (Fr. Jone, 1951, p. 155). Conversely, merely holding hands with a member of the opposite sex may be sinful if this seemingly innocent activity leads to voluntary delectation in unlawful venereal pleasure. Frs. Hagmaier, C.S.P., and Gleason, S.J. (1959, pp. 63–64), have noted that sexual thoughts are not *in se* sexually impure thoughts, nor are they necessarily sinful. Thoughts and fantasies about sex are an inevitable part of growing up and maturing. Only when these thoughts either lead to unlawful desires and actions or are indulged in for their own pleasure rather than for healthy exploration, do they become immoral. Fr. J. L. Thomas, S.J. (1958, p. 31), has written " . . . there is a tendency [by Catholics] to look upon the physical aspects of the reproductive drive as sinful and to lose sight of the fact that the sinfulness of unchaste actions is a quality of the act of consent, not of the venereal pleasure involved." Fr. Jone, O.F.M. Cap. (1951, p. 155), a moral theologian, said: "One should not readily consider young people guilty of grave sin when they kiss and embrace in their games and merrymaking."

Sex Education in the School

If youths are to develop and mature properly and fully, they must have adequate sex education. Fr. Haley, C.S.C. (1957, p. 50), has remarked that "it is imperative that an enlightened and conscientious program of instructing to [sexual] purity be inaugurated." Eugenie A. Leonard's conclusion (1932, p. 126) from her study on the problems of freshman college girls is still relevant for all young people: "There no longer seems any doubt that every girl should have full, detailed, and scientific information regarding sex. The girls themselves feel the need very keenly." There is an urgent need for accurate, well-rounded sex education. Cavanagh and Fr. McGoldrick, S.J. (1958, p. 177), wrote: "Improper or deficient education in sex matters may contribute to sexual maladjustments and cause unnecessary psychic pain." Fr. VanderVeldt, O.F.M., and Odenwald (1957, p. 400) made the following remark concerning sex crimes: "One cannot help wondering how much of this condition is the result of faulty sex education, of a bizarre attitude on sex, of a moral penury bred of puritanism." Fr. Ewing, S.J. (1964, p. 249), has observed that the role of the school in sex education and guidance supplements or makes up for deficiencies in the sex education and guidance provided by parents. Few parents have full or accurate sex information to provide their offspring; certainly they do not have charts or models which facilitate sex education. A host of studies have revealed that *de facto* parents fail to perform their rightful function of primary teacher in the sexual development of their children. Fleege's study (1945, p. 272) revealed that the father and mother ranked very low as the sources of a youth's sex knowledge (sixth and seventh, following, in descending order, companions, the street, books, magazines, and clergymen).

Much current sex education and guidance, particularly in Catholic circles, is detrimental to the development of proper sexual growth and healthy attitudes toward sex. As Frs. Hagmaier, C.S.P., and Gleason, S.J. (1959, pp. 62–63), have stated: "Perhaps the greatest single shortcoming of our [Catholic] sexual attitudes is the lack of down-to-earth, positive preparation for sexual maturity. For every sentence in Catholic literature which prepares the young person to enjoy and appreciate the sexual aspects of love, there are hundreds of sentences which define precisely and often realistically the threatening and dangerous aspects of man's sexual life." Often Catholic literature and Catholic school people use guilt-inducing or connotative words such as "self-abuse" for masturbation. Fr. Adam (1958, p. 180) noted in this connection that an undue sense of shame "may lead in one person, to inhibitions and excessive scruples and, in another, to a violent recoil, ending in destruction of all inner standards." Negative sex education can easily lead to sexual frigidity in a woman. Cavanagh and Fr. McGoldrick, S.J. (1958, p. 545) noted that 60 to 80 per cent of women in marriage are frigid, i.e., either do not receive sexual pleasure or even experience a revulsion for sexual relations. Frigidity is almost always psychic in origin.

Proper and effective sex education should include both factual information and the development of healthy attitudes. The older Catholic view of sex education and sex guidance maintained that the physiological details of human generation and intercourse should be omitted (see Fr. Vermeersch, S.J., 1919, p. 206). Modern Catholic experts agree, however, that for coping with the problems which sexual capacity brings, as well as for the integration of sexual development into one's total optimum personality development, it is crucial to know the essential facts and the relevant information. Girls and boys should know about menstruation and nocturnal emission. Erroneous concepts, such as the invalidism of the girl during her menstrual period or the pouring away of the life juices of the boy during nocturnal emission, should be discarded. Frs. Hagmaier and Gleason (1959, p. 13) have remarked that adequate preparation of boys and girls for nocturnal emissions and menstruation, respectively, helps them view these physical developments as evidence of their new maturity in which they should take justified pride, rather than "fearsome mysteries which must be puzzled out amid evasive explanations and garbled half-truths." Sister M. Kathleen Flynn (1946, p. 343) has noted that sex education for girls should concentrate on sex maturation problems of girls but include education and guidance on physiological and psychological developments within boys, so that girls can fully grasp their relationships with boys in their totality and learn to face sympathetically common problems of both sexes. There should be parallel sex education for boys.

In sex education medicophysical and anatomical details should be given but this information should be integrated with a sound philosophy of sex and human development. As the United States bishops observed in their 1950 annual statement, adequate sex education consists in more than merely imparting information; rather it comprises the development of attitudes, or integrating sex information into personality development.

An effective sex education program involves a team effort on the part of guidance workers, teachers, and administrators. Administrators plan an organized program of sex education. Teachers integrate sex guidance in their classes in a healthy, developmental manner. Finally, an adequate program of sex education must be continuous; certainly it cannot be accomplished in one or two class periods. The school must encourage and cooperate with the home in promoting sex education and sex guidance. For example, parents of primary school children should be urged to refer to sexual organs and the processes of elimination by their correct, dictionary terms rather than employing bowdlerisms or oblique circumlocutions in the family vocabulary. Small children are quick to conclude that when sexual organs and processes are described in hushed, couched language, there must be something wrong and dirty connected with them. As a result, false and perverted sex education and sex guidance result.

In any program of sex education for Catholic students, spiritual helps such as prayer, Mass, and Communion should never be neglected. And most important, chastity must never be overstressed at the expense of the other virtues. Rather, the virtue of charity and love of God should occupy the principal focus of emphasis, for as St. Thomas (*Summa Theologica,* I–II, q. 62, a. 4) has remarked, a person who has love possesses all other virtues.

Guidance workers, particularly those who are religiously committed, should deal with students in such a fashion that they are spurred on by hope. Hope eases the suffering and sorrow which every human being endures. When a person has hope, he has greater success in enduring pain and in effecting a successful recovery. But hope tends to vanish or at least to be obscured when certain needs, such as the need to belong and the need to believe, are lost. In his efforts to make hope optimally operative in the student, the guidance worker should so organize the environment that these needs are met and hope may thus be nourished. To paraphrase Karl Menninger (1959, p. 215), no matter how much a student is failing to self-actualize or how serious his problems are, he cannot help but hope; the task of the guidance worker is to assist him to hope more accurately, more congruently with reality, and to give him greater reason for hoping.

Nor should guidance workers hold out any less hope to students who exhibit sexual weaknesses. This is merely one type of human weakness and indeed is a small vice when compared with such major ones as serious uncharitableness or grave injustice. Liertz (1924, p. 112) has observed: "Men of excellent character in all other respects may manifest unbelievable weakness in the area of sexual morality, while spotless sexual morality may be found among people whose general morality leaves much to be desired." As Christ Himself said (Luke 7:47) of St. Mary Magdalen, "her sins, many as they are, shall be forgiven her because she has loved much." Fr. Adam (1958, p. 121) has compassionately and wisely written: "The sex-ridden individual is more likely to be humble, loving and meek; therefore despite many weaknesses, he is often of greater moral stature than one who, for no physical reason is virginal but lacks the oil of love."

RELIGIOVOCATIONAL DEVELOPMENT

Religiovocational development guidance is assistance to the student concerning the eventual attainment of his lifeway. Lifeway, or "state in life," is here considered from the religious perspective. Canon 107 of the *Corpus Juris Canonici* (Code of Canon Law) states that by Divine institution there are only two divisions of persons within the Church, viz., clerics and laity. A cleric is defined as one who has received first tonsure. Cutting across both divisions is the religious state of life. The religious state is a stable mode of common life in which the faithful, besides observing the commandments, undertake to observe the evangelical counsels by taking the vows of poverty, chastity, and obedience. The religious state, unlike clerical life, is of ecclesiastical origin and not of Divine institution. Fr. McFarland (1953, p. 119) notes that the state of perfection as lived through observing the evangelical counsels was offered to everyone; legislation on specifics of the common life as led by religious institutes constitutes ecclesiastical institution. Religious may be either lay persons or clerics; thus brothers or sisters are canonically lay persons even though they are also religious. Further, not all clerics (e.g., diocesan priests) are members of religious institutes. Religious institutes constitute only one of three juridic states of formally living the evangelical counsels within the Church today. The other two juridic states are secular institutes and societies with a common life but no vows (Fr. Goyeneche, C.M.F., 1962, p. 141; Fr. Ristuccia, C.M., 1958). These last two states unfortunately are not sufficiently known by a large segment of the Catholic population. The religious life, as well as the other lifeways which demand adherence to the three evangelical counsels, are only a *means* to sanctity and not an end. As St. Thomas (*Summa Theologica,* II–II, q. 184, a. 31) observed, the perfection of the Christian life consists essentially in charity and only secondarily in the observance of the evangelical counsels.

The lay vocation

All too many Catholic school people seem to consider the term *vocation* as reserved exclusively for the clerical or religious life, or both. A sort of Neo-Gnosticism which equates a vocation to the clerical or religious life with entrance into the ranks of the elite, into an inner sanctum, has arisen. Thus there is lost the true Christian emphasis of the religious, the cleric, and the layman as engaged in different types of apostolate, each vital to the Church's mission and each independent of the person's worth and holiness in the sight of God. Catholic literature customarily refers to the religious life as the "state of perfection," possibly giving rise to the notion that the lay life is a state of imperfection. Thus one sister (Sister M. de L. McMahon, S.C., 1955, p. 386) decried the dating practices of a Catholic high school girl who had aspirations to the religious life, alleging that such activities might diminish her aspirations and "compel her to remain in a condition of mediocrity," i.e., the lay life. Many religiovocational posters displayed in Catholic schools convey the false concept that those in a religious or clerical state are the only true apostles. Numerous posters read "Will you give your life to God?" with a picture of a priest, brother, or sister underneath. Quite a few lay people have given themselves totally to God; one need only think of St. Thomas More, St. Elizabeth of Hungary, Jacques Maritain, Dorothy Day, Catherine de Hueck, and, of course, St. Joseph and the Virgin herself.

A comparison of the dignity of the religious vocation with that of the lay vocation has, historically, yielded three different conclusions. The *traditional, now outmoded, view* is that both objectively and subjectively the religious vocation is superior to the lay vocation. The *contemporary view,* held by most theologians today, is that while the religious vocation is objectively superior to the lay vocation, it is not subjectively superior. This is to say that in the objective order the religious vocation is higher, but a person might become more holy and fulfill God's will more perfectly as a layman. The objective order is only an abstraction, while the subjective order represents the individual in the concrete existential situation; hence it is the subjective order which must occupy the concern of the guidance worker. The *egalitarian or most recent view* is that both objectively and subjectively the religious vocation is neither superior nor inferior to the lay vocation (see Fr. Gerkin, S.J., 1963).

A related question arises relative to the valuation of virginity as compared with marriage. In itself marriage is superior to virginity, since virginity represents a lack of fulfillment in a vital area of human development. Virginity is superior to marriage only when consecrated to God; i.e., the consecration, not the virginity as such, is the ennobling factor. This has been the consistent teaching of the popes. What is to be said, however, of the dignity of consecrated virginity as compared with that of a marriage totally consecrated to God? Even if the former were superior in the objective order, would the same hold true in the all-important subjective order in which each person works out his own salvation? Thus, for example, in its commentary on St. Paul's Letter to the Corinthians VII:7, the Catholic Biblical Association (1952, p. 459) noted that this text implies that "one who is married may have a special grace superior to spiritually motivated virginity."

There is a vocation to the lay state; i.e., one is called to the lay state just as one is called to be a priest or religious, or both. Pope Paul VI (1964) thus speaks of the layman as a person with a definite ecclesiastical vocation. To be a layman is to occupy a sacred state within the Church. The layman is not a person left behind, a person who does not enter the clerical or religious life. The lay state is not a concession to human weakness; a person is called to the lay state. Further, the Christian concept of vocation means that all vocations, not merely the clerical and religious vocations, are precious in the sight of God. Guidance workers should consequently not present the religious or clerical life as *necessarily* implying a greater love for God than the free election of the lay state. A person shows his love for God by conforming to His will, and God has called many to the lay state. Often religiovocational development guidance leads youths to believe that if they do not have a vocation to the clerical or religious life, they do not have a vocation.

The Christian layman, by virtue of his Baptism and Confirmation, as well as his vocation, is at once priest, prophet, and ruler. The layman is priest because he possesses "the quality which enables a man to come before God to gain His grace, and therefore fellowship with Him, by offering up a sacrifice acceptable to Him" (Fr. Congar, O.P., 1957, p. 145). As Fr. Meyer, M.M. (1956, p. 197), has noted, the laity "have a share in Christ's priesthood given by baptism and confirmation, and these confer on them a specific position with its corresponding function in the Mystical Body. The clergy are not the only other Christs: the laity are also in their own particular way." The layman is prophet because, with the help of the Holy Spirit, he knows God and the purpose of His grace and makes these known to others (Fr. Congar, 1957, p. 258). The layman is ruler because, through Christ, he exercises spiritual dominion over himself and over the world (Fr. Congar, 1957, pp. 222–238).

If the Church has a mission because of its Divine call, the laity for the same reason also has a mission. A basis for this doctrine is a vitally important statement which Pope Pius XII made to the Second World Congress of the Lay Apostolate: "You [laymen] are the Church."

The layman can most fruitfully exercise his threefold mission in the Church by being a dynamic lay apostle. Yet there is evidence which indicates that Catholic schools are not sufficiently stimulating their students in this direction. Donnellon's nationwide investigation (1954, p. 253) of Catholic men's colleges revealed that, of the 11 most common religious activities carried on by extracurricular groups, not a single one was directed at fostering an understanding of the lay apostolate; sponsoring vocations to the clerical and religious life was an important activity of these groups. Some dynamic Catholic universities have established special offices which encourage and coordinate lay missionary activities, but such instances are not common in American Catholic higher education (see Sheehan, 1963). The noblest and most fruitful form of the lay apostolate is Catholic Action, the participation of the laity in the apostolate of the hierarchy through a special mandate of the bishop. While European bishops and priests have established Catholic Action groups, the majority of American hierarchy and clergy have either opposed or ignored them, despite statements of the popes on the question. As Msgr. Civardi (1936, p. 178) has noted, the clergy must first study what Catholic Action really is and then implement it in the schools and parishes.

Fr. Saalfield (1958, p. 101) has observed that the Catholic school's religiovocational director should be interested not only in fostering vocations to the clerical or religious life, or both, but also in assisting the students to prepare optimally for a vocation in the lay state. Priests, customarily the school's religiovocational directors, generally do not fully understand lay life. Their seminary life, isolated as it was, allowed them only brief contact with peer group laymen and so prevented their experiencing how the layman actually forges his living synthesis between life and Christianity (Lee & Putz, 1965). A review of research by Fr. Meyers (1963, p. 23) concluded that the question of the theology of the layman is treated inadequately in theology courses in the seminary. Fr. J. Newman (1962, p. 161) could observe that "it is very hard to expect seminarians to take the matter of lay apostles seriously, if it is not treated as part of their normal course in theology." The presence of dynamic lay teachers and guidance workers in the Catholic school affords pupils living lay models worth emulating from the spiritual point of view.

Clerical and religious vocations

The statements of the recent popes have indicated one of the tasks of the Catholic schools is to promote vocations to the clerical and religious life. The research (cf. Fr. Drolet, 1959, p. 84; Sister M. U. Grimes, 1961, p. 247) shows that Catholic schools spend considerable time in actively fostering vocations. Time allotted for this purpose does not appear to need upgrading; what is imperative is drastic improvement of the quality of religiovocational development.

The Nature of Clerical and Religious Vocations

A vocation to the priesthood or to the religious life is not a special illumination or whispering of Christ to "come, follow Me," so often depicted in overpietistic holy cards. As Fr. Farrel, O.P. (1952, pp. 15–28), has noted, the concept of a vocation as a mystical element infused by the Holy Spirit and felt in the depths of the soul, making the recipient profoundly certain that God has called him to the clerical or religious life, is no longer held by most theologians and in fact has been condemned by Rome. The magisterium has never made a pronouncement on the *source* of a religious vocation. Throughout the course of history, there have been four theories on its source: attraction theory, external vocation theory, general vocation theory, and special internal vocation theory (Fr. Farrel, 1952, pp. 15–28). Most theologians and indeed Rome itself are of the opinion that a person has a religious vocation when *all* the following are present: (1) an intellectual and volitional attraction to the sacerdotal or religious state; (2) a right and worthy intention; (3) mental, physical, emotional, moral, and spiritual aptitude; (4) a lack of moral or canonical impediments; and (5) a free and expressed call to orders or to final vows by the bishop or religious superior. In one sense, as Canon Lahitton (1922) noted, the call from the bishop (or religious superior) is sufficient for a vocation, even in the absence of the other four elements.

Catholic school people should be mindful of these five elements. They should also attempt to assist students to the realization that God gives certain individuals grace to be disposed to be attracted to the priesthood or religious life not because of their own merits but because of God's will (Fr. Carr, O.F.M. Conv., 1950, pp. 7–15, 51–100).

Many vocation recruiters possibly drive away more numerous prospects than they attract. First, as Fr. R. Butler, O.P. (1961, p. 8), has noted, far too much religiovocational promotion tends to exaggerate obscurity by urging the young person to listen to some "inner voice" or to look deeply into his or her "heart of hearts." For example, Sister M. Alician's study (1949) of Catholic high school girls revealed that 75 per cent believed God would give them a special sign if they had a vocation to the religious life. Second, recruiters often fail to realize that choice of the priesthood or religious life is a developmental process which spans many years in the youth's maturation. His or her ultimate decision is profoundly affected by a series of influences, actions, and occurrences, each dependent in some measure upon preceding ones.

Clerical and Religious Careers

A person's lifeway and particular lifework within that lifeway form the core around which a social adjustment and personal satisfaction are woven. State of life and career are not mere adjuncts or accessories to living. The pattern of career development of a child and a youth prior to entry into that career is a growth process in which he learns about careers, attains some sort of career identity, finds out more about himself, discovers his self-concept, and attempts to bring this concept into congruence with reality. The early stages of all career development consist in exploration, reality testing, and actual attempts characterized by trial and error. In the case of religious development, realism is particularly important. Numerous vocation recruiters paint overglamorous accounts of the clerical and religious life. As a result many children and youths think of and often select the clerical and religious life on a fantasy choice rather than on a choice based on the reality of the career. Such youths enter the seminary and novitiate; later when they discover that their fantasy choices were indeed fantasies, they either leave or sail undisturbed through ordination, novitiate, and their careers, living a life of ecclesiastical romanticism while the realities of the world and of the laity they are supposed to serve pass them by.

Religiovocational guidance should keep in mind the following principles: First, the student should develop internal rather than external criteria of success in the clerical or religious career; e.g., the cleric with the wealthiest parish is not necessarily the most successful priest. Second, the student should come to an awareness that the clerical or religious career is a service profession, with emphasis on both the service and the professional aspects. Third, he should see the nature of the living out of a religiovocation as a development process. Fourth, he should perceive religiovocational choice as an essential thrust and active unfolding of an individual's unique personality.

For a student to make a wise choice concerning a religiovocation, it is essential that he have adequate information. The proper selection of a religious community, a secular institute, or diocesan clergy involves far more than a desire to be a religious or a priest. A religious vocation necessarily involves occupational selection. There are religious and priests who work in hospitals, who teach, who do parochial work, and each in a wide variety of settings, e.g., mission countries, the South, urban areas. Each community and diocese has its own spirit and emphasis. The task of religiovocational development is to give the interested student information and other types of assistance to aid him in selecting the community or diocese that will best help him fulfill his personality. It is morally indefensible to attempt to steer pupils into the order of which one is a member. Career-day lectures, homeroom discussions, and vocational guidance activities should provide the student with information on a wide variety of careers in the religious, clerical, and lay life. Such lectures and discussions should be characterized by general information rather than "hard-sell" pressures to enter the convent or seminary, since students wishing seriously to investigate this type of life usually prefer to conduct their investigations privately with a trusted school guidance worker. As a matter of fact, students quite often do not wish their classmates or teachers to know that they are thinking of becoming a priest or religious.

Some Factors Conducive to Clerical and Religious Vocations

Human beings, particularly children, tend to identify with ministering adults. Since for many years a child is ministered to by his parents and family group, it is only natural that he will introject their views, including their attitudes toward careers. Kinnane and Pable (1962) indicate that a young person's family influences are critical in the development of his work values. This finding is heightened by related results of Kinnane and Pable's own study which discovered that the work values of pupils, with the exception of the heuristic-creative type, are not significantly related either to general intelligence or to school curriculum. Many investigations indicate that the influence of the mother on her children's self-concept is a strong factor in affecting their vocational interest. For example, L. H. Stewart's study (1959, p. 202) came to a conclusion similar to Erik Erikson's theory; viz., the mother transmits the male ideal of *her* parents to her son. White's study (1963) discovered that a girl's vocational aspirations were greatly influenced by the mother's role in the formation of her daughter's self-concept and in the determination of social roles the daughter would follow. Religious vocation experts from many European countries have testified that family Catholic Action groups inevitably produce a greater number of religious vocations than do families which are not in Catholic Action (Fr. Houtart, 1962, pp. 40–41). An investigation by Sister Miriam de Lourdes McMahon, S.C. (1955, p. 388), concluded that fathers more frequently opposed their daughters' entering the convent than did mothers. An investigation by Malnig and Cristantiello (1956) of the interests of freshman students in a Catholic all-male college, however, revealed that parents played a minor role in influencing vocational goals. But the body of research supports the contention that family influence has considerable effect on children's vocational goals. It behooves the Catholic school to cooperate more closely with parents in fostering vocations to the clerical and religious life.

A second influence on religious and clerical vocations is the personality and behavior of priests and religious with whom the youth comes in contact, both in the parish and, particularly, in the school. A study by Sister Mary Mark Barrett (1960) concluded that the greatest influence encouraging or discouraging a Catholic high school girl to enter or not to enter the religious life is the conduct, attitudes, and personality of sisters with whom she comes in contact. By the same token, antihumanistic, overstrict, and ultrarigid personalities of religious and clerical teachers can discourage potential vocational prospects. A study by Sister Rose Matthew Mangini, I.H.M. (1958, p. 251), concluded that "[religious] vocations will not increase unless the religious life is attractive to the prospective candidate who has a right to expect a minimum of humanistic value in the work of the religious teacher. When the students observe incompetence and immaturity which are the obvious results of insufficient training, the sister teacher will alienate the students rather than encourage [religious] vocations among them." One religiovocational study (Fr. J. J. Campbell, S.J., 1952, p. 416) concluded that Catholic boys and girls "often accused priests and sisters of not being as inspiring, encouraging, or approachable as they would wish." A third influence on religious and clerical vocations is socioeconomic status. The Notre Dame study of major seminarians revealed that 62 per cent of the seminarians came from families of the lower-middle economic class, and 13 per cent from families of the lowest economic class (Fr. Fichter, S.J., 1961, p. 79). A fourth influence on clerical and religious vocations seems to be family size. A study made by Fr. (later Bishop) Hagan (1945) revealed that women religious born between 1885 and 1894 came from families whose average size was between five and six children. Then, however, families tended to be larger than they are today.

A fifth influence on clerical and religious vocations appears to be type of school attended. It is generally assumed that Catholic schools are more productive of vocations to religious and clerical life than non-Catholic schools, but there is not much research evidence on this subject. A comprehensive review of the research by Sister M. Celestine, S.C.C. (1962), plus her own study, concluded that single-gender Catholic high schools produce more numerous candidates to the religious life than do Catholic coeducational high schools. A ten-year study by Sister Mary Teresa Francis (1960) of the sources of vocations to the sisterhood concluded that, in the secondary schools taught by her community, single-gender institutions yielded a higher vocation count than those which were coeducational. On the other hand, a study by Brother Bertram Coleman (1960) concluded that there was no appreciable difference between boys' high schools and coeducational high schools as to the vocation yield for the seminary or novitiate.

Studies of single-gender versus coeducational high schools usually fail to evaluate two crucial elements. First, how many students from various types of high schools remain in the seminary or novitiate through ordination or final profession? Second, what is the quality of the students from these different groups who entered the seminary or novitiate? Do candidates from relatively sheltered girls' Catholic high schools who enter the convent at eighteen really understand the world in its material and heterosexual nature so as later to assume their roles in preparing young people to live in that world which they perhaps have never fully experienced? Many schools emphasize overconformity and overdocility; it might be questioned whether such traits produce the religious whose apostolate demands that he be oriented to the modern world.

The primary purpose of a school is not to furnish religious vocations; rather it is to educate youth to grow in truth, whole and entire. Unfortunately all too many clergy and religious regard the main purpose of schools as arsenals for recruiting vocations to their orders. One study (Sister R. M. Mangini, I.H.M., 1958, p. 264) relates of a religious who believed that Catholics should open junior colleges—the only reason she advanced for this proposal was that junior colleges have "a high vocation potential." If Catholic schools have not achieved their educational possibilities, perhaps one reason is that the needs of the student are placed second to the vocation recruitment requirements of the order conducting the school. Of interest in this connection is a study (Sister M. Celestine, 1962, pp. 528–533) which discovered that while 88 per cent of the priests surveyed believed that single-gender high schools were superior to coeducational high schools for promoting vocations to the clerical life, nevertheless 32 per cent of the same priests conceded that a central diocesan coeducational high school was best for the optimum development of adolescent personality.

Selection of Candidates for the Clerical and Religious Life

Selection refers to the total process whereby a diocese or a community systematically appraises a candidate to ascertain whether his developmental need patterns will be adequately fulfilled in the clerical or religious life and whether he is minimally suitable for this life. Emphasis is both on the individual's needs and on the needs of the diocese or community. Selection is often referred to as "screening," but this word has a pejorative connotation, implying that the process is to sift out the unworthy chaff.

The problem of systematic selection for the clerical and religious life first came to the fore when the celebrated Catholic psychiatrist Dom Thomas Vernor Moore (1936) discovered that a disproportionately high percentage of priests and religious suffer from certain types of mental illness. He attributed this circumstance to the fact that the clerical and religious life seems to have a special attraction for prepsychotic persons. He urged that selection devices be developed and utilized. This recommendation led Dom Moore's students to inquire whether the personality and interests of the clergy and religious differ to a significant degree from those of average lay persons. Summing up the research findings, T. N. McCarthy (1960a, p. 44) states: "The results of several interrelated studies gave an affirmative answer to this question. These studies consistently pictured the typical religious-in-training as a person somewhat more submissive, dependent, introspective, and self-conscious than the average American. Further, compared with college students and students preparing for the professions of law, medicine, and dentistry, all of whom deviate from the average, the seminarian was found to be the most deviant."

On a nonempirical level, Fr. Gleason, S.J., (1960), has observed that many religious (and candidates for the religious life) have sought in the religious life a refuge from the conflicts of the outside world. Such persons often were raised in "a Jansenistic twilight of fear [and] can never really learn to devote themselves fully and generously to a community." Frs. Evoy, S.J., and Christoph, S.J. (1963), have observed that the religious life is highly attractive to overdominated persons.

Selection of one sort or another precedes a candidate's entrance into the seminary or novitiate. Currently, psychological tests have been incorporated into the selection procedure. As Fr. Vaughn, S.J. (1957, p. 65), has observed, psychological testing of aspirants does not offer any direct information about the workings of grace within them. Nonetheless, since grace builds on or, more precisely, flows through nature, it is vitally important that the person's nature be assessed in terms of both the ability of the clerical or religious life to meet his developmental needs and the suitability of the candidate for this new way of life. Aspirants have mixed motivations in their religio-vocational choice. The clinically trained guidance specialist, e.g., the school psychologist, is in a position to make valid judgments about the dominance and prevalence of these motivations.

Father Bier, S.J. (1956), and others have used as their basis for psychological selection the Minnesota Multiphasic Personality Inventory. Others have used the Strong Vocational Interest Blank. The Strong blank attempts to ascertain whether a person has the same interests as successful individuals in particular occupational fields. Fr. Lhota, O.F.M. (1948), has developed a modified Strong blank for diocesan priests; Fr. D'Arcy, M.M. (1954), one for missionary priests; Brother Alfred Kolb, S.C. (1952), one for religious teaching brothers; and Sister Mary David Olheiser (1962), one for women religious.

The psychologist's role in the assessment program is not to make a decision about the candidate. Rather his function is to present pertinent information to the bishop or religious superior so that he or she may have facts on which to base the final decision. It is hoped that the bishop or religious superior bases his or her decision on the total picture. The bishop or religious superior, like the psychologist, is ethically bound to secrecy concerning the results of the personality assessment.

The School's Religiovocation Director

One of the Catholic school's staff can serve in the capacity of religiovocation director. The functions of this post include the following:

1. Work with the school guidance director to incorporate and synchronize the religiovocation development thrust into the school program.

2. Coordination of the school's efforts in the sphere of religiovocational development.

3. Encouragement of student interest in the conscious and mature selection of the clerical, religious, or lay life.

4. Making the school religiovocational-minded, not merely in the sense of fostering vocations to the religious or clerical life exclusively but in that of assisting school people to help students think seriously about a career and lifeway best suited to their unique developmental needs.

5. Interviewing students who wish to self-actualize religiovocationally or who have religiovocational difficulties. In not a few cases a student comes to the counselor hoping to have this guidance worker confirm his vocational choices. The counselor should not deny the pupil this support.

6. Maintenance of a library of information on various dioceses, religious communities, secular institutes, lay missionary societies, and careers in the lay apostolate. This library should not contain solely or chiefly information about the religious order conducting the school; such a practice is indirect coercion and thwarts the basic educational aim of helping the student grow according to his unique developmental pattern.

7. Work with counselors in planning career days. These days should include lectures and discussions on the lay, clerical, and religious lifeways and not merely on the last two.

8. Acting as an adviser to teachers, counselors, administrators, and coordinate staff on religiovocation development matters.

9. Observing "prudently," to use Fr. Saalfield's words (1958, p. 103), "undue influence and unhealthy relationships in vocational direction, since

undue influence is forbidden and since excessive attachment to some teacher may lead to an unwise decision."

10. Work with faculty advisers of various religiovocation clubs.

11. Development of Catholic Action cells to help students become aware of what the living of a vibrant lay life entails.

12. Assisting parents in developing within the students a sense of career. As Fr. Saalfield has noted (1958, p. 103), "in all cases parents ought to be consulted before, rather than after, a vocational decision."

13. Work with pastors and with groups such as the Christian Family Movement.

14. Cooperation and maintenance of close liaison with the vocation officials of the diocese and religious orders, as well as with leaders of lay apostolate groups, in developing and implementing the school's religiovocation development activities.

15. Keeping records of former students who have entered the seminary and novitiate, including those who complete their training and those who withdraw. In addition, the director should maintain records on those graduates who marry, separate, and divorce.

16. Attendance, if possible, at the marriage, investiture, profession, and ordination of former students.

The Catholic school should encourage vocations to the clerical and religious life, but this is not the same thing as to use high-pressure tactics. Fostering vocations to the clerical and religious life is a noble work and should never degenerate into the deliberate maneuvering of a student into convent or seminary. Sister M. Berchmans, R.D.C. (1961, p. 93), has commented that the guidance office is not a recruitment office for the clerical or religious life.

Some forward-looking religiovocational directors interviewing a boy or girl interested in the seminary or novitiate avoid suggesting any course of activities which insulates that student from the world. Realizing that the seminary or novitiate itself overinsulates youths from the world, these alert directors advise the young person to participate in activities of the school and community, including dating. In this way unsuitable prospects are screened before they formally apply for admission and those who enter have an accurate, healthy view of the layman's life. Alert religiovocation directors also suggest to a student interested in the seminary or novitiate that he or she give thought to a wide variety of religious congregations and dioceses, as well as careers in the lay life. Sometimes they are accused by reactionary Catholic school people of "discouraging vocations" or "being disloyal to the congregation or diocese." Quite the contrary is true, because they are attempting to assist youth to select that place in life most suitable to their personality fulfillment and therefore to God's glory. Any other course of action constitutes religiovocational chauvinism and immoral maneuvering.

part **5**

RETROSPECT AND PROSPECT

17

A PROSPECTUS FOR
IMPROVED GUIDANCE SERVICES

The need for adequate guidance

Responses to the need for comprehensive guidance services run from the bald assertion that guidance is merely an educational frill to the more subtle contention that guidance is useful only insofar as it renders pupils more pliant and docile to school rules. Between the two poles of this continuum range positions which overtly or covertly *deny* the need for a total program of school guidance services: First, an effective guidance program ensures that each student sees the counselor for a fifteen-minute period every month or two. "Bullet interviews" of this type enable every student to have the opportunity of presenting his problems to the counselor and having these problems solved promptly and without waste of time. Second, guidance is needed only when the student manifests reasonably serious problems, usually in the area of overt aggression and hostility. Third, the totality of school guidance services is handled by the counselor, whose basic function is to patch up temporarily the problems of students experiencing some difficulty. Thus the counselor is a sort of Mr. Fix-it who administers the same guidance aspirin to all clients. Fourth, guidance aims at assisting pupils to adapt to the jungle world in which they must live rather than actualize their ideals within their individual social milieu. As one hard-bitten counselor (Gendel, 1963) replied to the goals proposed by guidance experts, "Come off it; the ideals of Uthant [sic], Gardner Murphy are wonderful, but we live in a world that listens to other drum beats." Fifth, vocational guidance is necessary only for early school leavers or those who terminate formal education after high school. Sixth, the core of school guidance, as Owen (1958) maintains, consists in telling the student at the outset of his school career that in order to remain in school he will have to work hard and will not be coddled. Seventh, the ultimate in guidance weaponry consists in suspension guidance and expulsion guidance. By being removed from systematic guidance assistance, the pupil is being signally aided in coming to grips with himself and in solving by and for himself that problem which the school confidently felt neither it nor indeed any agency in the school system could help solve. Chapman (1962), a staunch advocate of this position, views suspension guidance as positive, cure-promoting therapy.

Most contemporary mature educators (cf. Lloyd-Jones, 1962, p. 17) and schoolmen regard guidance not only as a necessary element of the school's total educational program but in fact as one of its central bearings. Guidance is not confused or identified with education as it was in the 1930s, when, for example, F. Smith (1936, p. 774) wrote: "Guidance is education and education should be ninety-nine per cent guidance." Rather guidance is regarded as one of the three indispensable services which comprise the total school program; the other two are instruction and administration. The important Trump Report (J. L. Trump & Dorsey Baynham, 1961), which will undoubtedly provide the basis and guideline for secondary education in the next generation, placed heavy emphasis on the centrality and pervasiveness of the guidance function in the school's total program. Of Conant's famous 21 recommendations (1959) for the improvement of American high schools, nearly half concern guidance. It might even be of some consolation to know that Berdie's review (1959) concluded that available evidence indicates that students who receive counseling remain in school longer than matched students who do not.

School guidance is of significant assistance in helping normal youths self-actualize, but it can also be a valuable aid in the prevention of more serious mental disorders. Thus a Catholic psychiatrist (Cavanagh & Fr. McGoldrick, S.J., 1958, p. 16) commented: "Most cases of mental disorder, including many of the psychoses, are the result primarily of unhealthy mental and emotional habits which proper home and *school* training could have prevented [italics supplied]." Many mental illnesses manifest themselves when persons are still in school. The highest rate of incidence in the onset of diagnosed schizophrenia is between one and twenty years of age (Kuntz,

1939, p. 173), while 60 per cent of manic-depressives become so between the ages of fifteen and twenty-five (Cavanagh & Fr. McGoldrick, 1958, p. 369). Certainly every school guidance worker has as one of his obligations the detection of signs of potential mental illness in the students. A nation-wide survey by the 1960 Golden Anniversary White House Conference on Children and Youth reported that prevention and treatment of juvenile delinquency ranked as the number one major concern in 45 states surveyed; the second most frequently mentioned major problem was the emotionally disturbed child and youth (Baer, 1961). School guidance not only ministers to the needs of the average student but also identifies and makes appropriate referrals of more severely troubled students.

The need for effective preparation of school counselors

Counseling has increasingly become recognized as a distinct profession. Wrenn (1957, p. 176) has remarked, perhaps a bit wryly: "Surely counseling now has fairly secure status. Clinical psychologists now wish to counsel also, as do supervisors, ministers, and social workers. We have financial counselors, pastoral counselors, residence counselors—there is no end. Counseling as a function (*or* as a label) is surely on the bandwagon." Unless steps are taken to upgrade the quality of counselor preparation programs, the selection of counselors, the conditions under which counselors work, and the level of counselor in-service programs, however, the profession of school counselor will be in danger of degenerating into busy work.

Recruitment, selection, course preparation, and in-service education of school counselors are determined by and dependent on the professional competence the school counselor is expected to possess. The policy statement of the American School Counselor Association (1963b) declared that to possess minimal professional competence the school counselor should:

1. Understand clearly the processes which characterize individual, educational and psychosocial development within our culture.

2. Understand the purpose, potential, and limitation of mass education in his society, and the implications for counseling programs.

3. Understand the basis for and characteristics of the philosophical conflicts which stem from the interaction of students, teachers, and administrators within the context of the school.

4. Understand the teaching relationship as experienced by teachers.

5. Understand counseling theory and procedures which will enable him to counsel effectively with students within relatively short-term circumstances.

6. Have sufficient understanding of educational and psychological measurement to enable him to plan for and implement student appraisal programs and procedures, and to interpret and use resulting appraisal data with maximum efficiency and meaning.

7. Have skills which will permit him to capitalize upon group procedures whenever appropriate and possible.

8. Have a broad knowledge of educational and vocational trends and information resources adequate to assure that students can obtain sufficient information regarding educational-vocational and psycho-social opportunities within the total school program.

9. Have a working knowledge of resources and opportunities for help available to students with special problems.

10. Have a knowledge of other pupil personnel services sufficient to allow him to maximize coordination and cooperation between his efforts and those of other pupil personnel specialists.

Some public and Catholic school educators seem to believe that counseling is like kissing; there is no need for special preparation prior to practicing the art. Most responsible schoolmen and counselor-educators, however, are of the opinion that what is urgently needed is an uncompromising evaluation of the recruitment, selection, preparation, and in-service education of the school counselor. Nearly all evaluative studies on this question are descriptive only in terms of what is occurring in counselor preparation programs, rather than of how effective such programs are in producing successful counselors. Since passage of the National Defense Education Act (NDEA) in 1958 a little, but only a little, more attention has been focused on research in counselor preparation.

Recruitment of School Counselors

G. E. Hill's review (1961, pp. 355–356) concluded that school counselors are drawn chiefly from the teaching rank and file, largely from the staffs of the schools in which they become counselors. Herein lies a capital difficulty in the recruitment of outstanding counselors, since the teacher shortage has made it possible for almost any college graduate, however unsuitable, to become a schoolteacher. In some Catholic schools it is not even necessary for a teacher to be a college graduate. While there are proportionately few lay counselors in Catholic schools, their number is definitely on the increase. Fr. Tracy's nationwide study (1958, pp. 301–340) of lay teachers in Catholic high schools reveals that the selection process for hiring lay teachers is neither systematic nor demanding; the reservoir for tapping potentially outstanding lay counselors is not rich. Relevant to this point are nine of his findings: (1) 53 per cent of the schools preferred as lay teachers single women to married women; (2) 71 per cent employed lay teachers only when religious were not available, and 75 per cent had a policy that the number of the lay teachers could never exceed that of the religious teachers; (3) the Catholic high schools discriminated against hiring the Negro lay teacher—in theory 22 per cent stated that they would absolutely refuse to hire a Negro lay teacher, while in practice extremely few schools had Negro teachers; (4) 55 per cent had no written contract with lay teachers, while those which did had only an annual contract; (5) of the schools investigated, not a single one had a tenure plan for lay teachers; (6) the turnover of lay teachers was heavy because of such unprofessional working conditions as excessive class size and many teaching periods per day; (7) the Catholic school seemed to be a training ground for public school teachers; (8) Catholic school administrators seemed somewhat reluctant to admit that lay teachers had made important contributions to Catholic education; and (9) most schools seemed to feature separate teacher societies for the lay and religious staffs.

Nor is the college situation very favorable. A study (Berg, 1958) of college professors in three academic disciplines concluded that a person's entry into the groves of Academe is in most cases a drifting toward the professorial lectern; as regards clerical and religious teachers in Catholic colleges, it usually is the result of appointment by the religious superior.

The relatively low prestige which school counselors hold in the eyes of professional psychologists is a barrier to recruitment from the ranks of those who would like to enter some branch of the psychological services. Granger's study (1959) of the prestige rankings of 20 psychological occupations as rated by psychologists revealed that the school counselor ranked eighteenth and the school psychologist fourteenth. To improve dramatically the quality of school counselor candidates, it is necessary to inaugurate a systematic program of recruitment among in-service and preservice teachers, undergraduates majoring in social and behavioral sciences, and others suited to a career in the helping professions.

Screening of School Counselors

Not all who desire to become counselors should enter the profession, both for their own welfare and for that of youths they would counsel. Careful selection procedures must be employed to ensure that suitable candidates are admitted and retained in counselor preparation programs. The American Personnel and Guidance Association (APGA, 1961, p. 405) has formally recommended that there be three stages in screening school counselors, viz., selective admission, selective retention, and endorsement for certification. These procedures are to be carried on by the counselor preparation institution in cooperation with appropriate school systems. Unfortunately counselor selection is usually confined to admission to the program. Except for course marks and practicum, little is done to provide evaluation throughout the stages of the candidate's preparation.

Santavicca's study (1959) revealed that 85 per cent of counselor education programs in the universities surveyed made the applicant's college undergraduate record the primary screening consideration. While rigorous and continuous evaluation during the program does not seem to have taken place, there is one happy note in that 72 per cent of these institutions consider the personal adjustment of the candidate in the overall selection procedure. The study did not, however, disclose how the candidate's personal adjustment was measured. Some counselor educators have proposed administering personality tests to prospective counselor candidates to screen persons who wish to enter counseling as a means of working out their own personality difficulties by and through counseling relationships with clients. As Lawton (1958) has noted, poorly adjusted counselors in the counseling relationship overemphasize, nonverbally seduce, deny sex, and exercise the Babbitt syndrome. Indeed some counselors are themselves in urgent need of deep-level counseling and perhaps of psychotherapy (Harper, 1958, pp. 33–38; Lawton, 1958, pp. 28–33). There is a difference between a poorly adjusted counselor working out his personality difficulties through the relationship and the well-adjusted counselor learning more of his own personality through the counseling interview, since most counseling theorists subscribe to the principle that the counseling relationship is a learning situation for both counselor and client. As Recktenwald (1960, pp. 508–509) has observed, by coming to an awareness of the psychographics of the client's personality or problems, or both, the counselor can more clearly perceive and assess the contours of his own self. The primary goal of the counselor, however, must always remain that of assisting the client; what the counselor learns about himself is a vital by-product but a by-product nonetheless.

A review of literature by Dispenzieri and Balinsky (1963) concluded there is some evidence about the personality characteristics necessary for effectiveness in counseling. Such an identification of characteristics is highly important, for if personality inventories of counselor candidates are to have any meaning, it is vital that scores be judged against a bench mark, viz., knowledge of precisely what personality traits characterize the successful counselor. Dispenzieri and Balinsky found that the most frequently discussed characteristics in the literature are tolerance and open-mindedness of counselor toward the client and the counselor's level of generalized anxiety. To apply such a finding to counselor selection, Kemp (1926b) investigated two groups of counselor trainees, one group closed-minded, i.e., possessing dogmatic tendencies, and the other group open-minded (as measured by the Rokeach Dogmatism Scale, Form E). The investigation concluded that the open-minded group "who have less need to narrow and distort, and who normally consider ideas on their own merits [rather than by appeals to authority or by a need to conform] are better integrated, experience less threat, have less anxiety, and are more permissive in their normal relationships" tend in the actual counseling situations to be more understanding and supportive in response to clients than closed-minded trainees. Dogmatism is characteristic of the authoritarian personality, or one who is "conventional, submits uncritically in the face of authority, is anti-intraceptive, superstitious, and stereotypic in his thinking, is preoccupied with the 'dominance-submission, strong-weak, leader-follower dimension,' over-emphasizes the conventionalized attributes of his ego, has exaggerated assertions of strength and toughness, is cynical and destructive, tends to believe that 'wild and dangerous things go on in the world,' has an exaggerated concern with sexual goings on" (Adorno et al., 1950, p. 7).

Catholic clerics, religious, and laymen frequently possess many attributes of an authoritarian personality. It is not Catholicism, however, but a Jansenistic and ultraplatonic type of Catholic thinking which has caused many Catholics to develop an authoritarian personality. The infusion of the "new theology" into Catholic schools, while slow in coming, nevertheless will have an impact in broadening the narrowness of many contemporary Catholic attitudes. Results of P. P. Grande's doctoral study (1964) are instructive in this regard. Studying the determinants of rapport in the school counseling relationship, Grande reported (1) Catholic secondary school clients counseled by laymen experienced consistently a higher degree of rapport measured by the R. P. Anderson and G. V. Anderson (1962) Rapport Rating Scale than did otherwise similar clients counseled by "religious counselors," i.e., priests, brothers, and sisters; (2) counselor personality traits identified as low authoritarianism, low moral rigidity, high spontaneity in human relationships, high ego strength, and a definite preference toward radicalism and away from conservatism were related to client rapport, regardless of the counselor's religious status; and (3) counselor personality traits identified as sensitivity, tender-mindedness, and orientation toward persons rather than things were related to client rapport only when the counselor was a layman and not when the counselor was a religious, even though layman and religious possessed the same "amount" of these traits. The investigator concluded that the religious role (i.e., habit) sets up a barrier between counselor and client so that the client is unable to perceive and to respond positively to the last-named personality traits. Grande conjectured that such a barrier serves to explain why clients counseled by laymen generally experienced a higher degree of rapport.

A measurement instrument which attempts to screen out unpromising counselor candidates must appraise the entire range of personality traits of the effective school counselor. G. E. Hill's review (1961) revealed that there has not as yet been developed a satisfactory instrument on which selection of counselor candidates can be based. As Hill points out, before such an instrument can be developed, there must be a thoroughgoing analysis of all characteristics of the successful school counselor; indeed most studies have unearthed the fact that essential traits are much the same as for graduate preparation in any field, viz., scholastic aptitude, desire to enter the profession, and personal qualities requisite for success in most areas.

University Preparation of School Counselors

University preparation, including both course work and other counselor-oriented experiences, is determined by three factors, viz., actual functions of the on-the-job counselor, recommendations of professional organizations, and state certification requirements for counselors, customarily influenced to a marked degree by the first two factors. A number of studies, like Hutson's (1962a), reveal that counselors engage in many sorts of guidance activities in addition to counseling. This suggests breadth in counselor preparation programs. The APGA, through both its Committee on Counselor Preparation and its Association for Counselor Education and Supervision (ACES) National Committee on Counselor Education Standards, has recommended standards for certification of school counselors. These recommendations actually suggest university preparation requisite for the minimally effective school counselor, with the hope that state certification will be based on such preparation. The committees stated that the undergraduate education of the future counselor should include a broad program of general education, with some specialization in the behavioral sciences, but that it should not include specialized courses in counseling skills and techniques. The committees recommended that the master's degree representing two years of graduate work be considered a requisite for counselor certification, since only through such a program can integrated and in-depth training be assured. Merely taking courses here and there for certification purposes does not lead to unified, integrated training. In considering the content of the master's program, the APGA Committee on Counselor Preparation (1958) recommended eight broad areas with which every counselor candidate should be conversant: (1) personality organization and development, (2) environmental factors in adjustment, (3) individual appraisal, (4) statistical and research methodology, (5) philosophical and professional orientation, (6) counseling, (7) group guidance, and (8) supervised practicum. The committee believed that the practicum constituted one of the most important aspects of the university preparation program and recommended a minimum of 120 hours for one semester. It recognized that the preparation for elementary school counselors should differ from that for secondary school counselors.

Most guidance experts stress the need for extensive work in psychology in the preparation of school counselors. Yet a study by Harmon and Arnold (1960) of a sample of school counselors revealed that they felt that as far as preparation for their guidance duties was concerned, psychology courses in general, with the exception of courses in individual testing and mental hygiene, were less valuable than were guidance or guidance-related courses. This suggests the possibility of investigating the entire relationship of psychology courses with the guidance sequence, especially with a view to more effective coordination and increased awareness of psychology for guidance majors as supportive of guidance rather than as the study of a distinct discipline appropriate for the preparation of future professors of psychology.

Any institution of higher learning wishing to establish a graduate program leading to a degree in guidance and counseling, expanding its present program, or applying for an NDEA guidance institute, should possess certain essential and indeed minimal characteristics: (1) institutional quality of at least superior caliber, not just that of another run-of-the-mill small college; (2) a faculty of well-trained leaders in the field at least on the regional level; (3) a program of sufficient breadth, rather than a bare minimum of course work for the degree, e.g., specialized course work and allied activities in personnel work in higher education; (4) adequate institutional resources for the program, including counseling centers with trained counselors available for supervisory observation, fully equipped guidance laboratories, an institutional library well supplied with books and periodical literature not only in guidance but in the guidance-related areas of the social sciences, the behavioral sciences, and the humanities, and, finally, such allied departments as psychology; (5) opportunities for internships and externships; (6) working relationships with public and private counseling and social service agencies in the community so as to broaden students' experiences; (7) definite selection procedures for screening candidates for the program; and (8) willingness and available resources to evaluate the guidance program which the institution is offering.

Most important, preservice counselors need a healthy block of supervised counseling experience. The *counseling practicum* consists in supervised counseling experience in which the trainee actually handles both individual and group cases on the university campus, usually in specially designed counseling cubicles with one-way-vision screens. Clients are pupils from local high schools or the university itself, whichever is more appropriate for the trainee's program. The interviews are usually recorded and are discussed either individually with the trainee or made the focus of a trainee group discussion. The practicum differs from laboratory experience and from the counseling externship. *Laboratory experience* consists in activities related to analysis of or participation in counseling-related experiences as part of the total counselor preparation program, e.g., observation of counseling interviews, testing of students, analyzing occupational or educational materials, group work, and engaging in role-playing activities. The *externship* consists in systematically supervised experience in a school setting. This involves cooperation between the sponsoring university and the school.

The chief advantage of the practicum, as the review of the research by W. J. Mueller, Claire M. Gatsch, and Jean K. Ralston (1963, p. 513) indicated, is that the future style of the counselor in an interview can be reasonably predicted from his behavior with other clients in previous interviews. Norris (1960) found that counselors who attained the master's degree from a large Midwestern state university during a ten-year period, most of whom were employed in guidance, believed that greater emphasis in the degree program should be placed on the counseling practicum and on courses in testing and statistics. The APGA (1963, p. 404) recommended that the practicum be part of every counselor preparation program. Despite the importance of both the practicum and the recommendation of the APGA, a surprisingly large number of university counselor preparation programs still either do not offer such a course or make it mandatory for all counselor trainees. A study by Harmon and Arnold (1960) of school counselors in the Northern, Eastern, and Western United States revealed that as many as 40 per cent had no supervised practicum. Dugan (1960a, p. 39), a noted guidance expert, has stated that the greatest weakness in counselor preparation programs is the poor quality or even lack of a supervised practicum. One reason for this situation is that the practicum is costly in terms of time, facilities, and ratio of counselor educators to students. Hence many institutions, particularly the smaller ones, are unwilling to inaugurate the practicum despite its vital importance. The externship, of course, is rarer still.

A new type of university counselor preparation program has arisen as a result of the National Defense Education Act of 1958. The purpose of this act is to ensure trained American manpower of sufficient quantity and quality to meet national defense needs. NDEA authorizes the United States Commissioner of Education to arrange for the establishment of guidance institutes to assist teachers to enter a university preparation program necessary for them to become certified counselors. These institutes are contracted through approved institutions of higher learning by the U.S. Office of Education. Courses are at the graduate level. There are two types, short-term institutes, normally held during the summer session; and long-term institutes, customarily lasting an academic year. Federally financed NDEA guidance institutes have had a strong and generally beneficial influence on upgrading guidance in secondary schools.

It is generally agreed that long-term guidance institutes are preferable to short-term institutes. Indeed Dugan (1960a) has expressed some concern about NDEA summer institutes. First, the emphasis accorded them on the national level might give the impression that counselor preparation requires only a short-term "crash program," particularly when teachers take most of their course work in the summer or religious jump on the guidance bandwagon without enough systematic preparation to ride that bandwagon successfully. Second, summer institutes tend to encroach gradually upon established university programs for counselor preparation. The full-year residence program, rather than the summer program, must still be regarded as the "normal" route for counselor preparation. Third, there still seems to be a lack of adequate involvement of the members of the sponsoring university's psychology department so as to ensure a satisfactory, integrative psychological underpinning for counselor preparation.

The preparation of the effective school counselor does not terminate with his preservice education. Indeed, if preservice preparation is not supplemented with in-service work, there is every likelihood that the counselor will grow stale and cease to be a successful guidance worker. Preservice preparation merely marks the conclusion of the *introductory stage* of the counselor's professional education, not its end.

The increasing professionalization of counselor preparation has led to something of a dilemma. On the one hand, high standards of selection and preparation can strike a crippling blow at attempts to alleviate the counselor shortage. On the other hand, insistence that every school have a realistic counselor-pupil ratio has led to a relaxation of standards in hiring counselors. Public and Catholic school administrators tend toward the attitude of "get a body to fill the vacancy and we'll worry about the qualifications later." In this connection Dugan (1960b, p. 108) has stated that "the problem of ersatz counselors will increasingly haunt state educational leaders," the very leaders who lower standards for hiring counselors because of the school population explosion.

Other guidance needs

There are many needs for the improvement of school guidance other than those discussed thus far. Four of the more pressing needs are the following: *First,* research on a large scale in the area of guidance and counseling is being neglected despite the urgings of most guidance experts. Of the outstanding leaders in the guidance field, none is primarily a researcher; usually they are either professors or practitioners who may engage in research in a part-time capacity. Doctoral programs in guidance often do not adequately stress research; indeed many doctoral candidates labor under the erroneous impression that the dissertation is a necessary and unpleasant hurdle. Guidance and counseling do not tend to attract candidates interested in the eremitical life which rigorous research often entails. Published research on guidance and counseling does not, in Dressel's words (1954, p. 100), "seem to have much apparent effect on counseling practice, or at least its effect is not immediately apparent." The cause of this unfortunate situation is difficult to pinpoint: perhaps it is the normal time lag between research findings and implementation, perhaps counselor ignorance of these findings resulting from a lack of in-service growth, perhaps the consequence of a hesitation to change present practices, perhaps the conflict of findings with closely prized ideas or attitudes, or perhaps a combination of all these factors.

Second, more attention must be accorded to guidance and counseling on non-secondary school levels. The old vocational guidance thrust with its attendant emphasis on secondary school guidance had until 1965 been reinforced by NDEA with its special stress on upgrading secondary school guidance personnel exclusively. Only in the 1950s did textbooks begin to appear widely in the area of preparation for elementary school guidance work; their content is often not very different from that of the standard secondary school–oriented work. Little attention is given to specialized training programs for personnel workers in higher education, since, with the exception of the large universities, anyone with a kindly mien is deemed *ipso facto* a good college student personnel worker.

Third, more heed must be paid guidance needs in small schools. Certainly it is difficult for schools with fewer than 1,000 pupils to have a well-developed guidance program (or, indeed, a well-developed instructional program). This problem confronts Catholic schools in particular. Each religious community wishes to have its own school in order to foster religiovocations to that community; hence Catholic high schools tend to be small institutions. Some alert Catholic schoolmen, however, have been erecting large schools, such as two in Philadelphia which can accommodate 4,000 and 5,000 students, respectively. In many rural communities large schools are virtually impossible to establish, and therefore special attention should be directed at developing guidance programs in such educational settings.

Fourth, there is still an insular posture with respect to certification of guidance workers. There should be national (but not federally controlled) certification standards for counselors and other guidance personnel, developed by professional associations. Such a situation would bring about reciprocity of guidance certificates among states and upgrade certification standards in more lax states. In the interests of professionalization, however, perhaps it would be wise for guidance practitioners, in addition to satisfactory completion of a university program leading to certification, to take an examination to practice, much as do physicians, dentists, and lawyers. Nor is it wise to have a single counselor certificate valid for elementary, junior high, and senior high schools, since the guidance needs of the pupils are different at each level.

Need for criticism of guidance practices

Over the past two decades and particularly since the enactment of NDEA, the quality of school guidance services and personnel has improved dramatically, but much more remains to be done in public and, especially, in Catholic schools to bring services to the level of adequacy. Unfortunately many persons prefer to suppress criticism of the present state of guidance services and personnel. McDonough (1960) has deplored the trend in guidance conferences and symposia to emphasize only the positive aspects of the state of the guidance movement and to refrain from all but obscurely negative comments. Such gagging, he asserts, can lead only to paralysis and stagnation of school guidance services.

Guidance literature rarely gives an account of a failure or an unsuccessful experimentation in guidance. Almost all interviews end with the student confidently self-actualizing or gaining perceptive insight. One gets the impression that the history of guidance programs is one endless success story, that all counseling interviews turn out with the client living happily ever after. Only when one reads transcripts of interviews by depth psychologists does he encounter failure to achieve the goals of the counseling relationship. What is needed in guidance literature and addresses is the truth, not merely favorable reports. Schoolmen too long have cushioned the public, and indeed themselves, from the hard truth.

If critics of the guidance situation in public schools are often branded as "enemies of public education," then critics of the guidance situation in Catholic schools are vehemently denounced as "disloyal to the Church." Apologists fail to grasp that real disloyalty to the Church consists in whitewashing incompetence and blunderings in the school situation. Such whitewashing not only has perpetuated poor school guidance services but has either failed to develop or possibly even ruined the potentialities of some students who have passed through the portals of Catholic schools. If as Fr. Küng (1962, p. 36) has observed, the motto of the Church is *"ecclesia semper reformanda"* (the Church is always in need of reform), then the motto of the Church's schools must be "the school is always in need of reform." Fr. Ward, C.S.C. (1959, p. 25), has noted: "The best thing going on today in American education is criticism and self-criticism. Self-criticism is the life of the schools as well as the life of man and of human institutions."

Catholic guidance experts should be in the forefront of the American school guidance movement, not lagging behind public school experts, as has in fact happened. Cardinal Suhard (1950, p. 102) wrote: "Your task, therefore, Christian thinkers, is not to follow, but to lead. It is not enough to be disciples, you must become masters; it is not enough to imitate, you must invent."

Religious school people and guidance workers often hesitate even to point out to their superiors shortcomings of the guidance situation in schools. Frequently the reason for their silence is the belief that the vow of obedience commands them to do as they are told, not to criticize practices (or the lack of them) which the superior in his or her wisdom has instituted. In this connection Cottle (1962, p. 90) has noted that there is no real conflict between the vow of obedience and the professional obligation of the religious to point out to his or her superior, to peers, or to the Catholic world in general unprofessional practices with a negative or hindering effect on the program of guidance services. Fr. Poorman, C.S.C. (1964), concluded that the concept of shared decision making (which should characterize every school) necessitates frank analyses and criticisms on the part of religious subordinates of poor educational practices and that such analyses are decidedly within the law and the spirit of the vow of obedience. His investigation also concluded that the notion of "blind obedience" is regarded by most contemporary theologians as a distortion of the true nature of the vow and in fact only serves to stultify and kill the vow's life-giving spirit. It may be of interest to note that E. E. Smith's investigation (1959) revealed that individuals who behave defensively in groups are low in insight.

THE GUIDANCE SITUATION
IN PUBLIC SCHOOLS

The school system

By the beginning of 1963 most public school systems throughout the nation had some sort of organized system of pupil personnel and guidance services. In most cases, however, this organization was far from complete in both comprehensiveness and manpower. Typical of the shortage of manpower is the situation of the school psychologists. While membership in the Division of School Psychologists of the American Psychological Association (APA) increased by 800 per cent in the period from 1951 to 1962, there remains an acute shortage of these vital specialists. Most small school systems have no full-time school psychologist, while even the largest systems are woefully understaffed. In 1961 New York City, with the largest public school system in the nation, had only 100 school psychologists, while Chicago had but 90 (Trachtman, 1961). The recommended ratio of school psychologist to pupils is 1:1,000. Further, as Powell (1960) has remarked, in school systems which have sufficient school psychologists, these specialists are seldom used to the greatest possible advantage. Sometimes well-trained psychologists are employed only for testing of a routine nature, while in other cases their chief function is to set up and develop a testing program in a particular school. They rarely work with teachers in giving the curriculum a psychologically based guidance orientation or in assisting them to develop a deeper psychological awareness.

The secondary school

The secondary school level has received most attention from the guidance movement since its inception. Much improvement has taken place at this level, to the extent that secondary school guidance is in a more advanced stage than is guidance at any other school level. Yet much remains to be done.

The guidance program

A 1953 national survey (A. J. Jones & L. M. Miller, 1954) revealed that less than 20 per cent of the nation's public high schools had an organized counseling service of any kind. Since then, particularly since NDEA, there has been considerable improvement not only in the area of counseling services but in the entire guidance program itself. Nonetheless, much remains to be done in organizing a guidance program, implementing it, and making it known to and used by students. While both school systems and local schools assume a large share of the blame for not having adequately organized guidance programs, state educational authorities bear some portion of guilt. By 1963 only 18 states made it compulsory for a secondary school to have a guidance program in order to qualify for state accreditation. Only 12 states made mandatory requirements or suggestions regarding the organization and administration of the local school guidance program. A mere 2 states suggested that the school have a guidance committee, and only 7 states emphasized the necessity of coordinating the guidance program with curriculum and teaching. Indeed by 1963, 12 states had only one professional person assigned on a full or part-time basis to state guidance activities. State educational authorities must exert more positive leadership to assist local school systems and local schools to upgrade the quality of guidance.

Gibson's study (1962) of representative public high schools in a tri-state area discovered that one-half of the students were not sure of what constituted the services and activities of the school guidance program; one-third reported that the guidance program had never been described, explained, or outlined to them. A study (Hartley & Hedlund, 1952, pp. 17, 48, 71) of selected public secondary school guidance programs in New York State revealed that pupil needs in personal, social, and vocational guidance were not served as well as needs in scholastic development guidance. Pupils felt that the school guidance program was remiss in helping them decide whether to remain in or leave school, in assisting in successful adjustment to the world of work, and in aiding in the solution of their problems. Although this study dates back to 1950, there seems to be sufficient evidence that school guidance programs still do not adequately meet these identified pupil needs. Guidance teamwork and organized guidance assistance could also be improved. For example, an investigation (Roemmich & Schmidt, 1962) of all secondary school graduates in a large Western city revealed that only 1 in 20 students received help from his teachers in selecting a specific college or in making college plans and only 1 in 10 received assistance from his counselor in this regard. Indeed 1 in 3 students made his selection on his own, without the assistance of any school worker. Carlin's investigation (1960) of college freshmen found that only 40 per cent had an occupations or occupations-related course in high school. Further, half of those who had such a course felt it had not been helpful. On the basis of his own experience with culturally deprived youths, Vincent Riccio (Riccio & Slocum, 1962) observed that school guidance programs are quite unrealistic in terms of the needs of these students; indeed the programs seem predicated upon a middle-class conception of life and life values.

Plant Facilities for Guidance

Much has been accomplished to provide adequate space for the counselor and guidance specialists, particularly in the new public secondary schools, but much still remains to be done. A study by K. H. Parker (1957) showed that 75 per cent of both counselors and building principals investigated were dissatisfied with present school plant facilities for guidance. In its policy statement, the American School Counselor Association (ASCA; 1963b, p. 197) recommended: "The school counselor should have physical facilities appropriate to his work, including a private counseling room, a storage facility for student records and environmental information, and a student waiting room." It is safe to say that many public secondary schools still fall short of this recommendation. In this area, as in the case of the guidance program in general, the state educational authorities are derelict in their duty. By 1963 only four states had provisions in their state accreditation standards for specific physical facilities, e.g., private counseling offices. Seven other states had several overall but rather vague and undefined provisions to the effect that the facilities should be adequate to serve the program.

Number and Qualifications of Counselors

Since the enactment of NDEA, great strides have been made in increasing the number of school counselors and reducing the counselor-pupil ratio. By the end of 1957, prior to the passage of NDEA, the U.S. Office of Education (R. J. Becker, 1963) estimated 12,000 full-time counselors were available to students in grades 7 to 12 in public secondary schools across the nation, or a counselor-pupil ratio of 1:924. By 1960 there were an estimated 18,739 counselors, or a ratio of 1:638, and by 1963 the number of counselors had risen to an estimated 26,947, or a ratio of 1:537. Improvement must still be made if the counselor-pupil ratio is to approximate the recommendation of 1:250 set forth by the ASCA (1963a, p. 201). No states have a ratio approaching this recommendation. A study by Farwell and Vekich (1959) revealed that in Ohio public secondary schools 57 per cent of all schools had no full-time, half-time, or less than half-time counselors. Of the 43 per cent which had counselors, nearly one-fourth had only half-time or less than half-time counselors.

Regional accrediting associations have tended to help upgrade the guidance situation relative to the number of counselors in public schools. Some associations, however, have not pressed with vigor in this area. By 1964 the North Central Association *recommended* a ratio of 1 counselor to 300 students, while the Northwest Association *required* 1:400, and the Southern Association *prescribed* 1:500. Other regional associations did not mention the counselor-student ratio. The Middle States Association stated that, in addition to provision for qualified counselors, each staff member should share the responsibility for both formal and informal guidance.

Froehlich's conclusion concerning the level of preparation of guidance counselors is similar to that of practically every investigation from 1930 to the present: "Surveys of employed guidance workers have revealed the great disparity between recommended training and that actually possessed by on-the-job-counselors." A study by Wendorf (1956) revealed that in 1955 only 14 per cent of the 727 guidance counselors in Ohio high schools held state certification for that position. The previously cited investigation by Farwell and Vekich (1959) concluded that in schools with counselors of any sort only 20 per cent of these guidance workers held state certification. The low percentage of certified Ohio counselors had by 1963 been rectified because of the impact of NDEA; nevertheless, much more upgrading needs to be done (Van Atta & Peters, 1963). An investigation by Acree and Marquis (1957) revealed that as late as 1955 there was not a single full-time guidance counselor in the Tennessee secondary schools studied; only 8 per cent of the schools had an expenditure of any sort for guidance in their budgets. As late as 1957 there were only 19 certified school counselors in the state of Oklahoma (Oklahoma Curriculum Improvement Commission, 1961, p. 35). The sorry state of the numbers and certification of counselors prior to 1958 was due largely to inaction by state educational authorities. It was not until the Federal government's interest in and financial subsidization of guidance and counseling that states began to press forward in earnest. As late as 1950 only 23 states had established mandatory certification requirements for school counselors, 18 of them between 1946 and 1950. By 1955 only 27 states had certification requirements. After NDEA the number increased, reaching 37 by 1960. In 1963 there were still 5 states which required no special certification for school counselors, thus permitting anyone, however untrained, to become a counselor (of interest is the fact that none of these states was located in the South). A national study by Weitz (1958) of persons in charge of guidance services in public schools concluded that relatively few states were ready to undertake an evaluation of counselor certification requirements by means of experimentation. This indicates there still is not the requisite dynamism or leadership at the state level in counselor certification. In only a few states is there a special certificate for teacher-counselors, which means that for practical purposes any teacher, however untrained in guidance, can serve as a teacher-counselor in schools.

Arbuckle (1957a, p. 61), a counselor educator at a large Eastern university, testifies that more than once he has been asked by a prospective student "What course in guidance should I take?" because "I have recently been appointed director of guidance [in my school] but I don't know anything about it."

Counselor Role as Perceived by Students and School People

Various investigations have revealed that school counselors fail to give pupils and school people adequate information as to the counselor's role, with the result that students all too often perceive the counselor's function as almost exclusively occupational and educational advisement. Pupil perceptions of the counselor's role are crucially important, since they not only cause many students to refrain from seeking couselor assistance in areas perceived to lie outside the role but also condition the degree of pupil self-actualization during the relationship itself, as self-actualization in counseling is partially contingent on what the student expects to derive from the relationship.

A study by Gibson (1962, p. 457) revealed that high school students felt that counselors were not adequately communicating the role of the guidance program or of guidance services available. These students perceived the counselor variously as an administrator, a disciplinarian, an activity director, and a part-time librairan. In fact, many students did not identify counseling as the major function of the school counselor. Grant's study (1954a) indicated that while students regarded counselors of significant help in educational and vocational planning, they perceived the counselor as playing a minor role in problems of a personal nature. Houghton's investigation (1956) of the counselor role as perceived by high school seniors, teachers, counselors, and administrators in selected public high schools revealed that all four groups have a similar perception of the role as almost exclusively in the area of scholastic development guidance. A New York State study (Hartley & Hedlund, 1952, pp. 38–39) of guidance programs in selected public secondary schools disclosed that 89 per cent of pupils had been helped in scholastic and educational areas by the counselor, but only 60 per cent in social and personal areas. The study concluded that in the last two very sensitive areas pupils did not clearly accept the counselor role. Rather, the study noted, with problems of a personal nature a pupil tends to seek the help of a teacher in whom he has confidence or with whom he has close acquaintanceship, regardless of the teacher's assignment on the school staff. Further, personal and social development counseling is not inherently less difficult than scholastic and educational development counseling; indeed, it is more difficult. The researchers recommended that teachers receive special training in counseling as part of their regular work to be certificated as teachers. Heilfron's investigation (1960) of high school youths' perceptions of the role of the counselor revealed that students expected counselors to devote themselves to individuals with overt problems of a more or less serious nature rather than to those who could use assistance not so much in overcoming problems as in discovering the best ways of utilizing to the full their own resources. In addition, this investigation disclosed that students tended to perceive both counselor and guidance specialist as "head shrinkers," persons to whom "nuts" go for help. These studies serve to reinforce the concept that students and school people need to be educated concerning the nature and role of the school counselor, the counseling service, and the guidance program in general.

What Counselors Actually Do

The counselor's chief role is to serve as a consultant in human development to students, faculty, administrators, and parents. Within this broad role are many subroles, including counseling. Indeed, every guidance association and almost every expert agree that counseling is the chief subrole, with counseling-supportive activities (e.g., research on needs of students) and cooperation with teachers and staff in the guidance effort comprising other pivotal functions. Yet in actual practice counseling consumes less than half of the counselor's time, primarily because he engages in or is compelled to engage in activities definitely outside his role and province. D. L. Arnold's survey (1949) of counselors and counseling deans in Ohio found that these guidance workers spent more time in attendance work, punitive disciplinary functions, recording tardiness, and other duties than in counseling. Purcell's study (1957a; 1957b) of counselors in a large suburban area revealed that 75 per cent personally administered standardized tests of various sorts, 55 per cent were responsible for assigning students to classes, 13 per cent recorded class marks on official transcripts, and 9 per cent were required to keep the school's daily attendance records. An investigation by Tennyson (1956) on utilization of time revealed that counselors thought they were spending too much time in collecting and filing occupational and educational information (which could be done just as efficiently by a nonprofessional, paid counselor aide) and too little time in research services.

At the opposite extreme are counselors who disdain any legitimate counselor function other than personal and social counseling. Hitchcock (1953), in a nationwide study of public secondary school counselors, found that 40 per cent of those who assist with occupational plans do not regard this as their proper function; nor do 41 per cent of those who assist failing pupils to improve study habits and to raise marks, 37 per cent of those who interpret test results to teachers, and 37 per cent of those who assist teachers to help students with problems. A study by K. B. Hoyt and J. N. Loughary (1958) revealed that counselors in metropolitan secondary schools neither were well acquainted with nor were making effective use of referral sources at their disposal. To counteract exclusivism, the ASCA (1963a, pp. 198–201) has delineated 10 distinct functions for the school counselor: (1) planning and development of the guidance program, (2) counseling, (3) pupil appraisal, (4) educational and occupational planning, (5) referral work, (6) placement, (7) parent help, (8) staff consulting, (9) local research, and (10) public relations.

The elementary school

At the present time, organized comprehensive guidance in the elementary school is a goal rather than an accomplished fact. Professional guidance periodicals such as the *Personnel and Guidance Journal* and the *National Catholic Guidance Conference Journal* (like its predecessor, the *Catholic Counselor*) do not contain a proportionate share of articles on elementary school guidance. Until 1965, NDEA excluded elementary schools from participation in its guidance funds. Much of the thinking about the prospects and forms of elementary school guidance seems unduly colored by the secondary school model. What is needed in this regard are a distinctive guidance approach, strategy, and program for elementary school guidance, not a carbon copy of the secondary school pattern.

There are few counselors in elementary schools. Instead, guidance personnel in elementary schools tend to consist of a cluster of guidance specialists, e.g., the school psychologist, the psychiatric social worker who visits pupils' homes, the pediatrician, and so forth (Willey, 1960, pp. 8–11). A major reason for the existence of a cluster of specialists in place of a group of counselors is that elementary school guidance has tended to concentrate on the atypical rather than the normal child. Little change in such an emphasis will likely occur until school system administrators change their attitudes in this regard. The training of these specialists, unlike the counselor's broad training, tends to lead to a narrow specialism. Anna Freud (1960a, p. 38) noted in this connection: "At present all [specialized guidance] workers in the children's services, whether in schools, hospitals, courts, or clinics, suffer from the effects of specialized training and lack of coordination and integration in the field." Unless there is a guidance worker with a general background as well as highly advanced professional knowledge in the dynamics of human development, it is difficult for teamwork in guidance to become a reality in the school.

Some experts in elementary school guidance oppose counselors in elementary schools, preferring guidance specialists and consultants. They base their opposition on three points: there is seldom an opportunity for pupils to select courses on the elementary level, vocational planning is not encouraged in the elementary school, and only a limited number of pupils have the verbal facility which counseling seems to demand. Assistance in course selection, however, is only one function of the counselor. Indeed, if the nongraded elementary school continues to increase in numbers around the nation, there would seem to be a definite need for counselors to assist the student, his teachers, and his parents in adumbrating what areas of study are most fruitful for him (Goodlad & Anderson, 1963). Second, vocational planning must be viewed as an intimate outgrowth of personality development and therefore be considered, at least seminally, on the elementary level. Third, counseling is more a matter of pupil perception and emotional acceptance than of adult maturity in intellectual self-diagnosis. The level of intellectual self-diagnosis, while crucially important, cannot be measured by adult standards but rather on the level appropriate for the child of an early age group.

It probably will be some time before there is anything resembling an adequate counselor-student ratio on the elementary school level. Teachers in fact do much of the interviewing with students, a situation made relatively easy by the more personal teacher-pupil contact possible in a self-contained rather than in a departmentalized classroom. Unfortunately very few teachers on the elementary school level have the requisite course work to enable them to be even minimally qualified to engage in such a relationship, viz., graduate courses in guidance foundations at the elementary level, child development, learning and behavioral disorders of children, family interaction, and guidance practicum.

Personnel work in higher education

Guidance in colleges and universities is customarily referred to as student personnel work. This entire aspect of the college or university educational program is weak. In fact, it is difficult to ascertain which area is in greater need, elementary school guidance or student personnel work in higher education. A review of pertinent literature by Lloyd-Jones and Smith (1963, p. 163) concluded: "Guidance services [in higher education], like many other services in education, are still offered largely on the basis of hope and faith." The reviewers observed that, despite the general recognition of the need to evaluate the personnel services program, there is little evidence to indicate that this need is being met in the nation's colleges and universities. Perhaps institutions of higher learning are too much preoccupied with issuing vague but catchy slogans about their commitment to excellence and their "distinctive" programs to pay attention to the more essential but less glamorous aspects of implementing these slogans.

As a general rule, the smaller the college, the weaker the organized program of personnel services. W. L. Scott (1960, p. 739) remarked that some colleges seem to think that coordination of whatever guidance and personnel services exists is almost automatic in a small institution and can easily be taken care of informally during a coffee break. His investigation concluded that small colleges (defined as those with an enrollment of less than 2,000) needed "some serious thinking about the methods they use in the functioning of their student personnel services and in the ways the services are coordinated with other areas of these institutions." Scott also noted the paucity of personnel literature concerned with or directed at small colleges. He gave three reasons for this fact: small colleges usually do not encourage publication, nor do they prize it highly as in large universities; personnel workers in small colleges are often untrained and are usually faculty members who spend additional time in personnel functions; and it is easier to conceptualize student personnel services as separate, specialized units, such as are found on large campuses. As a result, concluded Scott, the workers' egoidentification is not with personnel services, and their means for gaining status within the college lies in areas other than in student personnel work; hence small college personnel workers have a tendency to spend less time thinking about and writing on personnel work.

Private liberal arts colleges, revered by tradition and wrapped in a veil of mystique, are quite weak in personnel services. A national survey by Arbuckle and Kauffman (1959) of representative private traditional arts colleges revealed that these institutions indeed recognized that counseling constituted the weakest area in their collection of personnel services; only 19 per cent of these colleges thought their counseling program satisfactory. The investigators found a tendency on the part of the colleges to consider the term *counselor* to include the college chaplain, selected faculty members, dean of students, dean of men, and dean of women, no matter what their qualifications or professional training. A review of student personnel literature by the same investigators concluded that very little research, reporting, or comment on student personnel services emanate from traditional liberal arts colleges.

While the most highly organized and most effective program of personnel services in a higher educational setting generally is found in large public institutions, all is not perfect there. Often, particularly in extremely large universities, the size of the institution thwarts adequate coordination of various personnel services and activities. A study by King and Matteson (1959) of student perception of the counseling center in a public university revealed that students feel free to take scholastic development problems to the counseling center; after scholastic development problems, the order is, in descending preference, vocational development problems, social development problems, and personal development problems. This study indicates that personnel workers have failed to communicate to the student body one of their central and pivotal roles, viz., assistance in personal problems. An investigation by Braden (1953) of 420 youths who either graduated from or dropped out of a fairly large public university concluded that university personnel and counseling services were not effective in facilitating postschool adjustment. Seeman (1959, p. 2) cites an investigation which revealed no significant personality differences (as measured by the MMPI) between clients of the university's counseling center and students in general. This *might* indicate that there are many students with serious personal problems who are not being counseled or that students' perception of the role of the counseling center is primarily scholastic, educational, and occupational, rather than social and personal. Finally, a rift born of large size and specialization seems to be growing in large university personnel staffs. In university counseling centers where there are many and indeed specialized counselors, a status distinction has arisen between the "upper-level" counselors engaged in therapy focused on personal problems and those workers on the "lower level" who counsel students experiencing vocational or scholastic difficulties. The lower-level worker sees his job as a stepping-stone to the upper level.

Colleges and universities, regardless of size and control (i.e., private or public), need to upgrade the quantity and quality of personnel services in residence halls. The purpose of residence halls is to provide a context of guided purposeful living in a school setting to attain the broad educational objectives of the school. One of these objectives is effective guidance brought about through a systematic, organized program of personnel services under the leadership of trained, qualified workers. As Williamson (1958a) has noted, the type and quality of leadership in residence halls is the basic key to their use as a goal-oriented, purposeful educational facility helping the student develop. Such qualified leadership, however, is lacking. A nationwide study by Kilbourn (1959) of member institutions in the Association of College and University Housing Officers which operated at least one residence hall for women students revealed the following data: First, only 17 per cent of the head residence officers had specialized college training in guidance, counseling, or personnel work, despite the fact that administrators of these institutions claimed to believe that course work in guidance and personnel services constituted the best academic preparation for the position of head resident officer. Second, only about half of the institutions required a bachelor's degree for the position of residence hall counselor, and 35 per cent stated they would hire a residence hall counselor without any college training whatever. Only one-fifth of the institutions required the master's degree for *new* residence hall officers. Larger institutions had higher academic standards for residence hall officers than did smaller colleges. Third, 65 per cent of the residence hall officers were over fifty years of age, with less than one-fourth being under forty. (Parenthetically, it might be noted that such personnel workers resemble house grandmothers more than they do house mothers.) On the other hand, 75 per cent of the administrators stated they preferred head residence officers less than fifty years of age. Fourth, 61 per cent of the residence officers were widows. The results of this investigation are more disheartening when one considers that less professionally minded institutions usually are not members of the Association of College and University Housing Officers and hence did not participate in the study. Kilbourn concluded his investigation with the recommendation that residence officers possess as a *minimal* training a bachelor's degree plus specialized preparation in guidance, counseling, and personnel services.

Certainly every residence officer should have at least a master's degree in personnel services, with concentration in the area of higher education. Both the National Association of Student Personnel Administrators (1957) and the National Association of Women Deans and Counselors (1957) have noted the need for upgrading the professional competence and status of residence hall workers if adequate services are to be afforded students. A study by the Committee on Student Personnel Work of the American Council on Education (1950) concluded that potentialities for fruitful and meaningful group living in the residence hall setting will never be attained until residence hall workers are given salary, status, and rank in keeping with the educational importance of their work. Unfortunately many administrators seem to think that residence hall work is little more than a form of baby-sitting and attendance inspection and hence have accorded residence hall personnel workers salary, status, and rank of such low level that few qualified persons seek the position.

Perhaps an even more neglected area than the professionalization of residence hall guidance workers is that of admissions officers. As indicated in Chapter 3, the admissions service is an integral part of a comprehensive guidance program. Consequently admissions officers should be qualified to fulfill their role as personnel workers. Minimal graduate training includes courses in principles of personnel work and guidance, tests and measurements, interviewing techniques, and cognate areas.

One of the newer and fastest-growing segments of higher education is the junior college. Junior colleges serve many functions, such as forming the more traditional upward extension of the finishing school, providing a new terminal institution, and offering students an opportunity for further school exploration to ascertain whether to continue formal education in a four-year college or a university. In any event, this type of institution of necessity has as an *essential* part of its program a guidance thrust. Despite this critical need for a highly developed guidance program, junior colleges are still quite remiss. Starr's survey (1960) of guidance practices in selected junior colleges in the Northwest concluded that there were a lack of professionally trained counselors, and excessive reliance on faculty members totally untrained in guidance, an almost exclusive dependence on the testing program as the major guidance vehicle, poorly developed programs fostering personal and social development, and little research evaluation on the effectiveness of the guidance program.

Everything considered, the evidence indicates that personnel and guidance services in publicly controlled educational institutions need improvement.

THE GUIDANCE SITUATION
IN CATHOLIC SCHOOLS

Great as the need is for upgrading guidance in public schools, it cannot begin to compare with the need which Catholic schools face in this crucial area. The guidance picture in Catholic schools is dismal. The only source of consolation is that it is impossible to fall off the floor, and therefore the situation must inevitably improve.

Perhaps the most pressing need is to convince Catholic school people that there *is* indeed an urgent need to upgrade guidance drastically and radically. Several reasons can be offered to explain why Catholic school people generally have not grasped the full import of the need. First, priests, who by and large control American Catholic education either by direct governance or by the influence of their example, have not come to a realization of the urgency of the situation. In large measure this is probably due to seminary training. Rarely in seminaries is there anything resembling an organized program of guidance services; the priest is often unfamiliar both with the concept of a guidance program and with the actual operations of such a program. Fr. Briggs, M.M. (1952, pp. 175–176), concluded that, according to both the standards of the regional secular accrediting agencies and the opinion of a jury of professional educators, insufficient time was provided for pupils in American minor seminaries to study or to think. As a result of their pressed schedule, little time was available for guidance activities, if such existed. Inadequate seminary libraries (Fr. Kortendick, S.S., 1963) at best provide an energetic seminarian with a paucity of works on guidance. Moreover, in his seminary days the priest often acquires the attitude that the collar, plus a knowledge of moral theology, plus the grace of the state of holy orders, automatically assures him of providing the most efficacious guidance possible, whether in the pastoral or in the school setting.

The second reason is the fact that the Catholic school is a creature of a Church which never changes its dogmas; this often tends to give a reactionary, antiprogressive cast to the responses of Catholic schoolmen to "new" educational developments such as guidance. If an organized guidance program did not exist in Catholic schools in bygone days, why is such a program necessary now? Indeed the unofficial motto of the American Church in general seems to be that of a famous ultraconservative Italian cardinal, viz., *"semper idem"* (always the same). Msgr. George Johnson's remarks made in 1924 (p. 576) anent Catholic schools and the new curricula then coming into existence are applicable today to the reaction of Catholic schools to organized guidance programs: "The public schools attempt some improvement; we [Catholic educators] react with charges of 'fad,' go in for sarcasm and ridicule, and end up by tardily accepting the improvement."

The third reason for the lack of Catholic awareness of the need to upgrade guidance drastically is a tendency among Catholic school people to believe that because a school is under Church auspices, it automatically provides the pupils with optimum guidance. There is no basis for this unwarranted inference even in the related area of instruction in religion. A study by Sister Katherine Paul Gregory, R.S.M. (1962), of five basal sets of religion textbooks used in Catholic secondary schools concluded that in only one was sufficient guidance information given to pupils on religioemotional problems.

The fourth reason is the all too common belief among Catholic school people that since rigorous selection procedures plus expulsion guidance assure most Catholic schools of having "good" pupils who are above average in intelligence, guidance is unnecessary. Guidance is regarded as rehabilitating "problem pupils"; students who are good and intelligent are neither troubled nor in trouble. The evidence seems to indicate, however, that this is true neither for modern Catholic school youths nor for youths in Catholic schools before World War II. An investigation by Sister Miriam de Lourdes McMahon, S.C. (1955, p. 391), disclosed that 65 per cent of Catholic high school students stated they felt the need for counseling. Fleege's celebrated study (1945) of Catholic high school boys revealed that 64 per cent of the seniors had not settled on the choice of a career and indeed felt that the school had been of no help in this area, 40 per cent thought they were not fitted for academic subjects they were studying in school, 80 per cent worried about their scholastic endeavors, 50 per cent felt depressed more or less frequently, 60 per cent believed at least occasionally that life was too difficult to understand, 30 per cent experienced difficulty in getting along with people, 60 per cent were dissatisfied with the social life opportunities offered by their parishes, and 50 per cent found leisure time wearisome.

The fifth reason is that Catholic school people are not only professionally insular in regard to the American school guidance movement but indeed tend to be unprofessional as well. Cottle (1962), a Catholic guidance expert, has noted that for much too long a time Catholic school people have hampered their educational programs by highlighting differences between their schools and public schools, as well as by withdrawal tendencies which cut them off from full professional life. The pitifully sparse representation of Catholic colleges and universities at the highly influential 1963 National Guidance Conference sponsored by the U.S. Office of Education (Lee, 1965) bears witness to Cottle's contention. Catholic guidance workers and authorities seldom contribute articles on guidance to non-Catholic journals. Before the *Catholic Counselor* appeared, there were disproportionately few articles on guidance in Catholic educational periodicals (Willett, 1955). Nor are Catholics availing themselves of the opportunities of participating fully in Federal moneys for guidance, a paradoxical development in view of the demand by the bishops for Federal aid for Catholic schools. By the spring of 1961, a total of 197 universities had held NDEA-sponsored guidance institutes, only 9 of which were conducted by Catholic institutions of higher learning. These institutes offered professional preparation to a total of 6,884 school counselors, of whom only 79 came from private secondary schools (which include not only Catholic schools but also schools conducted by Lutherans, Episcopalians, Jews, and nonsectarian groups). Hence NDEA has had comparatively little impact on Catholic secondary schools (Hunter, 1961, p. 138).

The sixth reason is that there is little or no stimulation or leadership on the national level for improving guidance services in Catholic schools. While there is a special branch for guidance in the U.S. Office of Education, as late as 1965 there was no special section or department for guidance in either the National Catholic Educational Association or the Department of Education of the National Catholic Welfare Conference. Nor had these bodies as late as 1965 actively furthered the goals of the National Catholic Guidance Conference.

In recent years not a few Catholic educators have been de-emphasizing the one essentially distinctive feature of the Catholic school, viz., the interpenetration of Catholic theology and the Catholic *Weltanschauung* into *all* areas of the school program. Whether this de-emphasis arises from an erroneous concept of the ecumenical spirit is difficult to determine. On the college level, the de-emphasis on Catholic interpenetration is possibly due more to a desire to enroll as many students as possible to pay the tuition necessary to support the institution's expansion program. Arthur E. Smith's nationwide study (1965) of Catholic colleges and universities offering master's degrees in guidance found that only 31 per cent of these institutions believed that the content in counselor preparation courses in Catholic institutions should differ from the content of similar courses in non-Catholic institutions. If Catholic schools on any level cease to be Catholic, it is difficult to understand why such institutions should continue to exist.

Almost all the evidence indicates that there is an urgent need to upgrade guidance drastically and dramatically in the nation's Catholic schools. This chapter cites some of the more important research not only to bolster this contention but to highlight the areas of particularly great need. A few Catholic schools have responded to the need in a professional manner, but the fact remains that such a positive response is the exception rather than the rule.

The nature of guidance

A prime need in Catholic schools is awareness by the Catholic school people as to the nature of guidance. All too often Divine guidance is confused with human guidance, so that in the main Catholic school people have come to believe that since the religious aspects of their school program (e.g., confession) provide Divine guidance, human guidance automatically follows. As Fr. C. F. Donovan, S.J. (1960, p. 89), has remarked, "One reason why at this hour in the day hostility to guidance can be found in some Catholic circles may be that we [Catholics] have relied too complacently on the mechanisms of divine guidance—the sacraments and the pastoral work of the Church." "Grace builds on nature" is an old Catholic maxim; unfortunately too many Catholics overstress the grace aspect while underplaying if not actually neglecting the nature factor. Inadequate guidance programs in Catholic schools, untrained religious, clerical, and lay guidance workers, and poor or nonexistent guidance facilities cannot be defended on the ground that since Catholic schools have the grace, they therefore also have the requisite nature. Catholic school people must attend to the nature element in guidance services and leave the grace primarily to God and to His priests in their sacerdotal functions.

Some priests and religious labor under the mistaken notion that their knowledge of philosophy and theology qualifies them as competent guidance workers. On this point a Catholic psychiatrist and a Jesuit philosopher (Cavanagh & Fr. McGoldrick, S.J., 1958, p. 16) have written: "Theology and philosophy are excellent studies, but an understanding of the nature of God, the mysteries of religion and other theological metaphysics, the knowledge of being, act and potency, the syllogism, even the study of abstract rational psychology leaves one completely ignorant of the technical art of helping people with emotional disturbances."

Occasionally certain segments of the diocesan press take editorial positions that guidance workers are perverting the young, that psychological testing represents an atheistic scientism and a lack of faith in the workings of God (Editorial, p. 1). Whether such editorial stands are taken in an attempt to defend the sorry state of guidance in Catholic schools is difficult to determine. At any rate, such editors—and Catholic school people in general—might well heed the words of Msgr. D'Amour (1959, p. 89):

> The picture insofar as guidance in our [Catholic] schools is concerned is far from bright. If we except the area of moral guidance, our [Catholic] schools are at their weakest in the field of guidance. . . . Too often, Catholic school administrators fail to recognize the scope of guidance. Perhaps this is a clerical failing which might be summed up in the attitude "We don't need guidance; we have the confessional." There is an unfortunate tendency to equate guidance in its entirety with religious and moral guidance. In addition, there is a tendency to feel that any priest and any religious is capable of guidance work and that our [Catholic] schools therefore have adequate guidance programs. School administrators often seem to lack a realization of the technical nature of guidance. Some of them, not realizing that guidance requires persons with special training and special skills, seem to think that guidance is merely a matter of sitting down and talking to a student.

Lee's review (1961a) of research indicates that guidance in Catholic schools is all too often conceived by the clerical and religious teachers and administrators "as steering the student toward a religious vocation, preferably to the order in charge of the school. The success of the school's overall guidance program is not uncommonly measured by the percentage of the graduating class entering the convent or seminary." Yet students in Catholic schools often have a different perception of what guidance should accomplish. For example, one study (Sister M. A. Signorelli, M.Z.S.H., 1956, p. 101) revealed that the students in a girls' Catholic high school perceived guidance as the presentation of occupational knowledge in areas in which students indicated an interest.

A mistaken notion of religion not infrequently hinders attempts at upgrading guidance in Catholic schools. Expressions such as "a noxious spirit of independence" and "a lack of submission to authority" are still quite common in much of Catholic spiritual and devotional literature. There seems little awareness in this literature that such manifestations of independence are due more to a pupil's need to fulfill his developmental tasks and to grow toward mature adulthood than to the satanic temptors. Indeed perhaps the only way a pupil can become himself amid the welter of arbitrary, ultrarigid, and sometimes downright silly rules which characterize much of Catholic school life is to manifest a heady independence.

The diocesan school system office

Most diocesan school superintendents fail to see the need for leadership on their part to assist Catholic schools under their jurisdiction to upgrade guidance. Fr. Drolet's nationwide study (1959) of diocesan superintendents revealed that only 13 dioceses had a diocesan guidance director, only 63 per cent of the superintendents favored the concept of a guidance director, little guidance assistance was offered by the superintendent's office to secondary schools, there was a "lingering skepticism" by superintendents as to a uniform diocesan testing program, and occupational guidance programs were not encouraged to any extent by the diocesan superintendent's office. Lee (1965) reported that no diocesan superintendent's office had an organized program of assistance for guidance services in Catholic secondary schools. Nor do diocesan superintendents seem to favor, much less inaugurate, experimental guidance programs.

Some educationally alert dioceses such as that of Pittsburgh have established diocesan child centers where individual psychological testing and other in-depth helping activities can be carried out. A study by Sister M. Ursula Grimes, S.S.J. (1961, p. 246), revealed, however, that parochial elementary school administrators and teachers in the Pittsburgh diocese made limited use of this center. As with most Catholic educational enterprises, not only are the guidance resources extremely limited but, regrettably, those which are available are not utilized to any significant degree.

The National Catholic Guidance Conference (NCGC) through its diocesan guidance councils attempts to compensate to some degree for the lack of leadership and school-wide guidance assistance by diocesan superintendents. The constitution of NCGC (1962, p. 103) lists the key objectives of the organization, objectives which also delineate the manner in which NCGC hopes to upgrade guidance services in Catholic schools: (1) to encourage development of student personnel services in American Catholic educational institutions, (2) to act as a coordinating and representative agency for Catholics in personnel and guidance work, (3) to foster participation in professional organizations and to serve as a liaison between the Catholic guidance movement and these professional organizations, (4) to stimulate the establishment and growth of diocesan guidance councils, (5) to publish an organ of communication (the *National Catholic Guidance Conference Journal,* formerly the *Catholic Counselor*) and to distribute in-service materials for Catholic guidance workers, (6) to sponsor an annual meeting for Catholic counselors in conjunction with the annual meeting of the American Personnel and Guidance Association, (7) to serve as a consulting agency to Catholic schools and dioceses wishing to improve personnel and guidance services, and (8) to integrate Catholic wisdom and principles with the best in modern personnel and guidance theory and practice.

The secondary school

The Guidance Program

On the whole, organized guidance programs in Catholic secondary schools are weak or nonexistent, according to a nationwide study by Fr. Hartnett, S.M. (1956, p. 69). A nationwide study by Cottle and Fr. Watson, O.S.B. (1957), revealed that only 27 per cent of American Catholic high schools had a formal guidance program, however poorly organized. An investigation by Brother Marion Belka, S.M. (1959, pp. 310–316), of selected secondary schools conducted by a religious order of men concluded that, of the seven identified major aspects of the total school program, the quality and quantity of the guidance service received the lowest rating by alumni and seniors. A study by Sister Violet Marie Custer, O.P. (1955), of the guidance situation in central Catholic high schools in a large Midwestern archdiocese concluded that counseling services were inadequate. A study by Brother Philip Harris, O.S.F. (1956, pp. 263–274), of New York State Catholic high schools offering business courses revealed that only one out of seven schools utilized a psychologist, psychiatrist, or school social worker, thus failing to supplement their guidance facilities by proper referrals; only about 35 per cent had an organized placement program; and only about 20 per cent had a follow-up program.

Perhaps the most complete survey of guidance programs in the nation's Catholic secondary schools was made by Fr. Stack (1958, pp. 155–182). His study, dedicated to St. Jude, concluded that public secondary schools have a more complete and highly organized program of guidance services than Catholic schools. Some conclusions of his study were as follows: First, preadmittance services were severely limited. Second, only 14 per cent of Catholic secondary schools had an orientation program for new students. Third, in less than one-fourth of the schools were guidance services organized under a school guidance director. Fourth, in only half of the schools were counseling services of any kind, however primitive, available. Fifth, in only one-third of the schools were behavior problems screened through a counseling interview. Sixth, Catholic high schools were seriously deficient in providing placement services. Seventh, there was a tendency for Catholic high school administrators to make faculty members untrained in guidance responsible for placement of students. Eighth, provisions for follow-up guidance services were three times less numerous in Catholic high schools than in public and other non-Catholic high schools. Ninth, less than half of the Catholic high schools had student government organizations, and in one-third of those schools which did the selection of student government members was made by administrative appointment or other nonelective methods. Tenth, there was a definite weakness in the number of services provided for guidance on further educational opportunities in college. Eleventh, only slightly more than half of the schools funished remedial work for students, and the schools in general were quite deficient in providing services to assist students scholastically. Twelfth, there was a noticeable emphasis on group guidance rather than on individual counseling.

As late as 1962 only 30 per cent of all American Catholic secondary schools were accredited by the regional accrediting associations (Gorham, 1963, p. 61). The highest percentage of accreditation occurred in Catholic secondary schools in the Pacific Northwest, while the lowest was in New England. If Catholic secondary schools wish to remedy this situation, they should give attention, among other things, to establishing an organized comprehensive program of guidance services, since such a program is normally a factor in attaining accreditation.

Plant Facilities for Guidance

As a general rule, facilities for guidance are extremely poor. Most of the older Catholic schools have no counselor suite, and many of the new buildings lack adequate space for guidance facilities. As a result, zealous principals sometimes have had to resort to such devices as converting oversized broom closets into counselor's offices. As Catholic school administrators begin to grow aware of the urgent need for proper and adequate guidance facilities and start assigning trained counselors to utilize these facilities, the situation in the new plants should very gradually improve.

Number and Qualifications of Counselors

Both the number and the qualifications of counselors in Catholic secondary schools are, in general, scandalously low. Fr. Blee's national study (1956) of selected Catholic high schools indicated that full-time trained counselors were still a rarity. An investigation by Brother Marion Belka, S.M. (1959), of selected secondary schools conducted by a religious order of men discovered that none of the counselors was certified by the state. A nationwide study by Cottle and Fr. Watson, O.S.B. (1958), disclosed that one-third of the "counselors" in Catholic secondary schools had never even taken a single graduate course in either guidance or psychology. The investigators concluded that this was one outgrowth of the common belief among Catholic school people that guidance, counseling, and religious formation are identical. Fr. Stack's study (1958) brought out that in less than half of the schools was there at least one full-time counselor, often in reality the spiritual director; only 18 per cent of all counselors were trained; counseling programs in Catholic high schools emphasized incidental or armchair counseling rather than professional counseling on the basis of definite case loads with trained counselors; only 14 per cent of those schools which had teacher-counselors gave them a reduced teaching load; and only 16 per cent of the schools had in-service training for teacher-counselors. There were no available data on the counselor-pupil ratio in Catholic secondary schools, but it was doubtless extremely high.

Fr. Blee reported that guidance workers were generally professionally unprepared for their positions. Such unpreparedness is probably due to three factors, viz., inadequate preservice preparation, inadequate in-service education, and a lack of the requisite broad experiencing of life and life situations.

The preservice education of guidance workers in Catholic secondary schools leaves a great deal to be desired. Most of these guidance workers, if they are indeed college graduates, have attended Catholic institutions of higher learning, either in the novitiate, the convent, the seminary, or a Catholic college. Most Catholic colleges do not offer guidance courses on the undergraduate level. A few religious congregations offer psychological training to seminarians, but this is not common, and even where it exists, it fails to give adequate preservice preparation to the religious guidance worker. In this connection it is interesting to note that a nationwide study (Givens & Peck, 1958) of representative accredited Protestant seminaries disclosed that nearly all the seminaries investigated offered at least one specialized course in psychological pastoral counseling; in more than 50 per cent of the cases such courses were taught by ministers who had professional training in both psychological counseling and in theology. Even the Sister Formation Conference, in attempting to upgrade dramatically the preservice preparation program for school sisters, has not provided a preservice program which offers a sufficient number of guidance courses to teachers, much less to those who become counselors (Everett Curriculum Workshop, 1956, pp. 91–98). In practice, most Catholic guidance workers, be they teachers, teacher-counselors, or counselors, assume their guidance positions first, then take courses while in service. Little thought is given to what ineffective if not harmful guidance work is taking place while these workers are becoming trained. An untrained counselor is often worse than no counselor at all.

Since the early 1960s swarms of sister-teachers have been taking in-service summer courses in guidance to fill the guidance gap in their schools, but as the nationwide study of Sister Rose Matthew Mangini, I.H.M. (1958, p. 259), concluded, "Sisters have been channeled into degree programs with little more than immediate need as qualification or background." Hunter

(1961, p. 141) made the following pertinent remarks about the manner in which Catholic school personnel are selected and trained for guidance work:

> A [Catholic school] principal writes "Send me four applications for your summer [guidance] institute. Several of our brothers have not yet been assigned, so I will send them to ———— [your university] for counselor training." Or when a sister writes, "I'm sixty-three and a teacher of mathematics. Last summer I attended a National Science Foundation Institute for Chemistry. This summer my superior wants me to attend your Guidance Institute." . . . Or a sister-teacher teaches eight periods a day, travels one and a half hours to the university, then falls asleep in class from exhaustion, and has no time for preparation outside of class.

Hunter concluded that religious superiors and school administrators have a professional and moral responsibility not to permit such an unprofessional situation to continue. Steimel (1961a, p. 146), a Catholic guidance expert, has noted that now that Catholic religious superiors are beginning to send their subjects to the universities for guidance training, the question must be raised whether Catholic schools are at this time willing "to go beyond this initial step and set up complete guidance programs under the direction of a fully-trained counselor." If Catholic school administrators and religious superiors are sincere about upgrading their guidance programs, they forgo the "good-man-can-do-anything" syndrome, select appropriate counselor candidates from among religious and laity, arrange for full-time preservice training, and only then assign them to guidance positions.

The third factor limiting adequate preparation of guidance workers in Catholic schools is lack of requisite broad experiencing of life and life situations. Most counselors in Catholic secondary schools are priests or religious whose rules and constitutions call for a withdrawal from the world. This creates the problem, though by no means insuperable, of attempting to assist lay students whose scope and range of experiences are sometimes far wider and of a different order from those of the religious and clerics. The constitutions of many religious communities prevent plunging directly into the students' milieu, the so-called world. A forward-looking modification of religious constitutions and of certain practices would go a long way in affording clerical and religious guidance workers that broad range of experiences crucial to a fruitful exercise of the school guidance apostolate.

At base, the real problem lies in coming to an awareness of the importance of professionalism in every facet of the educational enterprise. It is widely known that the greatest forces for upgrading the quality of Catholic schools and school personnel have come not from inside Catholic educational circles but from the outside, e.g., from regional accrediting agencies. Such outside forces have compelled Catholic schools at least to begin to improve their condition. Notwithstanding these beneficial influences, a nonprofessional or an unprofessional attitude still pervades Catholic education, perhaps because of the belief that since the Church operates the schools, it will also supply the necessary professionalization. Such an interpretation is quite unwarranted and certainly goes beyond even the broadest and most lenient interpretation of the famous Canon 209 of the *Corpus Juris Canonici*. It might seem difficult to believe that, in a day and age of strong public school awareness of the need for professionalization, nearly 40 per cent of the sisters teaching in Catholic secondary schools in 1957 did not have the requisite academic degrees to qualify minimally for high school work in a public school in their respective states (Sister R. M. Mangini, I.H.M., 1958, p. 257). Sister M. Ralph Fahey's nationwide study (1960, pp. 118–119) concluded that some religious communities still assign their nuns on the *agere contra* principle, i.e., giving them school positions not on the basis of their abilities and desires but on the basis that it is good for the sister's spiritual growth if she is assigned to a school position for which she has a distaste and little natural inclination. Apparently in such communities insufficient thought is given to moral responsibility for the welfare of each child with whom such a sister will come in contact.

Justice is a cardinal virtue, one on which many other virtues hinge. Certainly it is a matter of justice, and indeed of moral responsibility, for Catholic secondary schools to supply students with adequate trained counselors. As Fr. Hogan, C.S.C. (1963), has suggested, Catholic communities of teaching religious should first staff well the schools which they now operate before undertaking to open new institutions. Indeed some alert diocesan superintendents have put a moratorium on new school construction until existing schools are adequately staffed with trained personnel.

The Catholic Layman as Counselor

It is an unusual situation in which a layman is a counselor in a Catholic secondary school. Cottle and Fr. Watson, O.S.B. (1958), reported that only 5 per cent of the counselors in Catholic secondary schools are laymen. Perhaps the reason for this scarcity of lay counselors is a rather simplistic notion of guidance and counseling prevalent in Catholic educational circles. Fr. P. F. Flynn (1961, p. 788) epitomized this notion: "More often than not, when a pupil is not living up to his potential in the educational realm, the basic cause is moral. For a priest, it is comparatively easy to settle the problem or at least to begin to settle it on the spot. . . . It is difficult to imagine any lay guidance director touching these problems so thoroughly; . . . the child not only doesn't resent the priest's invasion, but rather expects it and in most cases welcomes it." There are several fallacies and weaknesses in this rather common Catholic position. First, problems arise from personality malfunctions, which may or may not be moral. Second, a priest by the mere fact that he is a priest has no special power to settle with comparative ease a youth's every problem or even begin to settle it quickly. This is particularly true if the priest is untrained in counseling. Third, a young person who *expects* others to invade his privacy is perhaps in more serious personality difficulty than Fr. Flynn imagines. Fourth, and most cogently, there is no reason why a trained lay counselor cannot effectively help a student solve his problems and self-actualize optimally. Indeed, P. P. Grande's investigation (1964), referred to earlier in this chapter, offers contrary empirical evidence.

The desirability of lay counselors in Catholic schools is linked to a deeper attitude on the part of clerical and religious administrators concerning the wisdom of having laymen in any capacity in Catholic schools. Study upon study of the status of the layman in Catholic schools has revealed that religious and clerical administrators do not usually welcome the idea of a lay staff member; indeed administrators are forced to "take in" lay personnel only when an insufficient number of religious are available. Fr. (later Msgr.) Novicky's study (1950) of laymen employed in Ohio Catholic schools disclosed they felt that (1) the religious did not appreciate the permanent role of the layman in Catholic education, (2) working conditions in Catholic schools were at variance with the principles of social justice espoused by the Church, and (3) religious school administrators failed to realize that lay school people cannot live adequately in the world on the basis of religious poverty. Fr. Tracy (1958, p. 301) sheds light on the attitude of some religious and clerical administrators vis-à-vis lay staff by citing what one priest-administrator of a Catholic school wrote him in connection with his nation-wide study: "Pray for an increase in religious vocations and keep lay teachers at a minimum. We do have some lay teachers of fine caliber, but the majority are a headache. They have disciplinary and professional problems which a well-trained religious rarely has. One little sister usually accomplishes more than two lay teachers combined." It is impossible to force laymen *into* Catholic education, but certainly it is easy to force them *out* of Catholic schools by shabby, ungrateful, unprofessional treatment. Happily, the National Catholic Guidance Conference passed an official resolution in 1964 urging the hiring of an increasing number of trained laymen as counselors in Catholic schools. The resolution further urged that these lay counselors be given salary, retirement benefits, professional status, and opportunity for advancement equivalent to those of comparable public school counselors.

This discussion of the need for lay guidance workers in Catholic secondary schools in no way minimizes the crucial importance of the guidance-trained priest-counselor. The priest fulfills his unique, sacramental function in the counseling relationship more directly than in classroom teaching of such subjects as mathematics, English, or Latin and certainly more than in school administration. A competent layman can be just as effective a classroom teacher or school administrator as a priest. Indeed this important fact should be integrated with Pope Pius XII's doctrine of subsidiarity; i.e., the priest should not perform functions which a layman can perform equally well. Counseling, however, is related to the sacramental ministry of the priest, for which he has special grace by virtue of his office. Through training in guidance principles and counseling techniques, grace can be effectively channeled into superior guidance work. Grace builds on nature; in this field, professional training and competence, gained from graduate preparation, provide the "nature" element. Upon such a nature, aptly disposed by sound professional training, grace is able to build.

Every Catholic secondary school should have a goodly number of lay counselors. Lay Catholics with apostolic leanings might well consider guidance work in Catholic schools as a career objective.

Occupational guidance

Numerous studies (Sister V. M. Custer, O.P., 1955; Sister M. C. Dyer, 1951; Fr. E. J. Fleming, 1955; Brother J. Winkler, F.S.C., 1953) of Catholic high schools and colleges concur that occupational guidance and placement constitute one of the weakest elements of the school's guidance program. Fr. Drolet's investigation (1959, p. 84) concluded that "occupational guidance programs do not appear to be receiving from the diocesan departments of education much support or encouragement." Fr. P. F. Harmon, S.J. (1962, p. 15), cited a study conducted by the sociology department of a New England Catholic men's college in which students were asked their attitudes toward work. The answers were divided into three categories: first, the positive attitude which viewed work as a value in itself and a source of personal fulfillment; second, the instrumental attitude, which perceived work merely as a means of gaining some material advantage; and third, the negative attitude, which regarded work as valueless in itself and in fact an unpleasant necessity. Only 21 per cent of students' responses fell in the first, or positive, category.

The lack of a developed theology of work in the Church is perhaps the primary cause of a lack of awareness of the importance of occupational guidance among Catholic school people. This view has translated itself into a faulty concept of work on the part of Catholic school students. Catholics on the whole do not think of work as a divinely impregnated act, something which of itself joins the person to God. Rather it is conceived of as something which may be offered up to God and hence sanctified by a religious intention. Until the Church develops a mature theology of work, Catholic schools will never give to occupational guidance its commensurate importance and dimension. Perhaps such a theology can proceed along the lines suggested by Fr. Teilhard de Chardin, S.J. (1960, p. 31), who observed that each labor, each work a person performs, *of itself* fulfills not only Christ's work but Christ Himself, for by work a person returns Christ to Christ.

Counseling methodology

Few Catholic guidance theorists have attempted to address themselves to counseling methodology. Catholic guidance practitioners, it is safe to say, still rely primarily on Divine illumination and heavy-handed advisement. Indeed, the posture of many, at least until very recently, was to oppose any counseling theory, e.g., nondirectivism, which ran counter to the hortatory method. Perhaps this is due to the frequent tendency of Catholics to be at best wary of new trends in the so-called secular world or at worst opposed to such trends. As a result the counseling *Zeitgeist* has passed many Catholic guidance workers by, leaving them with a primitive identification of counseling with advisement. As Nordberg (1960a, p. 316) has remarked in a related context, "Where we [Catholics] should be joyfully leading, we are often following and even resisting."

Some Catholic guidance experts ignore or brush aside counseling method as functionally insignificant. Thus, for example, one priest–guidance expert (Saalfield, 1958, p. 76) wrote: "Much discussion and debate have occurred in recent years over the relative merits of directive and nondirective techniques. The counselor in a Catholic secondary school will not be unduly concerned with this debate if he remembers that counseling is largely the work of the Holy Spirit. He will choose accordingly the method or technique that prudence and the other gifts of the Holy Spirit suggest. The power of the grace of God and the sincere interest of the counselor will constitute the best elements of any counseling technique."

In the past few decades there has been a new emphasis in the Church on the kerygmatic method of teaching religion. This method emphasizes joy, the good news of salvation, the sacramentality of all reality. What is needed now is kerygmatic counseling. Unfortunately counseling is still conceived of by many Catholic school people as advisement on how to avoid evil and the snares of the "world." On the other hand, there is a hopeful trend among more advanced Catholic guidance thinkers to integrate a joyful, world-acceptant, human-oriented attitude into counseling theory and practice.

The elementary school

Organized guidance programs in Catholic elementary schools are at an even lower stage of development than those in high schools. Typical is the conclusion of an investigation by Sister M. Ursula Grimes, S.S.J. (1961), viz., that in a large, educationally alert, and progressive Eastern diocese not a single Catholic elementary school surveyed (86 per cent of the total) had a formally organized guidance program, nor did any school have a single full-time trained counselor. Compounding this sorry state of affairs, the principals and teachers in these schools attached little value to nonschool referral services, services which could have assisted the schools in partially overcoming their own severe guidance limitations. While from some standpoints there is greater need for organized guidance programs on the secondary level, there can be no justifiable reason for the failure or reluctance of Catholic elementary schools to inaugurate guidance programs staffed with trained personnel.

Personnel work in higher education

Catholic colleges and universities are in need of a well-developed program of personnel services. A nationwide study by Cottle and Fr. Watson, O.S.B. (1958), revealed that 77 per cent of responding Catholic institutions of higher learning stated that they had formal personnel programs. This figure was deceptively sanguine, however, since the respondents considered any sort of loosely organized services, such as collection of information about students by means of College Entrance Examination Board scores, alumni follow-up for funds and promotion, and so forth, as comprising a "formal program." A nationwide investigation by Sister M. Claver Ready, R.S.M. (1958, p. 307), concluded that personnel services were still carried out in a rather primitive way in most American Catholic colleges for women and indeed were handled chiefly by untrained personnel, usually on a part-time basis. A national survey by Arbuckle and Kauffman (1959, p. 298) of traditional liberal arts colleges revealed that Catholic institutions tended to be better satisfied with their present counseling services and scholastic guidance services than were other colleges. Until Catholic college and university administrators recognize that their institutions need drastic upgrading in personnel services, there is little likelihood of more than surface improvement.

McMurray's nationwide study (1958, pp. 130–156) of personnel services in Catholic women's colleges revealed that preadmittance services were very weak in most colleges and that only about half of the institutions had an orientation course continuing through the first semester. A parallel nationwide investigation by Brother John J. Jansen, S.M. (1955, pp. 188–222), of Catholic men's colleges reached almost identical conclusions. McMurray (1958, pp. 130–156) also reported that in the area of misbehavior the majority of Catholic women's colleges did not consider personal counseling (judging by the extent of its use) an effective means of helping the student develop insight, come to grips with her personality, and formulate a plan for self-improvement. Only 42 per cent of these colleges stated that overt misbehavior cases were screened through at least one "counseling" interview with some school person, whether personnel worker, faculty member, or administrator. Brother Jansen (1955, pp. 188–222) found that less than one-half of the Catholic men's colleges indicated that overt misbehavior cases were screened through at least one counseling interview.

Lee (1961b) observed that Catholic women's colleges do not afford students adequate social life opportunities, thus stunting personal and social growth. Generally speaking, the better the social life program in a particular Catholic women's college, the more the sister-administrator feels the program is inadequate and strives for improvement; conversely, the weaker the program, the more the sister-administrator believes it is utopian. This lack is doubtless one reason why some Catholic girls attend a non-Catholic college or university which combines a vibrant social life program with high academic standards. Shinn's nationwide study (1959) of Catholic women's colleges concluded that social life is not encouraged and that student efforts to improve the relatively stagnant situation are often met with resistance.

Catholic colleges and universities often fail to provide meaningful experiences in student government to help students grow in self-responsibility and healthy independence. McMurray (1958, pp. 141–144) found that in only 3 per cent of Catholic women's colleges surveyed did the student government function as an executive, legislative, and judicial body within limits set by the administration. In most cases the students' role in student government was amorphously labeled "serving as a liaison between the administration, faculty, and students." The investigator hinted that the role of the student government vis-à-vis administration in Catholic women's colleges appears analogous to the position of those who argue for the complete separation of church and state. She suggested that administrators re-evaluate their position on the role of student government, mindful of the growth opportunities which real (as opposed to mock) participation in management of the institution offers.

The investigation by Brother John J. Jansen (1955) disclosed that vocational guidance and occupational placement services in many Catholic men's colleges were not integrated with the total educational objectives of the colleges or adequately staffed to meet the vocational and placement needs of the majority of students. He also reported that only 41 per cent of these colleges indicated that vocational choices were considered when placing students in part-time jobs and that only 59 per cent of these colleges kept an active file of employers and job openings. McMurray (1958) found similarly that occupational guidance in Catholic women's colleges was not well integrated with total educational aims. Only 20 per cent of the colleges stated that students' vocational choices were considered in placing them in part-time jobs, while only 40 per cent maintained an active file of employers and job openings.

Sister Anne Frances Hoey's study (1957) of self-defined problems in matched groups of Catholic students in selected Catholic colleges and in Newman clubs of secular universities determined that Catholic college students reported a higher average number of problems than did Newman Club students. Students in Catholic colleges reported more numerous problems in the academic, personal, and sociosexual areas than Newman Club girls. This study indicates that the entire educational milieu in Catholic colleges should be examined to ascertain if inherent causes produce or induce these problems and if so what can be done to rectify the causative factors.

Brother Jansen (1955) reported that the counseling service in Catholic men's colleges failed to assure the majority of students of personal attention and help. The nationwide study of Catholic women's colleges by Sister M. Claver Ready (1958) disclosed that only half kept "counseling" records, while only one-fourth had adequate physical facilities for counseling. Few Catholic men's or women's colleges have a full-time clinical psychological or psychiatric specialist; instead their catalogues customarily list the name of a local Catholic practitioner to whom the administration occasionally sends students it deems seriously disturbed.

Student Personnel Workers

Regrettably Catholic college administrators can and do hire anyone they wish for personnel work without particular regard for the depth or extent of his professional training. One cause of this situation is lack of awareness that personnel work in general and counseling in particular are specialized services which require professional competence. All too often any faculty member who sits down and talks with a student is considered a "counselor." Similarly an administrator who might supervise a student activity is often regarded as a counselor. Until administrators become professionally aware in this matter, there is little hope of radically improving the present state of affairs.

In his study, Brother Jansen (1955) found that nearly half of the formally designated personnel workers had little or no professional preparation in guidance or psychology. Only 48 per cent of Catholic men's colleges had at least one full-time counselor, trained or untrained. The principal role of the teacher-counselor, usually untrained, was to assist the students in selecting courses prior to registration. Finally, those services which personnel workers offered did not meet the spectrum of individual needs commonly found in student groups. McMurray's parallel study (1958) of Catholic women's colleges came to much the same conclusions, with the exception that these colleges had fewer full-time counselors, trained or untrained. Sister Ready (1958) reported, in her survey of personnel services in Catholic women's colleges, that 50 per cent of the respondents declined to answer items which inquired into whether personnel workers had advanced preparation in guidance or psychology. The investigator also discovered that (1) counseling was still done chiefly by part-time counselors in most of the colleges; (2) most part-time counselors were religious, generally untrained in counseling and personnel work; and (3) full-time counselors were not totally relieved of their teaching duties (indeed, in 18 colleges the full-time counselor taught between six and fourteen hours per week). Fr. John T. Byrne's study (1957, p. 109) of representative Catholic men's colleges concluded that college personnel were inadequate as counselors in connection with scholastic problems, an area in which they might appear to be qualified, and that these colleges assumed only limited responsibility for assisting students in the solution of occupational problems.

Those student personnel workers with some professional preparation as well as those without such preparation seem to be remiss in keeping alert professionally. Sister Ready (1958) found that only 6 Catholic women's college student personnel workers were members of the American Personnel and Guidance Association, while only 15 regularly read the *Personnel and Guidance Journal.*

The lack of adequate professional preservice and in-service education of most personnel workers in Catholic colleges has resulted in ineffective services. One area in which this condition is most evident is the degree to which students take problems to the workers, surely an index of how students perceive these workers to be capable of assisting them. A study by Sister Mary Elaine Rogers, R.S.M. (1957), of counseling preferences of matched college students in sophomore and senior years revealed that students in public colleges consulted counselors about problems more frequently than did Catholic college students. Sister Anne Frances Hoey (1957) discovered that "despite the seeming availability of counseling in the various problem areas, the use of the college counseling facilities by the students in Catholic colleges for women was limited, since they reported using them in considerably less than half of their problems." Fr. Byrne's investigation (1957) revealed that 38 per cent of students in Catholic men's colleges who reported having problems did not discuss their difficulties with anyone; of the remaining students with problems who did discuss their difficulties with someone, only 35 per cent talked with school personnel. These studies indicate that the majority of students in Catholic colleges feel it is not beneficial to present their problems to a teacher or personnel worker.

Student Housing

For college students who do not live at home, there are two chief types of housing, viz., the institutional residence hall and off-campus housing. College personnel workers customarily favor residence hall living because it provides a malleable environment conducive to promoting optimum student development in all areas of personal and social living. In theory, living in residence halls avails the students of opportunities both of communal living and of living in a milieu in which all the college's personnel services are fructified and actualized in the concrete order. Unfortunately the evidence seems to indicate that dormitory life has not had the intended effect on resident students. Sister Anne Frances Hoey (1957) found that resident students in Catholic women's colleges had more numerous problems than non-resident students. Indeed the number and seriousness of the problems of the resident students grew from freshman to senior year, thus suggesting that dormitory life not only failed to help students self-actualize but perhaps prevented them from doing so. Further, 15 per cent of senior residents complained that problems came about because the person in charge of the dormitory did not trust students committed to her care. The parallel study of Catholic men's colleges by Fr. J. T. Byrne (1957) reached similar conclusions.

These studies seem to point to the need for college administrators to use every means to eliminate causes of student problems specifically connected with campus living. A comprehensive, organized, and professional program of personnel services is necessary if residence hall living is to assist students to self-actualize. All too often Catholic college administrators believe that merely dwelling in a residence hall topped by a cross ensures student self-actualization. Sometimes, in the recent expansion of Catholic colleges, these institutions build new residence halls without further thought as to their purpose, methods of providing effective services, and so forth. The only concern seems to be to get a greater number of students into the college. The halls are usually staffed by persons whose chief duties lie outside residence hall personnel work, e.g., teaching and library work. Indeed residence hall staffs usually regard their positions as supervising and watching students so that there is no rowdyism or other unseemly behavior. Hence they look upon their role as a negative one of student containment rather than a positive one of professionally influencing students to self-actualize. Rarely are professionally trained residence hall counselors and officers hired; ancient laymen or laywomen, retired religious or priests, are not infrequently the dormitory "personnel workers."

Away-from-home students who are unwilling or unable to live in college dormitories usually occupy apartments or furnished rooms near the campus or in the town in which the college is situated. Studies by McMurray (1958, pp. 130–156) and Brother Jansen (1955, pp. 188–222) concluded that supervision of off-campus student housing has been greatly neglected. Colleges have an obligation to extend personnel services to residents in off-campus housing.

The Junior College

There are few definitive data on the numerous junior colleges under Catholic auspices. Available evidence suggests that, despite the essential guidance thrust presupposed by the *raison d'être* of these institutions, they possess an even less adequate program of personnel services than do Catholic four-year colleges. The study by Cottle and Fr. Watson (1958) revealed that only about one-third of Catholic junior colleges had any sort of formal program of personnel services, however loosely organized. There is need to upgrade personnel services in junior colleges. As Kohlbrenner (1963) has remarked, the current critical reassessment of Catholic higher education could have as one result the expansion and development of Catholic junior colleges.

Conclusion

Probably no area in all of Catholic education from the elementary school level to the university level is in such dire need of improvement as guidance and personnel services. Apostolic laymen, as well as student-oriented priests and religious, could perform a signal service for the Church by entering this sensitive area as professionally prepared and alert workers. The field is white for the harvest. The costs and the efforts are certainly not exorbitant; the returns are far beyond expectation.

AUTHOR INDEX AND REFERENCES

Numbers which appear in parentheses indicate pages in this book on which reference is made to the work cited.

ABBO, J. A., & HANNAN, J. D. *The sacred canons.* Vol. 1. St Louis: Herder, 1952. (446)

ACKERMAN, GLADYS H. An effective orientation program for seventh graders. *Sch. Couns.*, 1962, **10**, 62–63. (321)

ACREE, N. E., & MARQUIS, B. Counseling in the secondary schools of Tennessee. *Personnel Guid. J.*, 1957, **36**, 279–281. (507)

ADAM, A. *The primacy of love.* (Tr. E. Noonan) Westminster, Md.: Newman, 1958. (379, 471, 472, 474, 475, 477)

ADEN, L. Distortions of a sense of guilt. *Pastoral Psychol.*, 1964, **15**, 16–26. (465)

ADLER, A. *The individual psychology of Alfred Adler.* H. L. Ansbacher & Rowena R. Ansbacker (Eds.) New York: Basic Books, 1956. (104)

ADORNO, T. W., ET AL. *The authoritarian personality.* New York: Harper & Row, 1950. (497)

AGNES, SISTER MARY, C.R.S.M. The role of the classroom teacher in guidance. *Bull. nat. Cath. educ. Ass.*, 1958, **55**, 212–215. (133)

AIKEN, W. *The story of the Eight-year Study.* New York: Harper & Row, 1942. (220, 433)

ALEXANDER, F., & FRENCH, T. M. *Psychoanalytic therapy.* New York: Ronald, 1946. (121)

ALICIAN, SISTER M. Want the $64 answers? *Faculty Adviser*, 1949, **12**, 1–5. (482)

ALLERS, R. *Character education in adolescence.* New York: J. F. Wagner, 1940. (448)

ALLERS, R. Psychiatry and the role of personal belief. In F. J. Braceland (Ed.), *Faith, reason, and modern psychiatry.* New York: Kenedy, 1955. Pp. 31–62. (76)

ALLPORT, G. W. Attitudes. In C. Murchison (Ed.), *A handbook of social psychology.* Worcester, Mass.: Clark Univer. Press, 1935. Pp. 798–844. (142)

ALLPORT, G. W. The psychological nature of personality. *Personalist*, 1953, **34**, 347–357. (76)

ALLPORT, G. W. *Becoming: basic considerations for a psychology of personality.* New Haven, Conn.: Yale, 1955. (49, 74, 335)

ALLPORT, G. W. Psychological models for guidance. *Harvard educ. Rev.*, 1962, **32**, 371–381. (336, 341)

ALLPORT, G. W., & POSTMAN, L. *The psychology of rumor.* New York: Holt, 1947. (206)

ALOIS, BROTHER, C.F.X. A high school guidance bulletin. *Cath. Couns.*, 1959, **4**, 8–9. (189)

ALSTETTER, M. L. Guidance services in two hundred secondary schools. *Occupations*, 1938, **16**, 513–520. (17)

AMERICAN COUNCIL ON EDUCATION. *Social competence and college students.* Washington: Author, 1940. (376)

AMERICAN COUNCIL ON EDUCATION. *The teacher as counselor.* Washington: Author, 1948. (*134, 204*)

AMERICAN COUNCIL ON EDUCATION. *The student personnel point of view.* (Rev. ed.) Washington: Author, 1949. (*16, 25*)

AMERICAN COUNCIL ON EDUCATION, COMMISSION ON TEACHER EDUCATION. *Helping teachers understand children.* Washington: Author, 1945. (*224*)

AMERICAN PERSONNEL AND GUIDANCE ASSOCIATION. A statement of policy. *Personnel Guid. J.*, 1958, **36**, 589. (*102, 209*)

AMERICAN PERSONNEL AND GUIDANCE ASSOCIATION. Standards for the preparation of school counselors. *Personnel Guid. J.*, 1961, **40**, 402–407. (*170, 190, 495*)

AMERICAN PERSONNEL AND GUIDANCE ASSOCIATION, COMMITTEE ON COUNSELOR EDUCATION STANDARDS IN THE PREPARATION OF SECONDARY SCHOOL COUNSELORS. Standards for counselor education in the preparation of secondary-school counselors. *Personnel Guid. J.*, 1964, **42**, 1061–1073. (*170*)

AMERICAN PERSONNEL AND GUIDANCE ASSOCIATION, COMMITTEE ON PREPARATION OF ETHICAL STANDARDS. *A proposed code of ethics for the American Personnel and Guidance Association.* Washington: Author, 1958. (*223*)

AMERICAN PSYCHIATRIC ASSOCIATION, COMMITTEE ON NOMENCLATURE AND STATISTICS. *Diagnostic and statistical manual of mental disorders.* Washington: Author, 1956. (*372*)

AMERICAN PSYCHOLOGICAL ASSOCIATION, DIVISION OF COUNSELING AND GUIDANCE, COMMITTEE ON COUNSELOR TRAINING. Practicum training of counseling psychologists. *Amer. Psychologist*, 1952, **7**, 182–188. (a) (*171*)

AMERICAN PSYCHOLOGICAL ASSOCIATION, DIVISION OF COUNELING AND GUIDANCE, COMMITTEE ON COUNSELOR TRAINING. Recommended standards for training psychologists at the doctorate level. *Amer. Psychologist*, 1952, **7**, 175–181. (b) (*27*)

AMERICAN PSYCHOLOGICAL ASSOCIATION, DIVISION OF COUNSELING PSYCHOLOGY. The scope and standards of preparation in psychology for school counselors. *Amer. Psychologist*, 1962, **17**, 149–152. (*174*)

AMERICAN SCHOOL COUNSELOR ASSOCIATION. Tentative guidelines for the implementation of the ASCA statement of policy for school counselors. *Personnel Guid. J.*, 1963, **42**, 198–203. (a) (*165, 170, 506*)

AMERICAN SCHOOL COUNSELOR ASSOCIATION. Tentative statement of policy for secondary school counselors. *Personnel Guid. J.*, 1963, **42**, 194–198. (b) (*69, 170, 195, 493, 506*)

ANASTASI, ANNE. Psychological tests: uses and abuses. *Teachers Coll. Rec.*, 1961, **62**, 389–393. (*230*)

ANASTASI, ANNE. *Psychological testing.* (2nd ed.) New York: Macmillan, 1962. (*230*)

ANDERL, S., & RUTH, SISTER M., F.S.P.A. *The technique of the Catholic action cell.* (3rd ed.) LaCrosse, Wis.: St. Rose Convent, 1945. (*146, 202*)

ANDERSON, ALICE, & DVORAK, BEATRICE. Differences between three generations in standards and conduct. In R. G. Kuhlen (Ed.), *Psychological studies of human development.* (2nd ed.) New York: Appleton-Century-Crofts, 1963. Pp. 442–446. (*368*)

ANDERSON, R. P., and ANDERSON, G. V. Development of an instrument for measuring rapport. *Personnel Guid. J.*, 1962, **41**, 18–24. (*297, 308, 497*)

ANDERSON, V. E. The evolving core curriculum. In H. R. Douglass (Ed.), *The high school curriculum*. (3rd ed.) New York: Ronald, 1964. Pp. 247–267. (*206*)

ANDRY, R. G. *Delinquency and parental pathology*. London: Methuen, 1960. (*365*)

ANGERS, W. P., & PAULSON, P. C. Cooperation between counseling and health services. *J. Sch. Hlth*, 1964, **34**, 49–53. (*180*)

ANNETTA, SISTER M., S.L. Guidance in the lower grades. *Cath. Sch. J.*, 1940, **40**, 105–107. (*22*)

APP, A. A. Guidance in English classes. *Cath. Couns.*, 1957, **1**, 19–21. (*149*)

AQUINAS, ST. THOMAS. *De veritate*. (*192, 440*)

AQUINAS, ST. THOMAS. *Summa theologica*. (*83, 134, 135, 140, 447*).

ARBUCKLE, D. S. *Teacher counseling*. Reading, Mass.: Addison-Wesley, 1950. (*91, 140*)

ARBUCKLE, D. S. *Guidance and counseling in the classroom*. Boston: Allyn and Bacon, 1957. (a) (*140, 154, 507*)

ARBUCKLE, D. S. The teacher as counselor. *High Sch. J.*, 1957, **40**, 285–289. (b) (*130*)

ARBUCKLE, D. S. Five philosophical issues in counseling. *J. counsel. Psychol.*, 1958, **5**, 211–215. (*97*)

ARBUCKLE, D. S. *Counseling: an introduction*. Boston: Allyn and Bacon, 1961. (*246, 247, 250*)

ARBUCKLE, D. S. Occupational information in the elementary school. *Voc. Guid. Quart.*, 1963–64, **12**, 77–85. (*408*)

ARBUCKLE, D. S., & KAUFFMAN, J. E. Student personnel services in liberal arts colleges. *Personnel Guid. J.*, 1959, **38**, 296–299. (*512, 528*)

ARCHER, C. P. In-service education. *Encyclopedia of educational research*. (3rd ed.) New York: Macmillan, 1960. Pp. 703–708. (*208*)

ARNOLD, D. L. Time spent by counselors and deans. *Occupations*, 1949, **22**, 391–393. (*509*)

ARNOLD, F. X. *Serviteurs de la foi*. Tournai, Belgium: Desclée, 1960. (*77*)

AUGUSTINE, SISTER M., R.S.M. Guidance through the school newspaper. *Cath. Sch. J.*, 1957, **57**, 305–306. (*151*)

AUSTIN, BROTHER E., F.S.C. An experiment in group guidance. *Cath. Couns.*, 1959, **4**, 10–12. (*322*)

AUSUBEL, D. P. *Theories and problems of adolescent development*. New York: Grune & Stratton, 1954. (*56, 60, 363, 370, 395*)

BACHRACH, P. B. The pseudo-vocational problem. *Voc. Guid. Quart.*, 1959, **8**, 93–95. (*395*)

BAER, M. F. Washington flashes. *Personnel Guid. J.*, 1961, **39**, 440–441. (*198, 441*)

BAER, M. F. Washington flashes. *Personnel Guid. J.*, 1962, **40**, 261–262. (*387*)

BAER, M. F. Washington flashes. *Personnel Guid. J.*, 1963, **41**, 500–501. (*417, 435*)

BALDWIN, A., KALHORN, JOAN, & BREESE, FAY H. Patterns of parent behavior. *Psychol. Monogr.*, 1945, **58**, 1–75. (*113*)

BALDWIN, BROTHER, F.S.C. Causes which demand vocational training in the United States. *Bull. Nat. Cath. educ. Ass.*, 1917, **14**, 376–386. (*8*)

BALDWIN, J. Baldwin rejects despair on race. *New York Times*, June 3, 1963, p. 19. (*457*)

BALES, R. F. *Interaction process analysis: a method for the study of small groups.* Reading, Mass.: Addison-Wesley, 1950. (*261, 311*)

BALES, R. F. The equilibrium problem in small groups. In T. Parsons, R. F. Bales, & E. A. Shills (Eds.), *Working papers in the theory of action.* New York: Free Press, 1953. Pp. 111–161. (*144*)

BALES, R. F., ET AL. Structure and dynamics of small groups. In J. Gittler (Ed.), *Review of sociology: analysis of a decade.* New York: Wiley, 1957. Pp. 391–417. (*145*)

BANDURA, A. Social learning through imitation. *Nebraska symposium on motivation.* Lincoln, Nebr.: Univer. of Nebraska Press, 1962. Pp. 211–269. (*367*)

BANY, MARY A., & JOHNSON, LOIS V. *Classroom group behavior.* New York: Macmillan, 1964. (*326*)

BARBASTE, A., S.J. Scrupulosity and the present data of psychiatry. *Theol. Dig.*, 1953, **1**, 180–184. (*466*)

BARDON, J. I., & KAPLAN, MILDRED. Mental health and the school nurse. *J. Sch. Hlth.*, 1961, **31**, 112–114. (*180*).

BARNABAS, BROTHER, F.S.C. Leisure time education of the adolescent. *Bull. Nat. Cath. educ. Ass.*, 1925, **22**, 232–243. (*13*)

BARRETT, G. B., S.M. A self-report of the personal ideals of Catholic high school boys at the tenth, eleventh and twelfth grade levels. Unpublished doctoral dissertation, Fordham Univer., 1958. (*450*)

BARRETT, SISTER MARY MARK. *A study of the influences of Catholic high-school experiences on vocational decisions to the sisterhood.* Washington: Catholic, 1960. (*484*)

BARRY, RUTH E., & WOLF, BEVERLY. A history of the guidance-personnel movement in education. Unpublished doctoral dissertation, Teachers Coll., 1955. (*6, 7, 17, 19, 25*)

BARRY, RUTH E., & WOLF, BEVERLY. *Modern issues in guidance personnel work.* New York: Teachers Coll., 1957. (*11, 83*)

BARRY, RUTH E., & WOLF, BEVERLY. *An epitaph for vocational guidance.* New York: Teachers Coll., 1962. (*245, 336, 392, 395*)

BASS, B. M. Effects of motivation on consistency of performance in groups. *Educ. psychol. Measmt*, 1959, **19**, 247–252. (*314*)

BATEMAN, MILDRED M., & JENSEN, J. S. The effect of religious background on modes of handling anger. *J. soc. Psychol.*, 1958, **47**, 133–141. (*354*)

BAUER, F. The junior rat race. *New York Times Magazine*, Dec. 2, 1962, p. 137. (*368*)

BECKER, A. J. A study of the personality traits of successful religious women of teaching orders. Unpublished doctoral dissertation, Loyola Univer., 1962. *(136)*

BECKER, R. J. Improving the quality of guidance services. Unpublished paper, Conf. State Supervisory Personnel and Counselor Educators, Providence, R.I., April, 1963. *(27, 506)*

BECKER, W. C., ET AL. Factors in parental behavior and personality as related to problem behavior in children. *J. consult. Psychol.*, 1959, **23**, 107–118. *(366)*

BELKA, BROTHER M. F., S.M. An evaluation of the educational program and of guidance and counseling in particular from 1941 to 1957 in nine selected secondary schools of the Society of Mary. Unpublished doctoral dissertation, Univer. of Notre Dame, 1959. *(520, 521)*

BELL, H. M. *Matching youth and jobs.* Washington: Amer. Council Educ., 1940. *(396)*

BENNETT, MARGARET E. Functions and procedures in personnel services. *Yearb. nat. Soc. Stud. Educ.*, 1959. Pp. 103–133. *(72)*

BENNETT, MARGARET E. *Guidance and counseling in groups.* (2nd ed.) New York: McGraw-Hill, 1963. *(310, 324)*

BENZ, S. *An investigation of the attributes and techniques of high-school counselors.* Lafayette, Ind.: Div. Educ. Ref., Purdue Univer., 1948. *(114)*

BERCHMANS, SISTER M., R.D.C. School guidance services and religious vocation recruitment. *Cath. Couns.*, 1961, **5**, 93–95. *(488)*

BERDIE, R. F. Factors associated with vocational interests. *J. educ. Psychol.*, 1943, **34**, 255–257. *(16)*

BERDIE, R. F. A program of counseling interview research. *Educ. psychol. Measmt*, 1958, **18**, 255–274. *(267, 274)*

BERDIE, R. F. Counseling principles and presumptions. *J. counsel. Psychol.*, 1959, **6**, 175–182. *(158, 492)*

BERDIE, R. F. The counselor and his manpower responsibilities. *Personnel Guid. J.*, 1960, **38**, 458–463. *(90, 198, 423)*

BERDIE, R. F., ET AL. *Testing in guidance and counseling.* New York: McGraw-Hill, 1963. *(230)*

BERDYAEV, N. *The meaning of the creative act.* (Tr. D. A. Lowrie) London: Gollancz, 1955. *(429)*

BERELSON, B., & STEINER, G. A. *Human behavior: an inventory of scientific findings.* New York: Harcourt, Brace & World, 1964. *(470)*

BERG, I. A. Comments on current books and the passing scene. *J. counsel. Psychol.*, 1958, **5**, 316–317. *(495)*

BERGER, E. M. The relation between expressed acceptance of self and expressed acceptance of others. *J. abnorm. soc. Psychol.*, 1952, **47**, 597–606. *(88)*

BERGER, E. M. Zen Buddhism, general psychology, and counseling psychology. *J. counsel. Psychol.*, 1962, **9**, 122–127. *(78)*

BERGSTEIN, H. B., & GRANT, C. W. How parents perceive the counselor's role. *Personnel Guid. J.*, 1961, **39**, 698–703. *(163)*

BERLIN, I. N. Teachers' self-expectancies: how realistic are they? *Sch. Rev.*, 1958, **66,** 134–143. (*154*)

BERNARD, H. W. *Toward better personal adjustment.* (2nd ed.) New York: McGraw-Hill, 1957. (*342*)

BERNARDO, SISTER MARIA DEL C., D.O.C. The religious knowledge, moral judgement, and personality structure of a selected group of Catholic delinquent girls. Unpublished doctoral dissertation, Fordham Univer., 1957. (*149*)

BERNARDONI, L. C. A culture fair intelligence test for the ugh, no, and oo-la-la cultures. *Personnel Guid. J.*, 1964, **42,** 545–557. (*232*)

BETTELHEIM, B. *Truants from life.* New York: Free Press, 1955. (*429, 431*)

BETZ, B. J., & Whitehorn, J. C. The relationship of the therapist to the outcome of therapy in schizophrenics. *Psychiatric Research Report No. 5: research techniques in schizophrenia.* Washington: Amer. Psychiat. Ass., 1956. Pp. 89–117. (*114*)

BEXTON, W. H., HERON, W., & SCOTT, T. H. Effects of variation in the sensory environment. *Canad. J. Psychol.*, 1954, **8,** 70–76. (*137*)

BIBER, BARBARA. Integration of mental health principles in the school setting. In G. Caplan (Ed.), *Prevention of mental health disorders in children.* New York: Basic Books, 1961. Pp. 323–352. (*347*)

BIEHN, SISTER M. IGNATA, S.C.C. Vocational practices in girls' high schools in nine Midwestern states. Unpublished doctoral dissertation, Loyola Univer., 1933. (*20*)

BIER, W. C., S.J. A comparative study of five Catholic college groups on the MMPI. In G. S. Welsh & W. G. Dahlstrom (Eds.), *Basic readings on the MMPI in psychology and medicine.* Minneapolis: Univer. of Minnesota Press, 1956. Pp. 586–609. (*486*)

BISCHOF, L. J. *Interpreting personality theories.* New York: Harper & Row, 1964. (*38*)

BLEE, E. C. A study of professional characteristics of counselors and guidance workers in a selected number of Catholic secondary schools. Unpublished master's thesis, Catholic Univer. of America, 1956. (*521*)

BLOCK, J., & BLOCK, JEANNE. An investigation of the relation between intolerance of ambiguity and ethnocentrism. *J. Pers.*, 1951, **19,** 303–311. (*109*)

BLOOM, B. S., & PETERS, F. R. *The use of academic prediction scales for counseling and selecting college entrants.* New York: Free Press, 1961. (*420*)

BLOOMFIELD, M. *The vocational guidance of youth.* Boston: Houghton Mifflin, 1911. (*5, 6*)

BLOOMFIELD, M. Vocational guidance. In *Industrial education: typical experiments described and interpreted. Yearb. nat. Soc. Stud. Educ.*, 1912. (*6*)

BLOOMFIELD, M. Preface. In M. Bloomfield (Ed.), *Readings in vocational guidance.* Boston: Ginn, 1915. (*5*)

BLOS, P. *The adolescent personality.* New York: Appleton-Century-Crofts, 1951. (*55*)

BLOS, P. *On adolescence: a psychoanalytic interpretation.* New York: Free Press, 1962. *(55)*

BLUHM, BROTHER H., S.C. A study of the direct and transfer effects on a developmental reading program at the ninth grade level. Unpublished doctoral dissertation, Fordham Univer., 1961. *(437)*

BLUM, M. L., & BALINSKY, B. *Counseling and psychology.* Englewood Cliffs, N.J.: Prentice-Hall, 1951. *(247)*

BOARD OF EDUCATION, NEW YORK CITY, CURRICULUM GUIDANCE CONFERENCE. *The core program.* New York: Author, 1955. *(206)*

BOFFA, C. H. *Canonical provisions for Catholic schools.* Washington: Catholic, 1939. *(197)*

BOGAN, W. J. Guidance in the public schools. *Occupations,* 1935, **14,** 101–104. *(15)*

BONNER, H. *Group dynamics: principles and applications.* New York: Ronald, 1959. *(327)*

BONNER, H. *Psychology of personality.* New York: Ronald, 1961. *(43, 353, 366)*

BONNEY, W. C., & MCGENEARTY, L. Non-test pupil data. *Voc. Guid. Quart.,* 1962, **11,** 68–72. *(236)*

BOOTH, G. In the consultation clinic. *Pastoral Psychol.,* 1961, **12,** 54–56. *(472, 473)*

BORDIN, E. S. A theory of vocational interests as dynamic phenomena. *Educ. psychol. Measmt,* 1943, **3,** 49–65. *(16)*

BORDIN, E. S. Implications of client expectation for the counseling process· *J. counsel. Psychol.,* 1955, **2,** 17–21. *(296)*

BOROW, H. The logic of counseling research. *J. counsel. Psychol.,* 1956, **3,** 292–296. *(87)*

BOROW, H. Curricular approaches to personal development: some problems of research. *J. counsel. Psychol.,* 1959, **5,** 63–69. *(204)*

BOROW, H. College courses in vocational planning. *Voc. Guid. Quart.,* 1960–61, **9,** 75–81. *(410)*

BOSTON, O. School social work services. *Yearb. nat. Ass. soc. Workers,* 1960, Pp. 517–523. *(178)*

BOTT, MARGARET M. Feminine identity and the educational-vocational plans and preferences of adolescent girls attending parochial schools. Unpublished doctoral dissertation, Michigan State Univer., 1962. *(404)*

BOTT, MARGARET M. Who shall find the valiant woman? *Cath. Counsel.,* 1963, **7,** 102–105. *(403)*

BOUSCAREN, T. L., S.J., & ELLIS, A. C., S.J. *Canon law: a text and commentary.* (2nd ed.) Milwaukee: Bruce, 1951. *(456)*

BOWER, E. M. Primary prevention in a school setting. In G. Caplan (Ed.), *Prevention of mental disorders in children.* New York: Basic Books, 1961. Pp. 353–377. *(359)*

BOWLBY, J. *Child care and the growth of love.* Baltimore: Penguin, 1961. *(47)*

BOWLES, F. H. The nature of guidance. *Personnel Guid. J.*, 1959, **38**, 112–120. (*83, 116*)

BOWMAN, H. A. *Marriage for moderns.* (4th ed.) New York: McGraw-Hill, 1960. (*379*)

BOY, A. V., ISAKSEN, H. L., & PINE, G. J. Multiple counseling: a catalyst for individual counseling. *Sch. Couns.*, 1963, **11**, 8–11. (*330*)

BRADEN, M. M. Former students evaluate guidance. *J. educ. Res.*, 1953, **47**, 127–133. (*512*)

BRAMMER, L. M., & SHOSTROM, E. L. *Therapeutic psychology: fundamentals of counseling and psychotherapy.* Englewood Cliffs, N.J.: Prentice-Hall, 1960. (*40, 172, 247, 250*)

BRAMS, J. M. Counselor characteristics and effective communication in counseling. *J. counsel. Psychol.*, 1961, **8**, 25–30. (*267*)

BRANSBY, BROTHER E., C.S.C. A study of guidance practices in nine Catholic high schools for boys. Unpublished doctoral dissertation, Fordham Univer., 1949. (*435*)

BRAYFIELD, A. H. Performance is the thing. *J. counsel. Psychol.*, 1962, **9**, 3. (*94, 106*)

BREEDLOVE, C. L. Nondirective counseling and material sin: the obligation of the counselor to instruct and correct. Unpublished master's thesis, Catholic Univer. of America, 1962. (*461*)

BRENDER, M. A critique of Walters' position. *J. counsel. Psychol.*, 1959, **6**, 163–165. (*73*)

BREWER, J. M. *The vocational guidance movement: its problems and possibilities.* New York: Macmillan, 1918. (*5, 6*)

BREWER, J. M. *Mental measurement in educational and vocational guidance.* Cambridge, Mass.: Harvard, 1924. (*9*)

BREWER, J. M. *Case studies in educational and vocational guidance.* Boston: Ginn, 1926. (*11*)

BREWER, J. M. *A history of vocational guidance.* New York: Harper & Row, 1942. (*10*)

BREWSTER, R. E., & GREENLEAF, L. A roll-call of counselors. *Occupations*, 1939, **18**, 83–89. (*18*)

BRIGGS, E. F., M.M. Incompatibility between class load and study time in the American minor seminary. Unpublished master's thesis, Fordham Univer., 1952. (*515*)

BRITTON, E. C. & WINANS, J. M. *Growing from infancy to adulthood.* New York: Appleton-Century-Crofts, 1958. (*53*)

BRONFENBRENNER, U. Socialization and social class through time and space. In Eleanor E. Maccoby, T. M. Newcomb, & E. L. Hartley (Eds.), *Readings in social psychology.* (3rd ed.) New York: Holt, 1958. Pp. 400–425. (*364*)

BRONFENBRENNER, U. Soviet methods of character education: some implications for research. *Relig. Educ., Res. Suppl.*, 1962, **57**, 45–61. (*369*)

BROOKS, R. M., O.Praem. The former major seminarian. *Bull. nat. Cath. educ. Ass.*, 1961, **58**, 45–52. (*108*)

BROWN, C. Guidelines for junior high school guidance. Unpublished doctoral dissertation, Columbia Univer., 1961. (*426*)

BROWN, F. G. Identifying college dropouts with the Minnesota Counseling Inventory. *Personnel Guid. J.*, 1960, **39**, 280–282. (*434*)

BROWN, F. J. Postwar education for ex-service personnel. *Adult Educ. J.*, 1943, **2**, 178–182. (*25*)

BROWN, F. S. The in-service training of teachers toward the more effective use of test results. In A. E. Traxler (Ed.), *Measurement and research in today's schools*. Washington: Amer. Council Educ., 1961. Pp. 76–87. (*221*)

BROWN, J. S. *The motivation of behavior.* New York: McGraw-Hill, 1961. (*342*)

BROWN, MARIAN R. Guidance and the classroom teacher. Unpublished doctoral dissertation, Teachers Coll., 1950. (*193*)

BROWNFAIN, J. J. Stability of the self-concept as a dimension of personality, *J. abnorm. soc. Psychol.*, 1952, **47**, 597–606. (*88*)

BRUNER, J., & GOODMAN, CECILE. Value and need as organizing factors in perception. *J. abnorm. soc. Psychol.*, 1947, **41**, 33–44. (*80*)

BRUNSON, MAY A. *An integrating process in higher education.* New York: Teachers Coll., 1959. (*203*)

BUBER, M. *I and thou.* Edinburgh: T. Clark, 1937. (*98*)

BUBER, M. *Between man and man.* London: Routledge, 1947. (*116*)

BUCHHEIMER, A., & BALOGH, S. C. *The counseling relationship.* Chicago: Science Research, 1961. (*297*)

BUCHWALD, LEONA, & FROEHLICH, C. Opinion poll results and a plan of reorganization. *Occupations*, 1951, **29**, 368–374. (*26*)

BUCKLEY, L. F. College women and the labor market. *Cath. Couns.*, 1963, **7**, 98–101. (*403*)

BUEHLER, R. E., & RICHMOND, J. F. Interpersonal behavior analysis: a research method. *J. Communic.*, 1963, **13**, 132–139. (*268*)

BUGENTAL, J. F. T. A method for assessing self and non-self attitudes during the therapeutic series. *J. consult. Psychol.*, 1952, **16**, 435–439. (*265*)

BUGENTAL, J. F. T. Humanistic psychology: a new break-through. *Amer. Psychologist*, 1963, **18**, 563–567. (*336*)

BURGESS, E. W., & WALLIN, P. *Engagement and marriage.* Philadelphia: Lippincott, 1953. (*383*)

BURGMEISTER, BESSIE B. *The permanence of interests of women college students: a study of personality development.* New York: Columbia, 1940. (*451*)

BURTON, W. H. Implications for organizing instruction and instructional adjuncts. *Yearb. nat. Soc. Stud. Educ.*, 1950, Part I. Pp. 217–255. (*427*)

BURTON, W. H. *The guidance of learning activities.* (2nd ed.) New York: Appleton-Century-Crofts, 1952. (*146*)

BUTLER, LORETTA M. *History of Catholic elementary education of Negroes in the diocese of Lafayette, Louisiana.* Washington: Catholic, 1963. (*450*)

BUTLER, R., O.P. *Religious vocation: an unnecessary mystery.* Chicago: Regnery, 1961. *(462)*

BUTLER, R., O.P. *God on the secular campus.* Garden City, N.Y.: Doubleday, 1963. *(446)*

BUTLER, W. R. An analytical study of factors associated with scholastic achievement in high and low achieving fraternities. Unpublished doctoral dissertation, Univer. of Kansas, 1956. *(139)*

BYRNE, J. A. (Recorder) Excellence in curriculum—a report. *Bull nat. Cath. educ. Ass.,* 1960, **57,** 153.

BYRNE, J. T. *A study of student problems in Catholic men's colleges.* Washington: Catholic, 1957. *(435, 472, 531, 532)*

BYRNE, J. T. Roger's counseling theory and the nature of man. *Cath. educ. Rev.,* 1960, **58,** 114–118. *(259)*

BYRNE, M. J. Integrating tests with the counseling process. In J. O'Connor (Ed.), *College counseling and testing.* Washington: Catholic, 1958. Pp. 135–146. *(233)*

BYRNE, R. H. Beware the stay-in-school bandwagon. *Personnel Guid, J.,* 1958, **36,** 493–496. *(433)*

BYRNE, R. H. *The school counselor.* Boston: Houghton Mifflin, 1963. *(245)*

CALDWELL, BETTYE M. The usefulness of the critical period hypothesis on the study of filiative behavior. *Merrill-Palmer Quart. behav. Develpm.,* 1962, **8,** 229–242. *(58)*

CALDWELL, E. *Group techniques for the classroom teacher.* Chicago: Science Research, 1960. *(136)*

CALLAHAN, D. Problems and possibilities. In J. O'Gara (Ed.), *The layman in the Church.* New York: Herder & Herder, 1962. *(138)*

CALLAHAN, D. *The mind of the Catholic layman,* New York: Scribner, 1963. *(196, 199, 448)*

CALLIS, R. Counseling. *Rev. educ. Res.,* 1963, **33,** 179–187. *(438)*

CAMPANELLE, T. *Psychology of education.* Philadelphia: Chilton, 1960. *(435)*

CAMPANELLE, T. A critique on Catholic higher education. *Cath. educ. Rev.,* 1963, **61,** 313–334. *(72)*

CAMPBELL, J. J., S.J. Eighty per cent said no. *America,* 1952, **86,** 414–416. *(484)*

CAMPBELL, P. E. The philosophy of discipline. *Homil. pastoral Rev.,* 1940, **40,** 655–661. *(194)*

CAMUS, A. *Notebooks, 1935–1942.* New York: Knopf, 1963. *(118)*

CAPLAN, G. *Concepts of mental health and consultation.* Washington: U.S. Dep. Hlth. Educ. Welf., Children's Bur., Soc. Security Admin. GPO, 1959. *(359)*

CAPLOW, T. *The sociology of work.* Minneapolis: Univer. of Minnesota Press, 1954. *(401)*

CARAVELLO, S. J. Effectiveness of high school guidance services. *Personnel Guid. J.,* 1958, **36,** 323–325. *(157)*

CARLIN, L. O. Vocational decisions and high school experiences. *Voc. Guid. Quart.,* 1960, **8,** 168–170. *(407, 505)*

CARMENA, SISTER ADRIENNE, C.S.J. Creativity in education. *Cath. educ. Rev.*, 1962, **60**, 249–256. *(430)*

CARNES, E. F., & ROBINSON, F. P. The role of client talk in the counseling interview. *Educ. psychol. Measmt*, 1948, **8**, 635–644. *(467)*

CARR, A., O.F.M. CONV. *Vocation to the priesthood: its canonical concept.* Washington: Catholic, 1950. *(482)*

CARTER, G. E. *Psychology and the cross.* Milwaukee: Bruce, 1959. *(451)*

CARTER, H. D. The development of vocational attitudes. *J. consult. Psychol.*, 1940, **4**, 185–191. *(16)*

CARTER, L. F., ET AL. The relation of categorizations and ratings in the observation of group behavior. *Human Relat.*, 1951, **4**, 239–254. *(144)*

CARTER, SISTER M. RAYMOND. A Catholic activity program—an experiment. *Cath. educ. Rev.*, 1946, **44**, 259–271. *(207)*

CARTWRIGHT, D., & ZANDER, A. (Eds.) *Group dynamics: research and theory.* (2nd ed.) New York: Harper & Row, 1960. *(311)*

CARTWRIGHT, ROSALIND D. Effect of psychotherapy on self-consistency. *J. counsel. Psychol.*, 1957, **4**, 15–22. *(103, 265)*

CASEY, D., S.J. *The nature and treatment of scruples.* Westminster, Md.: Newman, 1948. *(468)*

CASHIN, BROTHER E. L., F.M.S. Paper delivered at First Annu. Marist Educ. Convention, Dec., 1963. *(145, 447, 450)*

CASSIDY, J. E., O.S.F.S. A study of the facilities for religious instruction and guidance in Catholic high schools in the United States. Unpublished master's thesis, Catholic Univer. of America, 1962. *(202)*

CATHERINE OF SIENA, ST. Cited by *Cath. Worker*, 1964, **30**, 6. *(105)*

CATHOLIC BIBLICAL ASSOCIATION. *A commentary on the New Testament.* n.c.: Author, 1952. *(479)*

CATHOLIC PROPERTY ADMINISTRATION. *Trends in Catholic education.* Author, 1964. P. 28. *(213)*

Catholic Vocational-counsel Conference proceedings. *Bull. nat. Cath. educ. Ass.*, 1931, **28**, 373–431. *(19)*

CATTELL, R. B. Extracting the correct number of factors in factor analysis. *Educ. psychol. Measmt*, 1958, **58**, 791–838. *(232)*

CATTON, W. R., JR. What kind of people does a religious cult attract? *Amer. sociol. Rev.*, 1957, **22**, 561–566. *(203)*

CAVANAGH, J. R. *Fundamental marriage counseling: a Catholic viewpoint.* Milwaukee: Bruce, 1962. *(387)*

CAVANAGH, J. R., & McGOLDRICK, J. B., S.J. *Fundamental psychiatry.* (2nd ed.) Milwaukee: Bruce, 1958. *(77, 79, 109, 137, 389, 459, 472, 473, 475, 476, 492, 493, 518)*

CAWLEY, SISTER ANNE, O.S.B. Guidance in Catholic schools. *Cath. educ. Rev.*, 1941, **39**, 219–228. (a) *(21)*

CAWLEY, SISTER ANNE, O.S.B. The present state of guidance in Catholic colleges. *Cath. educ. Rev.*, 1941, **39,** 275–283. (b) *(21)*

CELESTINE, SISTER M., S.C.C. Religious vocations and school environment. *Cath. educ. Rev.*, 1962, **60,** 518–537. *(485)*

CENTI, P. Should Catholic colleges provide reading programs? *Cath. Couns.*, 1957, **2,** 13–15. *(437)*

CHAFETZ, M. E., & DEMONE, H. W. *Alcoholism and society.* Fair Lawn, N.J.: Oxford, 1962. *(469)*

CHAMBERS, F. M. Empathy and scholastic success. *Personnel Guid. J.*, 1957, **36,** 282–284. *(416)*

CHAPMAN, R. W. School suspension as therapy. *Personnel Guid. J.*, 1962, **40,** 731–732. *(492)*

CHARLES, MOTHER THERESE, O.S.U. Forming the pupil to witness. *Sower*, 1963, **218,** 92–97. *(146)*

CHARTERS, W. W., & NEWCOMB, T. M. Some attitudinal effects of experimental increased salience of a membership group. In Eleanor E. Maccoby, T. M. Newcombe, & E. L. Hartley (Eds.), *Readings in social psychology.* (2nd ed.) New York: Holt, 1958. Pp. 276–281. *(367)*

CHAUTARD, J. B. *The soul of the apostolate.* (Tr. J. A. Moran, S.M.) Trappist, Ky.: Mission Press, 1945. *(456)*

CHENAULT, JOANN, & SEEGARS, J. E. The interpersonal diagnosis of principals and counselors. *Personnel Guid. J.*, 1962, 118–122. *(195)*

CHOUINARD, A. J. Extracurricular activities in Catholic high schools. Unpublished master's thesis, Catholic Univer. of America, 1927. *(13)*

CIVARDI, L. *A manual of Catholic Action.* (Tr. C. C. Martindale) New York: Sheed, 1936. *(202, 480)*

CLUTTON-BROCK, SIR ARTHUR. Cited by J. Maritain, *Education at the crossroads.* New Haven, Conn.: Yale, 1943. *(104)*

COHEN, A. A school dental health program can be dynamic. *J. Sch. Hlth.*, 1964, **34,** 116–122. *(180)*

COHEN, A. K. *Delinquent boys: the culture of the gang.* New York: Free Press, 1955. *(375)*

COHN, B., ET AL. Group counseling: an orientation. *Personnel Guid. J.*, 1963, **42,** 355–358. *(329)*

COHN, B., OHLSEN, M., & PROFF, F. Roles played by adolescents in an unproductive counseling group. *Personnel Guid. J.*, 1960, **38,** 724–731. *(327)*

COLE, LUELLA. *Student's guide to effective study.* (4th ed.) New York: Holt, 1960. *(143)*

COLEMAN, BROTHER B. A comparative study of boy-girl relations as a factor of interest of boys in religious vocations. Unpublished master's thesis, Immaculate Heart Coll., 1960. *(485)*

COLEMAN, J. C. *Abnormal psychology and modern life.* Chicago: Scott, Foresman, 1956. *(349, 350)*

COLEMAN, J. S. *The adolescent society.* New York: Free Press, 1961. *(81)*

COMBS, A. W. Counseling as a learning process. *J. counsel. Psychol.*, 1954, **1**, 31–36. *(31, 130)*

COMBS, A. W., & SNYGG, D. *Individual behavior: a perceptual approach to behavior.* (2nd ed.) New York: Harper & Row, 1959. *(36, 37, 39, 41, 395)*

COMMITTEE FOR COUNSELOR PREPARATION, AMERICAN PERSONNEL AND GUIDANCE ASSOCIATION. Professional training, licensing, and certification. *Personnel Guid. J.*, 1958, **37**, 162–166. *(18)*

COMMITTEE ON POSTWAR EDUCATION. Report. *N. central Ass. Quart.*, 1946, **20**, 301–335. *(25)*

COMMITTEE ON STUDENT PERSONNEL WORK, AMERICAN COUNCIL ON EDUCATION. *The housing of students.* Washington: Author, 1950. *(513)*

CONANT, J. B. *Modern science and modern man.* Garden City, N.Y.: Anchor Books, Doubleday, 1955. *(73)*

CONANT, J. B. Cited by J. W. M. Rothney et al., *Guidance practices and results.* New York: Harper & Row, 1958. *(81)*

CONANT, J. B. *The American high school today.* New York: McGraw-Hill, 1959. *(116, 492)*

CONGAR, Y. M. J., O.P. *Lay people in the church.* (Tr. D. Attwater) Westminster, Md.: Newman, 1957. *(199, 480)*

CONGAR, Y. M. J., O.P. *Laity, Church, and world.* (Tr. D. Attwater) Baltimore: Helicon, 1960. *(138)*

CONNELL, F. J., C.Ss.R. Juvenile courtships. *Amer. eccles. Rev.*, 1955, **132**, 181–190. *(385)*

CONNELL, F. J., C.Ss.R. The instruction on coeducation. *Amer. eccles. Rev.*, 1958, **138**, 289–293. *(380)*

CONNERY, J. R., S.J. Steady dating among adolescents. *Theol. Stud.*, 1958, **19**, 73–80. *(385)*

CONNORS, C., C.S.Sp. Teen-agers "going steady": whose problem? *Homil. pastoral Rev.*, 1957, **18**, 249–254. *(385, 386)*

COOK, J. J. Silence in psychotherapy. *J. counsel. Psychol.*, 1964, **11**, 42–46. *(267)*

CORRELL, P. T. Student personnel workers on the spot. *J. counsel. Psychol.*, 1962, **9**, 232–235. *(194)*

CORTALE, M. J. Counselors and discipline. *Personnel Guid. J.*, 1961, **39**, 349–351. *(193)*

COSGROVE, BROTHER C., S.C. A study of the extent and relationship between the theoretical knowledge and practical knowledge of religious and moral truths and principles among Catholic elementary school children. Unpublished doctoral dissertation, Fordham Univer., 1955. *(80)*

COSTER, J. C. Some characteristics of high school pupils from three income groups. *J. educ. Psychol.*, 1959, **50**, 55–62. *(368, 409)*

COTTLE, W. C. Administrator-counselor relationships in Catholic schools. *Cath. Couns.*, 1962, **6**, 89–90. *(503, 516)*

COTTLE, W. C. Changing the client's self image. *Cath. Couns.*, 1963, **8**, 3–7. *(35)*

COTTLE, W. C., & DOWNIE, N. M. *Procedures and preparation for counseling.* Englewood Cliffs, N.J.: Prentice-Hall, 1960. *(220, 221, 227, 244)*

COTTLE, W. C., & WATSON, E. P., O.S.B. Counseling and guidance services in Catholic schools. *Cath. Couns.*, 1957, **2**, 43–45. *(520, 521, 524, 528, 532)*

COWEN, E. L., ET AL. A preventive mental health program in the school setting: description and evaluation. *J. Psychol.*, 1963, **56**, 307–356. *(179)*

COWEN, P. A. *Factors related to the college plans of high school seniors.* Albany, N.Y.: Univer. of the State of New York, 1960. *(151)*

COX, RACHEL D. New emphases in vocational guidance. *Voc. Guid. Quart.*, 1961, **10**, 11–15. *(410)*

CRIBBIN, J. J. Analysis of the theological, philosophical and sociological principles of guidance presented in textbooks published since 1935. Unpublished doctoral dissertation, Fordham Univer., 1951. *(30, 98, 99)*

CRIBBIN, J. J. Hindsight, insight, and foresight in college student personnel work. *Cath. educ. Rev.*, 1954, **52**, 238–248. *(30)*

CRIBBIN, J. J. Critique of the philosophy of modern guidance. *Cath. educ. Rev.*, 1955, **53**, 73–91. *(336)*

CRONBACH, L. J. *Essentials of psychological testing.* (2nd ed.) New York: Harper & Row, 1960. *(230)*

CROOKSTON, B. B. Selectivity as a factor in fraternity scholastic achievement. *Personnel Guid. J.*, 1961, **40**, 355–357. *(433)*

CUMMINGS, J. E. Problems of Catholic education. *Cath. Sch. J.*, 1939, **39**, 16–18. *(22)*

CUNNINGHAM, W. A., C.S.C. *General education in a liberal college.* St. Louis: Herder, 1953. *(106)*

CURRAN, C. A. *Counseling in Catholic life and education.* New York: Macmillan, 1952. *(98, 244, 336)*

CURRAN, C. A. Guidance and counseling in the educational process. *Cath. Couns.*, 1956, **1**, 17–19. *(65)*

CURRAN, C. A. Religious factors and values in counseling. *Cath. Couns.*, 1958, **3**, 4–5. *(95, 97)*

CURRAN, C. A. The counseling relationship and some religious factors. *J. counsel. Psychol.*, 1959, **6**, 266–269. *(302)*

CURRAN, C. A. The concept of guilt and sin in psychotherapy. *J. counsel. Psychol.*, 1960, **7**, 192–197. (a) *(302)*

CURRAN, C. A. Some ethical and scientific values in the counseling psychotherapeutic process. *Personnel Guid. J.*, 1960, **39**, 15–20. (b) *(91)*

CUSTER, SISTER VIOLET M., O.P. *An evaluative study of the guidance program of the archdiocesan high schools of St. Louis.* Washington: Catholic, 1955. *(520, 526)*

CUTTS, NORMA E. (Ed.) *School psychologists at midcentury.* Washington: Amer. Psychol. Ass., 1955. *(178)*

CUTTS, NORMA E., & MOSELEY, N. *Teaching the disorderly pupil.* New York: Longmans, 1957. (*28*)

DALTON, J. V., S.J. Spiritual non-direction. *Cath. Couns.,* 1962, **7,** 13–16. (*460*)

D'AMOUR, O'N. C. Father D'Amour sums it up. *Cath. Couns.,* 1959, **3,** 89–91. (*518*)

DANSKIN, D. G. Roles played by counselors in their interview. *J. counsel. Psychol.,* 1955, **2,** 22–27. (*267*)

DANSKIN, D. G. & BURNETT, C. W. Study techniques of those superior students. *Personnel Guid. J.,* 1952, **31,** 181–185. (*426*)

DANSKIN, D. G., & ROBINSON, E. P. Differences in degree of lead among experienced counselors. *J. counsel. Psychol.,* 1954, **1,** 78–83.

DANTEC, F. *Love is life: a Catholic marriage handbook.* (Rev. by A. Schlitzer, C.S.C.) Notre Dame, Ind.: Univer. of Notre Dame Press, 1963. (*390*)

D'ARCY, P. F., M.M. Constancy of interest factor patterns within the specific vocation of foreign missioner. *Cath. Univer. Stud. Psychol. Psychiat.,* 1954, no. 9. (*487*)

DARLEY, J. G. *Clinical aspects and interpretations of the Strong Vocational Interest Blank.* New York: Psychological Corp., 1941. (*16*)

DARLEY, J. G. The faculty is human, too. *Personnel Guid. J.,* 1956, **35,** 225–230. (*173*)

DAUBNER, E. V. Teacher as counselor. *Cath. educ. Rev.,* 1964, **62,** 91–99. (*155, 438*)

DAVIS, ANNETTE. The home counseling visit. *Inst. appl. Psychol. Rev.,* 1961, **1,** 42–45. (*178*)

DAVIS, D. A. An experimental study of potential dropouts. *Personnel Guid. J.,* 1962, **40,** 799–802. (*432*)

DAVIS, J. B. *Vocational and moral guidance.* Boston: Ginn, 1914. (*4, 5, 6*)

DAVIS, J. B. *The saga of a schoolmaster: an autobiography.* Boston: Boston Univer. Press, 1956. (*139*)

DAVIS, K. Mental hygiene and the class structure. *Psychiatry,* 1938, **1,** 55–65. (*65, 73*)

DAWSON, J. The present status of the lay teacher in the Catholic elementary and secondary schools of Nebraska. Unpublished master's thesis, Catholic Univer. of America, 1962. (*196*)

DAY, DOROTHY. *The long loneliness.* New York: Harper & Row, 1952. (*74, 149, 285*)

DE CHARDIN, T., S.J. *The divine milieu.* New York: Harper & Row, 1960. (*74, 98, 406, 439, 529*)

DEFERRARI, R. J. *Some problems of Catholic higher education.* Boston: Daughters of St. Paul, 1963. (*447*)

DE HUECK, CATHERINE. *Friendship house.* New York: Sheed, 1946. (*458*)

DE HUECK, CATHERINE. *Dear seminarian.* Milwaukee: Bruce, 1950. (*458*)

DE LA BEDOYÈRE, M. *The layman in the Church.* London: Burns & Oates, 1954. (*137*)

DEMENT, ALICE L. Good students want counseling too. *J. counsel. Psychol.,* 1957, **4,** 113–118. (*292*)

DENNEY, T. Catholics in public high schools. *Cath. educ. Rev.*, 1962, **60**, 145–162. *(143)*

DE ST. JOSEPH, L. M. Spiritual direction—its nature and dimensions. *Theol. Dig.*, 1958, **6**, 39–44. *(460)*

DEUTSCH, HELENE. *Psychology of women.* Vols. I & II. New York: Grune & Stratton, 1944. *(382)*

DEUTSCH, M. A theory of cooperation and competition. *Human Relat.*, 1949, **2**, 129–152. *(362)*

DEWEY, J. *Democracy in education.* New York: Macmillan, 1916. *(92)*

DEWEY, J. The religious in experience. In J. Ratner (Ed.), *John Dewey, Intelligence in the modern world.* New York: Modern Library, 1939. Pp. 1003–1037. *(441)*

DIAMOND, ESTHER E. *Preparing students for college.* Chicago: Science Research, 1962. *(409)*

DIAZ, CARMEN V. A study of the ability of eleventh-grade girls to apply the principles of the moral law to actual and hypothetical life situations. Unpublished doctoral dissertation, Fordham Univer., 1952. *(448)*

DIENER, C. L. Similarities and differences between over-achieving and under-achieving students. *Personnel Guid. J.*, 1960, **38**, 396–400. *(433)*

DIETZ, J. W. Quoted by E. A. Lee, Critical issues in guidance and personnel. *Occupations*, 1937, **15**, 691. *(63)*

DIFFENBAUGH, D. J., & BOWMAN, D. J. Guidance services at the intermediate level. *Personnel Guid. J.*, 1962, **41**, 25–28. *(184)*

DIGGS, B. J. *Love and being.* New York: Vanni, 1947. *(440)*

DI MICHAEL, S. G. Increase in knowledge in how-to-study resulting from a how-to-study course. *Sch. Rev.*, 1943, 353–359. *(426)*

DISPENZIERI, A., & BALINSKY, B. Relationship between the ability to acquire interviewing skills and authoritarianism and manifest anxiety. *Personnel Guid. J.*, 1963, **42**, 40–42. *(496)*

DITTES, J. E. Galvanic skin response as a measure of a patient's reaction to the therapist's permissiveness. *J. abnorm. soc. Psychol.*, 1957, **15**, 295–303. *(112)*

DOLE, A. A. Educational choice is not vocational choice. *Voc. Guid. Quart.*, 1963, **12**, 30–35. *(411)*

DONDERO, BROTHER A., F.S.C. Interpersonal aspects of counseling. In E. C. Stefic (Ed.), *Psychological counseling in high school and college.* Washington: Catholic, 1961. Pp. 39–51. *(124)*

DONIGER, S. Editor's note on the consultation clinic: on masturbation. *Pastoral Psychol.*, 1961, **12**, 53. *(472)*

DONNELLON, J. A. The administration of Catholic-Action groups in Catholic colleges for men in the United States. Unpublished doctoral dissertation, Fordham Univer., 1954. *(456, 480)*

DONOVAN, C. F., S.J. Christian humanism and Catholic guidance. *Cath. Couns.*, 1960, **4**, 87–95. *(75, 99, 110, 132, 460, 517)*

DONOVAN, J. D. Family socialization and faculty publication. *Amer. Cath. sociol. Rev.*, 1963, **24**, 115–126. *(80)*

DONOVAN, J. D. *The academic man in the Catholic college.* New York: Sheed, 1964. *(418)*

DOYLE, MOTHER HORTENSE, R.S.C.L. The self-concept studied in relation to the culture of teen-age boys and girls in Canada, England, and the United States. Unpublished doctoral dissertation, St. Louis Univer., 1960. *(80)*

DOYLE, SISTER MARGARET M. *The curriculum of the Catholic women's college.* Notre Dame, Ind.: College Press, 1932. *(113)*

DRASGOW, J., & MCKENZIE, J. College transcripts, graduation, and the MMPI. *J. counsel. Psychol.*, 1958, **5**, 196–199. *(416)*

DRESSEL, P. L. Implications of recent research for counseling. *J. counsel. Psychol.*, 1954, **1**, 100–105. *(501)*

DREWS, ELIZABETH. (Ed.) *Guidance for the academically talented student.* Washington: Nat. Educ. Ass. and Amer. Personnel and Guid. Ass., 1961. *(428, 430)*

DRIVER, HELEN I. *Multiple counseling.* Madison, Wis.: Monona, 1954. *(330)*

DROLET, H. V. *A study of the services facilitating guidance provided by the diocesan superintendent's office of education in the United States.* Washington: Catholic, 1959. *(30, 481, 519, 526)*

DUGAN, W. E. The impact of N.D.E.A. upon counselor preparation. *Personnel Guid. J.*, 1960, **39**, 37–40. (a) *(500)*

DUGAN, W. E. The organization and administration of guidance services. *Rev. educ. Res.*, 1960, **30**, 105–114. (b) *(501)*

DUNN, FRANCES E. Two methods for predicting the selection of a college major. *J. counsel. Psychol.*, 1959, **6**, 15–27. *(426)*

DUNNE, W. J., S.J. University relations through the president's eyes. Unpublished address, 1961. *(447)*

DYER, SISTER M. CELESTINE. A student evaluation of the present twelfth grade guidance programs in Catholic high schools for girls in California. Unpublished master's thesis, Catholic Univer. of America, 1951. *(526)*

ECKELBERRY, R. H. Postwar planning. *J. higher Educ.*, 1944, **15**, 315–318. *(25)*

EDGERTON, A. H., & HERR, L. A. Present status of guidance activities in public schools. In *Vocational guidance and vocational education for the industries. Yearb. nat. Soc. Stud. Educ.*, 1924, Part II. Pp. 3–27. *(11)*

EDITORIAL COMMENT. Eliminate the loafers. *Cath. Sch. J.*, 1926, **25**, 471. *(76)*

EDITORIAL STAFF. Catholic guidance: a brief history. *Cath. Couns.*, 1963, **7**, 45–50. *(32)*

Editor's Note. *Cath. Sch. J.*, 1921, **21**, 13. *(13)*

EDUCATIONAL POLICIES COMMISSION. *Moral and Spiritual values in the public schools.* Washington: Author, 1951. *(156)*

EDWARDS, N., & RICHEY, H. G. *The school of the American social order.* (2nd ed.) Boston: Houghton Mifflin, 1963. *(32)*

EGAN, BROTHER J. M., F.S.C.H. Guidance councils on the diocesan level. *Cath. Couns.*, 1956, **1**, 3–5. *(31)*

EGAN, BROTHER J. M., F.S.C.H. Ten commandments for counselors. *Cath. Couns.*, 1958, **2**, 78–80. *(125, 299)*

EGAN, BROTHER J. M., F.S.C.H. Techniques in the counseling interview. In J. W. Stafford. C.S.V. (Ed.), *Counseling in the secondary school.* Washington: Catholic, 1960. Pp. 126–134. *(116)*

EGAN, BROTHER J. M., F.S.C.H. Acceptance and the counselor's concept of his role. In E. C. Stefic (Ed.), *Psychological counseling in high school and college.* Washington: Catholic, 1961. Pp. 18–28. (a) *(78)*

EGAN, BROTHER J. M., F.S.C.H. Acceptance counselor roles and the Christian concept of man. *Cath. Couns.,* 1961, **5,** 79–86. (b) *(246)*

EHRMANN, W. *Premarital dating behavior.* New York: Holt, 1959. *(380)*

EICHHORN, SISTER MARY F. Analysis of fourth-, fifth-, and sixth-grade history texts according to Christian social principles. Unpublished master's thesis, Catholic Univer. of America, 1962. *(207)*

EISERER, P. E. *The school psychologist.* Washington: Center Appl. Res. Educ., 1963. *(178)*

ELKIN, F. *The child and society.* New York: Random House, 1963. *(46)*

ELKIN, F., & WESTLEY, W. A. The myth of adolescent culture. *Amer. sociol. Rev.,* 1955, **20,** 680–684. *(370)*

ELLENBERGER, H. F. A clinical introduction to psychiatric phenomenology and existential analysis. In R. May, E. Angel, and H. F. Ellenberger (Eds.), *Existence.* New York: Basic Books, 1958. Pp. 92–124. *(34)*

ELLIS, J. T. The American Catholic and the intellectual life. *Thought,* 1955, **30,** 351–358. *(80, 418)*

ELY, SISTER AIMEE, F.C.S.P. *The youth problem and education.* Washington: Catholic, 1940. *(204)*

ENGLEHARDT, SISTER M. ROSWITHA, I.H.M. Parent-teacher relations in selected Catholic elementary schools of metropolitan Detroit. Unpublished master's thesis, Fordham Univer., 1957. *(199, 201)*

ENGLISH, O. S., & PEARSON, G. H. J. *Emotional problems of living.* New York: Norton, 1945. *(43)*

ERASMUS, D. *Handbook of the militant Christian.* (Tr. J. P. Dolan, C.S.C.) Notre Dame, Ind.: Fides, 1962. (a) *(136)*

ERASMUS, D. Cited by J. P. Dolan, C.S.C., Introduction. Erasmus, *Handbook of the militant Christian.* Notre Dame, Ind.: Fides, 1962. (b) *(136)*

ERB, E. D. Conformity and achievement in college. *Personnel Guid. J.,* 1961, **39,** 361–366. *(417)*

ERIKSON, E. H. *Childhood and society.* New York: Norton, 1950. *(43, 47, 56)*

ERIKSON, E. H. The problem of ego identity. *J. Amer. psychoanal. Ass.,* 1956, **4,** 56–121. *(395)*

ERIKSON, E. H. *Identity and the life cycle.* New York: International Universities Press, 1959. *(34, 44, 47, 48, 50, 57)*

ESTELLE, SISTER MARY, S.S.N.D. Student personnel work in the Catholic schools, 1900–1950. *Cath. Sch. J.,* 1951, **51,** 144–146. *(8)*

ESTELLE, SISTER MARY, S.S.N.D. Tips and techniques. *Cath. Couns.,* 1957, **2,** 28–29. *(421)*

EVERETT CURRICULUM WORKSHOP. *Report.* Seattle: Heiden's Mailing Bur., 1956. *(522)*

EVOY, J., S.J., & CRISTOPH, VAN F., S.J. *Personality development in the religious life.* New York: Sheed, 1963. *(145, 486)*

EWING, J. F., S.J. Sex education: role of the school. In W. C. Bier, S.J. (Ed.), *Personality and sexual problems in pastoral psychology.* New York: Fordham, 1964. Pp. 241–250. *(475)*

FAHEY, SISTER MARY RALPH, S.N.D. The in-service training of religious secondary school teachers in congregations of women in the United States. Unpublished doctoral dissertation, Fordham Univer., 1960. *(94, 212, 524)*

FALLON, R. L. An evaluation of selected high school religion textbooks. Unpublished master's thesis, Fordham Univer., 1958. *(207)*

FARIES, MIRIAM, & PERRY, J. Academic acceleration and the college student. *Personnel Guid. J.,* 1960, **38,** 563–566. *(436)*

FARNSWORTH, D. L. Mental health education: implications for teachers. *Teachers Coll. Rec.,* 1961, **62,** 264–273. *(356)*

FARRELL, E., O.P. *The theology of religious vocation.* St. Louis: Herder, 1952. *(481)*

FARSON, R. E. Introjection in the psychotherapeutic relationship. Unpublished doctoral dissertation, Univer. of Wisconsin, 1955. *(115)*

FARWELL, GAIL F., & VEKICH, ANNE M. Status and certification of counselors in Ohio schools. *Personnel Guid. J.,* 1959, **38,** 285–289. *(506, 507)*

FAUNCE, R. C., & BOSSING, N. L. *Developing the core curriculum.* (2nd ed.) Englewood Cliffs, N.J.: Prentice-Hall, 1958. *(118, 206, 424)*

FEDDE, N. A., & KOVER, A. J. The screening and referral function in a university study skills office. *Personnel Guid. J.,* 1960, **39,** 145–146. *(415)*

FEDDER, RUTH. *Guiding homeroom and club activities.* New York: McGraw-Hill, 1949. *(150)*

FEDER, D. D. Perspectives and challenges. *Personnel Guid. J.,* 1961, **40,** 6–10. *(119)*

FEIGL, H. The scientific outlook: naturalism and humanism. In H. Feigl & May Brodbeck (Eds.) *Readings in the philosophy of science.* New York: Appleton-Century-Crofts, 1953. Pp. 8–18. *(452)*

FENICHEL, O. *The psychoanalytic theory of neurosis.* New York: Norton, 1945. *(348)*

FERREE, W., S.M. *Introduction to Catholic Action.* Washington: Nat. Cath. Welf. Conf., n.d. *(202)*

FESTINGER, L., SCHACHTER, S., & BACK, K. The operation of group standards. In D. Cartwright & A. Zander (Eds.), *Group dynamics, research and theory.* (2nd ed.) New York: Harper & Row, 1960. Pp. 241–259. *(312)*

FICHTER, J. H., S.J. *Southern parish.* Chicago: Univer. of Chicago Press, 1951. *(450)*

FICHTER, J. H., S.J. *Social relations in the urban parish.* Chicago: Univer. of Chicago Press, 1954. *(448)*

FICHTER, J. H., S.J. The Americanization of Catholicism. In T. T. McAvoy, C.S.C. (Ed.), *Roman Catholicism and the American way of life.* Notre Dame, Ind.: Univer. of Notre Dame Press, 1960. Pp. 113–127. *(449)*

FICHTER, J. H., S.J. *Religion as an occupation.* Notre Dame, Ind.: Univer. of Notre Dame Press, 1961. (*484*)

FICHTER, J. H., S.J. A comparative view of the parish priest. *Paper given at Fifth World Congr. Sociol.,* 1962. (*459*)

FIEDLER, F. E. Quantitative studies on the role of therapists' feelings toward their patients. In O. H. Mowrer (Ed.), *Psychotherapy: theory and research.* New York: Ronald, 1953. Pp. 296–315. (*250*)

FIEDLER, F. E. Leadership, group composition, and group creativity. *Paper given at Amer. Psychol. Ass.,* 1960. (*430*)

FINDLAY, J. F. The origin and development of the work of deans of men. *Secretarial notes, Nineteenth Annu. Conf. Nat. Ass. Deans Advisers of men,* 1937. (*12*)

FINE, B. *1,000,000 delinquents.* Cleveland: World Publishing, 1955. (*373*)

FISHMAN, J. A. Flies in the psychometric ointment. *Teachers Coll. Rec.,* 1961, **62,** 595–601. (*232*)

FITZGERALD, MAUREEN P. Self-disclosure and expressed self-esteem: social distance and areas of the self revealed. *J. Psychol.,* 1963, **56,** 405–412. (*317*)

FLANAGAN, J. C., & DAILEY, J. T. Project talent—the identification, development, and utilization of human talents. *Personnel Guid. J.,* 1960, **38,** 504–505. (*232*)

FLEEGE, BROTHER U. H., S.M. *Self-revelation of the adolescent boy.* Milwaukee: Bruce, 1945. (*475, 516*)

FLEEGE, BROTHER, U. H., S.M. Issues and problems facing Catholic secondary education. *Cath. educ. Rev.,* 1946, **54,** 356–363. (*29*)

FLEMING, E. J. A survey of personnel programs in twenty-two Catholic colleges for men located within the states of New Jersey, New York, Maryland, and Washington, D.C. Unpublished doctoral dissertation, St. John's Univer., 1955. (*526*)

FLYNN, SISTER M. KATHLEEN, O.S.U. A plea for the adolescent boy. *Cath. educ. Rev.,* 1946, **44,** 342–345. (*476*)

FLYNN, P. F. Needed in every guidance program. *Cath. Educator,* 1961, **21,** 788–790. (*524*)

FORD, D. H. Research approaches to psychotherapy. *J. counsel. Psychol.,* 1959, **6,** 55–60. (*307*)

FORD, D. H. Group and individual counseling in modifying behavior. *Personnel Guid. J.,* 1962, **40,** 770–777. (*322*)

FORD, J. C., S.J. *What about your drinking?* New York: Deus, 1961. (*469*)

FORREST, A. L. Counseling talented students on college choice. *Personnel Guid. J.,* 1960, **40,** 42–48. (*451*)

FORREST, A. L. Persistence of vocational choice of the merit scholarship winners. *Personnel Guid. J.,* 1961, 466–471. (*423*)

FOSTER, R. G., & WILSON, PAULINE P. *Women after college.* New York: Columbia, 1942. (*389*)

FRANCIS, J. A., S.V.D. An analysis of errors on the sacraments made by high school pupils. Unpublished master's thesis, Catholic Univer. of America, 1962. *(448)*

FRANCIS, SISTER MARY TERESA. Sources of vocations. *Sister Formation Bull.*, 1960, **6**, 7–12. *(485)*

FRANK, G. H., & SWEETLAND, A. A study of the process of psychotherapy: the verbal interaction. *J. consult. Psychol.*, 1962, **26**, 135–138. *(266)*

FRANK, J. D. *Persuasion and healing: a comparative study of psychotherapy.* Baltimore: William & Wilkins, 1961. *(265)*

FREIDAN, BETTY. *The feminine mystique.* New York: Dell, 1963. *(404)*

FREIDEL, SISTER M. PRISCILLA, S.N.D. Guidance practices in fifty Catholic high schools. Unpublished doctoral dissertation, Fordham Univer., 1933. *(21)*

FRENKEL-BRUNSWIK, ELSE. Differential patterns of social outlook and personality in family and children. In M. Mead & M. Wolfenstein (Eds.), *Childhood in contemporary culture.* Chicago: Univer. of Chicago Press, 1958. Pp. 369–401. *(365)*

FRENKEL-BRUNSWIK, ELSE. Adjustments and reorientation in the course of the life span. In R. G. Kuhlen & G. G. Thompson (Eds.), *Psychological studies of human development.* (2nd ed.) New York: Appleton-Century-Crofts, 1963. Pp. 161–171. *(55)*

FREUD, ANNA. *The ego and the mechanisms of defense.* New York: International Universities Press, 1946. *(348)*

FREUD, ANNA. The child guidance clinic as a center of prophylaxis and enlightenment. In J. Weinreb (Ed.), *Recent developments in psychoanalytic child therapy.* New York: International Universities Press, 1960. Pp. 207–238. (a) *(510)*

FREUD, ANNA. *Psychoanalysis for teachers and parents.* Boston: Beacon Press. 1960. (b) *(47, 51, 105)*

FRIEDERICHS, R. W. Alter versus ego: an exploratory assessment of altruism. *Amer. sociol. Rev.*, 1960, **25**, 496–508. *(442)*

FRIESENHAHN, SISTER M. CLARENCE. *Curricular offerings in secondary schools of the province of San Antonio, Texas.* Washington: Catholic Education Press, 1930. *(21)*

FRISON, B., C.M.F. *Coeducation in Catholic schools: a commentary on the instruction on coeducation.* Boston: Daughters of St. Paul, 1959. *(380, 381)*

FROEHLICH, C. P. Counselors and guidance officers in public secondary schools. *Occupations*, 1948, **26**, 522–527. *(27)*

FROEHLICH, C. P. *Evaluating guidance procedures.* Washington: GPO, 1949. *(72)*

FROEHLICH, C. P. *Guidance workers' qualifications.* Washington: GPO, 1951. *(506)*

FROEHLICH, C. P. *Guidance services in schools.* (2nd ed.) New York: McGraw-Hill, 1958. *(125)*

FROMM, E. *Escape from freedom.* New York: Holt, 1941. *(106)*

FROMM, E. *Man for himself.* New York: Holt, 1947. *(103)*

FUERST, A. N. Education in Catholic grade school inadequate to solve problems on high school level. *Cath. Sch. J.*, 1954, **54**, 253–255. *(75)*

FUERST, A. N. What's wrong with religion teaching in the U.S.A.? *Cath. educ. Rev.*, 1963, **61**, 380–381. *(150)*

FUND FOR THE ADVANCEMENT OF EDUCATION. *They went to college early.* New York: Author, 1957. *(436)*

GABRIELINE, SISTER M., I.H.M. Techniques in interviewing parents. *Cath. Sch. J.*, 1955, **55**, 113–114. *(228)*

GALLEN, J. F., S.J. Questions and answers. *Rev. for Religious*, 1957, **16**, 188–192. *(144)*

GALLEN, J. F., S.J. Questions and answers. *Rev. for Religious*, 1962, **21**, 53–64. *(144, 195)*

GANSIRT, SISTER M. CLAIRE, O.P. The status of vocational guidance in 274 large Catholic high schools. Unpublished master's thesis, Univer. of Notre Dame, 1933. *(21)*

GARDNER, R. W., ET AL. *Cognitive control: a study of individual consistencies in cognitive behavior.* New York: International Universities Press, 1959. *(233)*

GARESCHÉ, E. F., S.J. The student counsellor. *Cath. educ. Rev.*, 1928, **26**, 541–547. *(14)*

GAZDA, G. M. Group counseling—a growing solution. *Cath. Couns.*, 1963, **8**, 17–26. *(330)*

GENDEL, H. What kind of hero, the counselor? *Personnel Guid. J.*, 1963, **41**, 634. *(462)*

GERKIN, J. D., S.J. *Toward a theology for the layman.* New York: Herder & Herder, 1963. *(479)*

GETZELS, J. W., & JACKSON, P. W. The meaning of giftedness. *Phi Delta Kappan*, 1958, **30**, 75–78. *(429, 430)*

GETZELS, J. W., & JACKSON, P. W. *Creativity and intelligence.* New York: Wiley, 1962. *(429)*

GIBB, C. A. Definitions of the group. In C. G. Kemp (Ed.), *Perspectives on the group process.* Boston: Houghton Mifflin, 1964. Pp. 241–259. *(312)*

GIBB, J. The effects of group size and threat reduction upon creativity in a problem-solving situation. Address to Amer. Psychol. Ass., 1951. *(144)*

GIBSON, R. L. Pupil opinions of high school guidance programs. *Personnel Guid. J.*, 1962, **40**, 453–457. *(149, 505, 508)*

GILES, H. H. *Teacher-pupil planning.* New York: Harper & Row, 1941. *(92)*

GINOTT, H. G. *Group psychotherapy with children: the theory and practice of play therapy.* New York: McGraw-Hill, 1961. *(330)*

GINZBERG, E. Toward a theory of occupational choice. *Occupations*, 1952, **30**, 491–494. *(399)*

GINZBERG, E. Guidance—limited or unlimited. *Personnel Guid. J.*, 1960, **38**, 707–712. *(166)*

GINZBERG, E., ET AL. *Occupational choice: an approach to a general theory.* New York: Columbia, 1951. *(399)*

GINZBERG, E., ET AL. *The Negro potential.* New York: Columbia, 1956. *(393)*

GIRLS' ACADEMY CHAPLAIN. Steady dating among teenagers. *Homil. pastoral Rev.*, 1957, **58**, 331–332. (*385*)

GIVENS, P. R., & PECK, B. Letters to the editor. *J. counsel. Psychol.*, 1958, **5**, 151–152. (*522*)

GLANZ, E. C., HAYES, R. W., & PENNY, J. F. The freshman psychology program as the basis for student personnel program. *Personnel Guid. J.*, 1959, **38**, 290–294. (*321*)

GLEASON, R. W., S.J. *To live is Christ: nature and grace in the religious life.* New York: Sheed, 1960. (*486*)

GLOVER, L. E. The teacher of marriage and the family as counselor. Unpublished doctoral dissertation, Univer. of Southern California, 1950. (*388*)

GLUECK, S., & GLUECK, ELEANOR. *Delinquents in the making.* New York: Harper & Row, 1952. (*105*)

GLUECK, S., & GLUECK, ELEANOR. *Predicting delinquency and crime.* Cambridge, Mass.: Harvard, 1959. (*373*)

GNAGEY, W. J. Do our schools prevent or promote delinquency? *J. educ. Res.*, 1956, **50**, 215–219. (*373*)

GODIN, A., S.J. *Le Dieu des parents et le Dieu des enfants.* Paris: Casterman, 1963. (*466*)

GOEBEL, E. J. Training boys and girls for a future social life. *Bull. nat. Cath. educ. Ass.*, 1933, **30**, 257–258. (*21*)

GOEBEL, E. J. Guidance in the classroom. *Bull. nat. Cath. educ. Ass.*, 1941, **38**, 374–377. (a) (*21*)

GOEBEL, E. J. Vocational guidance. *Cath. educ. Rev.*, 1941, **39**, 73–76. (b) (*238*)

GOLD, F. A counselor's time study. *Sch. Couns.*, 1962, **10**, 68–70. (*162*)

GOLDBURGH, S. J., & PENNY, J. F. A note on counseling underachieving college students. *J. counsel. Psychol.*, 1962, **9**, 133–138. (*89, 431, 432*)

GOLDEN ANNIVERSARY WHITE HOUSE CONFERENCE ON CHILDREN AND YOUTH. *Recommendations: composite report of forum findings.* Washington: GPO, 1960. (*27, 493*)

GOLDMAN, L. *Using tests in counseling.* New York: Appleton-Century-Crofts, 1961. (*231*)

GOLDMAN, L. Group guidance: content and process. *Personnel Guid. J.*, 1962, **40**, 518–522. (*320*)

GOODLAD, J. I., & ANDERSON, R. H. *The nongraded elementary school.* (Rev. ed.) New York: Harper & Row, 1963. (*208, 437, 510*)

GORDON, I. J. *The teacher as a guidance worker.* New York: Harper & Row, 1956. (*134, 145*)

GORDON, I. J. Action research improves an aspect of elementary school guidance. *Personnel Guid. J.*, 1958, **37**, 65–67. (*200*)

GORDON, J. E. *Personality and behavior.* New York: Macmillan, 1963. (*353*)

GORDON, T. Group-centered leadership. Boston: Houghton Mifflin, 1955. (*319*)

GORHAM, J. Secondary education notes. *Cath. educ. Rev.*, 1963, **61**, 341–343. (*521*)

GOSLIN, D. A. Accuracy of self-perception and social acceptance. *Sociometry,* 1962, **25**, 283–296 (*318*).

GOWIN, E. B., & WHEATLEY, W. A. *Occupations: a textbook for the educational, civic, and vocational guidance of boys and girls.* Boston: Ginn, 1916. (*6*)

GOYENECHE, S., C.M.F. The states of perfection in the world today. In G. R. Poage, C.P., & G. Liévin, C.Ss.R. (Eds. & Trs.), *Today's vocation crisis.* Westminster, Md.: Newman, 1962. Pp. 133–146. (*478*)

GRANDE, BROTHER L. M., F.S.C. Teaching dangerous/difficult fiction in the secondary school. *Cath. educ. Rev.,* 1962, **60**, 1–9. (*149*)

GRANDE, P. P. *The relationship between counselor characteristics and rapport.* Unpublished doctoral dissertation, Univer. of Notre Dame, 1964. (*497, 525*)

GRANDE, P. P., & PALLONE, N. J. Client rapport and counselor religious status: an exploration. *Nat. Cath. Guid. Conf. J.,* 1965, **9**, 209–220. (*297*)

GRANGER, S. G. Psychologists' prestige rankings of 20 psychological occupations. *J. counsel. Psychol.,* 1959, 183–187. (*495*)

GRANT, C. W. The counselor's role. *Personnel Guid. J.,* 1954, **33**, 74–77. (a) (*163, 296, 508*)

GRANT, C. W. How students perceive the counselor's role. *Personnel Guid. J.,* 1954, **32**, 383–389. (b) (*163*)

GRATER, H. A. Behavior standards held by university females and their mothers. *Personnel Guid. J.,* 1960, **38**, 369–372. (*470*)

GRAU, A. F., S.J. Counseling theory and procedures. *Cath. Couns.,* 1958, **2**, 32–34. (*99, 286*)

GRAU, A. F., S.J. The Pope's remarks and the limits of counseling. In W. C. Bier, S.J., & A. A. Schneiders (Eds.), *Selected papers from the ACPA meeting of 1957, 1958, 1959.* New York: Amer. Cath. Psychol. Ass., 1960. Pp. 71–77. (*113*)

GRAY, SUSAN S. *The psychologist in the schools.* New York: Holt, 1963. (*178*)

GREELEY, A. M. *Strangers in the house.* New York: Sheed, 1961. (*109*)

GREEN, A. W. Social values and psychotherapy. *J. Pers.,* 1946, **14**, 199–228. (*97*)

GREEN, D. A. School dropouts a matter of philosophy. *Voc. Guid. Quart.,* 1960–61, **9**, 75–81. (*408*)

GREENSPOON, J. S. The reinforcing effect of two spoken sounds on the frequency of two responses. *Amer. J. Psychol.,* 1955, **48**, 409–416. (*265*)

GREGORY, SISTER KATHERINE P., R.S.M. An evaluation of the treatment of emotions in five basal sets of religion texts for Catholic secondary schools. Unpublished master's thesis, Catholic Univer. of America, 1962. (*515*)

GRENNAN, SISTER M. JACQUELINE, S.L. Crisis and commitment in the education of a Catholic. Paper given at Webster Coll., 1963. (*207*)

GRIBBONS, W. D. Changes in readiness for vocational planning from the eighth grade to the tenth grade. *Personnel Guid. J.,* 1964, **42**, 908–913. (*407*)

GRIFFITTS, C. H. *Fundamentals of vocational psychology.* New York: Macmillan, 1924. (*9*)

GRIGG, A. E. Client responses to counselors at different levels of experience. *J. counsel. Psychol.*, 1961, **8**, 217–222. (*270*)

GRIGG, A. E., & GOODSTEIN, L. D. The use of clients as judges of the counselor's performance. *J. counsel. Psychol.*, 1957, **4**, 31–36. (*267, 270*)

GRIMES, SISTER M. URSULA, S.S.J. An evaluative study of the guidance services provided for eighth grade pupils in the diocese of Pittsburgh. Unpublished doctoral dissertation, Univer. of Notre Dame, 1961. (*209, 481, 519, 527*)

GROLLMES, E. E., S.J. Programs for superior students in American colleges. *Cath. educ. Rev.*, 1964, **42**, 34–38. (*436*)

GRONLUND, N. E. *Sociometry in the classroom.* New York: Harper & Row, 1959. (*229*)

GRONLUND, N. E., & WHITNEY, A. P. Relation between pupils' social acceptability in the classroom, in the school, and in the neighborhood. *Sch. Rev.*, 1956, **64**, 267–271. (*369*)

GROSS, M. L. *The brain watchers.* New York: Random House, 1962. (*240*)

GUARDINI, R. Cited by Dorothy Day, *The long loneliness.* New York: Harper & Row, 1952. (*454*)

GUSTAD, J. W. The definition of counseling. In R. F. Berdie (Ed.), *Roles and relationships in counseling.* Minneapolis: Univer. of Minnesota Press, 1953. Pp. 3–11. (*87*)

HAAS, V. P., O.P. Counseling the Catholic student for secular education. *Cath. Couns.*, 1964, **8**, 79–83. (*219, 446*)

HAGAN, J. R. Some factors in the development of religious vocations of women. *J. relig. Instruction*, 1945, **15**, 621–628. (*484*)

HAGMAIER, G., C.S.P., & GLEASON, R. W., S.J. *Counseling the Catholic.* New York: Sheed, 1959. (*91, 99, 461, 473, 474, 475, 476*)

HAHN, M. E., & MACLEAN, M. S. *Counseling psychology.* (2nd ed.) New York: McGraw-Hill, 1955. (*250*)

HALEY, J. E., C.S.C. *Accent on purity: a guide to sex education.* (4th ed.) Notre Dame, Ind.: Fides, 1957. (*475*)

HALKIDES, GALATIA. An experimental study of four conditions necessary for therapeutic change. Unpublished doctoral dissertation, Univer. of Chicago, 1958. (*123*)

HALL, C. S., & LINDZEY, G. *Theories of personality.* New York: Wiley, 1957. (*79*)

HALL, W. E. Basic approaches to mental health: the program at the Nebraska Human Resources Research Foundation. *Personnel Guid. J.*, 1958, **32**, 276–281. (*122*)

HAMBLIN, R. L., MILLER, K., & WIGGINS, J. A. Group morals and competence of the leader. *Sociometry*, 1961, **24**, 295–311. (*320*)

HAMBURGER, M. Counselor: professional or technician? Paper presented at annual meeting of New York State Counselors Ass., New York City, 1962. (*60, 164*)

HANCOCK, MARGIE. A visual aid for group test interpretation. *Voc. Guid. Quart.*, 1962, **10**, 113–114. (*323*)

HARDEE, MELVENE D. *The faculty in college counseling.* New York: McGraw-Hill, 1959. (*156*)

HÄRING, B., C.Ss.R. Rethinking the sacrament of matrimony. *Cath. World*, 1963, **197**, 359–365. (*382*)

HARLOW, H. F., & ZIMMERMAN, R. K. The development of affectional responses in infant monkeys. *Proc. Amer. phil. Soc.*, 1958, **102**, 501–509. (*124*)

HARMAN, P. F., S.J. Conscience of American Catholic college. *Cath. educ. Rev.*, 1962, **60**, 10–24. (*310, 526*)

HARMON, D., & ARNOLD, D. L. High school counselors evaluate their formal preparation. *Personnel Guid. J.*, 1960, **39**, 303–306. (*498, 500*)

HARPER, R. A. Neurotic interactions among counselors. *J. counsel. Psychol.*, 1958, **5**, 33–38. (*496*)

HARRIS, A. J. *How to increase reading ability.* (3rd ed.) New York: Longmans, 1956. (*177*)

HARRIS, BROTHER P., O.S.F. A survey of the guidance services provided for business students in selected Catholic secondary schools in New York State. Unpublished doctoral dissertation, Fordham Univer., 1956. (*281, 520*)

HARRIS, BROTHER P., O.S.F. Establishing a diocesan guidance service. *Cath. Couns.*, 1958, **2**, 36–38, 66–67. (*187*)

HARRIS, BROTHER P., O.S.F. Assisting parents in their guidance functions. *Cath. Couns.*, 1960, **4**, 49–51. (a) (*198*)

HARRIS, BROTHER P., O.S.F. Organizing the counseling program. In J. W. Stafford, C.S.V. (Ed.), *Counseling in the secondary school.* Washington: Catholic, 1960. Pp. 10–20. (b) (*245*)

HARRIS, I. D. *Normal children and mothers.* New York: Free Press, 1959. (*51*)

HARRIS, I. D. *Emotional blocks to learning.* New York: Free Press, 1961. (*417, 432*)

HART, C. A. *Metaphysics for the many: a Thomistic inquiry into the act of existing.* Washington: Catholic, 1956. (*336*)

HARTLEY D., & HEDLUND, P. A. *Reactions of high school seniors to their guidance programs.* Albany, N.Y.: Univer. of the State of New York Press, 1952. (*116, 505, 508*)

HARTNETT, J. L., S.M. A study of guidance practices in the Catholic secondary schools of the United States. Unpublished master's thesis, Catholic Univer. of America, 1956. (*520*)

HARTSHORNE, H., & MAY, M. A. *Studies in deceit.* New York: Macmillan, 1928. (*442*)

HARVEY, MOTHER MARIE EDMUND, R.S.H.M. A study of religious attitudes of a group of Catholic college women. Unpublished master's thesis, Fordham Univer., 1954. (*447*)

HARVEY, O. J., & RUTHERFORD, JEANNE. Status in the informal group: influence and influencibility at differing age levels. *Child Develpm.*, 1960, **31**, 377–385. (*370*)

HAVEMANN, E., & WEST, PATRICIA. *They went to college.* New York: Harcourt, Brace & World, 1952. (*378, 418*)

HAVIGHURST, R. J. *Human development and education.* (2nd ed.) New York: Longmans, 1953. *(43, 44, 53, 59)*

HAVIGHURST, R. J. Youth in exploration and man emergent. In H. Borow (Ed.), *Man in a world at work.* Boston: Houghton Mifflin, 1964. Pp. 215–235. *(400)*

HEILFRON, MARILYN. The function of counseling as perceived by high school students. *Personnel Guid. J.,* 1960, **39,** 133–136. *(508)*

HEINE, R. W. A comparison of patient reports in psychotherapeutic experience with psychoanalytic, nondirective, and Adlerian therapists. Unpublished doctoral dissertation, Univer. of Chicago, 1950. *(123)*

HEMPHILL, J. K. Relations between the size of the group and the behavior of "superior" leaders. *J. soc. Psychol.,* 1950, **32,** 11–22. *(146)*

HENNESSY, T. C., S.J. A study of the changes and the permanence of changes in the religious ideals of Catholic high school students after a closed retreat. Unpublished doctoral dissertation, Fordham Univer., 1962. *(462)*

HENNIS, R. S., JR. Basic psychological generalizations underlying the core concept. *High Sch. J.,* 1962, **45,** 306–313. *(206)*

HERLIHY, SISTER EMERENTIA, B.V.M. A study of some causal factors of overachievement in high schools girls. Unpublished master's thesis, Catholic Univer. of America, 1962. *(419)*

HERMAN, L. M. & ZEIGLER, M. I. The effectiveness of interpreting freshman counseling-test scores to parents in a group situation. *Personnel Guid. J.,* 1961, **40,** 143–149. *(322, 425)*

HERESY, J. *The child buyer.* New York: Knopf, 1960. *(173)*

HICKS, J. M. The influence of group flattery upon self-evaluation. *J. soc. Psychol.,* 1962, **58,** 147–151. *(316)*

HIGHBAUGH, SISTER M. ASSUNTA, O.S.B. A study of the cause of drop-outs in the Catholic secondary schools of Indianapolis, Indiana. Unpublished master's thesis, Catholic Univer. of America, 1960. *(381)*

HIGHTOWER, P. R. *Biblical information in relation to character.* Iowa City, Iowa: State Univer. of Iowa, 1930. *(442)*

HILDUM, D. C., & BROWN, R. W. Verbal reinforcement and interviewer bias. *J. abnorm. soc. Psychol.,* 1956, **53,** 108–111. *(265)*

HILL, G. E. The selection of school counselors. *Personnel Guid. J.,* 1961, **39,** 355–356. *(89, 356, 494, 497)*

HILL, G. E., & GREEN, D. A. The selection, preparation, and professionalization of guidance and personnel workers. *Rev. educ. Res.,* 1960, **30,** 115–130. *(497)*

HILL, G. E., & MORROW, R. O. Guidance and the drop-out rate in 19 southeastern Ohio schools. *Voc. Guid. Quart.,* 1957, **5,** 153–155. *(203)*

HILL, G. E., & NITZSCHKE, D. F. Preparation programs in elementary school guidance. *Personnel Guid. J.,* 1961, **40,** 155–159. *(355, 356)*

HILL, R. E., JR. Scholastic success of college freshman from parochial and public secondary schools. *Sch. Rev.,* 1961, **69,** 60–66. *(418)*

HITCHCOCK, W. L. Counselors feel they should. *Personnel Guid. J.,* 1953, **32,** 72–74. *(509)*

HOEY, SISTER ANNE F., S.N.D. *A comparative study of the problems and guidance resources of Catholic college women*. Washington: Catholic, 1957. (*196, 378, 529, 531*)

HOFFMAN, A. E. An analysis of counselor sub-roles. *J. counsel. Psychol.*, 1959, **6**, 61–67. (*69, 267, 274*)

HOFFMAN, M. L. The role of the parent in the child's moral growth. *Relig. Educ., Res. Suppl.*, 1962, **57**, S18–S33. (*200*)

HOFINGER, J., S.J. *The art of teaching Christian doctrine*. Notre Dame, Ind.: Univer. of Notre Dame Press, 1957. (*149*)

HOFINGER, J., S.J. (Ed.) *Teaching all nations*. (Rev. & Tr. C. Howell) New York: Herder & Herder, 1961. (*149*)

HOFLICH, J. E. The ungraded primary. *Bull. nat. Cath. educ. Ass.*, 1960, **57**, 8–25. (*208, 437*)

HOGAN, W. F., C.S.C. School or convent? *Cath. educ. Rev.*, 1963, **61**, 322–327. (*202, 524*)

HOLLAND, J. L. Some explorations of theory of vocational choice. *Psychol. Monogr.*, 1962, No. 545. (*400*)

HOLLAND, J. L. Explorations of a theory of vocational choice and achievement. *Psychol. Rep. Monogr.*, 1963, Suppl. 4–VI. (*400*)

HOLLAND, J. L. A theory of vocational choice. *Voc. Guid. Quart.*, 1963–64, **12**, 93–98. (*401*)

HOLLAND, J. L. Major programs of research on vocational behavior. In H. Borow (Ed.), *Man in a world at work*. Boston: Houghton Mifflin, 1964. Pp. 259–284. (*401*)

HOLLIS, J., & ISAACSON, L. E. How school counselors spend their time. *Sch. Couns.*, 1962, **9**, 89–95. (*162*)

HOLLISTER, W. G. Current trends in mental health programming in the classroom. *J. soc. Issues*, 1959, **15**, 50–58. (*356*)

HOPKE, W. E. The measurement of counselor attitudes. *J. counsel. Psychol.*, 1955, **2**, 212–216. (*250*)

HOPKE, W. E. How are school counselors counseling? *Couns. Educ. Supervis.*, 1964, **3**, 162–165. (*270*)

HOPKINS, G. M., S.J. As kingfishers catch fire. In W. H. Gardner (Ed.), *Poems of Gerard Manley Hopkins*. (3rd ed.) London: Oxford, 1948. (*103*)

HOPKINS, R. W., & McDANIEL, SARAH W. Critical problems in pupil personnel administration. *Personnel Guid. J.*, 1961, **40**, 240–246. (*191*)

HOPPOCK, R. What is the "real problem"? *Amer. Psychologist*, 1953, **8**, 124. (*338*)

HOPPOCK, R. *Occupational information*. (2nd ed.) New York: McGraw-Hill, 1963. (*325, 402*)

HORA, T. The process of existential psychotherapy. *Psychiat. Quart.*, 1960, **34**, 495–503. (*77*)

HORROCKS, J. E., & BUKER, MAE E. A study of the friendship fluctuations of preadolescents. *J. genet. Psychol.*, 1951, **78**, 131–144. (*368*)

HOSINSKI, SISTER MARION, S.S.M. The counseling role of the college faculty member. *Cath. Couns.*, 1963, **8**, 13–16. (*157*)

HOSINSKI, SISTER MARION, S.S.M. Self, ideal self, and occupational role: preceptual congruence in vocationally committed college women. Unpublished doctoral dissertation, Univer. of Notre Dame, 1964. (*404, 412*)

HOUGHTON, H. W. The role of the counselor as perceived by seniors, administrators, teachers, and counselors in selected New York State public high schools. Unpublished doctoral dissertation, Syracuse Univer., 1956. (*163, 508*)

HOUTART, F. The sociology of vocations. In G. Poage, C.M., & G. Liévin, C.Ss.R. (Eds.), *Today's vocation crisis*. Westminster, Md.: Newman, 1962. Pp. 21–48. (*484*)

HOYT, D. P., & NORMAN, W. T. Adjustment and academic predictability. *J. counsel. Psychol.*, 1954, **1**, 96–99. (*416*)

HOYT, K. B. What the school has a right to expect of its counselor. *Personnel Guid. J.*, 1961, **40**, 129–133. (*172*)

HOYT, K. B. Guidance: a constellation of services. *Personnel Guid. J.*, 1962, **40**, 690–697. (*162*)

HOYT, K. B., & LOUGHARY, J. N. Acquaintance with the use of referral sources by Iowa secondary school counselors. *Personnel Guid. J.*, 1958, **36**, 388–391. (*509*)

HUMPHREYS, J. A., TRAXLER, A. E., & NORTH, R. D. *Guidance services*. (2nd ed.) Chicago: Science Research, 1960. (*72, 182, 421*)

HUNTER, GENEVIEVE P. Improving counselor preparation in Catholic education. *Cath. Couns.*, 1961, **5**, 138–144. (*516, 522, 523*)

HURLOCK, ELIZABETH B. *Developmental psychology*. (2nd ed.) New York: McGraw-Hill, 1959. (*49, 363, 364, 368*)

HUTSON, P. W. *The guidance function in education*. New York: Appleton-Century-Crofts, 1958. (*121*)

HUTSON, P. W. Another "position" paper. *Couns. Educ. Supervis.*, 1962, **2**, 21–24. (a) (*498*)

HUTSON, P. W. Foundations of the curriculum for the education of homeroom teachers. *Personnel Guid. J.*, 1962, **60**, 698–702. (b) (*150*)

INTERNATIONAL CONFERENCE ON PUBLIC EDUCATION. Recommendation No. 56 to the Ministries of Education concerning the organization of educational and vocational guidance. *Personnel Guid. J.*, 1963, **42**, 321–324. (*181*)

IVEY, A. E. Role conflict in counseling: its effect on college student attitudes. *J. counsel. Psychol.*, 1962, **9**, 139–143. (*154, 156*)

JACOB, P. E. *Changing values in college*. New York: Harper & Row, 1957. (*75, 443*)

JACOBS, J. N. An evaluation of certain measures of aptitude and achievement in the prediction of scholastic success. Unpublished doctoral dissertation, Michigan State Univer., 1957. (*419*)

JAHODA, MARIE. *Current concepts of positive mental health: a report of the Joint Commission on Mental Illness and Health*. New York: Basic Books, 1958. (*342*)

JANET, SISTER MARY, S.C. *Catholic secondary education: a national survey*. Washington: Nat. Cath. Welf. Conf., 1949. (*29, 30*)

JANSEN, BROTHER J. J., S.M. *Personnel services in Catholic four year colleges for men.* Washington: Catholic, 1955. *(188, 452, 528, 529, 530, 532)*

JENSEN, V. H. Influence of personality traits on academic success. *Personnel Guid. J.*, 1958, **36**, 497–500. *(415)*

JERSILD, A. T. *In search of self.* New York: Teachers Coll., 1952. *(107)*

JERSILD, A. T. *The psychology of adolescence.* (2nd ed.) New York: Macmillan, 1963. *(58)*

JERSILD, A. T., & HELFANT, K. *Education for self-understanding.* New York: Teachers Coll., 1953. *(107, 115)*

JOAN, SISTER MARY, O.P. & NONA, SISTER MARY, O.P. *Guiding growth in Christian social living.* Vols. 1–3. Washington: Catholic, 1944–46. *(207)*

JOEL, D. E. Post-graduation vocational plans of college women. *Cath. Couns.*, 1963, **7**, 77–79. *(383)*

JOHN XXIII, POPE. In praise of the retreat movement. *The Pope Speaks*, 1959, **5**, 406. *(462)*

JOHN OF ST. THOMAS. *The gifts of the Holy Ghost.* (Tr. D. Hughes, O.P.) Sheed, 1951. *(135)*

JOHNSON, A. C., JR. Our schools make criminals. *J. criminal Law Criminol.*, 1942, **33**, 310–315. *(374)*

JOHNSON, G. The reform of the curriculum. *Bull. nat. Cath. educ. Ass.*, 1924, **21**, 570–578. *(515)*

JOHNSON, G. The activity curriculum. *Cath. educ. Rev.*, 1941, **39**, 65–72. *(206)*

JOHNSON, M., JR., BUSAKER, W. E., & BOWMAN, F. *Junior high school guidance.* New York: Harper & Row, 1961. *(109)*

JOHNSON, MARY H. *The dean in the high school: a record of experience and experiment in secondary schools.* New York: Professional & Technical Press, 1929. *(6)*

JOHNSON, W. F., STEFFLRE, B., & EDELFELT, R. A. *Pupil personnel and guidance services.* New York: McGraw-Hill, 1961. *(186)*

JOHNSTON, H. *A philosophy of education.* New York: McGraw-Hill, 1963. *(42)*

JONE, H., O.F.M. CAP. *Moral theology.* (Tr. U. Adelman, O.F.M. Cap.) Westminster, Md.: Newman, 1951. *(468, 474, 475)*

JONES, A. J., & MILLER, L. M. The national picture of pupil personnel and guidance services in 1953. *Bull. nat. Ass. secondary-Sch. Principals*, 1954, **38**, 118–123. *(504)*

JONES, ANNA M. The first fifty years of the New York City Personnel and Guidance Association. *Personnel Guid. J.*, 1959, **38**, 70–73. *(7)*

JONES, MARY C. A study of socialization patterns at the high school level. *J. genet. Psychol.*, 1958, **93**, 87–111. *(370)*

JONES, PATRICIA. Delinquency as aggression. *Nat. Cath. Guid. Conf. J.*, 1964, **9**, 76–77. *(372)*

JORDAAN, J. P. Exploratory behavior: the formation of self and occupational concepts. In D. E. Super et al., *Career development: self-concept theory.* New York: College Entrance Examination Board, 1963. *(398)*

JOSEPH, E. (Ed.) *The talented student in a democratic society.* Dayton, Ohio: Marianist, 1963. *(428)*

JOSEPH, BROTHER L., F.M.S. Guided group discussion: a homeroom guidance technique. *Cath. Couns.*, 1958, **3**, 47–49. *(104)*

JOYCE, A. R. The role of a psychiatrist in a mental health program. *Cath. Couns.*, 1959, **3**, 71–75. *(179)*

JOYCE, A. R. Psychiatric concepts of emotional maturity. *Cath. Couns.*, 1960, **4**, 120–126. *(343)*

JUDITH, SISTER M. Report on the Sister Formation Conference's vocation survey. *Sister Formation Bull.*, 1956, **3**, 1–7. *(208)*

JUNG, C. G. Cited by M. Buber, *The eclipse of God.* New York: Harper & Row, 1952. *(452)*

JUNG, C. G. *The development of personality.* (Tr. R. F. C. Hull) New York: Pantheon, Bollingen Ser., 1954. *(104)*

JUNGMANN, J., S.J. *Handing on the faith.* (Rev. & Tr. A. N. Fuerst) New York: Herder & Herder, 1959. *(149)*

KACZKOWSKI, H., GEORGE, C., & GALLAGHER, P. The influence of an exploratory shop course. *Voc. Guid. Quart.*, 1963, **11**, 202–204. *(409)*

KAGAN, H. E. Psychotherapy as religious value. *J. counsel. Psychol.*, 1959, **6**, 263–266. *(465)*

KARDINER, A. *The individual and his society.* New York: Columbia, 1939. *(79)*

KATZ, M. *Decisions and values: a rationale for secondary school guidance.* New York: College Entrance Examination Board, 1963. *(166)*

KAUTH, PRISCILLA, & BROWN, B. F. The non-graded high school in Melbourne, Florida. *Bull. nat. Ass. secondary-sch. Principals*, 1962, **56**, 127–134. *(208, 437)*

KAYE, JANET. Fourth graders meet up with occupations. *Voc. Guid. Quart.*, 1960, **8**, 150–153. *(408)*

KELLER, F. J., & VITELES, M. J. *Vocational guidance throughout the world.* New York: Norton, 1937. *(10)*

KELLEY, JANET A. *Guidance and curriculum.* Englewood Cliffs, N.J., Prentice-Hall, 1955. *(203)*

KEMP, C. G. Counseling responses and need structures of high school principals and counselors. *J. counsel. Psychol.*, 1962, **9**, 326–328. (a) *(194)*

KEMP, C. G. Influence of dogmatism on the training of counselors. *J. counsel. Psychol.*, 1962, **9**, 155–157. (b) *(496)*

KEMP, C. G. Bases of group leadership. *Personnel Guid. J.*, 1964, **42**, 760–766. *(318)*

KENOYER, SISTER MARIE FRANCIS, S.L. The influence of religious life on three levels of perceptual processes. Unpublished doctoral dissertation, Fordham Univer., 1961. *(81)*

KERINS, F. J. No priority for guidance. *Cath. educ. Rev.*, 1957, **55**, 82–88. *(83, 116)*

KERLINGER, F. N. *Social psychological definitions and concepts.* New York: Dep. Psychol., Sch. Educ., New York Univer., 1962. *(317)*

KERLINGER, F. N. *Foundations of behavioral research.* New York: Holt, 1964. *(308)*

KEVANE, E. Improving religion program in Catholic high school. *Cath. educ. Rev.*, 1963, **61**, 217–237. *(219)*

KILBOURN, D. W. A study of the status and roles of head residents in college and university residence halls for women. Unpublished doctoral dissertation, Michigan State Univer., 1959. *(513)*

KIMBALL, BARBARA. The sentence completion technique in a study of scholastic underachievement. *J. consult. Psychol.*, 1952, **16**, 353–358. *(432)*

KIMBLE, G. A. *Conditioning and learning.* (2nd ed.) New York: Appleton-Century-Crofts, 1961. *(265)*

KING, P. T., & MATTESON, R. W. Student perception of counseling center services. *Personnel Guid. J.*, 1959, **37**, 358–364. *(512)*

KINNANE, J. F., & PABLE, M. W. Family background and work value orientation. *J. counsel. Psychol.*, 1962, **9**, 320–325. *(405, 483)*

KINNANE, J. F., & SUZIEDELIS, A. Work value orientation and inventoried interests. *J. counsel. Psychol.*, 1962, **10**, 144–148. *(405)*

KINSEY, A. C., Pomeroy, W. B., & MARTIN, C. E. *Sexual behavior in the human male.* Philadelphia: Saunders, 1948. *(470)*

KIRK, BARBARA A. Test versus academic performance in malfunctioning students. *J. consult. Psychol.*, 1952, **16**, 213–216. *(416, 432)*

KIRK, BARBARA A. Counseling Phi Beta Kappas. *J. counsel. Psychol.*, 1955, **2**, 304–307. *(292)*

KIRKENDALL, L. A. Values and premarital intercourse—implications for parent education. *Marriage and Family Living*, 1960, **22**, 317–322. *(470)*

KIRKPATRICK, C. Religion and humanitarianism: a study of institutional implications. *Psychol. Monogr.*, 1949, **63**, 1–23. *(442)*

KIRSCH, F. M., O.F.M. CAP. *Sex education and training in chastity.* New York: Benziger, 1930. *(473)*

KISKER, G. W. *The disorganized personality.* New York: McGraw-Hill, 1964. *(346, 359)*

KITSON, H. D. *The psychology of vocational adjustment.* Philadelphia: Lippincott, 1925. *(10)*

KLAPMAN, J. W. *Group psychotherapy: theory and practice.* (2nd ed.) New York: Grune & Stratton, 1959. *(330)*

KLEIN, A. *Role playing in leadership training and group problem solving.* New York: Association Press, 1956. *(142)*

KLEIN, RUTH A. The school nurse as a guidance functionary. *Personnel Guid. J.*, 1959, **38**, 318–321. *(180)*

KLINGERHOFER, E. L. The relationship of academic advisement to the scholastic performance of failing students. *J. counsel. Psychol.*, 1954, **1**, 125–131. *(438)*

KNAPP, R. H., & GOODRICH, H. B. *Origins of American scientists.* Chicago: Univer. of Chicago Press, 1952. *(418)*

KNOEBBER, SISTER M. MILDRED, O.S.B. *The self-revelation of the adolescent girl* Milwaukee: Bruce, 1937. *(20)*

KOHAKE, C., O.S.B. Co-operative campus living. *Cath. educ. Rev.*, 1963, **61**, 37–51. *(119)*

KOHLBRENNER, B. J. Whither Catholic higher education? *Cath. educ. Rev.*, 1963, **61**, 593–600. *(533)*

KOHLBRENNER, B. J. The talented student in a democratic society: historical perspectives. In F. R. Cyphert, E. W. Harmer, Jr., & A. C. Riccio (Eds.), *Teaching in the American secondary school: selected readings.* New York: McGraw-Hill, 1964. Pp. 394–402. *(428)*

KOILE, E. A., & TREAT, CAROL L. Identifying student oriented teachers. *Personnel Guid. J.*, 1961, **40**, 344–348. *(141)*

KOLB, BROTHER A., S.C. Vocational interests of the Brothers of the Sacred Heart. Unpublished master's thesis, Catholic Univer. of America, 1952. *(487)*

KOLESNIK, W. B. *Educational psychology.* New York: McGraw-Hill, 1963. *(437)*

KOOB, C. A., O. PRAEM. Pious talk no substitute for religious instruction. *Cath. Wkly*, Mar. 22, 1963, p. 1. *(457)*

KOOB, C. A., O. PRAEM. Cited by Richard C. Dierenfield, The curriculum in religious secondary schools. In H. R. Douglass (Ed.), *The high school curriculum.* (3rd ed.) New York: Ronald, 1964. Pp. 651–688. *(207)*

KOOS, L. V. *Private and public secondary education.* Chicago: Univer. of Chicago Press, 1931. *(418)*

KORBIN, S. The conflict of values in delinquency. *Amer. sociol. Rev.*, 1951, **16**, 653–661. *(367)*

KORTENDICK, J., S.S. *The library in the Catholic theological seminary in the United States.* Washington: Catholic, 1963. *(515)*

KOTHEN, R. *Marriage: the great mystery.* (Tr. E. J. Ross) Westminster, Md.: Newman, 1947. *(390)*

KOWITZ, G. T., & KOWITZ, NORMA G. *Guidance in the elementary classroom.* New York: McGraw-Hill, 1959. *(51)*

KRASNER, L. Studies of the conditioning of verbal behavior. *Psychol. Bull.*, 1958, **55**, 148–170. *(265)*

KRECH, D., CRUTCHFIELD, R. S., & BALLACHEY, E. L. *Individual in society.* New York: McGraw-Hill, 1962. *(49, 229, 362)*

KÜNG, H. *The council, reform, and reunion.* New York: Sheed, 1962. *(453, 454, 503)*

KÜNG, H. *That the world may believe.* New York: Sheed, 1963. *(465)*

KUNTZ, L. F. *The elements of abnormal psychology.* Ann Arbor, Mich.: Edwards, 1939. *(492, 493)*

KVARACEUS, W. C. Delinquent behavior and church attendance. *Sociol. soc. Res.*, 1944, **28**, 284–289. *(442)*

KVARACEUS, W. C. *The community and the delinquent.* New York: Harcourt, Brace & World, 1954. *(373)*

KVARACEUS, W. C. The counselor's role in combatting juvenile delinquency. *Personnel Guid. J.*, 1957, **36**, 99–103. *(372)*

KVARACEUS, W. C., ET AL. *Delinquent behavior*. Washington: *Nat. Educ. Ass.*, 1959. (*372*)

LAHITTON, J. *La vocation sacerdotale*. (7th ed.) Paris: Beauchesne, 1922. (*481*)

LANDIS, J. T. The teaching of marriage and family living courses in college. *Marriage and Family Living*, 1959, **21**, 36-40. (*388*)

LANDIS, P. H. Research on teen-age dating. *Marriage and Family Living*, 1960, **22**, 266-267. (*470*)

LAWLER, J. G. *Catholic dimension in higher education*. Westminster, Md.: Newman, 1959. (*118*)

LAWLER, J. G. Federal aid and freedom. *Commonweal*, 1962, **75**, 451-454. (*450*)

LAWTON, G. Neurotic interaction between counselor and counselee. *J. counsel. Psychol.*, 1958, **5**, 28-33. (*283, 496*)

LAYTON, W. L. Constructs and communication in counseling: a limited theory. *J. counsel. Psychol.*, 1961, **8**, 3-7. (*102*)

LEANMAN, BROTHER B., S.C. An investigation of the problems of eighth grade boys attending Catholic parochial elementary schools in the United States. Unpublished doctoral dissertation, Fordham Univer., 1956. (*379, 432, 435*)

LECKY, P. *Self-consistency: a theory of personality*. New York: Island Press, 1945. (*38*)

LECLERQ, G. *La conscience du chrétien*. Paris: Aubier, 1946. (*460*)

LEE, J. M. A new role for the high school. *Bull. nat. Ass. secondary-Sch. Principals*, 1959, **43**, 102-105. (*68, 116, 117, 424*)

LEE, J. M. Professional criticism of Catholic high schools. *Cath. World*, 1961, **194**, 7-12. (a) (*29, 518*)

LEE, J. M. Social life in Catholic women's colleges. *Cath. educ. Rev.*, 1961, **59**, 323-337. (b) (*378, 379, 529*)

LEE, J. M. Notes toward lay spirituality. *Rev. for Religious*, 1962, **21**, 42-47. (*454*)

LEE, J. M. Counseling vs. discipline: another view. *Cath. Couns.*, 1963, **7**, 114-119. (a) (*120, 193*)

LEE, J. M. *Principles and methods of secondary education*. New York: McGraw-Hill, 1963. (b) (*81, 83, 92, 102, 118, 130, 138, 139, 142, 205, 206, 221, 225, 227, 310, 324, 328, 356, 406, 424, 426, 433*)

LEE, J. M. Guidance in Catholic high schools: recent research data. *Nat. Cath. Guid. Conf. J.*, 1965, **9**, 109-117. (*516, 519*)

LEE, J. M., & PUTZ, L. J., C.S.C. (Eds.) *Seminary education in a time of change*. Notre Dame, Ind.: Fides, 1965. (*481*)

LEE, W. S. *God bless our queer old dean*. New York: Putnam, 1959. (*116, 117*)

LEHMAN, E. W. The American Catholic college students' orientation to the world: an exploratory study of student autobiographical sketches. Unpublished master's thesis, Fordham Univer., 1959. (*453*)

LEHMAN, H. C. *Age and achievement*. Princeton, N.J.: Princeton, 1953. (*436*)

LEMAY, C. J., S.J. Helping the graduate of the Catholic high school to make the most intelligent and profitable transition from Catholic high schools to Catholic colleges. *Bull. nat. Cath. educ. Ass.*, 1932, **29**, 266-267. (*21*)

LENSKI, G. *The religious factor.* Garden City, N.Y.: Doubleday, 1961. (*80, 405, 418*)

LEONARD, A., O.P. Personality growth through the life of Christ. Paper read at Inst. for Local Superiors, Univer. of Notre Dame, 1963. (*108, 115, 379*)

LEONARD, EUGENIE A. *Concerning our girls and what they tell us.* New York: Teachers Coll., 1930. (*197*)

LEONARD, EUGENIE A. *Problems of freshman college girls.* New York: Teachers Coll., 1932. (*475*)

LEONARD, EUGENIE A. Current practices in guidance in Catholic women's colleges. *Cath. educ. Rev.*, 1943, **41**, 220–228. (*21*)

LEONARD, EUGENIE A. Counseling in Catholic secondary schools. *Cath. educ. Rev.*, 1946, **54**, 280–284. (*29, 31*)

LEONARD, EUGENIE A., & TUCKER, A. C. *The individual inventory in guidance programs in secondary schools.* Washington: GPO, 1941. (*17*)

LEONELLA, SISTER M., C.S.C. The school council in the grade school. *Bull. nat. Cath. educ. Ass.*, 1963, **60**, 1–16. (*455*)

LEPP, I. *The Christian failure.* Westminster, Md.: Newman, 1962. (*99, 108, 453*)

LEPP, I. *The psychology of loving.* Baltimore: Helicon, 1963. (*345*)

LEVINE, L. S., & KANTOR, R. E. Psychological effectiveness and imposed social position: a descriptive framework. *Personnel Guid. J.*, 1962, **40**, 418–425. (*115*)

LEVINSON, B. M. The dog as co-therapist. *Ment. Hyg.*, N.Y., 1962, **41**, 59–65. (*200*)

LHOTA, B. G., O.F.M. *Vocational interests of Catholic priests.* Washington: Catholic, 1948. (*487*)

LICHTER, S. O., ET AL. *The drop-outs.* New York: Free Press, 1962. (*433, 434*)

LIEBERMANN, F. Cited by G. Hagmaier, C.S.P., & R. W. Gleason, S.J., *Counseling the Catholic.* New York: Sheed, 1959. (*460*)

LIERTZ, R. *Wanderungen durch das Seeleben.* Munich: Herder, 1924. (*477*)

LIFTON, W. M. The role of empathy and aesthetic sensitivity in counseling. *J. counsel. Psychol.*, 1958, **5**, 267–274. (*295*)

LIFTON, W. M. *Working with groups: group process and individual growth.* New York: Wiley, 1961. (*311, 324*)

LIGUORI, ST. ALPHONSUS. *Theologia moralis.* Lib. 6. (*385*)

LIPPITT, R., ET AL. The dynamics of power: a field study of social influence in groups of children. In Eleanor E. Maccoby, T. M. Newcomb, & E. L. Hartley (Eds.), *Readings in social psychology.* (3rd ed.) New York: Holt, 1958. Pp. 251–265. (*370*)

LIPPITT, R., & WHITE, R. K. An experimental study of leadership and group life. In Eleanor E. Maccoby, T. M. Newcomb, & E. L. Hartley (Eds.), *Readings in social psychology.* (3rd ed.) New York: Holt, 1958. Pp. 496–511. (*318*)

LIPTON, A., & FEINER, A. H. Group therapy and remedial reading. *J. educ. Psychol.*, 1956, **47**, 330–334. (*312*)

LLOYD-JONES, ESTHER. *Social competence and college students.* Washington: Amer. Council Educ., 1940 (*106, 147*)

LLOYD-JONES, ESTHER. Implications of the Wrenn Report for counselor education. *Couns. Educ. Supervis.*, 1962, **2,** 17–20. (*492*)

LLOYD-JONES, ESTHER, & SMITH, MARGARET R. Higher education programs. *Rev. educ. Res.*, 1963, **33,** 163–170. (*511*)

LOCKE, H. J. *Predicting adjustment in marriage.* New York: Holt, 1951. (*366*)

LOUGHARY, J. W. Some considerations regarding fulltime counselor versus teacher-counselor assignments. *Educ. Admin. Supervis.*, 1959, **45,** 199–205. (*157*)

LOUGHARY, J. W. *Counseling in secondary schools.* New York: Harper & Row, 1961. (*268*)

LOW, CAMILLA M. Determining the nature of the needs of youth. *Yearb. nat. Soc. Stud. Educ.*, 1953, Part I. Pp. 22–43. (*204*)

LUCKEY, ELEANORE B. Relationship of marriage counseling and family life education. *Personnel Guid. J.*, 1963, **41,** 420–424. (*388*)

LURIE, W. A., GOLDFEIN, J., & BAXT, R. An intensive vocational counseling program for slow learners in high school. *Personnel Guid. J.*, 1960, **39,** 21–29. (*435*)

LYTTON, G. J., KNOBEL, M., & MACNEVEN, R. W. The function of a psychiatric diagnostic unit in the school system. *Amer. J. Orthopsychiat.*, 1960, **30,** 581–587. (*359*)

MCARTHUR, C. C. Distinguishing patterns of student neuroses. In G. B. Blaine & C. C. McArthur (Eds.), *Emotional problems of the student.* New York: Appleton-Century-Crofts, 1961. Pp. 54–75. (*34, 54, 395*)

MCAULIFFE, D. M., O.P. PAVLA in Salina. *Cath. educ. Rev.*, 1962, **60,** 538–544. (*203*)

MCCALL, R. J. Invested self-expression: a principle of human motivation. *Psychol., Rev.*, 1963, **70,** 289–303. (*62, 298*)

MCCARTHY, R. G., & DOUGLAS, E. M. *Alcohol and social responsibility: a new educational approach.* New York: Crowell, 1949. (*467*)

MCCARTHY, T. N. Psychological assessment and the religious vocation. *Cath. Couns.*, 1960, **4,** 44–49. (a) (*486*)

MCCARTHY, T. N. Understanding student behavior. *Cath. Couns.*, 1960, **4,** 110–115. (b) (*423, 435*)

MCCLEARY, L. E. Restructuring the interpersonal relations of a junior high school class. *Sch. Rev.*, 1956, **64,** 346–352. (*314*)

MCCLELLAND, D. C. Motivation to achieve: some clinical approaches. In G. Watson (Ed.), *No room at the bottom.* Washington: Nat. Educ. Ass., 1963. Pp. 63–75. (*374*)

MCCLELLAND, D. C., ET AL. *The achievement motive.* New York: Appleton-Century-Crofts, 1953. (*198*)

MCCLUSKEY, N. G., S.J. The dinosaur and the Catholic school. *Bull. nat. Cath. educ. Ass.*, 1960, **57,** 232–238. (*29*)

MACCOBY, ELEANOR E. Class differences in boys' choices of authority roles. *Sociometry*, 1962, **25,** 117–119. (*317*)

MACCOBY, ELEANOR E., GIBBS, PATRICIA K., & HUMAN DEVELOPMENT LABORA-
TORY STAFF. Methods of child-rearing in two social classes. In Celia Stendler
(Ed.), *Readings in child behavior and development.* (2nd ed.) New York: Har-
court, Brace & World, 1964. Pp. 272–287. *(365)*

MCCULLOUGH, MOTHER MARYGRACE. Liturgy in adolescent personality growth.
Insight, 1963, **2**, 18–28. *(45, 357)*

MCCULLY, C. H. Developments of a decade of VA counseling. *Personnel Guid. J.*,
1957, **36**, 21–27. *(23)*

MCCULLY, C. H. The school counselor: strategy for professionalization. *Personnel
Guid. J.*, 1962, **40**, 681–689. *(160)*

MCDONOUGH, T. E. The need for negative criticism. *Personnel Guid. J.*, 1960, **39**,
228–229. *(502)*

MCFARLAND, N. F. *Religious vocation: its juridic concept.* Washington: Catholic,
1953. *(478)*

MCGOVERN, J. D. The emotionally disturbed child as scapegoat. *Nat. Cath.
Guid. Conf. J.*, 1964, **9**, 75–76. *(357)*

MCGRATH, SISTER M. BERNARD. *The compatibility of Catholic schools and democratic
standards.* Washington: Catholic, 1948. *(194)*

MCGUCKEN, W. J., S.J. *Jesuit secondary education.* Milwaukee: Bruce, 1932. *(14)*

MCGUCKEN, W. J., S.J. *The philosophy of Catholic education.* New York: America
Press, 1942. *(107)*

MCGUIRE, W. P. A., S.M. *Brooklyn diocesan curricular offerings in high schools.*
Washington: Catholic Education Press, 1932. *(21)*

MCINTYRE, J. P., S.J. Counselor-centered acceptance. *Cath. educ. Rev.*, 1958, **56**,
229–305. *(297)*

MCKENNA, B. H. Greater learning in smaller classes. *NEA J.*, 1957, **46**, 437–438.

MCKENNEY, C. R., S.J. *Moral problems in social work.* Milwaukee: Bruce, 1951.
(113)

MCKEOUGH, M. J., O. PRAEM. Coeducation in the North Central area. *Bull. nat.
Cath. educ. Ass.*, 1954, **51**, 295–297. *(381)*

MCKINNEY, F. *Psychology of personal adjustment.* (3rd ed.) New York: Wiley, 1960.
(343)

MCKOWN, H. C. *Homeroom guidance.* (2nd ed.) New York: McGraw-Hill, 1946.
(150)

MCKOWN, H. C. *Extra-curricular activities.* (3rd ed.) New York: Macmillan,
1956. *(151, 433)*

MCLAUGHLIN, M. A., S.J. Factors in pre-vocational training. *Bull. nat. Cath. educ.
Ass.*, 1915, **12**, 312–320. *(8)*

MCMAHON, SISTER MIRIAM DE LOURDES, S.C. An investigation of the religious
vocational concepts of high school girls. Unpublished doctoral dissertation,
Fordham Univer., 1955. *(455, 478, 484, 516)*

MCMURRAY, HELEN B. *Personnel services in Catholic four year colleges for women.*
Washington: Catholic, 1958. *(188, 194, 447, 451, 452, 528, 529, 530, 532)*

McQUARY, J. P. Preferred counselor characteristics. *Couns. Educ. Supervis.*, 1964, **3**, 145–148. *(296)*

MALINOWSKI, B. *Sex and repression in savage society.* London: Routledge, 1927. *(391)*

MALLERY, D. *Developing student responsibility.* Boston: Nat. Ass. Independent Sch., 1961. *(119)*

MALLERY, D. *High school students speak out.* New York: Harper & Row, 1962. *(119)*

MALNIG, L. R., & CRISTANTIELLO, P. D. A deeper look into freshman interests. *Cath. Counsel.*, 1956, **1**, 6–9. *(423, 484)*

MANGINI, SISTER ROSE MATTHEW, I.H.M. Professional problems of sister teachers in the United States. Unpublished doctoral dissertation, Fordham Univer., 1958. *(436, 485, 522, 524)*

MANN, H. H., & MANN, CAROLA H. Role playing experience and interpersonal adjustment. *J. counsel. Psychol.*, 1959, **6**, 148–152. *(328)*

MANN, K. W. Religious factors and values in counseling: their relationship to ego organization. *J. counsel. Psychol.*, 1959, **6**, 259–262. *(445)*

MARCEL, G. *The mystery of being.* Vols. 1 & 2. Chicago: Regnery, 1960. *(109)*

MARGOLIN, R. J., & Williamson, A. C. *Case conferences in education.* Boston: Humphries, 1961. *(229)*

MARIE, SISTER ERNEST, C.S.J. Womanhood: a value concept. *Cath. Counsl.*, 1960 **5**, 34–36. *(382)*

MARINER, A. S., ET AL. Group psychiatric consultant with public school personnel, a two year study. *Personnel Guid. J.*, 1961, **40**, 254–258. *(179)*

MARITAIN, J. *Education at the crossroads.* New Haven, Conn.: Yale, 1943. *(104)*

MARTINO, T. P. Comparison of the Christian concept of humility and the self-concept according to Rogers. Unpublished master's thesis, Catholic Univer. of America, 1963. *(103)*

MASLOW, A. H. *Motivation and personality.* New York: Harper & Row. *(62, 113)*

MATHEWSON, R. H. The general guidance counselor. *Personnel Guid. J.*, 1954, **32**, 544–547. *(45, 246)*

MATHEWSON, R. H. School guidance: a four-dimensional model. *Personnel Guid. J.*, 1961, **39**, 645–649. *(84)*

MATHEWSON, R. H. *Guidance policy and practice.* New York: Harper & Row (2nd ed., 1955; 3rd ed., 1962). *(84, 216, 246, 258, 339, 364)*

MAUREEN, SISTER VIRGINIA, S.S.N.D. The teaching of science. In Correspondence. *America*, 1964, **110**, 270. *(207)*

MAURIN, P. *The green revolution.* (2nd ed.) Fresno, Calif.: Academy Guild Press, 1961. *(455)*

MAVERICK, L. A. *The vocational guidance of college students.* Cambridge, Mass.: Harvard, 1926. *(11)*

MAY, R., ANGEL, E., & ELLENBERGER, H. B. *Existence.* New York: Basic Books, 1958. *(77, 93)*

MEAD, MARGARET. Adolescence in primitive and modern society. In Eleanor E. Maccoby, T. M. Newcomb, & E. L. Hartley (Eds.), *Readings in social psychology.* (3rd ed.) New York: Holt, 1958. Pp. 341–350. *(52)*

MEAD, MARGARET. Marrying in haste. *Columbia Univer. Forum*, 1960, **3**, 31–34. (*57, 371*)

MEEHL, P. E. *Clinical vs. statistical prediction*. Minneapolis: Univer. of Minnesota Press, 1954. (*238*)

MEEHL, P. E. Religious factors and values in counseling: some technical and axiological problems in the therapeutic handling of religious and vocational material. *J. counsel. Psychol.*, 1959, **6**, 255–259. (*444*)

MENDELSOHN, G. A., & GELLER, M. H. Effects of counselor-client similarity on the outcome of counseling. *J. counsel. Psychol.*, 1963, **10**, 70–77. (*297*)

MENNES, A. H. Orientation of new students to high school. *Sch. Rev.*, 1956, **64**, 64–66. (*321*)

MENNINGER, K. A. *Love against hate*. New York: Harcourt, Brace & World, 1959. (*477*)

MENNINGER, K. A. *Theory of psychoanalytic technique*. New York: Science Editions, 1961. (*92*)

MEREI, F. Group leadership and institutionalization. *Human Relat.*, 1949, **2**, 23–39. (*368, 370*)

MERRILL, R. M., & MURPHY, D. T. Personality factors and academic achievement in college. *J. counsel. Psychol.*, 1959, **6**, 207–210. (*431*)

MERTON, T. The general dance. *Jubilee*, 1961, **9**, 9–11. (*95*)

MEYER, B. F., M.M. The lay vocation. In G. L. Kane (Ed.), *Meeting the vocation crisis*. Westminster, Md.: Newman, 1956. Pp. 194–204. (*480*)

MEYERS, W. F. The role of the lay teacher in Catholic education. Unpublished doctoral dissertation, Univer. of Notre Dame, 1963. (*481*)

MICHONNEAU, G. *Revolution in a city parish*. Westminster, Md.: Newman, 1948. (*108, 440, 460*)

MIDDLETON, R., & PUTNEY, S. Religion, normative standards, and behavior. *Sociometry*, 1962, **25**, 141–152. (*442*)

MILLER, A. D. The role of the school system in a mental health program. In M. Krugman (Ed.), *Orthopsychiatry and the school*. New York: Amer. Orthopsychiat. Ass., 1958. Pp. 135–140. (*355*)

MILLER, C. H. *Foundations of guidance*. New York: Harper & Row, 1961. (*363*)

MILLER, F. W. *Guidance principles and services*. Indianapolis: Bobbs-Merrill, 1961. (*337*)

MILLER, J. H., C.S.C. *Fundamentals of the liturgy*. Notre Dame, Ind.: Fides, 1959.

MINK, O. G., & SGAN, M. Does counselor approach really matter? *Voc. Guid. Quart.*, 1963, **11**, 204–206. (*270*)

MITCHELL, O. J. A study of pupil elimination from Gonzaga High school from 1923–1937. Unpublished master's thesis, Catholic Univer. of America, 1940. (*204*)

MOFFITT, J. W., & STAGNER, R. Perceptual rigidity and closure as functions of anxiety. *J. abnorm. soc. Psychol.*, 1956, **52**, 354–357. (*347*)

MOLNAR, S. G. *The future of education*. New York: Fleet, 1961. (*76*)

MONAHAN, T. P. Family status and the delinquent child: a reappraisal and some new findings. *Soc. Forces*, 1957, **35**, 250–258. (*373*)

MOORE, G. D. An investigation of certain aspects of a guidance program. *Personnel Guid. J.*, 1960, **38**, 558–562. (*69*)

MOORE, T. V., O.S.B. The problem child in the Catholic school. *Bull. nat. Cath. educ. Ass.*, 1930, **27**, 398–408. (*20*)

MOORE, T. V., O.S.B. Insanity in priests and religious, Parts I and II. *Amer. eccles. Rev.*, 1936, **95**, 485–496, 601–612. (*486*)

MOORE, T. V., O.S.B. *The driving forces of human nature and their adjustment.* New York: Grune & Stratton, 1950. (*45, 344*)

MORAN, BROTHER G., F.S.C. Hope: foundation of religious education. *Cath. educ. Rev.*, 1963, **61**, 302–312. (*117*)

MORENO, J. L. *Who shall survive? Foundations of sociometry, group psychotherapy and sociodrama.* Beacon, N.Y.: Beacon House, 1953. (*17, 229, 329*)

MORENO, J. L. Role. In J. L. Moreno et al., *The sociometry reader.* New York: Free Press, 1960. (*328, 329*)

MOROCCO, R. R. A study of the ideals expressed by a selected group of parochial and public school students. Unpublished master's thesis, Catholic Univer. of America, 1957. (*447*)

MORRIS, V. C. Conformity, rebellion, and the authentic life: a look at contemporary guidance theory. *Teachers Coll. Rec.*, 1959, **61**, 46–50. (*105, 356*)

MORRISON, J., O.S.B. Warped attitude of Catholic students toward the Negro. *Cath. Educ. Rev.*, 1946, **46**, 285–291. (*449*)

MORTENSON, D. G., & SCHMULLER, A. M. *Guidance in today's schools.* New York: Wiley, 1959. (*244*)

MOSER, L. E., & MOSER, RUTH S. *Counseling and guidance.* Englewood Cliffs, N.J.: Prentice-Hall, 1963. (*243, 335*)

MOTTO, J. J. A reply to Drasgow on underachievers. *J. counsel. Psychol.*, 1959, **6**, 245–247. (*438*)

MOUNIER, E. *A personalist manifesto.* (Tr. monks of St. John's Abbey) New York: Longmans, 1938. (*82, 109*)

MOUROUX, J. *I believe: the personal structure of faith.* (Tr. M. Turner) New York: Sheed, 1959. (*465, 466*)

MOWRER, O. H. "Q technique"—description, history and critique. In O. H. Mowrer (Ed.), *Psychotherapy theory and research.* New York: Ronald, 1953. Pp. 316–375. (*307*)

MOWRER, O. H. *Learning theory and personality dynamics.* New York: Ronald, 1960. (*54, 93*)

MOYNIHAN, J. F., S.J. Pastoral counseling. *Personnel Guid. J.*, 1958, **36**, 327–331. (*259*)

MOYNIHAN, J. F., S.J. Problems and procedures in making referrals. *Cath. Couns.*, 1962, **6**, 91–94. (*169*)

MUELLER, KATE H. Theory for campus disicipline. *Personnel Guid. J.*, 1958, **36**, 302–309. (*193*)

MUELLER, KATE H. Criteria for evaluating professional status. *Personnel Guid. J.*, 1959, **37**, 410–417. (*89*)

MUELLER, W. J., GATSCH, CLAIRE M., & RALSTON, JEAN K. The prediction of counselor interview behavior. *Personnel Guid. J.*, 1963, **41**, 513–517. (*499*)

MUELLER, W. J., & ROTHNEY, J. W. M. Comparisons of selective, descriptive, and predictive statements of superior students, their parents, and their teachers. *Personnel Guid. J.*, 1960, **38**, 621–625. (*227*)

MULLEN, J. J. *Psychological factors in the pastoral treatment of scruples.* Washington: Catholic, 1927. (*467*)

MUNGER, P. E., MYERS, R. A., & BROWN, DARINE F. Guidance institutes and the persistence of attitudes: a progress report. *Personnel Guid. J.*, 1963, **41**, 415–419. (*500*)

MURPHY, G. The cultural context of guidance. *Personnel Guid. J.*, 1955, **34**, 4–9. (*95*)

MURPHY, G. *Freeing intelligence through teaching.* New York: Harper & Row, 1961. (a) (*92*)

MURPHY, G. New vistas in personality research. *Personnel Guid. J.*, 1961, **40**, 114–122. (b) (*114*)

MURPHY, V. M. Achievers vs. non-achievers: which way is "over"? *Cath. Couns.*, 1964, **8**, 52–56. (a) (*415, 416*)

MURPHY, V. M. Psychological approaches to the Catholic delinquent: a task for the guidance function? *Nat. Cath. Guid. Conf. J.*, 1964, **9**, 77–78. (b) (*373, 374*)

MURRAY, E. Work: a neglected resource for students. *Personnel Guid. J.*, 1962, **41**, 229–233. (*437*)

MURRAY, J. B., C.M. College students' concepts of psychologists and psychiatrists: a problem in differentiation. *J. soc. Psychol.*, 1962, **17**, 161–168. (*179*)

MURRAY, SISTER TERESA G., O.S.B. *Vocational guidance in Catholic secondary schools.* New York: Teachers Coll., 1938. (*9, 20, 21, 22*)

[MURRAY], SISTER TERESA G., O.S.B. How to set up a guidance program in a Catholic secondary school. *Bull. nat. Cath. educ. Ass.*, 1940, **37**, 376–389. (*133*)

MURSELL, G. R. A study of religious training as a sociological factor in delinquency. Unpublished doctoral dissertation, Ohio State Univer., 1930. (*442*)

MUSSEN, P. H. *The psychological development of the child.* Englewood Cliffs, N.J.: Prentice-Hall, 1963. (*44*)

MUSSIO, J. K. The Catholic teacher. *Bull. nat. Cath. educ. Ass.*, 1959, **56**, 207–215. (*141*)

MUTHARD, J. E. The relative effectiveness of larger units used in interview analysis. *J. consult. Psychol.*, 1953, **18**, 184–188. (*267*)

NATIONAL ASSOCIATION OF STUDENT PERSONNEL ADMINISTRATORS, COMMITTEE ON TRAINING RESIDENCE HALL ADMINISTRATORS. *Thirty-ninth annual conference.* n.c.: Author, 1957. (*513*)

NATIONAL ASSOCIATION OF WOMEN DEANS AND COUNSELORS, COMMITTEE ON RESIDENCE HALLS. *The residence hall for students.* Washington: Author, 1957. (*513*)

NATIONAL CATHOLIC GUIDANCE CONFERENCE. Constitution. *Cath. Couns.*, 1962, **6**, 103–107. (*319*)

NATIONAL COMMITTEE FOR MENTAL HYGIENE. Cited in H. W. Bernard, *Human development in Western culture.* Boston: Allyn and Bacon, 1962. (*342*)

NATIONAL EDUCATION ASSOCIATION. Pupil behavior as related to school factors. *NEA Res. Bull.*, 1956, **34**, 65–69. (*192*)

NATIONAL EDUCATION ASSOCIATION, COMMISSION ON THE REORGANIZATION OF SECONDARY EDUCATION. *Vocational guidance in secondary education.* Washington: GPO, 1918. (*5*)

NATIONAL EDUCATION ASSOCIATION, EDUCATIONAL POLICIES COMMISSION. *Manpower and education.* Washington: Author, 1956. (*23*)

NATIONAL EDUCATION ASSOCIATION, PROJECT ON INSTRUCTION. *Schools for the sixties.* New York: McGraw-Hill, 1963. (*204*)

NATIONAL SOCIETY FOR THE STUDY OF EDUCATION. *Education for the gifted. Yearb. nat. Soc. Stud. Educ.*, 1958, Part II. (*428*)

NATIONAL STUDY OF SECONDARY SCHOOL EVALUATION. *Section G, guidance services.* Washington: Author, 1960. (*214*)

NEAL, RUTH. Counseling the off-campus woman student. *Personnel Guid. J.*, 1958, **36**, 342–343. (*412*)

NEEDHAM, J., STODOLA, Q., & BROWN, DARINE F. Improving test interpretation through films. *Voc. Guid. Quart.*, 1963–64, **12**, 141–144. (*323*)

NELSON, R. O. Early vs. developmental vocational choice. *Voc. Guid. Quart.*, 1962, **11**, 23–27. (*406*)

NELSON, J. O. The source of eagerness in daily work. *Voc. Guid. Quart.*, 1963, **11**, 162–166. (*411*)

NEWMAN, J. *The Christian in society.* Westminster, Md.: Newman, 1962. (*481*)

NEWMAN, J. H., CARDINAL. *On consulting the faithful in matters of doctrine.* New York: Sheed, 1961. (*199*)

NOLAN, J. R. M. The problem of scruples. In E. F. O'Doherty & S. D. McGrath (Eds.), *The priest and mental health.* New York: St. Paul, 1963. Pp. 87–97. (*467*)

NOLL, V. H. Preservice preparation of teachers in measurement. In A. E. Traxler (Ed.), *Measurement and research in today's schools.* Washington: Amer. Council Educ., 1961. Pp. 65–75. (*230*)

NORDBERG, R. B. Additive and non-additive mental measurement. *Cath. educ. Rev.*, 1955, **52**, 145–157. (a) (*233*)

NORDBERG, R. B. Evaluation: the ideal and the actual. *Cath. educ. Rev.*, 1955, **53**, 533–546. (b) (*233*)

NORDBERG, R. B. Problems in additive measurements. *Cath. educ. Rev.*, 1955, **53**, 373–383. (c) (*233*)

NORDBERG, R. B. Counseling: non-directive or non-coercive? *Cath. educ. Rev.*, 1958, **56**, 40–44. (*258, 259*)

NORDBERG, R. B. Behavioral science revisited. *Cath. educ. Rev.*, 1960, **57**, 313–322. (a) (*336, 527*)

NORDBERG, R. B. The march to holism—where are we? *Cath. educ. Rev.*, 1960, **58**, 240–247. (b) (*336*)

NORDBERG, R. B. Creativity: craze or crown? *Cath. educ. Rev.*, 1963, **61**, 588–592. (a) (*430*)

NORDBERG, R. B. Empathy: by-product of connaturality. *Cath. Couns.*, 1963, **7**, 106–108. (b) (*259*)

NORDBERG, R. B. Is there Christian counseling? *Cath. educ. Rev.*, 1963, **61**, 1–6. (c) (*98, 258*)

NORDBERG, R. B. Personality integration and mental health. *Cath. Couns.*, 1963, **8**, 8–12. (d) (*336*)

NORRIS, WILLA. The history and development of the NVGA. Unpublished doctoral dissertation, George Washington Univer., 1954. (*7*)

NORRIS, WILLA. More than a decade of training guidance and personnel workers. *Personnel Guid. J.*, 1960, **39**, 287–291. (*499*)

NOVICKY, W. N. The present status of the lay teacher in the Catholic schools of Ohio. Unpublished master's thesis, Catholic Univer. of America, 1950. (*525*)

NOVICKY, W. N. A study of the attitudes of fraternal charity in Catholic children differing in educational backgrounds. Unpublished doctoral dissertation, Fordham Univer., 1959. (*450*)

NURNBERGER, J. I., FERSTER, C. B., & BRADY, J. P. *An introduction to the science of human behavior.* New York: Appleton-Century-Crofts, 1963. (*43, 349, 351*)

NUTTIN, J. *Psychoanalysis and personality.* New York: New American Library, Mentor-Omega, 1962. (*45, 345*)

NYE, F. I. Child adjustment in broken and unhappy broken homes. *Marriage and Family Living*, 1957, **19**, 356–361. (*367*)

O'BRIEN, J. A. *Catholics on the secular campus.* New York: America Press, 1961. (*446*)

O'BRIEN, K. J., C.SS.R. *The proximate aims of education.* Milwaukee: Bruce, 1958. (*83*)

O'DEA, T. F. *American Catholic dilemma: an inquiry into the intellectual life.* New York: Sheed, 1958. (*80, 418, 423*)

O'DOHERTY, E. F. *Religion and personality problems.* Staten Island, N.Y.: Alba House, 1964. (*354*)

O'HARA, R. P., & TIEDEMAN, D. V. Vocational self-concept in adolescence. *J. counsel. Psychol.*, 1959, **6**, 292–301. (*402*)

OJEMANN, R. H. Basic approaches to mental health: the human relations program at the State University of Iowa. *Personnel Guid. J.*, 1958, **37**, 198–206. (*121*)

O'KANE, J. P. A critical analysis of the religious content from 1865 to 1914 of the American history textbooks widely used in the public secondary schools of the United States. Unpublished master's thesis, Catholic Univer. of America, 1962. (*207*)

O'KELLY, L., & MUCKLER. F. A. *Introduction to psychopathology.* (2nd ed.) Englewood Cliffs, N.J.: Prentice-Hall, 1955. (*347*)

OKLAHOMA CURRICULUM IMPROVEMENT COMMISSION. *A handbook for the improvement of guidance and counseling in Oklahoma schools, grades K–12.* Oklahoma City, Okla.: Oklahoma State Dep. Educ., 1961. *(507)*

OLHEISER, SISTER MARY DAVID. Development of a sister-teacher interest scale for the "Strong Vocational Interest Blank" for women. Unpublished doctoral dissertation, Boston Coll., 1962. *(487)*

OLMSTED, M. *The small group.* New York: Random House, 1959. *(311)*

OLSEN, LeR. C. Success for new counselors. *J. counsel. Psychol.*, 1963, **10**, 350–355. *(293)*

ONG, W. J., S.J. *Frontiers in American Catholicism.* New York: Macmillan, 1957. *(118)*

OOLE, ZELMA M. Guidance through creative writing on the secondary school level. Unpublished doctoral dissertation, Teachers Coll., 1959. *(149)*

OPPENHEIMER, O. Some counseling theory: objectivity and subjectivity. *J. counsel. Psychol.*, 1954, **1**, 184–187. *(124)*

ORAISON, M. *Union in marital love.* New York: Macmillan, 1958. *(390)*

OREGON DEPARTMENT OF EDUCATION. *Guidance services for Oregon schools.* Salem, Ore.: Author, 1961. *(76)*

OSTLUND, L. A. Group functioning under negative conditions. *J. educ. Psychol.*, 1956, **47**, 32–39. *(319)*

OSTOW, M., & SCHARFSTEIN, B. *The need to believe: the psychology of religion.* New York: International Universities Press, 1954. *(465, 466)*

O'SULLIVAN-BARRA, J. The Catholic school and vocational preparation. *Integrity*, 1955, **9**, 21–29. *(405)*

OWEN, G. H. Does counseling mean coddling? *Educ. Forum*, 1958, **22**, 359–362. *(83)*

PALLONE, N. J. The psychiatric social worker's role in a college mental health program. *Cath. educ. Rev.*, 1960, **58**, 589–594. *(188)*

PALLONE, N. J. Effects of short- and long-term developmental reading courses upon S.A.T. verbal scores. *Personnel Guid. J.*, 1961, **39**, 654–657. (a) *(437)*

PALLONE, N. J. The emotional matrix of reading difficulty. *Cath. Couns.*, 1961, **5**, 37–42. (b) *(437)*

PALLONE, N. J. Preparation for guidance and counseling. *Cath. Couns.* 1961, **6**, 24–27. (c) *(111)*

PALLONE, N. J. Vocational development and curriculum structure. *Cath. educ. Rev.*, 1961, **59**, 257–262. (d) *(245, 409, 419)*

PALLONE, N. J. Education and its subprocesses of teaching and guidance. *Cath. educ. Rev.*, 1962, **15**, 615–621. (a) *(83, 339)*

PALLONE, N. J. Toward a rationale for counseling services. *Cath. Couns.*, 1962, **6**, 99–100. (b) *(271)*

PALLONE, N. J. Adjustment, adaption, and the sane society. *Cath. Couns.*, 1963, **8**, 2. (a) *(336)*

PALLONE, N. J. "Career" motherhood: implications for guidance. *Cath. Couns.*, 1963, **7**, 71–76. (b) (*383, 403*)

PALLONE, N. J. The case for vocational guidance. *Cath. Couns.*, 1963, **7**, 92. (c) (*358, 396*)

PALLONE, N. J. Psychometric "lawfulness" and the prediction of behavior. *Cath. educ. Rev.*, 1963, **61**, 433–442. (d) (*232*)

PALLONE, N. J. Social authority and perceptual modification in the closed society. Doctoral dissertation, New York Univer., 1963. (e) [Published as: Explorations in religious authority and social perception: the collar and conformity. *Acta Psychol.* (Netherlands), 1964, **22**, 321–337.] (*81, 314*)

PALLONE, N. J. The phenomenal self, person, and the Catholic counselor. *Insight*, 1964, **2**, 20–26. (*259, 336*)

PALLONE, N. J., & GRANDE, P. P. *Facilitation of communication of problem related content in the school counseling interview.* Notre Dame, Ind.: Dep. Educ., Univer. of Notre Dame, 1964. (a) (*164, 262, 270*)

PALLONE, N. J., & GRANDE, P. P. Public perception or client need: counselor "role" or image? *Cath. educ. Rev.*, 1964, **62**, 39–46. (b) (*161, 162*),

PAPANEK, E. *The Austrian school reform.* New York: Fell, 1962. (*10*)

PARKER, H. J. Seventh graders choose parents for guidance. *Voc. Guid. Quart.*, 1963, **12**, 61–62. (*407*)

PARKER, K. H. Location of guidance facilities within the school plant. *Personnel Guid. J.*, 1957, **36**, 253–254. (*195, 506*)

PARSONS, F. *Choosing a vocation.* Boston: Houghton Mifflin, 1909. (*5*)

PARSONS, F. The vocation bureau's first report to the executive committee and trustees. In J. M. Brewer, *A history of vocational guidance.* New York: Harper & Row, 1942. Pp. 303–308. (*94*)

PASCAL, B. *Pensées.* New York: Dutton Everyman, 1908. (*457*)

PASSOW, A. H., ET AL. *Planning for talented youth.* New York: Teachers Coll., 1955. (*428*)

PATTERSON, C. H. Client expectations and social conditioning. *Personnel Guid. J.*, 1958, **37**, 136–138. (a) (*299*)

PATTERSON, C. H. The place of values in counseling and psychotherapy. *J. counsel. Psychol.*, 1958, **5**, 216–223. (b) (*97*)

PATTERSON, C. H. The counselor's responsibility in rehabilitation. Cited by D. S. Arbuckle, Counseling: philosophy or science? *Personnel Guid. J.*, 1960, **39**, 11–14. (*88*)

PATTERSON, C. H. *Counseling and guidance in schools: a first course.* New York: Harper & Row, 1962. (*94, 155, 250*)

PATTERSON, C. H. Control, conditioning, and counseling. *Personnel Guid. J.*, 1963, **41**, 680–686. (*275*)

PATTERSON, C. H. A note on the evaluation of the effectiveness of counseling and psychotherapy. *Couns. Educ. Supervis.*, 1964, **3**, 129–131. (*307*)

PAUL, H. A., O.S.F.S. Counseling and student use of high school record. *Cath. educ. Rev.*, 1961, **59**, 376–381. *(239)*

PAUL VI, POPE. Cited by Y. M. J. Congar, O.P., Lendemain d'élection. *Le monde*, 23–24 juin, 1963. (a) *(453)*

PAUL VI, POPE. Cited by *Time*, Atlantic ed., June 28, 1963. (b) *(479)*

PAUL VI, POPE. Letter to Antonio Cardinal Caggiano, 1964. *(453)*

PECK, R. F., ET AL. *The psychology of character development*. New York: Wiley, 1960. *(448)*

PEIXOTTO, HELEN E. The teacher looks into the home. *Cath. educ. Rev.*, 1960, **58**, 106–113. *(375)*

PEPINSKY, H. B., & KARST, T. O. Convergence: a phenomenon in counseling and in psychotherapy. *Amer. Psychologist*, 1964, **19**, 333–338. *(297)*

PERRY, W. G., & ESTES, S. G. The collaboration of client and counselor. In O. H. Mowrer (Ed.), *Psychotherapy: theory and research*. New York: Ronald, 1953. Pp. 95–119. *(261)*

PETERS, H. J. Interferences to guidance program development. *Personnel Guid. J.*, 1963, **42**, 119–123. *(192)*

PETERS, H. J., & FARWELL, GAIL F. *Guidance: a developmental approach*. Chicago: Rand McNally, 1959. *(152, 174)*

PETERS, H. J., & MUELLER, W. J. The counseling function. *Rev. educ. Res.*, 1960, **30**, 131–139. *(339)*

PIERSON, G. A. Aesop and the school counselor. *Personnel Guid. J.*, 1954, **32**, 544–547. *(164)*

PIERSON, G. A., & GRANT, C. W. The road ahead for the school counselor. *Personnel Guid. J.*, 1959, **38**, 208–209. *(154)*

PIERSON, L. R. High school teacher prediction of college success. *Personnel Guid. J.*, 1958, **37**, 142–145. *(134)*

PITTENGER, R. E. The first five minutes—its significance in mental health. *J. Communic.*, 1963, **13**, 132–139. *(297)*

PIUS XI, POPE. *Christian education of youth*. Washington: National Catholic Welfare Conference, 1936. *(380)*

PIUS XII, POPE. *Guiding Christ's little ones*. Washington: Nat. Cath. Welf. Conf., 1944. *(197)*

PIUS XII, POPE. *Counsel to teaching sisters*. (Tr. Nat. Cath. Welf. Conf.) Washington: Nat. Cath. Welf. Conf., 1951. *(135, 140)*

PIUS XII, POPE. *Problems of understanding youth*. Cited by P. Hug, O.F.M., Understanding the adolescent. *Cath. Couns.*, 1960, **5**, 25–28.

POFFENBERGER, T. Individual choice in adolescent premarital sex behavior. *Marriage and Family Living*, 1960, **22**, 324–330. *(471)*

POHLMAN, E. Changes in client preference. *Personnel Guid. J.*, 1961, **40**, 340–343. *(94)*

POHLMAN, E. Should clients tell counselors what to do? *Personnel Guid. J.*, 1964, **42**, 456–458. *(269)*

POHLMAN, E., & ROBINSON, F. P. Client reaction to some aspects of the counseling situation. *Personnel Guid. J.*, 1960, **38**, 546–551. *(307)*

POLICIES COMMITTEE, SECONDARY SCHOOL DEPARTMENT, NATIONAL CATHOLIC EDUCATION ASSOCIATION. The objectives of Catholic secondary education in the United States. *Cath. high Sch. quart. Bull.*, 1944, **2**, 22–28. *(83)*

POORMAN, R. O., C.S.C. An analysis of the relationship between shared decision-making and the vow of obedience in religious institutes in Catholic higher education. Unpublished doctoral dissertation, Univer. of Notre Dame, 1964. *(503)*

POWELL, M. Help wanted for school psychologists. *Personnel Guid. J.*, 1960, **38**, 662. *(504)*

PRESCOTT, D. A. *The child in the educative process.* New York: McGraw-Hill, 1957. *(50)*

PRESSEY, S. L. Educational acceleration: occasional procedure or major issue? *Personnel Guid. J.*, 1962. **41**, 12–17. *(436)*

PRITCHARD, D. H. The occupational exploration process: some operational implications. *Personnel Guid. J.*, 1962, **40**, 674–680. *(410)*

PROCTOR, W. M. *Psychological tests and guidance of high school pupils.* Bloomington, Ill.: Public School, 1923. *(9)*

PROUTY, HELEN. Personality factors related to over- and under-achievers. *Amer. Psychologist*, 1955, **10**, 139–141. *(466)*

PRUITT, W. Group size and organizational planning. *Personnel Guid. J.*, 1960, **38**, 626–632. *(317)*

PRÜMMER, D. M., O.P. *Handbook of moral theology.* (Tr. G. W. Shelton) New York: Kenedy, 1957. *(469, 474)*

PRY, H. C. Evaluate your home-room guidance program. *Bull. nat. Ass. secondary-Sch. Principals*, 1961, **45**, 95–100. *(324)*

PRYER, MARGARET W., FLINT, A. W., & BASS, B. M. Group effectiveness and consistency of leadership. *Sociometry*, 1962, **25**, 391–397. *(319, 320)*

PULLIAS, E. V. Masturbation as a mental hygiene problem—a study of the beliefs of 75 young men. *J. abnorm. soc. Psychol.*, 1937, **23**, 216–222. *(473)*

PUMPINATZI, D. *Les deux copains de natation de l'Éden Roc.* Cap d'Antibes, France: Hautjour, 1963. (a) *(149)*

PUMPINATZI, D. *La plage et les rochers.* Au-Bord-de-la-Mer, France: Leciel, 1963. (b) *(302)*

PURCELL, FLORENCE E. Counseling assignments and efficiency. *Voc. Guid. Quart.*, 1957, **5**, 111–113. (a) *(509)*

PURCELL, FLORENCE E. Counselor duties—a survey. *Sch. Couns.*, 1957, **4**, 35–38. (b) *(509)*

RAAB, E., & LIPSET, S.M. *Prejudice and society.* New York: Anti-Defamation League, B'nai Brith, 1959. *(318)*

RADHAKRISHNAN, S. *An idealist way of life.* (Rev. ed.) London: G. Allen, 1937. *(78)*

RAHNER, K., S.J. *Kirche der Sünder.* Freiburg-im-Bresgau: Herder, 1948. *(454)*

RAHNER, K., S.J. *Free speech in the church.* New York: Sheed, 1959. *(196, 460)*

RAMIREZ, A., O.F.M. Personality disorders and their therapy according to the client-centered theory. In *The mind of modern man.* Washington: Franciscan Educ. Conf., 1959. Pp. 161–202. *(42)*

READY, SISTER M. CLAVER, R.S.M. Training and functions of counselors in Catholic colleges for women in the United States. Unpublished doctoral dissertation, Fordham Univer., 1958. *(528, 530, 531)*

RECKTENWALD, L. N. Beyond the visible data. *Cath. Couns.,* 1957, **1**, 23–24. *(117)*

RECKTENWALD, L. N. The counselor's self-concept. *Personnel Guid. J.,* 1960, **38**, 508–509. *(496)*

REDDEN, J. D., & RYAN, F. A. *A Catholic philosophy of education.* (Rev. ed.) Milwaukee: Bruce, 1956. *(113)*

REDL, F., & WATTENBERG, W. W. *Mental hygiene in teaching.* (2nd ed.) New York: Harcourt, Brace & World, 1959. *(345, 359, 362, 375)*

REDL, F., & WINEMAN, D. *The aggressive child: children who hate.* New York: Free Press, 1957. *(373, 431)*

REED, H. J., & STEFFLRE, B. Elementary and secondary school programs. *Rev. educ. Res.,* 1963, **33**, 152–162. *(120, 192, 193)*

REIK, T. *Listening with the third ear.* New York: Farrar, Straus & Cudahy, 1948. *(91)*

REIK, T. *The need to be loved.* New York: Farrar, Straus & Cudahy, 1963. *(78, 123)*

REISS, I. L. Consistency and sexual ethics. *Marriage and Family Living,* 1962, **24**, 264–269. *(389)*

REISSMAN, F. *The culturally deprived child.* New York: Harper & Row, 1962. *(432)*

REYNOLDS, W. F., SCHWARTZ, M. M., PAVLIK, W. P., AND CARLOCK, J. Individual differences in response to verbal reinforcement: a preliminary report. *Psychol. Rep.,* 1963, **12**, 546. *(266)*

REZLER, AGNES G. Personal values and achievement in college. *Personnel Guid. J.,* 1960, **39**, 137–143. *(419, 422, 423)*

RICCIO, A. C. The status of the autobiography. *Peabody J. Educ.,* 1958, **36**, 33–36. *(226)*

RICCIO, A. C. The parochial school graduate in the secular university. *Cath. educ. Rev.,* 1962, **60**, 236–241. (a) *(117)*

RICCIO, A. C. Teacher education students evaluate the Ten Commandments. *Relig. Educ.,* 1962, **57**, 448–450. (b) *(454)*

RICCIO, V., & SLOCUM, B. *All the way down.* New York: Simon and Schuster, 1962. *(505)*

RICHARDSON, H., & BOROW, H. Evaluation of a technique of group orientation for vocational counseling. *Educ. psychol. Measmt,* 1952, **12**, 587–597. *(322)*

RICKARD, H. C., & DINOFF, M. A follow-up note on verbal manipulation in a psychotherapeutic relationship. *Psychol. Rep.,* 1962, **11**, 506. *(266)*

RIEGERT, N. Professional stimulation through diocesan guidance councils. *Cath. Couns.,* 1959, **3**, 86–88. *(186)*

RIESMAN, D. *Constraint and variety in American education.* Lincoln, Neb.: Univer. of Nebraska Press, 1956. *(76)*

RIFFEL, P. A., S.J. The detection of scrupulosity and its relation to age and sex. Unpublished master's thesis, Fordham Univer., 1958. *(467)*

RIFFEL, P. A., S.J. Sex and scrupulosity. In W. C. Bier, S.J. (Ed.), *The adolescent: his search for understanding.* New York: Fordham, 1963. Pp. 39–51. *(468)*

RISTUCCIA, B. J., C.M. *Quasi-religious societies.* Washington: Catholic, 1958. *(478)*

ROBINSON, F. P. The dynamics of communication in counseling. *J. counsel. Psychol.,* 1955, **2**, 163–196. *(264)*

ROBINSON, F. P. *Effective study.* New York: Harper & Row, 1961. *(143)*

ROCCHIO, P. D., & KEARNEY, N. C. Teacher-pupil attitudes as related to non-promotion of secondary school pupils. *Educ. psychol. Measmt,* 1956, **16**, 244–252. *(432)*

ROCKWELL, P. J. Social concepts in the published writing of some pioneers in guidance, 1900–1916. Unpublished doctoral dissertation, Univer. of Wisconsin, 1958. *(6)*

ROE, ANNE. *The psychology of occupations.* New York: Wiley, 1956. *(399)*

ROE, ANNE. Early determinants of vocational choice. *J. counsel. Psychol.,* 1957, **4**, 212–217. *(399)*

ROE, ANNE. Personality structure and occupational behavior. In H. Borow (Ed.), *Man in a world at work.* Boston: Houghton Mifflin, 1964. Pp. 196–214. *(396, 400)*

ROEBER, E. C., SMITH, G. E., & ERICKSON, C. E. *Organization and administration of guidance services.* (2nd ed.) New York: McGraw-Hill, 1955. *(182)*

ROEMMICH, H., & SCHMIDT, J. L. Student perceptions in assistance provided by counselors in college planning. *Personnel Guid. J.,* 1962, **41**, 157–158. *(505)*

ROESCH, R. A., S.M. A study of the personal experiences and attitudes of high school boys and girls as related to their transfer from a Catholic to a public secondary school in the city of New York. Unpublished doctoral dissertation, Fordham Univer., 1954. *(75, 204, 377, 434)*

ROGERS, C. R. *The clinical treatment of the problem child.* Boston: Houghton Mifflin, 1939. *(225)*

ROGERS, C. R. *Counseling and psychotherapy.* Boston: Houghton Mifflin, 1942. *(17, 246, 247, 252, 254, 297)*

ROGERS, C. R. *Client-centered therapy.* Boston: Houghton Mifflin, 1951. *(36, 37, 38, 39, 93, 247, 252, 254, 318, 343)*

ROGERS, C. R. Some directions and end points in therapy. In O. H. Mowrer (Ed.), *Psychotherapy: theory and research.* New York: Ronald, 1953. Pp. 44–68. *(39)*

ROGERS, C. R. Some issues concerning the control of human behavior. *Science,* 1956, **124**, 1060–1064. *(38)*

ROGERS, C. R. The necessary and sufficient conditions of therapeutic personality change. *J. consult. Psychol.,* 1957, **21**, 95–103. (a) *(96)*

ROGERS, C. R. A note on the "nature of man." *J. counsel. Psychol.,* 1957, **4**, 199–203. (b) *(77, 252)*

ROGERS, C. R. The characteristics of a helping relationship. *Personnel Guid. J.*, 1958, **37,** 6–16. (*115, 124, 356, 444*)

ROGERS, C. R. Lessons I have learned in counseling. In W. E. Dugan (Ed.), *Counseling points of view.* Minneapolis: Univer. of Minnesota Press, 1959. Pp. 14–26. (a) (*252*)

ROGERS, C. R. A theory of therapy, personality, and interpersonal relationships as developed in the client-centered framework. In S. Koch (Ed.), *Psychology: a study of a science.* Vol. 3. *Formulations of the person and the social context.* New York: McGraw-Hill, 1959. Pp. 184–256. (b) (*96*)

ROGERS, C. R. *On becoming a person.* Boston: Houghton Mifflin, 1961. (*39, 41, 55, 96, 154, 175, 236, 252, 253, 257, 297*)

ROGERS, C. R. The interpersonal relationship: the core of guidance. *Harvard educ. Rev.*, 1962, **34,** 416–429. (*95*)

ROGERS, SISTER MARY E., R.S.M. The attitude of college sophomores and seniors toward counseling procedures with reference to certain personality factors and personal problem frequency. Unpublished doctoral dissertation, St. Louis Univer., 1957. (*531*)

RONDET, H., S.J. Towards a theology of sin. *Theol. Dig.*, 1956, **4,** 171–176. (*463, 464*)

ROONEY, J. R. *Curricular offerings in 283 Catholic high schools.* Washington: Catholic Education Press, 1931. (*21*)

ROSAIRE, SISTER XAVIER. Guidance functions in a diocesan secondary school. *Cath. educ. Rev.*, 1944, **42,** 24–37. (*195*)

ROSE, FRANCES. Training courses in guidance. *Voc. Guid. Magazine*, 1932. **10,** 319–322. (*18*)

ROSEN, B. C. Family structure and achievement motivation. *Amer. sociol. Rev.*, 1961, **26,** 574–585. (*80, 368*)

ROSEN, B. C. Race, ethnicity and achievement. *Amer. sociol. Rev.*, 1963, **24,** 47–60. (*368*)

ROSENTHAL, J. Changes in some moral values following psychotherapy. *J. consult. Psychol.*, 1955, **19,** 431–436. (*97*)

ROSSBERG, R., & JACQUES, MARCELINE. The role of the group in patient evaluation, counseling, and management. *Personnel Guid. J.*, 1961, **40,** 135–138. (*329*)

ROTH, R. J., S.J. The importance of matter. *America*, 1963, **109,** 792–794. (*74*)

ROTH, R. M., & MEYERSBURG, H. A. The non-achievement syndrome. *Personnel Guid. J.*, 1963, **41,** 535–540. (*417*)

ROTHNEY, J. W. M., & FARWELL, GAIL F. The evaluation of guidance and personnel services. *Rev. educ. Res.*, 1960, **30,** 168–175. (*192*)

ROUSSEVE, R. J. Updating guidance and personnel practices. *J. Negro Educ.*, 1962, **31,** 182–183. (*286*)

ROUTH, T. A. The importance of "body" language in counseling. *Voc. Guid. Quart.*, 1958, **6,** 134–137. (*268*)

ROWAN, HELEN. Creativity. *Carnegie Corp. N.Y. Quart.*, 1961, **9,** 2–5. (*78*)

Rubinfeld, W. A., & Hoppock, R. Occupations course evaluated eight years later. *Voc. Guid. Quart.*, 1961, **10**, 45–47. (*409*)

Rudikoff, Lynn C., & Kirk, Barbara A. Goals of counseling: mobilizing the counselee. *J. counsel. Psychol.*, 1961, **8**, 243–249. (*247*)

Rudin, S. A. Academic anti-intellectualism as a problem in student counseling. *J. counsel. Psychol.*, 1958, **5**, 18–23. (*203*)

Ruesch, J. *Therapeutic communication.* New York: Norton, 1961. (*268*)

Rupp, U., S.M. Counseling and conscience. *Cath. Couns.*, 1957, **1**, 2–3, 12. (*299*)

Ruth, Sister M., F.S.P.A. *The technique of the Catholic Action cell.* (3rd ed.) La-Crosse, Wis.: St. Rose Convent, 1945. (*202*)

Ruth, R. A. Readability of occupational materials. *Voc. Guid. Quart.*, 1962, **11**, 7–11. (*409*)

Ryan, C. J. The Catholic central high school. Unpublished doctoral dissertation, Catholic Univer. of America, 1927. (*14*)

Ryan, C. J. Catholic education and the laity. *Cath. Sch. J.*, 1951, **51**, 141–143. (*28*)

Ryan, J. J. "Reply" to Albert Muntsch, S.J. Vocational guidance. *Bull. nat. Cath. educ. Ass.*, 1913, **10**, 266–267. (*8*)

Ryan, Mary P. *Are parochial schools the answer?* New York: Holt, 1964. (*207, 394*)

Saalfield, L. J. *Guidance and counseling in Catholic schools.* Chicago: Loyola, 1958. (*75, 99, 112, 388, 443, 480, 487, 488, 527*)

Sacopulos, Eugenia. Vocational guidance through fact and fiction. *Personnel Guid. J.*, 1961, **39**, 670–671. (*409*)

Sacra Congregatio de Religiosis. Instructio de juvenum utriusque sexus promiscua institutione. *Acta Apostolicae Sedis*, 1958, **50**, 99–103. (*140, 380*)

St. John-Stevas, N. Cited in Brother E. L. Cashin, F.M.S., Address to First Annu. Marist Educ. Convention, 1963. (*449*)

Salinger, M. D., Tollefson, A. L., & Hudson, R. I. The catalytic function of the counselor. *Personnel Guid. J.*, 1960, **38**, 648–652. (*244*)

Sandmel, S. The evasions of modern theology. *Amer. Scholar*, 1961, **30**, 366–379. (*405*)

Sanford, N. Developmental status of the freshman. In N. Sanford (Ed.). *The American college.* New York: Wiley, 1962. Pp. 253–282. (*57, 363, 413, 419*)

Santavicca, G. G. Supervised experience and selection of counselor trainees. *Personnel Guid. J.*, 1959, **38**, 195–197. (*495*)

Santopolo, F. A. The priest: a projective analysis of role. Unpublished doctoral dissertation, Fordham Univer., 1956. (*459*)

Sawrey, J. M., & Telford, C. W. *Dynamics of mental health.* Boston: Allyn and Bacon, 1963. (*341, 349, 350, 352*)

Saylor, J. G., & Alexander, W. M. *Curriculum planning for better teaching and learning.* New York: Holt, 1954. (*205*)

Scanlon, Kathryn I. Student government in Catholic colleges for women. Unpublished doctoral dissertation, Fordham Univer., 1955. (*30*)

SCARPITTI, F. R., ET AL. The "good" boy in a high delinquency area; four years later. *Amer. sociol. Rev.*, 1960, **25**, 555–558. (*372*)

SCHACHTER, S. Deviation, rejection, and communication. *Group dynamics* (2nd ed.) New York: Harper & Row, 1960. Pp. 260–285. (*314*)

SCHMIDT, A. G., S.J. Psychiatry and the Catholic school. *Bull. nat. Cath. educ. Ass.*, 1935, **32**, 220–228. (*20*)

SCHMIDT, L. D. Concepts of the role of secondary school counselors. *Personnel Guid. J.*, 1962, **40**, 600–605. (*190*)

SCHNEIDER, P. E. The failure of the present rural secondary curriculum. *Cath. educ. Rev.*, 1943, **41**, 129–138. (*204*)

SCHNEIDERS, A. A. *Personality adjustment and mental health*. New York: Holt, 1955. (*39, 42, 341*)

SCHNEIDERS, A. A. Emotional problems and academic performance in college students. *Cath. Couns.*, 1957, **1**, 4–7. (*420*)

SCHNEIDERS, A. A. Mental hygiene in the classroom. *Cath. Couns.*, 1960, **4**, 96–97. (*132*)

SCHNIEDERS, A. A. Counseling and moral values in the church-related college. *J. Coll. Student Personnel*, 1963, **5**, 35–38. (a) (*294, 299*)

SCHNIEDERS, A. A. The limits of confidentiality. *Personnel Guid. J.*, 1963, **42**, 252–254. (b) (*294*)

SCHNIEDERS, A. A. "Discussion" of Noel Mailloux, O.P., Scrupulosity in pastoral work. In W. C. Bier, S.J. (Ed.), *Personality and sexual problems in pastoral psychology*. New York: Fordham, 1964. Pp. 81–82. (a) (*467*)

SCHNIEDERS, A. A. Emotional conflicts in adolescents: developmental or pathological? *Nat. Cath. Guid. Conf. J.*, 1964, **9**, 75–76. (b) (*357*)

SCHRIER, H. The significance of identification in therapy. *Amer. J. Orthopsychiat.*, 1953, **23**, 585–604. (*445*)

SCHUYLER, J. B., S.J. Religious institutions and cultures changing morality. *Relig. Educ.*, 1962, **57**, 439–444. (*450*)

SCHWEBEL, M. Counselor intervention in resistance and ignorance. *Personnel Guid. J.*, 1960, **39**, 480–485. (*92, 267*)

SCHWEBEL, M. Some missing links in counseling theory and research. *Personnel Guid. J.*, 1962, **41**, 325–331. (*160*)

SCHWEBEL, M., KARR, L., & SLOTKIN, H. Counselor relationship competence: a unifying concept applied to counselor trainees. *Educ. psychol. Measmt*, 1957, **19**, 515–537. (*297*)

SCOTT, J. P. Critical periods in the development of social behavior in puppies. *Psychosom. Med.*, 1958, **20**, 42–54. (*44*)

SCOTT, W. L. Student personnel services: principles and practices for small colleges. *Personnel Guid. J.*, 1960, **38**, 737–739. (*511*)

SEARLES, A., JR. The effectiveness of limited counseling in improving the academic achievement of superior college freshmen. *Personnel Guid. J.*, 1962, **40**, 630–633. (*438*)

SEARS, R. R., MACCOBY, ELEANOR, E., & LEVIN, H. *Patterns of child rearing.* New York: Harper & Row, 1957. (*366*)

SEASHORE, H. G. Understanding the student through testing. In J. O'Connor (Ed.), *College counseling and testing.* Washington: Catholic, 1958. Pp. 105–134. (*231*)

SEASHORE, H. G. Women are more predictable than men. *J. counsel. Psychol.*, 1962, **9**, 261–270. (*419*)

SECHREST, CAROLYN A. *New dimensions in counseling students.* New York: Teachers Coll., 1958. (*248*)

SEEGARS, J. E., JR., & ROSE, HARRIETT A. Verbal comprehension and academic success in college. *Personnel Guid. J.*, 1963, **42**, 295–296. (*437*)

SEELEY, J. R. Basic approaches to mental health: the Forest Hill Village human relations classes. *Personnel Guid. J.*, 1959, **37**, 424–434. (*204*)

SEEMAN, J. Counselor judgments of therapeutic process and outcome. In C. R. Rodgers and R. Dymond (Eds.), *Psychotherapy and personality change.* Chicago: Univer. of Chicago Press, 1954. Pp. 99–108, (*123*)

SEEMAN, J. Editorial comment on normality for counselors. *J. counsel. Psychol.*, 1959, **6**, 2. (*512*)

SEGAL, S. J. Religious factors and values in counseling: the role of the counselor's religious values in counseling. *J. counsel. Psychol.*, 1959, **6**, 270–274. (*444*)

SEIGEL, ALBERTA E., & SEIGEL, S. Reference groups, membership groups, and attitude change. In D. Cartwright & A. Zander (Eds.), *Group dynamics: research and theory.* (2nd ed.) New York: Harper & Row, 1953. Pp. 232–240. (*367*)

SIEGMAN, A. W., & POPE, B. An empirical scale for the measurement of therapist specificity in the initial psychiatric interview. *Psychol. Rep.*, 1962, **11**, 515–520. (*266*)

SEITZ, P. F. D. Infantile experience and adult behavior in animal subjects: II. Age of separation from the mother and adult behavior in the cat. *Psychosom. Med.*, 1959, **21**, 353–378. (*341*)

SELLIN, T. A sociological approach to the study of crime causation. In M. E. Wolfgang, L. Savitz, & N. Johnson (Eds.), *The sociology of crime and delinquency.* New York: Wiley, 1962. Pp. 2–9. (*372*)

SEYMOUR, J. C., & GUTHRIE, FAIN A. A summer program combining freshman orientation, counseling, and counselor preparation. *Personnel Guid. J.*, 1962, **40**, 477–478. (*321*)

SHAFFER, L. F., & SHOBEN, E. J., JR. *The psychology of adjustment.* (2nd ed.) Boston: Houghton Mifflin, 1956. (*41, 339, 347*)

SHARP, B. L. College achievement: its relationship to high school achievement experiences and test scores. *Personnel Guid. J.*, 1962, **41**, 247–250. (*431*)

SHARP, W. H. Educational counseling. In J. W. Stafford, C.S.V. (Ed.), *Counseling in the secondary school.* Washington: Catholic, 1960. Pp. 53–64. (*54*)

SHAW, M. C., & BROWN, D. J. Scholastic underachievement of bright college students. *Personnel Guid. J.*, 1957, **36**, 195–199. (*431*)

SHAW, M. C., ET AL. The self-concept of bright underachieving high school students as revealed by an adjective check list. *Personnel Guid. J.*, 1960, **39**, 193–196. (*382, 416, 417*)

SHAW, M. C., & GRUBB, J. Hostility and able high school underachievers. *J. counsel. Psychol.*, 1958, **5**, 263–266. (*416*)

SHAW, M. E., & PENROD, W. T., JR. Does more information available to a group always improve group performance? *Sociometry*, 1962, **25**, 377–390. (*320*)

SHEED, F. *Are we really teaching religion?* New York: Sheed, 1952. (*448*)

SHEEHAN, F. X. Blueprint for lay missionary program in Catholic colleges. *Cath. educ. Rev.*, 1963, **61**, 105–112. (*480*)

SHEEHY, M. S. Tendencies in Catholic higher education. *Bull. nat. Cath. educ. Ass.*, 1928, **25**, 174–191. (*14*)

SHEEHY, M. S. *Problems of student guidance.* Philadelphia: Dolphin, 1929. (*13, 21, 192*)

SHEERER, ELIZABETH T. The relationship between acceptance of self and acceptance of others. *J. consult. Psychol.*, 1949, **13**, 174–175. (*297*)

SHERIF, M. The concept of reference groups in human relations. In M. Sherif & M. O. Wilson (Eds.), *Group relations at the crossroads.* New York: Harper & Row, 1953. Pp. 203–231. (*314*)

SHERIF, M., & SHERIF, CAROLYN W. *Groups in harmony and tension.* New York: Harper & Row, 1953. (*370*)

SHERIF, M., & SHERIF, CAROLYN W. *An outline of social psychology.* (2nd ed.) New York: Harper & Row, 1956. (*38, 311, 361*)

SHERIF, M., & SHERIF, CAROLYN W. Varieties of social stimulus situations. In S. B. Sells (Ed.), *Stimulus determinants of behavior.* New York: Ronald, 1963. Pp. 82–106. (*312, 313*)

SHERTZER, B., & STONE, S. C. The school counselor and his publics: the problem of role definition. *Personnel Guid. J.*, 1963, **41**, 687–693. (*164*)

SHEVIAKOV, G. V., & REDL, F. *Discipline for today's children and youth.* (Rev. by S. Richardson) Washington: Ass. Supervis. Curriculum Develpm, Nat. Educ. Ass., 1956. (*138*)

SHINN, HAZEL A. *Social living in Catholic four year colleges for women.* Washington: Catholic, 1959. (*378, 529*)

SHOBEN, E. J., JR. Personal responsibility, determinism, and the burden of understanding. *Personnel Guid. J.*, 1961, **39**, 342–348. (*73*)

SHOBEN, E. J., JR. The counselor's theory as personal trait. *Personnel Guid. J.*, 1962, **40**, 617–621. (a) (*249*)

SHOBEN, E. J., JR. Guidance: remedial function or social reconstruction? *Harvard educ. Rev.*, 1962, **32**, 430–443. (b) (*249, 355*)

SHULIM, J. I. The role of placement services in a liberal arts college. *J. Coll. Student Personnel*, 1962, **3**, 106–125. (*411*)

SHURE, G. H., ET AL. Group planning and task effectiveness. *Sociometry*, 1962, **25**, 263–282. (*313*)

SHURR, W., S.J. Themes of redemption in modern literature. *Cath. educ. Rev.*, 1963, **61**, 388–402. (*194*)

SIEGEL, M. Group orientation and placement counseling. *Personnel Guid. J.*, 1960, **38**, 659–660. (*322*)

SIGNORELLI, SISTER MARY ANTONINE, M.Z.S.H. The imperative needs of girls in a Roman Catholic high school. Unpublished master's thesis, Fordham Univer., 1956. (*377, 435, 518*)

SINGER, S. I., STEFFLRE, B., & THOMPSON, F. W. Temperament scores and socioeconomic status. *J. counsel. Psychol.*, 1958, **5**, 281–283. (*80*)

SINICK, D. The developmental character of counseling. *Cath. Couns.*, 1961, **5**, 33–34. (*245*)

SKINNER, B. F. *Walden II.* New York: Macmillan, 1948. (*108*)

SLECHTA, JOAN, GWYNN, W., & PEOPLES, C. Verbal conditioning of schizophrenics and normals in a situation resembling psychotherapy. *J. consult. Psychol.*, 1963, **27**, 223–227. (*266, 267*)

SLIEPCEVICH, ELENA M. *School health education study: a summary report.* Washington: Nat. Educ. Ass., 1964. (*180*)

SLOYAN, G. S. Catechetical renewal. *Worship*, 1963, **37**, 96–102. (*150*)

SMITH, A. E. The present and future in counselor preparation in Catholic institutions. *Nat. Cath. Guid. Conf. J.*, 1965, **10**, 102–108. (*517*)

SMITH, B. O., STANLEY, W. O., & SHORES, J. H. *Fundamentals of curriculum development.* (Rev. ed.) New York: Harcourt, Brace & World, 1957. (*424*)

SMITH, E. E. Defensiveness, insight, and the K scale. *J. consult. Psychol.*, 1959. **23**, 275–277. (*504*)

SMITH, F. College as a guidance experience. *Occupations*, 1936, **14**, 773–775. (*492*)

SMITH, G. E. *Counseling in the secondary school.* New York: Macmillan, 1955. (*245*)

SMITH, G. J. W., SPENCE, D. E., & KLEIN, G. S. Subliminal effects of verbal stimuli. *J. abnorm. soc. Psychol.*, 1959, **59**, 167–176. (*463*)

SMITH, SISTER M. LEONITA, O.P. Catholic viewpoints about the psychology, social role, and higher education of women. Unpublished doctoral dissertation, Ohio State Univer., 1961. (*204*)

SMITH, MARY E. Problems of freshmen college girls in relation to levels of education. Unpublished master's thesis, Catholic Univer. of America, 1950. (*377*)

SMITH, V. E. *The school examined.* Milwaukee: Bruce, 1960. (*76, 148*)

SNYDER, W. U. An investigation of the nature of non-directive psychotherapy. *J. genet. Psychol.*, 1945, **33**, 193–223. (*267*)

SNYGG, D. The need for a phenomenological system of psychology. *Psychol. Rev.*, 1941, **48**, 404–424. (*36*)

Some aspects of steady dating. *Theol. Dig.*, 1958, **6**, 136–138. (*384*)

SONNE, T. R., & GOLDMAN, L. Preference of authoritarian and equalitarian personalities for client-centered and eclectic counseling. *J. counsel. Psychol.*, 1957, **4**, 129–135. (*269*)

SOUTHARD, C. W. Effect of student-selection of adviser on rapport. *Personnel Guid. J.*, 1960, **38**, 614–620. (*75*)

SOUTHEASTERN CURRICULUM COMMITTEE. *Teachers guide*. St. Augustine, Fla.: Author, 1956. (*150*)

SPEER, G. S. Certifications of counselors and psychological services by professional organizations. *Occupations*, 1949, **27**, 311–316. (*26*)

SPEISMAN, J. C. Depth of interpretation and verbal resistance in psychotherapy. *J. consult. Psychol.*, 1959, **23**, 93–99. (*266*)

SPIELBERGER, C. C., WEITZ, H., & DENNEY, J. P. Group counseling and the academic performance of anxious college freshman. *J. counsel. Psychol.*, 1962, **9**, 195–204. (*438*)

SPITZ, R. A. Hospitalism: an inquiry into the genesis of psychiatric conditions in early childhood. *The psychoanalytic study of the child*. Vol. 1. New York: International Universities Press, 1945. Pp. 53–74. (*123*)

SPITZ, R. A. *A genetic field theory of ego formation*. New York: International Universities Press, 1959. (*47*)

SPRINGER, R. H., S.J. Adolescent steady dating: is marriage the sole justification? *Homil. pastoral Rev.*, 1959, **19**, 333–338. (*385*)

SPURGEON, SISTER MARY A., G.N.S.H. Implications of teacher-pupil relations in the supervision of sister teachers. Unpublished doctoral dissertation, Fordham Univer., 1959. (*136, 140, 145*)

STACK, P. L. *A national study of the guidance services in Catholic secondary schools*. Washington: Catholic, 1958. (*434, 520, 522*)

STAFFORD, J. S., C.S.V. Understanding the student—a psychological approach. In E. C. Stefic (Ed.), *Psychological counseling in high school and college*. Washington: Catholic, 1961. Pp. 3–10. (*346*)

STANCIOFF, MARION M. Parents and vocational guidance. *Integrity*, 1955, **9**, 2–9. (*405*)

STANTON, E. S., S.J. Formation of Christian social leaders. *Cath. educ. Rev.*, 1962, **60**, 433–441. (*449*)

STARR, J. M. Guidance practices in selected junior colleges in the Northwest. *Jr. Coll. J.*, 1960, **31**, 442–446. (*514*)

STATON, T. F. *Dynamics of adolescent adjustment*. New York: Macmillan, 1963. (*40, 43, 50*)

STEFFLRE, B. What price professionalization? *Personnel Guid. J.*, 1964, **42**, 654–659. (*164*)

STEIMEL, R. J. The role of testing in counseling. In J. W. Stafford, C.S.V. (Ed.), *Counseling in the secondary school*. Washington: Catholic, 1960. Pp. 82–95. (*230*)

STEIMEL, R. J. Counselor preparation in Catholic institutions. *Cath. Couns.*, 1961, **5**, 145–147. (a) (*523*)

STEIMEL, R. J. Psychological tests in counseling. In E. C. Stefic (Ed.), *Psychological counseling in high school and college*. Washington: Catholic, 1961. Pp. 61–72. (b) (*233*)

STEINKE, BETTY K., & KACZKOWSKI, H. R. Parents influence the occupational choice of ninth grade girls. *Voc. Guid. Quart.*, 1960–61, **9**, 101–103. (*407*)

STELLWAG, HELEN W. F. Impressions of traveling through the United States in search of the counselor. *Personnel Guid. J.*, 1961, **40**, 60–62. (*174*)

STEVENS, NANCY D. A concept of placement readiness. *Voc. Guid. Quart.*, 1962, **10**, 143–149. (*411*)

STEWART, C. C. A bill of rights for school counselors. *Personnel Guid. J.*, 1959, **37**, 500–503. (*193*)

STEWART, J. A. Factors influencing teacher attitudes toward and participation in guidance services. *Personnel Guid. J.*, 1961, **39**, 729–734. (*133*)

STEWART, L. H. The relationship of self concept and mother-son identification to vocational interests. Unpublished monograph. Cited by Becky J. White, The relationship of self concept and parental identification to women's vocational interests. *J. counsel. Psychol.*, 1959, **6**, 202–206. (*483*)

STOKES, W. R. Our changing sex ethics. *Marriage and Family Living*, 1962, **24**, 269–271. (*471*)

STONE, L. J., & CHURCH, J. *Childhood and adolescence.* New York: Random House, 1957. (*48*)

STONE, S. C., & SHERTZER, B. The militant counselor. *Personnel Guid. J.*, 1963, **42**, 342–347. (*167, 242*)

STOOPS, E., & WAHLQUIST, G. L. *Principles and practices in guidance.* New York: McGraw-Hill, 1958. (*213*)

STRANG, RUTH. *Counseling technics in college and secondary school.* (2nd ed.) New York: Harper & Row, 1949. (*224*)

STRANG, RUTH. *Group work in education.* (3rd ed.) New York: Harper & Row, 1958. (*311, 369*)

STRANG, RUTH. *An introduction to child study.* New York: Macmillan, 1959. (*46*)

STRANG, RUTH. Group guidance as students view it. *Sch. Couns.*, 1961, **8**, 142–145. (*319*)

STRANG, RUTH, ET AL. *Unity within guidance.* Syracuse, N.Y.: Syracuse Univer. Press, 1953. (*191*)

STREITFELD, J. W. Expressed acceptance of self and others by psychotherapists. *J. consult. Psychol.*, 1959, **23**, 435–441. (*297*)

STRODBECK, F. L. Family interaction, values, and achievement. In D. C. McClelland (Ed.), *Talent and society.* Princeton, N.J.: Van Nostrand, 1958. Pp. 135–191. (*418*)

STRONG, S. R. Verbal conditioning and counseling research. *Personnel Guid. J.*, 1964, **42**, 660–669. (*264, 265*)

STUARDI, J. E. A study of pupil transfer from Catholic schools to public schools in the diocese of Mobile. Unpublished master's thesis, Catholic Univ. of America, 1947. (*204*)

SUBCOMMITTEE ON VOCATIONAL GUIDANCE, WHITE HOUSE CONFERENCE ON CHILD HEALTH AND PROTECTION. *Vocational guidance.* New York: Appleton-Century-Crofts, 1932. (*17, 18, 20*)

SUHARD, E., CARDINAL. *Growth or decline.* (3rd ed.) Notre Dame, Ind.: Fides, 1950. *(79, 109, 110, 453, 503)*

SULLIVAN, H. S. *The interpersonal theory of psychiatry.* New York: Norton, 1953. *(76)*

SULLIVAN, P. J., C.S.C. Aspects of participation in parish organization. Unpublished master's thesis, Fordham Univer., 1959. *(202)*

SULZER, E. S. Research frontier: reinforcement and the therapeutic contract. *J. counsel. Psychol.*, 1962, **9**, 271–275. *(92)*

SUNDBERG, N. D., & TYLER, LEONA E. *Clinical psychology: an introduction to research and practice.* New York: Appleton-Century-Crofts, 1962. *(217, 237)*

SUPER, D. E. Group techniques in the guidance program. *Educ. psychol. Measmt,* 1949, **9**, 496–510. *(69)*

SUPER, D. E. Comments on current books. *J. counsel. Psychol.*, 1954, **1**, 73–75. *(79)*

SUPER, D. E. Transition: from vocational guidance to counseling psychology. *J. counsel. Psychol.*, 1955, **2**, 3–9. *(157, 358)*

SUPER, D. E. *The psychology of careers.* New York: Harper & Row, 1957. *(56, 174, 257, 275, 383, 396, 397, 398, 403, 404)*

SUPER, D. E. Some unresolved issues in vocational development research. *Personnel Guid. J.*, 1961, **40**, 11–15. *(232)*

SUPER, D. E. To the editors: guidance—an examination. *Harvard educ. Rev.*, 1963, **33**, 237–238. (a) *(248, 264, 267)*

SUPER, D. E. Vocational development in adolescence and early adulthood: tasks and behaviors. In D. E. Super et al., *Career development: self-concept theory.* New York: College Entrance Examination Board, 1963. Pp. 79–93. (b) *(397, 398)*

SUPER, D. E., ET AL. *Vocational development: a framework for research.* New York: Teachers Coll., 1957. *(397, 398)*

SUPER, D. E., ET AL. *The vocational maturity of ninth-grade boys.* New York: Teachers Coll., 1960. *(166, 397, 398, 405, 425)*

SUPER, D. E., & CRITES, J. O. *Appraising vocational fitness by means of psychological tests.* (2nd ed.) New York: Harper & Row, 1962. *(230)*

SYMONDS, P. M. *The dynamics of human adjustment.* New York: Appleton-Century-Crofts, 1946. *(340, 343)*

TANQUEREY, A., S.S. *The spiritual life: a treatise on ascetical and mystical theology.* (2nd ed.) Tournai, Belgium: Desclée, 1930. *(468)*

TANQUEREY, A., S.S. *Synopsis theologiae dogmaticae, tomus I.* (26th ed.) Tournai, Belgium: Desclée, 1937. *(452, 466)*

TAUBER, L. E., & ISAACSON, L. E. Group-need therapy—an approach to group planning. *J. counsel. Psychol.*, 1961, **8**, 260–262. *(326)*

TAULBEE, E. S. Relationship between certain personality variables and continuation in psychotherapy. *J. consult. Psychol.*, 1958, **22**, 83–89. *(75)*

TENNYSON, W. W. An analysis of the professional guidance position of certified secondary school counselors in Missouri. Unpublished doctoral dissertation, Univer. of Missouri, 1956. *(415, 509)*

TENNYSON, W. W., BLOCHER, D.H., & JOHNSON, R. H. Student personnel records: a vital tool but a concern of the public. *Personnel Guid. J.*, 1964, **42**, 888–893. *(239, 241)*

TENNYSON, W. W., & MONNENS, L. P. The world at work through elementary readers. *Voc. Guid. Quart.*, 1963–64, **12**, 85–88. *(408)*

TERMAN, L. M. *The intelligence of school children.* Boston: Houghton Mifflin, 1919. *(9)*

THELEN, H. A. Group dynamics in instruction: the principle of least group size. *Sch. Rev.*, 1949, **57**, 139–148. *(143)*

THELEN, H. A. *Dynamics of groups at work.* Chicago: Univer. of Chicago Press, 1954. *(144)*

THIBAUT, J. W., & KELLEY, H. H. *The social psychology of groups.* New York: Wiley, 1959. *(311)*

THOMAS, E. J. Effects of facilitative role interdependence on group functioning. *Human Relat.*, 1957, **10**, 347–366. *(362)*

THOMAS, E. J., & FINK, C. F. Effects of group size. *Psychol. Bull.*, 1963, **60**, 371–384. *(317)*

THOMAS, J. L., S.J. *The American Catholic family.* Englewood Cliffs, N.J.: Prentice-Hall, 1956. *(474)*

THOMAS, J. L., S.J. The place of sex. *Cath. Mind*, 1958, **56**, 30–38. *(472)*

THOMAS, L. *The occupational structure and education.* Englewood Cliffs, N.J.: Prentice-Hall, 1956. *(411)*

THOMPSON, G. S. Do values belong in psychology? *Cath. psychol. Rev.*, 1963, **1**, 11–16. *(122)*

THORNDIKE, E. L. *The original nature of man.* New York: Teachers Coll., 1923. *(10)*

THORNDIKE, E. L. *The psychology of wants, interests, and attitudes.* New York: Appleton-Century-Crofts, 1935. *(15)*

THORNDIKE, R. L., & HAGEN, ELIZABETH. *Ten thousand careers.* New York: Wiley, 1959. *(232)*

THORNDIKE, R. L., & HAGEN, ELIZABETH. *Measurement and evaluation in psychology and education.* (2nd ed.) New York: Wiley, 1961. *(230)*

THORNE, F. C. *Principles of personality counseling.* Brandon, Vt.: *J. clin. Psychol.*, 1950. *(25, 257)*

THORNE, F. C. Critique of recent developments in personality counseling theory. In J. F. McGowan & L. D. Schmidt (Eds.), *Counseling: readings in theory and practice.* New York: Holt, 1962. Pp. 340–353. (a) *(255, 257)*

THORNE, F. C. Principles of directive counseling and psychotherapy. In H. J. Peters et al. (Eds.), *Counseling: selected readings.* Indianapolis: Bobbs-Merrill, 1962. Pp. 111–125. (b) *(257)*

THRASHER, F. M. *The gang.* Chicago: Univer. of Chicago Press, 1936. *(370)*

TIEBOUT, H. M. The misnamed lazy student. *Educ. Rec.*, 1943, **24**, 113–129. *(432)*

TIEDEMAN, D. V. Decision and vocational development: a paradigm and its implications. *Personnel Guid. J.*, 1961, **40**, 15–21. *(401)*

TIEDEMAN, D. V., & FIELD, F. L. Guidance: the science of purposeful action applied through education. *Harvard educ. Rev.*, 1962, **32**, 483–501. (*91*)

TIEDEMAN, D. V., & O'HARA, R. P. *Career development: choice and adjustment.* New York: College Entrance Examination Board, 1963. (*401*)

TODD, W. B., & EWING, T. N. Changes in self-reference during counseling. *J. counsel. Psychol.*, 1961, **8**, 112–115. (*265*)

TOLBERT, E. L. *Introduction to counseling.* New York: McGraw-Hill, 1959. (*244*)

TOOKER, E. D. Counselor role: counselor training. *Personnel Guid. J.*, 1957, **36**, 263–267. (*164*)

TORRANCE, E. P. Current research on the nature of creative talent. *J. counsel. Psychol.*, 1959, **6**, 309–311. (*139, 430*)

TORRANCE, E. P. Cited by Sister Patrick Anne, C.S.J., Creatives in conflict. *Cath. Couns.*, 1961, **6**, 12–15. (*430*)

TORRANCE, E. P. Cited by Sister M. Michel, I.H.M., College residence hall guidance program. *Cath. Couns.*, 1962, **6**, 95–98. (a) (*81*)

TORRANCE, E. P. *Guiding creative talent.* Englewood Cliffs, N.J.: Prentice-Hall, 1962. (b) (*129, 429*)

TOWNSEND, J. C. *Introduction to experimental method for psychology and the social sciences.* New York: McGraw-Hill, 1953. (*232*)

TRACHTMAN, G. M. New directions for school psychology. *Exceptnl. Child.*, 1961, **38**, 159–163. (*504*)

TRACY, H. M. Status of the lay teacher in Catholic high schools in the United States. Unpublished doctoral dissertation, Fordham Univer., 1958. (*494, 525*)

TRAVERS, J. F. Learning theory—animal or human? *Cath. educ. Rev.*, 1961, **59**, 227–238. (*341*)

TRAVERS, J. F. Educational problems of delinquency: III. Theories on causes of delinquency. *Cath. Sch. J.*, 1964, **64**, 42–44. (*373*)

TRAXLER, A. E. *How to use cumulative records.* Chicago: Science Research. 1947. (*220*)

TRAXLER, A. E. *The nature and use of anecdotal records.* (2nd ed.) New York: Educ. Rec. Bur., 1949. (*225*)

TRAXLER, A. E. *Techniques of guidance.* (2nd ed.) New York: Harper & Row, 1957. (*221*)

TREACY, J. P. Educational and vocational guidance. *Cath. Sch. J.*, 1935, **35**, 256–257. (*6*)

TROUT, D. M. Why define counseling in medical terms? *Personnel Guid. J.*, 1954, **32**, 520–521. (*245*)

TRUMP, J. L., & BAYNHAM, DORSEY. *Guide to better schools.* Chicago: Rand McNally, 1961. (*142, 492*)

TUMA, A. H., & GUSTAD, J. W. The effects of client and counselor personality characteristics on client learning in counseling. *J. counsel. Psychol.*, 1957, **4**, 136–141. (*155*)

TURK, H., HARTLEY, E. L., & SHAW, D. M. The expectation of social influence. *J. soc. Psychol.*, 1962, **58**, 23–29. (*314*)

TURNER, G. Teacher looks at himself. *Cath. educ. Rev.*, 1963, **61**, 73–77. *(132)*

TWOMEY, L. J., S.J. Is Catholic education meeting the challenge of the modern crisis? *Coll. Newsltr nat. Cath. educ. Ass.*, 1961, **24**, 1–3. *(206, 449)*

TYLER, LEONA E. Theoretical principles underlying the counseling process. *J. counsel. Psychol.*, 1958, **5**, 3–10. *(102, 246)*

TYLER, LEONA E. *The work of the counselor.* (2nd ed.) New York: Appleton-Century-Crofts, 1961. *(73, 86, 227, 237, 246, 247)*

UGUREL-SEMIN, R. Moral behavior and moral judgment of children. *J. abnorm. soc. Psychol.*, 1952, **47**, 463–447. *(80)*

U.S. DEPARTMENT OF LABOR. *Manpower challenge of the 1960s.* Document 0-542270. Washington: Author, 1960. *(393, 403)*

USEEM, RUTH. Changing cultural concepts in women's lives. *J. nat. Ass. Women Deans and Counselors*, 1960, **24**, 35–38. *(403)*

UTTON, A. C. Recalled parent-child relations as determinants of vocational choice. *J. counsel. Psychol.*, 1962, **9**, 49–53. *(399)*

UZZELL, O. Influencers of occupational choice. *Personnel Guid. J.*, 1961, **39**, 666–669. *(407)*

VACCARO, J. J. Motivating the person for psychological assistance. *Cath. Couns.*, 1964, **8**, 43–46. *(169)*

VAN ATTA, R. E., & PETERS, H. J. Professional staffing of guidance positions. *Personnel Guid. J.*, 1963, **41**, 509–512. *(507)*

VANCE, F. L., & VOLSKY, T. C., JR. Counseling and psychotherapy: split personality or Siamese twins? *Amer. Psychologist*, 1962, **17**, 565–570. *(264)*

VANDERVELDT, J. H., O.F.M., & ODENWALD, R. P. *Psychiatry and Catholicism.* (2nd ed.) New York: McGraw-Hill, 1957. *(250, 252, 344, 467, 475)*

VAN KAAM, A. L., C.S.SP. Phenomenal analysis: exemplified by a study of the experience of "really feeling understood." *J. indiv. Psychol.*, 1959, **15**, 66–72. *(297)*

VAN KAAM, A. L., C.S.SP. Counseling from the viewpoint of existential psychology. *Harvard educ. Rev.*, 1962, **32**, 403–415. *(93, 253)*

VAUGHAN, R. P., S.J. Moral issues in psychological screening. *Rev. for Religious*, 1957, **16**, 65–78. *(486)*

VAUGHAN, R. P., S.J. Referring students to psychiatrists and psychologists. *Cath. Couns.*, 1959, **3**, 36–37. *(169)*

VERMEERSCH, A., S.J. *De castitate et de vitiis contrariis.* Rome: Pontificia Universita Gregoriana, 1919. *(476)*

VERNICE, SISTER M., S.N.D. The sister in service and her reading. *Cath. educ. Rev.*, 1959, **57**, 289–301. *(135)*

VERPLANCK, W. S. The control of the content of conversation: reinforcement of statements of opinion. In Eleanor E. Maccoby, T. M. Newcomb, & E. L. Hartley (Eds.), *Readings in social psychology.* New York: Holt, 1958. Pp. 32–39. *(265)*

VIDEBECK, R. Self-concept and the reactions of others. *Sociometry,* 1960, **23**, 351–359. *(295)*

VINCENT, C. E. *Unmarried mothers.* New York: Free Press, 1961. (*147*)

VON HILDEBRAND, D. *Marriage.* New York: Longmans, 1942. (*390*)

VON HILDEBRAND, D. *Transformation in Christ.* New York: Longmans, 1948. (*440*)

VON HILDEBRAND, D. *Christian ethics.* New York: McKay, 1953. (*106, 122*)

VON HILDEBRAND, D. *True morality and its counterfeits.* New York: McKay, 1955. (*112*)

VON HILDEBRAND, D. Marriage and overpopulation. *Thought*, 1961, **36,** 81–100. (*390*)

WAGGONER, G. R. The gifted student in the state university. *J. higher Educ.*, 1957, **28,** 414–424. (*434*)

WALKER, D. E., & PEIFFER, H. C., JR. The goals of counseling. *J. counsel. Psychol.*, 1957, **4,** 204–209. (*244*)

WALL, H. W. A counseling program for parents of college freshmen. *Personnel Guid. J.*, 1962, **40,** 774–778. (*200*)

WALSH, MARY B., & LEONARD, EUGENIE A. Opinions of college administrators regarding lay counselors in Catholic women's colleges. *Cath. educ. Rev.*, 1946, **54,** 169–172. (*31*)

WALSH, SISTER MARY MARJORIE, R.S.M. The problems and needs of adolescent girls in Catholic secondary schools in New England. Unpublished master's thesis, Catholic Univer. of America, 1955. (*377*)

WALTERS, SISTER ANNETTE, & O'HARA, SISTER KEVIN. *Persons and personality.* New York: Appleton-Century-Crofts, 1953. (*53*)

WALTERS, O. S. Metaphysics, religion, and psychotherapy. *J. counsel. Psychol.*, 1958, **4,** 243–250. (*73, 76*)

WARD, L. R., C.S.C. Introduction. In J. G. Lawler, *Catholic dimensions in higher education.* Westminster, Md.: Newman, 1959. (*503*)

WARMAN, R. E. Differential perceptions of counseling role. *J. counsel. Psychol.*, 1960, **7,** 269–274. (*163, 296*)

WARREN, PHYLLIS A. Vocational interests and occupational adjustment of college women. *J. counsel. Psychol.*, 1959, **6,** 140–147. (*383*)

WASSELL, B. B. *Group psychoanalysis.* New York: Philosophical Library, 1959. (*330*)

WATSON, D. E., RUNDQUIST, R. M., & COTTLE, W. C. What's wrong with occupational materials? *J. counsel. Psychol.*, 1959, **6,** 288–291. (*409*)

WATSON, G. The problem: an introduction. In G. Watson (Ed.), *No room at the bottom.* Washington: Nat. Educ. Ass., 1963. Pp. 1–6. (*373, 393*)

WATSON, GLADYS H. Emotional problems of gifted students. *Personnel Guid. J.*, 1960, **39,** 98–105. (*428*)

WEBER, F. J. The bulletin apostolate. *Worship*, 1964, **38,** 174–175. (*462*)

WEBER, G. P. *Chaplain's manual, Christian Family Movement.* Chicago: Chicago Federation of the Christian Family Movement, 1952. (*146*)

WECHSLER, D. *The measurement and appraisal of adult intelligence.* (4th ed.) Baltimore: Williams & Wilkins, 1958. (*234*)

WEHMEYER, D. J. A study to investigate the effects of utilization of guidance services in high school on academic adjustment in the first semester in college. Unpublished master's thesis, Univer. of Notre Dame, 1959. *(434)*

WEIGEL, G., S.J. American Catholic intellectualism: a theologian's reflections. *Rev. Politics*, 1957, **19**, 275–307. *(418)*

WEISS, R. F., KRASNER, L., & ULLMAN, L. Responsivity of psychiatric patients to verbal conditioning: "success" and "failure" conditions and patterns of reinforced trials. *Psychol. Rep.*, 1963, **12**, 423–426. *(266)*

WEISS, R. F., & PASAMANICK, B. Individual and group goals: a factor analysis. *J. soc. Psychol.*, 1962, **58**, 131–139. *(312)*

WEITZ, H. The role of the guidance worker in the schools. *Personnel Guid. J.*, 1958, **37**, 266–272. *(160, 507)*

WENDORF, R. A. Qualifications of guidance counselors in Ohio high schools. *Personnel Guid. J.*, 1956, **34**, 569–571. *(507)*

WERLING, N. G., O. CARM. Why teenagers go steady. *Amer. eccles. Rev.*, 1959, **140**, 319–324. *(386)*

WESSELL, ALICE, & FLAHERTY, SISTER M. RITA. Changes in CPI scores after one year in college. *J. Psychol.*, 1964, **17**, 235–238. *(381)*

WHEELIS, A. *The quest for identity.* New York: Norton, 1958. *(34, 37, 395)*

WHITAKER, C. A., WARKENTIN, J., & MALONE, T. P. The involvement of the professional therapist. In A. Burton (Ed.), *Case studies in counseling and psychotherapy.* Englewood Cliffs, N.J.: Prentice-Hall, 1959. Pp. 218–256. *(96)*

WHITE, BECKY. The relationship of self concept and parental identification to women's vocational interest. *J. counsel. Psychol.*, 1963, **4**, 202–206. *(483)*

WHITE, N. J. The educational whirl: I taught them all. *Clearing House*, 1938, **12**, 151, 192. *(148)*

WHITE, R. W. The dangers of social adjustment. *Teachers Coll. Rec.*, 1961, **62**, 288–297. *(376)*

WHITE, R. W. *The abnormal personality.* (3rd ed.) New York: Ronald, 1964. *(391)*

WHITE, V., O.P. Can a psychologist be religious? *Commonweal*, 1953, **53**, 583–584. *(408)*

WILD, J. *Plato's modern enemies and the theory of the natural law.* Chicago: Univer. of Chicago Press, 1953. *(77)*

WILKOW, M. E. A description of parents' frames of reference concerning a high school guidance program. Unpublished doctoral dissertation, Teachers Coll., 1962. *(197)*

WILLETT, J. E. A comparative survey of articles on guidance in education by Catholic and non-Catholic authors during the period 1949 to 1954. Unpublished master's thesis, Catholic Univer. of America, 1955. *(516)*

WILLEY, R. DeV. *Guidance in elementary education.* (Rev. ed.) New York: Harper & Row, 1960. *(510)*

WILLEY, R. DeV., & STRONG, W. M. *Group procedures in guidance.* New York: Harper & Row, 1957. *(206, 310)*

WILLIAMS, H. E. The guidance attitudes and understandings of a selected group of elementary school teachers. Unpublished doctoral dissertation, Univer. of Colorado, 1958. *(132)*

WILLIAMS, J. E. Changes in self and other perceptions following brief educational-vocational counseling. *J. counsel. Psychol.*, 1962, **9**, 18–28. *(103, 416)*

WILLIAMS, W. O. Public relations as a function of guidance officers in secondary schools. Unpublished doctoral dissertation, Teachers Coll., 1954. *(72)*

WILLAMSON, E. G. *How to counsel students.* New York: McGraw-Hill, 1939. *(17 88, 255, 256, 297)*

WILLIAMSON, E. G. *Counseling adolescents.* New York: McGraw-Hill, 1950. *(25, 88, 255)*

WILLIAMSON, E. G. Students' residence: shelter or education? *Personnel Guid. J.*, 1958, **36**, 392–397. (a) *(513)*

WILLIAMSON, E. G. Value orientation in counseling. *Personnel Guid. J.*, 1958, **36**, 522–523. (b) *(97, 130)*

WILLIAMSON, E. G. The meaning of communication in counseling. *Personnel. Guid. J.*, 1959, **38**, 6–14. *(122, 461)*

WILLIAMSON, E. G. *Student personnel services in colleges and universities.* New York: McGraw-Hill, 1961. (a) *(245)*

WILLIAMSON, E. G. Student personnel worker's responsibility for students' expression on social issues. *Personnel Guid. J.*, 1961, **40**, 123–127. (b) *(119)*

WILLIAMSON, E. G. The counselor as technique. *Personnel Guid. J.*, 1962, **41**, 108–111. *(95, 256, 257, 297)*

WILLIAMSON, E. G. An historical perspective of the vocational movement. *Personnel Guid. J.*, 1964, **42**, 854–859. *(410)*

WILLAMSON, E. G. Vocational counseling: trait-factor theory. In B. Stefflre (Ed.), *Theories of counseling.* New York: McGraw-Hill, 1965. Pp. 193–214. *(256)*

WILLAMSON, E. G., & DARLEY, J. G. *Student personnel work.* New York: McGraw-Hill, 1937. *(117, 143)*

WILLINGHAM, W. W. College performance of fraternity members and independent students. *Personnel Guid. J.*, 1962, **41**, 29–31. *(433)*

WILLIS, B. The contribution of guidance to the high school educational program. *Personnel Guid. J.*, 1957, **35**, 489–494. *(132)*

WIMSATT, W. R., & VESTRE, N. D. Extra-experimental effects in verbal conditioning. *J. consult. Psychol.*, 1963, **27**, 398–404. *(265)*

WINFREY, J. K. Implications of the Wrenn Report to the school counselor. *Couns. Educ. Supervis.*, 1962, **2**, 45–48. *(120)*

WINKLER, BROTHER J. F.S.C. An appraisal of guidance programs in Christian Brothers' high schools in the United States. Unpublished doctoral dissertation, St. Louis Univer., 1953. *(526)*

WISE, W. M. Residence halls and higher learning. *Personnel Guid. J.*, 1958, **36**, 398–401. *(512, 513)*

WITRYOL, S. L., & BOLY, L. F. Positive diagnosis in personality counseling of college students. *J. counsel. Psychol.*, 1954, **1**, 63–68. *(113)*

WITTY, P. The mental health of the teacher. In National Society for the Study of Education, *Mental health in modern education*, Fifty-fourth Yearb., Part II. Chicago: Univer. of Chicago Press, 1955. Pp. 307–333. *(147)*

WOLF, J. M. The relation between religious practices and moral practices. *Bull. nat. Cath. educ. Ass.*, 1930, **27**, 459–482. (*442*)

WOLFBEIN, S. L. Transition from school to work: a study of the school leaver. *Personnel Guid. J.*, 1959, **38**, 98–105. (*433*)

WOLFBEIN, S. L. Labor trends, manpower, and automation. In H. Borow (Ed.), *Man in a world at work*. Boston: Houghton Mifflin, 1964. Pp. 155–173. (*393, 411*)

WOLFF, W. *Contemporary psychotherapists examine themselves*. Springfield, Ill.: Charles C Thomas, 1956. (*97*)

WOLFLE, D. *America's resources of specialized talent*. New York: Harper & Row, 1954. (*425*)

WOODCOCK, LOUISE P. *Life and ways of the two-year old*. New York: Dutton, 1941. (*48*)

WOYWOD, S., O.F.M. *A practical commentary on the Code of Canon Law*. (Rev. ed.) New York: J. F. Wagner, 1957. (*446*)

WRENN, C. G. The ethics of counseling. *Educ. psychol. Measmt*, 1952, **22**, 161–177. (*122*)

WRENN, C. G. Status and role of the school counselor. *Personnel Guid. J.*, 1957, **36**, 175–183. (*164, 493*)

WRENN, C. G. The self concept in counseling. *J. counsel. Psychol.*, 1958, **5**, 104–109. (*102, 425*)

WRENN, C. G. Counselor orientation: theoretical or situational? *J. counsel. Psychol.*, 1960, **7**, 40–45. (*249*)

WRENN, C. G. *The counselor in a changing world: a preliminary report of the project on guidance in American schools*. Washington: Commission on Guid. Amer. Sch., Amer. Personnel and Guid. Ass., 1961. (*309*)

WRENN, C. G. *The counselor in a changing world*. Washington: Amer. Personnel and Guid. Ass., 1962. (*118, 163, 174, 190, 311, 358, 375, 403*)

WRIGHTSTONE, J. W. *How to be a better student*. Chicago: Science Research, 1956. (*143*)

WRIGHTSTONE, J. W. The discovery and stimulation of culturally talented youth. *Teachers Coll. Rec.*, 1958, **9**, 23–28. (*432*)

XAVIER, SISTER MARY, O.S.U. Fostering security of youth through guidance programs. *Cath. educ. Rev.*, 1960, **58**, 34–43. (*251*)

XAVIER, SISTER MARY, O.S.U. A Catholic philosophy of counseling oriented toward secondary schools. *Cath. educ. Rev.*, 1962, **60**, 93–105. (*251*)

YABLONSKY, L. The delinquent gang as a near-group. *Soc. Problems*, 1959, **7**, 108–117. (*370*)

YOUNG, K. *Personality and problems of adjustment*. (2nd ed.) New York: Appleton-Century-Crofts, 1952. (*340, 350*)

ZELLER, W. W. Understanding and accepting ourselves. *Insight*, 1963, 41–48. (*42*)

ZERAN, F. R., & RICCIO, A. C. *Organization and administration of guidance services*. Chicago: Rand McNally, 1962. (*192*)

ZIEGLER, SISTER M. EUGENIA, C.S.A.C. A comparative study of the problems, personality adjustments, and values of Catholic adolescent girls in two types of secondary schools. Unpublished doctoral dissertation, Fordham Univer., 1958. (125, 450, 451)

ZILBOORG, G. Clinical variants of moral values. *Amer. J. Psychiat.*, 1950, **106,** 744-747. (103)

ZILBOORG, G. Some denials and affirmations of religious faith. In F. J. Braceland (Ed.), *Faith, reason, and modern psychiatry.* New York: Kenedy, 1955. Pp. 99-121. (76)

ZILBOORG, G. The sense of guilt. In W. C. Bier, S.J. (Ed.), *Personality and sexual problems in pastoral psychology.* New York: Fordham, 1964. Pp. 44-50. (465)

ZINNER, E. M. The role of the speech correctionist as a colleague in the school health team. *J. Sch. Hlth*, 1963, **33,** 193-195. (177)